PARLIAMENT

PARLIAMENT

BY

SIR IVOR JENNINGS

SECOND EDITION

CAMBRIDGE
AT THE UNIVERSITY PRESS
1970

Published by the Syndics of the Cambridge University Press
Bentley House, 200 Euston Road, London N.W. 1
American Branch: 32 East 57th Street, New York, N.Y. 10022

© Cambridge University Press 1957

International Standard Book Numbers:
0 521 07056 2 clothbound
0 521 09532 8 paperback

First edition 1939
Second edition 1957
Reprinted 1961
First paperback edition 1969
Reprinted 1970

Printed in Great Britain
at the University Printing House, Cambridge
(Brooke Crutchley, University Printer)

268376

CONTENTS

CONTENTS

CONTENTS

A NOTE ON REFERENCES

Parliamentary papers referred to only occasionally are given their titles as well as their serial numbers. Papers quoted frequently are referred to by their serial numbers only. The most important are the following:

H.C. 378 of 1914	Report (with Minutes of Evidence) of the Select Committee on the Procedure of the House of Commons.
H.C. 255 of 1920	Report from the Select Committee on Members' Expenses (with Minutes of Evidence).
H.C. 257 of 1920	Report from the Select Committee on the Procedure governing Bills which involve Charges (with Minutes of Evidence).
H.C. 158 of 1930	Report from the Select Committee on Private Bills.
H.C. 161 of 1931	Special Report from the Select Committee on Procedure on Public Business (with Minutes of Evidence).
H.C. 162 of 1936	Report of the Committee on Common Form Clauses in Private Bills.
H.C. 112 of 1937	Report from the Select Committee on Private Bill Procedure (Local Legislation Clauses) (with Minutes of Evidence).
H.C. 122 of 1944	Eleventh Report from the Select Committee on National Expenditure, Session 1943–4.
H.C. 9 of 1945–6	First Report from the Select Committee on Procedure (with Minutes of Evidence).
H.C. 58 of 1945–6	Second Report from the Select Committee on Procedure (with Minutes of Evidence).
H.C. 93 of 1945–6	Report from the Select Committee on Members' Expenses (with Minutes of Evidence).
H.C. 189 of 1945–6	Third Report from the Select Committee on Procedure (with Minutes of Evidence).
H.C. 310 of 1953	Report from the Select Committee on Delegated Legislation (with Minutes of Evidence).
H.C. 72 of 1954	Report from the Select Committee on Members' Expenses, etc. (with Minutes of Evidence).
Cmd. 4060	Report of the Committee on Ministers' Powers.

PARLIAMENTARY DEBATES

These are referred to by their official modes of reference.

E.g. Parl.Deb. 4 s.   The Parliamentary Debates (Authorised Edition), Fourth Series.

H.C.Deb. 5 s.   The Parliamentary Debates (Official Report), Fifth Series: House of Commons.

H.L.Deb. 5 s.   The Parliamentary Debates (Official Report), Fifth Series: House of Lords.

STANDING ORDERS

The Standing Orders are referred to as follows:

S.O.   Standing Orders of the House of Commons: Part I (Public Business).

S.O. (C.)   Standing Orders of the House of Commons: Part II (Private Business).

Lords' S.O.   The Standing Orders of the House of Lords relating to Public Business.

S.O. (L.)   Standing Orders of the House of Lords relative to the bringing in and proceeding on Private Bills and Bills for confirming Provisional Orders or Certificates and relative to the proceedings in relation to Special Orders and proceedings in relation to India and Burma Orders.

BOOKS

Books quoted frequently have 'short titles' and are as follows:

Cabinet Government   Jennings, *Cabinet Government* (2nd edition).

Durell   Durell, *Parliamentary Grants*.

Epitome   Epitome of the Reports from the Committees of Public Accounts, 1857 to 1937 (H.C. 154 of 1938).

May   Sir Erskine May, *Parliamentary Practice*. (References are to the 15th ed., except where otherwise expressly stated.)

Redlich   *The Procedure of the House of Commons*, 3 vols. (All references are to the English translation except where expressly stated.)

PREFACE

The first edition of this book, which was published in 1939, was to have been the second of three books surveying the British Constitution as it operated in practice. The first book, *Cabinet Government*, regarded the Constitution from the angle of the Government. It was published in 1936 and reprinted in 1937 and 1947; a second edition, much revised, was published in 1951. *Parliament* sought to analyse the parliamentary institutions of the United Kingdom as pieces of constitutional machinery. Notes for a new edition were prepared in 1949, but it was impossible to complete the revision until after my return to England in the summer of 1954. The ambition to write the third book, *Party Politics*, persists. It soon became apparent that a different technique was required. An analysis of the functioning of parties and the conduct of elections would not in itself be adequate. Each of the parties represents layers of tradition which influence current political emotions. Those traditions have developed continuously since the seventeenth century and there was no great change (as there was in respect of Cabinet Government) in the period of the first Reform Act. Nor is it as easy to deal with political emotions as it was to deal with constitutional machinery. For these reasons, and because of other preoccupations, *Party Politics* remains an ambition, though some tentative conclusions arising out of my study were published in *The British Constitution* (published 1941; third edition 1950).

The revision of *Parliament* after eighteen exciting years has presented many difficulties. The framework of the book remains unaltered. The latter part of Chapter II has been rewritten because of the material to be found in the election studies of Nuffield College, Oxford, and the work of Dr Ross and Mr R. T. McKenzie, and because of the increasingly unrepresentative character of the House of Commons through high taxation and low salaries. The problem of the accountability of the nationalised industries did not fit easily into the framework of the book and has therefore been dealt with in a new Chapter X. An additional section has been inserted into the chapter on 'Delegated Legislation'.

Elsewhere the changes have been numerous: of the 526 pages of the first edition only 138 required no alteration. Many of these changes are minor and incidental, but there has been much rewriting in Chapter I, the third section of Chapter III, the third and fourth sections of Chapter IV, the first section of Chapter V, the first section of Chapter VI, the fourth section of Chapter VIII, the second and third sections of Chapter IX, Chapter XII (formerly Chapter XI), and Chapter XV (formerly Chapter XIV). The example of a guillotine resolution in Appendix III has been removed, since the procedure is now better known. It has been replaced by an example of a 'Shadow Cabinet'.

The question whether to replace pre-war examples by post-war examples where there has been no change of practice has caused some difficulty. In the first edition the examples were taken mainly from the Hansards of 1935 to 1937, and they necessarily dealt with political controversies of which many younger readers will be ignorant and which older readers will remember but vaguely. On the other hand, more modern examples would produce the same conclusions, would require much research, and would 'date' as quickly. Generally speaking I have left in a reference where the point made was clear enough to those who had not an intimate knowledge of the political circumstances which produced the example. This is particularly obvious in Chapter VII and Appendix II, which were based mainly upon technical periodicals to which I no longer have access.

W. IVOR JENNINGS

TRINITY HALL
CAMBRIDGE
28 May 1956

CHAPTER I

AUTHORITY TRANSCENDENT AND ABSOLUTE

'Of the power and jurisdiction of the Parliament, for making of laws in proceeding by Bill,' said Sir Edward Coke,[1] 'it is so transcendent and absolute, as it cannot be confined either for persons or causes within any bounds. Of this Court it is truly said : *Si antiquitatem spectes, est vetustissima, si dignitatem, est honoratissima, si jurisdictionem, est capacissima.*' Blackstone[2] and Dicey[3] used language to the same effect. Such propositions were not accepted by the American colonies, who denied that Parliament could impose legislation on them; but though the American revolution broke up the first British Empire, the law was maintained. 'The King's Majesty,' said the Declaratory Act of 1766,[4] 'by and with the Advice and Consent of the Lords Spiritual and Temporal, and Commons of Great Britain, in Parliament assembled, had, hath, and of right ought to have, full Power and Authority to make Laws and Statutes of sufficient force and Validity to bind the Colonies and People of America, Subjects of the Crown of Great Britain, in all cases whatsoever.'

This statute remains in the books and is commonly understood to express the law not only for subjects of the Crown in America but for British subjects everywhere. The legislative authority of Parliament extends to all persons, to all places and to all events; but the only legal systems which it can amend are those which recognize its authority. The courts of the United States of America, or the Republic of Ireland, or India or Pakistan or Burma would not admit the argument that, because the Parliament of the United Kingdom had once exercised jurisdiction over their respective countries, it could at any time resume that jurisdiction. Similarly, the courts of the Union of South Africa would not recognise an Act of Parliament which purported to apply to

---

[1] 4 Co. Inst. 36.
[2] 1 Bl. Comm. 160, 161.
[3] *Law of the Constitution* (9th ed.), pp. 38–40.
[4] 6 Geo. III, c. 12, s. 1.

South Africa in breach of section 4 of the Statute of Westminster, 1931. In other words, the authority is transcendent and absolute only by English law, and that law can be changed by Act of Parliament. It is true that Lord Coke said that 'Acts against the power of the Parliament subsequent bind not';[1] but it is certain that, when once Parliament has withdrawn its claim to legislate for a territory, only those who remain within its jurisdiction are likely to admit a claim to withdraw the withdrawal. It is not even certain that the English or the Scottish courts would not recognise that section 4 of the Statute was a limitation on the power of Parliament, in spite of observations to the contrary in the Privy Council.

The power inherent in Parliament is a power recognised by law. It is merely a principle determining the action of judicial authorities. It does not determine whether Parliament could in practice enact anything, or would if it could, or could secure enforcement if it did. De Lolme's statement that 'Parliament can do everything but make a woman a man, and a man a woman' is, as perhaps Blackstone meant to suggest,[2] beside the point; Parliament is not legally subject to any physical limitation. Law deals in convenient general propositions which are not too remote from realities but which do not necessarily bear any very close relation to the facts of social and political life.

Indeed, we are talking in fictions or concepts even when we mention 'Parliament'. Parliament is not an institution. The ordinary enacting clause: 'Be it enacted by the Queen's most excellent Majesty, by and with the advice and consent of the Lords Spiritual and Temporal, and Commons, in this present Parliament assembled, and by the authority of the same'—is much nearer the truth. It indicates that 'Parliament' consists of two, if not three, distinct bodies.

> Aux murs de Westminster on voit paraître ensemble
> Trois pouvoirs étonnés du nœud qui les rassemble.[3]

As a matter of strict law this is not quite correct. Parliament consists not of the Queen, the House of Lords, and the House of Commons,

---

[1] 4 Co. Inst. 42. [2] 1 Bl. Comm. 161.
[3] Quoted by J. Barthélemy, *Le Travail Parlementaire*, p. 233.

but of the Queen in Parliament, the Queen sitting with the Lords Spiritual and Temporal, and with the Commons standing at the Bar, though in practice, which is authorised by law,[1] the Queen's assent is given in Parliament by Commissioners acting on her behalf. This is, however, a mere picturesque formality, not the whole process of enactment, but its formal termination. The effective decisions are taken by the Lords Spiritual and Temporal sitting separately as the House of Lords, and the Commons sitting separately as the House of Commons. To speak of these two Houses as parts of the same institution is to introduce an element of fiction. They have different functions and different characteristics. These differences are evident even when the Government has a majority in both Houses; they are even more obvious when the Government has to face a hostile majority in the House of Lords.[2] In popular language, which often expresses the substance more clearly than lawyers' language, 'Parliament' usually means the House of Commons; but when it is used to describe both Houses it refers not to two parts of the same institution but to two different institutions. The consent of both is required for legislation, except when the Parliament Acts otherwise provide; in no other sense are they one.

The fact that legislation has to pass both Houses does, however, emphasise one important point. For reasons hereinafter discussed,[3] it is technically easier for persons who are not members of the Government to secure the passage of Bills in the House of Lords than in the House of Commons. Yet all such Bills, in order to become law, have also to pass through the House of Commons. There it is that the technical difficulties arise, and it is there, too, that the main political issues, if there are any, have to be fought. The predominance of the lower House is as marked in legislation as it is in other spheres of activity.

In emphasising the 'transcendent and absolute' authority of Parliament we tend, moreover, to stress too strongly the legislative functions of both Houses. Legislation is not the sole or even the more important function of the House of Lords. That House is rather an assembly for

---

[1] 33 Hen. VIII, c. 21.   [2] See Chapter XII.
[3] See Chapter XII.

the debate of the less technical and, in the party sense, less 'political' issues of government. Because the fate of the Government does not depend on its votes and because of the preponderance of one party, the House of Lords can debate in a less obviously partisan manner the principles of foreign and imperial policy; and because it is not kept at work by the pressure of the whips and, often, gives perfunctory consideration to legislative proposals, matters of some general but mostly non-political importance can be discussed at leisure; and because the peers have no constituents to placate, no meetings to address, and, often, no speeches to make, they can devote more time to the less spectacular but often useful technical functions of legislative control.

The House of Commons cannot afford to be so leisurely. It is in that House that the essential business of legislation is carried out. Apart from the necessary financial proposals, certain Bills must be passed every year. If the Expiring Laws Continuance Bill is not passed the temporary laws scheduled to it will lapse. If the Public Works Loans Bill is not passed the functions of the Public Works Loan Commissioners—whose work is necessary to local government among other purposes—will come to an end. Temporary laws providing subsidies for industry and agriculture have to be renewed from time to time. The process of administration shows defects in the law which have to be remedied as parliamentary opportunities arise, and there are always 'departmental Bills' on the waiting list.[1] Above all, every party in the State has a declared policy of social amelioration or reconstruction. Proposals of a general kind are made in election manifestos and must be carried out if the party attains power. Groups of interests seek to show that measures are necessary for their own and the national interest.[2] Emergencies and new problems arise which can be met only by new legal prohibitions or new administrative powers.

Thus, the Government always has more proposals for legislation than the House can find time to debate. The Departments 'fight for time'

[1] 'There are Bills waiting, and which have been waiting for years and years, on the doorstep of the House of Commons, which cannot get through simply because there is no particular drive behind them.' Lord Eustace Percy, H.C. 161 of 1931, Q. 2090. See also H. Morrison, *Government and Parliament*, pp. 235–7.
[2] See Chapter VII.

4

before the Future Legislation Committee of the Cabinet at the beginning of the session and a programme is drawn up.[1] No matter what kind of Government is in power, there are always more items on the programme than can possibly be put forward. There are always departmental projects whose chance of realisation is so small that they are not even put in the programme. Always there are new problems arising which have to be met by immediate legislation even though the programme reserves no place for them. Finally, unless the pressure is so great that the House consents to Government business having precedence throughout the session, certain opportunities are given to private members to occupy the time of the House with their own proposals.[2]

Even so, the time of the House is by no means wholly occupied by legislation. Table I (p. 6) gives a detailed analysis, made by Sir Gilbert Campion, K.C.B., Clerk of the House of Commons, of the distribution of time according to function from 1906 to 1913 and from 1919 to 1938. It will be seen that the House spends only about one-half of its time on the discussion of legislation. It is true that legislation also results from some of the other functions. The ten per cent of the time allocated to the control of finance consists of the debates in Committee of Ways and Means on the Budget Resolutions, which precede the Finance Bill, and the proceedings on the Finance Bill itself: but though these discussions lead to the enactment of the annual Finance Act they are in pith and substance debates on the financial and economic policy of the Government. Similarly, the debates on Estimates, Supplementary Estimates and Consolidated Fund Bills lead to the enactment of the Appropriation Act and two or more Consolidated Fund Acts, but the debates on Estimates and Supplementary Estimates are in truth debates on various aspects of Government policy, selected by the Opposition; and any subject that does not require legislation may be discussed as a Consolidated Fund Bill. In short, though the House is technically discussing financial legislation it is in fact debating the policy and administrative efficiency of the Government.

[1] H. Morrison, *op. cit.* pp. 223–4, 234–7. The practice of drawing up a programme has to a large extent abolished the practice which used to be known as 'the massacre of the innocents' at the end of a session. Better control by the whips' office also is important, see *post*, pp. 85–7.

[2] See Chapter IV, § 1, and Chapter XI.

Indeed, much of the discussion on legislative proposals is not really of a legislative character. It is characteristic of the British parliamentary system that all important Bills, and most other Bills which actually pass, are produced by the Government. The powers of private members are rigidly limited.[1] It is the responsibility of the Government as much to initiate legislation as to conduct administration. The two are inextricably entwined, for the Cabinet recognises no essential difference between proposals involving legislation and those involving administrative action.[2]

TABLE I. *House of Commons. Distribution of Time according to Functions*[3]

Functions	1906–13 Days	%	1919–29 Days	%	1929–38 Days	%	General Average Days	%
I. Control of Finance Budget Resolution and Finance Bill	16·4	11·0	12·3	9·2	16·9	10·7	15·0	10·3
II. Control and Formulation of Policy	56·9	38·2	57·8	43·5	61·1	38·7	58·5	40·2
1. Address in Reply to King's Speech	6·7		5·2		5·8		5·8	
2. Estimates, Supplementary Estimates and Consolidated Fund Bills	30·5		34·6		31·2		32·3	
3. Adjournment Returns	3·4		6·4		7·7		5·9	
4. Substantive Returns	15·3		11·5		16·4		14·2	
5. East India Revenue Account	1·0		0·1		—		0·3	
III. Legislation	75·7	50·8	62·8	47·3	79·7	50·6	71·9	49·5
1. Public Bills	72·6		59·7		73·9		67·9	
2. Private Bills	3·1		2·2		2·1		2·4	
3. Delegated Legislation	—		0·9		3·7		1·6	
Length of Session	149		132·9		157·7		145·4	

Accordingly, the attitude of the House towards legislation is the same as its attitude towards administrative action. Proposals for legislation require positive approval; proposals for administration usually

[1] See Chapter IV, *post*, pp. 95–9, and Chapter XI.
[2] *Cabinet Government*, pp. 214–5.
[3] H.C. 189 of 1946, p. xxix. Percentages have been added. See also H. Morrison, *op. cit.* p. 337.

do not. The technique of parliamentary procedure is therefore different; but the purpose is the same. The supporters of the Government give general support or make gentle criticism. The Opposition criticises the Government for all that it has done and for all that it has refrained from doing. In substance Parliament controls legislation as it controls administration, by debating and ultimately approving the policy of the Government.

The element of control is indeed slight. The function of the Government is to govern; that of its supporters is to support it; and that of its opponents is to criticise it. In the last resort the House can compel the Government either to resign or to dissolve Parliament. The last resort is, however, far, far away if the Government possesses a party majority. The British Government is one of the strongest, if not the strongest, in the world. It normally has at its command a stable parliamentary majority whose support is based on loyalty to the personnel and acceptance of the principles of the party from which the Government is drawn, upon dislike of the alternative which would be drawn from the Opposition, and upon the big stick of dissolution which the Government can, if need be, wield. The choice for a private member on the Government side is between support for the Government, on the one hand, and, on the other hand, either a resignation or a dissolution at the choice of the Prime Minister. Either branch of the latter alternative is, normally, worse than the former alternative. Emphasis need not be placed on the 'big stick'; like all big sticks it is intended never to be used; its mere existence, however, comes to the aid of all the other psychological influences that induce a private member to remain loyal to the Government. Though in one sense it is true that the House controls the Government, in another and more practical sense the Government controls the House of Commons.[1]

The true function of the House is to question and debate the policy of the Government. In so doing it can bring home to the Government the unpopularity of a particular line of policy. Democratic Governments rest upon public opinion. A change in a small section of opinion, representing a few hundred thousand votes in the key constituencies, can bring in a new Government at the next election. No one who has

[1] See *Cabinet Government*, ch. XIV; and see Chapters IV, V and VIII of this book.

within a few years seen one of the strongest Governments of this century bow to criticism in the House and withdraw the Unemployment Assistance Regulations (1934), denounce the Hoare-Laval agreement (1934), withdraw the Coal Mines Bill (1936), withdraw the proposals for a National Defence Contribution (1937), and radically amend the Population Bill (1937), can doubt the influence of parliamentary debate upon Government proposals. It is reasonably certain, however, that not one of these policies would have been rejected if the Government had insisted. It is not the control of the Government by the House but the fact that its dislikes are often a representation of electoral dislikes that makes debate important.

The influence of the various factors in relation to each kind of business is discussed in subsequent chapters. Here it is necessary to emphasise that, when the Government has a majority in both Houses, the 'transcendent and absolute' authority of Parliament is the authority of the Government. It is not really transcendent and absolute. Behind the Government and behind the House of Commons stands public opinion. This vague and elusive phenomenon cannot be discussed here.[1] Though it is difficult to say what exactly it is, there can be no doubt of its existence. The fact that no Government could secure powers to kill all blue-eyed babies is not due to any legal limitations in the power of Parliament but to the fact that both the Government and the House of Commons derive their authority from the people.

Within the limits of physical possibility and the limits of public opinion, Parliament can decide anything. This does not imply, however, that any member of the House of Commons can make any motion at any time that he considers convenient to himself. The necessity of maintaining an order in the conduct of business and of dealing with the most pressing subjects has compelled strict adherence to a programme which is, for the most part, in the control of the Government.[2] The private member may ask questions; he may move the adjournment of the House (if the Speaker will let him and he has the support of forty members) for the discussion of a definite matter of urgent public importance; he may take part in debates on motions introduced by the

---

[1] See Chapter xv for some remarks.
[2] See Chapter IV, § 4, *post*, pp. 121 *et seq.*

Government or other members; he may ballot for the privilege of moving motions, introducing Bills, or moving amendments when the Speaker is about to be moved out of the Chair when the House first goes into Committee of Supply on the Naval, Army, Air and Civil Service Estimates respectively; and he may raise matters for discussion if there is any interval between the end of opposed business and the rising of the House.

This may seem a great deal; but expressed in time it is very little. Leaving aside the question hour, which occurs four times a week during the session, only about eight per cent of the time of the House is controlled by private members. Though the rules rarely distinguish between ministers and others, and though the existence of the 'Front Benches' is due to custom and not to the rules (Mr Cobden on one occasion occupied the seat of the leader of the Opposition, Sir Robert Peel, and refused to give it up), in practice parliamentary procedure is a conflict between Her Majesty's Government and Her Majesty's Opposition. It is, in other words, a conflict between Her Majesty's present Government and Her Majesty's alternative Government, with private members joining in. The practice of the House provides that, between one general election and another, Her Majesty's Government shall always defeat Her Majesty's Opposition.

Nevertheless, the Government recognises the right of the Opposition to criticise, and is therefore willing and indeed bound by convention to allow ample time for such criticism to be made effective. Table II, prepared by Sir Gilbert Campion, shows the distribution of time in the periods 1906 to 1913 and 1919–38, according to where the initiative fell. The periods during which the Budget and the Finance Bill were debated are placed as 'indeterminate' because, though the initiative rested with the Government, the Opposition had by convention wide opportunities for choosing the sections of financial policy that they wished to criticise. It will be seen that, even if the 'indeterminate' period be included, the Government took on the average less than two-thirds of the time of the House, but that the Government and the Opposition between them took some eighty-six per cent of the time. By using its majority the Government can, however, deprive private members of their time; and this was in fact done in 1928–9,

Table II. *House of Commons. Distribution of Time according to Parties*[1]

	1906–13 Days	%	1919–29 Days	%	1929–38 Days	%	General Average Days	%
I. Private Members' Time	18·0	12	19·3	14	21·8	14	19·9	14
1. Private Members' Bills	10·5		11·4		12·2		11·4	
2. Private Members' Motions	4·9		5·0		6·9		5·6	
3. Ditto in Government Time	1·6		0·9		0·2		0·9	
4. Adjournment Motions	1·0		2·0		2·5		2·0	
II. Opposition Time	40·7	27	46·5	35	46·5	29	44·6	31
1. Address in Reply to King's Speech	6·7		5·2		5·8		5·8	
2. Adjournment Motions	2·4		4·4		5·2		3·9	
3. Opposition Motions in Government Time	1·1		2·3		4·3		2·6	
4. Supply	30·5		34·6		31·2		32·3	
III. Indeterminate	20·5	14	14·6	11	19·0	12	17·7	12
1. Budget and Finance Bill	16·4		12·3		16·9		15·0	
2. Private Bills, etc.	4·1		2·3		2·1		2·7	
IV. Government Time	69·8	47	52·5	40	70·4	45	63·2	43
1. Public Bills	62·1		48·3		61·7		56·5	
2. Government Motions	7·7		3·3		5·0		5·1	
3. Delegated Legislation	—		0·9		3·7		1·6	
Days in Session	149		132·9		157·7		145·4	

1931–2, 1934–5, 1945–6, 1946–7 and 1947–8, in addition to the war years.[2]

The importance of the 'transcendent and absolute' legal authority of Parliament is that, there being no constitutional limitation on legislation, there is no subject which the House of Commons cannot, on an appropriate occasion, discuss. This does not mean that all matters can be discussed with equal facility. The time of the House is so much in the hands of the Government that it is not easy for a private member to find a suitable occasion to initiate a debate. The Opposition has greater freedom, partly because it has control over the subjects debated on the Estimates, and partly because of the convention that the Government will find time for a vote of censure. Even the Opposition, however,

[1] H.C. 189 of 1946, p. xxxi.
[2] H.C. 189 of 1946, p. 1 and Appendix.

can secure debate on legislative proposals only by the courtesy of any of its members who are successful in the ballot for private members' time. Moreover, most proposals for legislation involve public expenditure. But by a rule which in one form or another goes back to 1713 the House refuses to proceed upon any motion for a grant or charge upon the public revenue unless it is recommended by a minister.[1] In other words, if a Bill involves expenditure it can proceed beyond second reading only if a minister introduces a financial resolution.[2]

There are, too, other self-denying ordinances. The conduct of the sovereign, the heir to the throne, the Governors-General of the Dominions, the Speaker, the Chairman of Ways and Means, members of either House, judges of the superior courts, or county court judges, cannot be discussed save on a substantive motion.[3] In recent years the tendency has been to confer governmental functions upon bodies which are not under the control of responsible ministers and whose actions cannot, therefore, be raised in Parliament in criticism of ministers. Thus, the Speaker has refused to allow an urgency motion to adjourn to consider the failure of the Port of London Authority to relieve traffic congestion and decasualise labour.[4] Ministers have refused to answer questions relating to marketing boards,[5] the Central Electricity Board,[6] the Sugar Commission,[7] and the National Coal Board. They will often do their best to obtain information from outside bodies such as the British Broadcasting Corporation and those controlling nationalised industries. Where Estimates have to be presented or Regulations approved, as in the case of the National Assistance Board, debate may be raised, and there are other occasions on which discussion may sometimes take place, as on the address in answer to the Queen's Speech and on the adjournment. There are, therefore, opportunities even for private members. But there is nothing whatever to prevent the Government

---

[1] 'This House will receive no petition for any sum relating to public service or proceed upon any motion for a grant or charge upon the public revenue, whether payable out of the consolidated fund or out of money to be provided by parliament, unless recommended from the Crown.' S.O. 78, laid down in 1713 and amended in 1852 and 1866. For the precise consequences, see *post*, pp. 253–67.

[2] See S.O. 79.   [3] May, p. 430.

[4] 41 H.C.Deb. 5 s., 816 (1912).

[5] 299 H.C.Deb. 5 s., 808, 1198; 317 H.C.Deb. 5 s., 2074.

[6] 265 H.C.Deb. 5 s., 1449.   [7] 322 H.C.Deb. 5 s., 360.

from introducing legislation on any subject-matter whatever. However 'independent' an authority may be it is, in the last resort, subject to the control of the Government. For if the Government has a majority in both Houses it can always secure legislation.

For this reason the 'transcendent and absolute' power of Parliament places enormous power in the hands of the Government. It is not a power which can be seriously abused; for abuse would lead to retribution at the hands of the House of Commons or the electorate. Because it is a democratic system, the British parliamentary system can afford strong Governments and does not require constitutional limitations upon parliamentary authority. The House of Lords could obstruct the immediate realisation of the positive plans approved by the electorate, though in so doing it would prejudice its own future. A Government with only a minority in the House of Commons has to secure what legislation it can. Subject to these qualifications, the Government can do as it pleases, and public opinion is the ultimate control.

CHAPTER II

HONOURABLE MEMBERS

I. THE IMPORTANCE OF BEING ANCIENT

The first Lord Brentford—then known to the world as Mr Joynson-Hicks and to his opponent as Bill Hicks—first entered Parliament as a result of a spectacular by-election. His opponent was Mr Winston Churchill, who had vacated his seat on his appointment as President of the Board of Trade.[1] Being not only a minister but also a renegade from the Conservative Party, Mr Churchill was pursued by all the venom which British parties reserve for their 'traitors'. The election thus became front-page news; and 'Bill Hicks', the successful but unknown solicitor, found himself at the centre of the political world. His success at the election was followed by scenes cheering to an ambitious but hitherto obscure individual. Not only North-West Manchester but the whole Conservative world acclaimed his victory. He was received in the House of Commons with loud and sustained cheering; nearly every member of the Conservative Opposition was anxious to meet him; he was the hero of an Albert Hall meeting organised by the Primrose League; he was presented to the King by a viscount. 'Bill Hicks' had indeed come to Town. But one by-election does not make a minister. When Mr Joynson-Hicks addressed the House he found it not yet ready to follow the lead of the member for North-West Manchester. 'The speech was devoid of that modesty which the House expects of a new colleague in his first utterance', said his biographer.[2] The *Daily Express* was less outspoken but more explanatory: 'It was good of Mr Joynson-Hicks to come and speak to the House this week.'[3]

The new member had not realised that a new member is like a new boy at school. He was, as he himself said later, unfortunate in coming in in so spectacular a manner.[4] Ordinarily a new member finds himself

[1] The law has since been altered: see Re-election of Ministers Act, 1926, and Ministers of the Crown Act, 1937.
[2] H. A. Taylor, *Jix—Viscount Brentford*, p. 101.
[3] *Ibid.*   [4] *Ibid.*

in the company of others equally inexperienced in the ways of the House. However important he may have appeared in his own constituency, he is a nonentity in the House. Though he will be saluted by the policemen as soon as they find out that he is a member, there are no other signs of his importance. When a popular subject is being debated he even has to get up early to secure a seat. He has nothing more than a locker in a corridor in which to place his papers, and he must prepare his speeches, if any, in a crowded library.

Moreover, all the forms and ceremonies of the House are used to persuade him that he is only a raw recruit. There are some places where he may not walk; there are rules about his hat; there are many things that he may not say; he must turn and bow to the Speaker ere he leaves the Chamber. The ceremonies that accompany the opening of Parliament help to teach him the atmosphere. Just as the new boy learns the traditions of the school and the raw subaltern the traditions of the regiment, so the new member learns the traditions of the House. Unimportant though he is, he is impressed with the importance of the House. When Black Rod comes to summon members to attend the Lords Commissioners, the door is shut and bolted because Charles I once came with a body of armed men and, to murmurs of 'privilege!', walked up the gangway to ask for the surrender of six members. The Queen and the Queen's men come in only by permission of the House. When the Lords Commissioners desire the House to choose a Speaker they are recalling the days when the House met in private and placed its petitions before the King through a representative standing at the Bar of the House of Lords. When Mr Speaker-elect leads the House to announce his election to the Lords Commissioners the mace that goes before him—in the arms and not over the shoulder of the Sergeant-at-Arms because he is only Speaker-elect—is the successor of the 'bauble' that Cromwell ordered to be taken away. When Mr Speaker, having been confirmed in his office, demands 'all their ancient and undoubted rights and privileges, especially to freedom of speech in debate, to freedom from arrest, and to free access to Her Majesty whenever occasion shall require, and that the most favourable construction shall be put upon all their proceedings', he is making a demand that has been made for centuries.

It must not be thought that the ancient ceremonies, the picturesque uniforms, and the odd antique language, are without importance. The dictatorships have come to recognise the propaganda value of 'circuses'. In these respects the British governmental system takes no lessons; it gives them. All public ceremonies, from a court or a coronation or a jubilee to the changing of the guard, are calculated, often deliberately but sometimes unconsciously, to stimulate the national patriotism and to maintain national unity. The ceremonies of the House of Commons are less for the public eye than for members themselves, though the pageantry of the 'opening' of Parliament reminds the country once a year that Parliament flourishes in spite of new ideologies. Their internal influence is, however, substantial. Particularly important are those affecting the Speaker.[1] He is, usually, a very ordinary member elected to the Chair because he has taken no very prominent part in controversy. His very substantial powers in themselves give him a prestige; even so, everything is done to enhance his position. The high precedence that he enjoys, the full-bottomed wig, the salary of £5000 a year free of tax, the charging of that salary on the Consolidated Fund so as not to compel an annual vote, the ceremonies attendant upon his election, the rule that he alone must be addressed, the rule that when he stands every member must sit, even his right to drive to the Queen's levee down the centre of the Mall with an escort of Life Guards—all these add to his dignity and importance.

Nor are other apparently useless rules without their utilitarian aspect. To be compelled to refer to another member as 'the honourable member for the Bleak Division of Blankshire', or 'the honourable and gallant member for Thamesmouth', or 'the honourable and learned member for Ambleton' takes the sharp edge off parliamentary criticism. The same idea underlies the complicated rules relating to 'unparliamentary' language. 'The use of temperate and decorous language', the standing authority on parliamentary procedure used to say, 'is never more desirable than when a member is canvassing the opinions and conduct of his opponents in debate.'[2]

The psychological effects of these influences are very substantial.

[1] See further Chapter III, § 2, *post*, pp. 63–71.
[2] May (13th ed.), p. 325, cf. 15th ed. p. 431 and Redlich, III, p. 62.

15

There are other characteristics no less important. The seats on the floor of the House are sufficient to accommodate only about one-half of the members. The side galleries are, technically, part of the House, and a member may speak from a seat there. In fact, however, such an event rarely happens. Nor, in any case, is the rule important. The House is rarely 'packed' except for a special occasion or a special speech, such as the introduction of the Budget. As soon as ordinary members begin to speak, the legions troop out to more attractive quarters, and the whips' difficulty is not to find seats but to find people to occupy them. The result, nevertheless, is that the members speak not in a vast hall but in a comparatively small Chamber. Flights of oratory were not unknown in the old Chamber, before the Palace was burned in 1834, and when the House was no bigger than it is to-day. Burke, Fox, Pitt, Sheridan and Canning gave magniloquent addresses which are no longer suited to the modern temperament.[1] Sir Robert Peel, said Disraeli,

gradually introduced a new style into the House of Commons, which was suited to the age in which he chiefly flourished, and to the novel elements of the assembly which he had to guide. He had to deal with greater details than his predecessors, and he had in many instances to address those who were deficient in previous knowledge. Something of the lecture, therefore, entered into his displays. This style may be called the didactic.[2]

Young Disraeli had to learn the lesson. His maiden speech was modelled on the oratory of the Golden Age. Some of the ironical laughter was due to Disraeli's change of party. O'Connell had supported Disraeli the Radical at High Wycombe in 1832. Three years later Disraeli attacked the Melbourne Government for having clasped 'the bloody hand of O'Connell'. His maiden speech in 1837 was an attack on O'Connell, and O'Connell led the 'hisses, groans, hoots, catcalls, drumming with the feet, loud conversation, and imitation of animals' with which the speech was interrupted.[3] Nevertheless, a reading of the speech in cold print suggests that for an alien-looking and strangely dressed renegade to use such colourful language in his first speech,

---

[1] Cf. Redlich, III, p. 67.   [2] *Life of George Bentinck*, p. 228.
[3] Monypenny and Buckle, *Life of Disraeli*, I, pp. 406–8; MacDonagh, *Parliament*, pp. 216–19.

especially in an attack upon the Irish, was to ask for trouble. 'I sit down now, but the time will come when you will hear me', he concluded; certainly the time did come; but though Disraeli's method of speaking could never be described as common or pedestrian, he learned to suit his mannerisms to his audience.

Macaulay may be said to have been the last of the orators, and he described it as 'the most peculiar audience in the world'. 'A place where Walpole succeeded and Addison failed; where Dundas succeeded and Burke failed; where Peel now succeeds and where Mackintosh failed; where Erskine and Scarlett were dinner-bells; where Lawrence and Jekyll, the two wittiest men, or nearly so, of this time, were thought bores, is surely a very strange place.'[1] The speeches which succeed are quietly spoken, tinged with humour, straightforward in argument. The extravagances of the political platform fall flat; even the methods of the law courts, strangely quiet and unemotional though they are when contrasted with those adopted in many other countries, are not sufficiently conversational. The House is a small and compact body. Its members are experienced in demagogy, and are impatient of it in their own proceedings. The speaker who 'catches the ear' of the House must speak well, but he must speak intelligently. Pathos is apt to turn to bathos and emotion to apathy. For some part of this insistence on quiet, unemotional and business-like speaking the smallness of the House is responsible.

Another reason is that there is no tribune. The member rises in his place with his notes in his hand. The minister or the member of the Front Opposition Bench can, it is true, lean on the box on the table and emphasise his points with his fist. But the set oration from on high is impossible. The speaker's friends are around him; his opponents are facing him. Moreover, he addresses the Speaker or Chairman and not the House. Those with soap-box experience know the difference. So when the leader of the Opposition castigates the Prime Minister he leans conversationally across the table, he speaks sufficiently loudly to be heard in the press gallery, he glances along the benches opposite to see that his points are going home, he looks around him to make sure that he is being followed on his own side, but he addresses the Speaker.

[1] MacDonagh, *op. cit.* pp. 213–14, quoting Macaulay.

'Sir,' he says, 'the right honourable gentleman says one thing, but I say the opposite.'

These various factors help to explain the peculiarities of the House of Commons. The 'atmosphere' is the product of a long and chequered history. It is impossible to convey an adequate idea of it by cold analysis. Perhaps a more impressionistic picture may be more successful.[1]

I must ask you to imagine a dull and rather small assembly hall, surrounded by galleries. Brought somewhat forward at one end stands a cheap-looking kind of throne. On it sits an impressive figure, wearing a full-bottomed wig, black gown, and court dress—velvet breeches, silk stockings, and shoes with silver buckles. In front of the throne is a table, at which sit three clerks, also wearing wigs and gowns. Conspicuous on the table is a large silver mace. At the two sides of the table are boxes and the rest of the space is filled with books. Stretching lengthwise down the hall, away from the figure on the throne, are benches. Men, and a few women, are sitting in all sorts of attitudes. The benches are so packed that there is not room for everybody. One of the members is standing in his place, leaning on the box on the table, speaking rather conversationally, occasionally referring to the papers in front of him, sometimes emphasising his points by lightly striking the box. Occasionally there is an interjection from the benches facing him. Probably it is a joke, for those in the neighbourhood laugh. Occasionally a cheer arises from the benches behind the person speaking. The House of Commons is in session; the Speaker, who does not speak, is in charge of the House; the Prime Minister is making an important speech; the House is unusually full.

Let me emphasise that the benches stretch straight down the room, away from the Speaker. The House is, therefore, divided into two parts, separated by a gangway. The members do not form a semicircle, each facing the Speaker, but two rectangles, the members in each of which face the members of the other. There is, therefore, no gradation from right to left; there is only a right and a left. On the right is the Government and its supporters; on the left is the Opposition. He who does not support the Government opposes it. A member who changes his party is said to 'cross the floor'. Actually, some supporters of the Government will be on the left. For the Government has a majority. If the House is full, all its supporters may not be able to find seats on their own side. They will, therefore, sit quite

---

[1] From a lecture prepared by the present writer for delivery at the International Summer University at Santander in 1936. Owing to the outbreak of rebellion in Spain it was never delivered. The personal pronoun appropriate to a lecture has been deliberately retained.

comfortably (in a metaphorical sense—for the House is not really comfortable) among the Opposition.

On the right, nearest the table, is the Treasury or 'Front' Bench. On it sit the members of the Cabinet. On the other side of the table is the 'Opposition Front Bench'. Its occupants are the leaders of the Opposition. They are 'His Majesty's Opposition'. For His Majesty needs not only a Government but also an Opposition. It is the duty of His Majesty's Government to govern and of His Majesty's Opposition to oppose. His Majesty's Opposition is, in fact, His Majesty's alternative Government. If at the next election they secure a little extra support, they will change places with the occupants of the Treasury Bench.

At the moment which we are imagining, the Prime Minister stands looking down on the leaders of the Opposition, explaining to them the Government's policy, meeting in advance the criticisms which they are formulating against him. Yet he is not addressing them directly. He is addressing the Speaker. 'But, Sir,' he is perhaps saying, 'the right honourable gentleman the member for Limehouse will say one thing, and the honourable and learned member for East Bristol will say another. I would prefer to use the language of my friend the honourable and gallant member for . . . .' For all members are 'honourable' if they are not 'right honourable'; all lawyers are 'learned'; all retired officers are 'gallant'; all lords and ladies are 'noble'; all supporters of the speaker are 'friends'; and every member is referred to by his office or his constituency.

When the Prime Minister sits down, the person facing him will rise. The Speaker will call 'Mr Attlee'; and the right honourable gentleman the member for Limehouse will pour out the criticisms that he has patiently been accumulating. When he in turn sits down, the Speaker will call on a member from the Government's 'back benches'. Neither Prime Minister nor back-bencher will come to a rostrum, or even approach the table. He will just stand in his place. When the back-bencher sits down the Speaker will call on one of the Liberals who have risen. So the debate will ebb and flow across the floor of the House.

Let me emphasise, too, the smallness of the House. Though perhaps 500 members will be present, they will be so close to each other that little more than a conversational tone is required, though a member must speak up if he desires to be heard by the reporters in the gallery. Such proximity might be thought to give rise to a contagion of excitement. But you must remember that here are phlegmatic Englishmen and dour Scots. The 'Celtic fringe' is too small to change the atmosphere, especially since the Irish went to enliven their own assembly in Dublin. Scenes are rare. There is no banging of desks; there are no desks to bang; and they would not be banged if there were. The moments of excitement are so rare that they go down in the political annals. Once a book was thrown at a minister; once a Prime Minister was shouted down; once a minister was called 'Judas' and a free fight developed; once a member walked off with the mace. The task of the Speaker is easy. A calm word, a humorous comment, usually restores order. He has no bell, no hammer. The Speaker rises, the members sit, and the House is quiet. An admonition cools tempers. If some member disregards the Speaker's authority, he is 'named' by the Speaker. The leader of the House at once proposes that 'the member be suspended from the service of the House'. The motion is put to the vote; it is carried, and the member leaves the House. Even this power is rarely exercised; and the suspension of the House for disorder is even less frequent. The truth is that the House is rarely exciting; usually it is deadly dull.

It must not be forgotten, too, that the House is not merely a debating assembly. It has a bar, a smoke-room, a dining-room, and a library. It has been called the 'best club in Europe'. It is not that; for one thing it contains too many bores—the clubman's most deadly enemy. It is, nevertheless, a kind of fellowship. It has traditions of its own, developed through the centuries. To be described as 'a good House of Commons man' is to be paid the highest tribute. Members of all parties talk to each other, share jokes in common, listen to each other's grumbles. It is a common sight to see one of the irreconcilables of the left laughing with the most fire-eating of the jingoes.[1]

[1] Let a 'wild Clydesider' speak for himself: 'I had often been warned by my Socialist friends against the "air" of the House of Commons, its friendliness, its tolerance, and its freedom from rancour. I found that the warning was necessary. One day after I had had a row in the House, old T. P. O'Connor, the "Father of the House", came up to me and said: "Don't do that sort of thing! I've been through it. It does no good. You might as well stick pins in a crocodile. These people have a code. They will listen to argument, but abuse does not interest them." Very early in my career I found how true that was. The "conventions" of the Commons are strong to bind. At first I thought they were nothing more than surface politeness. They are not. They are the foundation of the parliamentary system. I have offended against these conventions very often. I am rough in speech and have never learnt the art of choosing my words or modifying my ideas. Sometimes I have been rebuked. I cared little for that. But rebuke is for the floor of the House. Outside in the Lobby it is not rebuke that rebukes. There is a courtesy and intimacy among members which I learnt to understand after many strange incidents.' David Kirkwood, *My Life of Revolt*, pp. 202–3. And, after giving examples: 'This atmosphere of good-nature among members does not in any way affect their attitude in the House itself. There, a man is expected to argue his point with strength and conviction. If he is sincere, he will be heard. If he is insincere or artificial, there will be such a coming and going, such a rustle of papers, and so many points of order that he can make no headway. The House of Commons is the most tolerant place in the world; but it will not tolerate insincerity.' *Ibid.* pp. 206–7.

This is, so to speak, the social atmosphere: but it is carried into the House itself. When a new member makes his first speech, he is listened to in silence. The next speaker—almost always from the opposite side of the House—will begin with a graceful tribute. He will congratulate the honourable member on the excellence of his matter and the grace of his manner; he will express the hope that the honourable member will contribute frequently to their discussions. When a new minister makes his first speech in office, an Opposition member will congratulate the right honourable gentleman on the high place to which he has been called. When the Opposition elects a new leader, the Prime Minister will take the first opportunity of welcoming his opponent.

I am trying to convey to you an impression of the normal working of this democratic system. It is a most difficult task. Let me give you some quotations. I will first take a debate on 24 February 1936, when the Labour Party criticised the Government for its inaction in respect of oil sanctions against Italy. Let me say first that this debate was arranged between the Government and the Opposition. The Opposition wished to criticise the Government and said, in effect, 'We want to attack you about oil sanctions next week.' The Government, in effect, said: 'Certainly; next Monday will suit us. Will it suit you?' The Opposition said that it would. So, on the Monday, the Government moved that the House be adjourned in order that, speaking to the motion, Mr Lees-Smith from the Opposition Front Bench might attack the Government's 'humiliating and vacillating policy'. He was heard almost in silence. The Foreign Secretary replied. He began by thanking 'the House and the Opposition for the arrangement by which they had made it possible to discuss this afternoon our foreign problems in their broader aspects'. He was interrupted once only. This was Mr Eden's first speech as Foreign Secretary. Accordingly, when he was followed by the leader of the Liberal party, that gentleman began: 'It is my privilege to be able to extend to the right honourable gentleman an expression of our gratitude and admiration for his clear and masterly survey of the whole field of foreign affairs in the compass of a comparatively short speech.' So the debate proceeded.

Nor is this interchange limited to the leaders. On 19 February 1936, a motion was moved on the training of unemployed juveniles. A recently elected Labour member delivered a 'maiden' speech. Viscountess Astor, a Conservative, followed him, and congratulated him on his 'moving' speech. 'When one hears what his experience was, one cannot blame him for being bitter. I myself feel that I should be desperately bitter if I had started work at eight years of age, and, much as I regret the bitterness, I do understand it.' She was followed by Mr Maxton, of the Independent Labour party, who joked with her about her age. 'I said to myself,' he added, 'the kind of education I want for the people of this country is an education which brings all the women of the same age...to the same stage in life with the same vitality, vigour and general health that the Noble Lady evidently enjoys.'

I have chosen my examples at random. I took one of the volumes of *Parliamentary Debates* for 1936 and glanced through it. I might have chosen any other volume and arrived at the same result. I do not want you to think, however, that political opposition is a sham or that the parties are not fundamentally opposed. On certain subjects, under certain conditions, there may be a large measure of agreement. But in most matters of ultimate policy there is little point of contact. The opposition between capitalism and socialism, between imperialism and pacifism, lies deep. Vigorous arguments can be used, hard words bandied across the gangway, fierce attacks be made and fiercely repelled. Yet the courtesies of debate are maintained. The Government governs and the Opposition opposes; yet both can laugh at a good joke and applaud a good speech. At the end of the debate men may vote in different lobbies but go home in the same taxi. In so doing, they do not abate one iota of their political opposition.

2. MEMBERS AND THEIR PARTIES

The fundamental physical characteristic of the House of Commons, the division into two parts separated by a gangway, has already been mentioned. It is fundamental because its maintenance indicates that the British parliamentary system assumes the existence of two parties. On the right of the Speaker sits Her Majesty's Government and its supporters; on the left sits Her Majesty's Opposition. Some members of the Government must be in the House of Lords. The conduct of Government business there must be in the hands of ministers; some peers are worthy of office by reason of merit and experience; some persons cannot accept the obligations of office and at the same time manage constituencies and therefore have to be made peers. All other ministers must by convention be members of the House of Commons, though exceptions are sometimes allowed in wartime.

This is in itself a factor of great importance. It lies at the root of Cabinet Government as the British Constitution understands it. It is the essential characteristic of the British parliamentary system—though that is to say the same thing in a different way. The ministers and officers of the Royal Household in the House of Commons number some sixty.[1] Each minister has an unpaid parliamentary private secretary, bringing the total number of persons with an official or quasi-official position up to more than one hundred. Where the parties are fairly evenly divided it follows that the Government secures the approval of its proposals only because its members vote for themselves.[2] In the Parliament of 1924 the Labour Prime Minister had only 191 supporters. Of these, fourteen were in the Cabinet and thirty-one were junior ministers. In other words the ministers and their parliamentary private secretaries comprised more than one-third of the regular supporters of the Government. The situation of a minority Government such as that of 1924 must necessarily be peculiar; but it must always be remembered that when 'control' by the House of Commons is spoken of, the House for this purpose includes the ministers. The Government not only persuades its supporters to vote for it; it also votes for itself.[3]

Facing the Government sits the Opposition. Fortunately, in spite of coalitions there has always been an Opposition, or at least since 1832. The nearest approach to a unanimous House was between 1914 and 1916, when the Conservative party for patriotic reasons ceased to oppose and even the irreconcilable Irish postponed their criticism until the end of the War, and from 1940 to 1945, when only a handful of left-wing members opposed Mr Churchill's Government. From 1916 to 1918, too, the Liberals who followed Mr Asquith could hardly be said to have been a regular Opposition. A national war provides an exception to all rules and practices of government, for the eternal conflict over political ends is for the time being substantially stilled by the effort to attain one immediate purpose, the defeat of the enemy, and

[1] In the Eden Government of 1955, fourteen of the eighteen members of the Cabinet were members of the House of Commons; also in that House were fifteen ministers not in the Cabinet, thirty junior ministers, whips and Household officers. Thus there were sixty-two 'official' members of that House, apart from parliamentary private secretaries. The corresponding number in 1938 was forty-two.

[2] Cf. Mr Baldwin in H.C. 161 of 1931, Q. 239; and see *Report from the Select Committee on Offices and Places of Profit under the Crown*, H.C. 120 of 1941.

[3] In 1941 a Select Committee recommended that not more than sixty holders of ministerial offices should sit and vote in the House of Commons; but, as will be seen from the previous footnote, this recommendation has not been acted upon. It was also recommended that a Government Department should have only one parliamentary private secretary, and this has since been done.

public debate is deprecated because it gives that enemy an impression of internal conflict. With this exception the House of Commons has been divided into two, the Government and the Opposition. Whig and Tory, Liberal and Conservative, Conservative and Labour—these have been and are the current coin of ordinary political discussion.

Yet it has never been the fact that the serried ranks of the party in power have been faced only by the serried ranks of the party in opposition. We are too apt to think of the House of Commons as being and as having always been a conflict between the supporters of Mr Gladstone and Mr Disraeli, their predecessors and successors. Parliamentary debate is not a perpetual Trojan war, with Priam inside the walls and Menelaus outside and with the sweets of office as the modern Helen. Though it may be a private fight it is, as the lamented Irish gladiators might have said, one in which anyone may join. Mr Gladstone himself, for much of his political career, was a Peelite or Liberal Conservative. But for the perverseness of the electors of Wycombe Mr Disraeli might have begun his parliamentary career as a Radical. There have always been third parties, sometimes between the Government and the Opposition and sometimes outside them. Radicals, Peelites, Liberal Unionists, Irish Nationalists, Labour members, Liberals, Independent Labour members, Liberal Nationals, National Labour members, Common Wealth, Scottish Nationalists, Communists and so on, have marred the symmetry of the parliamentary battle and attacked indiscriminately the parties to the Westminster duel.[1]

The rules of the House do not recognise parties as such. Indeed, they rarely recognise ministers as such. All proposals creating a financial charge must be made on behalf of the Crown, and must therefore be made by a minister. On certain days of the week Government business has precedence over other orders of the day. Subject to these

---

[1] Names can, however, mislead. According to *The Times Guide to the House of Commons, 1955*, the Government majority in 1955 was made up of Conservatives, Ulster Unionists, Conservative and National Liberals, National Liberals and Conservatives, Conservative and Liberals, Liberal and Conservatives, and National Liberals. Except the first two, these names were all devices for securing to the Conservative party as much as possible of the Liberal vote which followed Sir John (afterwards Viscount) Simon in the National Government of 1931, and to capture as much as possible of the Liberal vote which followed Sir Herbert (now Viscount) Samuel out of that Government in 1932.

and a few minor qualifications, all members are theoretically equal. In practice, however, parliamentary procedure is dominated by the party spirit. In the first place, the minor qualifications are important. In substance, private members have very little opportunity either to initiate legislation or to open discussions on administrative questions. Nine-tenths of the business of the House is Government business, initiated by ministers, or by the Opposition leaders by agreement with the Government whips. In the second place, much of the so-called private members' business is in fact suggested by the party whips. In the third place, even on private members' business the Government usually expresses an opinion, and the Government whips are sometimes put on. 'Free votes' for Government business are very rare; for private members' business they are not essential. Practically every discussion in the House terminates in a division where the whips act as tellers and the supporters of the Government are in one lobby and the Opposition in the other. Though the rules of the House do not contemplate the two-party system, practical politics consist of conflicts between Government and Opposition with minor parties and independent members intervening.

3. MEMBERS AND THEIR CONSTITUENCIES

It may seem strange to consider members as party politicians before considering them as elected representatives. The reason is, however, clear. Nearly all members are elected because they are party politicians. The extension of the franchise has not only wiped out the 'pocket boroughs' owned by private persons before 1832; it has also diminished almost to nothing the importance of 'influence'. Even at the General Election of 1880 'Marlborough was traditionally Liberal, and was little more than a pocket borough of the Bruce family'.[1] In 1865 Mr G. O. Trevelyan bought for £61,000 the Cherton estate, whose farmers and tenants always voted for the owner. Mr Trevelyan was thus elected for the borough of Tynemouth and then sold the estate.[2] That system has now practically disappeared. The influence of a great landowner, such as the Earl of Derby or the Marquis of Salisbury, may secure

[1] Sir Charles Petrie, *Walter Long and his Times*, p. 28.
[2] *Life of Sir George Trevelyan*, pp. 71–2.

nomination by the local Conservative association and so enable the person nominated to acquire a safe seat; but the seat is safe because the great majority of the electors normally vote Conservative, and not because of the influence of the landowner. Similarly, the safe miners' seats are in substance in the nomination of the National Union of Mine-workers, but only because the divisional Labour party accepts the nominee of the Union and the great majority of the electors can be trusted to vote Labour.

A general election is in fact an election of a Prime Minister. Its result depends upon the floating vote that is not firm for either party. In 1955, eighty-eight per cent of the candidates supported either the Government or the Labour party; ninety-six per cent of the votes were cast either for the Government or for the Labour party, and ninety-nine per cent of the members returned to Parliament either supported the Government or belonged to the Labour party. In general, the electors vote not for a candidate but for a party. A bad candidate may lose a few hundred votes and a good candidate may gain a few hundred. Except in a comparatively few marginal constituencies, a few hundred votes either way make no difference. There are many seats which simply cannot be lost by a candidate no matter how incompetent he may be. Most members of Parliament are chosen not by the electors but by the parties; the elector's own choice becomes important only in those marginal constituencies where the normal party support is fairly evenly balanced and in those constituencies where the intervention of a third candidate destroys the simplicity of the two-party conflict.

The elected member must, however, maintain his majority. Nothing that he can do can prevent a 'landslide' caused by the incompetence of his own party leaders, changes in economic circumstances, or waves of emotion. No amount of nursing in a constituency could have prevented the average Conservative from being defeated in 1905 or 1945. The 'Wee Frees' who had not the coupon ticket in 1918 did not fail to secure return merely because they had neglected to pay enough attention to the interests of their constituents. The two hundred Labour members who were defeated in 1931 were probably among the most careful of nurses.

Nevertheless, the average member never knows when a few hundred votes may not become important. The margin moves according to waves of public opinion; some of the safest seats in 1900 became unsafe in 1905, and constituencies which gave huge left majorities in 1929 moved suddenly to the right in 1931, while in 1945 the 'swing' went much further left than in 1929. For this reason, apart from others, the member must maintain contact with his constituency. It expects to be visited regularly. Even before 1924 many members were compelled to visit their constituencies nearly every week. Since the institution of the free railway pass in 1924 local party organisations have considered themselves even more entitled to demand the presence of their representatives. It is most difficult to keep a House on a Friday.[1] Nor is visiting the member's only duty. Evidence given before the Select Committee of 1920 suggested that the average member had to reply to at least fifty letters a week from his constituents.[2] Evidence given before the Select Committee of 1946 showed that in this respect the members' obligations had increased. In a single week in December 1945 it was estimated that 50,000 letters had been addressed to members[3]—an average of 80 if allowance be made for university members. Members thought that they spent from £25 to £250 per annum on postage, the average being £100 per annum.[4] A member who had to write only seventy letters a week was thought to have 'trouble-free constituents'.[5] Most letters require not merely answers but also action. The member must take up with the appropriate minister the complaint which is addressed to him. Will the Minister of Pensions explain why John Smith's military pension has been reduced? Will the Minister of National Insurance explain why Richard Robinson has received no insurance benefit? Will the Minister of Housing and Local Government see that Mrs Parke's excellent tenement house is not condemned under a slum-clearance order? Will the Home Secretary reduce the sentence passed on James Doe by the Blankshire magistrates? If no satisfactory answer is forthcoming from the Department a question must be asked in the House. If the member thinks that some flagrant injustice is being perpetrated he must open a debate on the adjournment.

---

[1] Cf. Mr Thomas Kennedy (Chief Whip), H.C. 161 of 1931, Q. 807.
[2] Report from the Select Committee on Members' Expenses (H.C. 255 of 1920), p. 19.
[3] H.C. 93 of 1946, Q. 120.　　　　[4] *Ibid.* p. 113.　　　　[5] *Ibid.* Qs. 416, 417.

There are, too, petitions to be presented, in spite of the fact that under the modern procedure the right of petitioning is of no use whatever. Matters of more general interest must be raised. Lancashire members must pay special attention to the plight of the cotton industry; members for rural constituencies must be interested in subsidies for farm products; fish are always either too scarce or too cheap for the members for fishing towns and the Government must be urged to do something about it; Coventry wants steel to be cheap and the steel-producing areas want steelworkers to have high wages; Scotland and Wales always want more from the United Kingdom; and every member has a special interest in better houses at cheaper rents.

All these and many other things the member has to do because he is a representative and because he must take care of those few hundred votes. Indeed, it is not merely a question of a few hundred votes. The tenure of the safest seat depends not on the member's capacity or qualifications but on the goodwill of his divisional party or association. He must be satisfactory to that body not only in the political but also in the personal sense. 'A good member' is not only in accord with the political views of the active party members; he is, also, ready and eager to satisfy their personal needs and ambitions. A Conservative member, for instance, must urge the claims of the most eminent of his constituents to honours. Birmingham used to be the City of Knights not only because of the eminence of its city leaders, but because at least one Chamberlain had influence with Conservative Governments for fifty years. Labour members, on the other hand, must secure the goodwill of the local trades council and the trade unions represented therein; for the local branches of trade unions are affiliated to the divisional Labour party and provide much of the revenue of the election fund.

Even so, it must not be thought that the member is no more than a representative of the local association or divisional party. He represents the constituency. He asks no questions as to the politics of those who enlist his support for the making of complaints and the redress of grievances. He is not expected to vote against his party except in an extreme case; but he is expected to urge the Government, by private representation, by debate, or by moving amendments, to forward the interests of his constituents. On those rare occasions when a free vote—

free from whips' influence, that is—is permitted, he has to balance his own views against those of his influential constituents. In the Prayer Book debates of 1928 and in the debates on the Marriage Bill in 1937, for instance, some members voted according to their own and some according to their constituents' consciences. No elector of Northampton would have expected Charles Bradlaugh to be a pillar of support for the Church of England; but a member who has no very strong views about the permanence of religious marriages may be expected to vote against extending the grounds for divorce if he has a large number of constituents who join in communion with the Church of Rome.[1]

The influence of constituents is, however, comparatively small. When 'log-rolling', 'distributing the pork barrel', and other problems of a like nature which are so evident in some foreign Constitutions are studied in relation to the British Parliament, it has always to be remembered that no proposal passes the House of Commons without the consent of a Government in which the Chancellor of the Exchequer plays a prominent part. No Government omits electoral conditions from its calculations; no Government fails to pay attention to suggestions from the whips that certain proposals would 'do their men good in their constituencies'. But one man's meat is another man's poison; or, to be more exact, one man's income is another man's expenditure. What the Government spends through one Department it must collect through the Exchequer. The electoral conditions which the Government keeps in mind are those of a very substantial part of the country. It is to be expected that a Conservative Government will look with more favour on agricultural districts than on mining areas, and that a Labour Government will pay more attention to industry than to seaside resorts. Even so, the constituencies which both have to gain or maintain are the marginal, wavering constituencies. No Conservative Government can make much impression by largess on industrial South Wales; no Labour Government can hope to win Bournemouth or Cheltenham. Electoral considerations may cause Birmingham to be happy under any Government; but the average private member finds that the Treasury has a heart of stone.

[1] Cf. Mr A. P. Herbert's attempts to persuade members to support his Marriage Bill: *The Ayes Have It*, p. 67.

4. MEMBERS AND THEIR INTERESTS

Mr Labouchere, the prize parliamentary cynic, was once asked why men enter Parliament. He replied:

'Some of them enter Parliament because they have been local Bulls of Bashan, and consider that in the localities where they have roared and pawed the ground, they will be even more important than heretofore; some because they want to be peers, baronets and knights; some because they have a fad to air; some because they want to have a try at climbing the greasy pole of office; some because they have heard that the House of Commons is the best club in London; some because they delude themselves that they are orators; some for want of anything better to do; some because they want to make a bit out of company promoting; and some because they have a vague notion that they are going to benefit their country by their devotion to legislative business.'[1]

The reference to company promoting betrays an age that is long since past. Membership of Parliament is too serious a business to be merely an asset on a prospectus. It is one of the professions to which no forty-hour-week rule applies. Nor is it now on the direct road to wealth. It may lead to office or honour, but it does not lead to riches. Indeed, there are more rapid ways to the House of Lords than that provided by the House of Commons. Political ambition in a democratic Constitution is a virtue. The less reputable corners of 'the City' provide the adventurer with greater opportunities and less work. Even respectability can be bought, and wealth opens more entrances to Society than membership of the House. Accordingly, whatever may have been the position in the great Gladstonian era, the great majority if not all of the members of the House are honest hard-working legislators.

It does not follow that no member has an axe to grind. It is, however, an axe required for purposes different from those which 'Labby' had in mind. A landowner in the golden age of the eighteenth century could increase his rent roll by securing the passage of an Act authorising him to inclose for quite inadequate compensation the lands of the neighbouring yeomen of England. The modern landowner can do nothing of the kind. What he can do is to urge upon the Government that, agriculture being the backbone of England and being moreover

[1] Thorold, *Life of Henry Labouchere*, p. 68.

an industry necessary for carrying on the next war, it is essential that the Government should by special legislation granting subsidies, obvious or concealed, strengthen the backbone and rehabilitate the industry. It is, in his view, necessary to the national welfare that more beef, milk, sugar-beet, potatoes, hops, wheat, barley and, indeed, everything else, should be produced and sold at higher prices.

It would be wrong to suggest that he is anxious to line his own pockets. He honestly believes that his proposals are in the national interest. His view of the national interest is, however, necessarily partial. The national interest and his own are inextricably mixed. Neither he nor anyone else can separate his public and his private motives. A lawyer may argue that property rights ought not to be interfered with except by judicial decisions without being wholly conscious that he wants to provide more fees for lawyers. A university teacher may favour increased university grants without considering too precisely whether the result might be to give him academic promotion and an increased salary.

The claims and desires of ordinary members have only an indirect impact on the Government. An opinion expressed by the Council of the Trades Union Congress, for instance, will have more influence with a Labour Government than the collective opinions of trade union representatives in Parliament. Similarly, the opinion of the National Farmers' Union or the constituent members of the Federation of British Industries will carry more weight than those of the agricultural and industrial members of the House. Nevertheless, many interests desire to secure representation in the House in order that their views may be made clear publicly. In any event it is important to consider the interests which are dominant in the House itself; for the character of those interests determines very largely the character of debate; and the character of debate determines to some extent the attitude of the Government.[1]

The interests of members depend partly on the bodies by whom they are nominated for election, partly on the sources from which they derive

---

[1] For the influence of debate on the Government, see Chapter I, *ante*, pp. 7–8, and Chapter V, *post*, pp. 132–47. For the influence of outside interests, see Chapter VII, *post*, pp. 201–23 and 227–34.

their income, partly on their previous experience, and partly on the special studies which they have made of public questions and the contacts which they have made in consequence. Information on any of these points is not easy to obtain and generalisation is necessarily difficult.

Conservative candidates are nominated by the local constituency associations. Such an association is a self-constituted body consisting of those persons resident in or connected with the constituency who accept the principles of the Conservative party and are sufficiently interested to contribute to its funds. Before the war it was often a small body dependent for its funds on a few wealthy contributors, including usually the prospective candidate himself. Since 1945, however, great efforts have been made to broaden the basis of the Conservative party as an organisation, to increase the income from small subscriptions, and to prevent the 'purchase' of seats by wealthy men. The membership of the party is now nearly three million. The actual work of the association, as in all voluntary bodies, is performed by a small group of active and enthusiastic committee members. These may not be, and often are not, in tune with the political opinions of the mass of the Conservative electors, but the divergence cannot be excessive, since in the Conservative party policy is laid down by the Leader, and he has to consider electoral prospects throughout the country. The orthodoxy of the association is maintained by the executive committee of the National Union of Conservative and Unionist Associations, whose approval is necessary for affiliation and which can at any time withdraw that approval.[1]

The parliamentary candidate is, generally speaking, chosen by the executive council of the association after examination of the field by a selection committee.[2] The candidate will, however, need the official endorsement of the Conservative party, as witnessed by a letter from the Leader; and the constituency association will require assistance in respect of 'literature' and speakers and possibly (if the constituency is a poor one) in respect of finance also. It is, therefore, necessary that the central organs of the party should be consulted at an early stage. The body officially concerned is the Standing Advisory Committee on

[1] R. T. McKenzie, *British Political Parties*, p. 242.   [2] *Ibid.* pp. 250–2.

Candidates of the National Union of Conservative and Unionist Associations;[1] but the Conservative Central Office is inevitably concerned and shows that concern through one of the Vice-Chairmen of the party organisation, who in turn is responsible to the Leader. The division of responsibility between him and the Advisory Committee is not very clear; he is not a member of the Committee but he is consulted by them. Moreover, two persons from the Central Office are members of the Committee. It may be assumed, therefore, that a candidate is not approved by the Advisory Committee unless he is also approved by the Central Office. Most candidates are, in fact, drawn from a list of approved candidates maintained by the Advisory Committee and sent to a constituency association at its request. Moreover, in order to avoid the difficulties which would arise if a candidate adopted by the constituency association were not approved by the Advisory Committee, the association is expected to consult the Committee in advance. What in fact happens in all normal cases is that the chairman of the executive council of the constituency association consults the Central Office and the office of the National Union before any names are submitted to the selection committee. That committee, in turn, recommends three or four names to the executive council, which asks the candidates to appear and votes on them. The candidate so selected becomes the prospective candidate and is formally 'adopted' as candidate after the date of the election is announced.

The Conservative member is, in theory, more free of constituency control than the Labour member. The policy which he is expected to follow is that of the Leader, and the constituency association has no power to give him instructions. On the other hand, the association finds the money and the votes; one Conservative candidate would do almost as well as another; the path of prudence therefore leads to close and friendly relations between the member and the comparatively few active Conservatives in his constituency. Members have occasionally defied their associations, stood as 'Independent Conservatives', and even won elections; but it is safer and more usual to be a dependent Conservative. Accordingly, the 'independence' of the Conservative member is something of a fiction.

[1] *Ibid.* pp. 216–19.

It seems that, in the Conservative party as in the Labour party, candidates are sometimes 'sponsored' by pressure groups in order that they may secure representation in Parliament. Before the war the National Farmers' Union, the British Medical Association and the National Union of Teachers contributed to the election expenses of candidates.[1] If this practice is still followed, it would have to be with the connivance of the constituency association, which is responsible for meeting the cost of the election. It is, however, doubtful whether expenditure by an outside interest is worth while. There are always farmers and medical practitioners, and usually there are teachers (though politically-minded teachers tend towards the Labour party) among the Conservative members of Parliament. Moreover a wide range of organisations follows the practice of inviting members of Parliament to 'take an interest' in their work. The members become patrons or vice-presidents, are invited to annual conferences and feasts, receive what is euphemistically called 'literature', and generally are given places of some prominence. If legislation affecting the organisation is introduced, the member takes care to be placed on the appropriate Standing Committee and is 'briefed' by the officials of the organisation. If he is successful in the ballot for private members' Bills the organisation may have a 'little Bill' ready for him. If general debate arises on an issue affecting the organisation, the member is able to speak with some technical knowledge and therefore with some authority. How helpful all this is towards success in a parliamentary career depends in large measure on the member himself; but it is noticeable that members who are active in this way often find themselves in the charmed circle of the Parliamentary Secretaries—not so charmed now that it is so inadequately remunerated—and sometimes are invited to join the Cabinet. This may be, however, the reason for being asked to 'take an interest', not its consequence.

The position in the Labour party is not fundamentally different, though there are variations in detail.[2] The question whether there shall

[1] See *Parliament*, 1st ed., pp. 33–6. The organisations are now more modest about their achievements. Thus, the report of the Political Fund Committee of the National Farmers' Union, even in an election year, is now compressed into one sentence: 'The Committee met for administrative purposes during the year.'

[2] R. T. McKenzie, *British Political Parties*, pp. 550–8.

be a Labour candidate at a parliamentary election in a constituency is in effect decided by the National Executive Committee of the Labour party, after consultation with the divisional (or constituency) party. The decision being in favour, it becomes the responsibility of the divisional party to produce a candidate acceptable to the N.E.C. As in the case of the Conservative party, a list of suitable candidates is maintained at Transport House (Labour party headquarters), but if a recommendation is sought by the local party it is usual to submit two or three names in order to avoid any suggestion that a candidate is being 'foisted' on the constituency. The trade unions, the Co-operative party and other affiliated bodies also have lists of approved candidates, who may be nominated by the local branches. Nominations may therefore be received by the local executive committee from the N.E.C., its own ward-committees, or its affiliated organisations. Where the candidate's name appears on the list of an affiliated organisation, the consent of the executive committee of that organisation must be obtained, apparently on the assumption that the organisation, in sponsoring the candidate, will contribute to the election fund.

The local executive committee may itself have names to suggest; but when all the names are in, it must consult the N.E.C. or its officers to determine the validity of the nominations. This means that the local committee must find out whether any of the candidates is not likely to be officially endorsed by the party. The local committee then ascertains the political views of the proposed candidates, either by questionnaire or by interview, and compiles a short list of the candidates who have not been locally nominated. This short list, with the list of candidates locally nominated, is submitted to the general management committee of the local party. The meeting of this body is attended by a representative of Transport House, whose duty it is to see that the procedure follows that laid down by the N.E.C. After listening to short speeches from the proposed candidates, the general committee ballots until one such candidate has obtained an absolute majority. The next step is to secure the endorsement of that candidate by the N.E.C. In special circumstances, and especially at by-elections, this procedure may be shortened.

It will be seen that there is little difference between the parties in the procedure employed, if allowance be made for the influence of affiliated organisations in the local Labour parties. The real difference is the open acceptance by the Labour party of the system of 'sponsored' candidates. There may be such candidates in the Conservative party; but there the sponsoring is both exceptional and *sub rosa*. In the Labour party sponsored candidatures are both numerous and open. The figures for the last three elections were:[1]

	1950	1951	1955
All Labour candidates	617	617	620
Sponsored by co-operative parties	36	38	38
Sponsored by trade unions	140	137	128

Thus, about twenty-eight per cent of Labour candidates were sponsored. There is, too, a tendency for the sponsoring organisations to choose the safer seats. The distribution of seats won in the same elections was:

	1950	1951	1955
All Labour seats	315	295	277
Members sponsored by co-operative societies	19	17	16
Members sponsored by trade unions	110	103	96

Thus, whereas sponsored candidates were only twenty-eight per cent of all Labour candidates, sponsored members are about forty-one per cent of all Labour members.

A local party is encouraged to accept a sponsored candidate by reason of the fact that sponsoring solves the problem of financing the election. In the Labour party the sponsoring organisation is allowed to spend up to eighty per cent of the election expenses, and in fact the average payment in 1955 was about £500 per candidate.[2] On the other hand, the sponsoring organisation usually seeks candidatures where its membership is considerable. The National Union of Mineworkers, for instance, is successful with so many candidatures because it chooses mining constituencies. Also, the trade union contributes to expenses both at the centre and, frequently, in the constituencies, even when it has no candidates of its own. Some unions, for instance, make a contribution to the election expenses of any member, even when he is not a sponsored candidate.

[1] H. G. Nicholas, *The British General Election of 1950*, p. 61; D. E. Butler, *The British General Election of 1951*, p. 42; D. E. Butler, *The British General Election of 1955*, p. 219.
[2] D. E. Butler, *The British General Election of 1955*, p. 217.

There is a further difference between the Labour members and the Conservative members. While the policy of the Conservative party is determined by the Leader, that of the Labour party is determined by the Annual Conference of the Labour party. It is true that timing and priorities are determined by the Parliamentary Labour party when the party is in Opposition and by the Cabinet when it is in office.[1] Nevertheless, a divisional Labour party which supports the Conference is in a stronger position *vis-à-vis* its member than a Conservative constituency party with ideas of its own, whether they have been accepted by the National Union of Conservative and Unionist Associations or not. The Conservative member is bound to accept leadership: the Labour member is bound, at least theoretically, by Conference decisions.

In thinking in terms of conflict, however, we are thinking of exceptions. The ordinary member and the ordinary constituency are both orthodox, and fierce conflicts over doctrine are unusual; they do not find it at all difficult to follow the party line, whether set by the Leader or by the Conference. Nor does the average member find it difficult to accept the particular prejudices of his constituents: if many of them live on the profits from the herring fishery it is as obvious to him as it is to them that the wholesale price of herrings ought to be high and that it is the responsibility of the Government to see that it is high, provided of course that the retail price is kept low in constituencies in which consumers of herrings vote the party ticket. Nor must the Government forget that the 'middle-men', objectionable though they are to producer and consumer alike, also have votes and are politically more powerful than their number would normally indicate. On the other hand, there comes a point in the political careers of some politicians in which a measure of unorthodoxy provides the path for the prudent or at least for the ambitious. One route to high office involves obeying the slightest behest of the whips; but the other route, though dangerous, produces more publicity. One does not for ever expect a Joseph Chamberlain to tread in the footsteps of a Gladstone; nor does Birmingham object to its member having a mind of his own: if 'our Joe' cannot persuade his own constituents, whose constituents can he persuade?

These principles, or perhaps platitudes, apply equally to the study

[1] R. T. McKenzie, *British Political Parties*, pp. 419–20.

of the social and economic background against which members formulate their opinions. Since the first edition of this work was published, much work has been done in this field.[1] It is, however, easy to exaggerate its importance. Between the wars (1918 to 1939) too much emphasis was laid upon social and economic status as determinants of opinion. If every politician based his policy upon his 'class interest' there would never be a Conservative Government and half the Labour members would be without seats, for in most constituencies the working-class holds the majority. The politician has to capture a seat by winning votes, and the parties have to adapt their policies to the prejudices of the electors. Social and economic status is an important factor in elections, but it is not the only factor.[2] The danger of a purely economic interpretation was being exhibited while the first edition of this book was going to press, for the Munich policy was widely understood (especially in the United States) as an expression of the Chamberlain prejudice for middle-class dictatorship, though now that the documents are available there is not the slightest sign of it. One might, however,

[1] Interest in this field was first stimulated by the late Professor H. J. Laski, who had the social composition of each Parliament investigated by his pupils. One of them, Dr J. A. Thomas, provided the material on the Parliaments of 1832 to 1901 used in the first edition of this work: *Parliament* (1st ed.), pp. 36–40. That material has since been published: J. A. Thomas, *The House of Commons, 1832–1901*. The figures for 1901 to 1936 given in the first edition (pp. 40–6) were compiled by me. Figures for 1918–35 have also been published, in much greater detail, by Dr J. F. S. Ross, *Parliamentary Representation*, 2nd. ed., 1948, pp. 1–83. In the second edition of that work figures for 1945 also were provided. In *Elections and Electors* (1955), Dr Ross published figures for the general elections of 1945, 1950 and 1951 based on a different (and more useful) method of analysis, and related them to the figures for 1918 to 1935 compiled on the same basis. See also the Nuffield College election studies: R. B. McCallum and Alison Readman, *The British General Election of 1945*, pp. 272–4; H. G. Nicholas, *The British General Election of 1950*, pp. 42–64; D. E. Butler, *The British General Election of 1951*, pp. 35–43; D. E. Butler, *The British General Election of 1955*, pp. 38–46. Each author has a different method of classification, mentions that the material at his disposal was not complete, and gives warning that there are subjective elements in his classification. Anybody who has tried, for instance, to discover whether a 'barrister-at-law' ought to be classified as a lawyer will appreciate the difficulty. Moreover, a company director may be a person of private means who attends a board meeting once a quarter, an active member of the liquor interest (which has disappeared from the later classifications though very much alive), a professional philanthropist, or an expert in the stock market. Even so, general conclusions can be drawn and an attempt to do so has been made in the text.

[2] Cf. R. S. Milne and H. C. Mackenzie, *Straight Fight*; M. Benney and P. Geiss, 'Social Class and Politics in Greenwich', *British Journal of Sociology*, vol. 1; A. H. Birch and P. Campbell, 'Voting Behaviour in a Lancashire Constituency', *ibid*.

select examples at random. Home Rule, for instance, cannot be explained in economic terms, and even the economic explanation of Conservative 'imperialism'[1] now appears far-fetched, especially when it is discovered that aggressive colonial 'nationalism' has almost exactly the same characteristics as the 'colonialism' which it seeks to overthrow.

It is not denied that the character of British politics depends in large measure on the character of British politicians, which in turn depends in part on their training and environment. It is important that the Prime Minister was educated at Eton and Balliol and was a company director, while the Leader of the Opposition was educated at Winchester and New College and was an academic economist before he became a professional politician; but these facts do not explain the difference between Conservative and Labour policy nor tell us very much (though they do tell us something) about the working of the parliamentary machine.

One element in the British parliamentary system which must not be forgotten is that of tradition. It has been the tradition since the reign of Elizabeth I that the great and the would-be great should sit in Parliament.[2] 'You will be of the House of Commons as soon as you are of age', wrote Lord Chesterfield to his son in 1749, 'and you must first make a figure there if you would make a figure in your country';[3] and Sir Lewis Namier, who quotes this passage, immediately adds: 'For several centuries the dream of English youth and manhood of the nation-forming class has remained unchanged; it has been fixed and focused on the House of Commons, a modified, socialised arena for battle, drive and dominion'; Labouchere, in the passage already quoted,[4] expressed the same idea more cynically and in the context of Victorian England. Today there are young men anxious to enter Cambridge (and perhaps other places too) who tell us that they 'would like to go into

---

[1] Cf. J. A. Hobson, *Imperialism*, which Lenin bowdlerized in his more famous pamphlet.

[2] Cf. J. E. Neale, *The Elizabethan House of Commons*, especially chs. i and xv: 'Most of the famous men in Elizabethan history sat in Parliament: statesmen, as a matter of course': *ibid*. p. 301.

[3] Quoted L. B. Namier, *The Structure of Politics at the Accession of George III*, p. 2.

[4] *Ante* p. 30.

politics', though they immediately add that they 'have no money'. They are not aware that there were 139 university men in the Parliament of 1563[1] and 328 in the Parliament of 1955,[2] but they do know that Cambridge provides one of the roads to Parliament, and it is a road which an ambitious young man may properly wish to follow.

The fact that the young men complain (like their older peers) that they 'have no money' is, however, another aspect of parliamentary service. It always has been so, and Parliament has usually consisted of comparatively wealthy men not because a particular class has striven to secure representation in order to improve its class position (though that has happened) but because only the comparatively wealthy or the adventurous can afford the expense of membership. The payment of members since 1912 has altered the nature of the problem but has not removed it. Indeed, as we shall see,[3] it has caused the character of the House of Commons to become warped.

Sir Lewis Namier divides the members of the House of Commons in 1761 into several categories.[4] First, there were the 'predestined Parliament men', for whom membership was a social duty, the eldest sons of politically active peers, who expected in due course to take their places in the House of Lords, the younger sons of the leading political families, and the country gentlemen who controlled boroughs. Secondly there was the 'country party', the sixty or eighty landowners of such respectable authority in their areas that they were elected for the counties and respectable boroughs by reason of their social standing and who, generally speaking, sought no offices or profits. Thirdly, there were the professional politicians and social climbers, some of whom could afford to buy their seats while others had to beg for Treasury seats or for boroughs owned by the mighty, and who would generally be found supporting the Government. Fourthly, there were members sent into Parliament by their relatives or friends in order that they might, by assiduous support of the ministry, find suitable places in the public service. Fifthly, there were the senior officers of the armed forces, the

---

[1] J. E. Neale, *op. cit.* p. 302.

[2] D. E. Butler, *The British General Election of 1955*, p. 42. The Cambridge men numbered ninety-four, and the Cambridge share is tending to rise; *ibid.* p. 44.

[3] *Post*, pp. 44–58.

[4] L. B. Namier, *The Structure of Politics at the Accession of George III*, vol. I, pp. 4–75.

civil servants and the lawyers, who hoped for promotion and preferment. Sixthly, there were the merchants and financiers, most of whom were seeking social prestige, and many of whom held Government contracts. One of the great advantages to the Government was that they could afford to contest the expensive constituencies, in which bribery and treating had to be practised on a large scale.

By 1832 the worst of these abuses had been removed, partly by legislation (notably Acts of 1782 and 1801) and partly by better administrative practice. In other respects the changes were only gradual. Nor had the Reform Act of 1832 any immediate effect on the membership of the House of Commons. The character of the county members had not changed, for the forty-shilling freeholders still dominated the counties and the tenants at will enfranchised by the Chandos clause were even more subservient to the 'landed interest' than the freeholders.[1] In most of the boroughs the freemen and other holders of 'ancient rights' were swamped by the £10 leaseholders[2] enfranchised by the Act; but there is no evidence that the character of the members elected was affected, except of course in respect of party affiliation. The 'nomination boroughs' in which nomination was equivalent to election had disappeared; but there were still 132 boroughs with less than 1000 electors[3] and in them 'influence' was no less strong. Speaking generally the effect of the Reform Act was to require that rich men be borough candidates, since the cost of bribery, treating and so forth, was greater in the enlarged urban electorates.[4] A Select Committee reported in 1835 that bribery was universal wherever there was a contest and 'influence' was not strong enough.[5]

There was in consequence no great change in the composition of the House of Commons until 1865.[6] The number of members having interests in land declined slowly from 464 in 1832 to 436 in 1865 and then the decline became more rapid, so that in 1901 there were only 198. The number of members who had had military or naval experience remained almost constant until 1874, and the decline afterwards was

[1] C. S. Seymour, *Electoral Reform in England and Wales*, p. 78.
[2] *Ibid.* p. 83.   [3] *Ibid.* p. 78.   [4] *Ibid.* p. 171.   [5] *Ibid.* p. 172.
[6] For what follows, in relation to the period 1832–1901, see J. A. Thomas, *The House of Commons, 1832–1901*.

slight. It must, however, be remembered that the character of the landed interest (with which the Army, if not the Navy, was closely associated) changed during the course of the century. The landed gentry acquired interests in banking, insurance, railways and mining as the stigma of 'trade' became less important than the prestige of wealth. The railway interest, which hardly existed in 1832, rose to its peak in 1865 and then declined. By the end of the century the number of members interested in finance (banking, insurance, etc.), was as large as the number of members interested in land, though of course many were interested in both. Shipping and transport, too, had a fair representation in the House, particularly in the later period. The most spectacular rise was, however, in mining and manufacturing: thirty-nine members had interests in them in 1832 and 219 in 1901. The character of industry had, however, changed. The 'business men' of the new generation were not proprietors working in their shirt-sleeves with their men, but frock-coated directors sitting in offices. By the end of the century, the classifications 'finance', 'manufacturing and mining', 'railways', 'shipping and transport' and 'merchants' were almost meaningless, for the same type of person was involved, and indeed the same person might be director of several companies engaged in different trades or industries. What is more, most of the business men were Conservatives. In the period after the Reform Act of 1832, while the landed interest dominated the Conservative party, there was a substantial and growing business interest in the Liberal party. Curiously enough, it was not substantially increased by the accession of the Peelites after the repeal of the Corn laws in 1846: on the contrary, the landed interest was proportionately stronger among the Peelites than among the rest of the Conservative party. When the Liberal Unionists seceded over Home Rule in 1886, however, they took a very substantial business element into the Unionist alliance. The two movements illustrate the dangers of the economic interpretation of history. By 1846 a large section of the landed interest was liberal in sentiment and willing to become Liberal in politics, even when Liberalism favoured cheap imported wheat. By 1886 many business interests were conservative in sentiment and willing to become Conservative in politics. The repeal of the Corn laws and the advocacy of Home Rule were occasions rather than causes.

The period between the Boer War and the War of 1914–18 was one of transition.[1] The Reform Acts of 1867 and 1884, like that of 1832, had had few immediate effects. The Act of 1832 raised the electorate from three per cent of the population to four per cent, that of 1867 from four to eight per cent, that of 1884 from nine to sixteen per cent. The working-class did not at once realise its power. In the rural areas, especially outside the Celtic fringe, the working-class vote was mainly Conservative, while in the industrial areas it was mainly, though by no means exclusively, Liberal. It began to use its industrial power in 1889 and its political power in 1899, dates which must no doubt be associated with the establishment of the board schools in 1870 and the adoption of compulsory education in 1881. The early years of the present century therefore saw both the beginning of the Welfare State and the foundation of the Labour party. The election of 1906 may be regarded as the triumph of the 'Nonconformist Conscience'; but thereafter it went into rapid decline because it was fundamentally lower middle-class. The decline was accelerated by the conflict between Mr Asquith and Mr Lloyd George after 1916, but it seems probable that it would have happened in any case. Though there were large exceptions, including as usual the Celtic fringe, Nonconformity had had no very strong hold on the working-class; and though the older workman continued to vote Conservative or Liberal for the good reason that he had always done so, the Labour party captured an increasing proportion of the younger voters so that, except for a comparatively slight drop in 1931 (considering the environment), the Labour vote increased steadily until 1951. The Labour members were not, however, exclusively working-class. The proportion of trade unionists has always been high, but there has also been a substantial representation of the middle-class elements which had given strength to the Liberal party after the secession of the Liberal Unionists—retailers, journalists, authors, teachers, and members of the newer professions.

Between the wars[2] the Conservative and Liberal parties consisted mainly of company directors, managers, and professional men, especially lawyers. The Labour party, too, had its share of professional men,

[1] See the figures in *Parliament* (1st ed.), pp. 41–2.
[2] J. F. S. Ross, *Parliamentary Representation* (2nd ed.), especially pp. 73–7.

though trade union officials counted for nearly half and trade union members a good deal more than half. Since the war the only considerable changes[1] have been an increase in the proportion of professional men in both parties and an increase in the number of farmers and stock-breeders. This second change may be more apparent than real, owing to the growing practice of using farming losses as a set-off against surtax on investment income. On the other hand, it may be merely a reflection of the growing prosperity of the farming industry under Government subsidies. The House of Commons now consists in the main of company directors, lawyers and other professional men, officers of the armed forces and of other services who have retired on pension, persons who supplement their incomes by broadcasting and journalism, and trade union members (many of them trade union officials).

5. MEMBERS AS PROFESSIONAL POLITICIANS

The House of Commons sits from 2.30 p.m. to 10.30 p.m. (or later) on four days a week, and from 11 a.m. to 4.30 p.m. on Fridays, during a session of approximately thirty-six weeks. Committees may function while the House is sitting, but time has often to be found in the morning for Standing Committees, Select Committees, party meetings, group meetings, etc. Every member has to spend a substantial part of each day on his correspondence, the cost of postage, telephones and telegrams averaging £100 per member per annum. Most members have to spend frequent week-ends in their constituencies. All members who make any serious attempt to carry out their duties have to spend many hours a week reading newspapers, blue books, white papers, party memoranda, agenda papers, and so forth. There are social functions to perform, both in London and in the constituencies, which are essential if the member is to keep his name before the public. From time to time questions, amendments and motions have to be drafted. From time to time speeches have to be prepared and delivered, both inside the House and outside. In fact, the average member has to spend

[1] J. F. S. Ross, *Elections and Electors*, ch. 26, especially p. 440; D. E. Butler, *The British General Election of 1955*, p. 43. Dr Ross and Mr Butler use different methods of classification.

more time on his parliamentary duties than he would normally spend in earning a living. There is no eight-hour day or forty-four-hour week. Nevertheless, even the latest Select Committee on Members' Expenses says that 'few would support the idea of a House of Commons composed principally of full-time politicians in the sense of men and women cut off from any practical share in the work of the nation'.[1] There is evidently some confusion of thought.

This theory, and indeed practice, has had a long innings. It derives from the fact that, in the Tudor period, when a seat in Parliament began to carry high prestige, wealthy landowners and their relatives and hangers-on were prepared to forego their parliamentary wages in order to encourage the electors, who would have to pay the wages, to elect them.[2] Moreover it became the duty of candidates to entertain their constituents,[3] to assume the responsibility for the payment of the customary fees to the election officials,[4] and even to bribe the electors.[5] Though these practices were not always approved, eighteenth-century Parliaments thought that members should be men of substance and not adventurers or men of straw. An Act of 1710 required that a knight of the shire should have an income of £600 a year derived from land, and a burgess an income of £300 a year.[6] The Act was amended in 1836[7] in favour of persons deriving incomes from personal property, but was not repealed until 1858. It was often evaded even before 1760 and was rarely enforced afterwards,[8] but it helped to maintain the tradition that members of Parliament ought to be persons who could pay for the privilege and did not need to earn their living.

There is no doubt that the 'country party', the landed gentry who owed nothing to the favour of the Crown or the patronage of borough-mongers, provided a solid block of independent opinion in a corrupt age, though not all of them could resist the temptation to sell votes for ribbons, baronetcies and peerages, nor the temptation to obtain places

---

[1] H.C. 72 of 1954, p. xxvii.
[2] E. Porritt, *The Unreformed House of Commons*, vol. 1, p. 153; J. E. Neale, *The Elizabethan House of Commons*, pp. 321–4.
[3] J. E. Neale, *op. cit.* pp. 328–30.   [4] E. Porritt, *op. cit.* pp. 181–203.
[5] *Ibid.* pp. 154–65.
[6] *Ibid.* pp. 166–9. The Act did not apply to Scotland.
[7] 1 & 2 Vict., c. 48.   [8] E. Porritt, *op. cit.* pp. 170–7.

and pensions for their relatives and retainers. Nevertheless, there were even in the eighteenth century many members who depended upon fees or salaries. The lawyers were not so numerous as they became in the nineteenth century, and even less numerous than they are now; but the law was a profession which enabled a person without great estate to earn a living in London and yet to spare the time to look into the House of Commons during the course of the evening;[1] and, moreover, membership of the House on the right side gave a claim (though it no longer does so) to preferment. Officers of the Army and Navy were prominent in the House until the Service Departments decided to take members of Parliament off the active list: since then most of the regular officers in the House have retired from service on pension. There were even civil servants in the House before the distinction between civil and political office was clearly drawn. There were, too, many persons drawing sinecures or offices whose duties could be performed by deputy. Moreover, there were representatives of financial interests anxious to secure contracts for loans, remittances, or the supply of goods. The theory that owners of inherited or acquired wealth were the most suitable legislators because they were independent and had a stake in the country was far from being carried out in practice; but the prestige of the country party, compared with the distrust of those who held places, pensions and contracts, did help to establish the tradition that service in Parliament ought to be honorary and indeed was a privilege that might reasonably be paid for.

In the nineteenth century it was impossible to maintain the principle that the landowners were enfeoffed by Providence in order that they might govern the country. Inherited or acquired wealth, or at least membership of a profession which provided time for legislative duties, was, however, still necessary. The development of the limited liability company, which provided commerce and industry with a new class of part-time directors, also provided the House of Commons with a new class of part-time legislators. Thus the theory that the United Kingdom could be governed by gifted amateurs while lesser breeds without the law employed professional politicians could be maintained. In fact,

---

[1] An Act of 1372 disqualified lawyers for election as knights of the shire, but the provision was forgotten and it was repealed in 1871.

however, all leading politicians were professionals in the sense that they made a business of politics and devoted their full time to it, though until 1911 they were paid only while they were in office and therefore had to have incomes large enough to subsist during periods of opposition; and it must be remembered that before 1914 official salaries, when related to the cost of living and the level of taxation, were very much higher than they are now. Most of our Prime Ministers and other elder statesmen entered Parliament as young men and lived on accumulated wealth; a few, but only a few, had first to accumulate capital in business or a profession; a few have had the good fortune to have private associations with public or private companies, so that out of office they could revert to the profession of company director; a few have found it necessary or convenient to capitalise their knowledge of affairs by writing their memoirs. These exceptions belong to the class of what census enumerators would call 'subsidiary occupations'. The fact that our senior politicians are now regarded as professionals, as indeed they always were, is shown by the pensions granted to former Prime Ministers and the salaries provided for Leaders of the Opposition. Since Mr Baldwin could rely on the profits of the family business while out of office he was able to appreciate the problems of a politician who had no such source of income and was able to recommend a change because he would not need to profit from it. Perhaps, too, he thought it undesirable that Ministers should speculate on the stock exchange or have to ask permission to use official papers in order to make profits out of their memoirs. At any rate, he admitted that Mr Attlee, Mr Asquith and Mr Lloyd George ought to be regarded as professional politicians; but there is really no reason for distinguishing the front bench from the back bench in this respect. Every member of Parliament who does his work properly is a professional politician, even when he has a subsidiary occupation.

It is probable that members of the working-classes would have been excluded until the end of the nineteenth century even if membership of the House had been a well-paid profession. Though many of them had the vote in 1868 a generation was needed to convince them and the electors that some of them ought to be in Parliament. Once that point was conceded, however, the payment of members either by the State or by outside organisations became inevitable, and the latter was rendered impracticable by the Osborne judgment. The miner could not go down the pit or the cotton operative work his loom while the House of Commons stood adjourned or Parliament was prorogued, and so earn enough to live while it was in session. It would have been astonishing if the dock-labourer from Stepney or the builder from Islington could, like the lawyer from the Temple, down tools after a day's work and make his way (at his own expense) to Westminster to do a night's work. Accordingly, a salary of £400 a year was voted in 1911. The little Welsh attorney who moved the motion, Mr Lloyd George, must have been well aware that others besides Labour members would have financial difficulties when they were not in office; he had tried to carry on his profession and had failed. In his speech[1] he emphasised the growth in the legislative programme, the expectations of the constituencies (which did not exist fifty years before) that their members would sit and vote and even speak, the demands for speeches in the constituencies, and generally the increase of parliamentary work. 'A member who does his duty to his constituents has very little time left for anything else.'[2] His main point, however, was the need to diversify membership. Apart from the Irish and the Labour members, the membership was largely confined to four classes: those with unearned income, barristers practising in the London courts, persons with well-established businesses who had efficient and accommodating partners, and those who were 'something in the City'. On the question of the amount of salary, Mr Lloyd George remarked:[3]

When we offer £400 a year as payment of members of Parliament it is not a recognition of the magnitude of the service, it is not a remuneration; it is not a recompense; it is not even a salary. It is just an allowance, and I think the minimum allowance, to enable men to come here, men who would render incalculable service to the State and whom it is an incalculable loss to the State not to have here, but who cannot be here because their means do not allow it. It is purely an allowance to enable us to open the door to great and honourable public service. . . .

The motion was opposed by the Conservative party, mainly on the ground that it would be a grave misfortune if the great majority of the

---

[1] 29 H.C.Deb. 5 s., 1365–83. [2] *Ibid.* 1372. [3] *Ibid.* 1383.

House were to be 'divorced from the life, the industry and the commerce of the country',[1] that payment would put members at the service of their constituents and destroy their independent position, and that payment would bring to the House members who had failed at everything else.

The question of the adequacy of £400 a year in view of the fall in the value of money during the war of 1914–18 was discussed by a Select Committee in 1920.[2] No increase was recommended, because of the financial position of the country, but a recommendation, carried out in 1924, was made that members be allowed free travel by railway between London and their constituencies. It was also recommended that free postage be provided for members' letters; but this recommendation was not accepted. The salary was increased to £600 a year in June 1937, on a motion proposed by Mr Neville Chamberlain.

The question was again raised in 1945, when another Select Committee was appointed.[3] Figures produced by the Board of Inland Revenue showed that 228 out of 534 members (i.e. the whole House less Ministers and others who had official salaries) were able to claim that their expenses were £600 a year, while another eighty-one claimed that their expenses were between £500 and £600.[4] The expenses included only cost of secretarial assistance, postage and telephones, and travelling and subsistence away from home. A group of Labour members, whose expenditure would probably be lower than that of most Conservative members, estimated their ordinary expenses as follows:[5]

Secretarial expenses	£250 (average)
Telephones, telegrams and postage	£100 (average)
Office accommodation	£26 to £100
Visits to constituencies	£6 to £150
Attendance at House	£150 (average)

Among other recommendations, the Committee suggested that the salary should be raised to £1000 a year, of which £500 should be tax-free as an expense allowance. The former proposal was accepted, the

---

[1] *Ibid.* 1460 (Mr Austen Chamberlain, who had been able to take to politics because of the family business).
[2] Report from the Select Committee on Members' Expenses, H.C. 255 of 1920.
[3] Report from the Select Committee on Members' Expenses, H.C. 93 of 1945–6.
[4] *Ibid.* p. 103.   [5] *Ibid.* p. 113.

latter rejected.[1] It was also recommended, and agreed, that season tickets for free travel might be issued to members travelling not less than four times a week between their homes and London.

In 1954 another Select Committee reported on the same subject.[2] It noted that the activities, political and social, of members had since 1911 'increased enormously', thereby making it increasingly difficult to combine outside work with membership of the House.

There are today a number of employments from which a member would be required to resign on his election to Parliament. Even in the professions it is difficult for a member to perform his work efficiently or adequately unless he can rely on partners or a competent staff. It is obviously impossible for any member to continue in full-time employment as a school teacher, engineer, miner, railwayman or in any executive or managerial position which requires his constant attendance at works, factory or office, especially out of London. Further, some firms and companies are reluctant to employ a member of Parliament even for full-time. Some members can, however, add to their income by directorships, by journalistic work, broadcasting, lecturing, consultative work, advising and similar tasks, which do not call for long absences from the House, and some are in receipt of payments made to them as officials of organisations.

Further, the expenses 'wholly, exclusively and necessarily incurred' in carrying out duties connected with membership had risen from an average of £550 in 1946 to £750 in 1953.[3] These expenses did not include those incurred by members for the use or maintenance of a car, purchasing books and papers, attending meetings and conferences, providing hospitality to constituents or donations to charity, nor expenses incurred by the member's wife in attending public and social functions in the constituency or elsewhere. A considerable number of members stated that they could not, on the parliamentary salary, afford the expenses necessitated by their parliamentary duties and maintain a reasonable standard of living for themselves and their families.

Some have sold or mortgaged their homes; the savings that others had made before entering Parliament are now exhausted and debts are accumulating:

[1] Members could, as before, prove that the expenses had in fact been incurred 'wholly, exclusively and necessarily' in the performance of their duties.

[2] Report from the Select Committee on Members' Expenses, etc., H.C. 72 of 1954.

[3] Twenty per cent of members were able to claim as expenses the whole parliamentary salary of £1000: H.C. 72 of 1954, p. 67.

others have sacrificed pension rights which they had established with a company or firm, in whose employ they were before entering Parliament, and are now at an age when it would be difficult, if not impossible, for them to find employment: for a long time some have not been able to afford lunch or dinner in the dining rooms of the House of Commons and use only the tea room.[1]

The Select Committee also pointed out that members could not afford to accumulate savings to provide for their retirement, loss of seat, or provision for widows and orphans in the event of death. In cases of extreme hardship, and in such cases only, grants could be made from the House of Commons Members' Fund established by an Act of 1939.[2]

By reason of its narrow terms of reference, the Select Committee did not consider the broader issues involved. It did report its opinion that

the payment made to members of Parliament should be of such an amount as to enable men and women from all walks of life to enter this field of public service without finding the financial sacrifice for themselves and their families too great. Your Committee believe that the enduring strength and authority of Parliament depend upon the quality of its members. The House of Commons must also be representative of the people, and should not be drawn from certain sections only; the field of choice should be wide. Few would support the idea of a House of Commons composed principally of full-time politicians in the sense of men and women cut off from any practical share in the work of the nation. It would be no less damaging to the country if the House were to become a place where members could not give of their best because of a dominating need to escape from financial pressure.[3]

The Committee did not, however, draw attention to the fact that the House was already unrepresentative and that it was likely to become more so over the next generation. The young men who 'have no money' are typical of their generation because heavy taxation makes both the accumulation and the inheritance of wealth difficult, so that the 'professional politicians' who relied on inherited wealth must become fewer. In 1954 only 190 persons had incomes, after tax, of more than £6000 per annum. No doubt many people benefited from capital

---

[1] H.C. 72 of 1954, pp. x–xi.   [2] Amended by an Act of 1948.
[3] H.C. 72 of 1954, p. xxvii.

appreciation, which is not subject to tax; but to produce an income of £2000 a year (subject to tax) a capital of £40,000 (assuming income of five per cent) is needed, and to inherit £40,000 a person must take the whole estate of a person dying possessed of £67,000. For a person paying surtax to accumulate £67,000 during a working life is impossible, except of course by capital appreciation. These figures perhaps exaggerate the problem, since a young member would normally be provided with an allowance by a living father. It is, however, obvious that the number of young men who can look forward to an unearned income of £2000 a year has diminished, is diminishing, and is likely to diminish still further. In other words, the class which produced the Pitts, Peels, Gladstones and Edens is virtually disappearing; nor will it be easy to adopt Disraeli's method of 'marrying money'.

According to Dr Ross,[1] the average number of members who were under 31 at first election between the wars was nineteen; but this figure was inflated by the general election of 1931, when an array of Conservative candidates who did not expect to be elected was in fact elected, and if that election be eliminated the average was fifteen. The average in the three elections between 1945 and 1951 was eleven. The comparable figure for 1955 is not available, but the number of members under 30 in that year was seven.[2] It does not follow that all these young men were not earning income, but there does seem to be a diminution in the number of young members. On the other hand, the average age of all new members has tended to decline because there has also been a decline in the number of elderly members entering for the first time.[3] Perhaps this is because the number of persons who have been able to accumulate enough capital to support the dignity of a member of Parliament is declining. If this is correct we are tending to get a 'middle-aged' parliament because in that age-group will be those who can hope to earn enough to maintain themselves by 'subsidiary occupations'.

It is noticeable, too, that there is a fairly rapid turn-over of members due not only to the vagaries of elections but also to the deliberate choice

[1] *Elections and Electors*, p. 388.
[2] D. E. Butler, *The British General Election of 1955*, p. 40.
[3] Ross, *op. cit.* p. 392.

of members. The number of members who did not seek re-election in some recent elections was as follows:[1]

Election	Conservative	Labour	Others	Total
1935	57	2	9	68
1945	86	29	14	129
1951	16	11	2	29
1955	23	17	2	42

The reasons are unknown, but they would obviously include age and ill-health as well as lack of means. The average length of service of members has not diminished since the war,[2] but this may be due in part to the rapid turn-over in the 1920's through the growth of the Labour party and to the general election of 1931, and in part to the fact that elections have become cheaper for Conservative candidates since 1950. Of the 630 candidates successful in 1955, 446 had first fought an election in 1945 or earlier.[3]

It is difficult to draw conclusions about the representative character of the House of Commons from the figures relating to education. The information is not complete and there are differences of opinion about classification.[4] The figures given by Dr Ross, however, for all elections from 1918 to 1951[5] do not suggest that there has been any very great change. When there is a Conservative majority the public schools provide more than half the members, and when there is a Labour majority over forty per cent.[6] In 1955, according to Mr David Butler[7] (who appears to use another method of classification), the percentage

[1] *The Times Guide to the House of Commons*, 1935, 1945, etc.
[2] Ross, *op. cit.* p. 402.　　　[3] Butler, *op. cit.* p. 39.
[4] The following are the figures for Conservative and Labour members in 1951, as given by Dr Ross and Mr Butler:

	Conservative		Labour	
	Ross	Butler	Ross	Butler
Elementary school	10	4	147	78
Secondary school	44	77	74	157
Public school	252	240	66	60

See Ross, *op. cit.* p. 405; Butler, *The British General Election of 1951*, p. 39.
[5] *Op. cit.* p. 407.
[6] 'Public schools' include the grammar schools represented on the Headmasters' Conference.
[7] *The British General Election of 1955*, p. 42. Mr Butler gives figures for the two large parties only.

was approximately fifty-two. It may be noted that among the defeated candidates, both in 1951[1] and in 1955[2] the distribution was very different, the percentages of public school products being respectively thirty and twenty-seven. This percentage is only partly accounted for by the larger number of Labour candidates defeated, for among the Conservative candidates defeated the percentages were only forty-two and forty-three. Since most of the successful candidates were members seeking re-election and on the average the unsuccessful candidates were younger, the inference would be that the secondary school product is coming into his own in the Conservative party as in the Labour party. The explanation is, in part, that the Conservative candidate has no longer to make a substantial contribution to election and party funds; but the figures also suggest that the older type of public school *rentier* is disappearing. This would accord with university experience: the 'new poor' are doing their best to send their sons to the public schools and then to the universities, even when they cannot obtain scholarships and maintenance grants, but the struggle to maintain standards is becoming increasingly difficult. A reduction in the proportion of public school products in the House of Commons would make it more and not less representative, but the next generation will probably see fewer professional politicians of the Eden (Eton and Christ Church) or Butler (Marlborough and Pembroke) type and many more secondary school products who have entered one of the few trades and professions compatible with membership.

The figures of university education tend to the same conclusion.[3] Oxford, which has had a traditional connection with the landed gentry, provides rather more than twenty per cent of the House when there is a Conservative majority and rather less when there is a Labour majority.

[1] *The British General Election of 1951*, p. 39.
[2] *The British General Election of 1955*, p. 42.
[3] There is less difference between Dr Ross and Mr Butler. The 1951 figures are:

	Conservative		Labour	
	Ross	Butler	Ross	Butler
Oxford	102	102	38	39
Cambridge	69	66	17	18
Other universities	43	42	74	65

Ross, *op. cit.* p. 418; Butler, *op. it.* p. 39.

Cambridge, which has been more accessible to the 'poor scholar' and the scientist, similarly provides around fifteen per cent. The contribution of other universities has been rising slowly, and is now between that of Oxford and that of Cambridge. Among the defeated candidates of 1955, however, the Oxford share was only eleven per cent, the Cambridge share was seven per cent, while the other universities claimed twenty-four per cent. These figures, too, are exaggerated by the large number of Labour candidates defeated. In the Conservative party, however, the figures were, Oxford eighteen per cent, Cambridge ten per cent, and other universities twenty per cent.[1] Thus, while Oxford and Cambridge are keeping their representation, other universities are increasing theirs.

Figures relating to occupational groups are even more difficult to compile and interpret.[2] It seems permissible, however, to make the following generalisations:

(1) The old-fashioned *rentier* has almost completely disappeared. For 1955, Mr Butler gives only eleven among elected members and only one defeated candidate.[3] This does not mean that members dependent upon inherited or accumulated wealth have almost disappeared. The 'landed

---

[1] Mr Butler points out (*op. cit.* pp. 44, 45) that of the candidates elected for the first time after the general election of 1951, Oxford provided twenty-five per cent and Cambridge twenty-eight per cent in the Conservative party, while each provided eight per cent in the Labour party.

[2] Comparison between the figures provided by Dr Ross and those provided by Mr Butler are again instructive. Those for 1951, where comparable, are as follows:

	Conservative		Labour	
	Ross	Butler	Ross	Butler
Barristers	54	61	26	28
Regular officers	46	32	2	2
Solicitors	11	11	10	12
*Clerks and secretaries	10	6	25	11
Journalists and authors	21	13	26	33
Teachers and lecturers	4	5	39	42
†Farmers and stockbreeders	30	15	—	2
Physicians and surgeons	4	4	6	9

* Clearly a difference of classification.

† Mr Butler seems to have classified 'gentlemen farmers' as 'Private means': cf. *The British General Election of 1955*, p. 42, n. 2.

[3] *The British General Election of 1955*, p. 43. There are two errors of arithmetic under 'Miscellaneous'.

interest' of the nineteenth century now appears not only under 'private means' but also under 'farming'. The *rentier*, depending on stocks and shares, usually appears as a 'company director'; and no doubt many appearing under other disguises depend in part upon unearned income.

(2) The largest group now consists of the company directors, and its size has been increasing, especially in the Conservative party. Dr Ross[1] shows that, according to his classification, there was an average of thirty-two per cent between the wars and that it had risen to forty-four per cent in 1951. Though Mr Butler's figures show a reduction in 1955,[2] the changes are probably due to increases under 'Professions' and 'Business' in respect of persons who are also directors of companies. There is also a considerable proportional increase in the Labour party.

(3) The number of Conservative lawyers has remained fairly steady, but there has been a considerable increase among Labour lawyers.[3]

(4) The number of former regular officers has declined slightly from the inter-war average, though there was an increase in 1955.[4] The figures in this group usually move with 'private means'.

(5) Taking the professional group as a whole, there has been a considerable increase from an average of forty-five per cent between the wars to over fifty per cent since.[5] Much the larger part has been in the Labour party. There was a further increase in 1955.[6]

(6) The middle-class and white-collar elements in the Labour party have shown a considerable increase, involving a comparable diminution in the proportion of manual workers.[7]

(7) The 'business' element has remained fairly stable, but this is due on the one hand to an increase among the company directors and on the other hand to a reduction among those engaged actively in office or factory.

(8) These tendencies are all shown very strongly among the persons who entered Parliament for the first time after the House first met in 1951.[8] It may therefore be assumed (subject to the usual vicissitudes) that they will be continued in future Parliaments.

None of these methods of analysis proves the assertion made above that the House of Commons is becoming increasingly unrepresentative.

---

[1] *Elections and Electors*, p. 444.

[2] *The British General Election of 1951*, p. 41; *The British General Election of 1955*, p. 43.   [3] Ross, *op. cit.* p. 444.

[4] Ross, *op. cit.* p. 433; Butler, *The British General Election of 1951*, p. 41, and *The British General Election of 1955*, p. 43.   [5] Ross, *op. cit.* p. 440.

[6] Butler, *loc. cit.*   [7] Ross, *op. cit.* p. 440.

[8] Butler, *The British General Election of 1951*, p. 44.

Indeed, it may be argued that the Labour party is becoming increasingly representative. As Mr Butler says:[1]

In 1955 the Labour party once again offered a more diverse, though not necessarily an abler group of candidates than the Conservatives. Women, Jews, nonconformists and manual workers seem to have had a decidedly better chance of getting into Parliament on the Labour than on the Conservative side; being an Etonian may have been no handicap to a would-be Labour candidate, but it was certainly an asset among Conservatives. On the other hand, youth seems to have had rather more opportunity with the Conservative party.

More important, perhaps, is that the Labour party is ceasing to be a 'class' party, because it now contains substantial elements from the professional classes and white-collar workers; and this accords with political realities.[2] On the other hand the Conservative party, which has always had a large working-class vote, has at last secured the election of a manual worker, and actually put up nineteen working-class candidates in 1955.[3] The severe restriction on payments to party funds, introduced by the Conservatives after their failure at the general election of 1945, has in fact opened the way to better representation in both parties. The fundamental defect of existing arrangements is that every member of Parliament, apart from the small and disappearing band of *rentiers*, has to find a part-time job. The position is not, as it used to be, that a minority of full-time employees (including the self-employed) could afford to be part-time politicians; it is that full-time politicians have to become part-time employees in order to live.

The Select Committee of 1954[4] recommended that the parliamentary salary should be raised from £1000 to £1500 and that there should be a scheme for the payment, at the age of 65, of pensions of £350 a year for a member who had completed ten years' service after the age of 45 and of £500 a year for those who had completed fifteen years' service after the age of 40. There would be increased contributions to a new Benevolent Fund, which would take over the assets of the Members' Fund, and which would be used for additional payments in cases of

[1] *The British General Election of 1955*, p. 45.
[2] See John Bonham, *The Middle Class Vote*, ch. 5.
[3] Butler, *op. cit.* p. 43.   [4] H.C. 72 of 1954, pp. xxviii–xxix.

hardship. Though the proposal to increase salaries, and a modified proposal to refer the pension scheme to the trustees of the Members' Fund, were carried on a free vote by 280 votes to 166, the Government refused to accept these proposals on the ground that there was not complete agreement. Eventually it was agreed between Government and Opposition that there should be a sessional allowance of £2 for every day on which Parliament sits, except Fridays. This would provide a gross payment of £288 a year, assuming a parliamentary session of 36 weeks.

Conservative opposition to the increase was largely political. It was put on the basis that the claims of members should be postponed to those of old age pensioners, widows, retired officers, and others whose incomes had been affected by inflation. In fact, however, the real question was not whether the members of the Parliament of 1954 were or were not justified in asking for increased salaries, but whether the country could not get better and more representative members than those in the House in 1954 if they were, like everybody else, paid 'the rate for the job'. In an age in which almost everybody has to earn his living, members of parliament must increasingly be drawn from the following groups:

(*a*) Persons whose inherited or accumulated wealth, family connections, or 'names', enable them to become company directors.

(*b*) Persons engaged in professional or business occupations in London who can leave their chambers or offices for a few hours every evening, or who have become semi-sleeping partners.

(*c*) Persons who have retired from the armed forces, other public services, and similar pensionable employments.

(*d*) Persons who have inherited wealth or have accumulated it through capital appreciation and who are prepared to live on capital.

(*e*) Trade union officials and others who can find part-time secretarial, administrative or advisory appointments in London.

(*f*) Persons of a journalistic frame of mind who can increase their incomes by journalism, broadcasting, or the writing of popular books.

The 'bright young men' who want to 'go into politics' but 'have no money' have to be advised accordingly.

CHAPTER III

PARTIES AND OFFICIALS

I. MAJORITY AND MINORITIES

Two fundamental principles govern the procedure of the modern House of Commons. They are, that the Government shall, so long as it can maintain a majority, be able to secure such legal powers as it considers necessary for administration, and that minorities, however small, shall be able to criticise that administration.[1] These principles imply respectively the right of the majority and the rights of minorities, for normally the majority is the Government. There have been, it is true, many examples of minority Governments;[2] they have, however, lasted but a short while unless they had firm support from parties which, with their own party supporters, in fact gave the Government a majority. As soon as a minority Government is refused the opportunity of governing it has no alternative but to resign; the art of managing the House becomes even more difficult. It has to carry on discussions not only 'behind the Speaker's Chair', but also outside the purlieus of the House. If it wishes to stay in power it must negotiate, and negotiate constantly, with a third party. The task is not easy, and it is glad of an opportunity either to resign or to dissolve Parliament. Minority Governments are heading either for coalition or for defeat. In the last resort the electors bring parliamentary government back to the two-party system. Parliamentary practice assumes that system, and it is the working of the system that we will discuss.[3]

Technically speaking, a Government with a majority has complete control of the House. The Standing Orders, as will presently be explained, protect minorities; but Standing Orders are merely resolutions of the House which can be swept away by a majority vote. In certain cases they can be suspended without discussion. For instance, the rule

---

[1] Cf. *Cabinet Government*, Chapter XIV; and see Chapter I of this book.
[2] See *Cabinet Government*, p. 27.
[3] On the working of minority Governments, see *Cabinet Government*, pp. 446–7.

that any business (other than exempted business) shall be brought to an end at ten o'clock at night may be waived by the carrying of a motion to that effect at the beginning of public business. No amendment to that motion may be moved, and no debate on it may take place.[1] Again, the rule as to Supply after ten o'clock may be waived on the motion of a minister, decided without amendment or debate.[2] But even where no such rule applies a Standing Order can always be waived by motion. Such a motion can be debated; but the closure can be moved, with the consent of the Speaker, in order to bring the debate to a close. Thus, though the Standing Orders provide certain days for private members' business, it is always possible for a motion to be passed at the request of a minister to take all the time for Government business. Perhaps one day is lost in debating this motion in order that the Government may gain twenty days. Similarly, any restrictive motion may be passed. If the Government moved to exclude all members of the Opposition, or to exclude all members of a particular party, that motion would be perfectly in order if put on the paper as a Government motion on a day on which Government business had precedence. It would be debated, and at length; no doubt, too, a long time would elapse before the Speaker was prepared to accept a closure motion. Nevertheless, so long as the Government's majority remained loyal the closure would ultimately be carried and the motion would then be carried too. Dictatorship could be introduced into the British constitutional system by a Government with a loyal majority in both Houses, without any technical difficulty whatever.[3]

All this is, however, essentially theoretical. Though the Government often uses its majority to suspend the ten o'clock rule, and though it sometimes takes all private members' time, it never seeks to interfere with the essential rights of minorities. Indeed, most of the rights of minorities arise not out of Standing Orders but out of pure practice. The only Orders which definitely protect minorities are the closure rule, which provides that the Speaker or Chairman need not put the closure if he thinks it 'an infringement of the rights of the minority',[4] and the 'kangaroo closure' rule which similarly enables the Speaker

[1] S.O. 1 (7).   [2] S.O. 16 (2).
[3] 9. H.C. 189 of 1945–6, Q. 2210.   [4] S.O. 29 (1).

or Chairman to refuse a motion that the question on a clause or new clause may be put.[1] In addition, the Committee of Selection is ordered, in nominating members of Standing Committees, to 'have regard to the composition of the House';[2] but this is sufficiently vague not to be any protection against a Government which really desired to take away minority rights.

In truth, the rights of minorities depend not upon express rules but upon the custom of the House. It is not a custom which goes back to immemorial antiquity. The impartiality of the Speaker, for instance, has lasted little more than a century—a short time in the history of Parliament. In the days when any minister was liable to be impeached after his fall, ministers in the full glory of their power were not tender of their opponents' rights. So long as the House was ruled by bribery and corruption the conventional rules implicit in a democratic system could not be developed. Much of the courtesy of debate and respect of opponents that now provide the dominant characteristic of the House came in under the amiable Lord North and the younger Pitt. Much of it was brought in by Peel. Though their history be short, however, these conventions have become firmly fixed in the conduct of proceedings. The Speaker and the Chairman do their best to attain impartiality. Proceedings are conducted by agreements 'through the usual channels', and even where those channels become temporarily congested the opposition which leads to an all-night sitting follows well recognised rules. In the ordinary process of debate a speaker on one side is followed by a speaker on the other, a leader on one side by a leader on the other. Select Committees and Standing Committees are appointed so as to represent all shades of opinion, while giving a majority to the Government. Professor Redlich has emphasised one example which is so much according to custom that an Englishman might be forgiven for failing to notice its importance. When a Select Committee was appointed to consider the amendments to the Standing Orders which Mr Parnell's most famous obstruction had made necessary,

---

[1] S.O. 29 (3). This is the old 'kangaroo closure', which is not often used. The word 'kangaroo' is now commonly used of the power to select amendments in S.O. 31. This power is not a closure at all.

[2] S.O. 58.

Mr Parnell himself was made a member of the Committee.[1] What is more, Mr Parnell followed a convention by behaving as if his sole function as a member of the Committee was to assist the House in coming to a conclusion. Nothing is more remarkable than the care taken both by members of and by witnesses before Select Committees not to make statements which may be taken in the sense of party controversy.

Breaches of these customary rules simply 'are not done'. Lawyers (if one of them may be permitted to say so) are too apt to assume that rules are obeyed because there is a policeman standing behind. It is not true that people refrain from killing their grandmothers because the law says that such an act is murder to be punished with death. Nor is it true that the rules of the House of Commons have any direct, or even obvious and indirect, sanction. They are followed because they are part of the tradition, because they are reasonable, and because they are essential to the working of a democratic system. There may be sanctions in the distant background; a Government which overrode all the rights of minorities would meet Nemesis at the next election— if it held an election of the kind which allowed that stern goddess to exercise the electoral rights of freeborn British citizens. If this be the sanction it operates only because other rules are obeyed. If a Government waives one set of rules it will not hesitate to waive another. Gradual encroachments upon minority privileges are a different matter. Some will say, as they said before the Select Committee on Procedure in 1914, that all the changes since 1877, including Mr Gladstone's, Mr Balfour's and Sir Henry Campbell-Bannerman's, have strengthened the hands of the Government and weakened the power of minorities. In this statement there is much truth. The changes were, however, inevitable consequences of the growth of the business of the State, the greater application of private members to their duties, and the added complication of the international situation. Mr Parnell's obstruction was the cause but not the reason. In all these changes care has been taken to leave to minorities ample opportunities for debate, while forbidding obstruction and enabling the completion of a reasonable amount of Government business.

[1] Redlich, I, p. 145.

Indeed there is evidence that small minorities are favoured. Sir Dennis Herbert said in 1930, and Mr Lloyd George agreed with him, that the Speaker or Chairman endeavours to secure the representation of all points of view. Members who will probably repeat the ideas of previous speakers are not called upon; and 'if a man is a crank he has a better chance of being called than anyone else'.[1] The Liberal party is given more speakers than its numbers on a strictly proportionate basis would warrant;[2] and Mr Rhys Davies said that 'when a Communist was in this House he could get up and speak at almost any time he liked'.[3] This last statement was denied by Mr Lloyd George; but observation suggests that in the Parliaments of 1935–45 and 1945–50 the Communist members had greater opportunities than anyone, simply because they represented a point of view that only they could express. The Select Committee of 1861 said that the old rules were 'a sure defence against the oppression of overpowering majorities'.[4] The rules have been altered but the essential principle remains unchanged; the practice of the House protects minorities from oppression by overpowering majorities.

2. THE SPEAKER AND THE CHAIRMAN

Care for the rights of minorities is evidenced by the deliberate exaltation of the office of Speaker. His power to protect is very narrowly limited. If a motion is properly proposed he has no option but to put it to the vote; and if it is passed he has no alternative but to see that it is carried out. But motions which deliberately interfere with minority rights are not moved; and Mr Speaker can warn the House of the consequences of motions which do not directly but might indirectly affect those rights. As often happens in British institutions, the Speaker's authority is greater than his power. The House takes great care to maintain and even to enhance his prestige.

It is unnecessary to consider here the powers that he exercises by long-standing practice. His essential function is to preside impartially over the debates of the House otherwise than in committee and to

[1] H.C. 161 of 1931, QQ. 986–7. [2] *Ibid.* Q. 978.
[3] *Ibid.* Q. 981.
[4] 1861 Report, p. xi, quoted Redlich, I, p. 103.

advise the House in its proceedings. British experience shows that it is by no means impossible for a fair-minded man deliberately to cast away his political bias and to attain a state of mind which is almost, if not quite, impartial. He is normally chosen, in the first instance, from among the Government majority. It is desirable that he should not have taken too prominent a part in party polemics. Mr Gladstone therefore insisted in 1871 that a Speaker ought not to be taken from the Treasury Bench.

It would not be wise or allowable [he said] to propose any candidate taken from the Treasury bench; upon these grounds especially, that it would be most difficult, at any rate at present, to relieve any such person from the suspicion of partiality; that precedent does not run in this direction; and that a resort to such a measure, in critical times, would not be without a tendency to lower the dignity of the Chair by giving rise to a suspicion that the disposal of it had been made use of to serve the purposes of the Government.[1]

Actually, Mr Brand, who had been a Liberal whip, was appointed—and a very good Speaker he made.

Nevertheless, the same principle was laid down by the Liberal Cabinet in 1895.

A great desire had been expressed on both sides of the House that Mr Campbell-Bannerman, who is universally popular, should be nominated; but the Cabinet felt that there were great objections on principle to taking a principal member of their own body and placing him in the Chair, thus making the Speakership a purely party appointment, a practice which has had such an evil result in the United States.[2]

Further, an attempt is made to secure agreement between Government and Opposition, and this attempt is usually successful. The exceptional cases, those of 1895 and 1951, prove the rule. In 1895 Sir William Harcourt discussed the matter with Mr Balfour, and they made joint representations to Mr Speaker Peel to induce him to remain. This failing, the Cabinet's choice fell upon Mr Courtney, a Liberal-Unionist who had been Chairman of Committees from 1886 to 1892. Mr Courtney found that he would be opposed by the Conservatives and not cordially supported by the Liberal Unionists, and accordingly he

[1] *Letters of Queen Victoria*, 2nd Series, II, p. 164.
[2] Sir William Harcourt to the Queen: *Letters of Queen Victoria*, 3rd series, II, p. 487.

refused.[1] The Government therefore nominated Mr Gully, 'who knows nothing and whom nobody knows',[2] and the Conservatives nominated Sir M. White-Ridley. The vote favoured Mr Gully, who made a not unsuccessful Speaker. In 1951 Mr Churchill had written to Mr Attlee, suggesting the names of Mr W. S. Morrison (who had been a Conservative Minister in the previous Conservative and Coalition Governments) and Mr Hopkin Morris (a Liberal). At a conference between the Leader of the House and the Leader of the Opposition, at which their deputies and whips were also present, the cases of Major Milner (who had been Chairman of Ways and Means under the Labour Government) and Sir Charles MacAndrew (a Conservative who had been Deputy Chairman) were mentioned. Since the Conservatives would probably not support Major Milner, it was agreed that Mr Morrison be nominated. The Labour Liaison Committee decided, however, to support Major Milner, and Mr Morrison was elected by a majority vote only. He was re-elected in 1955 without opposition.[3]

The result of this practice is that the Speaker is often, like Mr Gully, an obscure back-bencher. He must not have taken part in acrimonious controversy; he must not be obnoxious to either side; he must not, therefore, have made himself too prominent. The qualities required of a Speaker are not really very high, and so great is the prestige of the office, and so careful are all parties to maintain his independence and authority, that any reasonable man can make a success of the office. As Lord Rosebery said, *à propos* the election of Mr Gully,

There is much exaggeration about the attainments requisite for a Speaker. All Speakers are highly successful, all Speakers are deeply regretted, and are generally announced to be irreplaceable. But a Speaker is soon found, and found, almost invariably, among the mediocrities of the House.[4]

Once a Speaker is appointed, he divests himself of his party character. He resigns from his party, has no communications of a party character,

[1] Sir William Harcourt to the Queen: *Letters of Queen Victoria*, 3rd series, II, p. 487.
[2] *Life of Sir William Harcourt*, II, p. 356.
[3] 493 H.C.Deb. 5 s., 2–22. The four previous Speakers had occupied the Chair as Chairman or Deputy Chairman of Ways and Means, whereas Mr Morrison had been a Minister. Mr Churchill had invited Mr Morrison to stand before the former was informed that the Labour party would oppose.
[4] Lord Rosebery to the Queen: *Letters of Queen Victoria*, 3rd series, II, p. 495.

and is prevented from advocating the claims of his constituents. This rule was definitely established early in the nineteenth century. Mr Speaker Manners Sutton had been in constant communication with the Duke of Wellington as to the changes involved after the 'dismissal' of Lord Melbourne in 1834. Lord Melbourne therefore said that his re-election ought to be opposed. 'I think the Speaker of the House of Commons should not take part in political changes, and particularly not in a change which there was every reason to believe was disagreeable to the majority of the House, of which he is the servant, and which involved its dissolution.'[1]

The re-election of Manners Sutton in 1835 was therefore opposed by the victorious Whigs, who were successful by eleven votes in carrying their candidate, Abercromby. But since then the convention has been established that a Speaker who wishes to continue shall be re-elected, even if the party from which he came is no longer in office. In 1841 some members of the Conservative party were in favour of opposing the re-election of Mr Speaker Shaw Lefevre; Sir Robert Peel declared himself in favour of re-election, for five reasons:

First, I do not think it for the public advantage that the election for the Chair should necessarily be made the object of a party.

Secondly, I do not think it would be just towards a Speaker who has shown himself well qualified for his office, and has in my opinion acted fairly and impartially, to reject him.

Thirdly, I think that the late Speaker, if he be re-elected with the general goodwill of the House, will have greater authority and power to preserve order than a Speaker elected after a party contest.

Fourthly, I do not think we have any person to propose who would appear to advantage as Speaker, all things considered, when compared with Lefevre.

Fifthly, it is not a very high or satisfactory ground to allege for opposing Shaw Lefevre that the Whigs and Radicals opposed Lord Canterbury [i.e. Manners Sutton in 1835]. We said it was unjust and unpolitic to oppose Lord Canterbury, and it seems to me more becoming to a great party to act upon its own principle, and even apply it against itself, than to say to its opponents, Though our principle was the right one, yet by way of retaliation we will adopt yours.[2]

[1] *Lord Melbourne's Papers*, p. 245.
[2] Parker, *Sir Robert Peel*, II, pp. 476–7.

A letter to *The Times*, ascribed to Mr Disraeli (though he denied authorship), attacked this decision.[1] But the re-election of Shaw Lefevre was proposed by Mr Disraeli himself in 1852. He then wrote to Lord John Russell asking him to provide a seconder, 'though this course may be unusual'. Lord John Russell agreed, and added that he did the same when he asked Lord Castlereagh to second the nomination of Manners Sutton.[2] It is now the invariable practice for the re-election of the Speaker in a new Parliament to be proposed by a speaker from the Government and seconded by a speaker for the Opposition.

It is, also, the normal practice not to oppose the re-election of the former Speaker at a general election. There have been three recent exceptions only.[3] In 1895 Mr Gully's re-election at Carlisle was opposed by the Conservatives, and Mr Balfour even wrote letters supporting his opponent. Sir William Harcourt thereupon wrote to Mr Gully:

As one who entertains profound regard for the established and honourable traditions of the House of Commons I cannot but deplore that the Leader of that House[4] should have thought it right to take part in an electioneering attack on the seat of the Speaker. Such a proceeding is contrary to the whole spirit and practice which has hitherto prevailed in our party contests, and cannot but have a most injurious effect upon our parliamentary life. It is without precedent in the past, and I sincerely trust may find no imitation in the future.

It is well known that the Speaker from the nature of the office he has lately filled cannot take an active part in the political contest, and this consideration is one which should restrain every one, and most of all the Leader of the House of Commons, from taking an unfair advantage of his situation.[5]

Mr Gully was re-elected to Parliament, and his re-election as Speaker was proposed by the Conservative Government. With the extension of the franchise it is not so easy to maintain Sir William Harcourt's principle as he indicated. The position is not merely that the constituency is disfranchised by having its representative as Speaker, but also that

---

[1] *Ibid.* II, p. 478.   [2] Monypenny and Buckle, *Life of Disraeli*, I, pp. 1205–6.

[3] In 1950 Colonel Clifton Brown was opposed by an Independent but supported by the Labour party; and in 1955 Mr W. S. Morrison was opposed by an 'Independent Labour' candidate who did not get the Labour party's endorsement.

[4] The Liberal Government had resigned after being defeated on the cordite vote, and Lord Salisbury had formed a Conservative Government and dissolved Parliament.

[5] Gardiner, *Life of Sir William Harcourt*, II, pp. 373–4.

3-2

it is most difficult to keep an organisation together for the event of the Speaker's retirement. The Labour party, in particular, relies for most of its electioneering on unpaid assistance rendered by enthusiastic supporters whose sole incentive is the hope of the ultimate election of their candidate. The highly complex organisation which any well-organised divisional party has to evolve is kept in existence between elections, and the process of 'nursing' is continuous. The election contest itself, even if obviously doomed to failure, is interesting and exciting. The supporters are willing to work hard even if the chance of election be remote. If, however, there is no election, the difficulty of maintaining the organisation is substantial. The honorary officers of the local parties are all the more discouraged if there is evidence that the political complexion of the constituency is changing. For these reasons the divisional Labour party at Daventry, supported by the central Labour organisation, decided to oppose Captain FitzRoy in 1935. They believed that, given an ordinary election, a Labour candidate would be returned. They believed also that, unless they could have an election, they could not keep an organisation together ready to seize the seat when the Speaker resigned, whereas the local Conservative association, relying mainly on paid labour, could improvise the necessary organisation. The decision was attacked by the other parties. Mr Speaker himself, feeling that he could not wage a campaign without taking part in politics, contented himself with sending out a strictly non-political election address; and leaders of the Conservative and Liberal parties spoke at meetings arranged to support his candidature. Mr Speaker was elected, and his re-election as Speaker was seconded by the Leader of the Labour party. The same considerations induced the Labour party to oppose Colonel Clifton-Brown at Hexham in 1945. He followed the example of Captain FitzRoy and was elected. The Labour Government nevertheless nominated him for re-election as Speaker. The possible disadvantages of making the Speaker a partisan are sufficiently great to outweigh the obvious disadvantages of following the well-established precedent. At the same time, there is no real answer to the suggestion which has been made that Mr Speaker should be given a fictitious constituency or, if fictions be disliked, should be empowered to sit in Parliament without a constituency.

The House itself has done its best to make the Speaker impartial. His salary of £5000 a year, free from all deductions and taxes,[1] and his official residence, are provided for by permanent legislation.[2] They are consequently not voted every year and no opportunity arises for criticism except on a formal motion.[3] In the House he is restrained by usage from taking part in debate. When the House is in committee he may do so according to numerous precedents; but the last instance quoted by May was in 1870,[4] and the right may perhaps be regarded as having fallen into desuetude[5].

The Speaker is thus for all practical purposes impartial, and the House can leave to him the important judicial function of deciding all points of order. One of the many ways in which the House differs from so many other legislative assemblies is, as Redlich points out,[6] that there are no debates on points of order. It is true that, in accordance with a rule laid down in 1604, 'if any doubt arise upon a bill, the Speaker is to explain but not to sway the House with argument or dispute'.[7] Accordingly, if the precedents are not clear, the Speaker leaves the matter to the House. But the ordinary interpretation of the rules and customs of the House is the function of the Speaker himself, and he will allow no debate or criticism of his decision except on a formal motion. If a member raises a point of order the Speaker gives his decision; he may permit questions to elucidate it and suggestions which may enable the member concerned to keep within the rules, but he allows no discussion.

The decisions of the Speaker, if made in the House, are recorded in the *Official Report* and in the Journals of the House. Many decisions are, however, taken privately, when matters are submitted to him by the Clerks-at-the-Table. Such decisions, too, are taken down and are printed

---

[1] There was some doubt in 1931 whether the Speaker was a 'servant of the Crown' whose salary was subject to deduction under the economy legislation of that year. Without prejudice to the legal position, Mr Speaker voluntarily accepted the deduction. The better opinion seems to be that he is elected by the House and approved by the Crown, and not nominated by the House and appointed by the Crown. If this is so, he is not a servant of the Crown.

[2] 2 & 3 Will. IV, c. 105; 4 & 5 Will. IV, c. 70. [3] May, pp. 234, 374.
[4] May (13th ed.), pp. 364–6. [5] May (15th ed.), p. 234. [6] Redlich, II, p. 146.
[7] *House of Commons Journals*, I, p. 187; Hatsell, *Precedents* (4th ed.), II, p. 239; see Redlich, II, p. 145, and cf. May, p. 235.

and circulated among the Clerks-at-the-Table and their assistants, though they are confidential and are not made generally available. These decisions, whether published or not, are so many precedents as closely followed as the precedents created by the law courts. Consequently, there is a body of rules which cannot be found in the Standing Orders but which form the practice of the House.[1] The Speaker is thus able to maintain the judicial character of his office by following strictly in the footsteps of his predecessors. If he is asked for a ruling on a difficult point he asks for time to 'consider' his opinion. With the assistance of the Clerks-at-the-Table and his Counsel he looks up the precedents and renders a considered judgment. Consequently, when once a practice has been adopted, only a resolution of the House can change it. This is of particular importance now that questions of some delicacy have to be determined by the Speaker. For instance, the Speaker has the duty under the Parliament Act, 1911, of deciding whether a Bill is a money Bill. This function has been exercised since 1911 by a series of Speakers with the assistance of members appointed by the Committee of Selection. Accordingly, there is a long series of precedents determining what kinds of provisions exclude a Bill from the definition of 'money Bill' contained in the Act. Unless the character of the Speaker's office is fundamentally changed, these precedents are binding on future Speakers; and whatever their political sympathies they would follow them.

It is impossible, however, to indicate by an enumeration of powers and immunities the prestige which the Speaker enjoys. Psychological influences can never be adequately explained in writing. Express rules, long custom, ancient ceremonial, and deliberate policy combine to give him an actual authority which none of these alone could confer. Here as elsewhere antiquity has its importance;[2] here, too, the flair for governmental technique, which is characteristic of the British peoples, comes to the assistance of custom and tradition. The 'scenes' of which newspapers write have to be coloured by journalistic art to make them arresting. The House is in truth a most orderly assembly and it grows

---

[1] Informally a distinction is drawn between the 'procedure' of the House, which is governed by Standing Orders, and the 'practice' of the House, which is governed by precedents. [2] Cf. Chapter II, *ante*, pp. 13–22.

more orderly from generation to generation. Nor is this due to English lack of emotion; there are, after all, always the Celtic fringes, and until recently one of them was much more than a fringe. The irrepressible Irish were very seriously restrained by the atmosphere of the House and the authority of the Speaker. How much this orderly character owes to historical accident and how much to design it is impossible to say. Tradition and deliberation combine to confer on the person who sits in the Chair a dignity and authority which could hardly be surpassed.

This authority spreads over and covers the Speaker's deputies. When the House goes into committee the Speaker leaves the Chair, and under the old procedure the House proceeded to elect a Chairman. But the Committees of Supply and of Ways and Means are set up at the beginning of each session and remain in existence throughout the session. The same Chairman is elected for both and therefore holds a quasi-permanent appointment. Until 1910 the leader of the House called upon a member to take the Chair. If another member were also nominated, the House resumed with the Speaker in the Chair and a motion was made. Since 1910, however, the Chairman of Ways and Means has been appointed at the beginning of each Parliament after motion made in the House by the leader of the House. Since 1841, also, the Chairman of Ways and Means has acted as Chairman of all other committees of the whole House.[1] Finally, Standing Orders have provided since 1855[2] that the Chairman of Ways and Means shall act as Deputy Speaker, and this is strengthened by the Deputy Speaker Act, 1855, which enables the Chairman to exercise the statutory functions of the Speaker.

Standing Orders have also provided since 1902[3] that at the commencement of every Parliament, or from time to time, as necessity may arise, the House may appoint a Deputy Chairman, who shall be entitled to exercise all the power vested in the Chairman of Ways and Means, including his powers as Deputy Speaker.

The older rule[4] provides that whenever the House shall be informed by the Clerk-at-the-Table of the unavoidable absence of Mr Speaker, the Chairman of Ways and Means shall perform the duties and exercise the authority of the Speaker in relation to all proceedings of the House, as

[1] For all this, see May, p. 237.   [2] See now S.O. 96.
[3] See now S.O. 96 (2).   [4] S.O. 96 (1).

Deputy Speaker, until the next meeting of the House, and so on from day to day, on the like information being given to the House, until the House shall otherwise order; but if the House adjourns for more than twenty-four hours the Deputy Speaker shall continue to perform the duties and exercise the authority of Speaker for twenty-four hours only after such adjournment. This rule is intended to be used, however, only during illness or absence for some other cause. The ordinary relief of the Speaker—essential since the lengthening of the proceedings and the abolition of 'the Speaker's chop' and the subsequent provision for a dinner-hour adjournment—is provided for by a newer rule[1] which enables the Speaker to call upon the Chairman or Deputy Chairman to take the Chair without any communication to the House.

For the purpose of providing Chairmen of Standing Committees, who may also act as deputies to the Chairman of Ways and Means, the Speaker sets up at the beginning of every session a Chairmen's panel of not less than ten members nominated by him.[2] The Chairman of Ways and Means and the Deputy Chairman are *ex officio* members, and it has power to report to the House on matters of procedure relating to Standing Committees. The Chairman of a Standing Committee is appointed from the panel by the Speaker, while if the Chairman of Ways and Means requires a member to act as temporary Chairman of a committee of the House, he requests some member of the Chairmen's panel to act. The members of the Chairmen's panel, it should be added, are chosen irrespective of party, and it is not uncommon for a member of the Opposition to preside over a Standing Committee which contains a Government majority and which is considering a Government Bill in charge of a minister. It is significant of the spirit with which the House conducts its proceedings that a member of the Opposition can, as Chairman, rule out of order an amendment moved or speech made by a minister. The minister will accept the Chairman's ruling as he would accept a ruling by the Speaker.

Thus the House uses the most fair-minded of its members to preside over all its proceedings from the House itself to the Standing Committees. The Chairman of a Select Committee is nominated *ad hoc* by the House, but his position is in substance the same. It should be added

[1] S.O. 96 (3).　　　　　　　　[2] S.O. 96 (4).

that, as will be more fully explained hereafter,[1] the Chairman of the Select Committee of Public Accounts, a most important body, is invariably a member of the Opposition, with ministerial experience if that is possible.

The dignity and prestige of the Speaker are carried over so as to cover all the Chairmen. These attributes are not deliberately emphasised by ceremonial and firm rules. The Chairman of Ways and Means and the Deputy Chairman are nominated by the Government and there is no tradition of re-election on change of Government. An attempt is, however, made to reach agreement with the Opposition so as to secure a unanimous vote, and since 1945 a member of the Opposition has been Deputy Chairman. The Chairman and Deputy Chairman of Ways and Means have salaries, but they are voted annually in the Estimates and not charged on the Consolidated Fund. There is no paraphernalia of ceremony and costume. The Chairman wears no wig; and when the House is in committee he sits at the Table and not in the Chair. But his conduct, or the conduct of a Deputy or temporary Chairman, cannot be challenged except on a substantive motion[2] and there is no appeal from his decision to the Speaker.[3] By custom, the Chairman and Deputy Chairman do not take a very active part in political debates even in the House itself. The Chairmen of Standing Committees are unpaid and they have none of the conventional protection accorded to the Speaker. Nevertheless, a Standing Committee is, in its relation to the Chairman, merely a miniature of a committee of the whole House. Absolute impartiality can never be obtained, but in all the proceedings of the House and its committees those who preside over the deliberations attain as near impartiality as human nature permits. This is one of the many problems of government which the British Constitution has solved by common sense and the exercise of a wise restraint.

3. THE PRIME MINISTER, THE LEADER OF THE OPPOSITION, AND THE WHIPS

The British Constitution has a way of creating offices without legislation and without any formal decision. Such an office is that of leader of the House of Commons. There is nothing in legislation or Standing

[1] See Chapter IX, § 9, *post*, pp. 332–38.   [2] May, p. 375.   [3] *Ibid.* p. 570.

Orders about it. The term itself apparently originated about the middle of the nineteenth century;[1] but the institution is really much older. Though the Government has only gradually obtained formal powers of control, especially since 1877, the business of the House has been substantially regulated by the Government at least since the time of the younger Pitt. When the Prime Minister was in the House of Commons he was necessarily the chief spokesman of the Government. In the days when it was possible for the Prime Minister to be in the House of Lords a leading minister had to take his place in the lower House. Thus, whether the term was used or not, Lord Althorp was leader of the House under Lord Melbourne until his succession to a peerage in 1834;[2] and the 'dismissal' of Lord Melbourne by William IV was largely due to the king's belief that Lord John Russell would not make an effective leader of the House with Sir Robert Peel, Lord Stanley and Sir James Graham in opposition. When the Whig Government was restored in 1835 Lord John Russell became leader of the House. Lord John Russell similarly acted under Lord Aberdeen, Mr Disraeli under Lord Derby, Mr W. H. Smith under Lord Salisbury, and Sir William Harcourt under Lord Rosebery. In recent times the pressure of business and political considerations have produced two developments. First, where the Prime Minister undertakes the lead of the House of Commons he sometimes appoints a deputy leader. Thus Mr Baldwin in 1935 appointed Sir John Simon to be Home Secretary and deputy leader of the House. In 1937, however, Mr Neville Chamberlain took the lead of the House without appointing a deputy, Sir John Simon acting informally as such while Chancellor of the Exchequer. Secondly, the Prime Minister may formally give up the lead to another Minister. In 1940 Mr Churchill decided to concentrate on the direction of the war as Prime Minister and Minister of Defence and therefore appointed Mr Attlee as leader of the House of Commons. Mr Attlee followed this precedent in 1945 when, as Prime Minister, he appointed Mr Herbert Morrison as Lord President of the Council and leader of the House of Commons. In October 1951, Mr Churchill became Prime Minister and Minister of Defence, Mr Eden became Foreign Secretary and Deputy Prime Minister,

[1] Redlich, 1, p. 120.
[2] But so were Castlereagh and Canning before him.

and Captain Crookshank became Minister of Health and Leader of the House of Commons. Captain Crookshank continued to be leader under Sir Anthony Eden until 1956, when Mr Butler was appointed Lord Privy Seal and leader of the House. This arrangement does not deprive the Prime Minister of his ultimate responsibility for the management of the House, but the leader of the House controls the whips and conducts the negotiations 'through the usual channels'.

The leader of the House, said Mr Gladstone, 'suggests, and in a great degree fixes, the course of all principal matters of business, supervises and keeps in harmony the actions of his colleagues, takes the initiative in matters of ceremonial procedure, and advises the House in every difficulty as it arises'.[1] The details of the arrangement of business are considered hereafter;[2] but it is necessary here to indicate why that function falls on the leader of the House.

Until 1939 Government business had precedence on all sitting days except certain Wednesdays and Fridays. Since 'private members' time' was restored in 1950 Government business has had precedence on all days except twenty Fridays, when private members' Bills and motions have precedence. The Friday sittings are short and are usually counted as half-days. On this basis Government business occupies nine-tenths of the time of the House. This really applies only to the time devoted to 'orders of the day', i.e. between about 3.30 p.m. and 10 p.m. on ordinary days and the whole of Friday (when only formal business may be taken before orders of the day). Also, Government business, like private members' business, may be interrupted by 'urgency' motions under Standing Order 9 and by opposed private business. On the other hand, any lengthening of the session does not extend private members' time proportionately. Moreover, the ten o'clock rule is often suspended under Standing Order 1 (10) so that Government business may go on after 10 p.m., and sometimes the House resolves after debate on a motion proposed by a minister to take the whole or some part of private members' time. In the sessions 1928–9 and 1931–2, and in the whole Parliament of 1945–50, for instance, the Government took the whole time of the House. Omitting the question-hour on all days of the week other than Friday, we shall not be inaccurate in assuming that the

[1] Gladstone, *Gleanings*, I, p. 241.　　[2] *Post*, pp. 95–9.

business of the House is determined by the Government for at least nine-tenths of the sittings.

The arrangement of Government business is the responsibility of the leader of the House, though the details are settled, subject to his control, by the chief whip. The legislation and other matters (such as statutory instruments) to be introduced are determined primarily by Cabinet decisions on proposals submitted by the departments. The programme for a session is, however, worked out by a Cabinet committee. Before the war this was the Home Affairs Committee,[1] which undertook the double task of supervising the programme of one session and planning the programme of the next. During the war these functions passed to the Home Policy Committee, which had wider functions until those wider functions were taken over by the Lord President's or Steering Committee, when a Legislation Committee was set up.[2] The Labour Government of 1945 had such a large volume of work to pass through Parliament that it decided to separate the two functions of planning the work of the session, which was assumed by the Future Legislation Committee,[3] and the supervision of the programme for the current session, which was retained by the Legislation Committee. Under the Labour Government[4] the Future Legislation Committee included the leader of the House of Commons as chairman, the leader of the House of Lords, the chief whip in the House of Commons, and the whip in the House of Lords. No departmental ministers were included because they were necessarily advocates for their own departments. They therefore stated their claims before the Committee but took no part in its decisions.

The main lines of a programme are always clear. Time has to be found for the debate on the Queen's Speech; the financial legislation must be completed by the beginning of August, and essential legislation, such as the Expiring Laws Continuance Bill and the Public Loans Works Bill, must be passed. Time must be found for such 'contingencies' as debates on votes of censure or on motions put down by the Government or the Opposition, adjournment debates under Standing Order 9,

[1] *Cabinet Government* (1st ed.), pp. 199–200.
[2] *Cabinet Government* (2nd ed.), pp. 239–40.
[3] H. Morrison, *Government and Parliament*, pp. 222–4.
[4] The names and functions of Cabinet committees are official secrets during the life-time of a Government.

opposed private Bills, and so forth. Within this framework there will be time for one large Bill embodying Government policy, or perhaps two such Bills, for a number of Departmental Bills of some complication, but not particularly contentious, for minor Bills which will go through without much debate, and for Consolidation Bills designed to clean up the statute book. Thus, a programme can be drawn up in some detail before the session opens, and on it the Queen's Speech is based. Since modifications will be needed during the session, the Future Legislation Committee, or some other committee exercising the like functions, meets during the session to make such alterations as may appear necessary. The business for each week is, however, negotiated with the Opposition through the usual channels, i.e. by consultation between the chief whips acting under the control of the respective leaders, and is announced by the leader of the House on Thursday in answer to a 'private notice' question by the Leader of the Opposition. The chief whip sees the leader of the House every morning to discuss the order of Government business for the next day.[1]

The function of the leader of the House is, however, not limited to the fixing of the subjects and order of Government business. Though much of the organisation of debate is left to the whips in so far as it is not the responsibility of the Speaker or Chairman, he is responsible for the action of the whips. He may give them directions, and they may consult him. Such questions as to the ministers who are to take charge of proceedings, the ministers who are to speak, and the point at which permission is to be sought to move the closure, have to be settled. On an important debate on general policy, for instance, he may have to decide whether one day or two days shall be allowed before the closure is moved, and whether it is desirable that the Prime Minister should speak. When a Bill is before the House, the appropriate departmental minister will be in charge, but the length of time to be devoted to each stage, the question whether a motion shall be moved ordering its reference to a committee of the whole House, the relation between ministers where the Bill affects two or more departments, and the question whether the Prime Minister shall speak, have all to be settled.

[1] The arrangement may be altered without notice: S.O. 14.

Moreover, questions of procedure often arise during the course of the debate. The minister in charge of a Bill may be pressed hard to accept the amendment. If it is not very important he will accept it on his own responsibility. If the matter ought to be considered by the Cabinet or by his advisers he will promise to consider the matter if the amendment is withdrawn. Sometimes, however, he will consult the Prime Minister or leader during the proceedings and accept or oppose the amendment on his responsibility. There have even been occasions on which the Prime Minister has intervened to accept proposals which the minister in charge has already resisted.[1] Again, if a debate on policy is going badly, he may be sent for to see what can be done about it, or, being present, he may decide to intervene to calm the fears of his supporters. The Opposition may be 'outraged' by a speech by a minister or by a breach of an understanding between the whips, and he may have to pour oil on the troubled waters either by intervening in the debate or by sending a message to the leader of the Opposition. In short, the leader of the House has usually to be present either in the House or in his room in order that a responsible decision may be taken as to the management of Government business.

Nor is he concerned with Government business alone. The Government must come to a decision on private members' motions and Bills. Usually, the Cabinet decides whether the whips are to be put on against the proposal, or even in support of the proposal, or whether the question shall be left to a free vote. Occasionally, however, urgent questions arise during the course of the debate and have to be settled by the leader or his deputy.

Similarly, certain questions are addressed to the Prime Minister or to the leader at question-time. As a result of answers given by other ministers, supplementary questions may be put. If for some reason the answers to questions are deemed inadequate, the Opposition may move the adjournment of the House for the discussion of a definite matter of urgent public importance; and if the Speaker accepts the motion it will be necessary to arrange for speakers on the adjournment motion later in the evening.

Finally, there are functions to be performed in the House which the

[1] See *Cabinet Government*, pp. 208–9.

Prime Minister cannot effectively delegate. In some respects he has taken the place of the Speaker. He speaks on behalf of the House when some event of national importance, especially one connected with the Royal Family, takes place. He makes sympathetic references to the death of a distinguished statesman, no matter to what party he belonged. He leads the House, behind the Speaker and in company with the leader of the Opposition, to listen to the Queen's Speech (which, probably, he drafted) in the House of Lords. He proposes the election or re-election of the Speaker and moves a vote of thanks when the Speaker retires. In short, when the House speaks as a corporate body he speaks on its behalf.

The leader of the Opposition similarly holds an office which arose out of practice and which has no official functions either according to legislation or to the rules of the House. Her Majesty's Opposition is Her Majesty's alternative Government. The leader of the Opposition is almost Her Majesty's alternative Prime Minister. Technically, however, he is only the leader for the time being of the chief Opposition party. The parties adopt somewhat different methods for this purpose. A Conservative Prime Minister is elected leader of the Conservative party at a meeting of the Conservative peers, Conservative members of the House of Commons, prospective Conservative candidates, and members of the Executive Committee of the National Union of Conservative and Unionist Associations. He remains leader of the party until he resigns, and so is leader of the Opposition in the House of Commons so long as the party is in opposition and he is in the lower House. Thus, Mr Balfour was leader of the Opposition from 1906 to his resignation in 1911, Mr Baldwin was leader in 1924 and from 1929 to 1931 and Mr Winston Churchill was leader from 1945 to 1951. It is not certain that any leader of the party would be appointed if the leadership fell vacant while the party was in opposition, and probably the old practice of electing a leader in each House would be followed. Thus, between the death of Lord Beaconsfield in 1881 and the appointment of Lord Salisbury as Prime Minister in 1885 there was no 'leader of the Conservative party'; but Lord Salisbury was elected by the Conservative peers to be their leader in the House of Lords, and Sir Stafford Northcote was similarly elected by the Conservative members to lead them in the House of Commons.[1] Similarly, on the resignation of Mr Balfour in 1911 the question of the leadership of the party was left open until the party took office, when it would have been decided by the King's appointment of a Prime Minister. Mr Bonar Law was elected as their leader by the Conservative members of the House of Commons, but he did not become leader of the party until he was chosen as Prime Minister in 1922.[2]

The Liberal party followed the same practice. Thus, when Mr Gladstone resigned in 1875 Lord Hartington was elected leader in the House of Commons and Lord Granville in the House of Lords.[3] When Mr Gladstone became Prime Minister in 1880 he again became leader of the party and so was leader of the Opposition from 1886 to 1892. On the resignation of Lord Rosebery in 1896 no successor was appointed, and Sir William Harcourt was elected leader of the party in the House of Commons only.[4] When he resigned in 1898 Sir Henry Campbell-Bannerman was appointed leader in the House of Commons by the three former leaders remaining, and this choice was ratified at a meeting of Liberal members of Parliament.[5]

The Labour party has no 'leader'. The National Executive Committee is elected by the Annual Conference, and the Committee chooses a chairman for the year. This chairman is not necessarily a member of Parliament, he is not normally re-elected, and there is no suggestion that he has any kind of claim to become Prime Minister or even to office of any kind. The Labour members of Parliament (who are organised into the 'Parliamentary Labour party') elect a chairman of the Parliamentary Labour party, or leader, every session, and he is usually re-elected. He has some considerable claim to appointment as Prime Minister. Thus, Mr Ramsay MacDonald became Prime Minister in 1924 and 1929. It was made clear when Mr Lansbury was elected in 1931, however, and still more clear when Mr Attlee was elected in 1935, that the Parliamentary Labour party reserved its full liberty of action to elect whom it pleased if the party secured a majority, and thus to

---

[1] *Life of Robert, Marquis of Salisbury*, III, p. 41.
[2] Sir Austen Chamberlain, *Politics from Inside*, p. 322.
[3] *Life of Sir Henry Campbell-Bannerman*, I, p. 212.
[4] *Life of Sir William Harcourt*, II, pp. 421–2.
[5] *Life of Sir Henry Campbell-Bannerman*, I, p. 212.

indicate to the King who was desired as Prime Minister. In 1945, however, the King sent for Mr Attlee (who had been Deputy Prime Minister in Mr Churchill's Coalition Government) and there was no formal election by the new parliamentary party. On the other hand, when Mr Gaitskell was elected chairman and leader of the Parliamentary Labour party at the end of 1955 it seems to have been assumed that he would be the next Labour Prime Minister.

The parties differ also in the power which is left to the leader of the Opposition. The Conservative and Liberal parties have had what came to be known as a 'Shadow Cabinet'. This institution goes back at least to 1876, when Sir William Harcourt objected to the 'late Cabinet' deciding the policy of the Liberal Opposition. He and Sir Henry James, who had been law officers, had been summoned only to consider the Slave Circular and not other matters.[1] The Conservative Opposition between 1906 and 1914 had a similar body.[2] For instance, Sir Austen Chamberlain in 1907 described to his father, Mr Joseph Chamberlain, a meeting of the Shadow Cabinet: 'All morning I fought with beasts, *very* nice beasts, I confess—not a soul with me except, I think, Linlithgow.'[3] The leader of the Opposition, like the Prime Minister, could summon whom he pleased to a meeting. Thus, Mr Bonar Law in 1911 invited Mr F. E. Smith, who as a Privy Councillor (nominated by Mr Asquith in spite of Mr Balfour's remonstrance) was technically entitled to sit on the Front Opposition Bench but had not done so, to take his place there, and accordingly he became a member of the Shadow Cabinet.[4] In 1924 and between 1929 and 1931, also, the Conservative party had a 'Policy Committee' which was really a Shadow Cabinet.

The Parliamentary Labour party adopts what it regards as a more democratic system. Not only the chairman and leader, but also the vice-chairman and the chief whip are elected, and are *ex officio* members of the Executive Committee, other members being elected by the members of the parliamentary party. Ex-ministers, as such, have no

---

[1] *Life of Sir William Harcourt*, 1, pp. 300–1.
[2] The term is used in a letter in 1907: Sir Austen Chamberlain, *Politics from Inside*, p. 84.　　　　　　　　　　　　[3] *Ibid*. p. 50.
[4] *Life of Frederick Edwin, Earl of Birkenhead*, 1, pp. 222–3.

right to a seat on the Front Bench. The leader and the chief whip of the Labour group in the House of Lords and one peer elected by that group are also members of the Committee, though they do not take part in discussions which relate only to the functions of the House of Commons. Members of the parliamentary committee in the Commons, and other members of the party, are assigned by the Leader of the Opposition to take charge of particular subjects, much as in the Government itself.[1]

The task of the leader of the Opposition is not so difficult as that of the leader of the House, but it is nevertheless of considerable public importance. Indeed, it is so important that under the Ministers of the Crown Act, 1937, he has a salary of £2000 a year charged on the Consolidated Fund.[2] It may seem strange that the Government should by taxation raise £2000 a year in order to enable its principal opponent to criticise it; but in truth opposition is an essential part of democratic government.[3] Opposition cannot be effective enough to paralyse the Government, because then the Opposition must become the Government. What is expected from an Opposition is effective criticism.[4]

The need for effective leadership is shown by the disorganisation of the Liberal Opposition in 1874. Mr Gladstone was wavering about resignation and absented himself from the House.

During what remained of the session of 1874, Mr Gladstone was a rare visitor to the House of Commons, and as he had appointed no lieutenant, confusion and disintegration soon made themselves felt among his diminished and discouraged followers. The rank and file abused the leaders for not giving a clear lead, failing to comprehend the difficulty in which the occupants of the front bench found themselves placed by the frequent absence of their chief.[5]

---

[1] See the Shadow Cabinet of 1956 in Appendix.

[2] Also, he has a room in the House—a precious privilege, since accommodation is so limited.

[3] See *Cabinet Government*, ch. XIV; and see Chapter 1 of this book.

[4] The fact that a salary is paid may give rise to an understanding that the leader of the Opposition has some responsibility to the House. When Mr Attlee went to Spain in December 1937 he gave the usual undertaking not to engage in propaganda. In view of a speech made by him, a vote of censure was put down by a Conservative member. See *The Times*, 9 December 1937. The motion was not moved, but Mr Attlee made a personal explanation, emphatically denying that he owed any responsibility except to his constituents: 330 H.C.Deb. 5 s., 821–4 (13 December 1937).

[5] *Life of Lord Granville*, II, p. 137.

Mr Goschen in the following year described the experience of the previous session:

We used to be pressed by a number of our party to settle the direction to be given to a debate on a given question. If we did not do so, we were accused of neglecting our duty, in fact we were effacing ourselves. If we did do so, we were taunted with attempting to lead where we had no authority.... The absence of a chief must necessarily lead a dispirited party to murmur against the innocent lieutenants; and I say frankly that Gladstone is placing us (in the House of Commons) in a humiliating and *intolerable* position, if he persists in the same course which he followed last year.[1]

'There are few positions less inspiriting than that of the leader of a discomfited party,' said Mr Disraeli (whose later experience confirmed his analysis). 'He who in the parliamentary field watches over the fortunes of routed troops must be prepared to sit often alone. Few care to share the labour which is doomed to be fruitless, and none are eager to diminish the responsibility of him whose course, however adroit, must necessarily be ineffectual.'[2] The post is indeed one of responsibility. Our Constitution assumes that at any moment, if the Government resigns, or is defeated, or breaks up, an alternative can be formed from the Opposition. Irresponsible opposition is not part of democratic government, though many democratic States have never learned that lesson. The Opposition is giving a hostage to fortune whenever it takes a decision. It may be called upon—it hopes that it will be called upon—to assume in a short time the burdens of government. Even when its chance of accession to office is remote, it is its duty to limit the extremity of the Government's action, to arouse public criticism of any dangerous policy, and to make the Government behave reasonably. It has at its disposal none of the technical knowledge that the resources of the civil service place at the disposal of the Government. It must, nevertheless, take decisions only less important because they will not immediately be carried out.

The Shadow Cabinet, however called, is thus an imitation, by no means too pale, of the Cabinet. The leader of the Opposition is, so to speak, the obverse of the leader of the House. The Shadow Cabinet decides the policy of the Opposition. The leader of the Opposition

[1] *Ibid.* pp. 138–9.   [2] Disraeli, *Life of Lord George Bentinck*, p. 7.

controls the Opposition whips, accepts responsibility for the course of negotiation about business with the Government, arranges the subjects for debate where (as in Committee of Supply) practice leaves the choice of subject to the Opposition, cross-examines the Prime Minister and other ministers, watches for encroachments on the rights of minorities, demands debates when the Government is trying to slide away without parliamentary criticism, arranges for the more important speakers to reply to ministers. He must be in his place even more constantly than the Prime Minister. He must be familiar with all the tricks of skilled parliamentarians and all the opportunities of the rules of the House. It is excellent training for the future occupants of the Treasury Bench, and essential for the effective operation of democratic government.[1]

The whips work under the control of the party leaders. Their functions differ somewhat according as their party supports the Government or is in opposition. The function of the Government whips, it has been said, is 'to make a House, to keep a House, and cheer the Minister'. Of the last of these we need say little: a minister who cannot get a cheer except out of his whips either is a poor speaker or has a poor case to justify: there are certain formulae, varying from party to party, which can always raise a cheer from the most depressed party member. Making and keeping a House is a more important duty. By a usage which dates from 1640, and which may be altered by resolution of the House, there is a quorum of forty members.[2] At the meeting of the House it is the Speaker's duty to see that a quorum is present. If a quorum is not present after prayers, he waits or retires from the House either until a quorum is present, or until four o'clock. At four o'clock he again counts the House, and if a quorum is not present he adjourns the House to the next sitting day without question put.[3] Accordingly, if the Government wishes any business to be done, the whips must see that a quorum is present. In practice, there is no difficulty, at least on a full day, for some members have questions to put and others wish to hear the answers and to put supplementary questions. Moreover, though the Government usually wants certain motions passed, the Opposition equally desires to criticise those motions.

---

[1] On the functions of Opposition, see Chapter VI.
[2] May, p. 311. [3] May, p. 312.

Keeping a House is not quite so easy. Once the House is sitting the Speaker takes no action unless his attention is drawn to the absence of a quorum, or unless there are not forty members voting in a division. If notice is taken that forty members are not present, the Speaker directs strangers to withdraw and members are summoned as if for a division. After the expiration of two minutes, the Speaker proceeds to count the House, the outer door being kept open during the proceedings. If the count is demanded before four o'clock, the Speaker adjourns until that hour or until the quorum is made up before that hour. If a quorum is not present at four o'clock, the House is adjourned until the next sitting day. If the count is demanded after four o'clock, and the quorum is not present, the House stands adjourned until the next sitting day. The same course is followed if forty members are not present at a division, except that if a division is taken between 7.30 p.m. and 8.30 p.m. (during which period a count may not be demanded) the business under discussion stands over and the next business is taken.[1]

It is obviously not necessary that members should be in the Chamber itself. They must be somewhere near the fount of oratory, but they need not drink. The visitor to the House is in fact impressed with the multifarious duties which members find to perform when an ordinary member is speaking in an ordinary debate. The honourable member may be addressing almost empty benches. A minister will be on the Treasury Bench. With him will be a whip. A few members, most of whom are anxious to speak, will be found dotted among masses of order papers. In the lobbies, members will be interviewing constituents or talking to friends or just gossiping. In the library others will be preparing speeches, or writing to constituents, or just reading. Some will be at the bar, some in the smoke room, some in the dining room or on the terrace. Upstairs, Select Committees (or even Standing Committees) and private members' committees will be sitting. When the bell rings these will all troop into the Chamber and be counted or walk into the division lobbies according as they are instructed by the whips. Consequently, all that the whips have to do to keep a House is to see that enough members are at hand. The result is that a count is rarely

[1] May, pp. 312–13.

successful when Government business is being taken; and counts are therefore rarely demanded.

On the other hand, the whips have no responsibility when private members' business is under discussion. If a member wishes to keep a quorum he must persuade enough friends to support him. This is especially difficult because private members' business is always taken on Fridays, when many members visit their constituencies.

Sometimes 'counting out' is deliberate, and on occasion it has been organised by the whips. If a private member decides to raise an inconvenient subject, there are several ways of dealing with him. If he is on the Government side the whips may persuade him not to raise it but to talk the matter over with a minister. If he persists, or is not amenable to persuasion because he comes from the other side, the whips can be put on against him and his proposal defeated. This does not, of course, stop the preceding discussion. Sometimes debate may be avoided by 'talking out' the previous subject by persuading members to go on discussing that subject until the time for the automatic adjournment of the House.[1] Sometimes members can be advised not to answer the division bell so that the House is counted out.

Making and keeping a House are not the most important functions of the Government whips. Primarily, their business is to secure the passing of Government motions with the least delay and difficulty possible. Accordingly, their essential function is to see that the Government has a majority in every division for which the whips are put on. Indeed, they do more, for they must never allow the Government majority to fall very low. It is considered that a narrow majority, and still more a defeat, even on a minor issue or in a 'snap vote', is damaging to the prestige of the Government. It creates the impression that Government supporters are not keen in their support or are failing in their parliamentary duties, and it encourages the Opposition, both in the House and outside. The psychological effect of low majorities and even of defeats is perhaps exaggerated. It is nevertheless true that Opposi-

---

[1] E.g. in April 1937 members opposed to (1) Sunday restrictions on the sale of ice-cream, and (2) amendment of the divorce laws, kept up a debate on a Road Traffic Bill in order to leave no time for a Shops (Sunday Trading Restriction) Bill and a Marriage Bill: see 323 H.C.Deb. 5 s., 757–60 (30 April 1937).

tion newspapers make the most of the situation. 'Government defeat' in the headlines encourages the party workers of the Opposition and discourages the party workers of the Government. A paragraph which begins: 'The growing unpopularity of this Government, even with its own supporters, is shown by the fact that last night its majority fell to...' is annoying, though the real explanation may be that Old Etonians were having a feast, or merely that a combination of circumstances kept a number of members away. There is some evidence, however, though it is not very strong, that some of the waverers who really determine elections tend, like rats, to leave a sinking ship.

On their side the Opposition whips do their best to keep the Government majority as low as possible. They, too, are therefore anxious to secure the largest possible attendance of their own supporters when a division takes place. The more important the division, the more members are required. Hence arises the practice, followed by both sides, of emphasising the importance of a division by underlining the request for attendance. A 'three-line whip' indicates that all other engagements should be put aside.

Some members must obviously be absent, through illness, pressing engagements, or the performance of ministerial duties. The Government whips can without qualms give permission for absence if an equal number of Opposition members will be absent; on their side, the Opposition whips can give permission for absence if they are sure that, by reason of the absence of Government members, the majority will not be increased. So arises the practice of 'pairing'. A member who wishes to be absent from a certain division asks his whip to find him a 'pair'. If twenty members from each side can thus find 'pairs', the forty members can leave the House with their consciences intact, their prestige with their whips unimpaired, and their duties at least partly performed. Absence without pairing does not necessarily call for a reprimand, but frequent ill-attendance will produce a circular letter from the whips pointing out the dangers of the situation. Reprimand is not in fact the normal weapon of the whips. It is their business to know their members, to talk to them in a friendly fashion, and to suggest rather than to demand more regular attendance. The whips succeed best if they persuade their members to say to each other: 'I don't want to let old Blank down.'[1]

Sometimes, however, if a whip sees a member trying to sneak away, he will explain that they are most anxious for his attendance that evening, that he has reason to believe that the Prime Minister has his eye on the member as one who may give great assistance to the Government in some ministerial capacity on a future occasion, and that it would not be wise to let the party down on this occasion of all others. This function was particularly onerous when, under Mr Balfour's reform, the short and casual interruption for dinner known as 'the Speaker's chop' was superseded by a formal adjournment for dinner at 8.15 p.m. on Tuesdays and Wednesdays. Mr Gulland, a Liberal whip, has explained to a Select Committee that from 7.30 p.m. to 8 p.m. he had to stand at the door to prevent men from going out to dinner, in case a division was called for.[2]

More serious than absence is the offence of voting in the wrong lobby. Absence counts one vote, while voting with the other side counts two. Moreover, a Government, particularly (though an Opposition equally dislikes to find its men voting with the Government), is weakened in public opinion if its proposals cannot secure the support of its own members. Here again the velvet glove is more effective than the mailed fist. If a whip finds that a member dissents strongly, he promises to draw the Prime Minister's attention to the complaint, suggests that perhaps some modification may be agreed or some inquiry made to satisfy the member's point of view, which he recognises to be one of great importance; and in the last resort he can always point out that the member could make his protest effective by abstaining from voting on the question. The mailed fist is seldom, if ever, employed. The efficient whip, to change the metaphor, rides his horse with free rein, and uses his whip only to keep off the flies. Of one famous whip, the Master of Elibank, it was said,

Persuasion tips his tongue when e'er he talks.[3]

In the debate which preceded the setting up of the Select Committee on Procedure in 1913 there was general agreement that reprimands

[1] The chief whip to the National Government which resigned in 1945 estimated that for a three-line whip as many as 150 or 200 members might be expected to be not available: H.C. 9 of 1945–6. This was in wartime, when the number of absentees would be larger than usual.
[2] H.C. 378 of 1914, Q. 1319.   [3] 50 H.C.Deb. 5 s., 667 (Sir J. D. Rees quoting).

were rare. Mr Arthur Ponsonby, who was by no means an orthodox party voter, said that he had frequently voted against the Government, and only once had any pressure or influence been brought to bear upon him. Then the chief whip sent him a note which began: 'May I say with what pain....' He had then been in the House for ten days only; and perhaps the whip thought that as a new boy he ought to be informed of the conventions of the school.[1]

Mr Spencer Leigh Hughes agreed with him:

I have voted against the Government sometimes, and I have never been reproached by the whips. If I were I should retort. Indeed, the only official communications I have had from the whips have been when they have approached me with great deference, almost with obsequiousness, asking me to go and speak at some by-election in the country. So that the tyranny of the whips, so far as I am concerned, is a fiction altogether, and I do not believe it exists.[2]

The evidence given to the Select Committee was to much the same effect. Mr Gulland, a Liberal whip, stated that he had never heard of a member being spoken to if he voted against the Government, though he thought that the practice might differ in the Conservative party.[3] Mr R. A. Sanders, a Conservative whip, said that if a whip saw a member moving towards the wrong lobby he would speak to him; if it was found that he was constantly voting against his party his local association would be communicated with; but no action would be taken in respect of a single instance.[4] Mr James Hope said that he had heard of a member who had received a letter from his chief whip beginning: 'It is with the greatest pain I note your vote last night.'[5] What usually happens, in fact, is that the local association or party asks the member to explain his conduct, and decides to seek a new candidate if his answers are not satisfactory. In 1914, for instance, Mr Martin of St Pancras twice voted against the Government, and his Radical association decided to seek a new candidate.[6] Similarly, Mr Mason of Coventry voted against the Government and his association refused to recognise him as a candidate.[7] Since 1914, however, the Liberal party has become more

---

[1] 50 H.C.Deb. 5 s., 642.
[2] 50 H.C.Deb. 5 s., 656.
[3] H.C. 378 of 1914, Q. 1615.
[4] Ibid. Qs. 1813–21.
[5] Ibid. Qs. 1616–17.
[6] Ibid. Q. 1511.
[7] Ibid.

'liberal' in its attitude to cross-voting. The Labour party has the strictest of machines. The party Constitution declares that 'any candidate who, after election, fails to accept or act in harmony with the Standing Orders of the Parliamentary Labour Party shall be considered to have violated the terms of this Constitution'.[1]

These Standing Orders state:[2] 'The privilege of membership of the Parliamentary Labour party involves the acceptance of the decisions of the party meeting. The party recognises the right of the individual member to abstain from voting on matters of deeply held personal and conscientious conviction.' They add that the whip may be withdrawn 'on account of things said or done' by members of the party. Further, 'serious or persistent breaches of party discipline' may be reported to the National Executive Committee of the Labour party, which has power to deprive a member of his party endorsement at the next election, and this means in practice his almost certain defeat if he chooses to defy the party and stand as an independent.

These Standing Orders were adopted while the Labour party was in office in 1929–31, in order to meet the difficulties caused by conflict between the Labour Government and the Independent Labour party, whose members were, as members of the Labour party, members of the Parliamentary Labour party but acted as a left-wing pressure group.[3] They remained in operation while the Labour party was in opposition from 1931 to 1940 and while it formed part of Mr Churchill's Coalition Government from 1940 to 1945. They were redrafted when the Labour Government took office in 1945,[4] but were suspended until the party was again in opposition in 1952, when they were reintroduced in their present form. This reintroduction was due to the fact that fifty-five members of the party, led by Mr Aneurin Bevan, disobeyed the Labour party whip to vote for the party's amendment, expressing approval of the Government's White Paper on Defence. The decision was taken at a meeting of the Parliamentary Labour party on 11 March 1952, when the following resolution was passed:[5]

[1] Clause VIII, 8 of the Constitution. See *Labour Party*, Report of the National Executive Committee, 1936, p. 125.
[2] R. T. McKenzie, *British Political Parties*, p. 599.
[3] See the text in *Parliament* (1st ed.), p. 81.   [4] R. T. McKenzie, *op. cit.* p. 598.
[5] *The Times*, 12 March 1952.

Believing that the disregarding of decisions arrived at by the Parliamentary party gravely damages the party as a whole, and makes it impossible for the Parliamentary party to discharge its duties as an effective Opposition, this meeting decides to impose such Standing Orders as will make it obligatory on all members to carry out decisions of the Parliamentary party, taking into account the traditional conscience clause.

The existence of the Standing Orders has, however, little effect. The left wing of the Labour party, like the right wing of the Conservative party, tends to be in disagreement with the main body of party opinion, particularly where the two parties are more or less in concord on a particular issue, and at times this lack of agreement is converted into open revolt. Actual cross-voting is more common in the Labour party than in the Conservative party, where the public-school tradition of loyalty to the 'team' is more evident. In the Conservative party the lack of agreement is more subdued and expresses itself in campaigns under slogans like 'Balfour must go', 'Baldwin must go', and so forth. The Parliamentary Labour party, being a formally organised body, holds a meeting to give expression to the controversy and, if need be, to take a decision which appears in the newspapers next morning. In either party steps can be taken to withdraw the whip and, in an extreme case, to cancel party endorsement. Neither party admits the right of persistent opponents to shelter under the party banner or to retain the privileges of the party label. The difference is one of machinery. In the Conservative party the whip is withdrawn by the leader and refusal of endorsement at the next election follows as a matter of course. In the Labour party there is a formal hearing before the Parliamentary Labour party before the whip is withdrawn and another formal hearing before the National Executive Committee before membership is cancelled. The 'discipline' of the Conservative party is as strong as that of the Labour party, though less attempt is made to formalise it and the machine operates more secretly and silently.[1]

Cross-voting is, however, uncommon. There are other and more effective methods of protesting against or influencing party or Government policy.[2] It is, in fact, one of the most important functions of the

---

[1] Mr Disraeli himself was refused the Conservative whip in 1844: see Parker, *Sir Robert Peel*, III, p. 144.　　[2] See Chapter IV.

whips to keep leaders, and especially ministers, informed of the currents of opinion among ordinary members of the party in the House. The Government whips especially are liaison officers, making the wishes of the Government known privately to members, and making the wishes of members known privately to the Government. This is part of the art of management which is discussed in the next chapter.

The functions of the Government whips and especially the chief whip in arranging Government business under the control of the leader of the House have already been described.[1] There are ancillary functions with which the leader is not directly concerned. The Government speakers, for instance, are arranged with the leader or minister in charge. The debate must, however, be sustained to the appointed time and must come to an end at that time. It is convenient for members to know that a division is expected at, say, 7 p.m. or 9.45 p.m. They can thus attend to their professional business, or go to the theatre, or speak at a public dinner, with reasonable certainty that their presence will not be missed. Provided that the subject has been fully discussed, the Speaker or Chairman will accept a closure motion; so that, provided that the debate is continued in the interval, the division—or rather, the two divisions, that on the closure and that on the motion—can be arranged for the appropriate time. In the meantime it is necessary to keep the debate going. Usually, it goes of its own accord, for there are more members wishing to speak than there is time for speeches. In such a case the whips do no more than indicate to the Speaker or Chairman that certain members desire to speak. Such a notification does not bind the presiding officer, even in practice. Moreover, most members personally inform the Speaker or Chairman of their desire to speak, and do not leave the whips to do it. There have been exceptional cases in which a Chairman, looking at his list, allowed a member to catch his eye when the member concerned was not present. Usually, however, he looks round to see who is 'up' and chooses that member who is most likely to add something to the debate.[2] We have already noted a tendency for minorities and persons of peculiar views to catch his eye

---

[1] *Ante*, pp. 75–7.

[2] In February 1937 a member was suspended for persisting in accusing the Deputy Chairman of choosing only those on the whips' list: see 320 H.C.Deb. 5 s., 1492 (18 February 1937).

more often than members who are likely merely to repeat in more halting language what has already been said more smoothly. Nevertheless, it is convenient for the Chairman to know who is most anxious to speak, and especially to know what maiden speeches are waiting to leave virginal lips—for maiden speeches are always given preference—and what ministers and ex-ministers are willing to speak.

If, however, there is likely to be any shortage of eloquence or if, before the appointed time, the fount of oratory threatens to dry up, the whips have to do some pumping. This can be done before the debate by suggesting that the leaders are very anxious to hear the views of a few of the more long-winded members. Moreover, there are always members—usually voted as prize bores, but even bores have their uses—who are capable of speaking at any length on anything. A couple of speeches will fill up the time until the prodigal sons and daughters return, not to eat of the fatted calf, but to express their views on the opinions they would have heard if they had attended the debate. In the last resort the prodigals must be brought back. It is the business of the whips to know where they are to be found. If an unexpected division appears likely, or if an expected division is about to take place at an unexpected time, some member must be put up to occupy the time while telephones ring 'in town to-night' and taxis disgorge members in Palace Yard. This function is a little more complicated during all-night sittings. If the Government has a substantial majority a system of relays can be provided. As the Opposition vote falls, Government supporters can be allowed to go home. All that is necessary is that the Government should maintain a majority. Accordingly, as supporters become anxious to go home to bed or breakfast, other supporters must be brought out of their beds or away from breakfast. It is not un-common for a member to be awakened at 5 a.m. by a telephone message asking urgently for his attendance.

The Government whips are, technically, junior ministers. The chief whip is Parliamentary Secretary to the Treasury. Until recently he was known as 'Patronage Secretary', a name which descends from the more expansive days when a majority was kept by patronage or influence or, as some would say, corruption. His functions in this respect have not entirely disappeared. He brings to the attention of the Prime Minister the names of members who are deserving of honours or whose support will be more effective if honour is accorded them. Members approach him to recommend those among their constituents who are most worthy of decoration, or whose decoration will make the members' seats rather safer. If, as is not always the case, he is treasurer of the party fund, he indicates to the Prime Minister those whose 'political and public services', as witnessed by the party fund, are most suitable for royal acknowledgment. It must be said, however, that something other than mere party advantage must now be shown, and that the Prime Minister is not informed of any contributions that may have been made.[1]

In addition, there are three or more Lords Commissioners of the Treasury. In January 1956, there were five paid and three unpaid Assistant whips. The Treasurer, Comptroller and Vice-Chamberlain of the Household are also Government whips. In other words, ten or twelve members on the Government side are whips, seven or eight of these being paid out of moneys provided by Parliament.[2]

The office of Parliamentary Secretary, said Mr Disraeli, 'requires consummate knowledge of human nature, the most amiable flexibility, and complete self-control'.[3] Knowledge of human nature and amiability are perhaps the most essential requirements of all whips. They must know all their members; they must be aware of every wind of opinion that blows; they must understand the temper and whims of the Opposition; they must know when to cajole, when to persuade, and when to threaten. The House must be treated on a large scale as a committee is treated on a smaller. Obstruction can be removed by a gentle conversation beforehand. Proposals will find acceptance if they are put to one man in one way and to another man in another way. Ruffled feathers must be smoothed and sensitive skins gently stroked. Much of the process of parliamentary management is conducted in the lobbies and smoke rooms, where indeed the only really dangerous opposition arises, as we shall see in Chapter V.

[1] See *Cabinet Government*, ch. XIII.
[2] Until the Civil List Act, 1936, the Household officers were paid out of the Civil List.
[3] *Life of Lord George Bentinck*, p. 227.

CHAPTER IV

THE FRAMEWORK OF ORATORY

I. HOURS OF LABOUR

Until quite recently the session began in February and ended in July or August. Occasionally Parliament sat through the summer. The opposition of the House of Lords to the 'confiscation of property' in the Municipal Corporations Bill of 1835, for instance, kept Parliament in session until September. The session of 1860, which lasted from 24 January to 28 August, was stated to be the longest for many years.[1] In 1887, owing to the Crimes Bill and Irish opposition, Parliament sat until the middle of September.[2] Even now Standing Orders contemplate that the session will begin in the spring. This is, however, by way of precaution only, because they proceed to indicate the course of business if it begins in the autumn.

Commencement in the autumn is, in fact, now the rule. Not only is seven months quite inadequate for the business which the Government desires the House of Commons to undertake, but also there is so much essential business to be done in February and March and between April and July, that very little time is left for ordinary legislation. For instance, between 14 February and 31 March 1912, the King's Speech occupied eight days, essential financial business twelve days, private members' business eight-and-a-half days, and the Government had only four-and-a-half days for its own legislation, which included the Army Bill.[3]

Moreover, the complications of the financial system and of international affairs have made it difficult to justify even the long interval between the end of July and the middle of October. In 1930 each House resolved at the end of July that the House should adjourn until October,

---

[1] Quoted Bell, *Palmerston*, II, p. 253.   [2] *Life of A. J. Balfour*, I, p. 131.
[3] H.C. 378 of 1914, Q. 1330 (Mr J. W. Gulland). Between 10 March and 31 March 1913: King's Speech, 5 days; finance, 9 days; Government Bill, 1 day; all private members' time was taken. Between 10 February and 31 March 1914: King's Speech, 8 days; finance, 14 days; private members, 11½ days; Government Bills, 2½ days.

but that if the Lord Chancellor and the Speaker respectively, after consultation with the Government, were satisfied that the two Houses should meet at an earlier time, they should give notice accordingly, and the Houses should meet at the time stated in the notice.[1] This procedure was followed in subsequent years and was embodied in Standing Orders in 1947. Standing Order 112 now provides that whenever the House stands adjourned and it is represented to Mr Speaker (or, if he is unable to act, the Chairman or Deputy Chairman of Ways and Means) by Her Majesty's ministers that the public interest requires that the House should meet at any earlier time during the adjournment, Mr Speaker, if he is satisfied that the public interest does so require, may give notice that he is so satisfied, and thereupon the House shall meet at the time stated in such notice. To enable this Standing Order to be used, if need be, Parliament is not prorogued in August, but the two Houses stand adjourned until October or November. After a short meeting Parliament is prorogued and is summoned to meet again almost immediately. In other words, the two Houses are now in continuous session, subject to a long adjournment in the summer and shorter adjournments at Christmas, Easter and Whitsuntide.

Except on Fridays, the House of Commons meets at 2.30 p.m. and sits until 10.30 p.m., though if Standing Orders are suspended the hour of adjournment may be later, and all-night sittings are not uncommon. Long sessions and long daily sittings often go together, since the cause is some acute political controversy or some unusual political situation. In the session of 1860, for instance, the House rarely rose before 2 a.m., and often continued until 3 a.m. or even 4 a.m.[2] In the summer of 1887 the House rose only twice before midnight, and the average hour was 2.15 a.m. Before the war of 1939–45 Standing Orders prescribed 11.30 p.m. as the time of rising, but during the war the blackout, evening air raids and transport difficulties rendered earlier sittings necessary. In 1945 it was decided not to revert to the late sitting, and the House now rises at 10.30 p.m. The Standing Orders can always be suspended by resolution; but, since neither side likes long sittings, it is generally

[1] 255 H.C.Deb. 5 s., 2638; 81 H.L.Deb. 5 s., 1311. This form of motion had been adopted on four previous occasions.
[2] Bell, *Palmerston*, II, p. 253.

possible to secure agreement for the termination of business at the time fixed.

The hours are, nevertheless, somewhat strange, though there is good reason for them. The new rules of 1902 provided for sittings to begin at 2 p.m., but this gave inadequate time for lunch. Accordingly, the time was fixed at 2.45 p.m. in 1906 and was not altered until the war of 1939–45 compelled the House to change its habits. When normal conditions were restored in 1945, however, the desirability of leaving the mornings free was emphasised, and the hours of 2.30 p.m. to 10.30 p.m. were fixed. One reason for this preference is indicated by the fact that even in the seventeenth century the Speaker often sent the Sergeant-at-Arms to fetch the legal members from the courts.[1] There has always been a fair number of lawyers in the House. The courts rise at 4.15 p.m. If, therefore, questions end at 3.30 p.m., the legal members can attend to their profession and yet perform a substantial part of their parliamentary duties. This is, however, one example only. Mr Swift MacNeill asserted that the beginning of sittings in the afternoon was due to the introduction of 'City gentlemen' into politics.[2] Certainly the House of Commons is not composed either wholly or in substantial part of professional politicians. Most members have businesses or professions to conduct. They can, therefore, attend to their own affairs in the day and the nation's in the evening. Indeed, provided that a quorum is left in the House and a majority on the Government side, they can also attend to their pleasure in the evening and obey the whip near 10 o'clock at night. It is usually possible to prevent an important division between 3.30 p.m. and 9.45 p.m. Tea, dinner and a theatre may thus be enjoyed in the interval, and taxis disgorge their loads at 9.45 p.m. to vote for or against the Government.

Immediately after prayers, the House proceeds to private business. This is now entirely formal. If a Bill is opposed it is set down on the instructions of the Chairman of Ways and Means for 7 p.m. on some day other than a Friday, and must then either be passed or rejected before 9 p.m., or be adjourned.[3] Otherwise, no private business may be taken after 2.45 p.m.[4] Questions begin immediately and may con-

---

[1] Redlich, II, p. 76.   [2] H.C. 378 of 1914, Q. 534.
[3] S.O. 7 (4) (5).   [4] S.O. 7 (2).

tinue until 3.30 p.m., after which no questions may be asked except those which have not been answered owing to the absence of the minister to whom they are addressed, and those which have not appeared on the paper, but which are of an urgent character and relate either to matters of public importance or to the arrangement of business[1] ('private notice' questions). Thus, something approaching an hour is given to questions. Motions for the adjournment of the House may then be made. The adjournment must be for the purpose of discussing a definite matter of urgent public importance; and if the motion is accepted by the Speaker and adequately supported, the adjournment is moved, not at once, as was formally the practice, but at 7 p.m. on the same day.[2] Public petitions may next be presented. The member presenting a petition must confine himself to a statement of the parties from whom it comes, of the number of signatures attached to it, and of the material allegations contained in it, and to the reading of the prayer of the petition.[3] No debate is now permitted, unless it complains of some present personal grievance for which there may be an urgent necessity for providing an immediate remedy. All other petitions presented are ordered to lie upon the Table and are referred to a committee on public petitions, by which they are, for all practical purposes, decently interred.[4] Consequently, the public petition no longer plays the great part in initiating debate that it played a century ago.

Unopposed motions for accounts or papers may next be moved, and notices of motion are given.[5] Motions for the appointment of Select Committees and motions for leave to bring in Bills may be moved on Tuesdays and Wednesdays, and may also be moved on Mondays and Thursdays if the notice is set down by the Government.[6] In practice, however, motions for Select Committees are rare, and motions for leave to bring in Bills under the 'ten minutes' rule' are used only by private members.[7] The House then proceeds to the orders of the day.

On Fridays, the House meets at 11 a.m. and adjourns for the week-end at 4.30 p.m. The time of the adjournment indicates the reason for this practice. Members wish to get away for the week-end, often to

---

[1] S.O. 8 (2) (3).   [2] S.O. 9.   [3] S.O. 91.   [4] S.O. 93–4.
[5] These are of no importance except as to private members' motions, for which see Chapter XI.   [6] S.O. 12.   [7] See Chapter XI.

their constituencies. Accordingly, Friday has a short sitting only. Indeed, since private members' business is taken on most Fridays, the attendance is usually thin. Ministers take the opportunity to do some departmental business, and members proceed to their constituencies. On Fridays no questions, except private notice questions, are taken; and after private business and petitions the House proceeds to the orders of the day.[1]

2. QUESTIONS

Of this preliminary business, only questions and their attendant adjournment motions are of real importance. The practice of asking questions, though now of the utmost constitutional importance, is of comparatively recent origin. The first formal question was asked, apparently, in 1721,[2] but the practice was not substantially developed until after 1832. The first question appeared on the notice paper in 1835, and a special part of the paper was not given to questions until 1869.[3] Until 1886 all questions were put orally; but since the resolution of 1886, embodied in Standing Orders in 1888, questions are put by the member simply rising in his place and calling out the number of his question.[4] Until 1882, also, a debate might arise immediately out of a question. The method of *interpellation* has never been used in the House of Commons, though something very similar is common in the House of Lords. It is a well-recognised rule in the lower House that a debate cannot arise except on a motion; but under the old practice no difficulty arose, for the member put himself in order by moving the adjournment of the House. As a result, the Irish members saw to it that the wrongs of Ireland were debated before the House proceeded to the orders of the day; and after 1882 the procedure was altered so that the modern 'urgency motion' was the only adjournment motion permitted at this stage. Even this did not prevent the continuance of questions until a late hour. In 1901, for instance, there was an occasion when a debate on a private Bill occupied nearly two hours, then there were 160 questions and finally an adjournment motion. The result was that public business

[1] S.O. 2. [2] Redlich, I, p. 117.
[3] *Ibid.* I, p. 117. The number of questions rose from 129 in 1847 to 6448 in 1901, when 'starring' was introduced: *ibid.* II, p. 244 n. [4] *Ibid.* I, p. 184.

was reached after 8 p.m.[1] Under the modern practice the urgency motion comes in at 7 p.m. and opposed private business is set down for an evening. Also, the question-hour is rigidly limited; and the House proceeds to discuss public business at 3.30 p.m. or as soon thereafter as private notice questions have been answered and motions on the order of business passed.

In order to minimise the inconvenience caused by this rigid rule and yet to give the question-hour its full constitutional importance, it was provided in 1902 that the answers to all questions not marked with an asterisk should be in writing and circulated in the *Official Report*.[2] It was thought that questions which merely sought information could thus be answered without occupying the time of the House. 'Starring' is in fact frequent, partly because many questions are in substance criticisms, and partly for other reasons. In particular, the departments take far more trouble to answer a starred question quickly. As Mr E. Brown said in 1930:

> Members have found in dealing with the departments that, when they want an answer, and want it rather urgently, if they star their question they get their answer within two or three days, whereas I have known it to be two or three weeks before an answer came to an unstarred question.[3]

The result is that there are usually more starred questions than can be answered in an hour. In 1909 the House resolved to limit the number of such questions to be asked by any member on any day to a maximum of eight; in 1918 the number was reduced to four; and in 1920 it was reduced again to three, the figure at which the rule now stands. Even this has not always enabled the House to secure oral answers to all starred questions, as the following figures show:[4]

	No. of Questions in the Paper	No. of Questions reached
Session 1935–6		
5 December 1935	105	68
18 December 1935	110	95
4 March 1936	90	90
29 June 1936	79	76
29 October 1936	54	54

[1] H.C. 378 of 1914, Q. 213 (Mr James Hope).
[2] See now S.O. 7.   [3] H.C. 161 of 1931, Q. 166.
[4] H.C. 58 of 1946, pp. 2 and 39.

	No. of Questions in the Paper	No. of Questions reached
Session 1936–7		
5 November 1936	103	80
9 December 1936	52	52
2 March 1937	68	67
28 June 1937	47	47
21 October 1937	93	92
Session 1937–8		
28 October 1937	115	75
8 December 1937	86	82
1 March 1938	60	60
27 June 1938	67	59
5 October 1938	48	48
2 November 1938	34	34
Session 1938–9		
10 November 1938	102	75
14 December 1938	115	85
1 March 1939	86	85
26 June 1939	71	71
Session 1945–6		
23 August 1945	182	64
16 October 1945	211	72
1 November 1945	154	80

It will be seen that before the war there was generally a large number of questions at the beginning of a session, but that all starred questions were usually reached towards the end of the session. In the post-war sessions, however, numerous questions arose out of demobilisation, insurance problems, housing, and so on, which made it impossible to reach more than a third of the starred questions. The Select Committee on Procedure of 1945–6 decided not to recommend a decrease in the maximum number of questions. Though before the war there were members who put down three questions every day for the sake of publicity—questions by Mr Harry Day, M.P., were sometimes met by the chant 'Another Day'—in the session 1945–6 a reduction in the maximum would have gained no more than fifteen to twenty questions out of 150 or so. Also, there has been no evidence in the post-war period of an abuse of the privilege.

Questions not disposed of orally are answered in writing, so that if a question is asked for the sake of information that information is forthcoming whether the question is answered orally or not. As will be seen presently, however, this is not always the purpose of a question. Since not all the starred questions may be reached, the Government arranges the departments on a rota. For instance, Foreign Office questions may be grouped near the top on Mondays and Wednesdays; the Prime Minister's questions come at No. 45; and so on.

A desire for information may not be, however, the reason for starring a question. It is true that some members really seek information, perhaps to provide material for a speech, perhaps to enable a friend to include hitherto unpublished material in a book,[1] or possibly merely out of idle curiosity. For purposes of information, however, an answer in writing is as good as an oral answer. Sometimes, indeed, the answer is already in a published return. For instance, Mr Ramsay MacDonald pointed out in 1930 that on the day on which he was giving evidence one question not only asked for information which had already been published but referred to the document in which it could be found.[2] Often the Clerks at the Table, acting under the authority of the Speaker, will disallow such a question.[3] Sometimes, however, the member desires less to possess information than to impart it. Questions such as 'Is the minister aware that...and does he propose to take steps to deal with the matter?' are not uncommon. Mr Ramsay MacDonald, in his evidence before the Select Committee of 1930, stated that more than half the questions were on debating points.[4] In other words, the question-hour is used by the Opposition as a means of embarrassing the Government. An instance may be selected at random. On 23 July 1937, the First Lord of the Admiralty stated in a public speech that the protection of ships carrying refugees from Spanish ports was as much 'intervention' in the Spanish civil war as any more obvious method. On 26 July 1937, the Secretary of State for Foreign Affairs found himself compelled to answer questions on whether the Government recognised as intervention the protection of refugees, and whether it was a policy of the Government to protect refugees. Obviously, neither questioner sought information. He was anxious to put into a difficulty the First Lord or the Foreign Secretary or, better still, both of them.

[1] By way of precaution it should be stated that the present writer has used many methods, but not this one.   [2] H.C. 161 of 1931, Q. 159.
[3] *Ibid*. Q. 168 (Mr E. Brown). Questions may be disallowed for other reasons.
[4] H.C. 161 of 1931, Q. 159.

So obviously is this the fact that in June 1937 it was suggested to the Labour party that some kind of central bureau should be set up for the examination of questions to be placed on the paper by Labour members. It was proposed that they should hand in questions to the bureau 'in order to prevent overlapping and to ensure that every afternoon ministers are subjected to a well-organised barrage'.[1] The art of questioning is part of the technique of opposition.

Sometimes, too, a question is the only means of securing redress of an individual grievance which a member has already put before the appropriate minister without securing satisfaction. The two points of view, the desire for redress and the desire to embarrass, are put in the following colloquy between Mr J. Chuter Ede and Sir Austen Chamberlain:

A starred question sometimes represents the following up of unsuccessful private representations to the minister, does it not, and it is a very powerful weapon for a private member to have in his hands to use if he does not get reasonable courtesy and consideration from a minister on an important personal matter relating to one of his constituents, that he can put the question in the House?—My experience is of a rather different kind. If I want to get a thing done I write to the minister, but if I want to make a row I put down a question. If my interest is in harrying a minister, I put down a question for the sake of the supplementaries I can put, but if my question is in the interests of a constituent, I write to the minister.[2]

The two points of view are really not very different. A member who desires to raise the claim of a constituent will normally write to the Department concerned not merely because a starred question is at this stage too heavy a weapon but also—at least if he is a supporter of the Government—because he does not wish to embarrass the Minister. Nor is it always good tactics to begin with the heavy weapons. If the Minister is compelled to answer a question in the House he may have to pledge himself publicly against a point of view which the member is urging on him; in other words, the parliamentary question is the last remedy, not the first.[3] The member proceeds to 'make a row' only if he cannot get what he wants in some other way. In any event, whether

---

[1] *The Times*, 23 June 1937.   [2] H.C. 161 of 1931, Q. 2526.
[3] H.C. 58 of 1946, Q. 1311.

the member wishes to redress a wrong or attack the minister, the power to ask a question is important. It compels the departments to be circumspect in all their actions; it prevents those petty injustices which are so commonly associated with bureaucracies. It compels the administrator to pay attention to the individual grievance. The citizen writes to his member, or to some other member (a member of the Opposition, for instance), and, if the grievance appears to be well founded, no fine promises or fair words will prevent, ultimately, an attack in the House of Commons. The foremost function of a civil servant is to protect his minister. The question-hour, said Mr Hacking, 'is dreaded more than any other hour by the civil servants, and it keeps them up to the mark much better than any other way which anybody could suggest'.[1]

There are disadvantages. The process of satisfying the curiosity and meeting the inquisition of ministers occupies much of the time of civil servants. Not only must investigations be made in the department, but also, if the questioning is likely to be strenuous and the minister likely to flounder, a civil servant must be in the 'box' with his files,[2] ready to pass an answer to the minister's parliamentary private secretary and thus provide the minister with defensive ammunition. Also, the constant inquisition is often destructive of departmental initiative. Since the minister must not be exposed to criticism, the department must not make mistakes; and since the department must not make mistakes, it often takes the line of least resistance and neglects to experiment. The administration of the Post Office under a responsible minister has been criticised on this ground.[3] It is difficult to conduct a business 'under the fierce light of publicity'.[4] This is one of the reasons suggested for the setting up of public service corporations.

[1] H.C. 161 of 1931, Q. 306.

[2] The 'box' is a row of seats at the end of the House to the right of and behind the Speaker's Chair. It is separated from the House by a low partition and is technically not part of the House. A member can, however, talk to an official over the partition, and notes may be passed into the House. For the benefit of readers abroad it should be mentioned that 'strangers' are not allowed within the bar or elsewhere within the House, so that there are no messenger boys to deliver notes.

[3] See Report of the Committee of Enquiry on the Post Office, Cmd. 4149/1932.

[4] A phrase used in the Report of the Special Board of Inquiry into certain statements made in *Lambert* v. *Levita*, affecting the British Broadcasting Corporation; Cmd. 5337, p. 29.

For the prevention of minor oppressions—often major oppressions so far as individuals are concerned—the process of questioning is, however, invaluable. A single well-known example will serve to illustrate. On 17 May 1928, Mr T. Johnston, by private notice, asked the Home Secretary 'whether he was aware that on Tuesday, the 15th May, at about 1.50 p.m., two police officers called at the place of business of Miss Savidge, and without affording her any opportunity of communicating with her parents or legal advisers...conveyed her to Scotland Yard, and that there she was questioned by two police officers for a period exceeding five hours; and whether such action was authorised by the right hon. gentleman in connection with his inquiry into the Sir Leo Money case?' The Home Secretary returned a soft answer, giving some information, and stating that he was making inquiries. Further questions followed, producing a telephoned message from Scotland Yard which, being read by the minister, was interrupted with cries of 'Shame!'[1] At the end of questions, Mr Johnston moved the adjournment of the House. The motion was accepted by the Speaker and was adequately supported. Thereupon a debate took place the same evening. The Home Secretary sent for the Director of Public Prosecutions and the police officers. While Mr Johnston was speaking to the adjournment motion, the minister's parliamentary private secretary secured a denial of some of the allegations from the police officers; nevertheless, the Home Secretary at once consented to a public inquiry.[2] The inquiry resulted in some criticism of the police,[3] and a Royal Commission then examined the whole question of police powers and practice.[4]

The acts of the police were described as 'third degree', though they would not have been recognised as such in some of the jurisdictions where that phrase originated. They were done by police officers in defence of brother officers accused, in substance, of perjury. They were good-humoured, and no force at all was used. Nevertheless, they were not in the tradition of British police administration. Being done by

---

[1] 217 H.C.Deb. 5 s., 1216–20. [2] *Ibid.* 1311–16.

[3] Report of the Tribunal appointed to inquire into the interrogation of Miss Savidge by the police, 1928, Cmd. 3147.

[4] Report of the Royal Commission on Police Powers and Procedure, 1929, Cmd. 3297.

metropolitan police officers, the Home Secretary was responsible; and by questions and debate the House called him to account. On such issues party divisions are forgotten, and members give chase at the mere scent of injustice like greyhounds after a hare.

One advantage of a starred question is that a rapid answer is secured. Until 1946 only two days' notice was given, and this in effect meant little more than one day's notice to the department. Thus, a question handed in on Monday would be circulated in the Order Paper on Tuesday (when it would first come to the notice of the department) and be answered on Wednesday. Where information had to be obtained from several departments and collated, or received by cable from abroad, the notice was sometimes insufficient. Accordingly, the Select Committee on Procedure in 1946 recommended[1] that two full days' notice be given to the department. Thus, a question handed in before the sitting of the House on Monday must be answered on Wednesday (unless a later reply is asked for), but a question handed in after the House begins sitting on Monday need not be answered until Thursday.

Originally, questions were asked in order to secure an answer. Today, they often serve as pegs on which to hang a more insidious 'supplementary'. The answers to questions on the paper are prepared by civil servants. Supplementary questions, however, may be put on the spur of the moment, and, though there may be a civil servant in the 'box' and a parliamentary private secretary in attendance ready to act as a channel of communication between the 'box' and the front bench, ministers usually have to answer supplementary questions out of their heads. Moreover, supplementaries need not be asked by the original questioner. Often a question produces a barrage of supplementaries. If two or three members rise, the Speaker usually calls on the original questioner. He is entitled, as Mr Baldwin once put it, 'to wring the last drop out of the orange before anyone else comes in'.[2] In fact, however, the function of cross-examination is thrown open. It is a public fight, and anybody can join in.[3]

The assumption is, first, that the minister probably knows nothing

[1] H.C. 58 of 1946, p. iv.   [2] H.C. 161 of 1931, Q. 312.
[3] Though the asking of a supplementary to some other member's question has been described as 'the lowest form of parliamentary activity': H.C. 58 of 1946, Q. 1537.

about the subject, and secondly, that if he does, he can probably be persuaded to say more than he intends. On their side, the minister and his advisers realise the purpose of the question; and it is the function of his civil service private secretary to see that the minister is provided not only with the answer to the original question but also with the answers to the probable supplementaries. In other words, the game of questioning is like a game of chess, in which all the moves are well known and each player thinks several moves ahead. Like chess, the game often ends in a draw. Though it would seem that the questioner has an advantage, in fact the winner is usually the minister. He is told by his private secretary not only what he may say but also what he must not say. Lord Eustace Percy once said that ministers are no more afraid of questions than a public speaker is afraid of hecklers; 'on the contrary, he prays for them in order that he may score off them'.[1] But his success depends on his quickness in repartee; there are some ministers, perhaps excellent administrators, who think of their best retorts in the bath next morning. On the other hand, there are ministers who jump into battle and do as much damage to themselves as to the other side. They have to face, not a single questioner, but serried ranks of critics. Each member of the Opposition delights in making a minister uncomfortable. Back-benchers on the Opposition side have no particular responsibility and need consider only the harm that they can do to the minister and to the Government and the quality of their wit. The minister's primary task is to say neither too little, so as to suggest that he is hiding something, nor too much. Smart repartee challenges a reply and hasty language is apt to annoy. The most successful minister in this ordeal is often he who says very little at great length and in a bland and confidential manner. Moreover, a junior minister answering for his chief must be appropriately humble.

The real difficulty of questions, from the ministerial point of view, is that in all ordinary circumstances some answer has to be given; and it is not always possible so to frame an answer as not to give the information desired. Particularly is this so where searching questions on the same subject follow daily with monotonous regularity. As Lord Eustace Percy has said: 'I have always found that the minister gets into a hole

[1] *Ibid.* Q. 1895.

as a result not only of supplementary questions, but of being driven by successive questions on successive days to divulge a little more.'[1]

It is easy to ignore a supplementary question. It is possible to refuse to answer a question on the paper. Where there is good cause for this course the House will acquiesce. Details about defence arrangements need not be disclosed; where delicate negotiations are in progress the minister will refuse to give particulars; the minister can be asked questions only about matters within his responsibility. No minister is responsible for the activities of foreign Governments or the Governments of independent members of the Commonwealth. In these cases the Minister will give information if he has it, but there is no obligation on him to get it. The Secretary of State for the Colonies is not responsible for the actions of colonial Governments within their sphere of self-government and he need do no more than give such information as he possesses; it is not his business to justify their action, though if a service is grant-aided from the United Kingdom he may be called upon to reply.[2] Many statutory corporations have been established—notably the British Broadcasting Corporation and the corporations controlling the nationalized industries—in order to limit the sphere of parliamentary control, and the member must so frame his question as to bring the subject-matter within the sphere of ministerial responsibility. If the member is genuinely seeking information, the minister may get it from the authority concerned and give it to the House, while disclaiming responsibility. Sometimes the information is obtained in a roundabout manner. Thus in 1937 there were many questions on the operation of social credit in Alberta. The Dominions Secretary satisfied members by requesting information from the High Commissioner for Canada, who presumably obtained it from the Government of Alberta. Ministers do their best to make some kind of answer, especially because the Opposition begins to suspect that something is wrong if answers are refused. If the minister thinks that the public interest requires him to refuse, he can normally make a successful appeal to the member not to ask— perhaps by telling him the answer confidentially. Sometimes, too, the member will find out privately what the answer will be and then decide that in the public interest the question ought not to be asked. For

[1] H.C. 161 of 1931, Q. 2022.   [2] 536 H.C.Deb., 5 s., 139.

instance, when Sir John Jellicoe was dismissed from the post of First Sea Lord in 1918, Mr Asquith asked Mr Bonar Law what the answer would be if a question were asked in the House. In view of the answer, Mr Asquith decided not to ask the question.[1] Many questions, too, are stopped by the Clerks-at-the-Table, on the ground that they are contrary to the practice of the House. As the Clerk of the House said in 1930:

If a question is put up to us that we do not like, we take it to the Speaker and he gives a ruling, which, if we consider it important, we record. We have a great many volumes. Some of [the precedents], of course, have been reported publicly in the House. The Speaker says: 'I did not allow this question', giving his reason, and that is on record. There are many others of which we have a record which the House has not.[2]

The fact that a question is asked does not necessarily mean that the member desires the answer. Quite often the minister desires to make a public pronouncement and requests the member to put the question down. The information may indicate a new policy, or it may be a move in a diplomatic manœuvre. For instance, in 1914 Colonel House was anxious that Argentina, Brazil, and Chile should enter with the United States into a Pan-American non-aggression pact. Chile could not easily be persuaded; and Colonel House thought that it might help if Great Britain and Canada expressed approval (like most Americans in 1914 he did not recognise that Canada meant Canada and not Great Britain). Accordingly, he asked Sir Edward Grey to get a question

[1] Bacon, *Life of Earl Jellicoe*, p. 384. In 1938 Mr Duncan Sandys, M.P., asked a question about anti-aircraft defences. The minister replied that the information was incorrect. Subsequently, Mr Sandys had a conversation with the Secretary of State and suggested that, before he asked another question, he should submit it to the minister. Accordingly, he sent a draft question containing full particulars of the arrangements made for defence and asking whether the minister was prepared to deny the facts. Instead of asking Mr Sandys not to ask the question, the Secretary of State consulted the Prime Minister, who advised him to send the papers to the Attorney-General, because the facts were accurate and could only have been known to Mr Sandys by reason of a breach of the Official Secrets Act by some person. The Attorney-General saw Mr Sandys and asked him to disclose the name of his informant. According to Mr Sandys—though this was denied by the Attorney-General—Mr Sandys was threatened with the penalties under the Official Secrets Act. Mr Sandys then raised the question of privilege in the House. In one of his statements in the House Mr Sandys said that he would not have asked the question in the House if the Minister had asked him not to do so. 'It was not the first time he had presented questions to ministers or withdrawn or withheld them at the request of ministers': *The Times*, 1 July 1938.

[2] H.C. 161 of 1931, Q. 4029 (Sir Horace Dawkins).

asked in the House of Commons in order that the Foreign Secretary might give the project his blessing.[1] Actually, the question was never asked; but the example shows that even in 1914 the technique was sufficiently well known to enable an American to suggest its use.

3. ADJOURNMENT MOTIONS

Mention has already been made of the use of adjournment motions to debate matters arising out of questions. It is convenient, however, to examine all so-called dilatory motions together. A distinction must be made between dilatory motions moved while a resolution is before the House and similar motions when no motion has yet been moved. If no question has been put to the House, the discussion on the motion to adjourn the House may relate to the reasons for suggesting the adjournment; that is, anything whatever (except matters already set down for discussion at some future date and proposals for legislation) may be debated. General debates could thus take place during or after questions or after public business was disposed of; and the Irish Nationalists naturally used such occasions to discuss the wrongs of Ireland. If, on the other hand, a motion was before the House or the House in committee, the purpose of a motion to adjourn the House, or to adjourn the debate, or (in committee) to report progress to the House, or that the Chairman leave the Chair, was to bring the debate on the motion before the House or to bring it to an end. Hence it was strictly not possible to debate any other subject on the dilatory motion, though in fact considerable laxity of practice prevailed. Such dilatory motions were pure obstruction, and were used by the Irish as such.

In 1882 and 1888 the rules on these matters were considerably tightened up. The Standing Orders now provide that when a motion is made for the adjournment of a debate, or of the House during any debate, or that the Chairman do report progress, or do leave the Chair, the debate thereupon must be confined to the matter of such motion; and no member, having moved or seconded any such motion, is entitled to move, or second, any similar motion during the same debate.[2] Also, if the Speaker or Chairman thinks that any such motion is an abuse of

---

[1] *Intimate Papers of Colonel House*, 1, pp. 233–5.   [2] S.O. 25.

the rules of the House, he may forthwith put the question without debate or refuse to propose the question.[1] In consequence, such motions are rarely moved except during an all-night sitting, when the chief whip is trying to get through more business than the Opposition is prepared to allow; the argument then proceeds on the basis that the House has had enough and that members ought to go to bed. Such motions are no longer of constitutional importance.

Adjournment motions are therefore important only when they are moved either before or after public business. Even here there are substantial restrictions. The motions before public business commences are the 'urgency motions' referred to above. Under the modern rule, adopted in 1882 and amended on three occasions since, no motion for the adjournment of the House may be made until all the questions asked at the commencement of business on each day (other than Friday) have been disposed of. Also, no such motion may be made before public business 'unless a member rising in his place shall propose to move the adjournment for the purpose of discussing a definite matter of urgent public importance'.[2] Accordingly, the Speaker has to decide whether the matter is definite and of urgent public importance. Successive Speakers have interpreted the Order very narrowly. There is a body of precedents as to what is 'definite', 'urgent', and of 'public importance',[3] and they have tended to restrict opportunities for discussion.

At first Mr Speaker decided only whether a motion was 'definite' and left it to the House to say (by supporting the motion) whether it was 'urgent' and of 'public importance'; but later Speakers assumed (more correctly) that it was their duty to say whether a motion came within the Standing Order.[4] Also, Speakers have apparently recognised that the growing pressure on the time of the House compelled them to interpret the Standing Orders more rigidly.[5] Table III[6] (p. 112) gives particulars of the use of the Standing Order between 1882 and 1939. It will be seen that the number of motions accepted by the Speaker has, on the whole, progressively declined, with the result that the number of motions has similarly declined.

---

[1] S.O. 26. [2] S.O. 9. [3] May, pp. 344–8.
[4] H.C. 189 of 1946, p. xxxix (Sir Gilbert Campion).
[5] *Ibid*. p. xxxviii. [6] *Ibid*. pp. liv–lv.

TABLE III. *Adjournment Motions under S.O. 9*

Period I, 1882–1901

Session	Government	Offered	Refused	Allowed
1882	Liberal	4	0	4
1883	Liberal	5	0	5
1884	Liberal	9	0	9
1884–5	Liberal	4	1	3
1886	Conservative	4	0	4
1887	Conservative	12	2	10
1888	Conservative	11	1	10
1889	Conservative	10	3	7
1890	Conservative	8	2	6
1890–1	Conservative	6	1	5
1892	Conservative	3	0	3
1893–4	Liberal	23	3	20
1894	Liberal	5	0	5
1895	Liberal	3	1	2
1896	Conservative	6	0	6
1897	Conservative	7	0	7
1898	Conservative	6	1	5
1899	Conservative	5	0	5
1900	Conservative	9	3	6
1901	Conservative	14	5	9
Totals		154	23	131
Annual average		8·1	1·2	6·9

Period II. 1902–20

Session	Government	Offered	Refused	Allowed
1902	Conservative	16	2	14
1903	Conservative	4	1	3
1904	Conservative	10	3	7
1905	Conservative	17	8	9
1906	Liberal	6	1	5
1907	Liberal	4	1	3
1908	Liberal	4	2	2
1909	Liberal	5	3	2
1910	Liberal	2	2	0
1911	Liberal	6	5	1
1912–13	Liberal	10	4	6
1913	Liberal	7	3	4
1914	Liberal	4	1	3
1914–16	Coalition	0	0	0
1916	Coalition	11	0	11
1917–18	Coalition	17	4	13
1918	Coalition	8	3	5
1919	Coalition	9	0	9
1920	Coalition	23	4	19
Totals		163	47	116
Annual average		8·6	2·5	6·1

TABLE III (*continued*)

Period III, 1921–39

Session	Government	Offered	Refused	Allowed
1921	Coalition	11	3	8
1922	Coalition	14	10	4
1923	Conservative	13	11	2
1924	Labour	7	5	2
1924–5	Conservative	6	6	0
1926	Conservative	10	10	0
1927	Conservative	1	1	0
1928	Conservative	5	3	2
1928–9	Conservative	1	1	0
1929–30	Labour	7	4	3
1930–1	Labour	6	5	1
1931–2	Coalition	6	6	0
1932–3	Coalition	6	6	0
1933–4	Coalition	4	3	1
1934–5	Coalition	4	4	0
1935–6	Conservative	3	2	1
1936–7	Conservative	4	2	2
1937–8	Conservative	2	0	2
1938–9	Conservative	4	4	0
Totals		114	86	28
Annual average		6·0	4·5	1·5

The working of the Order may be illustrated by examples drawn from two sessions of the Parliament of 1931–5.[1] On 8 December 1932, questions were raised about the action of the Persian Government in cancelling the concession of the Anglo-Persian Oil Company. Mr G. Lansbury (leader of the Opposition) suggested that the answers showed that in certain circumstances the British Government would take armed measures against Persia and, at the end of questions, he moved the adjournment. The Speaker stated that the motion was based on a hypothetical consideration and refused to accept it.[2] On 15 February 1933, Mr Batey complained that he had been prevented by the Government from raising the question of the operation of the means test in Durham on the ordinary evening adjournment, and sought to move an urgency motion for the adjournment. The Deputy Speaker ruled that as the circumstances complained of had existed for some time and might have been raised previously, he could not accept the motion.[3]

[1] Sessions 1932–3 and 1933–4.   [2] 272 H.C.Deb. 5 s., 1795–6.
[3] 274 H.C.Deb. 5 s., 1013–5.

Six days later, Mr Lansbury asked a private notice question on the outbreak of war in Manchuria, and Major Nathan moved the adjournment
because the Government proposed to await action by the League of
Nations before prohibiting the export of arms to Japan. The Speaker
refused to accept the motion, apparently because the matter was not
urgent.[1] On 25 April 1933, Mr Lansbury moved the adjournment to
discuss the decision of the Government to place an embargo on Russian
imports to this country. The Speaker refused to put the motion because
the decision was taken under powers recently conferred for that purpose
by Act of Parliament.[2] On 11 May 1933, Mr Lansbury sought to move
the adjournment on the ground that certain fascist propagandists had
been allowed to land; but the Speaker refused the motion without giving
reasons.[3] On 26 July 1933, Brigadier-General Spears moved the adjournment to discuss an assault by three police officers on an Air Force
officer. The Speaker refused to accept the motion because the subject
could be discussed on the Appropriation Bill that day.[4]

On 28 November 1933, Mr David Kirkwood sought to move the
adjournment to discuss the slowness of the negotiations between the
British and Russian Governments. The Deputy Speaker said that the
matter was not urgent.[5] On 20 December 1933, Mr Buchanan sought
to move the adjournment to discuss the action of the Government in
restricting imports of beef. The Speaker refused to accept the motion
because the House proposed to adjourn for the Christmas recess on
the following day, and the question could then be discussed on the
adjournment motion.[6] Finally, on 11 June 1934, questions as to the
action or inaction of the police at a Fascist meeting were raised in the
House, and the Home Secretary made a statement. Thereupon Mr V.
Adams asked leave to move the adjournment 'to call attention to the
violence accompanying the Blackshirt meeting at Olympia on Thursday,
7th June'. The Speaker refused leave on the ground that the matter
was not definite.[7]

The period covered by these examples was selected at random, and
they produce a fair impression of the difficulty of securing a debate on

[1] 274 H.C.Deb. 5 s., 1601–2.　　[2] 277 H.C.Deb. 5 s., 27–8.
[3] 277 H.C.Deb. 5 s., 1703–6.　　[4] 280 H.C.Deb. 5 s., 2597–8.
[5] 283 H.C.Deb. 5 s., 699–700.　　[6] 284 H.C.Deb. 5 s., 1300–1.
[7] 290 H.C.Deb. 5 s., 1348–9.

an urgency motion for the adjournment. The circumstances in which the motion will be allowed are indicated by the case of Miss Savidge[1] and by the motion moved on 15 July 1937.[2] To end a deadlock on the Non-Intervention Committee in respect of the Spanish civil war, the Government announced its intention of making a proposal including, among other matters, the recognition of belligerent rights to the insurgent Government. This fact having been ascertained by questions, and the Committee being about to meet that afternoon, Mr Attlee asked leave to move the adjournment, and the Speaker accepted the motion.[3]

In nearly all the examples mentioned above, the question for discussion was definite—that of Mr Adams apparently failed to be definite owing to a defect in drafting only. Most of them were matters to which public attention was directed and were well worthy of being discussed. Some of them failed because other opportunities for debate were available. Even where such opportunities can be utilised, there is some advantage in an urgency motion. If the question is discussed in Committee of Supply, or on the Appropriation Bill, or on an ordinary adjournment motion, it is necessarily mixed up in other things. It may be sandwiched between a short debate on destruction by rats and mice and another on the United Nations. If it stands alone its importance is enhanced. On the other hand, it is undesirable to interrupt business as arranged between the whips except for matters of real public importance. Accordingly, while it is generally recognised that the course of precedents has narrowed the opportunities too strictly, no very substantial modification of the rule would prove acceptable.

The example of Miss Savidge shows how effective an adjournment motion is when it is allowed. It compels a scurry in Whitehall, a conclave of advisers, a collection of files, and a concerted movement to Westminster by those affected. The rule is, therefore, an important addition to the question-hour. Even the infrequency of its operation does not restrict substantially its effect as a sanction. The programme has been arranged a week in advance and its outlines were settled by

---

[1] *Ante*, p. 105.   [2] 326 H.C.Deb. 5 s., 1491.

[3] On 23 June 1938, Mr Attlee obtained leave to move the adjournment to call attention to the sinking of British ships by Spanish insurgent aircraft and the failure of the Government to afford protection to such ships: *The Times*, 24 June 1938.

the Government at the beginning of the session. It was suggested before the Select Committee of 1945–6 that the earlier practice of leaving the House to decide 'urgency' and 'public importance' might be restored; but this was rejected by the Select Committee because it would involve frequent breaks in the programme. The suggestion that the debate should be limited to two hours was rejected because if a matter was both urgent and of public importance a longer debate would almost certainly be necessary. The Select Committee agreed, however, that when such a motion was debated the superseded business should be 'exempted business' for as long as the adjournment debate lasted;[1] and this recommendation has been embodied in the Standing Orders.[2] The effect of this decision is that the motion, if accepted, does not interfere with the Government's programme.

If the motion is accepted by the Speaker, it must either be supported by forty members or by the House itself on a division. In practice, the whole Opposition supports the motion; and once it has passed the Speaker its future is assured. Before 1902 the question was discussed immediately; but in order to give time for preparation of the cases for the mover and the minister, the motion is now taken at 7 p.m. the same evening.[3]

The third kind of adjournment motion is that which is moved every evening at the end of public business. Formerly there were no limits (except the ordinary limits of debate) to the discussion of matters on the adjournment. But in 1888 the rule was made that the House should adjourn at 12.30 a.m. without question put unless 'exempted business' was under discussion. In 1906 the time was altered to 11.30 p.m. and remained so fixed until the war of 1939–45. When the normal procedure of the House was restored, it was decided to bring the hour for the completion of the business on the paper forward to 10 p.m. and to provide that there should always be half an hour between the end of that business and the adjournment of the House, thus giving private members the opportunity to raise grievances.

Accordingly, Standing Order 1 provides that at 10 p.m. the proceedings or any business then under consideration shall be 'interrupted'; and, if the House be in committee, the chairman shall leave the chair,

[1] H.C. 189 of 1946, p. xviii.   [2] S.O. 9 (2).   [3] S.O. 9.

and report progress and ask leave to sit again. If a motion has been made before 10 p.m. for the adjournment of the House, or of the debate, or in committee that the chairman do report progress or do leave the chair, every such motion shall lapse. On the interruption of business the closure may be put; and this means that, if the closure is carried, the consequential motions may be made.

There is, however, no interruption if 'exempted business' is under discussion. This includes the proceedings on a Bill originating in Ways and Means, proceedings in pursuance of any Act of Parliament,[1] proceedings in pursuance of Standing Order 87 (contracts to be approved by resolution), and the proceedings on the reports of the Committee of Ways and Means and of the committees authorising the expenditure of public money (except the Committee of Supply). Debate on 'exempted business' may continue after 10 p.m., and any item of 'exempted business' may be begun after 10 p.m. even if opposed.

Further, a Minister of the Crown may at the commencement of public business move either of the following motions:

(*a*) That the proceedings on any specified business be exempted; or

(*b*) That the proceedings on any specified business be exempted for a specified period after 10 p.m.

This motion must be decided without amendment or debate and, if it is carried, there is no interruption at 10 p.m. and any business so exempted may be taken up even if opposed. If, however, the second of the two motions is carried, the exemption ceases after the period fixed has elapsed.

Subject to these exemptions, no opposed business may be taken after 10 p.m. The effect is, therefore, that the motion that the House do not adjourn is moved by a whip at one of the following times:

(i) at 10 p.m.; or

(ii) when the closure motion has been moved and carried and the consequential decisions taken; or

(iii) exempted business has been completed; or

(iv) unopposed business has been completed.

---

[1] It includes Church Assembly Measures, special orders and motions for the approval of or prayers against statutory instruments. See Chapter XIV.

Any such adjournment motion may be debated for half an hour, and then Mr Speaker adjourns the House without putting the question.

This formulation of the rule gives private members the half-hour adjournment on every day, whereas under the old rule the House was adjourned without question put at 11.30 p.m. unless exempted business was under discussion or the 11 p.m. rule had been suspended. In other words, the half-hour was available only if there was no exempted business or the 11 p.m. rule was not suspended.

The position on Fridays is much the same. The House meets at 11 a.m. and business is interrupted at 4 p.m.[1] It is, however, not the practice to suspend the 4 p.m. rule and it is rare to take exempted business after 4 p.m.

The short debate on the adjournment is generally used to raise individual grievances. In practice the member must notify the minister concerned beforehand, otherwise he will not be present to reply and the chief whip will merely say that he regrets that the minister was not able to be present and that he personally knows nothing whatever about the question. If the minister says that he cannot be present, the member can do no more than choose another day. Debates on the adjournment also have the disadvantage that they are rarely reported in the newspapers, so that the member does not get the publicity which he desires. Finally, the member cannot on the adjournment discuss any question which requires legislation. In spite of these difficulties, debates are frequent. They allow a member to raise a question which cannot be dealt with by question and answer, and they add a little to the efficacy of question-hour. It is not uncommon for a member who has received an answer which he regards as unsatisfactory to announce that he will raise the matter on the adjournment at the earliest opportunity. The demand for the use of the adjournment became so heavy during the war that it had to be controlled. Since there was a queue every day, it was decided in 1945 to have a ballot. The result was that many members put down their names whether they had 'grievances' to raise or not, and the whips began compiling lists of appropriate subjects.

Adjournment for the week-end does not require the passing of a formal resolution. Adjournment for a longer period, such as the

[1] S.O. 2.

Christmas, Easter and Whitsuntide and Summer recesses, requires a formal motion which is put on the order paper. These motions enable any question, except one of legislation, to be raised by members. In practice, however, the subjects are arranged beforehand. The official Opposition has the right to raise the first question, and the Opposition whip therefore informs the Speaker and the chief whip, the latter arranging for the appropriate minister to be present. Other members inform the Speaker of their wish to raise questions. The list is reported to the whips who can, no doubt, make representations to the Speaker. The Speaker himself makes the choice and informs the whips so that the necessary ministers and Opposition speakers can be available.[1]

Consequently, the debate takes the form of short discussions on a variety of matters of topical importance. For instance, on the motion to adjourn for the Easter recess in 1935, the Labour front bench raised the question of water supplies. The debate lasted for an hour and fifteen minutes, the Parliamentary Secretary to the Ministry of Health replying for the Government. A Liberal member then raised certain questions relating to the business of the House, the chief whip and others taking part in a debate which lasted for an hour. A Labour member then introduced a criticism of the Government for setting up a Royal Commission on Merthyr Tydfil, and the Parliamentary Secretary to the Ministry of Health replied. A Conservative member next discussed the speed limit in built-up areas, a Labour member and the Parliamentary Secretary to the Ministry of Transport took part, and then the House adjourned.[2]

It will be convenient at this point to refer to the other occasions on which 'open debate' may take place, though since they relate primarily to the opportunities available for private members, they will be discussed elsewhere.[3] The only occasions on which unrestricted debate may take place are the discussions on the address in answer to the Queen's Speech at the beginning of the session. Between six and eight days are usually allowed, and the debates range over the whole field of government, legislation as well as administration. Though the subjects for each day are in fact arranged 'through the usual channels', there is nothing to

---

[1] 318 H.C.Deb. 5 s., 1037. [2] 300 H.C.Deb. 5 s., 2011–64.
[3] See *post*, Chapter XI, pp. 355–64.

prevent any member who catches the Speaker's eye from discussing anything he pleases.

The only other occasions for general debate are the second and third readings of Consolidated Fund Bills. These Bills grant money to the Crown, and any question relating to the services for which the money is provided may be debated. Proposals for legislation may not be made, but every aspect of administration may in theory be raised. In practice, the subject is chosen by arrangement between the Government and Opposition whips; and the only difference between discussion on these Bills in the House and discussion on the Estimates in Committee of Supply is that on the former any member who catches the Speaker's eye may bring in any other question of administration. In practice this is done but rarely, partly because such frolics are frowned upon by the whips, and partly because no minister will be ready to reply unless notice is given.[1] In any case, the opportunities do not arise very frequently, since there are usually only three Consolidated Fund Bills (including the Appropriation Bill) during each session.

Finally, it has to be mentioned that under the old practice of the House known as the rule of 'anticipation' it was possible for a member to prevent discussion on any motion whatever by putting down a motion of his own on that subject. The rule was that when a motion was put down that motion could not be 'anticipated' by a motion, or an amendment to a motion, or a motion for the adjournment of the House. It was immaterial that the member who had put the motion down had no real intention or opportunity of moving it. Consequently, motions were often put down to 'block' any motion being put down by the other side. For instance, in the days when the Unionists were uncertain whether they approved free trade or not they could (and did) prevent the Liberals from raising the embarrassing question by putting down an anticipatory motion and so blocking any Liberal motion. A well-known example may be taken from 1911. The Government proposed to move a resolution authorising the payment of £400 a year to members of the

---

[1] E.g. when Mr A.P. Herbert wanted to attack the functions of the King's Proctor, he gave notice to the Attorney-General. As a result, both Law Officers had to 'hang about the House' (i.e. in the Smoking Room). The day being hot and the general debate long, Mr Herbert got tired of waiting and took the Law Officers down to Wapping on his boat: A. P. Herbert, *The Ayes Have It*, p. 79.

House of Commons, and the Chancellor of the Exchequer put down a motion to that effect. Four Conservative members, however, anticipated him by putting down motions for Bills on the same subject. Consequently, the Government motion could be moved only because, after an appeal by the acting leader of the Opposition, the four members withdrew their motions. As a result of this and other incidents, a Standing Order was made in 1914 requiring that, in determining whether a discussion is out of order on the ground of anticipation, Mr Speaker should have regard to the probability of the matter anticipated being brought before the House within a reasonable time.[1] There being usually very little probability, blocking motions have almost entirely disappeared.

4. GOVERNMENT BUSINESS AND THE CLOSURE

Questions and urgency motions are the cocktails before the oratorical feast. At 3.30 p.m., or very shortly thereafter, the House gets down to public business. In theory, the House itself settles the order of its business; but here as in many parts of the Constitution practice has long since swept theory aside. In the early years of the nineteenth century Government business had no precedence over private members' business. A minister was just a member, with no greater rights than the most timid and tongue-tied of his followers. Custom allowed two days a week to Government business, but these two days were not formally allotted until 1846. Usually, a third day was given by resolution towards the end of the session.[2]

In the early years of the present century Government business had precedence on all days except Tuesdays after 8.15 p.m. up to Easter, Wednesdays up to Whitsuntide and after Michaelmas, Fridays up to Whitsuntide, and the third and fourth Fridays after Whit Sunday. Between the wars the Government took the whole of Tuesdays and the Standing Order was so drafted that the private members had about eight Wednesdays for motions and about thirteen Fridays for Bills. Since private members' time was restored in 1950, they have had twenty Fridays, motions and Bills being taken in alternate weeks.[3]

[1] Now S.O. 11.   [2] Redlich, I, p. 102.   [3] S.O. 4 (1).

The rest of the time of the House, subject to questions, adjournment motions, and private Bills, is taken by the Government. Even this niggardly allowance to private members is subject to the exception 'unless the House otherwise directs'. What the House directs is really what the Government directs. If the Government finds that it cannot complete its programme, a motion is made that Government business have precedence at all sittings throughout the session or the remainder of the session. The Government's majority supports the motion and it is carried. Such motions are not usual.[1] Private members dislike having their opportunities for publicity and public service cut down, and except in an emergency the Government frames its programme to suit the time available.

The opportunities of private members to raise during the course of Government business the pet notions which they are anxious to propagate are also strictly limited. The restrictions imposed on adjournment motions and other dilatory motions have already been mentioned.[2] These are, however, merely examples of a general tendency to restrict discussion to the matter on the order paper. As Mr Balfour once said, 'there was a time when the state of Europe could be debated on the motion that candles be brought in'.[3] In the present rules the phrase which most constantly appears is 'without question put'. Since the House cannot debate except on a question, the effect of such words is to prevent debate. When, for instance, an Order of the day is read for the House to resolve itself into committee (other than a committee on a Bill), the Speaker must leave the Chair without putting any question unless on a day on which the Committee of Supply stands as the first order of the day a Minister moves 'That Mr Speaker do now leave the Chair' for the purpose of enabling a motion on going into Committee

---

[1] It will be seen from Appendix 1 that there were no days for private members' motions in 1928–9, 1931–2 and 1934–5 and no days for private members' Bills in 1928–9 and 1934–5. In 1931–2 there was only one day for private members' Bills. The whole time of the House was also taken by the Government between 1914 and 1918 and between 1939 and 1949. In 1949–50 no time was allowed for private members' motions.

[2] *Ante*, pp. 110–21.

[3] H.C. 378 of 1914, Q. 1258. This motion was in fact necessary until 1717, when the Sergeant was charged with the duty of having the House lighted when 'daylight be shut in'. Now the Speaker or Chairman directs that the lights be switched on: May (13th ed.), p. 263 n.

of Supply to be moved as an amendment to the question.[1] Again, when the Chairman has been ordered to make a report to the House, he must leave the Chair without question put; and the report must be brought in without question put.[2]

The most important restrictions, apart from those applying to adjournment motions, are, however, those relating to the Committee of Supply. Formerly, the House sat in Committee of Supply until all the Estimates had been disposed of. In 1887, for instance, the Civil Estimates alone were considered for 27 days. The Government could carry Supply only by sitting into August and suspending the twelve o'clock rule every night so as to wear down the Opposition by lack of sleep. This gave private members a substantial power of coercion; for though they were kept out of their beds and away from their holidays, the ministers, who needed sleep and rest even more, had to stay in the House with them, especially when the Government had such a small majority as it had between 1892 and 1895. The private member thus had a remedy which would now be called that of a 'sit down strike', though 'stand up' would be more appropriate.[3] In 1896, when the Conservatives (who had been foremost in using this method) were in office, the modern Supply rule was made by sessional order, and it became a Standing Order in 1902.

This rule provided that only twenty days should be allotted for the consideration of the Estimates, though by resolution three extra days might be added. Extra days were of course required for Supplementary Estimates and four days were required for moving the Speaker out of the Chair when the four main groups of Estimates were first to be discussed. In order to give greater flexibility to the debates in Supply, which have become debates by which the Opposition criticises Government policy, and to prevent the discursive debates on Supplementary Estimates, the Select Committee on Procedure of 1945–6 recommended, and the House agreed in principle, that the Supply days, the days for moving the Speaker out of the Chair, and the days allocated for Supplementary Estimates should be amalgamated.

[1] S.O. 16.   [2] S.O. 51.
[3] H.C. 378 of 1914, Qs. 136–43 (Lord Hugh Cecil—who had experience).

Accordingly, Standing Order 16 allocates twenty-six days before 5 August for supply, which is given a wider definition. It includes proceedings on motions 'That Mr Speaker do now leave the chair'; supplementary or additional Estimates for the current financial year; excess votes; votes on account; main Estimates whether for the coming or the current financial year; and the consideration of reports from the Committee of Public Accounts and the Select Committee on Estimates; but it does not include votes of credit or votes for supplementary or additional Estimates for war expenditure. In effect, it includes all the normal financial business of the year except proceedings in Ways and Means and the proceedings on the Finance Bill, the Appropriation Bill and the Consolidated Fund Bills.

As has been said, these twenty-six days are opportunities for the Opposition to criticise the Government, and the vote to be put down is decided through the usual channels. Theoretically, however, the subject of discussion is the particular vote, so that proposals for legislation cannot be debated. This has often produced an artificial restriction on debate. This restriction may, however, be overcome by means of an amendment to Standing Order 17 made in 1948. As has been mentioned above, if an order of the day provides for the House to go into supply, Mr Speaker leaves the Chair without question put except—and this is the amendment made in 1948—when a Minister moves 'That Mr Speaker do now leave the Chair' for the purpose of enabling a motion on going into Committee of Supply to be moved as an amendment to that question. It is further provided that where that amendment is under discussion, Mr Speaker may permit such incidental reference to legislative action as he may consider relevant to any matter of administration then under debate, when enforcement of the prohibition would, in his opinion, unduly restrict the discussion of such matters. For instance, if the Opposition wishes to discuss full employment, it may have the National Insurance Vote put down in Supply; but if it wishes to criticise the Government for not having altered the law of National Insurance it must ask the Government to move 'That Mr Speaker do now leave the Chair' and itself move an amendment relating to full employment.

Supply is still technically the voting of money, and the Government must have the funds voted reasonably quickly. Some of these votes, including the votes covering expenditure between 1 April and the giving of the royal assent to the Appropriation Bill, must be passed before 1 April. The others must be passed before the House rises in August. Accordingly the Standing Orders provide for two 'guillotines' (which must not be confused with the guillotine motion which is passed in order to get a Bill through Committee by a fixed date). The first of these guillotines falls on the seventh allotted day or on some later allotted day before 31 March. At 9.30 p.m. on that day the Chairman must put every question necessary to dispose of the vote then under discussion. Next he will put the question relating to any vote on account (i.e. until the Appropriation Act is passed) and all such navy, army and air force votes for the coming financial year as may have been put down. Then he must put the question on Supplementary Estimates put down seven clear days previously. Finally he must put the question on all outstanding excess votes. All these clear up the financial business for the financial year which is just expiring, and provide for the early part of the coming financial year until the Appropriation Act takes effect in August. The following day all these resolutions in Supply are reported to the House and all outstanding questions are put, without amendment or debate, from 9.30 p.m. onwards.

The guillotine falls again on the last but one of the allotted days, the House being again in Committee of Supply. This time all the votes for the current financial year are put from 9.30 p.m. onwards. These are reported to the House on the next Supply day and at 9.30 p.m. all the outstanding questions are put by Mr Speaker.

Thus on four days in the year members may tramp through the lobbies voting for or against numerous motions for supplying money to the Crown. By so doing they are able to increase the number of divisions which they are recorded to have attended and so help to satisfy their constituents, if not the whips, that they have been assiduous in their attention to their parliamentary duties.

The amount of time available even for Government business is strictly limited. Though in a full session the Government may have over 120 full days and perhaps ten Fridays, much of this must necessarily be occupied by regular annual business. The address in answer to the Queen's Speech at the opening of the session occupies between five and eight days. Annual Bills like the Public Works Loans Bill and the Expiring Laws Continuance Bill, must be passed. Two or more full days are spent in discussing miscellaneous questions on the adjournment for a recess. By far the largest block of essential business is, however, the financial business. Before the financial year ends in March, at least eight Supply days must be taken, and there will be eighteen such days between 1 April and 5 August. The Budget will occupy at least three days in Committee of Ways and Means and possibly another day in the House before the Finance Bill is introduced. The number of days occupied by the Finance Bill depends upon its length and complication and upon the element of controversy in its provisions. In the meantime a Consolidated Fund Bill will have been passed in order to give effect to the votes on account necessary to authorise expenditure between the beginning of the financial year and the passing of the Consolidated Fund (Appropriation) Bill. This Bill itself will take two days. Altogether financial business occupies at least forty full days. With a session of 120 full days and thirty-one Fridays, only about sixty full days and eleven Fridays are available for Government legislation.

The task of arranging business is even more difficult than this recital suggests. Most Government Bills have six stages at which discussion may take place—second reading, financial resolution, report of financial resolution, committee, report, and third reading. There is no financial resolution if the Bill contains no money clause; there is usually no debate on the report stage of a financial resolution; the committee stage may be taken upstairs to a Standing Committee, except on a money Bill. The ways and means resolutions which authorise appropriation of moneys voted in Supply are not usually discussed. Nevertheless, it is obvious that arrangement of business is an art to which attention must be paid.

The arrangement is undertaken by the chief whip under control of the leader of the House. He has in his hands the remedy of the closure. In the last resort he can secure the passing of a 'guillotine' resolution for closure by compartments, so as to be assured that a Bill passes its various stages at times fixed beforehand.[1] Difficulties due to a host of

---

[1] See *post*, pp. 241–6.

amendments can be overcome by the use by the Speaker or Chairman of his power to select amendments, or 'kangaroo' power.[1] These last means of expediting business relate primarily to legislative procedure and are considered elsewhere. The remedy of the closure is of general application.

In the spacious days of the early nineteenth century the House had no means of limiting debate except an individual motion that a member 'be no longer heard'. Until the Irish began to realise the possibilities of parliamentary procedure and to obstruct all legislation that did not apply to Ireland because they wanted legislation for Ireland, and all legislation that related to Ireland because they did not like it,[2] such means were hardly necessary. Though it is often said that it is only in recent years that the front benches have monopolised parliamentary time, the reverse is the truth. Until well into the nineteenth century ordinary members neither thought of themselves as of 'Cabinet timber' nor considered that their constituents required a regular output of oratory. A scion of a great house, like the Marquis of Hartington, who intervened even once in debate was marked down for ministerial office; and though men of small estate like Mr Gladstone and Mr Disraeli had to show greater assiduity, it was not difficult for them to find opportunities to distinguish themselves from the mass. The private member became a professional orator when the franchise was extended to working men who thought that grievances could be remedied by speeches.

The Irish Nationalists finally broke down the notion that the House could do its business even when every member had the right to talk at any length on any subject. The immediate cause of the closure—or the 'clôture' as those who disliked it usually called it—was the obstruction on the Coercion Bill of 1881. This Bill was announced in the Queen's Speech in January 1881. The debate on the address began on 6 January and ended on 20 January after eleven sittings. On 24 January the Irish Secretary asked leave to bring in the Bill, but the House had to adjourn without the question being put. On the following day Mr Gladstone moved to suspend Standing Orders and to give the Bill priority over all

---

[1] See *post*, pp. 240–1.

[2] It is not suggested that the Irish invented obstruction; they made it an art: see *post*, pp. 149–51.

other business, and this motion was carried after a debate lasting twenty-two hours. On the 27th the contents of the Bill were disclosed by an indiscretion; as a result the sitting which began at 4 p.m. on Monday, 31 January, ended after forty-one-and-a-half hours at 9.30 a.m. on Wednesday, 2 February, and then only because, after consultation with the Prime Minister and the leader of the Opposition, the Speaker closed the debate on his own responsibility,[1] and leave to bring in the Bill was at last given.

It was part of the arrangement between the Speaker and Mr Gladstone that steps should be taken to deal with obstruction. Mr Gladstone then introduced the 'emergency procedure' which, while the resolution creating it was in force, enabled the Speaker to regulate the procedure. Among the emergency rules made by the Speaker in consequence was one enabling him to put a closure motion on his own responsibility and, if it was approved by a sufficient majority, to put the question under debate forthwith. A rule similar in principle was made a Standing Order in 1882. In 1887 the initiative was taken from the Speaker and transferred to any member of the House, though the Speaker's consent was necessary before the closure motion was put. Subject to a slight modification in 1888, the rule has since remained unaltered.

The present closure rule applies to the House, committees of the whole House, and Standing Committees. The closure cannot be moved in the House unless the Speaker is in the Chair (except when the unavoidable absence of Mr Speaker has been previously announced, in which case the Deputy Speaker may accept a closure motion), nor in committee of the whole House unless the Chairman of ways and means or the deputy Chairman is in the Chair. Any member may claim to move 'That the question be now put'. Unless the Chairman considers that the motion is an abuse of the rules of the House, or an infringement of the rights of the minority, it must be put forthwith and decided without amendment or debate. It will not be regarded as carried unless 100 members—or in a Standing Committee twenty members—have supported it. If, however, it is carried, the question under discussion is put forthwith.[2]

[1] Redlich, I, pp. 152–3; *Life of Gladstone*, III, pp. 52–3; 257 Hans. Deb. 3 s., 2032–3.
[2] S.O. 29 and 57 (5).

It is not unusual for the Speaker to refuse to accept a closure motion, whether it is moved by a Government whip or by any other member.[1] In the period 1887–99 the closure was claimed on an average sixty-two times a session and was allowed thirty-six times. For 1900–13 the corresponding figures are seventy-five and fifty-six, and for 1919–32 they are sixty and forty-two. Within each period there are considerable fluctuations. In 1893–4 the closure was claimed 168 times and carried seventy-three times, whereas in 1898 it was claimed twenty-three times and carried thirteen times. In 1909 it was claimed 156 times and carried 124 times, whereas in 1910 it was claimed twenty-eight times and carried thirteen times. In 1929–30 it was claimed on 139 occasions and carried on ninety-six, whereas in 1931–2 it was claimed seven times and carried on five occasions.[2] The occasions would be more frequent but for the fact that the whip usually consults the Speaker before moving.[3] But if the motion is moved by the Government and accepted by the Speaker, its passing is as assured as the passing of any other Government motion. The Government whips are put on and members vote in accordance with their party affiliations. Occasionally, as Mr E. Brown once put it,[4] the Government is 'caught napping' either because the whips have not kept a hundred members in the House, or because the Opposition has brought up secret reserves. A defeat on a closure motion is not important, because the debate is merely continued until the whips have collected a majority; but, naturally, any kind of snap vote is an unspoken criticism of the whips' efficiency, and they do their best not to be 'caught napping'.

[1] 'Mr Ede: Is there ever a case of the Government having been beaten on the closure when the Government has asked for it?—Mr Lloyd George: No, but there have been many cases where the Speaker has refused and intimated that he would not put the closure if it were moved.' H.C. 161 of 1931, Q. 997.

[2] G. F. M. Campion, 'Methods of Closure in the Commons', Journal of the Society of Clerks-at-the-Table in Empire Parliaments, I, p. 20. These figures should be considered in the light of the growth in the use of the guillotine and the kangaroo. Also, the figures relate to the House itself and not to the committee of the whole House, as to which see ibid.

[3] See Mr Lloyd George's remark, above, n. 1. 'The closure is never moved now unless it is thought that the Speaker or Chairman will accept it. If he says "I will not accept a closure just now", you never move it': H.C. 161 of 1931, Q. 126 (Mr R. MacDonald); see also H.C. 378 of 1914, Q. 1458 (Mr J. W. Gulland) and G. F. M. Campion, loc. cit. I, p. 21.

[4] H.C. 161 of 1931, Q. 999.

Unless the ten o'clock rule has been suspended or exempted business is under discussion, the Government must in fact carry the motion, otherwise the matter under discussion will be 'talked out' by the Opposition, and the guillotine will fall at 10 p.m. or, on Fridays, 4 p.m. under Standing Orders. Since the amendment made in July 1948, however, a closure motion may be made after 10 p.m. Consequently, talking out a Government motion is even rarer than it was before the rule was amended. Even before the war it was so rare that the Prime Minister, Mr Ramsay MacDonald, suggested in 1930 that a division was quite unnecessary. 'When the closure is moved,' he said, 'the result is a foregone conclusion.... What does the division mean? It means nothing at all. I would therefore suggest that the closure should be given without a division. It is only a waste of time.'[1] Mr Baldwin did not agree, but for a very curious reason. 'If you have a Bill when the closure is often being used, especially in the month of July when the weather is hot and tempers are getting a little frayed, and everyone is tired, putting on the closure always makes the House a little uneasy and disagreeable, and I think that a walk through the lobbies is a very good thing. They come back much cooler and much quieter. I think that if you were to carry straight on you would very quickly lose the ten minutes you would save in the lobbies.'[2] This reads rather like Blackstone's justification of the anomalies of the common law, especially when it is remembered that the closure motion is followed not by one division but by two divisions, since the division on the closure leads to an immediate division on the question under discussion.

The proposal and the reason for opposing it indicate, however, that in Government business the closure is almost automatic, once it is granted by the Speaker. Combined with the powers already discussed, it places a very considerable power in the hands of the Government.[3]

---

[1] H.C. 161 of 1931, Q. 115.   [2] *Ibid.* Q. 206.

[3] It is unnecessary to do more than refer to the other kind of closure, which is now provided by S.O. 29 (3) and which enables debate on a clause to be brought to an end and amendments not yet considered to be excluded. This closure, the original 'kangaroo closure', is rarely used. Between 1887 and 1932 it was used only seven times in the House and forty-six times in committee. Between 1919 and 1932 it was used only twice in committee and not at all in the House. It is no longer necessary because of the regular use of the modern 'kangaroo' since 1919. See Campion, *loc. cit.* I, p. 20. Its abolition was recommended by the Select Committee of 1932: H.C. 129 of 1932, p. 14.

The Government takes by Standing Orders nine-tenths of the time of the House and it can, by resolution, take the whole. It can arrange its business as it thinks fit. Much of its financial business is exempted from the ten o'clock rule and it can always suspend that rule by resolution. As soon as any question has been adequately discussed, it can move and carry the closure. Debates in Committee of Supply, which might go on for ever, are inevitably brought to an end by the automatic guillotine on the seventh, eighth, twenty-fifth and twenty-sixth days. If the debate on a Bill is taking too long, the House can, by resolution, fix dates by which the various stages are completed. On every question submitted by it to the House the Government must, within very wide limits of reasonableness, prove successful. In other words, the Government determines what shall be discussed, when it shall be discussed, how long the discussion shall take, and what the decision shall be. So long as its party majority holds, the Government is in complete control of the House of Commons. 'Parliament', said Mr Lloyd George, and he ought to know, for few Prime Ministers have been so dictatorial, 'has really no control over the Executive; it is a pure fiction.'[1] One who has been almost a permanent critic of Mr Lloyd George, Lord Eustace Percy, made much the same remark:

As to the final control over executive action, I think its control over executive action is got by retaining or throwing out the Government. I do not think there is any good in suggesting that the House of Commons has control of the executive action of a Government which it wants to keep in power.[2]

Yet sovereignty is never without its limitations; the strongest despot has his weaknesses. The British Government is not despotic; it has to govern with and through the House of Commons. Its authority rests on its majority, and its majority on the people. To keep its majority and to use that majority with the greatest ease are the most important parts of the art of management.

[1] H.C. 161 of 1931, Q. 450.   [2] *Ibid.* Q. 2040.

CHAPTER V

THE ART OF MANAGEMENT

I. THE MANAGEMENT OF A MAJORITY

The effective power of a Government depends essentially on its majority. If it has no majority it may be able to maintain itself in power for a short time by manœuvre or intrigue, but it is doomed as soon as the rest of the House combines against it.[1] Mr Pitt, whose appointment as Prime Minister in 1783 was met with 'shouts of derisive laughter',[2] manœuvred for a few months and then secured a majority at a general election. Lord Melbourne's Government from 1839 to 1841 had no coherent Opposition, and the difficulty of the Queen's Ladies prevented Sir Robert Peel from taking any steps to secure office. The Whigs from 1846 to 1852 could rely on Peelite support. The Conservatives in 1852 and in 1858–9 lasted only a few months. In 1866 to 1868 they stayed in only by Mr Disraeli's adroit management, and because the Cave of Adullam had split the Liberal party. The Conservatives in 1885–6 were merely awaiting a Redistribution Bill and Mr Gladstone did not seek to turn them out. Mr Gladstone in 1886 resigned as soon as the Liberal Unionists joined with the Conservatives to out-vote him. From 1886 to 1892 the Conservatives had the support of the Liberal Unionists; and the Liberals had the support of the Labour party and the Irish from 1910 to 1914 and of all parties from 1914 to 1915. The Labour Government resigned in 1924 as soon as the Liberals and Conservatives joined on a motion which the Government regarded as one

---

[1] See *Cabinet Government*, ch. xiv. Before the Indian Congress party decided to accept office in certain Indian Provinces, Sir Tej Bahadur Sapru and other leaders quoted passages from that book to show that according to British practice minority Governments were not uncommon. The essential difference between those examples and the Indian situation between April and July 1937 was that in the British examples no party had a majority, whereas in the Indian examples the Congress party had majorities. As *The Pioneer* (Lucknow, 7 April 1937) pointed out, the book showed that according to British practice a Government defeated on a vote of no-confidence would resign at once.

To some extent the material and arguments set out in that book are here repeated. The difference is one of angle of approach.

[2] May, *Constitutional History of England* (1st ed.), I, p. 61.

132

of censure; and the Labour Government of 1929–31 reigned uneasily with the discriminating support of the Liberal party.

So long as the Government can control business it can control the House. If it is a minority Government, it can control business only if it can make backstair arrangements with a third party. Such a situation is essentially unstable. It has a weapon, the threat to resign or dissolve, which to some extent enables it to compel the acquiescence of the third party.[1] But unless the third party fears the lion in opposition more than the lamb in office, as between 1886 and 1892, the situation cannot last long. It is the inevitable result of any breach with the two-party system—and hence a fundamental objection to any electoral system that encourages the break-up of parties—that government is weak and ineffective.

A Government with a majority can be overthrown by the House of Commons only if a split occurs in its majority. In 1866, for instance, Robert Lowe led the Cave of Adullam against Mr Gladstone's Reform Bill, and the Government resigned. This division among the Liberals disappeared when Mr Disraeli produced the even more radical Reform Bill of 1867. The Conservatives remained in office because the Adullamites were succeeded by the Tea-Room party, Whigs who did not want to bring Lord Russell or Mr Gladstone back into office, and who therefore supported Mr Disraeli against Mr Gladstone.[2] This disappeared in the Radical successes of 1868, to appear again in the split that destroyed Home Rule in 1886. Since 1886 there has been no serious party cleavage with a Government in office except that for which Mr Joseph Chamberlain was responsible in 1903, and then Mr Balfour's finesse managed to keep a majority together until it went down in the Radical gale of 1905. The last majority Government to be ejected by a vote of the House was the Liberal Government of 1895, which need not have been defeated or have accepted the defeat as a vote of no-confidence, but resigned because Lord Rosebery, the 'dark horse' in the gilded stables of the House of Lords, could not work with Sir William Harcourt, the 'gay crusader' who led the battle which really mattered in the House of Commons. Mr Asquith resigned in 1915 because he thought he had lost Conservative support and Mr Lloyd George in 1922 because he really

[1] *Cabinet Government*, pp. 446–7. [2] *Life of Gladstone*, II, p. 228.

had lost it. Each was ejected by Mr Bonar Law and neither waited to be defeated in Parliament. Mr Neville Chamberlain resigned in 1940 because the Labour party and some Conservative members voted against him: but he had a majority in the House of Commons and he resigned only because he regarded virtual unanimity as necessary in wartime.[1]

Not only is it rare for a Government to be defeated in the House of Commons; it is even rare for a Government supporter to vote against the Government. To some extent this characteristic has been over-emphasised in recent years, since majority Governments have for all but six of the years since 1919 rested on the strength of the Conservative party, which is little inclined to be rebellious in public, though it often says a good deal in private. Between 1945 and 1951 Labour members voted against the Government on several occasions,[2] though never in such a manner as to defeat the Government. There is, nevertheless, good reason for it. However much a member may criticise individual proposals of the Government, he is even more critical of the Opposition. Potential rebels are usually to be found on the extreme wings. Those Conservatives who disliked the extensive powers proposed by the Government in the Government of India Bill, 1935, disliked still more the policy of the Labour party, which was to grant even more extensive powers. Those Conservatives who disliked the proposals of the Coal Mines Bill, 1936, were even less anxious to nationalise the mines, as recommended by the Labour party. Those who criticised the original National Defence Contribution in 1937 would have been even more critical not only of any tax proposed by the Labour party in its place but also of the use to which the Labour party would have put the money. During the Labour Government of 1945–51 those members who disliked the foreign policy or the defence policy of the Labour party would have liked that of the Conservative party even less. These last were occasions on which it was reasonably safe for Labour members to vote against the Government because the Government was reasonably sure of Opposition support. There are occasions when 'progressive' or left-wing opinion in the Conservative

[1] See the details in *Cabinet Government*, Appendix 1.
[2] E.g. on conscription in March 1947: McKenzie, *British Political Parties*, p. 450; and in the other cases mentioned *ibid.* p. 451, n. 2.

party sympathises with right-wing opinion in the opposite party; but in such a case the Government is reasonably sure of a majority.

Normally, therefore, the danger to a Government arises not from a possible union of opponents in the division lobby, but in discontent which shows itself in other ways among its supporters in the House and outside. As Mr Lloyd George said, referring to 1915: 'The Opposition lobbies...were not overcrowded with malcontents. Real parliamentary opinion can rarely be gathered from a perusal of division lists. There were sinister grumblings in the corridors and tea-rooms.'[1] When Mr Lloyd George wrote these words he had had bitter experience of their truth. The vote which sent him into authorship was taken not in the House of Commons but in the Carlton Club.

Invited by the Government to demand a Northcliffe peace, the country had given Mr Lloyd George [in 1918] the largest and worst majority that any Prime Minister ever found behind his back. Mr Lloyd George was the victim of this atmosphere in two senses. Partly he was afraid of his majority. The majority was not so much behind his back as on his back. There came a moment in the negotiations [over the Peace settlement], when, realising the consequences of throwing too great a burden on Germany, he tried to prepare the English people for concessions. The answer came in the famous telegram from the House of Commons holding him to his promises, and he found, like Hernani in Meredith's poem, that he had filched the prize, forgetting the horn of the old gentleman.[2]

It was this 'largest and worst' majority, and not the Opposition, which Mr Lloyd George had to fear and, in fearing, manage, for three more years, until it decided at the Carlton Club in 1922 to turn him loose. Similarly, Mr Baldwin's greatest struggle was not with the Labour party either in or out of Parliament, but the 'Empire Free Trade' movement led by the press lords and followed by some of his supporters in the Parliament of 1924–9.

The management of a majority is thus not an easy task. There are weapons available, the weapon of refusing the whip especially. A member of Parliament, however insignificant, likes his seat, or he would not be there. He possesses it only because he wears a party label. Deprived

---

[1] Lloyd George, *War Memoirs*, II, p. 741.
[2] J. L. Hammond, *C. P. Scott*, p. 259.

of his label he would, in the great majority of cases, sink into the comparative insignificance that his character probably merits. The label is thus of great value to him, and though the threat to take it away is rarely used and still less rarely carried out, the fact that it is available helps to maintain his party loyalty.

There is, too, another weapon which applies to the majority in the mass. A defeat of the Government on a major issue may produce its resignation: but whether it does or not it will certainly produce a dissolution of Parliament. If the Government does not dissolve to restore its majority, the Opposition will dissolve to acquire one. A dissolution is what the average member dislikes most. This sanction is rather weaker now than it was before the war, because most members have most of their election expenses paid for them and the maintenance of a seat is so costly. Even so, there is no certainty of re-election and an election involves an unpleasant three weeks. Accordingly, what forces private members to support the Government is not so much the threat to resign as the threat to dissolve;[1] or, as one member put it, 'an implied threat of resignation with a dissolution to follow'.[2] So clearly was this recognised in 1914 that in evidence before the Select Committee of that year (which was set up because private members complained of encroachments by the Government upon private members' opportunities[3]) two members[4] suggested that Parliament should sit for fixed periods and not be subject to dissolution within those periods.

It must not be forgotten, too, that the Government has a very useful weapon in the party machinery. The whips themselves do little more than gently persuade;[5] but the member has to seek re-election through a body of constituents who voted for his label and would, with equal facility, vote against him if he lost it. The whip, or label, is rarely taken away by the party leader; but the label itself may be lost in the constituency. The member must be nominated by the committee of his local association or party. This consists of keen party men who are usually orthodox, and perhaps rather more than orthodox. They keep an eye on their member, and a gentle hint from headquarters or a fairly

[1] H.C. 378 of 1914, Qs. 187–8 (Mr J. Wedgwood).
[2] *Ibid.* Q. 302 (Mr F. W. Jowett).   [3] 50 H.C.Deb. 5 s., 588–667.
[4] Mr T. Lough and Mr F. W. Jowett.   [5] *Ante*, Chapter III, pp. 84–90.

obvious tendency towards independence in the member will produce a summons from the constituency and a demand for personal explanation.

Mr Asquith referred in 1913 to the 'watch and ward which the electorate keep over their representatives... to see that on the whole members do not give way to the vagaries of individual judgment, but keep abreast of the general movement of their own party and their own cause'.[1] Mr Bonar Law agreed with him:

I do think that owing to the action of the electors belonging to our different parties in the constituencies more than in the House, there has been a tightening of discipline which, on the whole, has not been an advantage.[2]

What was true in 1913 is even more true today; and the lax ways of the older parties would be disapproved by the stern disciplinarians of the Labour party. The Standing Orders of the Parliamentary Labour party provide for a member being reported to the National Executive Committee in 'cases of serious or persistent breaches of party discipline'. This means that the National Executive Committee may, after enquiry, deprive the member of his party membership, which automatically makes him incapable of standing as a Labour candidate.

There is, in any event, always the appeal to loyalty. Some persons choose their parties with an eye on their prospects;[3] but most begin with opinions which the company they keep does nothing to dispel. Private conversations are far more effective than public discussions. If a conservative hears in public an attack on the capitalist system he dismisses it as 'politics': if quietly he is asked whether he does not think that banks are a nuisance, landlords a curse, and profiteers dangerous to the community, he will often agree, provided that he is not a banker, a landlord, or a profiteer. In similar circumstances, the average socialist will show that he is by nature a conservative. If a person of no great independence of judgment finds himself constantly associated with people of the same bias, he will be confirmed in his own opinions.

---

[1] 50 H.C.Deb. 5 s., 610.   [2] *Ibid.* 618.

[3] It is interesting to speculate what would have happened if Mr Disraeli had not made the unfortunate mistake of first standing as a Radical and a friend of O'Connell. Perhaps Sir Robert Peel would have put him in the Government of 1841; he would then have voted for the repeal of the Corn Laws; he would have been in Lord Palmerston's Government; and—well, how long would it have been before he led a Cave of Adullam against Mr Gladstone?

Discussions in the tea-room and the lobby have therefore far more influence than debates in the House. A member is, however, necessarily thrown into the company of his political brothers rather than into that of his opponents. Not only is he induced to believe, and therefore conform, but also he feels it treachery to leave his friends in the lurch. A 'traitor' is not only an opponent; he is also an enemy. He has to begin a new political life in an atmosphere of suspicion. 'Crossing the floor' is therefore rare; and in many cases members are right to suspect a personal motive. But a knowledge that motives will be suspected makes the transition all the more difficult. Life is easier and more pleasant for those who conform than for those who protest.

So, Governments can usually rely on their followers. They can, within wide limits, force unpopular measures through a sullen House. Yet there are limits to endurance. Sir Robert Peel knew that even the old Tories would support his Maynooth proposals:[1] but he could not repeal the Corn Laws without breaking his party. A Prime Minister owes a duty to his country, but he cannot carry out his duty if he has no party. As Mr Disraeli said, 'if we were not partisans we should not be ministers'.[2] Peel's great crime, in Disraeli's eyes, was not that he had repealed the Corn Laws but that he had broken up the Conservative party. To orthodox Liberals Mr Gladstone was the embodiment of political virtue; but the Whigs never knew whether introducing Home Rule or breaking up the party was the greater crime. Mr Lloyd George was forgiven much; but the old guard never forgot that he split the Liberal party into fragments. Mr Ramsay MacDonald's defection was always remembered and his earlier services to the Labour Movement invariably forgotten. A Prime Minister, it has been said, has three duties, to his Queen, his country, and his party; and it is never certain which is the correct order in the scale of values.

The maintenance of party unity is not the supreme object of political activity; yet obviously a Prime Minister will hesitate before he creates or encourages a break. British parties are not just collections of ambitious politicians. Their differences are based upon contrasted views of public policy. Usually, the weight of public opinion is almost equally divided between left and right, and a comparatively small turn-over of

[1] *Peel Papers*, III, p. 175.   [2] *Life of Disraeli*, I, p. 1658.

votes will deprive a party of opportunities for power for perhaps a generation. The result of the repeal of the Corn Laws in 1846 was that the Conservative party did not again obtain a majority until 1874. Though the Radical accession to the Liberal party in 1886 and Mr Gladstone's enormous prestige enabled a Liberal Government to be formed in 1892, it had but a small majority, and after 1895 it spent ten years in Opposition. At no time since 1918 has the Liberal party appeared to be anything more than a small minority. The triumphal progress of the Labour party was stopped by Mr Ramsay MacDonald in 1931, and a new generation came to the franchise before it obtained a majority.

Parties may appear to split suddenly over some great issue, as in 1866, 1886 and 1931; but regarded historically these great issues were rather the immediate reasons than the ultimate causes; they represented deep-seated tendencies. The task of managing a party is not merely to secure agreement on such issues, but to maintain such a balance between action and opinion that the party remains solidly behind its leaders. This demands a quality in leadership which the most eminent statesmen do not necessarily possess; Mr Disraeli, Mr Balfour, and Mr Baldwin, for instance, possessed it in greater measure than the abler Prime Ministers, Sir Robert Peel, Mr Gladstone, and Mr Lloyd George.

The skill which is required for this purpose would not be placed high among the political virtues. Its exercise is, nevertheless, a matter of some delicacy. It requires a sensitiveness to party opinion which neither Mr Gladstone nor Mr Ramsay MacDonald—to take contrasting examples—possessed in any marked degree. But all Prime Ministers must keep their ears to the ground. The whips inside the House and the party organisers outside act as microphones. This explains why 'whip' is really an inappropriate name. They do not compel; they do not even persuade; rather, they suggest. They keep members friendly to their leaders and the leaders familiar with their followers.

It is not without significance that the chief whip is still known in the House of Commons as the 'Patronage Secretary'. It is part of his function to keep an eye on those members who have some influence with their fellows, and to recommend their appointment to minor Government posts or, where these are not available, to advise the conferment of titles and honours. Brigadier-General Page Croft calculated that of the members of the 1910–18 Parliament (in which there were 80 Irish and 40 Labour members), no less than 290 received posts or honours.[1] Admittedly this was the longest Parliament since the Long Parliament that Cromwell closed, and there was a generosity about Mr Lloyd George's distribution of patronage which none of his predecessors or successors has equalled; it was, in short, an exceptional case. But every Honours list contains the names of a few of the Government supporters knighted or belted for 'political and public services'.

The distribution of patronage helps, but it is not very important. The fundamental problem is to keep members in accord with the policy of the Government. Significant whispers in the lobbies must be shut up. If members return from the weekly pilgrimage to the constituencies, or (in the case of a Conservative Government) from the weekly board meetings, or (in the case of a Labour Government) from the monthly trade union meetings, with complaints or criticisms, they must be listened to and their grievances met. For parties really split over a multitude of small complaints. The murmurs swell to a roar until the storm bursts. It must again be emphasised that the actual turn-over of votes required to defeat a Government is small. In all normal elections a transfer of one million votes from the Government to the Opposition will produce a change of Government. Consequently, no Government can afford to ignore even a comparatively small minority. The Catholic vote, the Nonconformist vote, the textiles interest, the miners' interest, the brewers' interest, the temperance vote, and many others, are all important. Though it is not possible to satisfy everybody all the time, it is possible partly to satisfy most of the people most of the time, and to see that the satisfied majority is not always the same.

Moreover each party has its back-benchers' sounding-board. In the Conservative party there is the Conservative Private Members' Committee, or 1922 Committee, so-called after the backbenchers' revolt which caused the break-up of Mr Lloyd George's Coalition and the creation of the Bonar Law Government of 1922.[2] Its officers are backbenchers, elected by the Conservative private members, and when the party is in office ministers do not attend except by invitation. There is

[1] 116 H.C.Deb. 5 s., 1339.   [2] R. T. McKenzie, *British Political Parties*, p. 58.

always a whip present, whose task is to report opinion to the Prime Minister. There are also 'functional' committees, consisting of private members interested in the various activities of government, which may report to the 1922 Committee when they have specific proposals or specific criticisms.

The Labour party, as usual, has rather more formal arrangements. The Parliamentary Labour party as a whole has regular meetings, at which policy and strategy are discussed; and when the Labour party is in office it elects a liaison committee or consultative committee to maintain contact with the Government.[1] There are also party groups interested in different activities of government and regional groups concerned with the special problems of groups of constituencies; with these groups the ministers concerned maintain greater or less contact, according to their habits and inclinations.

Members of Parliament are not always good judges of opinion. They are drawn, as we have seen,[2] from specialised and often unrepresentative groups. What is being said in the City and in the corridors of the Royal Courts of Justice is not necessarily what is being said in the pubs and the 'tubes'. Many members, especially the wealthier Conservatives and the Labour 'intellectuals' live in worlds of their own cut off from the real world: the subjects of discussion in the Carlton Club and the Fabian Summer Schools may be completely foreign to the subjects of discussion in less select circles. There is evidence, for instance, that nationalisation, its merits and defects, has never interested the electorate, which is, however, equally unconcerned with the merits and defects of 'free enterprise'. Nor are the constituency organisations, with which most members are in close contact, always good judges of the electorates whose votes they hope to catch. On the other hand, private members are usually better judges than ministers working hard in an official environment, because each private member has to pay attention to those movements of opinion which will affect the safety of his own seat. Fortunately, public opinion in Britain is both homogeneous and vocal, and it soon becomes clear whether the Government is losing support rapidly or slowly—it rarely gains it because the pendulum is always swinging against it.

[1] *Ibid.* pp. 428–41.   [2] *Ante*, pp. 44–58.

The result is that the British system is very far from the dictatorial system that it is sometimes represented to be. The Government possesses in its majority an instrument that gives it as great a strength as any Government in the world. Nevertheless, it is extraordinarily responsive even to small changes in public opinion. It is, perhaps, slow in coming to conclusions. Though it must lead it must also follow. Even the War Governments of 1914–18 acted more slowly than their enemies, and people like Colonel House contrasted the slowness of the British Government with the rapidity with which the President of the United States could take decisions.[1] Nevertheless, once a lead has been given to opinion and opinion has expressed itself, no Government in the world can think or act more quickly or more certainly. Then, the Government has a majority in Parliament and a majority in the country. Having reached a conclusion by democratic means, all democrats whether in the majority or the minority will accept the conclusion. In such a case the Opposition does not obstruct, it merely opposes: there is no Congress to say nay, and no revolutionary minority to put down.

This result is achieved, it will be noticed, by reason of the two-party system. The Government's majority in the country is made up of heterogeneous elements. The party is made up not of minds with but a single thought and hearts that speak as one, but of minds that produce different ideas and hearts that, in private, engage in cross-talk. The resultant policy is not, however, a highest common factor (which is necessarily low) but a lowest common measure. Each minority receives ample consideration because a party is necessarily catholic and catholicity necessarily implies tolerance and mutual assistance; or, to put it in a more realistic way, minorities have votes and all votes are important. One result—though this is not the place to prove the point—is that the effective differences between the immediate policies of the two great parties are never very great. The position would be very different if a system of proportional representation produced a variety of parties, each with its one-track mind. A system of bargaining would then be necessary. Each party would drive its engine to the junction and the

---

[1] On the other hand, the speed with which the Cabinet took decisions during the Atlantic Conference of 1941 astonished the Americans: *The White House Papers of Harry L. Hopkins*, I, p. 162.

drivers would adjourn to the signal-box to debate at length in what order they should cross the points. If the meat went first the coal would go home and the people would have raw meat for lunch or, more probably, nothing.

The control of the party in the House is one aspect only of this problem, but it is an important aspect; for it is in the House that the currents of opinion are most obvious. The Governments since 1931 have shown how necessary it is to bow to opinion in the House even when no immediate loss of majority is to be feared. During that period the Government has been defeated in the House on two occasions only.[1] On the motion to go into Committee of Supply for the Civil Estimates in 1936, a private member's amendment that equal pay should be given to men and women in the civil service was moved and carried.[2] There was a rather thin House, partly because the vote was taken on the first Wednesday in the session which was not a private member's day. The vote was reversed by a substantial majority in the following week.[3] In 1951, on a prayer to annul an order reducing the cheese ration the Labour Government was defeated by 237 votes to 219. A new order was made and, after it was explained that there was not enough food in the country to maintain the ration, the prayer for its annulment was withdrawn.

On the other hand, there have been many occasions on which Governments have given way to criticism, in spite of the large and fairly docile majorities by which they have been supported. A few outstanding examples of 'bowing to the storm' will suffice.

The Incitement to Disaffection Bill had already been attacked outside the House before it came up for second reading on 16 April 1934. The Council for Civil Liberties, then containing supporters, and even members of Parliament, of all parties, had recently been set up, and its first task was to lead the attack on the Bill. The Attorney-General therefore knew before he moved the second reading that it was regarded with a considerable amount of dislike. Hardly anything was said in its favour

---

[1] Defeats on private members' Bills and motions, when the whips are not put on, are ignored.

[2] 310 H.C.Deb. 5 s., 2017–80. The amendment was carried by 156 to 148; but when the amendment was put as a substantive motion it was lost by 149 votes to 134.

[3] 310 H.C.Deb. 5 s., 2441–566; carried by 361 votes to 145.

on either side of the House, except by the Law Officers. It was, never-theless, passed by 263 votes to 61, no Conservative voting against it.[1] Under Standing Orders it was committed to a Standing Committee consisting of fifty members, of whom forty-two supported the Govern-ment. The small minority of eight members fought the Bill almost line by line. They challenged twenty-nine divisions, in all of which they were unsuccessful. One Conservative member voted with them on one occasion, but with this exception they found a solid phalanx of Govern-ment supporters against them. It is perhaps significant of the lack of enthusiasm on the side of the Government that the Government's support never exceeded twenty-eight, and on one occasion fell as low as fifteen. Twice the Government failed to secure a quorum, and on several other occasions the Committee was counted out. Including these delays, the Committee stage occupied sixteen days, and on several occasions the Committee sat all day. The Bill was very considerably modified; but the Attorney-General was always sure of his majority when he chose to resist. On Report, the highest vote for the Opposition was seventy-nine, and the Bill passed its third reading by 241 votes to 65. It was a very different Bill from that read a second time, and clearly the amendments were not made because the Attorney-General could not rely on his majority, but because so many people, both outside and inside the House, had, as the Solicitor-General put it, expressed 'appre-hensions' about some of its terms.

The Coal Mines Bill, 1936, provides an example of a different kind. Its main purpose was to compel a better organisation of the coal mining industry. It therefore aroused opposition from the industry itself and from its numerous representatives in the House of Commons. The Labour party opposed it for the very different reason that it did not accord with the policy of nationalising the mines adopted by that party —and the miners are very strongly represented in the House of Com-mons. Here, too, there was much opposition before the second reading came on. The Bill had a 'bad press'. 'The present bill...has been fiercely attacked by the coalowners within the last few days, and more than a dozen of their henchmen in the House put down a motion for rejection.'[2] Before the motion for the second reading came on, the

[1] 288 H.C.Deb. 5 s., 739–850.   [2] *Manchester Guardian*, 19 May 1936.

Cabinet found it necessary to accept amendments. 'It was recognised that if the Bill was to be passed into law this session important concessions would have to be made, and Mr Runciman was authorised to announce them when he moved the second reading of the measure.'[1] Mr Runciman (contrary to the practice of the House—but some latitude is allowed to a minister) read his speech, indicating that three important amendments would be proposed when the Bill went into committee. Objection was at once taken that these went to the root of the Bill, and the adjournment of the House was moved from the Labour front bench and supported by the Liberal party. Speakers on the Government side, while not all supporting the adjournment, admitted that they had been placed in a position of 'some difficulty'. As Mr Maxton said, 'if this motion [i.e. the adjournment] were taken to the division lobbies the Government would probably win', but appeals came from both sides to adjourn the debate. The Secretary for Mines was put up to try to persuade the House to discuss the Bill, but many members showed that they were not satisfied. The Prime Minister therefore agreed that there should be an additional day provided for the second reading, and that in the interval a White Paper should be issued showing the proposed changes. The adjournment motion was then put and defeated by 255 votes to 117, only one supporter of the Government voting with the Opposition. The Government thus maintained its prestige, and a small House carried on a desultory debate on such of the Bill as was left.[2] The further discussion of the second reading was never taken, and an amended Bill was not reintroduced until the end of 1937, nearly two years later.

In this instance the general objection to the Bill was confused with the particular objection to the procedure. No such confusion arose over the National Defence Contribution proposed in the Budget of 1937. The scheme outlined by the Chancellor of the Exchequer was criticised on all sides of the House. He nevertheless pressed it for several weeks (during which he became Prime Minister). There was vociferous opposition from all the 'interests' outside, and before the division on the second reading of the Finance Bill was taken it was

[1] *The Times*, 19 May 1936.
[2] For the debate, see 312 H.C.Deb. 5 s., 853–970.

withdrawn, a new scheme being substituted later. The Finance Bill was read a second time and carried by 340 votes to 149.

These examples show that, no matter how great the Government's effective majority, it can be compelled to give way to a combination of criticism in the House, complaint in the lobbies, and agitation outside. With a Conservative Government the strongest force rests with the 'interests' which dominate the industrial and commercial field; with a Labour Government the trade unions are perhaps even more important.[1] It is difficult to separate interests outside and opinion inside; for most members represent somebody besides their constituents.[2] Also, the constituents themselves have economic interests which affect their attitude to the Government and therefore affect their representatives in Parliament. Even if a Labour member representing a mining constituency is not the nominee of a miners' trade union he is necessarily in close touch with the local branches of the union and, for all practical purposes, their views are his. Similarly, Birmingham manufacturers are represented in Parliament not only by the representatives of the Federation of British Industries and its sectional bodies, but also by the Conservative members for Birmingham. For these reasons it is not possible to weigh one influence against another: they are in substance the same.

Even where no economic interest is affected, there are cultural and propaganda bodies, also represented in the House, which can arouse public opinion. There were, for instance, no economic interests directly affected by the Incitement to Disaffection Bill. Such propaganda bodies are particularly important in the sphere of foreign affairs. Public opinion, both organised and unorganised, compelled the Government to withdraw the Hoare-Laval proposals,[3] and to modify its attitude to the 'blockade' of Bilbao in the spring of 1937 and to alter its Suez policy in 1956.

Other examples might be drawn from any Parliament. Within a few months after the general election of 1955 the Eden Government was so much on the defensive that a formal statement had to be issued from Downing Street that the Prime Minister did not intend to resign. It had

---

[1] For the influence of 'interests', see further Chapter VII.
[2] See *ante*, pp. 30–44.   [3] *Cabinet Government*, pp. 365–7.

been alleged by a section of the Conservative press (not to mention the Opposition press) that it was weak and indecisive. Its efforts to control inflation were alleged to have been dilatory and ineffective; to the demand for self-determination for Cyprus it had moved from never to somehow, sometime; riots had occurred in Jordan because of negotiations for the adhesion of that country to the Baghdad Pact; it had withdrawn a scheme for a subsidy to the white fish industry under pressure from the interests concerned and had suspended a proposal for the prohibition of the manufacture of heroin. Examples might also be drawn from the experience of the Labour Government of 1945–51, particularly of left-wing pressure (i.e. 'Keep Left' and 'Bevanite'). Every Government has its troubles; it is far from true that everybody behind the Treasury bench is happy. Indeed, members who have helped to win a general election seem often to have made themselves excessively optimistic by the exuberance of their own verbosity; they have all said so much that turns out to be mere wishful thinking. Nor is it unknown for back-benchers to believe that Cabinet timber of a better quality could be found on the back-benches, that new blood is wanted on the front bench, that somebody else should have a chance to bat, that more drive is wanted at the centre, and so through the whole list of hackneyed metaphors. Of course, a Government is not perpetually on the defensive. It needs to lead public opinion at least as much as it is led by it. But it is clear that one of the main functions of the whips is to keep the Government informed of the criticisms that are not uttered in the House and to give explanations that cannot be made in the House. 'Our men will not like it' is one of the most potent arguments that a whip can address to a minister; and 'frankly, the minister is doing his best for you, but I assure you that there are considerable difficulties with other people not so reasonable as yourself', is far more persuasive to a member than any speeches in the House.

2. BEHIND THE SPEAKER'S CHAIR

Though the Government's control of the House of Commons became effective as a result of Irish obstruction, the powers conferred by the reforms since 1882 would in any event have been inevitable. The

¹ *Ibid.* pp. 81–2.

expansive days of the middle of the nineteenth century have long since disappeared. The 'condition of the people' is no longer merely a question of the price of wheat; foreign affairs do not follow the leisurely development of a long-term diplomacy; administrative problems are not limited to the 'economical reform' of Burke. The Industrial Revolution—or rather, Revolutions, for the invention of the telegraph and the internal combustion engine were as revolutionary as the invention of the steam engine—and the consequent extension of the franchise have fundamentally modified the nature of politics. The development of a democratic local government was followed by the development of a bureaucratic central government, and a host of new authorities' attempts to meet problems which in substance were unknown a generation ago. The existence of a world economy has produced a new world order. The Concert of Europe has been converted into world disharmony. There is always a war, hot or cold.

There are, therefore, more numerous and urgent problems to be debated in Parliament. The removal of the Irish in 1921 has left fewer people to debate them, but there are more members anxious and indeed insistent upon speaking. In 1833, 395 members out of 658 spoke in the House, and among them they made 5765 speeches. Fifty years later there were over 21,160 speeches. In 1954–5 the *Official Report* occupied over 13,000 columns, and this excludes the Standing Committees. Members are elected to speak and they do speak. They have to satisfy a large body of constituents who consider that the function of a member of Parliament is to assist in the government of the country by taking part in debate. 'What does he do when he gets there?' is one of the most devastating questions that the election canvasser has to answer.

On the other hand, speeches are much shorter than they used to be. The set oration of several hours' length has disappeared. Front bench speakers rarely talk for more than an hour, and twenty minutes is the usual time for a private member,[1] even in the House. In Committee, speeches of five or ten minutes are quite common. So many members are anxious to speak that they complain if others monopolise the time.

---

[1] 'The number of people who exceed twenty minutes in the House is very small, except on the Front Bench': H.C. 161 of 1931, Q. 736 (Capt. Bourne); 'The vast majority of speeches run from ten to twelve minutes': *ibid.* Q. 739 (Capt. Bourne).

Moreover, the Government is always anxious to push its business through and to limit speaking on its own side. As Mr Baldwin said:

When a Government is in, they want to get legislation through, and they do not encourage their men to talk. I suppose they feel the men on the front bench, and, perhaps, one or two behind them, are quite sufficient to answer the points that are put. They expect the Opposition to raise the difficulties. They do not want their own supporters to raise difficulties.[1]

Or, as Mr A. P. Herbert put it:

The rules of parliamentary procedure have one chief purpose, to prevent people talking too much. The tact and cunning of the Government whips are mainly directed to the same end, to prevent people talking too much, especially when the Government do not want people to talk at all.[2]

It is interesting to compare the evidence given by Mr Ramsay MacDonald before the Select Committees of 1914 and 1931. Before the former he was leader of a small minority; before the latter he was Prime Minister. In 1914, therefore, he was anxious to extend the opportunities of private members; in 1931 he was concerned primarily to get his business through the House. In 1914, for instance, he was a strong opponent of the guillotine; in 1931 he thought that it should be applied to all Bills.

The opportunities of the Opposition have been restricted by Standing Orders. The ten o'clock rule, the Supply rule, and the closure, in particular, have enabled the Government very stringently to limit debate; the kangaroo has considerably restricted the number of amendments to Bills; and if legislation threatens to take a long time there is always the remedy of the guillotine. Even so, if an Opposition wishes to be obstructive it can easily find the means. The Government has no difficulty with Supply. Individual debates are brought to an end by the ten o'clock rule, and if the Government wants a decision at once it can apply the closure. At the end of twenty-six days all the Supply motions remaining are put through without debate. Legislation presents greater difficulty. Debates on second and third readings can be brought to an end by the closure; but the committee and report stages can go on almost for ever. If the Opposition likes to debate every statutory

[1] H.C. 161 of 1931, Q. 271.
[2] A. P. Herbert, *The Ayes Have It*, p. 40.

instrument that requires express approval and to put down a prayer against every statutory instrument that does not, there is little to stop them. Even under the present rules, and even with the ultimate remedy of the guillotine—a remedy which cannot be used except after a motion itself preceded by a debate—there are plenty of opportunities for obstruction.

Obstruction as a parliamentary device has now quite a respectable history. Redlich goes back to the debate on the Grand Remonstrance in the Long Parliament of 1641, and obstructive tactics were used by Burke in 1771. In 1806 Castlereagh made long speeches to stop the Radicals from obtaining Liberal legislation from the Fox-Grenville Cabinet. Obstruction was used on the Reform Bill in 1831, by O'Connell on the Coercion Bill of 1833, and on the Arms Bill in 1843.[1] Parnell justified his obstruction by reference to Gladstone's tactics on the Matrimonial Causes Bill of 1857.[2] It was used by the Conservatives on the Ballot Bill of 1870 and by 'the colonels' against the Army Purchase Bill of 1871.[3] It was then used by the Fourth Party under Lord Randolph Churchill as a general parliamentary device.[4] From the Fourth Party it was taken over by Parnell, and this general use of obstruction led to the reforms of 1882.[5] The Radicals under Labouchere used obstruction against the Estimates in 1886, and this led to the Supply rule and the modern closure.[6] But even with the Government armoury filled with weapons it could still be used by the Conservatives against the Finance Bill of 1909, the Parliament Bill of 1911 and the Home Rule and Welsh Church Bills of 1912–14.

There was no obstruction during the war of 1914–18, and since 1919 the weapon has been used only on rare occasions. One reason was that the Labour party provided the Opposition for the whole period between the wars, except for the brief intervals of 1924 and 1929–31. The Labour party has always held firmly to the principle of majority rule in its own

[1] Redlich, I, pp. 138–9.
[2] *Life of Lord Granville*, I, p. 231; *Life of Lord Sherbrooke* (Robert Lowe), II, p. 164.
[3] *Life of Sir Charles Dilke*, I, p. 98; *Letters of Queen Victoria*, 2nd series, II, p. 134; Guedalla, *The Queen and Mr Gladstone*, p. 284.
[4] *Life of Lord Randolph Churchill*, I, p. 213. The device of blocking motions (*ante*, p. 120) was invented to prevent Churchill from moving frivolous motions: *ibid*.
[5] *Ante*, pp. 127–8.
[6] *Life of Lord Randolph Churchill*, II, p. 150.

assemblies, from the divisional party and trade union branch to the Annual Conference and the Trades Union Congress, and it applied that principle to proceedings in Parliament. In opposition it was led by men like Mr Ramsay MacDonald, Mr George Lansbury and Mr Attlee, who were little inclined to battle and who were in any case mere chairmen who carried out decisions made coolly in party meetings however heated the atmosphere of the House itself became.

These decisions were taken in the knowledge that a Labour victory at the polls depended in large measure on a middle-class 'floating vote' whose members doubted—especially after 1931—Labour's fitness to govern. Most Labour members in opposition were sober and solid trade unionists of the type of Mr Clynes and Mr Henderson, not bright young men of the 'Fourth Party' type. Most of the Labour members, too, went home by bus or underground and desired no late sittings.

It is also important that from 1923 to 1937, with short intervals, Mr Baldwin was the effective leader of the Government. By nature indolent and peaceful, he was always ready to compromise and to meet opposition half-way. The result of all these factors was a far closer relationship between Government and Opposition than was the case when the Liberals carried through the preliminaries of social reform, as well as Home Rule, the Parliament Bill and Welsh Church Disestablishment, in the Parliaments of 1906 and 1910. The same practice seems to have dominated Parliament since 1945. Obstruction is now rarely necessary because Government business is arranged by the party leaders through the party whips or, to use the parliamentary euphemisms, 'behind the Speaker's Chair' and 'through the usual channels'. Exceptional occasions like the debates on the Trade Unions and Trade Disputes Bill of 1927 apart, obstruction is necessary only where agreement cannot be reached, and it is then carried on only for a single all-night sitting. Provided that the demands of the Government are not unreasonable, the Opposition will usually acquiesce.

This method of arranging business through the usual channels was of course known long before 1919.[1] Thus, a Liberal whip gave evidence

---

[1] Cf. the arrangement between Lord Palmerston and Lord Derby between 1860 and 1866, whereby, as it was said, England was governed 'en société anonyme': Guedalla, *Gladstone and Palmerston*, p. 150; Saintsbury, *Lord Derby*, ch. VIII.

before the Select Committee of 1914 that the Prime Minister on the advice of the whips arranged days for the various stages of legislation. The whips discussed the matter with the Opposition whips, the whips of the other parties, and the officers of the House. For instance, that evening the debate suddenly collapsed. The whips went to the Opposition whips and suggested that two or three small measures might be taken and that the House should rise early. This proposal was agreed to within five minutes and was carried out.[1]

Some examples will indicate how the system works, and why it sometimes breaks down. When the Conservatives were in opposition in 1906, Mr Austen Chamberlain wrote:

This afternoon we agreed to finish the third reading of the Irish Town Tenants Bill on the condition that the Government took only two other little Departmental Bills—one of which I was pressing for in the interest of my constituency. For the purpose of shortening debate it was arranged that we should not provoke the Irish, on condition that the Government was very mild and did nothing to provoke us. In spite of this Cherry, the Irish Attorney-General, made an ill-tempered speech which caused Balcarres [Conservative whip] to tell Whiteley [Liberal whip] that it justified us in throwing up the agreement. To which Whiteley replied, 'So it does, but I hope you won't. You fellows play the game, but ours are such d——d fools that they can't play it even when it is explained to them.'[2]

In May 1907, the Government chief whip went to the Conservative whip and asked him to enable them to get on faster. 'Why should I?' he replied, 'You never helped us.'[3] In March 1911, there was an agreement between the Government and the Opposition that there should be 'full opportunity for discussion' and that the House should sit only 'a little late'. The former undertaking was broken (apparently by mistake) by Mr Winston Churchill (then of course a Liberal minister). The House therefore sat all night, and at 10 a.m. had passed only one more clause than might have been obtained at 12.30 a.m. without discussion. Mr Austen Chamberlain's comment was: 'I have never known such an episode before, for it was a clear breach of one of those

---

[1] H.C. 378 of 1914, Qs. 1454–8 and 1462 (Mr J. W. Gulland).
[2] Sir Austen Chamberlain, *Politics from Inside*, pp. 39–40.
[3] *Ibid.* p. 85.

parliamentary undertakings which all leaders have hitherto so carefully guarded.'[1]

Most all-night sittings are due to the fact that an agreement cannot be reached. At certain periods of the year, especially in March, the Government is much pressed for time. It therefore asks the Opposition to let more and more business through. The more the Opposition gives way, the more the Government whips urge on them, until there comes a moment when the Opposition must make a stand for what it conceives to be its rights. Thus, in February 1936, the Opposition considered that the Government was asking the House to pass too many supplementary estimates[2] in a single sitting. Accordingly, it proceeded to discuss every item in detail. The first item was a supplementary estimate for the Office of Works. It was not easy to debate such an estimate, for the Office of Works was responsible only for the buildings and not for the use to which they were put. The first Opposition speaker was called to order for discussing employment exchanges when he was permitted to discuss only the buildings. Then he remembered that there was no lavatory accommodation near the Employment Exchange at Newcastle, and for more than an hour the Opposition expatiated on the hardship of the unemployed in having to walk a hundred yards to the nearest public lavatory. The next Office of Works vote related to buildings to be erected as anti-gas stations. Here discussion was easy on the subject of air-raid precautions, and it went on for two hours. Next came a supplementary estimate for Home Office schools. Penal reform was ruled out of order, but a desultory discussion, punctuated by rulings by the Chairman, was carried on for an hour. A supplementary estimate for the Colonial Office, required because of the war between Italy and Ethiopia, provided easy matter for debate. The subject of the internment of Italian deserters being mentioned, and the Attorney-General entering the House at that moment, he was called upon to explain the rules of international law on that question. Since he obviously knew nothing about them, a member of the Opposition moved the adjournment. This being lost, a Labour lawyer explained the rules of international law. This debate lasted an hour-and-a-half.

[1] *Ibid.* p. 329.
[2] Supplementary estimates are now included in Supply days.

It is needless to continue. At 12.55 a.m., the leader of the Opposition moved the adjournment to find out how much longer the Government intended to continue. The chief whip regretted that the ordinary channels had not functioned on this occasion, and explained that he was willing to make a reasonable arrangement. An attempt was apparently made through the usual channels to come to agreement. This failing, the Opposition again made an appeal to the Government. The chief whip then explained publicly what arrangement he was willing to make, but the Opposition rejected his offer. At 7.52 a.m. the leader of the Opposition made a new appeal without success. The debate on this motion for the adjournment alone lasted two hours. At about mid-day, an arrangement was at last made. Two orders of the day were read without further debate, the rest were postponed, and the House rose after more than twenty hours' debate.[1]

The debate, as a debate, was futile. Whether it was necessary for tactical reasons only the whips can say: but, clearly, unless the Opposition is always to accept what the chief whip proposes, they must at times show that they are ready to use their power to obstruct. Nearly all obstruction is now of this character.

I have noticed, as we have all noticed, that business sometimes comes to a standstill; we sit for hour after hour during which no progress appears to be made; there are motions to report progress, and to ask leave to sit again, and so on; it goes on hour after hour, and then suddenly something happens, and everything goes quite smoothly, and everybody becomes happy. What really happens is that the usual channels have been operating, and have come to an agreement. Would you not agree that a definition of obstruction is: a failure of the usual channels to function?[2]

Occasions for such protests rarely arise more than once a session. Mr Baldwin, for instance, was always careful of the rights of the

---

[1] 309 H.C. Deb 5 s., 689–974.

[2] H.C. 161 of 1931, Q. 1458 (Mr Herbert Morrison). '*Capt. Bourne*: Would not you also say that a certain amount of what you call obstruction arises when there is disagreement through the usual channels as to the total amount of time which should be allotted to a Bill?—*Mr T. Kennedy* (Chief Whip): That is the time when attempts at agreement would break down naturally. *Capt. Bourne*: It probably is a genuine disagreement between the Government and the Opposition as to what is a fair time to give to any Bill, but is it not a fact that often an amount of obstruction will take place in the early stages, then an agreement is arrived at, and, after that, the thing goes through quite smoothly?—*Mr T. Kennedy*: Yes.' H.C. 161 of 1931, Qs. 772–3.

Opposition, and Mr Ramsay MacDonald protested his constant desire to follow the same practice.[1] There is, however, another kind of obstruction, directed to the delay of those measures to which the Opposition is fundamentally opposed. Irish obstruction on Coercion Bills was of this character, and so was the opposition of the Conservative party to the major legislation of the period 1910 to 1914. The opposition to the Parliament Bill, 1911, illustrates both the method of the obstruction and the Government's power of meeting it. The question that leave be given to introduce the Bill was discussed for two days and passed. The second reading debate was brought to an end after four days by a closure motion. Eight instructions to the committee were then put on the paper, but seven were ruled out of order. The Bill, which contained only six clauses, some of them very short, was in committee for thirteen days. A vast number of amendments were put down, but many of them were ruled out of order, and many more were passed over by the Chairman under his kangaroo power. It was even sought to amend the long title, the short title, and the preamble. The closure was moved and carried twenty-nine times. The eleven o'clock rule was suspended on nine of the thirteen days, and only on two of these nine days was the House able to rise before midnight. On one night the debate continued until 4.40 a.m. Before the report stage was reached, a guillotine motion was passed allotting time to the report stage and third reading, and the Bill passed the House under the guillotine. The Bill was amended in the House of Lords, but the Government then announced that the King had consented to create sufficient peers to pass it in the form in which it had left the House of Commons. When the Prime Minister sought to move in the House of Commons that the Lords' amendments be considered, he was shouted down by the Opposition. The leader of the Opposition then made an attack, but when the Government sought to continue the debate the Speaker had to adjourn the House on account of grave disorder. A vote of censure on the Government was moved and defeated. Ultimately, the Lords' amendments, with a few excep-

---

[1] 'I have never tried to set a time limit for a discussion of anything without trying to come to an arrangement, because I think the House of Commons ought never to be driven, but it ought always to be a sort of co-operation between us so far as time is concerned': H.C. 161 of 1931, Q. 50.

tions, were defeated, and the Bill passed the House of Lords under the threat to create peers.

Such opposition was purely obstructive, owing to the revolution, as the Opposition put it, that the Government was effecting in the Constitution (Lord Hugh Cecil's remark that the ministers were guilty of high treason was one of the mildest comments). Obstructive opposition has not necessarily this purpose. It may be directed towards wearing down the resistance to amendments which the Opposition considers reasonable. Even if the Government will not give way altogether, it may possibly propose a compromise in order to get the Bill through at a reasonable speed. In particular, private members on the Government side dislike all-night sittings even more than the Opposition. There is some amusement and excitement to be obtained out of the making of long speeches, the proposing of dilatory motions, and generally walking the narrow line that separates what is in order from what is not. Government supporters are compelled to sit mute and dispirited on uncomfortable benches, or to sleep in such comfort as they can find within the precincts of the House and to wait for the division bell to summon them to a count. After a time they begin to think that perhaps the Government might compromise; the whips fear that they may not be able to keep a majority of supporters out of their beds; and accordingly ministers give way. As a Conservative member, Lord Robert Cecil, said in 1914:

The Opposition now...does undoubtedly indulge in proceedings the legitimate object of which is to secure that any particular amendment shall be brought over and over again before the House....When the Opposition is really anxious to amend a Bill, its only means of doing so is, first, to move an amendment, and then, when it is inevitably defeated in the Division Lobby, if possible to bring it up again and again, and gradually to induce the supporters of the Government to put pressure on the Government.[1]

Obstruction is thus an ordinary part of parliamentary procedure. Every whip, it has been said, 'collects those members who are parti-

---

[1] H.C. 378 of 1914, Q. 737. Possibly suggested by the debate on the Budget in 1912 about which Sir Austen Chamberlain said: 'I was up till four on Monday night and till three on Tuesday. We wrung some concessions from Lloyd George, who yielded sooner than have us sit up and on to the bitter end.' *Politics from Inside*, p. 490.

cularly and specially ingenious for the purpose of obstruction'.[1] Thus, Captain Crookshank was said to be 'the Prince of obstructive practices',[2]—though he denied the charge—and in fact his blue blood was extraordinarily degenerate when compared with that of his royal predecessors.

It must be emphasised, however, that obstruction is quite exceptional. The arrangements through the usual channels are a regular procedure. The chief whip submits to the leader of the House at the beginning of the week a draft programme for the following week. The outline might be: Monday, second reading of a Government Bill; Tuesday and Thursday, Supply; Wednesday, private members' motions; Friday, private members' Bills. This having been approved, it is submitted to the Opposition whips. The Opposition chooses the votes to be debated in Supply. The Opposition whips would perhaps suggest that the Foreign Office vote should be put down for Tuesday and the Ministry of Labour vote for Thursday. The chief whip was exceedingly sorry, but the Minister of Labour had an engagement for Thursday: would they prefer to take the Labour vote on Tuesday, or postpone it for the following week? In due course, agreement is reached and is approved by the respective leaders. On Thursday afternoon the leader of the Opposition will rise in his place to ask the leader of the House what business will be taken in the following week. The leader of the House reads out the agreed agenda, and so the whole House knows what arrangement has been made for the following week.

Once or twice a session the Opposition feels so strongly on a particular question, such as the rise in the cost-of-living, or the failure of the Government to stop the war between Brobdingnag and Lilliput, or its incompetent handling of the Utopian problem, that it decides to move a vote of censure. There is a recognised convention that the Government will always find time for such a vote.[3] Accordingly, the Opposi-

---

[1] H.C. 161 of 1931, Q. 1420 (Mr Leach).

[2] *Ibid.* Q. 2943 (Mr Leach).

[3] This is probably subject to the condition that the question cannot be effectively discussed in some other way. Once when Mr Austen Chamberlain thought of putting down a vote of censure he refrained, one reason being that as the question could be raised on the Consolidated Fund Bill, Mr Asquith could and probably would refuse: Sir Austen Chamberlain, *Politics from Inside*, p. 234.

tion whip will take the motion to the chief whip and 'demand a day'. Probably something like the following conversation will take place:

Chief Whip: We are willing to do our best for you. But look here, old man, we've an awful lot of business to get through. Can't you raise this on one of your Supply days, or wait until we bring in the Consolidated Fund Bill next week?

Opposition Whip: I'm afraid not. Our people want to talk about Education on the Supply day; and they won't wait for the Consolidated Fund Bill.

Chief Whip: Well, I'll make you an offer. If you'll close down the debate on the Shrimp Industry Reorganisation Bill at seven on Monday and let us have a couple of small Bills the same evening, we'll let you move your vote of censure on Tuesday.

Opposition Whip: Will that mean suspending the ten o'clock rule on Monday?

Chief Whip: I'm afraid so, but I'll try to stop our men from talking if you'll do the same.

Opposition Whip: Very well, thanks very much.

So on Monday the chief whip moves to suspend the ten o'clock rule. For form's sake this is opposed by the Opposition, but carried (without debate, of course). Members on both sides find that they are not encouraged to talk about shrimps; and as those representing the industry insist on carrying on the debate, the chief whip moves the closure at 7 p.m. For form's sake, the motion is opposed, but is carried. Whereupon the House proceeds to discuss the small Bills. Agreement having been reached already, they are opposed but not obstructed, and the House rises at the usual time. On Tuesday, therefore, the House proceeds to consider whether the Government ought to be censured for not imposing an embargo on exports of oil to Brobdingnag.

The absurdity of a system in which the Government postpones its own business in order to let the Opposition threaten death and damnation is only apparent. The Opposition is not just a nuisance to be tolerated, but a definite and essential part of the Constitution. Once it is accepted that opposition is not only legitimate but essential to the maintenance of democratic government, the need for arrangements behind the Speaker's Chair follows naturally. Standing Orders and the practice of the House enable each side to exercise its proper functions.

If either pressed its rights to the uttermost, the parliamentary system would come to an end.

Sometimes, indeed, the practice of consultation goes further than mere arrangements about business. It is recognised, for instance, that matters relating to the Crown should, if possible, be settled by agreement. Lord Melbourne failed to communicate with Sir Robert Peel about the Prince Consort's annuity in 1840, with the result that the allowance was reduced by £20,000 and, had it not been for the Prince's good sense, serious difficulties might have arisen when the Conservatives secured a majority. Lord Melbourne's justification was that Peel was 'a very bad horse to go up to in the stable'.[1] Mr Disraeli made the same mistake when he agreed to the assumption by Queen Victoria of the title of Empress of India.[2] Since then the rule has been strictly followed, notably when Mr Baldwin consulted the leader of the Opposition and the leader of the Liberal party on the abdication of King Edward VIII.[3]

In matters of defence and foreign affairs, too, there is often consultation. The Duke of Wellington was often consulted by the Whigs.[4] Mr Joseph Chamberlain tried to persuade Sir Henry Campbell-Bannerman to support his policy against Kruger in 1899: 'It would be a game of bluff, and it was impossible to play that game if the Opposition did not support the Government.'[5] Mr Balfour was consulted by Mr Asquith as to the various defence schemes in 1908.[6] At the outbreak of war in 1914, paraphrases of despatches were sent to the Opposition to be read in the Shadow Cabinet.[7] Mr Austen Chamberlain assisted the Allied War Conferences on financial questions, and discussed the first War Budget with Mr Lloyd George.[8] In 1915 Conservative leaders were summoned to the War Council to secure their agreement to the

[1] *Life of Lord Granville*, II, pp. 160–1. A remark, incidentally, attributed by Mr Augustine Birrell to Lord Rosebery, with reference to Lord Morley: see Birrell, *Things Past Redress*. [2] *Ibid.*
[3] Jennings, 'The Abdication of King Edward VIII', *Politica*, II, p. 292.
[4] E.g. in 1836: *Lord Melbourne's Papers*, pp. 342–3.
[5] C.B.'s version: *Life of Sir Henry Campbell-Bannerman*, I, pp. 233–5.
[6] *Life of Lord Oxford and Asquith*, I, pp. 243–7; *Esher Papers*, II, pp. 316–17, 364.
[7] Beaverbrook, *Politicians and the War*, I, p. 51.
[8] Lloyd George, *War Memoirs*, I, pp. 105–6, 119.

promise that Constantinople should go to Russia after the War.[1] In 1938 and 1939 the Labour Opposition was frequently consulted by Mr Neville Chamberlain and in 1949 Mr Attlee consulted Mr Churchill. As was pointed out on the last of these occasions, an Opposition leader who receives information in this way may effectively be stopped from disclosing it in the House, even though he could have obtained it from other sources. On the other hand, if the Government decides to 'go it alone', it must expect opposition as fierce as the opposition to the Eden Government's Suez policy in 1956.

There are other examples of consultation directed towards the minimisation of opposition. The famous long sitting of 1881[2] was brought to an end after agreement between Government and Opposition.[3] After the Phoenix Park murders in 1882, Sir Stafford Northcote took the initiative in indicating his willingness to support the Government in any action they proposed.[4] The dispute over the Reform Bill of 1884 was settled by agreement.[5] There were secret negotiations between Mr George Wyndham and the Irish over the Irish Land Bill of 1903.[6] The Labour Government in 1929–31 could maintain office only by consultations with the Liberals.[7] In July 1931, the Government consulted leaders of the Opposition parties as to the financial crisis.

These consultations are not strictly 'behind the Speaker's Chair'. They indicate, however, that the Government has always to bear in mind that there is an Opposition, and that certain matters cannot effectively be settled except by agreement.

[1] Beaverbrook, *op. cit.* I, p. 59; they refused to accept responsibility, but did not oppose: Churchill, *World Crisis*, 1915, pp. 198–9.

[2] *Ante*, p. 127.

[3] *Letters of Queen Victoria*, 2nd series, III, pp. 187–95.

[4] *Life of Gladstone*, III, p. 68.

[5] *Ibid.* III, pp. 135–8. The dispute was really between the two Houses. See also *Cabinet Government*, pp. 285–6.

[6] W. S. Blunt, *My Diaries*, 1888–1914, p. 463.

[7] Snowden, *Autobiography*, II, pp. 879–89.

[8] *The Times*, 14 October 1937.

3. THE HOUSE AND THE COUNTRY

The House of Commons is far more than a debating assembly in which proposals are discussed with a view to their acceptance, rejection, or amendment. Indeed, it is almost a fiction to say that this function is exercised at all. With insignificant exceptions the motions are proposed or opposed by the Government. If they are amended, it is because the Government accepts the amendments. Otherwise, the motions are accepted or rejected at the Government's decision by the application of the Government's majority. Sir Austen Chamberlain has said:

I hold that there is nothing so untrue as to say that votes are not changed by speeches. Again and again, any one of us who has been long in the House has seen a proposal withdrawn or amended out of recognition as a result of debate, even though it were a Government question, even though the Government whips were going to be put on, because the back-benchers, the supporters of the Government, have shown uneasiness, growing uneasiness, as they have seen that all the weight of argument was on this other side, and that their own chiefs had not got a case, and the whips have come in from the Lobby and said: 'Look here, there is a rot set in, and we do not know where we shall be'; so the Leader of the House is sent for to pull his colleague out of the difficulty into which he has got, and he says he will reconsider this matter before Report, and so on. If you go into a debate, in spite of your whips, the debate will have a great influence on the shaping of the principles which are accepted.[1]

This is, however, not quite what happens. There is no real possibility that the Government will be defeated. The debate does not change votes; it changes, or perhaps settles, opinions. The Government gives way because the 'sense of the House', a sense which would not be noticeable in the division lobbies, is against it. The process is part of the technique of managing the majority, and is not due to any real fear of defeat.[2]

---

[1] H.C. 161 of 1931, Q. 2375.

[2] It frequently happens, however, that a minor defect is pointed out in the House, so that the minister in charge accepts an amendment, or undertakes to consider the matter. More often than not this decision is taken *before the speech about it is made*. The minister's advisers consider the amendment on the paper and recommend either that it ought to be accepted or considered, or that no harm would be done if it were accepted. See further Chapter VII, § 3.

This is all the more obvious from the fact that very few members sit through much of a debate. Sir Austen Chamberlain's evidence shows by implication how spacious is the area of the Treasury Bench. The whip *sends for* the Prime Minister to get *his colleague* out of a hole. The minister in charge of the motion, his parliamentary secretary, if he has one in the House, his parliamentary private secretary, and the inevitable whip, represent Her Majesty's Government. Facing them are the equivalent members of the Shadow Cabinet. Behind them, on both sides, are those waiting to speak or having nothing better to do. The average candidate no doubt thinks of himself as expressing the opinions of South Blankshire to the assembled statesmen of the nation; he will in fact address rows of empty benches and piles of discarded order papers.

On this point the general opinion is represented by a member of long experience, Earl Winterton:

There is no doubt that fewer members listen to debates than was formerly the case. In old days when an important subject was under discussion both Front Benches were well occupied. Today it often happens that, even when a big issue is under review, the Minister in charge of the debate and the ex-Minister of the Department concerned, together with a whip on each Bench, are the only occupants of the Front Benches for hours at a time, whilst the Back Benches are mainly occupied by a handful of members waiting to speak. When I first entered the House it was a rule of etiquette that any member, of whatever status, who had spoken in a debate should, after he had sat down, remain in the Chamber to hear the next two or three speeches. This custom has apparently fallen into desuetude, since members now frequently hurry from the Chamber immediately after they have spoken.[1]

The converse is true where the result is not a foregone conclusion, so that speeches may affect votes. But this is possible only where the Government whips are not put on and the question is left to a free vote. By common consent the debates on the Prayer Book Measure in 1928 possessed this character. Sir Archibald Sinclair was one witness among many:

I think that by common consent one of the most effective debates was the debate on the Prayer Book Measure, and I think that was due to two things: first of all, the House addressed itself to a broad issue of principle, and,

[1] H.C. 161 of 1931, Q. 3377.

secondly, we had a free vote, and every member who made a speech knew that his speech might actually influence votes and decide the issue; and the speeches were listened to with, I think, greater attention and by a more crowded House than I have ever seen, although the debate went on over two days.[1]

Such debates are as rare as a hot summer in England.

Is a debate, then, entirely or almost entirely without value? The answer is in the negative. A private member's speech usually has one of two objectives, to indicate his ability to his party leaders, or to obtain publicity outside. In the mass, the latter is the more important, and it applies to all members, on the Front Benches as well as behind. We shall see that the primary function of Opposition is to appeal to public opinion, partly to coerce the Government, but mainly to induce the electorate to give the Opposition a majority at the next election.[2] It is equally the function of the Government to appeal to public opinion, and the debate is arranged to that end. Mr Swift MacNeill, whose membership of the Irish Nationalist party did not prevent him from understanding the British Constitution, said in 1914 that debates in the House were primarily addressed to public opinion,[3] and Cobden said long ago that the best platform from which to address the country was the floor of the House.[4]

For the private member this is entirely true; for the minister it is not wholly accurate. The *Official Report* does not find its way into every household, and the average voter knows nothing of what is said in the House except what he reads in his newspaper. It often happens, however, that a platform speech in the country by a prominent politician is better reported than a speech in the House. This is not because the speech outside is better or more significant than the speech inside. In some respects it is worse, because there is no reply to the platform, and extravagances which would be ridiculed in the House meet with loud applause in the garden party or the public hall. Extravagances are, of course, better news than plain common sense, just as a death is not important unless it is a tragedy. The real reason is, however, one of

---

[1] H.C. 161 of 1931, Q. 1077.   [2] *Post*, Chapter VI.
[3] H.C. 378 of 1914, Q. 935.
[4] Sir Austen Chamberlain, *Politics from Inside*, p. 199.

pure newspaper mechanics. Whatever the news, the same space is available to report it. When the House is sitting there is not one speech but a dozen. Not all the dozen will be mentioned, yet some of them must be. Accordingly, the prominent politician, instead of getting his column or half-column, has to share it with others of almost equal prominence.

In any case, politics have to compete for space with many things far more interesting and even exciting. In spite of the great controversy over the Parliament Bill,[1] a recent writer has pointed out that for several reasons there was no great public interest in it:

It was the year of the Coronation, and the pageantry which attended that event naturally made a greater appeal to the man-in-the-street than an arid controversy regarding the powers of the House of Lords. Then, again, the months when the political struggle was being waged most strenuously witnessed a number of events calculated to arrest public attention. Such were the 'battle of Sidney Street', the Clapham Common murder, the embarrassed circumstances of the Birkbeck Bank, the formal inauguration of the Queen Victoria Memorial with the new Mall and the Admiralty Arch; and the production of *Kismet*. Save at rare intervals, these distracted the popular notice from politics, and, as was certainly not the case in 1832, it was against a background of general indifference that the battle over the latest change in the Constitution was fought.[2]

There is, too, another difficulty. Though habits have changed a little lately, the ordinary working man, especially in the provinces, reads an evening newspaper. Unless he has to travel a considerable distance in the morning, he has no time to read a morning paper. In the evening he comes home, takes off his boots, his collar and his coat, and reads the evening newspaper through from the sporting page to the advertisements. By that time, the House of Commons has hardly begun, and there is certainly no time to report any of the debates. In any case, no popular newspaper dares to make too much of a feature of politics. 'I am a journalist, and it is the view of the newspaper world that if you want to kill a newspaper you put politics into it.'[3] Or, as another member put it: 'During a generation when journalistic technique has

[1] *Ante*, p. 155
[2] Sir Charles Petrie, *Walter Long and his Times*, p. 148.
[3] H.C. 161 of 1931, Q. 3174 (Commander Kenworthy).

been steadily tending in the direction of picturesque compression, parliamentary debates have been no less steadily tending in the direction of disjointed discursiveness.'[1] The rule of modern journalism is that all the news must be put into the first paragraph; and if it cannot be so compressed it is not news and will be cut out.

Finally, there is the difficulty that the popular morning papers are produced in London and despatched to the provinces quite early in the night. This difficulty has in part been met by rearranging the order of debate. In the nineteenth century the leaders spoke late in the evening, probably at the end, so that the debate led up to the great climax, the duel between Mr Gladstone and Mr Disraeli. Now, it is almost necessary that the leaders should speak early.[2] Consequently, the fire is extinguished before the members have warmed to their task, and after the initial speeches on either side, the House proceeds to a desultory conversation which would lead almost inevitably to a count out but for the fact that a division is taken before the adjournment and enough members to make a quorum will therefore be found somewhere within the precincts.

Nor is publicity always an advantage. A stray thought given casual expression by a minister may explode all the T.N.T. in Europe. He will, therefore, take care to have everything of significance put down in writing, and will read from his manuscript. Though this is technically out of order, great latitude is given to a minister. This tendency is accentuated by the complication and difficulty of many of the questions which over-worked ministers are called upon to explain. They tend to rely more and more on their departmental briefs, and to read to a dispirited House an excellent essay by a bright young, or careful old, civil servant. A brief can be read without being understood either by the audience or by the speaker himself.[3]

The influence of debates should not, however, be underestimated. The ways of public opinion are devious. The gossip writer and the lobby correspondent send impressions when sub-editors cannot find

[1] *Ibid.* Q. 1886 (Lord Eustace Percy).
[2] Sir Austen Chamberlain, *Politics from Inside*, p. 86: H.C. 161 of 1931, Q. 2366 (Sir Austen Chamberlain).
[3] H.C. 161 of 1931, Q. 2453 (Sir Austen Chamberlain).

space for facts. Even when it is not put into print, the word goes round that Mr A. is a failure or Mr B. a success. The quality of the Opposition or, more probably, the majority's view of the quality of the Opposition, becomes a part of common knowledge. Moreover, when great issues arise on which the public feels strongly, especially some moral issue, a debate has very great influence. This is not the place to consider the value of parliamentary institutions:[1] it is, however, clear that in the last resort all debate is intended for the enlightenment and persuasion of public opinion. A Government cannot lose its authority in the House and yet maintain its prestige in the country.

[1] See *post*, Chapter xv.

CHAPTER VI

THE TECHNIQUE OF OPPOSITION

1. THE PURPOSES OF OPPOSITION

The reader will already have grasped the leading ideas of the technique of parliamentary opposition. In the previous chapter, however, the process of debate was regarded from the angle of the Government, and it is desirable now to regard the same process from the angle of the Opposition. The Government tends to regard the Opposition as the brake on a car going uphill; whereas the Opposition thinks that the car is going downhill. 'Uphill' and 'downhill' are terms relative to some notion of 'level', and there is no recognised standard by which the impartial person, if there were such a person, could determine his conclusions. The Heaven of the Right is the Hell of the Left, and it is only in totalitarian States that the populace can be induced to cry 'Excelsior' whether the Government moves forwards or backwards (or both at the same time).

Tierney said that the duty of an Opposition was to propose nothing, to oppose everything, and to turn out the Government. Lord Randolph Churchill confessed that the function of an Opposition as he understood it was to oppose and not to support the Government. Both statements sound and are old-fashioned. The real function of an Opposition is much more complicated.[1]

Strict party alignments and the conditions explained in the previous chapters make it reasonably obvious that the Opposition cannot turn out the Government. The Government can lose its party majority in one of two ways only, by a general election or by a party split. An Opposition never hesitates to put a finger into any crack in the party front against it. Usually, however, the intervention of the Opposition has no effect except to cement together sections that seemed likely to part. Sometimes the cry 'Come over here' is heard from the

---

[1] Tierney's dictum would be received with greater reverence if his opposition to Tory rule had been more effective. It may indeed be said, to extend Canning's rhyme, that Fox was to Tierney as Pitt to Addington or London to Paddington.

Opposition benches; but more often the dissident minority on the Government side is at the further extreme from the Opposition. The Conservative party is more likely to split on its right, and the Labour party on its left; intervention by the other party merely shows the rebels that their rebellion is likely to let in the outside enemy and therefore has the effect of strengthening the common front.

The tactics of the Opposition are therefore directed to the conversion not of the Government's party but of the electorate outside. A comparatively small turn-over of votes at the next election will turn out the Government and place the Opposition in power. This is not the place to examine the reasons; but analysis of election returns shows that at every election since 1884 (the elections of 1918 and 1931 excepted) the electorate has been divided into two almost equal camps, for and against the Government. The chief Opposition party has usually secured a somewhat lower vote than the Government, but the difference is never very great.

The difference in 1950 was 800,000 votes, or 2·6 per cent of the votes cast; in 1951 the Conservatives won a small majority of seats though the Labour party won 200,000 more votes; in 1955 the difference was just under 900,000, or 3·3 per cent of the votes cast. These figures relate to safe seats as well as to the minority of marginal seats which really determined the election. In 1945, at an election taking place after ten years which included the war, the difference in votes was just over 2,000,000: but there would have been a Conservative majority if the Conservatives had won 104 marginal constituencies, and those constituencies would have been won if 136,000 Labour voters had been persuaded to vote Conservative. In 1955 the Labour party would have won if it had gained thirty-five marginal constituencies, and these would have been won if 18,000 Conservative voters had been persuaded to vote Labour. Calculations of this kind are of course unrealistic, for two reasons. First, elections are not necessarily won by a turn-over from Labour to Conservative or vice versa, because in all marginal constituencies those who do not vote hold the balance, and a constituency can be won or lost by increasing or decreasing the number of non-voters. Secondly, owing to the political homogeneity of the United Kingdom, a turn-over of votes in the marginal constituencies is merely a part of a general turn-over which is equally obvious in the safe seats. For instance, the turn-over needed to give the Conservatives a majority in 1945 was 4800 votes per seat, which would require a total turn-over of approximately 400,000 votes.[1] Even so, it is plain that only a small shift in opinion is needed to turn out any Government. Indeed, there need be no shift. Approximately one-fortieth of the electorate changes every year as the older people die and the younger come on the register. At an election held after four years there are over three million new electors. Normally they seem to distribute themselves between the parties,[2] but their votes have to be won. It appears, in fact, that each of the parties has a solid core of convinced supporters, with a fringe of potential supporters who may or may not vote for it, and some of whom may even be persuaded by events (as in 1931) to vote against it. There is, too, a solid bloc of probable non-voters, who may be induced by events to vote for or against the party. Finally, there are the new electors who have to be persuaded. It is convenient to describe the doubtful electors, those who may or may not vote for either party, according to the course of events and the movement of opinion, as the 'floating vote'.[3]

[1] It may be that Mr David Butler's 'swing', which is the increase or decrease in the departure from the average of the Conservative or Labour vote, expressed as a percentage of the total Conservative and Labour vote, is a better approximation: cf. *The British General Election of 1951*, p. 242. Neither method is accurate because the various sections of the electorate do not 'turn over' or 'swing' uniformly. There is, however, a general tendency, due to political homogeneity, which justifies the assumption that a large gain in Cheltenham or Salford will be followed by large gains the same way in London or Cornwall or Caithness and Sutherland.

[2] With, apparently, some preference for the Labour party; but this preference may not have existed in 1955.

[3] The use of this term in the first edition (p. 155) and in *The British Constitution* gave rise to some misunderstanding. It was not assumed that the defeat of a Government was occasioned by a transfer of a 'floating vote' to the Opposition, because the operation was obviously more complicated. The electorate consists of:

(1) the solid Conservative vote;
(2) the solid Labour vote;
(3) the certain non-voters (who may include Liberal electors who would not vote except for a Liberal candidate);
(4) the doubtful Conservative vote;
(5) the doubtful Labour vote; and
(6) the doubtful non-voters (i.e. those who may vote Conservative or Labour or for some other candidate or not at all).

The floating 'vote' consists of groups (4) to (6). It must be appreciated, however,

Estimates, or perhaps guesses, of the size of the floating vote vary from ten per cent to twenty per cent of the electorate, though obviously the size depends on the length of the period since the last election. The longer the period, the larger the number of new electors and, what is more, the greater the chances of events changing the sluggish minds of the electors. It is obvious that the floating vote was much greater in 1945 than in 1935 or 1951. It is nevertheless clear that parliamentary activity, envisaged as a process of electioneering, is a process of persuading a minority. The Government must do nothing to alienate its solid bloc of supporters: it cannot afford to offend its right in order to placate its left, or to offend its left in order to placate its right. It must follow a middle path which gives reasonable satisfaction to everybody. It must, in addition, try to maintain the allegiance of that part of the floating vote which gave it a majority, or which might give it a majority in the future. It is on the defensive because Governments always tend to lose votes. The 'swing of the pendulum'[1] is a consequence of the criticisms which have built up against it during its period of office, because no Government can hope to solve all its problems to the satisfaction of all its supporters.[2] Highly exceptional circumstances apart, no party expects to hold office for more than ten years, or has done so since the Reform Act.[3] The Opposition, while maintaining the support of its solid core of voters, has to make itself attractive to the floating vote, by keeping up a fire of sound and statesmanlike criticism and, if need be, by taking as its own policy, with embellishments and improvements, those items of Government policy which seem most popular. In spite of their claims to represent different traditions—

that the groups are not static. Not only are the new electors added and dead electors subtracted between elections, but also there are other changes due to changing opinion. Strictly speaking, the 'floating vote' should be assessed immediately after a general election, and then again before the next election campaign opens.

[1] See Jennings, *The British Constitution* (3rd ed.), p. 30; *The Times Guide to the House of Commons* (1955), p. 254.

[2] It may, however, be able to dissolve Parliament at a particularly favourable moment, as in 1955. The swing away from Labour, shown in 1951, had not been completed because the election of 1951 was held so soon after the election of 1950. The young voters, in particular, seemed to tend towards Conservatism in accordance with a general ideological movement. Hence the unusual spectacle of a Government gaining seats.

[3] The Conservative party was in power from 1931 to 1945, but there had been no general election after 1935.

which are not unjustified when they refer only to traditions—there is inevitably a very high common factor in the policies of the two parties.

The purpose of parliamentary opposition is, therefore, to appeal to the floating vote. The Opposition does not expect to be able to follow Tierney's advice and 'turn out the Government' by its vote. It hopes to persuade the floating vote to do so at the next election. So long as the Government majority holds, the Government cannot be defeated except on a snap vote. It is the function of the Government so to mould its policy and manage its forces that it never runs the risk of defeat. It can always reverse a decision by sending out an urgent whip and marshalling its majority; but it is recognised that a defeat is damaging to its prestige[1]—is damaging, that is, in the eyes of the floating vote—and it is the purpose of the Opposition to show that it could manage the affairs of the nation much more competently.

There are other methods by which the same conclusion can be suggested. There is less loss of prestige in withdrawing an unpopular proposal than in being beaten on it. Indeed, the Government press may assert that it is a merit in the Government if it 'bows to the popular will' even if the popular will for this purpose means the Stock Exchange or the Federation of British Industries[2] or the Trades Union Congress. Nevertheless, the discerning elector (and he is many-headed) realises that a Government that introduces a proposal and then withdraws it is not very efficient, and if it is done often enough he may gradually be persuaded to transfer his vote. Even if the Government persists, and even if, as is almost certain, its proposals are carried, the effect of the debate may be to bring home to some sections of the electorate that undesirable or dangerous proposals are being made.

Nor is the process carried on only by debate. The mere ascertainment of facts is an extremely useful function. When the House of Commons is in recess, the country is dependent upon such information as the Government chooses to disclose to the press or upon such information as is available elsewhere. The decision of the Government not to renew the permits of three German journalists in the summer of 1937 is an

---

[1] H.C. 161 of 1931, Q. 1156 (Sir Archibald Sinclair).
[2] Cf. the withdrawal of the Coal Mines Bill, 1936, *ante*, p. 144; and of the original National Defence Contribution in 1937, *ante*, p. 145.

example in point. It was explained that they had engaged in activities other than journalism, but no further information was forthcoming. If the House had been sitting, the Home Secretary would have been pressed for further information day after day. In the end he would certainly have said something, if only to persuade the Opposition to let the matter drop and to justify his action to his own supporters.

Though in the last resort the Government can always carry its policy if it insists, the existence of the Opposition provides a most valuable outlet for minority opinions. This was most clearly demonstrated in the summers of 1936 and 1937. Memory being short, it may be forgotten what profound distress there was among radical opinion at the outbreak of the Spanish Civil War in 1936 and the intervention of other powers. Criticism of the British Government from this point of view was immediate. It had, however, no effective means of expression, and there was general relief when the House of Commons met again. This was not because it was thought that the Government would be defeated, but because it was thought that certain things needed to be said publicly and forcibly, because the House was the only place where they could be said effectively, and because it was believed—rightly as it happened—that the pressure of public opinion brought to bear in Parliament would compel the Government to modify somewhat the emphasis of its policy if not the policy itself. This anxiety for parliamentary discussion in the summer of 1936 was followed in 1937 by an anxiety lest the Government should seize the opportunity of the recess to adopt a different policy. It was suspected that the Government intended to accord recognition of belligerency to the Spanish insurgents, and it was believed that this step could be prevented if Parliament were sitting.

This example, like others already cited,[1] shows that the function of Opposition is not merely to discredit the Government in the eyes of the floating vote, but also to induce it to modify its policy. The two purposes cannot be separated. The Government is as aware as the Opposition that its authority rests only on the electorate, and that if it wishes to keep its majority it must maintain its electoral support. The effect of Opposition criticism is therefore to maintain a close relation between Government policy and public opinion. The Opposition's

[1] Chapter v.

action is one of enlightened self-interest. In seeking support for itself it compels the Government to maintain its own support. In appealing to public opinion it compels the Government to rest its policy on public opinion. Far from being 'unpatriotic' in criticising even foreign policy, it is intensely 'patriotic' because it insists that public opinion and not a group of senior civil servants shall determine national policy.

Public opinion, however, is not something clearly formed and precisely defined. It has to be led as well as followed. In a totalitarian state it can be led quite easily because the Government has the means for inducing it to follow the Government's direction. There are always at least two views as to what is desirable. In a totalitarian state one is chosen by the Government. In a democratic state all views can be expressed and put before the people, who choose rationally or instinctively that which seems to it to be most desirable. The British electoral system, the difficulties of party organisation, and the fact that electors prefer to choose a party that might form a Government rather than one that could not, are factors which in practice restrict the choice to one of two. The most remarkable fact is that in the United Kingdom the people have been divided into two almost equal parts for at least seventy years.

Even so, the actual divergence is not very great. It was possible for the extreme left of the Gladstonian Liberal party to join with the Conservative party to defeat Mr Gladstone, for an Opposition whose virulence knows no parallel in this country to make common cause under Mr Asquith, whom they had shouted down four years before, against a common enemy, for a Labour Prime Minister to invite his opponents into his Cabinet and to urge the electors to vote against the Labour party, and for the Conservative and Labour parties to work in close harmony from 1940 to 1945. Accordingly, there is always substantial agreement on many questions, especially on foreign affairs and defence. It is sometimes alleged that in foreign affairs there is a 'principle of continuity'. It can hardly be suggested, however, that the Liberal Government of 1880 accepted Lord Beaconsfield's foreign policy, or that Lord Salisbury continued the policy of Mr Gladstone's Government. Lord Rosebery followed Lord Salisbury in 1892 and Sir Edward Grey followed Lord Lansdowne in 1905; but in 1924 Mr Austen

Chamberlain rejected the Geneva Protocol and substituted Locarno,[1] and it was alleged that Sir John Simon's attitude to disarmament was different from that adopted by Mr Arthur Henderson. Nevertheless, when once a situation has been created there is often only one reasonable policy to be followed, and it is then considered undesirable that the Opposition should indulge in too many recriminations. This explains the split between the 'Imperialists' and the 'Pro-Boers' in the Liberal party in 1900. Both were agreed that the actions of Mr Joseph Chamberlain had provoked the Boer War, but they were disagreed as to whether the situation required support in the prosecution of the war or constant criticism of the Government in order to compel what was described in a later war as 'peace without victory'. Similarly, there was a split in the Labour party between 1914 and 1918 over the attitude to the war, in 1937 and 1938 over rearmament, and in 1950 over attitudes to the Soviet Union. There may be differences of opinion as to whether an Opposition must support the Government in carrying out the inevitable consequences of what it considers to be the Government's ineptitude. On the other hand, it is not 'unpatriotic' but intensely 'patriotic' to try to prevent the Government from adopting a policy which the Opposition regards as dangerous. Patriotism in this sense requires not blind support of any policy that may be adopted, but guidance of that policy into directions which are regarded as leading towards justice.

The Opposition is compelled by the logic of the parliamentary system to adopt a responsible attitude. It is not only Her Majesty's Opposition but also Her Majesty's alternative Government. It presents itself to the electorate in that capacity; it asks for a mandate to govern. It must, therefore, show its capacity to govern in the parliamentary arena. Promises sown broadcast produce a harvest that has to be reaped. Wild obstruction frightens the timid into calmer waters. All Oppositions are, to their opponents, factious and irresponsible; but the word goes round whether they are good or bad.

The Opposition's appeal is inevitably to the electorate. In the main its eyes are directed on the next election. But so are the eyes of the Government, and the effect is to produce an immediate reaction to any

---

[1] The late Sir Austen Chamberlain repeated to me in 1935 this alleged 'principle of continuity', though I forbore to make the obvious comment.

stimulus supplied by public opinion. Accordingly, the Opposition can appeal at once from the House to the country, knowing that the views of the House and the Government can be modified by constituents individually or in the mass. Such a reaction by the people to the course of parliamentary proceedings implies that the constituents are aware of the discussions in Parliament. There are few sources of information other than the newspapers, which are necessarily partisan. The partiality tends, too, to lead to one side. During the Munich period, for instance, only two morning papers and one evening paper of all those published in London could be said to be at all favourable to the Opposition. Such a situation is inevitable so long as newspapers depend upon advertisements for their revenue and, to a large degree, upon circulation among readers in the higher income-groups. The rise of the Labour party shows that it is possible to achieve a large measure of support even with a completely hostile press. Moreover, the popular newspaper reports only so much of parliamentary proceedings as is 'news'. Not much of a debate reaches the high standards of Fleet Street, but it does appear from the news columns if not from the leading articles that there are two sides to every question. Broadcasts, too, help to redress the balance; for the British Broadcasting Corporation gives a considerable part of the news time to parliamentary news and tries to state it impartially. It may be suspected that a higher proportion of the electorate takes its parliamentary information from the B.B.C. than from the newspapers.

Parliamentary debate is, however, only one of the instruments of the Opposition. The Opposition is a party outside the House of Commons as well as inside. It has a complete series of central and local organisations all engaged in propaganda. The Labour party, in addition, makes up for the deficiency of its newspaper support by maintaining close contacts with the trade unions, which again have several complete series of national and local organisations. The Conservative party has no such advantage, though it is naturally easier for the Conservative point of view to be put before such non-political bodies as Chambers of Commerce, Rotary Clubs and Women's Institutes, and before bodies like Ratepayers' Associations which are associated with the Conservative party.

The result is a constant flow of propaganda, often both in favour of and against the Government, but sometimes setting in one direction. There is a constant educative process which at the same time gives guidance to Government and Opposition. Nor must it be forgotten that the most effective propaganda is that which has no propaganda aim—the casual remark, the incidental conversation, the right word at the right moment. If, therefore, the Government has a bad case, it soon knows it; if it has a good case, the Opposition soon knows it. The details of decisions, the niceties of policy, do not proceed very far. The man who insists on distinguishing the French political parties when the question under discussion is 'What will win the 2.30?' is commonly voted a bore. Even so, the notion that the Government is weak and the Opposition excellent, or vice versa, soon spreads. The ways of public opinion are devious and the methods of its influence obscure. Its importance can hardly be overrated; and it is to public opinion that parliamentary opposition is directed.

There is, however, one feature of opposition which has little connection with the electoral process. The importance of Parliament as an instrument for the redress of individual grievances has already been mentioned. It is the function of every member to raise such questions as are brought to his notice, especially by his constituents—and he asks no questions as to his informant's political affiliation. Nevertheless, the Opposition naturally takes a special interest in them because they may be the consequence of defective policy or bad administration—defects which it is the duty of the Opposition to expose. On such issues, however, the debate rarely runs on party lines. The minister concerned usually welcomes the fullest possible investigation.

2. THE METHODS OF OPPOSITION

Something has already been said about the organisation of the Opposition.[1] It does not differ radically from the parliamentary organisation of the Government. Its primary purpose, however, is not to justify but to criticise. There is, therefore, much greater scope for the back-bencher who, provided that he does not emulate the 'Fourth party' by seeking to give 'ginger' to his own front bench, is given

[1] *Ante*, pp. 79–82.

greater freedom of debate and greater initiative. Each member of the Opposition can, for instance, think out his own questions and line of cross-examination by supplementaries. If out of any question there appears to arise a 'definite matter of urgent public importance', he can move the adjournment without consultation with his leaders and, provided that the leaders have not already made some arrangement with the Government—as for instance to debate the matter on a Supply day —he can be certain of the support that the Standing Order requires.

For the official policy of the Opposition (subject to party decisions in the case of the Labour party) the 'Shadow Cabinet' or its equivalent, or the leader of the Opposition on its behalf, accepts responsibility. There is the same kind of complaint if the leader takes decisions without the consent of the Shadow Cabinet as there is if the Prime Minister ignores his Cabinet. Thus, Mr Walter Long wrote a long memorandum of protest to Mr Balfour in 1910, complaining that Mr Balfour was leaving too much to the Opposition whips, and suggesting weekly meetings of the Shadow Cabinet and the allocation of specific members to 'watch specific ministers'.[1] For the Budget of 1909 the Conservatives organised forty or fifty members into four committees to deal each with a section of Mr Lloyd George's proposals.[2]

As the Labour party grew up in opposition it developed a more formal technique.[3] It is organised into a party which holds weekly meetings, and has its own secretary, who is not a member of Parliament but has a room in the House of Commons. The leader of the Opposition is elected for each session by the parliamentary party, and he is chairman of the party and a member of its executive committee (he is also *ex officio* a member of the National Executive Committee of the Labour party— i.e. the national party organisation outside the House). A deputy chairman, the chief whip, and the executive committee (twelve in number—to which must be added the chairman and deputy chairman, the chief whip and three peers) are similarly elected by the party at the beginning of every session, or preferably at the end of a session, so as to take office during the next session. The party itself holds weekly

[1] Sir Charles Petrie, *Walter Long and his Times*, pp. 149–52.
[2] Sir Austen Chamberlain, *Politics from Inside*, p. 176.
[3] The process was gradual, but it is convenient to describe the practice followed since 1931. For the Conservative practice, see pp. 180–2.

meetings during the session, and the executive committee reports to the party meeting. It is provided by the party's Standing Orders[1] that 'for the purpose of securing concerted action in the House, members should consult the officers of the parliamentary party before tabling any motion, amendment or prayer, or other proposal which may involve party policies or decisions'—which means that differences of opinion in the party should be discussed at party meetings and not on the floor of the House. Resolutions of the party meetings are recorded in the minutes and are binding on the executive committee and on members. Subject to such resolutions the executive committee is given authority to arrange for the execution of the functions of opposition. But all matters of principle are settled by the party meeting itself, and the weight of the executive committee depends on the ability of its members and the confidence which Labour members generally feel in the committee which they have elected. Moreover, the majority rule is recognised, as it is throughout the Labour movement, as being essential to democratic action. Accordingly, members are expected to follow the party decisions even if they do not agree with them. Standing Orders permit a member to abstain from voting if he has conscientious scruples; but otherwise he is expected to vote with the party.

In this way the conduct of opposition is placed by the Labour party on a democratic basis and is yet highly organised. As is usual in a democratic system, there are inevitable defects. The process of decision is slower than that adopted in the nineteenth century and, in the present century, by the Conservative party. The leader of the Opposition has less responsibility and his position is less assured. He cannot take important decisions without consultation, and the consultation required is not merely that of the Labour equivalent of the 'Shadow Cabinet', but of the parliamentary party as a whole. The individual member, too, is given less scope than the member of the Conservative party in opposition. Free-lances like Lord Randolph Churchill, Mr F. E. Smith, Lord Hugh Cecil and Captain Crookshank are not encouraged. Their work is, in the main, determined for them by the party. They have, it has been said, more democracy and less liberty.

[1] R. T. McKenzie, *British Political Parties*, p. 599.

Other causes make a Labour Opposition less intransigent than a Conservative Opposition. By nature most Labour members are not of the spectacular fighting breed. Dour trade unionists skilled in negotiation have immense capacity for obstinacy, but they are not handy with the rapier. The tub-thumping idealist is usually neither a skilled obstructionist nor a smart tactician—Mr Maxton was the obvious exception and he, be it noticed, broke with the Labour party because he would not accept the dictation of the majority. Moreover, the Labour party differs from the Conservative party in opposition, because it usually accepts Government proposals, especially on social legislation, as instalments of its own policy. It usually does not want to obstruct because it wants the legislation to be passed; it usually objects to some of the proposals, but it rarely objects to them all; and its main cause of complaint is that they do not go far enough. Yet another reason is purely personal. Obstruction implies long sittings and most Labour members are comparatively poor men who have to live in the cheaper and therefore more remote suburbs, and they cannot afford taxi fares. If a debate is kept up beyond midnight, they miss the last underground trains and omnibuses. One result, incidentally, is that long sittings are usually all-night sittings which do not break up before breakfast time. Such sittings are much more of a physical strain than ordinary long sittings, and there is every incentive for making them infrequent.

Again, a student of the Labour movement must be impressed by the importance of the majority decision. The Government is, after all, a majority representing a majority of the people. Psychologically, therefore, Labour members cannot be too intransigent. It is their business to wring concessions if they can. If they cannot, obstruction or persistent opposition is, in their minds, not capable of justification. Finally, the electoral aspect has to be considered. Conservative propaganda necessarily capitalises the fears that the prospect of change induces in timid men—and especially timid women. All those who are able to apply the popular epithet 'comfortable' to themselves tend to fear that changes may be for the worse. The standard of living being higher in England than in most European countries, even working men and women realise that they have something to lose. 'Workers of the world, unite; you have nothing to lose but your chains' is not a slogan which can have a very wide popular appeal in Great Britain. There are, as the Conservative Central Office has discovered, too many who might lose the deposits paid on building society mortgages, or savings bank deposits, or even little patches of garden. Consequently, much of the Conservative propaganda for a century has consisted of a series of bogies associated with the names (most of which are now quite respectable, though originally they were terms of abuse) of 'democracy', 'socialism', 'communism', and 'bolshevism'. It is easier to associate revolutionary changes with a 'forward' policy than one in which mild reforms only appear to be contemplated. A Conservative Opposition is concerned primarily with opposition: a Labour Opposition advocates more extensive reforms. Accordingly, history has shown that Conservative Oppositions for nearly a century—that is, since Disraeli pocketed the crown that fell from the head of Sir Robert Peel—have been the most intransigent and effective and, in popular phrase, the 'dirtiest' Oppositions that the British parliamentary system has seen. Even when leaders like Lord Derby, Lord Salisbury, Mr Balfour and Mr Baldwin have toned down the official Opposition, there have been gallant highwaymen prepared to frolic; and with such a leader as Mr Bonar Law (assisted by very able lieutenants) opposition has degenerated from a gentlemanly swearing match to a public-house brawl. The Labour party, on the other hand, has to prove to the timid floating vote that it is essentially respectable. It has, so to speak, to go regularly to chapel in its Sunday suit and to frown on such of its members as would like to go hiking. Since it may be accused of revolutionary tendencies, it must show itself more strictly constitutional than any.

In spite of the more elastic methods of their party, the Conservative Oppositions of 1924 and 1929–31 found it necessary to follow some way along the path of Labour development. Mr Baldwin had been chosen Prime Minister by the King in 1923 and had in consequence become leader of the Conservative party. In accordance with the practice of that party, he remained leader until his resignation in 1937, and was therefore leader of the Opposition while the Labour Governments were in office, and no new election was necessary. The pre-war practices were followed so far that the whips and the Policy Committee, which was in reality the 'Shadow Cabinet', were appointed by him. It was considered necessary, however, for the whips to organise committees for the study of Government policy and the organisation of opposition. Private committees of Conservative members had developed on their own initiative during 1922, and some of these were converted into semi-official Opposition committees. Others were created, so that each department of government had facing it a committee of Opposition members. The committee appointed its own chairman and honorary secretary. Usually, however, the chairman was a leading member of the party who had been the appropriate departmental head in the previous Conservative Government. He was, therefore, usually a member of the Policy Committee. No attempt was made to draft amendments to Bills, nor was there any suggestion that any member could not put down what motions and amendments he pleased. No member was prevented from taking a strong line in opposition, provided that he voted with the party where the Policy Committee adopted a definite line of action. The general practice of Conservative opposition was therefore not fundamentally changed, and the only results of the committee system were to occupy members and to provide for better and more organised examination of the Government's proposals.

The Conservative party was again in opposition between 1945 and 1951. Mr Winston Churchill, as the former Prime Minister, was *ex officio* leader, and he chose the Shadow Cabinet, assigning to its members fields of activity corresponding with those of ministers. Various 'subject' committees were formed, usually with former ministers as chairmen, and meetings of these chairmen might be held in a 'Business Committee' which was rather larger than the Shadow Cabinet. Mr Churchill did not, however, devote so much time to parliamentary duties as had his Labour predecessors; nor was there any 'ginger group' of back-benchers. The tradition of co-operative opposition developed by Mr Baldwin and the Labour party was therefore followed by the Conservatives. Since the supporters of the Labour Government, in a majority for the first time, tended to be noisy and provocative, there was some criticism of the 'spinelessness' of the Opposition; but the tactics may no doubt be defended by referring to the fact that the Labour party lost its majority in 1951, after only six years of office.

The task of an Opposition is not merely to see that such of the Government's proposals as are objectionable are opposed by voice and vote, to secure concessions on Government Bills, to compel the Government by all the methods of propaganda to modify its general policy, and finally to create the necessary public opinion against the Government ready for the next election; it must take part also in the actual process of parliamentary government. The Opposition parties choose the votes to be put down on Supply days. By arrangement with the Government whips, the main subjects to be discussed on the Addresses to the Crown, the long adjournments, and the Consolidated Fund Bills, are determined by the Opposition whips acting on behalf of the 'Shadow Cabinet' or party meeting. In addition, the Labour party takes an active part in the work which technically falls to private members. The subjects to be debated when the House first goes into Committee of Supply on the navy, army, air force and civil estimates are normally determined by the party meeting in case a Labour member is successful in the appropriate ballot. Lists of motions are drawn up and lists of desirable Bills compiled in order of precedence, so that the most may be made of private members' motions and Bills. Consequently, when Labour members are successful in the ballots for private members' time, they are expected to take their motions or Bills from the office of the secretary to the parliamentary Labour party. There have been cases where members have insisted on their right to choose. Mr Snowden in 1923 insisted on a general debate on socialism.[1] In the main, however, private members' time is, so far as the Labour party is concerned, Labour party time. Here, as in many other matters, the Labour party has departed from the traditions of its predecessors.

[1] Snowden, *Autobiography*, II, p. 581.

CHAPTER VII

WHO MAKES THE LAWS?

I. VOX POPULI

This chapter is appropriately headed by a question, for it is easier to ask than to answer. The lawyer evades difficulties by refusing to go behind the constitutional authority and by answering 'Parliament', or, if he be a pedant, 'the Queen in Parliament'. For one who seeks the substance rather than the form, that will not do. Parliament has but small concern with the matter. The ardent reformer who demands that 'the Government' put a stop to it or do something about it is nearer the truth; but he goes only one stage further back, and he, too, uses a mystic symbol. Perhaps the lady in the back street, who insists that *They* ought to do something about it, has the greatest constitutional perspicacity. They ought, and they do.

Democracy, we are told, is government of the people, by the people, and for the people. Yet it was Lincoln himself who pointed out that there are 'fancy people' as well as 'plain people'. He went on to assert that there are more 'plain people' than 'fancy people'; but a little reflection serves to raise doubts whether indeed there are any 'plain people'. The lady in the back street is probably a member of a co-operative society, a subscriber to a burial club, a contributor to a 'provident society', the wife of a trade unionist, a pedestrian and the wife of a ratepayer. The man on the Clapham omnibus, the 'ordinary reasonable man' so beloved of the private lawyers, is a fiction of their imagination. Certainly there are men on Clapham omnibuses, ordinary reasonable men; but the type is obtained by emphasising one aspect alone of their social status. The man on the Clapham omnibus may be anything from a company promoter to an errand boy, an archbishop to a member of the Ethical Union, a clubman to a darts player, a professor to a mechanic.

Yet the lawyer's method has reason in it. For certain kinds of law men are considered as ordinary reasonable men. The law of torts makes no distinction among men of full age and understanding. The same people may be considered by the Landlord and Tenant Act as landlords or tenants, by the Moneylenders Acts as lenders and borrowers, by the Pawnbrokers Acts as pledgers and pledgees, by the Road Traffic Acts as motorists, cyclists and pedestrians; and so for a thousand branches of the law. The plain people of one category are the fancy people of many more categories. The man on the Clapham omnibus may be not only an ordinary reasonable man, but also an archbishop, a landlord, a tenant, a shareholder, a clubman, and a member of more learned and philanthropic societies than his secretary can keep track of. The law does not consider all his capacities, but it takes account of many of them. Fancy people are built, so to speak, on a foundation of plain people, each of whom complicates his social relationships by adding a superstructure of fancy characteristics. The individual has as many legal 'personalities' as the Sunday edition of the *New York Times* has sections.

Government for the people, then, means government for the people in a host of different capacities. The legislative function is by definition exercised in the national interest; but the national interest is nothing more than the sum total of the interests of individuals. The phrase no doubt needs elaboration—no nation can neglect the possible requirements of future generations, and a system of government that claims to be founded on justice cannot neglect the claims of humanity in general—but it is adequate enough for present purposes. The sum total of the interest of individuals means, however, not the interests of individuals in isolation but the interests of individuals in groups. It involves not merely the interests of ordinary reasonable men but also the interests of landlords and tenants, motorists, cyclists and pedestrians, lenders and borrowers, churchmen and atheists, publicans and temperance reformers, porters, printers and professors.

These group interests, it should be emphasised, are not necessarily selfish. Some of the members of a church, for instance, may have selfish motives in advocating changes in the legal situation of their church. The archbishop on the omnibus would find it difficult to separate his motives when he advocates the protection of the property of the Church of England, just as professors find difficulty in distinguishing between the advancement of learning and the advancement of professors; nevertheless, few of the societies to which the archbishop belongs are concerned with the personal interests of their members. The primary interest of most individuals is their own happiness, and material well-being plays a large part in the achievement of that state; nevertheless, most of them have interests whose development involves no material advantage to themselves.

The advancement of group interests is most easily obtained through organisation. It has been said that wherever two or more Englishmen are gathered together there exists a club. British society as a whole is a mass of clubs and associations. The State itself operates through collective enterprises—Government departments, local authorities, judicial tribunals, bodies like the National Coal Board, the British Transport Commission, the British Electricity Authority, the Gas Council, and the British Broadcasting Corporation. Within and among these bodies others may be created which the State recognises but does not endow with legal functions—the civil service associations, the local authorities' associations, the associations of local government officers, and the Magistrates' Association. Other collective enterprises are established by private initiative but are recognised by the State; British social and economic life is dominated by collective enterprises which have sought 'incorporation'. Some of them are given express governmental powers. The device of the public utility corporation was much used during the century which preceded the war of 1939–45, and a host of associations representing their views was developed. Since 1945, however, the tendency has been to vest their functions in national boards. Some professional organisations, too, are either created by statute or have had statutory functions imposed upon them for the protection of their professional interests. Among them are the General Medical Council, the Dental Board, the Law Society, the Central Midwives Board, the General Nursing Council and the Architects Registration Council.

The industrial and commercial enterprise of the nation is becoming vested more and more in incorporated companies. In any particular trade or industry they are usually in competition, though the Reports of the Royal Commission on Monopolies show that very often the existence of 'rings' prevents free competition even for public tenders, and the very general use of price-fixing agreements limits the operation of 'consumers' choice'. Even where free competition exists, however, the particular trade or industry is united in desiring advantages for the trade or industry as a whole and in seeking protection against any action (including legislation) that may restrict its operation or limit its profits. Accordingly, there is hardly a trade or industry that is not organised for mutual protection and advantage. There are hundreds of national associations and federations of this kind. If we take the agricultural interest and its associated trades by way of example we find that there are twenty or thirty. Thus, the National Farmers' Union during a few years conducted negotiations or arranged joint action with the following bodies:

The Central Landowners' Association, the National Farmers' Union of Scotland, the Ulster Farmers' Union, the National Association of Corn Merchants, the Brewers' Society, the Fertilisers Manufacturers' Association, the Agricultural Engineers' Association, the Animal Medicine Makers' Association, the Co-operative Managers' Association, the Dutch Bulb Exporters' Association, the National Federation of Fruit and Potato Trades Ltd., the National Association of Cider Makers, the Horticultural Trades Association, the National Poultry Council, the National Federation of Fishmongers, the National Traction Engine Owners' and Users' Association, the National Association of British and Irish Millers, the National Association of Corn and Agricultural Merchants, the Home Grown Timber Merchants' Federation, the Co-operative Wholesale Society, the Federation of Grocers' Associations, the Amalgamated Master Dairymen Ltd., the National Federation of Young Farmers' Clubs, the National Pig Breeders' Association, the National Cattle Food Trades Association, the Merchants' Association of the United Kingdom, the British Glasshouse Produce Marketing Association, the National Federation of Meat Traders' Associations, the Livestock Traders' Association, and the National Cheese Council.

Lists of this kind might be multiplied twentyfold. For instance, the following were among the bodies whose representatives submitted evidence to the Royal Commission on Transport, 1928–31:

The Accident Offices Association, the Association of British Chambers of Commerce, the Canal Association, the Commercial Motor Users' Association, the Dock and Harbour Authorities' Association, the Electric Vehicle Committee of Great Britain, the Federation of British Industries, the Furniture Warehousemen and Removers' Association, the London Chamber of Commerce, the London and Provincial Omnibus Owners' Association, the Long-Distance Road Haulage Committee of Inquiry, the Municipal Tramways and Transport Association, the National Council for Inland Waterways, the National Farmers' Union, the National Federation of Iron and Steel Manufacturers, the National Road Transport Employers' Federation, the National Traction Engine Owners' and Users' Association, the Railway Companies' Association, the Scottish Chamber of Agriculture, the Shipowners' Parliamentary Committee, the Society of Motor Car Manufacturers and Traders, Ltd., and the Tramways and Light Railways Association.

Those bodies which represent the major trades and industries of the country are justly entitled to consider that their representations—whether they are representations to the Government, to Royal Commissions and Departmental Committees, or to the public generally—should be given emphasis. Among such bodies are the Chamber of Shipping, the National Farmers' Union, the National Federation of Iron and Steel Manufacturers, and the Society of Motor Manufacturers and Traders. Moreover, wherever there are likely to be special problems affecting a section of the country's economic life either permanently or temporarily, a joint committee may be formed.

Charitable and philanthropic bodies are at least as numerous, though they are not so well organised for joint action. There is, for instance, a group of societies concerned with the protection of animals. The Charity Organisation Society lists 150 charity organisations and similar societies in Great Britain. The Consultative Committee on the Welfare of the Deaf-Blind contains representatives of the National Institute for the Blind, the National Institute for the Deaf, and the Royal Association in Aid of the Deaf and Dumb, as well as of local associations for the Blind. There are bodies like the Central Association for Mental Welfare, the National Council for Mental Hygiene, the National Association for Promoting the Welfare of the Feeble-minded, the National Society for Epileptics, the National Association for the Prevention of Tuberculosis, and many more. The National Council for Social Service has a council representing fifty-two associations concerned with various aspects of social service.

The professional associations cover all the hundreds of professions, and sometimes fall into the category of educational bodies concerned with research in or the development of the particular techniques of the profession, though more often they are at least as much concerned with maintaining the social and economic status of their members. These last are hardly distinguishable from trade unions, and often are organised as such, though they are not affiliated to the Trades Union Congress unless they accept the political views of that body. Against the employees' federations must be set the employers' federations, though their influence is not so great as the associations for trade and industry.

With trade unions, however, we enter a wider field, since they represent some eight million members. A characteristic so general approaches that of the 'plain man'. Indeed, if the trade unions represented all 'workers by hand and by brain' they would represent nearly everybody. The representation of the other interests of ordinary people is far more difficult. There is an Income-Tax Payers' Society, but it represents only a small proportion of income-tax payers. The Pedestrians' Association represents only what may be called the persistent pedestrians. The Ratepayers' Associations, nearly all federated in the National Union of Ratepayers' and Property Owners' Associations, represent a section of ratepayers only, and in fact the federation is an ancillary of the Conservative party. On the other hand, the Automobile Association and the Royal Automobile Club between them contain a large proportion of motorists, and are correspondingly influential.

Organisation in such a wide field is inevitably difficult. Where an interest is so common that it is that of a large section of the nation it merges into that of the nation as a whole. The organisation of eight million workers into trade unions with a common organ in the General Council of the Trades Union Congress is really an achievement. Where employees have not been so organised, steps have been taken, by the formation of trade boards under statutory authority, to provide means for the settlement of conditions of employment, though the trade boards do not take an active part in the wider propagation of group interests. The trade unions are, however, an exceptional case. Plain people as owners or tenants of landed property are not organised, since the bodies federated into the National Union of Ratepayers' and Property Owners' Associations are not really representative; and representative groups of tenants are to be found only in small and compact areas, such as municipal housing estates. Still less is it possible to organise plain people as consumers; and because some representation of consumers' interests is frequently necessary—as when monopolies are conferred upon nationalised industries or organisations of producers like marketing boards—Consumers' Councils have been formed under statutory authority.

The achievement of the aims of a group interest does not necessarily involve taking part in the controversies of party politics. Some associations have considered that their policies are so much a matter of 'politics' that they have become associated with the parties. The trade unions were foremost in the foundation of the Labour party and still form its main strength. The National Farmers' Union gives discriminating support to the Conservative party, and the National Union of Ratepayers' and Property Owners' Associations is a subsidiary of that party. Most of the employers' associations and the commercial and industrial groups are necessarily more sympathetic to that party than to the Labour party. They are more influential in the former, and their propaganda, even when it strictly has no political aims, is generally antagonistic to the latter. Most of them, however, do not openly give support to the Conservative party, and many of them take great care not to appear to be politically biased. Their function, as they see it, is to advance the interests of their members. Usually, this involves stimulating a Conservative Government and fighting against a Labour Government; but quite often they are compelled to oppose specific proposals of the former and to support specific proposals of the latter. Nor are they always on one side. When the manufacturers want more tariffs the commercial interests may want less. Consequently, the industrial and commercial interests are rarely unanimous in favour of the proposals of a Conservative Government or against the proposals of a Labour Government. The charitable and philanthropic associations are more often unanimous or, even more often, uninterested in each other's proposals. Sometimes a group of them finds convenient the establishment of a joint committee for specific purposes. The Education Act, 1936, for instance, was due largely to the agitation of a substantial group of educational interests, acting through a joint committee, which compelled both parties to adopt the proposal for raising the school-leaving age. Moreover, organisations may be established for the temporary purpose of achieving specific reforms, such as that established in 1956 for the abolition of capital punishment.

With the technique for securing the aims of group interests we shall presently be concerned. For the moment it is enough to emphasise that the national interest is an amalgam of hundreds of group interests. The people who vote at elections, who therefore determine the composition of the House of Commons and the political character of the Government, and for whose benefit the government of the country is carried on, are also the groups of which an account has been given above. It is true that some of the most common interests, as those of tax-payers, ratepayers, consumers, tenants, and the like, can be effectively represented only by members of Parliament. They are interests so wide that any Government or political party must pay even more attention to them than to the organised group interests. Nevertheless, it must always be remembered that, though the voice of the people is made audible in party meetings and at general elections, it is heard also through a large number of organised bodies. Often the voices clamour for different things. The national interest is a compromise which, in the view of the Government, will maintain its majority at the next general election, or which, in the view of the Opposition, will give it a majority at the next general election.

2. THE INSPIRATION OF MEMBERS

A public Bill can be introduced in the House of Commons only by a member, and in the House of Lords only by a peer. A Bill must pass both Houses, but whereas the House of Lords has always ample time for legislation, except at the end of the session, when Government Bills arrive thick and fast, the time of the House of Commons is strictly limited. Private members of that House can secure debates on their Bills only on ten Fridays in each session, and for the privilege of using that time they have to ballot. They can secure the passage of other Bills only if not one member is prepared to oppose them—so that the Bills go through as unopposed business after ten o'clock at night. Bills first introduced in the House of Lords otherwise than on behalf of the Government have no greater opportunity in the House of Commons than private members' Bills; they must either be taken on Fridays or go through as unopposed Bills. It matters little for present purposes whether a Government Bill is introduced first in the House of Lords or in the House of Commons, and we may ignore the House of Lords so far as private members' Bills are concerned.

When a private member is successful in the ballot, or when he introduces a Bill which will, he hopes, pass as an unopposed measure, it may be that he has been anxious for years to be a legislator. Mr A. P. Herbert went to the House of Commons with the deliberate intention of proposing a measure for the reform of the Divorce Laws. As he was not successful in the ballot either in 1936 or in 1937 he secured the passage of the Bill only because he found another member ready to take it over. Mr Herbert had other Bills in his pocket: but he was an exceptional member, and it may be assumed that few members who ballot really have Bills whose subjects they have thought out for themselves.

Often, in fact, the private member who ballots really has not the least idea what Bill he will introduce if he is successful. If he is a Labour member the subject will almost certainly have been determined by a party meeting. If he is not, he can always ask the whips to provide him with a Bill, and often the Government Departments provide the whips with useful small measures that they have not found time to introduce themselves. All this is discussed in greater detail in a later chapter.[1]

For present purposes it is important to notice that many private members' Bills are 'inspired' by interests outside. Many such interests have representatives in the House.[2] If Sir Robert Gower introduced a Bill for the protection of animals it was certain that the Royal Society for the Prevention of Cruelty to Animals was concerned in it; indeed, almost any Bill of that kind may be traced to the Society,[3] which is one of the most persistent and successful of legislators because its proposals are rarely opposed. When the late Sir Henry Jackson introduced a Bill to compel local authorities to provide superannuation schemes for their

---

[1] See Chapter XI, § 3, *post*, pp. 364–73. [2] See Chapter II, § 4, *ante*, pp. 30–44.
[3] 'The Dogs Amendment Act, which received the Royal Assent yesterday, was introduced by Sir Robert Gower on behalf of the Royal Society for the Prevention of Cruelty to Animals': *The Times*, 14 April 1938. 'Sir Robert Gower asked leave to introduce the Protection of Animals (No. 3) Bill....He said that the Bill was promoted by the Royal Society for the Prevention of Cruelty to Animals': *The Times*, 14 July 1938.

officials, it needed no effort of imagination to arrive at the conclusion that the mover was the mouthpiece of the National Association of Local Government Officers.[1] If a Trade Marks Bill is introduced by a private member, its source can probably be traced to the Trade Marks, Patents, and Designs Federation.[2] A Bill relating to the sale of alcoholic liquor in clubs may be assumed to be promoted by the Association of Conservative Clubs. Unless it is a Government measure, a Rivers Pollution Prevention Bill will come from the Central Council for Rivers Protection, perhaps after consultation with other bodies.[3]

An interest is extraordinarily lucky if its permanent representative, or one of its permanent representatives, in the House of Commons is successful in the ballot among, perhaps, 250 members balloting. A representative can introduce the Bill and hope that it will pass as an unopposed Bill. Often the interest forms a parliamentary committee— the representative summons a private meeting of members, at which the officers of the association put their case. If the Bill is put down for second reading after ten o'clock but is opposed by a member, an attempt can be made to meet the criticisms of that member by amending the Bill (which involves the introduction of a new Bill) or promising to accept an amendment in committee, or even by persuading the member that he has misunderstood the Bill. The Bill (or a new Bill) may then be again put down for second reading, and possibly it will pass this time. It is, however, quite possible that the Bill is never expected to pass as an unopposed measure. It is introduced partly to satisfy the members of the association that their officers are active in promoting the association's interest, and partly as a means of propaganda in order to persuade the appropriate minister that the association has a case and that Government legislation should be introduced. This is the case particularly where the

---

[1] See *post*, pp. 218–19.   [2] Cf. *British Industries*, XIII, p. 93 (1930).

[3] Amendment of the law was proposed by the Joint Advisory Committee on River Pollution, 1930. The recommendations were embodied in a Bill drafted by the Central Council for Rivers Protection. This Bill was discussed at a conference at the Ministry of Health of representatives of the Council, the associations of local authorities, the Federation of British Industries, the British Waterworks Association and the Institute of Sewage Purification. After discussions, the Bill became an agreed measure and was introduced as the Public Health (Drainage of Trade Premises) Bill in 1935. Owing to lack of time, it proceeded no further, but was introduced with modifications and passed in 1936–7. See *Municipal Review*, v, pp. 88–93 for the earlier history.

Bill is introduced under the ten minutes' rule,[1] since the short statement of the case made by the member introducing and the attendant publicity may assist in the formation of a public opinion in favour of the Bill. In any case, the introduction of a Bill shows on the one hand what support can be obtained and on the other hand what opposition has to be faced. The Government will often introduce a Bill provided that no substantial parliamentary time will be taken up. Government time is so limited that a department cannot expect to be able to introduce more than one very contentious Bill in a Parliament unless there are substantial electoral interests at stake. All its other Bills must be substantially non-contentious. It will never secure from the Cabinet permission to occupy much time with a Bill which is primarily for the benefit of small sectional interests, even though there is also some general public advantage, unless it can assure the chief whip that there will be no real opposition. Accordingly, the interest promoting the Bill must try to come to terms with its opponents. The introduction of a private member's Bill enables it to find out who its opponents are.

If, however, the interest is serious in its attempt to get a measure through as a private member's Bill and there is no prospect of getting it through after ten o'clock as an unopposed measure, it must secure second reading on a Friday by a member successful in the ballot. One method is to circularise members beforehand asking for their promise to introduce the Bill if they are successful in the ballot. The attempt of the National Association of Local Government Officers to secure compulsory superannuation for local government officers, which is set out at length later in this chapter,[2] provides several examples. For many years the Association's efforts were directed towards persuasion of the Government. In 1921, however, it was decided to proceed by private member's Bill, and the branches were asked to appeal to their local members of Parliament to take part in the ballot and, if successful, to introduce a superannuation Bill. Many promises were received, including one from the member for Ealing, Sir Herbert Nield, K.C.

---

[1] See *post*, pp. 250–1.

[2] See *post*, pp. 215–20. My information is taken from a memorandum prepared by the Association in celebration of the enactment of the Local Government Superannuation Act, 1937, and hereinafter referred to as *Superannuation*. The Association is now known as the National and Local Government Officers' Association.

The Association was very fortunate, for it was successful at its first attempt:

> The General Secretary was in the Committee Room of the House of Commons when the ballot took place. His excitement when the first name to come out of the hat was that of Sir Herbert Nield can be imagined. This was an unprecedented piece of good fortune. No time was lost in getting hold of Sir Herbert, who was probably more surprised than anyone to learn that he had promised his place to the Association.[1]

Sir Herbert was then supplied with the form of the notice of presentation and, after a series of conferences (for he had apparently promised his place rather casually), he agreed to introduce a Bill giving local authorities power to establish superannuation schemes. This Bill was drafted by the Association and introduced and, after considerable parliamentary vicissitudes, was passed as the Local Government and Other Officers' Superannuation Act, 1922.[2] In 1923 the Association desired certain amendments of the Act, and another attempt was made to secure a place in the ballot. None of the members whose aid had been promised was successful, but the Bill was introduced as an unballoted Bill by Mr Isaac Foot in 1924; naturally, it suffered the usual fate of unballoted Bills.[3] Branches were again asked to approach their local members in 1925, and several members promised to introduce the Bill if successful, while many others promised support. But in the ballot 'the Association [sic] failed to secure a favourable position and efforts to win the support of successful members did not succeed'.[4] The Association then concentrated on the task of making superannuation schemes compulsory, and for this purpose brought pressure to bear on the Government. In 1931 the Association asked private members to promote any one of three measures. The Association's branches were advised to send deputations to the local members. As a result, twenty-six members undertook to introduce legislation, if successful.[5] In 1934 another attempt was made, and thirty-three members promised support; but the Government took all private members' time.[6] The Bill of 1937 was introduced by the Minister of Health as a Government measure.

[1] *Superannuation*, p. 13. [2] *Ibid.* p. 14.
[3] *Ibid.* p. 20. [4] *Ibid.* p. 21.
[5] National Association of Local Government Officers: Reports, etc., 1932, pp. 75–6, where the terms of the circular letter are set out. [6] *Ibid.* 1935, p. 15.

Another method is to get into touch with members who have been successful in the ballot. This implies rapidity of action, for notices have to be given almost at once. Consequently, the representatives of the interest in the House of Commons are the most appropriate persons to make the attempt. Being themselves unsuccessful, and having the Bill in their pockets, they can at once call on one of the successful members and inform him that they have 'a very good Bill' which he can introduce. Rear-Admiral Sir Murray Sueter, M.P., has described his own experience:

Immediately my good luck in taking first place in the ballot became known my letter-bag grew and grew. Everybody interested in a particular Bill begged my support to place it upon the statute book.[1]

In fact, however, he had a Bill of his own arising out of his own experience in the Navy.[2]

Yet another method is to get in touch with the Labour party in the hope that the Bill may be put on the Labour party's list. Associations of a non-political character are naturally reluctant to do this, since the Labour party is concerned primarily with the political aspects of a Bill. However, the Hire Purchase Act, 1938, was passed in this way. A group of persons concerned with social work in the East End of London recommended the proposal to the Labour party. The Bill was drafted on behalf of the Haldane Society (then a body of barristers and solicitors affiliated to the Labour party) and was introduced by Miss Ellen Wilkinson, M.P., who secured a high place in the ballot.[3]

[1] *The Evolution of the Tank*, p. 277.   [2] See also Chapter xi, *post*, pp. 364–73
[3] In 1938 the Society had sub-committees on the following matters: Rent Restriction Acts, Organisation of the Police Forces, Land Nationalisation Bill, National Legal Service for Persons of Moderate Means, Reform of Law relating to Aliens, Amendment of Representation of the People Act. Members drafted or were drafting the following Bills in addition: Iron and Steel Nationalisation Bill (at the request of the New Fabian Research Bureau—another Labour organisation); Forty-Hour Week Bill (at the request of the Labour party), Workmen's Compensation (Increase of Payments) Bill (at the request of the Labour party), Bill to Remedy 'Snowball' Trading (at the request of the Labour party). *Haldane Society*: Annual Report, 1937–8, pp. 6–7. The Report also mentions that 'The Society has continued to keep a careful watch on all pending legislation, and, where necessary, to draft amendments for the use of the Parliamentary Labour party. Amendments were drafted in particular to the Government's Rent Restriction Bill....Members of the Society have attended the House of Commons to render assistance to Labour M.P.'s in the debates on hire purchase, rent restriction and company law reform.'

Whatever method be used, it is always wise to obtain as much agreement as possible both outside and inside the House. Indeed, the two are to a substantial degree the same. If other interests are in opposition their representatives in Parliament will oppose. If the claims of other interests can be met, it will generally be found that there is no opposition in the House unless, for instance, the Bill runs counter to the principles of the Labour party or may be alleged to be 'socialism' so as to arouse opposition from members of the Conservative party. Where opposition from members not representing interests is to be feared, it can sometimes be prevented by circulating explanatory memoranda to members, as is often done, or by holding special meetings of members at which officials of the association concerned can dispose of objections, or by setting up a special parliamentary committee to use persuasion and to issue whips, or by securing the support of one of the existing private members' committees.[1]

Two examples will suffice. Before any efforts were made to secure legislation about superannuation, the National Association of Local Government Officers tried to reach agreement with the local authorities' associations. Moreover, though the first Bill was introduced by a private member, the responsibility for the second was taken over by the Minister of Health as soon as all the interests were substantially agreed.

A longer recital may be permitted in the case of the two Bills which became the Architects Registration Acts, 1931 and 1938, because the example admirably illustrates the technique of promoting Bills through private members. The Act of 1931 provided a system of registration for qualified architects. The need for such a system had been discussed among architects for a period approaching forty years, and the Royal Institute of British Architects produced three drafts before reasonable agreement was reached among the interests. The third draft was introduced in 1927 by a private member who had been successful in the ballot, and he stated at the outset that it was 'promoted by the Royal Institute of British Architects'.[2] He asserted that it was supported also by the Royal Sanitary Institute and the Royal Institute of Public Health (though the representative of the latter in the House at once

---

[1] For these committees, see *post*, pp. 374–80.
[2] 204 H.C.Deb. 5 s., 2431.

pointed out that its support had been withdrawn).[1] It was found, however, that other interests were opposed. An unsuccessful attempt was made to meet the claims of the co-operative societies, and in fact their representative moved a 'wrecking' amendment. The opposition of the University of Cambridge was withdrawn after negotiations in which the senior burgess for the University took part.[2] Negotiations with the County Councils Association similarly resulted in a withdrawal of opposition. The representative of the Incorporated Association of Architects and Surveyors, however, stated that his Association (which had set up a special committee under his chairmanship to consider the Bill) was firmly opposed to it.[3] Another member objected on behalf of the Institution of Civil Engineers,[4] and it was mentioned by the member in charge of the Bill that the Institute of Builders was opposed. After a long debate, the Home Secretary suggested as *amicus curiae* that the Bill should be referred to a Select Committee. This being done, the Committee took evidence from twenty organisations and reported against it by a majority of one. It should be said, however, that this was a very unusual procedure.

The Bill was again introduced in 1928 by another member who had been successful in the ballot.[5] The amendments recommended by the Select Committee were included, and negotiations with the Institute of Builders resulted in their withdrawing opposition provided that certain amendments were accepted in committee. The opposition of the Institution of Civil Engineers also had been withdrawn. The rejection was moved, however, by the representative of the Incorporated Association of Architects and Surveyors, and the House was counted out before a division could be taken. In the following year the Bill was introduced in the House of Lords and passed without amendment, but the dissolution of Parliament prevented its being considered by the House of Commons. Finally, it was introduced in the House of Commons in 1930 by yet a third member who had been successful in the ballot. The member representing the Incorporated Association of Architects and Surveyors had been defeated at the general election, and the new Bill passed without substantial opposition.

[1] *Ibid.* 2436.   [2] *Ibid.* 2439.   [3] *Ibid.* 2473.   [4] *Ibid.* 2485.
[5] 214 H.C.Deb. 5 s., 755–87.

The Act of 1931 established an Architects Registration Council. This body had no power to spend money on the promotion of Bills, but it established a parliamentary committee representing all the architects' associations except the Incorporated Association of Architects and Surveyors, whose representative had found a new constituency and was back in the House. The Bill passed the House of Lords in 1937, but was talked out in the House of Commons. In the 1937–8 session it was taken over by a private member who had been successful in the ballot and, in spite of the opposition of the representative of the Incorporated Association, it passed both Houses and became law.

Private members' time is thus used by interests for the promotion of Bills for their own advancement or the advancement of causes which they have in view. Apart from the inevitable restrictions on time—and it will have been seen how easy it is for contumacious members to obstruct private members' Bills—there are two serious limitations in respect of subject. In the first place, no such Bill can pass if the Government thinks fit to stop it. Normally, the whips are not put on against private members' Bills. There is no doubt, however, that they would be put on whenever the Government thought the issue serious enough. For instance, in 1949 a Labour member who had been successful in the ballot introduced a Bill to compel local authorities to provide clinics for women in child-birth. The Bill was enthusiastically supported by the Conservative Opposition because it implied a criticism of the Government's National Health Service. It was opposed by the Government for the same reason, and the whips were put on in order to defeat it. Usually a less formidable but equally effective device is used. A Government whip suggests to a few members that this Bill ought to be opposed and makes certain that enough members attend to vote against it or to talk it out. Also, a junior minister is put up to explain that, though the Government whips will not be put on, the view of the Government is that the Bill ought not to pass. A nod is as good as a whip, and it is reasonably certain that the Bill will not obtain a second reading. If it does, it is not difficult so to obstruct it in committee that it never again sees the light of day. In the case of a Bill brought forward after ten o'clock, the procedure is even easier; it is necessary only to suggest to one member that he shout 'Object!' when the Speaker puts the question. The Bill thus becoming an opposed Bill, it cannot proceed.[1] Yet another method, which is, however, not available where members of the Opposition are concerned, is to suggest to the member that the Bill has so many defects that it ought to be withdrawn. The following extracts from a letter to *The Times* written by Sir Arnold Gridley, M.P., and relating to the Motor Drivers (Signals) Bill, 1938, are self-explanatory:

It was 'blocked' by the Ministry of Transport by friendly arrangement between the Minister and myself in order that it might be further considered between us and by those who have given me legal advice, and by the legal advisers to the Ministry....

In view of the fact that the Bill has the full support of all parties in the House, of the R.A.C., the A.A., the Society of Veteran Motorists, and of the technical press associated with the industry, I am not without hope that, with the friendly co-operation and assistance of the Minister of Transport and his advisers, this little, but important, Bill may yet find its way to the statute-book.[2]

Far more important, however, is the fact that for practical purposes many Bills sought by interests cannot be introduced at all by private members. The agricultural interests, for instance, hardly ever promote Bills through private members. The explanation is that usually they

---

[1] As in the case of the Local Government Superannuation Bill of 1934. 'One of the reasons why the Government whips opposed the second reading of Sir Henry Jackson's Superannuation Bill last session was that the Treasury took the view that compulsory superannuation for local government officers and servants was a matter of such importance that there should be a debate on second reading.' See National Association of Local Government Officers, Reports, etc., 1935, p. 15. Nevertheless, the promotion of this Bill had important consequences. 'It was presented night after night, but was always opposed by self-appointed national economists. Nevertheless, when two persistent people meet, something is bound to happen, and the Association's efforts resulted in an important telephone call to [the Association's offices] something to this effect:
Voice: How far do you expect this Bill of yours to go?
Answer: As far as we can possibly push it.
Voice: But you surely don't expect to make any progress under the present conditions in the House, and it is rather an inconvenience to us.
Answer: If you wish us to withdraw the Bill, what do you offer?
That was too much for the dignity of a prominent civil servant. The conversation ended by our saying that N.A.L.G.O. would withdraw this Bill only on condition that the Government made a move that session by the presentation of Sir Henry Jackson's Bill.' The result was the beginning of the discussions which ended in the presentation of the Government's Bill of 1937. See *Superannuation*, pp. 25–6.

[2] *The Times*, 9 March 1938.

want something involving grants from public funds or taxation. They seek financial assistance for nearly everything that they produce; and if they cannot get adequate financial assistance they want substantial restriction of imports. In either case Standing Orders require a 're-commendation from the Crown'. In other words, there must be a motion to which the Queen's recommendation is signified.[1] In practice such a recommendation is never given except to a motion moved by a minister. Moreover, though the motion may be moved after the Bill has been read a second time, it is so well understood that finance is a matter for the Government that a private member very rarely introduces a Bill imposing a charge; and, indeed, even reputable works assert that a private member cannot introduce such a Bill. Though this is not the case, the assertion does represent the practice. In any case, it is not possible for a Bill imposing a charge to pass through the House of Commons unless it is actively supported by the Government.

These two restrictions produce one of the most important charac-teristics of responsible government. If interests want to dig their hands into the national money-bag they must persuade the Treasury to hold the mouth open. Where log-rolling takes place the Chancellor of the Exchequer captains the team. The pork-barrel is kept locked up in 11 Downing Street, and those who want to take part in the distribution must stand on the door-step and prove their credentials. Or, to leave metaphors, private interests must prove that the use of public funds for their benefit is also for the national benefit—or the Government's benefit—and the Government has to raise the money as well as spend it, to rob Peter to pay Paul, and to consider whether Paul brings more votes than Peter. It has been said that every interest is represented in the American House of Representatives except the national interest; what British interests have to show is that they themselves are the national interest. In the last resort the responsibility for all legislation, especially financial legislation, rests with the Government; and there is no financial legislation except Government legislation.

[1] See Chapter VIII, *post*, pp. 254–7.

3. THE INSPIRATION OF THE GOVERNMENT

Most legislation and, with occasional exceptions like the Marriage Bill of 1937, all important legislation, is introduced on behalf of the Government. If we are asked why such legislation and not some other legislation is introduced, we can give no simple answer because there are several factors to be considered.

First in importance, though its importance is not often realised, is the factor of time. When a minister answers a request for a Bill by regretting that the state of the parliamentary programme renders legislation on this topic impossible in the present session of Parliament, he is not being dilatory and he really means what he says. The Government rarely has more than eighty days, including some Fridays, for all legislation other than the annual financial legislation. Subject to an allowance for contingencies, this time is allotted at the end of the previous session. When it is urged that something ought to be added to the programme the simple and correct answer is that, unless it can be made non-contentious, there is no time for it. The question of the desirability of the Bill is therefore academic, and the Cabinet is too busy to consider academic questions. Towards the end of the session, it may be necessary to consider whether it should be included in the programme for the next session; but for the time being the apparently dilatory answer is the correct one. There are two morals to be drawn by those who are anxious for legislation on a particular topic. The first is that there is much more chance of getting time if the Bill can be made comparatively uncontentious, for then not much time will be wanted and it may possibly be squeezed in. The second is that whether the Bill is uncontentious or not the Cabinet should be impressed with its desirability.

Much of the available time is taken up by annual and consequential legislation. Apart from those hardy annuals the Finance Bill and the Consolidated Fund Bills, Parliament must pass every year the Expiring Laws Continuance Bill, the Isle of Man (Customs) Bill, and the Public Works Loans Bill. These are departmental Bills with no particular background. Other Bills are required to continue existing legislation which was originally intended to be temporary, or to make the provisions consequential upon previous legislation. Of the fifty-five Government Bills passed in 1936–7, eight were annual Bills and eight were consequential upon previous legislation.[1] The Government rarely proposes, for instance, that subsidies to particular interests or industries shall be granted in perpetuity. The general idea is that subsidies will be required to tide over a difficult period, or to enable the industry to effect economies by reorganisation. Experience suggests that the idea is never carried out; but the fiction is maintained by passing temporary Acts from time to time. Thus, the British Shipping (Continuance of Subsidy) Act, 1937, continued for one more year the subsidy for shipping, and the Milk (Amendment) Act, 1937, continued for a further period and subject to amendment of conditions subsidies originally granted in 1934 pending a long-term programme for British agriculture. Subsidies to local authorities come into the same category, for though there is in this case no pretence that they are temporary, the Treasury is careful to maintain control by having the exact amounts fixed from time to time. Thus, the Local Government (Financial Provisions) Act, 1937, and the Local Government (Financial Provisions) (Scotland) Act, 1937, fixed the amounts of grants originally laid down in 1929 and modified in 1933. The Empire Settlement Act, 1937, was of the same character, though the subsidy in this case was in aid of emigration to the Dominions. The India and Burma (Existing Laws) Act, 1937, was passed to remove a doubt in the Government of India Act, 1935; the Unemployment Assistance (Temporary Provisions) (Amendment) Act, 1937, was consequential upon a modification in the Unemployment Act, 1934, effected by temporary legislation in 1935; and the National Health Insurance (Amendment) Act, 1937, was necessitated by a mistake in the National Health Insurance Act, 1936. The Post Office and Telegraph (Money) Act, 1937, must be associated with the category of temporary laws, because the Post Office is not given general power to borrow for capital expenditure, but must come to Parliament from time to time.

The Bills for these purposes were necessarily produced by the appropriate departments. The fact that temporary laws are coming to an end makes it essential for the department to consider whether they shall be continued. Mistakes or doubts in existing legislation are probably

[1] See Appendix II, where a full analysis of the legislation of 1936–7 is set out.

discovered by the departments themselves. Nevertheless, even such Bills are not necessarily the product of the departments alone. The continuance of the shipping subsidy, for instance, was pressed on the Government by the shipping industry and by their representatives in the House of Commons. The continuance of the milk subsidy was emphatically demanded by the National Farmers' Union and its representatives in Parliament. The local government grants were reconsidered in 1937 because the local authorities had insisted in 1929 that a provision for consultation with them should be inserted in the legislation; and there were in fact long consultations in which the associations of local authorities and bodies such as the Institute of Municipal Treasurers and Accountants took part. The Dominions were naturally consulted about the Empire Settlement Bill.

Some Bills, then, are required every year because they are enacted only from year to year or because they are enacted for short periods only. For the rest, the Cabinet can do as it pleases. It is not a question of determining what Bills are desirable, but rather a question of deciding what desirable Bills can be introduced and passed in the little time available. It is rarely possible to secure the passage of more than two long and controversial measures. When it was decided in 1935 that the Government of India Bill and the Housing Bill should be passed, it was obviously futile for any other minister to suggest that, for instance, a Factories Bill or a Coal Mines Bill should be introduced. A Factories Bill, in fact, had been in and out of the Home Office for ten years, though it never got to Parliament until 1937; and the need for a Coal Mines Bill was obvious as soon as it was found that Parliament had emasculated the Coal Mines Bill of 1930.

The determination of priorities in such circumstances is obviously difficult. To a considerable degree the result depends upon the source from which the demand springs. The Government is dependent primarily upon its vote in the House of Commons, and its vote in the House is dependent on the support of the constituencies. Throughout its period of office it must remember that it will have to seek re-election. If, therefore, it can be said that the electorate, or that section of it which supports or is likely to support the Government, wants legislation of a particular kind, then it is the business of the Government to supply the need. Actually, it is rarely possible to say that the electorate wants anything very definitely. Nevertheless, the parties think so, and develop elaborate programmes for future legislation. Early in a Parliament, accordingly, the major legislative proposals are taken from the party programme. In the case of the Labour Government of 1945, indeed, the whole Parliament was occupied, so far as major measures were concerned, by Bills taken from the party programme.

In the case of a Conservative Government, and particularly one which has been in office for many years, this source is not so important. In any case, every party has to meet needs arising suddenly through changes in the political situation of the world or sudden economic changes. Thus in 1936–7 two Acts were due to the Spanish civil war, one Act was produced to meet fascist agitation in this country, and two Acts were consequent on the abdication of Edward VIII. This was an unusually high proportion, but there are always a few measures of this kind, and there are often international treaties to be given legislative effect. Moreover, where a party has been in office for a number of years the electoral policy cannot be dissociated from the experience of its members as ministers, and it is impossible to say whether the party policy comes from the departments or the departmental policy from the party.

There is, however, often a departmental policy which varies but little from Government to Government. The process of rationalising agricultural marketing by means of marketing boards was apparently developed by the Ministry of Agriculture and Fisheries as a means for meeting some of the demands of the agricultural interests without resorting to subsidies, quotas and tariffs, which the interests wanted. The first Act was passed with a Labour Government in office. A policy of low tariffs and to a limited extent of quotas and subsidies was adopted by the National Government, but the departmental policy of providing marketing boards was continued so far as the agricultural interests would accept it. The second Act, therefore, was passed while the National Government was in office. Similarly the Ministry of Housing and Local Government has a fairly consistent long-term policy in relation to housing, a policy which has to be modified in its details or held up temporarily owing to economic conditions or changes of Government, but which in substance continues to flourish while ministers pass through the office on their way to higher things. Other examples, like the policy of the Board of Trade in respect of trade agreements, could be quoted.

Before we leave the policy aspect to deal with the departmental aspect, however, it must be noted that the choice of priorities depends in part on the ministers at the head of the various departments. Ministers in the House of Commons are naturally ambitious. They wish to develop their political prestige or at least to leave some mark on history. When a minister takes office, therefore, he is apt to look round for a subject for legislation. The minister in charge of the main measure of the session holds the centre of the parliamentary stage and, like all other actors, ministers like to have good parts and to put their names at the top of the bill. In part, accordingly, the competition for time is a competition between ministers. A minister who tops the bill in one session can hardly expect to top it again in another. As a former Minister of Transport said when the Road Traffic Bill of 1930 was introduced by his successor:

Every Government wishes to pass more legislation than there is time for, and if a Department has had one big measure allotted to it in the course of a Parliament, it is considered to be lucky. We in the Ministry of Transport had the Electricity Act [of 1926]. Naturally, all the other ministers make it their business to see that one Department does not get more than one Bill of that importance in order that their own Departments may have opportunities.[1]

Examination of the legislative programmes of the National Governments between 1931 and 1939 shows that the rule is not followed invariably. The Ministry of Health under Sir Kingsley Wood had more than its share; but this is an exception which proves the rule, for Sir Kingsley Wood was an active minister whose prestige stood high. Also, the Ministry of Transport had rather more than its share of the limelight while Mr Hore-Belisha was minister. Not many ministers can claim to have secured the passage in two years of three measures so important as the London Passenger Transport Act, 1933, the Road and Rail Traffic Act, 1933, and the Road Traffic Act, 1934—though the first of these had been introduced in the previous Parliament. Again this is an exception which proves the rule.

[1] 235 H.C.Deb. 5 s., 1226–7.

The annual legislation, the consequential legislation, and the major political measures take up most of the time devoted to Government legislation. There remains time only for a dozen or more small 'departmental' Bills. Every department has noted a large number of desirable reforms, usually of a minor character, which can be effected if time is granted. Sometimes the acceptance of a major proposal enables minor matters to be slipped in. Thus, the decision of the Chancellor of the Exchequer in 1928 to reduce the rates on industry and agriculture enabled the Ministry of Health to insert in the Local Government Bill of that year a large number of amendments which had been in contemplation for years and had nothing to do with 'de-rating'. From time to time the ministry in charge of local government manages to secure time for a Public Health Bill, and then inserts a wide variety of minor reforms. The Home Office amasses suggestions for amending factory legislation and obtains time for a Bill perhaps every ten or twenty years. Sometimes specific changes can be made by private members' Bills 'inspired' by the departments. Sometimes the necessary impetus can be obtained by setting up a Departmental Committee to examine and report on a question. All the major departments are thus lined up ready to introduce minor Bills if only the Cabinet will give them the opportunity; nor is the principle of the queue adopted— a department with a minister prepared to fight for time seizes its opportunity and, as the schoolboy puts it, 'hogs it'.

The chances of getting a Bill introduced are much greater if the whips and the Cabinet can be assured that not much time will be taken because the proposals are not contentious. If the interests affected are likely to object no such assurance can be given. Moreover, it is naturally desired that the Act, when passed, shall be capable of taking effect with the least possible delay and controversy. In addition, if a Bill receives the expert criticism of those who know something about the subject it is certain to operate better and to require little amendment in the future—and amendment is difficult because of the lack of parliamentary time. For these reasons it is the practice, whenever new provisions have to be made, to consult the appropriate outside interests. Evidence to that effect was given before the Select Committee on Procedure in 1930[1]

[1] H.C. 161 of 1931, Qs. 1043, 1065, 1964.

and the Committee on Ministers' Powers in 1931;[1] yet such evidence is hardly necessary, for the procedure can be seen constantly in operation. It is particularly obvious in respect of local government legislation, which is always a substantial part of the legislation of every session. Thus, the principles of English local government legislation are discussed with the County Councils Association, the Association of Municipal Corporations, the Urban District Councils Association, and the Rural District Councils Association. Education Bills are discussed with the first two of these and with the Association of Education Committees.[2] Where technical questions are concerned, the appropriate technical associations are consulted either directly by the department or indirectly through the local authorities' associations. Where a special class of officials is concerned, there is also discussion with the appropriate organisation, such as the National Union of Teachers and the National and Local Government Officers Association. *Ad hoc* joint committees are often appointed by two or more of these bodies. For instance, the Ministry of Health suggested a joint committee of the local authorities' associations, the London County Council, the National Association of Local Government Officers and the Trades Union Congress to discuss the question of compulsory superannuation,[3] and the principles agreed upon by this committee formed the basis of the Local Government Superannuation Act, 1937. The County Councils Association and the Association of Municipal Corporations have joint standing committees for Blind Welfare. There are bodies such as the Central Association for Mental Welfare, the National Institute for the Deaf, the National Institute for the Blind, and the Council for the Preservation of Rural England, on which the local authorities' associations as well as voluntary organisations are represented. There is, in short, a whole network of organisations available for consultation.

[1] Minutes of Evidence, II, pp. 8, 131.
[2] 'No President of the Board of Education would dream of introducing any measure into this House which had not been discussed *ad nauseam* with the three Associations of Educational authorities and the National Union of Teachers': H.C. 161 of 1931, Q. 1964 (Lord Eustace Percy). In 1937 the Parliamentary Secretary to the Ministry of Health even advised the House to reject a private member's Bill on the ground that the associations had not been consulted: *The Times*, 4 December 1937.
[3] National Association of Local Government Officers, Reports, etc., 1935, p. 14.

It is not usual to submit the terms of a proposed Bill, though there have been cases where this was done,[1] and there have also been cases where draft Bills have been published for criticism.[2] More often, only the principles of the proposals are submitted, or observations are invited upon a scheme notified publicly. For instance, the Minister of Transport announced to the House of Commons his intention of introducing the Bill which became the Trunk Roads Act, 1936. Thereupon his Department communicated to the County Councils Association a brief outline of the proposals, with a request for a conference.[3] The decision of the Government to accept the proposals outlined in the McGowan report on Electricity Distribution was similarly announced publicly and followed by a confidential memorandum to the local authorities' associations[4] and to the bodies representing the electricity distributors, with the result that it came into the hands of members of Parliament associated with these bodies and that questions were asked in the House of Commons.

The purpose of these prior consultations is to attempt to reach agreement before the Bill is introduced. The financial proposals of the Air-Raid Precautions Bill, 1937, were the subject of long discussion between the local authorities' associations and the Government, and substantial concessions were made. Sometimes, indeed, the associations are asked to formulate a policy in consultation with the departments. This method was adopted with the provisions which became the Local Government (Financial Provisions) Act, 1937. Here, however, consultation was specifically provided for by statute (in a provision of the Local Government Act, 1929, which had been inserted, it may be noticed, at the request of the associations of local authorities). On occasion, observations are requested on proposals made by a committee of inquiry or by interested parties. The majority report of the Royal Commission on

[1] E.g. the Rating and Valuation Bill, 1925: see Committee on Ministers' Powers, Minutes of Evidence, Vol. II, p. 131 (Ministry of Health evidence); and also see the Agriculture Bill, 1937: *Municipal Review*, 1937, p. 352.

[2] E.g. the Road Traffic Bill, 1927, ultimately passed as the Act of 1930.

[3] *County Councils Association Official Gazette*, 1936, p. 381. The Council of the County Councils Association appointed a special sub-committee which contained representatives of the County Accountants' Society and the County Surveyors' Society: *ibid.* p. 481.

[4] *Municipal Review*, 1937, p. 300; *County Councils Association Official Gazette*, 1937, Supplement, p. 140.

Tyneside, 1937, for instance, contained observations of general application about regional government, and the Minister of Health requested the associations to send in their views. Again, representations were submitted to the Board of Trade by the Fruit and Vegetable Canners' Association, and supported by the Grocers' Federation, for an amendment of the Sale of Food (Weights and Measures) Act, 1926, and the Department asked the County Councils Association for observations.[1]

Organisations representing trade and industry are less often consulted, perhaps because they are so numerous. The Federation of British Industries is consulted on all matters affecting industry generally, such as factory legislation,[2] rating of industrial hereditaments, industrial service conditions, and the like. Usually, the need for Budget secrecy prevents consultation on proposals for taxation, but proposals of a technical character are usually submitted to the Council of the Federation. Similarly, the Association of British Chambers of Commerce and the London Chamber of Commerce are consulted on matters affecting trade. Much of modern legislation is concerned, however, with specific trades and industries. The Chamber of Shipping, the National Farmers' Union, the Joint Committee of Cotton Trade Organisations, the Corporation of Lloyds, and similar bodies, are frequently consulted. Where legislation affects conditions of labour, the advice of the General Council of the Trades Union Congress is sought. Naturally, the relation between the Government and the trade unions is closer when a Labour Government is in power. Consultation between the Government and the Trades Union Congress was partly responsible for the split in the Labour Government in 1931, since it was found that the economy proposals of a Cabinet Committee were not acceptable to the trade unions. But in 1929 the Labour Government refused to establish a formal liaison with the Trades Union Congress 'because it would give

---

[1] *County Councils Association Official Gazette*, 1937, Supplement, p. 120.

[2] E.g. the Factories Act, 1937, was based on a Bill drafted originally in 1924 and redrafted in 1926. Consultations between the Government on the one hand and the Federation of British Industries and the Trades Union Congress were held from time to time. A confidential report was submitted to both bodies in 1936 by the Home Office. The Federation of British Industries appointed a special sub-committee which was authorised to meet representatives of the National Confederation of Employers' Organisations. See *British Industries*, XIX, p. 274 (1936).

countenance to the idea that the Government was under outside dictation'.[1]

The Coal Mines Act, 1930, provides an example of consultation of this kind carried to extremes. A Labour Government, without a majority, was in office, and at the election of 1929 the Labour party had pledged itself to a decrease in miners' hours of labour without a decrease in wages. The ordinary socialist remedy of nationalising the mines was not available, since it was certain that such a proposal would not be accepted by either House. Accordingly, the Government accepted the principle of 'rationalisation', or compulsory amalgamation of mining companies which would, it was believed, produce sufficient economies to enable hours of labour to be reduced without increasing costs of production. A Cabinet Committee obtained a plan on these lines from the Mines Department and sought to secure the approval of the Mining Association on the one hand and the Mineworkers' Federation of Great Britain on the other. The usual practice is for consultations to take place between the interests concerned and the minister or (more often) an official on the basis of a memorandum. On this occasion the Cabinet Committee kept the negotiations in its own hands and sought a round-table conference. Consultations took place separately before memoranda were circulated;[2] but these were subsequently circulated and were criticised by both sides.[3] A joint meeting was then summoned, but the Mining Association refused to send representatives because the Bill dealt with wages, a subject which they had not been empowered to discuss.[4] The Mineworkers' Federation, on the other hand, summoned a delegate conference which accepted the heads of proposals in principle.[5] At this stage the Prime Minister and the Foreign Secretary (Mr A. Henderson) were added to the Cabinet Committee, but the Mining Association remained adamant.[6] The Central Marketing Committee of Coalowners was also called into consultation by the Cabinet Committee.[7] The Government decided to introduce the Bill without securing agreement, but consulted the Liberal leaders so as to obtain a parliamentary majority.[8]

[1] Snowden, *Autobiography*, II, p. 762.
[2] *Iron and Coal Trades' Review*, 1929, pp. 554, 647.
[3] *Ibid.* p. 694.   [4] *Ibid.* p. 732.   [5] *Ibid.*
[6] *Ibid.* p. 776.   [7] *Ibid.* p. 858.   [8] *Ibid.* p. 894.

It must not be assumed, however, that the impulse always springs from the Government. When a new problem arises, or when a substantial section of public opinion calls for a change in the law, or when an old problem becomes insistent, or even when a department realises that some change is necessary, the department is not always ready with an immediate solution. Civil servants have to undertake a vast amount of day-to-day administration and have neither the time nor, always, the capacity, to work out new schemes.[1] The Treasury does not recognise the need of persons concerned primarily with thought. It may suspect, and certainly members of Parliament are prone to suspect, that people with instructions to think are likely to be people who do nothing. The British Constitution has therefore developed a technique of public inquiry.[2] Formerly, the task lay with the House of Commons, which set up Select Committees to examine propositions put before it or problems which required solution. At the present day the initiative more often rests with the Government, which sets up a Royal Commission or a Departmental Committee to examine any question for which it cannot find, or does not want to find, an immediate solution. Very often, knowledge of the facts upon which policy could be formulated is lacking. The great Royal Commissions of the last century, such as those which preceded the development of poor law, public health, local government, housing, and factory legislation, had first to ascertain the facts and then to suggest remedies. The central departments now have vast stores of factual material ready at hand. The index of published statistics alone occupies 340 pages, and much information remains embedded in departmental files. The fact-finding function remains important; but more important still is the recommendation of remedies. Few years pass without at least half-a-dozen reports from commissions and committees, and most of these are in due course translated into legislation.[3]

[1] An exception must be made in the cases of the Service Departments, each of which has a Chief of Staff concerned primarily with the formulation of policy; and defence policy as a whole is studied by the Defence Committee and its sub-committees. But as the Machinery of Government Committee pointed out (Cd. 9230, 1930 reprint, p. 6), the problems of these Departments are essentially dissimilar. In any case, they seldom require legislation.

[2] On one aspect, see Clokie and Robinson, *Royal Commissions of Inquiry* (1937).

[3] The above statement is limited in terms to Bills; it must be realised, however, that a Bill may be built up of a large number of clauses each with its separate history. For

Such Royal Commissions and Departmental Committees are set up to examine specific questions: but since the Report of the Machinery of Government Committee emphasised the need, most departments have established advisory committees—some statutory, like those of the Ministry of Education; and some not, like those of the Colonial Office —to advise the departments on the exercise of their functions. These committees bring the experts in the department into touch with the experts outside, especially those in the universities, local government and trade and industry.[1] The whole educational system was reformed between the wars and given statutory effect by the Education Act, 1944, as the result of the work of the Consultative Committees established under the Education Act, 1921. Usually, however, these committees are concerned with administration, and they result in the production of legislation incidentally.

Normally, Royal Commissions, Departmental Committees and advisory committees contain a large proportion of members representing outside interests in the wide sense in which that term is used in this book.[2]

instance, clause 6 (2) of the Food and Drugs Bill, 1938, was in substance recommended to the Departmental Committee on the Composition and Description of Food (1928) by the Food Manufacturers' Federation, Patent and Proprietary Foods Section. It was approved by the Departmental Committee and was therefore 'noted for enactment at a suitable opportunity' by the Ministry of Health. When the law of Food and Drugs was examined by the Local Government and Public Health Consolidation Committee this sub-clause was brought up, was approved by the Committee, incorporated in the Bill drafted by the Committee, and ultimately enacted in the Food and Drugs Act, 1938. See Local Government and Public Health Consolidation Committee, Third Interim Report, Cmd. 5628, p. 18. Other provisions of the same Bill were based on recommendations of the Royal Commission on Local Government (Final Report). Further, it has to be remembered that a large part of local government legislation is based on experiments made by local authorities and approved by Parliament in local Acts. These are adopted by other local authorities and gradually generalised, until they are ultimately adopted into general legislation: see on this point Chapter XIII, *post*, pp. 462–4. In the Public Health Bill, 1936, twenty-three clauses were taken in whole or in part from local Acts; and in the Food and Drugs Bill, 1938, ten clauses (nine of them stated to be 'common form') were similarly taken from private Acts.

[1] The Royal Commission on Common Land, 1955, included the Secretary of the National Association of Parish Councils, the President of the Royal Forestry Society, a member of the National Parks Commission, the chairman of the Wool Marketing Board, the President of the International Federation for Housing and Town Planning, a member of the Welsh Agricultural Land Sub-Commission, and the Director of the Land Utilisation Survey.

[2] Any example will do, but the Report of the Departmental Committee on Street Lighting happens to be at hand. The Committee was unusually loaded with civil servants,

Partly this is because they are the experts outside the civil service, and partly because generally the legislation cannot effectively be carried out without the collaboration of those interests. Any local government committee, for instance, will contain representatives of the local authorities' associations concerned. If an agreed report is produced, as usually happens, the proposals are reasonably certain of acceptance by the interests if they are accepted by the Government, though even in this case the interests are consulted.[1] Indeed, the interests take the report into consideration and make recommendations to the minister before the Government's view is made known. Sometimes, however, the diversity of interests prevents an agreed report. The Sankey Coal Commission of 1919, and the Royal Commission on Licensing in 1932, are obvious examples, and it is significant that neither led to legislation.

of whom there were four. In addition there was one county council official, two county borough council officials, and two representatives of electrical and gas industries. Among the bodies submitting evidence were the motoring and pedestrians' associations, the Joint Gas Lighting Committee (representing four bodies), the associations concerned with electricity supply, two bodies representing engineering officials, the Chief Constables' Association, and the Metropolitan Police. The Committee has been criticised for making administrative proposals without consulting the local authorities' associations. See *Local Government Chronicle*, 27 November 1937. The local authorities' associations are frequently asked to nominate members to serve on Departmental Committees.

[1] The Final Report of the Royal Commission on Transport (1931) was submitted by the Minister of Transport to five associations of local authorities, fifteen transport undertakings associations, four motoring associations, four trade unions, the Association of British Chambers of Commerce, the Federation of British Industries, the Mansion House Association on Transport, and the National Federation of Iron and Steel Manufacturers. Their replies were published: Royal Commission on Transport: Communications received from certain Organisations..., Cmd. 4048 (1932). The interests were not agreed, and in particular the views of the railway companies and of the road transport associations were in direct opposition. The minister set up a conference with four representatives and an independent chairman which produced an agreed scheme, though the representatives were not able to bind their organisations and in fact the road transport representatives had their agreement repudiated. The Road and Rail Traffic Bill departed in some respects both from the Royal Commission Report and from the Conference Report. It may be noted that there was active lobbying on this Bill, both sides sending memoranda, and both setting up parliamentary groups. The second reading debate was almost entirely taken up by the representatives of interests, including representatives of the Railway Companies Association ('As a member of the Railway Companies Association, I have been asked by them to put the position with regard to this Bill as the railways see it': 277 H.C.Deb. 5 s., 904), the National Union of Railwaymen, the road transport interests, two 'railway towns', and the Port of Bristol (which, as a municipally owned port, objected to a Bill which might increase the trade of the railway-owned port of Cardiff).

These cases apart, the interval of time between the report and the subsequent legislation is now quite short.[1]

The committee's task is generally to produce proposals, not Bills. There have been exceptional cases. The Crown Proceedings Committee of 1927 was asked to produce a Bill. The Committee on the Simplification of the Law of Income Tax produced a Consolidation Bill. Similarly, the Local Government and Public Health Consolidation Committee, which was asked to make recommendations intended to facilitate consolidation of the law of local government and public health, decided that its work would be hampered unless it had before it 'rough drafts of clauses indicating the form which the law would assume if our recommendations were accepted'.[2] Accordingly, it produced three draft Bills which became, with slight amendments, the Local Government Act, 1933, the Public Health Act, 1936, and the Food and Drugs Act, 1938.

These devices show that there may be sources of inspiration behind and outside the departments. There are, however, other sources. Legislative changes are often due to representations made directly to the departments by outside interests of the kind already described. Frequently they are groups of reformers either combined in a permanent organisation or acting through an *ad hoc* committee. The Education Act, 1936, had its source in a general belief among educational reformers that an increase in the maximum school-leaving age was desirable. Finding that their opinions were widely held but were not canalised, they formed a special committee to approach the Government and to direct a publicity campaign in order to convince or coerce those in authority. In other words, the technique which led to the passing of the Eighteenth (Prohibition) Amendment to the Constitution of the United States is well known in this country; but it has the significant difference that a publicity campaign must generally be directed towards the Government, which alone in most cases has the means to secure the enactment of the necessary legislation. It is part of the technique to circularise members of Parliament, to initiate questions and debates in

---

[1] See, as to Royal Commissions, Clokie and Robinson, *op. cit.* pp. 143–7. It must be remembered that Royal Commissions usually deal with more contentious matters than Departmental Committees.

[2] (First) Interim Report, Cmd. 4272, p. 8.

the House, and even to secure the introduction of a private member's Bill. But generally speaking the purpose is not to secure a majority— only the Government has a majority—but to create an opinion both among the Government's majority and in the public outside. The responsible Government of a democratic state, and especially the British Government, is so susceptible to public opinion, especially when it is expressed in the lobbies of the House, that all the batteries of publicity are directed upon the House: but it is the Government, not the House, which is sought to be persuaded.

The technique is well illustrated by the Local Government Superannuation Act, 1937, to which reference has already been made. Here there was a definitely organised body, the National Association of Local Government Officers, which desired the enactment of the proposals. Where there is no such body, the first step is to form one. In many cases, too, wider publicity is required. This is, however, a simple case which illustrates on the one hand that it is necessary to persuade the Government and on the other hand that it is easy to persuade the Government once competing interests are agreed.

A London Municipal Officers' Association was formed about 1896; and from its inauguration it repeatedly sought parliamentary approval for a superannuation Bill which might be adopted by the authorities concerned with London government.[1] In 1905 the National Association of Local Government Officers was formed, and one of its main efforts was to secure superannuation for all local government officers. Early in 1906 a sub-committee was set up to consider the drafting of a Bill, and in 1907 the principles of a Bill were approved. Approaches were made to the President of the Local Government Board, but the opinion was expressed that 'there appeared to be little hope, through the congested state of parliamentary business, that the Government would take up the Bill'.[2] The Association then sought the support of the Association of Municipal Corporations, but without success. A draft Bill was produced in 1908, and an attempt was made to enlist the support of the National Union of Teachers and the Association of Municipal Corporations. The latter asked for further and better particulars. At the general election of 1910, however, a questionnaire was sent to all

---

[1] *Superannuation*, p. 1.   [2] *Ibid.* p. 3.

parliamentary candidates, and 130 of the members elected promised to support a Bill when presented to Parliament.[1] The negotiations with the Association of Municipal Corporations were extended in the same year to the County Councils Association and the Urban District Councils Association. The next step was to ask for interviews with the Chancellor of the Exchequer and the President of the Local Government Board. The latter first asked for further information, and ultimately stated that the suggestions of the Association had been noted, but that the Government was unable to hold out any hope of legislation at the present time and that the minister saw no advantage in troubling a deputation to wait upon him. Nevertheless, the President of the Association saw the President of the Local Government Board and the Solicitor-General. 'The minister was not enthusiastic.'[2]

It was proposed in the Association that the next step should be the introduction of a private member's Bill. The proposal was not adopted, but instead branches were urged to interview their local members of Parliament. The result was 'most satisfactory'.[3] In the meantime, amendments were suggested by the Association of Municipal Corporations and the County Councils Association. A new Bill was drafted, and consultations took place with the trade unions as to the inclusion of 'workmen'. In 1914, the President of the Local Government Board at last agreed to receive a deputation. The minister admitted that the Association had just cause for its claims, but pointed out certain difficulties. The war then intervened, and it was not until 1918 that another deputation raised the question before the President of the Local Government Board. It being ascertained that no Government grants were required, the President expressed his agreement with the general principle, and a Departmental Committee was set up to consider whether it was desirable to introduce a scheme.[4] The committee reported in favour of the suggestion, and six weeks later the Minister of Health invited the Association to submit its observations.[5] In 1920 the minister agreed to receive a deputation urging immediate progress. The minister admitted the justice of the claim, but no action was taken.

Every member of Parliament was sent a statement of the Associa-

[1] *Ibid.* p. 5. [2] *Ibid.* p. 6. [3] *Ibid.* p. 7.
[4] *Ibid.* p. 10. [5] *Ibid.*

tion's case, and in 1921 a meeting of members of Parliament was convened in the House of Commons by Mr Neville Chamberlain and other members, who were drawn from all parties. Seventy members were present, and it was agreed to send a deputation to wait upon the Prime Minister or other members of the Government.[1] The Minister of Health consented to receive a deputation, but explained that the condition of the national and local finances prevented any action which would add to the rates.[2] The Association, in desperation, turned to the device of having a private member's Bill introduced, as has already been described.[3] The Bill was read a second time without a division. In Standing Committee, the Minister of Health proposed an amendment which would have made a local poll a preliminary to the adoption of a superannuation scheme. This being strenuously opposed by the promoters, the minister suggested that they should hold a conference with him to see if a compromise could be reached. It may be noted that members of the Association were present at this conference, as well as officials of the Government departments concerned. Eventually, the Bill was limited to posts 'designated' for superannuation purposes by the local authority. As a result, the Bill passed through Committee.[4]

On the day before the Bill came back to the House for report, the member in charge was conferring with two officials of the Association, when the door of the room was opened and the stentorian voice of the policeman cried: 'Who goes Home?' The House had adjourned because of the assassination of Field-Marshal Sir Henry Wilson. The assassination was therefore discussed for most of the next day. Eventually, the Bill came on. But Sir Frederick Banbury tried to obstruct the measure until the automatic adjournment at four o'clock. Sir Frederick spoke seventeen times, 'on each occasion slowly sorting his papers, with probably no idea of what he was going to say. But he remained cool and collected throughout, in contrast to Sir Herbert Nield, anxiously watching the clock with flushed excited face'. The last amendment was disposed of at one minute to four o'clock. Sir Herbert Nield at once moved that the Bill be read a third time; but Sir Frederick Banbury immediately arose and talked out the Bill. It appeared that Sir Frederick

---

[1] *Ibid.* p. 12.
[2] *Ibid.* p. 13.
[3] *Ante*, p. 196.
[4] *Superannuation*, pp. 15–16.

Banbury was merely obstructing the next Bill on the order paper, the Railway Fires Act (1903) Amendment Bill, and that as chairman of the Great Northern Railway Company he did not intend to let that Bill through.[1]

There remained one more Friday for private members' legislation. The Bill not having been passed the previous week, it now appeared third on the Order paper. Nevertheless, it received its third reading in spite of Sir Frederick Banbury. After considerable delays, the Bill also passed the House of Lords, but with amendments. These amendments required the consideration of the House of Commons: but the Government then announced that all private members' time would be taken until after the summer recess. The leader of the House proved adamant until a large number of members put their names to a petition asking for Government time. The Government then agreed, provided that there was no opposition. The Bill duly appeared as a Government Bill on the Order paper, but rumours circulated to the effect that the whips were suggesting postponement until after the recess. The Association's parliamentary agent, without consulting the member in charge, at once interviewed the chief whip. The chief whip pointed out that it would take half-an-hour for the Speaker to read the amendments and suggested that postponement until the autumn would not hurt the Association: but the agent remarked that there might be 'no Autumn'. He arranged to have a copy of the Order paper prepared for the Speaker, indicating the nature of each amendment. The amendments were reached at 11.30 p.m., and the Speaker got through them very rapidly and finished at midnight. On the following morning the Bill received the royal assent, and the Houses then adjourned 'until Tuesday, November 14'. During the recess, however, Parliament was dissolved and a new Government took office. There was thus 'no Autumn'. So the adoptive Local Government and Other Officers' Superannuation Act, 1922, was passed.[2]

The Association next tried to secure an amending Bill. Being unsuccessful in the ballot for private members' Bills, an unballoted Bill was introduced by Mr Isaac Foot, but the Bill made no progress. An interview was sought with the Minister of Health, who agreed that amendments were desirable. It was suggested that a Bill might be brought in

[1] *Ibid.* p. 17.   [2] *Ibid.* pp. 18–20.

after eleven o'clock and read a second time without discussion: 'but the Minister deemed this undesirable, since other Government Departments would wish to put forward their views and a full discussion should be allowed'. On the other hand, a Government Bill could not be introduced for lack of time. The Minister therefore suggested appointing another Departmental Committee.[1] This Committee did not report until 1928, but, subject to conditions, it recommended a compulsory system of superannuation. In the meantime, the Association gave evidence to the same effect before the Royal Commission on Local Government. In 1930, evidence was given also before the Departmental Committee on the Qualifications, Recruitment, Training and Promotion of Local Government Officers.

In 1930, also, the Minister sent to the Association a memorandum outlining proposed amendments to the Act of 1922, but the economic crisis of 1931 prevented further progress for some years. The Association therefore decided to prepare another private member's Bill, which was introduced by Sir Henry Jackson, but opposed by the whips.[2] In 1934, the Secretary of the Ministry of Health invited a deputation to discuss the whole issue. It was made clear that substantial agreement must be reached with the local authorities' associations before legislation could be introduced. Accordingly, a conference was held, at which were present representatives of the Ministry of Health, the Scottish Office, the associations of local authorities, the London County Council, and the Association. At a second conference representatives of the Trades Union Congress also were present. A joint committee was appointed to consider certain questions and, when agreement was reached, the Association was asked to secure the drafting of a new Bill. A joint letter was sent to the Prime Minister announcing that agreement had been reached, and asking for Government time during the current session. The Prime Minister replied that it was impossible to give an undertaking, and that there were still points which required examination. A joint letter to the Minister of Health produced a list of the points still requiring elucidation. Early in 1936, the parliamentary secretary received a deputation from the joint committee and announced that a Bill would be produced in the next session. The joint committee continued

---

[1] *Ibid.* p. 22.   [2] See *ante*, pp. 198–9, especially footnote 1, p. 199.

work on the details, and ultimately the Minister of Health introduced two Bills, which became law without real opposition as the Local Government Superannuation Act, 1937, and the Local Government Superannuation (Scotland) Act, 1937.[1]

This long disquisition has been necessary because it provides examples of most of the devices used by interests to obtain legislation. Twenty-one years' work was necessary to secure the aim which the National Association of Local Government Officers had in view. Most of it, it will be noticed, was directed towards persuading the Government; and the first approaches to the House of Commons itself were directed to ensuring that there would be support in the House for a Government proposal. It was not to be expected that the Government itself should be particularly active in the matter: while there were substantial administrative advantages to be obtained, no votes were to be won, and some opposition was to be expected in view of the prospect of increased cost to local authorities. Accordingly, it was necessary not merely to persuade the Government that there were governmental advantages, but also that not much time would be occupied in the House, to the prejudice of what the Government regarded as more important legislation. Hence the subsequent process of popularisation, involving reports by Departmental Committees and evidence before other governmental inquiries. Hence also the final procedure of securing as much agreement as possible from other interested parties, particularly the local authorities themselves. In the meantime, the Association used the private member's Bill procedure to obtain a permissive Bill and to keep the matter before the public. The 'representatives' of the Association in the House assisted considerably by introducing the Bills, leading deputations to the minister, and calling a meeting of private members.

The National Farmers' Union may be taken as another example because, though legally a trade union, its purposes and its methods are quite different. It is an organisation not of employees concerned with conditions of service, but of primary producers anxious to secure the maximum profit for themselves. To effect this purpose it has to seek protection from foreign competition by import restrictions and subsidies and protection from the reduction of prices created by too much

[1] *Superannuation*, pp. 26–9.

internal competition. Nearly every piece of legislation which it requires must be proposed by the Government, not only because it is of great social importance as affecting the supply and cost of agricultural produce to the consumer, but also because it must contain financial provisions which cannot in practice be inserted in private members' legislation. Accordingly, the Union is concerned primarily to bring pressure to bear on the Government and it can rarely use the device of the private member's Bill. Nor can it be contended that the legislation can be passed without political controversy. Neither the Labour party nor the Liberal party is sympathetic to the chief aims of the Union. If the legislation is to be obtained at all, it must be obtained from a Conservative Government, though it may be noted that the Agricultural Marketing Act, 1931, was passed under a Labour Government. The Union cannot pretend and does not pretend that it is impartial in the party sense. Its support is extremely useful to Conservative members in rural areas, some of whom are, or have been, supported financially; others are given propaganda assistance; and all are anxious not to arouse opposition.

The Union could go further and establish its own party, and suggestions to that end have been made in the past.[1] They have never been approved, because the putting up of separate candidates would almost certainly result in the defeat of some Conservative members and, perhaps, the return of a Labour Government. The Union no longer publishes particulars of its political fund. There is a Political Fund Committee, whose annual report discloses only that 'the Committee met for administrative purposes during the year'. In 1937 the Union had a political fund of over £68,000, a sum exceeding by one-half the total assets in the Union's general fund. This political fund could be used for any of the following purposes:

(*a*) The payment of any expenses incurred either directly or indirectly by a candidate or prospective candidate for election to Parliament or to any public office,[2] before, during or after the election in connection with his candidature or election.

---

[1] National Farmers' Union, Annual Report, 1937, p. 73.

[2] 'Public office' is defined to mean the office of member of any county, county borough, district, or parish council, or board of guardians or of any public body who have power to raise money either directly or indirectly by means of a rate. It is understood that this power is not in fact exercised.

(*b*) The holding of any meeting or the distribution of any literature or documents in support of any such candidate or prospective candidate.

(*c*) The maintenance of any person who is a member of Parliament or who holds a public office.

(*d*) In connection with the registration of electors or the selection of a candidate for Parliament or any public office.

(*e*) The holding of political meetings of any kind, or the distribution of political literature or political documents of any kind, unless the main purpose of the meetings or of the distribution of literature or documents is the furtherance of statutory objects within the meaning of the Act, that is to say, the regulation of the relations between workmen and masters, or between workmen and workmen or between masters and masters, or the imposing of restrictive conditions on the conduct of any trade or business, and also the provision of benefits to members.

How far powers of this kind have been used since 1945 is not known. The Parliamentary Committee of the Union reported[1] that on the announcement of the general election of 1955 it made 'a detailed review of the procedure adopted by the Union at previous general elections'. Its method was to interview candidates with a list of questions, but it is not stated what was done with the answers, though the results showed that the decision to recommend this system was 'fully justified'. After the election the Committee made a study of the results and noted that the results in farming areas 'did not show a well-defined trend although it did appear that the Conservative party did not increase their majorities to the same extent in the rural constituencies as they did in the urban areas'. In the main, however, the Parliamentary Committee was concerned to keep a watch on Government policy and to make representations for the sort of legislation that the Union liked and against the sort of legislation of which it disapproved. The Union 'continued to use the established channels of communication with the Parliamentary Agricultural Committees of the major political parties; and as occasion required, the principal officers and staff of the Union attended meetings of those committees and their representatives to discuss the issues arising.

The Union is closely associated with the Federation of British Industries in matters of common interest and there are frequent references to collaboration with the Country Landowners Association.

[1] National Farmers' Union, Annual Report, 1956, p. 31.

For instance, there has for some time been a campaign for the abolition of the 'de-rating' of agricultural and industrial hereditaments, whose rates were reduced by legislation in 1928 when agriculture and industry were both depressed. In 1951 the Union prepared a memorandum setting out the case for continuing this particular subsidy to agriculture, and similar action was taken by the Federation of British Industries and the Country Landowners Association. Nevertheless, a resolution in favour of abolishing de-rating was passed by the County Councils Association in 1955. Thereupon the Union revised its memorandum and circulated it; and similar action was taken by the Federation of British Industries and the Country Landowners Association.[1] The matter was considered at the annual meeting of the Union in January 1955 and 'steps were taken to ensure that the Government and Parliament were fully seised of the strength of the Union's opposition to the proposal'.[2] Many examples could be shown of pressure being brought to ensure advantages or to prevent disadvantages to members of the Union. For instance, the Union secured the inclusion in the Agricultural (Miscellaneous Provisions) Act, 1954, of a provision securing the indefinite continuance of the grant-in-aid of field drainage and farm ditching schemes.[3]

4. DRAFTSMEN

To say what a Bill is required to do is one thing; to put it in a proper form is another. Bills have to be drafted for lawyers to interpret and administrators to put into force. Mr Balfour spent much time on the clauses for the Education Bill, 1902. The draftsman to whom they were shown said: 'You have written a very good popular account of the Bill.'[4] A good popular account will not do; it must be written by lawyers for lawyers.

The private member must arrange for the drafting of his own Bills. Sir Alan Herbert's Marriage Bill, which passed as the Matrimonial Causes Act, 1937, was based on a Bill placed in charge of Mr Holford Knight so long before that the name of the draftsman has been for-

[1] National Farmers' Union, Annual Report, 1955, p. 175.
[2] National Farmers' Union, Annual Report, 1956, p. 36.
[3] National Farmers' Union, Annual Report, 1955, p. 173.
[4] *Life of A. J. Balfour*, I, p. 324.

gotten. To it was added a clause drafted by Sir Alan himself, 'very crudely and badly'. A friend then introduced him to Lord Kilbracken, an expert draftsman, who offered his aid. Mr Claude Mullins, a Metropolitan Police magistrate interested in social reform, suggested amendments and additions. Sir Alan himself wrote the preamble, and so the Bill was introduced in his first session.[1] In his second session it was again introduced, this time by Mr De la Bere (who had won a favourable place in the ballot and was persuaded by Sir Alan to take over the Bill). It appearing during the second reading debate that the House was in favour of its principles, the Government offered the assistance of the Attorney-General and Solicitor-General, though it was to remain a private member's Bill. Accordingly, a preliminary conference was held at which the promoters, the Attorney-General, the Treasury Solicitor and the First Parliamentary Counsel attended. The two Law Officers were members of the Standing Committee, and the Treasury Solicitor and a member of the Parliamentary Counsel's Office sat behind.[2]

This was a somewhat unusual procedure, but if the Government does not oppose a Bill the appropriate minister usually refers it, through the Treasury, to the Parliamentary Counsel's Office;[3] and after examination both there and in the department suggestions are made to the member as to suitable amendments. It has been said, however, that 'it may happen, under existing arrangements, that a Bill, bad in substance or in form, or in both, slips through Parliament because it is not the duty or interest of any one in particular to stop or improve it'.[4]

All Government Bills, except Scottish Bills and certain annual Bills which do not vary substantially in form, are drafted in the Office of Parliamentary Counsel to the Treasury. This office was established by Treasury minute in 1869.[5] The earliest Acts of Parliament were drafted by judges on the basis of parliamentary petitions; and even when legislation by Bill became the practice the judges sometimes assisted. But it appears that by the end of the eighteenth century the drafting was

[1] A. P. Herbert, *The Ayes Have It*, pp. 53–66.
[2] *Ibid.* pp. 98, 103.
[3] Sir Courtenay Ilbert, *Legislative Methods and Forms*, pp. 90–1.
[4] *Ibid.* p. 91.   [5] For what follows, see *ibid.* pp. 77–85.

undertaken by lawyers or other persons in the department concerned. Thus, Mr Pitt's financial Bills were drafted by a lawyer who was described as Parliamentary Counsel to the Treasury, and who sometimes undertook work for other departments. This office disappeared about 1837; but about the same time the Home Office, which at this time was concerned most with initiating legislation, appointed counsel for the purpose of drafting. Possibly the most eminent of the draftsmen, Mr Henry (afterwards Lord) Thring, was appointed counsel to the Home Office in 1860. He drafted most of the important Cabinet measures of his time, but other Bills were drafted in the departments or by counsel employed specially for the purpose. This not only involved increased cost, but also prevented uniform language being used[1] and hindered any kind of Treasury control over legislative proposals. The Office of Parliamentary Counsel to the Treasury was therefore established in 1869 as a subordinate department of the Treasury. Mr Thring was appointed Parliamentary Counsel, and an assistant and office staff provided. 'The Parliamentary Counsel was to settle all such departmental Bills, and to draw all such other Government Bills (except Scotch and Irish Bills) as he might be required by the Treasury to settle and draw. The instructions for the preparation of every Bill were to be in writing and sent by the heads of the Departments to the Parliamentary Counsel through the Treasury, to which latter Department he was to be considered responsible. On the requisition of the Treasury he was to advise on all cases arising on Bills or Acts drawn by him, and to report in special cases referred to him by the Treasury on Bills brought in by private members. It was not to be part of his duty to write memoranda or schemes for Bills, or to attend Parliamentary committees, unless under instructions from the Treasury.'[2]

Besides the First and Second Parliamentary Counsel, there are four other counsel, two junior counsel, and a number of assistant counsel. Normally, one of the senior members and a junior member work together. Such joint action is rendered necessary by the difficulty of the

[1] The Reform Bill of 1867 was drafted by Mr Baxter, of Baxter, Rose & Norton, the firm which advised Mr Disraeli personally and managed his elections. It was referred to Thring, who criticised its drafting, and it was thereupon committed to Thring for drafting: *Life of Disraeli*, II, pp. 251–2.
[2] Sir Courtenay Ilbert, *Legislative Methods and Forms*, pp. 84–5.

task. 'You must have someone working with you at your elbow to see that you do not make too many mistakes.'[1] Only very small Bills are undertaken by the juniors without assistance.

Once the department has made up its mind that a Bill is necessary, has secured the approval of the Cabinet, and has consulted the appropriate interests, the drafting can proceed. A note is sent to the Treasury asking for a Bill to be drafted on the lines stated. The Treasury thereupon instructs Parliamentary Counsel.

The instructions thus given are of a general and indefinite character. They may or may not be accompanied by more specific instructions from the minister or department principally concerned, in the form either of a short note, or of reference to the report of a Commission or Committee, or of papers showing the circumstances which appear to render legislation expedient.[2]

Usually, the information thus provided is not in itself sufficient, and the Parliamentary Counsel consults the minister,[3] or the permanent secretary, or the senior civil servant charged with the preparation of the Bill. With a complicated measure, 'it is often necessary to prepare memoranda, stating the existing law, tracing the history of previous legislative enactments or proposals, or raising the preliminary questions of principle which have to be settled. The first draft may take the form of a rough "sketch" or of "heads of a Bill".'[4] Sometimes ten or fifteen drafts have to be prepared, and the Bill goes backwards and forwards between the department and the Office until agreement is reached. With a really complicated Bill at least three months are required for this stage.

When the Bill has been introduced and published, it is in the hands of Parliament and not of Parliamentary Counsel. He must, nevertheless, continue to be responsible for the language, and take steps to inform the

---

[1] Sir William Graham-Harrison, H.C. 161 of 1931, Q. 4409.

[2] Sir Courtenay Ilbert, *op. cit.* p. 87.

[3] But ministers can rarely find much time to deal with the matter. Ministers like Mr Gladstone and Mr Balfour spent much time studying and improving the texts of their Bills. Modern ministers have delegated this function, and it is evident that often they know little more than is contained in their departmental briefs. Cf. the Population (Statistics) Bill, 1937; and see Sir William Graham-Harrison, 'An Examination of the Main Criticisms of the Statute Book and of the Possibility of Improvement', *Journal of the Society of Public Teachers of Law*, 1935, p. 44.   [4] *Ibid.* p. 88.

minister of any errors which he discovers or which are pointed out by others. Amendments of substance may be proposed to the minister by the interests affected,[1] or put on the Order paper by members. These will be discussed between the department and the Office, accepted where possible, drafted where required, and fitted into the Bill. When amendments are made, consequential amendments must be drafted. Though the Bill is under the control of Parliament, the Parliamentary Counsel remains responsible for the form; and the only effect of parliamentary control is that every amendment must be moved by a member, even if it is concerned only with drafting.

Thus, there may be doubt as to who makes the laws in substance, but the Parliamentary Counsel determines the form of all Government Bills, and in part of all private members' Bills which are submitted to him.

5. AMENDMENT IN PARLIAMENT

It is well known that statistics, if properly selected, can be made to prove almost anything. It is certainly possible to exaggerate the influence of members of Parliament, and of the House of Lords, in the framing of legislation, by indicating the number of amendments in both Houses. Undoubtedly, many Bills suffer a considerable transformation. Private members' Bills are often turned inside out, and in this case much of the amendment is due to members themselves. A balloted Bill has little chance of being read a third time and passed unless it passed fairly rapidly through the Standing Committee. The member in charge must, therefore, show evidence of a spirit of accommodation; and the simplest means of doing so is to go to those who are leading the opposition and ask, 'What can I do to meet your point of view?' Agreed amendments can thus be inserted, contentious clauses deleted, and safeguarding provisos added. Usually this process goes on, if not behind the Speaker's Chair, at least behind the Chairman's back; but on occasions amendments are put down by members and accepted by the member in charge. The appropriate minister is, however, a more powerful opponent than any combination of private members. At his word the whips are put on, and an obstinate member finds either that his Bill is amended against

[1] See *post*, pp. 228–31.

his will or, what is worse, defeated on third reading. The Bill as it passes second reading—and it does not pass unless the minister thinks fit—is subjected to scrutiny in the department and, at the minister's request, in the Office of Parliamentary Counsel. Frequently the member in charge is invited to see the appropriate departmental adviser, or the draftsman to whose tender mercies the Bill is committed, or both. Out of these discussions proceeds a series of amendments designed to make it acceptable to the minister and which, probably, will make it acceptable to the House.

Such considerations do not apply to a Government Bill, which is, if not a thing of beauty and a joy for ever, at least as perfect as the combined wisdom of the department and the draftsmen can make it. Draftsmen are usually compelled to work at high pressure. As one of them has said, they must bear in mind the Horatian exhortation, *nocturna versate manu, versate diurna*[1], for what appeared to the tired eye in the watches of the night to be without blemish may be full of errors and inconsistencies under the cold light of morning. Moreover, as the departmental officials begin to understand, perhaps through criticism in the House or elsewhere, what it is that they and their minister and the Cabinet have approved, they may be appalled at what they have asked Parliament to accept. Other officials, perhaps in other departments, cast a wary eye over the sections likely to affect them; for no official ever trusts another. For these reasons the process of departmental amendment may proceed as long as the Bill is before either House, though every such amendment must be moved in and accepted by the House. Nevertheless, this is not the most fruitful source of ministerial amendments. The importance of organised interests in the initiation of legislation has already been stressed; their importance as critics of legislative proposals is even greater. Economic interests, especially, are organised primarily for protection, and such protection involves close examination of all Bills in order to prevent, if possible, the passing of adverse or restrictive legislation. Organisations directed towards improved social conditions, on the other hand, are more likely

---

[1] Sir William Graham-Harrison, 'An Examination of the Main Criticisms of the Statute Book and of the Possibility of Improvement', *Journal of the Society of Public Teachers of Law*, 1935, p. 45.

to suggest increased governmental powers or, what is not always the same thing, additional restrictions on private action. In between may be placed bodies like the associations of local authorities, who on the one hand seek to protect the kind of local authority which they represent, and on the other hand are always anxious to make their own powers more effective.

The practice of prior consultation frequently avoids the necessity for amendment; and where there is such consultation it may generally be assumed that the minister in charge is not open to further private pressure, and that action must be taken through private members. Also, where the report of a commission or committee proposes legislation which will necessarily affect the interest concerned, that interest gets in on the ground floor by sending in a memorandum and, perhaps, asking for an interview before the Bill is prepared. Frequently, however, neither process is possible because the interest is affected only incidentally or because it is not the particular kind of interest which is usually consulted. For instance, a Trunk Roads Bill, 1936, was introduced without prior consultation with the National Association of Local Government Officers, and the Association pressed, unsuccessfully, for an amendment to be proposed by the minister for compensating any local government officer displaced as a result of the transfer of trunk roads from county councils to the Minister of Transport.[1] Certain amendments were made in the Local Government Bill, 1933, as a result of representations to the Minister of Health by the Conjoint Conference of Public Utility Associations,[2] and by the Bribery and Secret Commissions Prevention League,[3] among other bodies. Bills in respect of which representations were made by the Federation of British Industries in a single year included the Rating and Valuation Bill, 1927,[4] the Company Law Amendment Bill, 1927,[5] and the Finance Bill, 1927.[6] Examples of similar action by the associations of local authorities are far too numerous even for representative examples to be noted.

[1] N.A.L.G.O. in 1936, p. 53.
[2] British Waterworks Association, *Official Circular*, 1934, pp. 405–6.
[3] News-Sheet of the Bribery and Secret Commissions Prevention League, 1936, p. 53; *Bribery, its Prevalence and Prevention* (3rd ed.), p. 9.
[4] *British Industries*, x, p. 53.　　　　　[5] *Ibid.* p. 253.
[6] *Ibid.* pp. 300, 304.

From this process it results that as soon as a Bill is published representations are made by all the interests affected, unless their concurrence has already been obtained. These representations are considered by the appropriate officials and, if necessary, deputations are received by a minister or by some senior official. If it is considered possible either to accept the amendments or to make amendments which to some extent meet the representations, the necessary amendments are drafted by the draftsmen and are moved by the minister in committee. The first and most effective step for any interest is thus to convince the department. There is, however, a second line of defence. It is always possible for the representatives of the interest in Parliament to put down the amendments.[1] At this stage the minister may have relented, or he may be persuaded to relent as a result of the debate.

For instance, the proposals of the National Association of Local Government Officers for the amendment of the Trunk Roads Bill, 1936—which are mentioned above and were rejected by the minister— were put down by two of the Association's parliamentary vice-presidents, and were pressed to a division, but were defeated.[2] On the other hand, amendments to the Housing Bill, 1935, proposed by the Association, were accepted by the minister in Standing Committee.[3] In respect of the Bill which became the Road Traffic Act, 1934, it is alleged that the representations of the Association resulted in the postponement of the measure for a session, the amendments being ultimately accepted in Standing Committee.[4] It is to be noted that in this case the Association communicated with the Opposition. Similar examples could be drawn from a wide range of interests.

It is evident that this method of operation verges upon a system of lobbying. It is a common practice for memoranda to be circulated to members and for meetings to be called by interested members in committee rooms. Sometimes pressure can be applied through the constituencies; but usually this can be done only where the subject is

---

[1] A member, 'as honorary vice-president of the Meat Traders' Association', suggested an amendment to the Food and Drugs Bill, 1938—but this was before a joint select committee: *The Times*, 11 May 1938.

[2] N.A.L.G.O. in 1936, p. 53.

[3] N.A.L.G.O., Reports, etc., 1936, p. 72.

[4] *Ibid.* 1934, pp. 53–4; 1935, p. 38.

of some general interest. Thus, as part of its agitation against the Incitement to Disaffection Bill, 1934, members of the National Council for Civil Liberties 'called out' their representatives by means of a 'mass lobby'. Here, however, we leave the process of securing amendment and approach that of obtaining the withdrawal of the Bill.

It must be emphasised that the aim is not to persuade members of Parliament but to coerce the Government. Parliamentary action is taken only if private representations to the department prove ineffective. Majority Governments are not defeated in the House and are rarely defeated in Standing Committees; if they are defeated in Standing Committees they can insist on the reversal of the vote in the House. The most effective method is to secure amendment before the Bill is introduced; the next most effective method is to persuade the Government before the committee stage is reached. Often the amendment is put down only by way of precaution, because negotiations are proceeding and it is believed that they will prove fruitful before the amendment is reached. If the minister does not give way beforehand, a debate may induce him to do so, or at least to agree to 'consider' the point, or to accept a compromise. It is his business to get the Bill through the House as easily as possible, without bringing too much pressure to bear on his followers, by peaceful persuasion rather than by the whip. Lobbying may prove effective by raising a public opinion in the House, but only because Governments are very susceptible to the pressure of opinion from their own supporters. Every Government does, in fact, insist on rejecting amendments which many of the majority would like to see accepted; for, in the last resort, the majority will line up to pass through the lobby where the Government whips are to be found. Members appeal to the minister to accept amendments; they do not compel.

The position is not quite the same in the House of Lords. There, amendments are quite frequently passed against the Government, and it is a regular practice when the Labour or Liberal party is in power. Insistence by the House of Lords involves a conflict between the two Houses. With a Conservative Government, the Lords do not insist on their amendments; with any other Government the question becomes one of tactics as between the Government on the one hand and the

Opposition (including the majority of the peers) on the other. If the amendment does not go to the root of the Bill, a game of bluff is played, the Government threatening that the Bill will be withdrawn, and the House of Lords that it will not be passed. If the amendment does go to the root of the Bill, it becomes a matter of pure politics.

When the minister finds an amendment on the paper, he is briefed as to his answer. If the sense of the House is against him, however, he may decide that he ought to give way. In order that his parliamentary instinct may not lead him to make undesirable concessions, and that he may give reasonably accurate replies to points raised in debate, a departmental official and the draftsman are seated in the 'box'[1] and communications pass through his parliamentary private secretary or 'fetch-and-carry man'.[2] 'It is a very precarious kind of contact, and the information they give is sometimes given in such circumstances that the minister cannot fully comprehend it. Little slips of paper are passed backwards and forward.'[3] In a Standing Committee the officials are even closer at hand, sitting at the table,[4] and the minister can turn to consult them directly. In either case it is sometimes necessary for the draftsman there and then to supply a form of words. 'Many an amendment so drafted has come out all right, but there is always a risk of disaster; happily, in late years there has been a considerable diminution

[1] The 'box' is a seat under the gallery, near the Treasury Bench, provided for the use of officials. Until 1906 this seat was at the opposite end of the House, and Sir Courtenay Ilbert, Parliamentary Counsel, drew public attention to the inconvenience in 1901 (*Legislative Methods and Forms*, p. 89). In the recess of 1906 the seats were altered: H.C. 161 of 1931, Q. 3377. The 'box' is technically not part of the House.

[2] Sir William Bull, who was parliamentary private secretary to Mr Walter Long, President of the Board of Trade and in charge of the Metropolitan Water Board Bill, 1902, has thus described his function:

'I sat behind the Ministry all through....Long never turns his head but gives directions this wise: Bull, ask the whips on the other side if we will give them two more representatives on the L.C.C. will they let the clause go through to-night.

See Sir A. Provis and see he approves of Amendment 51.

Stanhope is outside—say I can't come out, and find out what he wants.

See what Gladstone said in 1886 about unconstitutional amendments.

Take a note of what Tim Healy is saying. I shall be back directly.' Sir Charles Petrie, *Walter Long and his Times*, p. 66.

[3] H.C. 161 of 1931, Q. 1804.

[4] *Ibid.* Q. 1805. The Chairman sits at a small table on a dais, with officials of the House on one side and the departmental officials and the draftsman on the other. The minister usually sits at the top of the table on the floor below, and thus near his advisers.

in impromptu amendment of this kind.'[1] Normally, the minister undertakes to consider the matter before report stage, or to secure the putting down of an amendment in 'another place'.

The result of this process is that from its inception to its passing a Government Bill is essentially under the control of a minister and the drafting under the control of Parliamentary Counsel to the Treasury. It is not only a Government Bill but the Government's Bill. The enacting clause, which states that it is enacted by the Queen 'by and with the advice and assent' of the two Houses and 'by authority of the same', is now wholly accurate only if by 'Queen' is understood the Government. It must be emphasised, however, that the 'authority' is more than formal. Though it is true that the Government can force through the House of Commons any legislation that it thinks fit, its close dependence upon public opinion compels it to give way to a clear expression of opinion, especially where that opinion is expressed in the House or in the lobbies. The Incitement to Disaffection Bill, 1934, and the Population (Statistics) Bill, 1937, are examples of measures which have been fundamentally modified by the Government because of adverse criticism; and the Coal Mines Bill, 1936, and the original National Defence Contribution of 1937 were withdrawn altogether after debate.

Where an interest is entirely opposed to legislation, therefore, its task is to rouse public opinion against it. The Coal Mines Bill, 1930, provides a good example, though it is rather complicated because the Labour Government had no majority in either House.[2] The process of consultation prior to the introduction of the Bill has already been explained.[3] Even before the Bill was introduced, however, the Mining Association made public pronouncements of its own views,[4] and other interests, such as Chambers of Commerce, the National Gas Council, and the National Association of Merchants and Manufacturers, gave public support.[5] The London Chamber of Commerce sent protests to members

---

[1] Sir William Graham-Harrison, 'An Examination of the Main Criticisms of the Statute Book and of the Possibility of Improvement', *Journal of the Society of Public Teachers of Law*, 1935, p. 31.
[2] The Coal Mines Bill, 1938, had a similar background, however.
[3] *Ante*, p. 210.
[4] *Iron and Coal Trades Review*, 1929, p. 732.
[5] *Ibid.* 1929, p. 858; *ibid.* 1930, pp. 61, 105 and *passim*.

of both Houses.[1] While the Bill was before Parliament, the Federation of British Industries, the National Federation of Iron and Steel Manufacturers, the Association of British Chambers of Commerce, the British Coal Exporters' Federation, and the Welsh Plate and Sheet Manufacturers Association, published memoranda or resolutions against what the Federation described as 'an attack upon the fundamental rights of property'.[2] In the House of Lords the lead against the Bill was taken by Lord Londonderry, Lord Gainford, Lord Melchett and Lord Joicey, who were described with truth as 'but a few of those members of the Upper House who have practical and first-hand knowledge of the business of coal-mining', and whose efforts resulted, after a conflict between the Houses, in radical amendment of the Bill.

Such a combination of vested interests can be successful against a Labour Government only because of the existence of the Conservative majority in the House of Lords. Where similar massed attack develops against a Conservative Government, the Government must give way. For though it cannot be contended, in view of the wide franchise, that the Conservative party is representative only of vested interests other than Labour, it is undoubted that its foundation rests, both electorally and financially, on private enterprise in trade, industry, and agriculture. Vested interests expect to be defended, not attacked, by a Conservative Government; and when such a Government proceeds further along the path of collectivisation than the interests think desirable in their own and (what is in their view the same thing) the national interest, they protest more in sorrow than in anger. They succeeded in compelling the Government to withdraw the Coal Mines Bill, 1936, and the original National Defence Contribution, partly by direct pressure on the Government by memoranda and deputations, partly by publicity outside Parliament, and partly by circularising and sending direct representations to members of Parliament.

[1] *Iron and Coal Trades Review*, 1930, p. 105.
[2] *Ibid.* 1930, pp. 188, 215, 262.

CHAPTER VIII

THE PROCESS OF LEGISLATION

I. GENERAL CHARACTERISTICS

It has already been emphasised[1] that such time as is available for the process of legislation is nearly all occupied by Government Bills or by Bills for which facilities are provided by the Government. Between 1925 and 1929 Government legislation occupied $267\frac{1}{2}$ days, while private members' Bills occupied seventy-three Fridays, the equivalent of $36\frac{1}{2}$ days. Comprehensive figures given to the Select Committee on Procedure in 1946[2] may be summarised as follows:

	Averages in Days	
Sessions	Government Bills	Private Members' Bills
1906–13	62·1	10·5
1919–29	48·3	11·4
1929–38	61·7	12·2
General Averages	56·5	11·4

It must be remembered, too, that in the later period more and more Government Bills were sent to Standing Committees and that the closure, the kangaroo and the guillotine accelerated the process of passing. The following figures[3] are averages:

Sessions	Legislative Days per Session	Statutes per Session	Statute Book Pages per Session	Pages per Legislative Day
1906–13	72·6	49·6	355	4·9
1919–29	59·7	57·7	641·8	10·75
1929–38	73·9	57·0	995	13·46

No private members' Bill goes through unless it secures an early place in the ballot or unless it is so non-controversial that not a single member desires to oppose it. Less than one-fifth of the Bills introduced by private members pass the House (see Table IV, p. 236); and the fact

[1] *Ante*, pp. 21–2.　　　　[2] H.C. 189 of 1945–6, pp. l–liii.
[3] *Ibid.* p. 356.

TABLE IV

The following table gives particulars for the Parliament of 1924–9:[1]

	Balloted Bills		Ten Minutes' Rule Bills*		Other Bills*	
Session	Introduced	Passed	Introduced	Passed	Introduced	Passed
1924–5	34	6	20	4	47	5
1926	31	8	19	2	31	3
1927	30	7	17	—	56	2
1928	24	8	27	3	45	4
1928–9†	—	—	19	2	30	6
Totals	119	29	102	11	209	20

*These proceed, if at all, as unopposed Bills.
†Government took all private members' time.

The following table marks the difference between private members' and Government Bills:

	Government Bills		Private members' Bills	
Session	Introduced	Passed	Introduced	Passed
1931–2	49	48	27	9
1932–3	44	41	62	14
1933–4	54	50	60	10
1934–5	49	44	10	3
Total for Parliament	196	183	159	36
1935–6	44	42	55	12
1936–7	60	59	51	13

that so many do not pass necessarily means that a great many more are never introduced.

Private members' Bills follow the same procedure as Government Bills, subject to certain qualifications. In the first place, a substantial number of private members' Bills are introduced under the Ten Minutes' Rule[2] for purposes of propaganda, whereas in practice Government Bills are never so introduced. In the second place, a private member cannot proceed beyond second reading with a Bill containing a money clause unless a financial resolution is moved in Committee by a minister of the Crown; and in practice such a Bill is not introduced by a private member.[3] In the third place, most private members' Bills are in practice

[1] See H.C. 161 of 1931, p. 439.   [2] See *post*, p. 250.   [3] See *post*, pp. 254–66.

taken in Standing Committee and not in Committee of the Whole House. Since in other respects they follow the same procedure as Government Bills, and since the time of the House is mostly occupied by the latter, it will be assumed in the present chapter that Bills are introduced and managed on behalf of the Government.

The law knows nothing of the legislative process. An Act which appears on the Roll of Parliament as having been enacted by the Queen on the advice of the two Houses, or of the House of Commons alone under the Parliament Acts, 1911 and 1949, is good law whatever the method adopted for its passage. The so-called *Statutum de Tallagio non concedendo* is an Act of Parliament even though it was never passed by Parliament, because it appears on the Parliament Roll and was decided in the *Case of Ship-money*[1] to be a statute. If it be true, as Burnet asserts,[2] that the Habeas Corpus Act, 1679, was passed only by counting a fat lord as ten lords, it is nevertheless an Act. The practice of having three readings in each House dates from time immemorial. It was in use when the Journals began in the sixteenth century, and seems to have followed close upon the beginning of the process of legislating by Bill.[3] Even now it is not provided, though it is assumed, by Standing Orders;[4] and there is nothing to prevent the House from suspending these Standing Orders by resolution, after debate.

The Standing Orders do not prevent all the stages of a Bill from being taken on the same day. Just before the outbreak of war, on 3 August 1914, the Chancellor of the Exchequer moved to suspend Standing Orders in order to consider a Bill authorising the Crown to suspend payments under bills of exchange and other obligations. Mr Speaker pointed out that the resolution was unnecessary. Mr Lloyd George asked leave to introduce the Bill; leave was granted and the Bill read a first and second time without debate. The House went immediately

---

[1] (1637) 3 St.Tr. 825.
[2] 'Lord Grey and Lord Norris were named to be the tellers. Lord Norris, being a man subject to vapours, was not at all times attentive to what he was doing; so a very fat lord coming in, Lord Grey counted him for ten, as a jest at first, but, seeing Lord Norris had not observed it, he went on with this misreckoning of ten; so it was reported to the House, and declared that they who were for the Bill were the majority, though it indeed went on the other side; and by this means the Bill passed': Burnet, *History of his own Time* (1724 ed.), I, p. 485.
[3] Redlich, I, p. 22.   [4] S.O. 35–54.

into Committee. The Bill had not been printed, and Mr Lloyd George read it out. It was passed through Committee without discussion, read a third time after a short debate, and sent to the House of Lords. It was there passed through all stages and received the royal assent the same evening.[1] The same procedure was followed on 5 August 1914, on the Prize Courts (Procedure) Bill,[2] and the Aliens Restriction Bill.[3] On 6 August 1914, the Currency and Bank Notes Bill was passed in the same way;[4] and the Electoral Disabilities (Removal) Bill[5] and the Police Reservists Allowances Bill[6] were passed through all stages in the House of Commons. On 7 August 1914, the Army (Supply of Food, Forage and Stores) Bill[7] and the Patents, Designs and Trade Marks Bill,[8] were enacted, and the Defence of the Realm Bill[9] passed through all stages in the House of Commons. On 8 August 1914 (a Saturday), Parliament passed the Unreasonable Withholding of Foodstuffs Bill,[10] and on 10 August the Special Constables (Scotland) Bill.[11] The same procedure was followed just before the outbreak of war in 1939.

These examples show that the House of Commons—and Parliament as a whole—can expedite its procedure when urgency is required. Normally, however, the procedure is leisurely, so leisurely that there is always complaint of lack of time. There used to be a process known as 'the slaughter of the innocents', which occurred at the end of the

[1] 65 H.C.Deb. 5 s., 1805–9. In the House of Lords the necessary Standing Orders were suspended, following the precedent adopted in 1883 on the Explosive Substances Bill. The Lords' Orders, like the Commons', do not insist on three readings, though they imply this rule. But by Lords' S.O. 41, no Bill shall be read twice the same day, nor reported on the same day as the committee goes through it, nor read a third time on the day that it is reported. The House had been adjourned, except for judicial business, but the Lord Chancellor held that it was properly constituted, since the meeting was merely the adjournment of the meeting for judicial business—an argument not easily followed. See 17 H.L.Deb. 5 s., 311–20. Actually, the proclamation authorised by the Bill had been issued on the previous day.
[2] 65 H.C.Deb. 5 s., 1985–6; 17 H.L.Deb. 5 s., 383–5.
[3] 65 H.C.Deb. 5 s., 1986–90; 17 H.L.Deb. 5 s., 386.
[4] 65 H.C.Deb. 5 s., 2101–7; 17 H.L.Deb. 5 s., 443–8.
[5] 65 H.C.Deb. 5 s., 2108–10; royal assent next day.
[6] 65 H.C.Deb. 5 s., 2138–9; royal assent next day.
[7] 65 H.C.Deb. 5 s., 2186; 17 H.L.Deb. 5 s., 456.
[8] 65 H.C.Deb. 5 s., 2187; 17 H.L.Deb. 5 s., 470.
[9] 65 H.C.Deb. 5 s., 2191–3; royal assent next day.
[10] 65 H.C.Deb. 5 s., 2212–13; 17 H.L.Deb. 5 s., 481–2.
[11] 65 H.C.Deb. 5 s., 2296–7; 17 H.L.Deb. 5 s., 497.

session when all the Bills for which time could not be found were regretfully dropped. The planning of the time-table by the chief whip[1] and by the Cabinet on the advice of the Future Legislation Committee[2] has made the process much less spectacular, so that some are tempted to believe that the House has ample time for what the Government requires it to do; in truth, however, there are few innocents to be slaughtered because most of the innocents are kept back in the departments, awaiting the day when they may be brought forth to meet their fate. The situation has not altered essentially since 1912, when Mr Asquith said:

> I do not exaggerate when I say that if you were to sit continuously during the whole twelve months of the year, and worked through them with unremitting ardour and assiduity, you would find at the end not only that there were still large arrears of legislation which you had not even attempted to overtake, not only enormous sums raised by taxation whose appropriation had never even been discussed, but that there were vast areas of the Empire— I do not now speak of the self-governing Dominions—for which we are still directly responsible as trustees, to whose concerns we had not been able to afford so much as one single night.[3]

That, as the Prime Minister added, was the case for Home Rule for Ireland. Yet it was the unanimous opinion of those who gave evidence on the point before the Select Committee of 1931 that the creation of the Irish Free State had not substantially relieved the pressure.[4] Though the closure and the kangaroo are now normal parts of the procedure, and the guillotine is available for use as occasion may require, the pressure is as great as ever; for the problems coming before Parliament are wider in scope, greater in intensity, and often more urgent in their need.[5] Apart from the deterioration in world affairs since 1931, the

---

[1] See *ante*, pp. 76–7.   [2] See *Cabinet Government*, pp. 199–200.
[3] 36 H.C.Deb. 5 s., 1405.
[4] 1931, H.C. 161, Q. 4 (Mr MacDonald); Qs. 210, 212 (Mr Baldwin); Q. 548 (Mr Lloyd George).
[5] The Factories Bill which formed the basis of the Factories Act, 1937, was introduced in 1924 but proceeded no further than the first reading. It was promised in the King's Speech for the session 1924–5 but was not introduced owing to lack of time. In 1926 it was promised for that Parliament; the 1924 Bill was, however, introduced as a private member's Bill, but rejected on the ground that it ought to be a Government Bill. Another Bill was introduced for purposes of discussion by the Government later in the session

intervention of the State in industrial and commercial legislation has required not only more legislation but legislation of a more complicated and detailed character.

The closure, the kangaroo and the guillotine are the instruments for driving legislation through at a reasonable pace. The closure is used on all kinds of motions, and has been discussed elsewhere;[1] the kangaroo and the guillotine are normally used for legislation only.[2]

Under the kangaroo power, the Speaker on the report stage, the chairman of Ways and Means in committee of the whole House, and the chairman of a standing committee, have power to select the new clauses or amendments to be proposed.[3] This power grew out of the 'kangaroo closure' which is still in Standing Orders, though it is rarely used.[4] Under the kangaroo closure a member may claim to move that the question that words stand part of a clause or that a clause stand part of a Bill be now put. This motion, if permitted by the Chairman and carried, ruled out all amendments not put. Occasionally the Chairman indicated that certain of the amendments were worth discussing while others were not: in other words, he intimated that he might accept the closure motion if it were not agreed that the unimportant amendments should be withdrawn, but would not accept it if they were.[5] In 1909 an amendment was made to Standing Orders permitting a motion to be made, with the assent of the Chair, empowering the Chair to select amendments. Such a motion had to be put without amendment or debate. The occasion for this change was the Finance Bill of 1909,

---

but not proceeded with. In 1927 the Prime Minister regretted that owing to pressure of business the Bill could not be introduced that session, but the Home Secretary promised that it should become law by 1928. In 1928 the Prime Minister regretted that it could not be introduced that session owing to lack of time, but hoped it would be passed in 1929. In the following session the Prime Minister regretted that time did not permit the introduction of the Bill in that session. It was promised in the King's Speeches of 1929–30 and 1930–1—but need the tale be continued?

[1] *Ante*, pp. 127–30.

[2] Though technically there is no reason why they should not be used on other occasions; see as to kangaroo the terms of S.O. 31.

[3] S.O. 57, applied to standing committees by S.O. 57 (5) (introduced in 1932).

[4] See S.O. 29 (3) and *ante*, p. 130, n. 3.

[5] See the examples quoted by Mr Asquith: 8 H.C.Deb. 5 s., 1214–16. Examples may be found in 315 Hans.Deb. 3 s., 1313; 41 Parl.Deb. 4 s., 129; 42 Parl.Deb. 4 s., 39; 74 Parl.Deb. 4 s., 519; 158 Parl.Deb. 4 s., 1511; 6 H.C.Deb. 5 s., 1663.

which had already been in committee for fourteen days, though only nine clauses had been carried. It was stated by a member that the amendments occupied 70,000 pages.[1] Mr Balfour, who was stated by a member to have spoken 'with moderation', described the rule as 'martial law'.[2] However, it was accepted by the House and was used on the remaining stages of the Bill, but only in respect of groups of amendments.[3] In 1919 the rule was altered to its present form,[4] which no longer requires a motion, but is an ordinary part of the procedure. It was extended to standing committees in 1932.

The Standing Order empowers the Chair to call upon a member to explain his amendment; and this is sometimes done, though usually the Speaker or Chairman consults the member privately if he does not know exactly what the amendment is intended to do.

Its effectiveness cannot be checked by figures. On a general impression it is most effective on the report stage of Bills, where it is chiefly used by the Speaker to dispose of amendments which have been adequately debated in committee. In committee it is more sparingly used, generally only for amendments which are of little substance or doubtfully in order—seldom for substantial amendments. It cannot deal with obstruction on an important Bill, or be a substitute for the closure. But it is very valuable where a Bill is being debated under the guillotine, in helping the House to make the best use of the time allotted by concentrating on the most important amendments.[5]

Its use is not, however, restricted to such occasions, since it is a recognised means of accelerating the consideration of Bills. The Speaker and the Chairman discuss all amendments carefully with the draftsman in order that the most suitable amendments may be selected.[6]

Closure by compartments, usually known as 'the guillotine', was introduced under the Urgency Rules made by the Speaker in 1881. The second series of these rules enabled a motion to be made, to be put

---

[1] 11 H.C.Deb. 5 s., 1049 (Mr George Toulmin). There were 16 pages of amendments to clause 11: 9 H.C.Deb. 5 s., 252. The statement is not credible.

[2] 8 H.C.Deb. 5 s., 1220.

[3] See, e.g., the first occasion, 9 H.C.Deb. 5 s., 111 (9 August 1909).

[4] The new rule was moved by Sir Gordon Hewart on behalf of Mr Bonar Law, Mr Balfour's successor in the Conservative leadership.

[5] G. F. M. Campion, 'Methods of Closure in the Commons', *Journal of the Society of Clerks-at-the-Table in Empire Parliaments*, I, p. 23.

[6] H.C. 189 of 1945–6, Qs. 3133–4.

without debate, for the Chairman to report the Bill by a certain date, or that consideration be concluded by a certain date. Such a motion, to be carried, required a majority of three to one: but, if carried, only one speech could be made on each new clause or amendment (or two speeches if the new clause or amendment were moved by the member in charge of the Bill).[1] A different method was used on the Criminal Law Amendment (Ireland) Bill of 1887. Mr W. H. Smith, leader of the House, moved on 10 June 1887 that if the Bill were not reported by 17 June, the Chairman should proceed to put the remaining clauses without debate.[2] Nineteen days had then been occupied in committee, and only five of the twenty clauses had been passed; but only one more clause was debated before the guillotine fell. The guillotine was used again on the Bill to set up the Parnell Enquiry Tribunal in 1888, though it had been in committee for three days only.[3]

The guillotine was used on the Home Rule Bill of 1893 and the Evicted Tenants (Ireland) Bill, 1894. The resolution was now more scientifically drafted; separate dates and times were fixed for the various clauses and stages; and authority was given for Government amendments to be moved and put without debate after the fall of the guillotine. Such a resolution was passed for the Education Bill, 1902.[4] This Bill had already been in committee for thirty-eight days; but the (Liberal) Opposition vehemently protested, and challenged a division on every possible occasion. One night members were obliged to tramp through the division lobbies twenty-two times between 11 p.m. and 3 a.m.[5] However, the new Liberal Government proposed a resolution when the Education Bill, 1906, had been in committee for six days only.[6] For the Old Age Pensions Bill, 1908, a guillotine resolution was passed before the House went into committee, and time was allocated for the various clauses in committee, on report, and third reading. It was said by a Conservative leader that this Bill was 'so severely guillotined that much

---

[1] Redlich, I, pp. 166–7.
[2] Redlich, I, pp. 180–1; see also *Life of W. H. Smith*, II, p. 199; *Life of Gladstone*, III, p. 378; *Life of Arthur James Balfour*, I, p. 135.
[3] *Life of Gladstone*, III, p. 401.   [4] Redlich, III, p. 274.
[5] *Life of Sir Robert Morant*, p. 196.
[6] For the text, see 158 Parl.Deb. 4 s., 1395. The guillotine was used also on the Licensing Bill, 1904, and the Aliens Bill, 1905.

of the Bill went undiscussed'.[1] The motion for the Licensing Bill, 1908, adopted the schedule form which has now become usual.[2] Mr Balfour then pointed out that the guillotine had been used twice between 1886 and 1892, twice between 1892 and 1895, not at all between 1895 and 1900, three times from 1900 to 1905 and ten times between 1905 and 1908.[3]

The National Insurance Bill, 1911, followed rather a peculiar procedure. After fourteen days in committee, Part II was committed to a standing committee, while the rest remained in committee of the whole House subject to a guillotine resolution.[4] Mr E. F. Wise, who watched the procedure as Clerk of the House and was afterwards on the Insurance Commission, said in 1931 that the parts which needed amendment soon afterwards were those discussed in the House, while those parts which went through the guillotine or were for some other reason not amended in the House required no amendment for several years.[5]

The guillotine was not used on the Finance Bill of 1909, but was used on the Finance Bill of 1909–10, for which a most complicated resolution was passed.[6] It covered not only all the proceedings on the Bill itself, but also on the preceding financial resolutions. Lord Snowden's statement that the guillotine was never applied to a Finance Bill before that of 1931 is correct if the peculiar Bill of 1909–10 be excluded.[7] The Government of Ireland Bill, 1912, was also passed under the guillotine. Of fifty-one clauses, only twenty were partly discussed, and only six were fully discussed.[8] Further examples need not, however, be given. It may be said generally that the Liberal Government of 1905–14 and the Labour Governments of 1929–31 and 1945–51 used the guillotine more frequently than any other Governments since 1881. The Labour Government of 1945–51 had an immense programme which could not have been completed without frequent use of the guillotine in standing committee as well as on the floor of the House.

The guillotine resolution is usually settled by the Government. It is believed, however, that in recent years an attempt has been made to

[1] Sir Austen Chamberlain, *Politics from Inside*, p. 127.
[2] 192 Parl.Deb. 4 s., 1235–40.
[3] *Ibid.* 1242.
[4] 30 H.C.Deb. 5 s., 111–15.   [5] H.C. 161 of 1931, Q. 2161.
[6] 16 H.C.Deb. 5 s., 1725–30.   [7] Snowden, *Autobiography*, II, p. 907.
[8] Colvin, *Life of Lord Carson*, II, p. 159.

secure agreement 'through the usual channels'. The need for a resolution on the Government of India Bill, 1935, was avoided by the setting
up of a committee representing all parties, which arrived at an agreement
as to the allocation of time under a time-table.[1] A certain amount of
latitude was allowed, and the committee remained in existence to make
any modifications that might be considered desirable.[2] Such meetings
were in fact held; and occasional appeals by the Chairman and goodwill
on all sides enabled the Bill to be passed without suspending the eleven
o'clock rule or the use of the guillotine or closure, though the kangaroo
was used somewhat drastically. The Bill was the longest ever placed
before Parliament, and was hotly contested by a section as large as the
old Irish party and, on some matters, by the Opposition as well.

It was suggested by Mr Winston Churchill, the leader of the unofficial opposition to the Bill, that this procedure might enable the
House to recover some of the flexibility in its procedure which it had
lost by the reforms since 1881. Mr Ramsay MacDonald suggested in
1931 that all Bills taken on the floor of the House should be subject to
the guillotine, but that the resolution should not be put until it had
been considered by an all-party committee.[3] In 1945 the Government
suggested a formal committee, consisting of the Speaker's Panel of
Chairmen and five other members, to allocate the time after a guillotine
resolution had been passed.[4] The Select Committee on Procedure of
1946 preferred to leave this to a sub-committee of the standing committee concerned,[5] and the Government accepted this alteration.
Accordingly Standing Order 64, introduced in 1947, provides that a
guillotine order relating to the committee stage of a Bill in standing
committee shall stand referred, without question put, to the business
sub-committee of the standing committee. This sub-committee reports
to the standing committee:

(a) the number of sittings to be allotted to the consideration of the Bill;

(b) the allocation of the proceedings to be taken at each sitting; and

(c) the time at which proceedings, if not previously brought to a conclusion, shall be concluded.

[1] 297 H.C.Deb. 5 s., 1710–11 and 1936–7.
[2] See the statement by the chairman of Ways and Means, 298 H.C.Deb. 5 s., 193–6.
[3] H.C. 161 of 1931, Q. 35.   [4] H.C. 9 of 1945–6, pp. xiii–xiv.
[5] Ibid. p. vii.

The sub-committee consists of the chairman of the standing committee and seven members nominated by Mr Speaker. When the sub-committee reports, its recommendations are decided upon by the standing committee without amendment or debate. If approved, they are deemed to be included in the guillotine order. If disapproved, they are referred back to the sub-committee.

It will be seen that this applies only to a Bill in standing committee; and in its Final Report[1] the Select Committee on Procedure agreed that a business committee, on the lines suggested by the Government, should be set up to allocate the time where a guillotine resolution applied to a committee of the whole House or on report. Standing Order 41 therefore sets up a business committee consisting of the chairmen's panel and five other members nominated by Mr Speaker. This Committee:

(1) shall, in the case of any Bill in respect of which a guillotine order has been made, allocating time in committee of the whole House or on report, divide the Bill and allot to each part so many days or portions of days;

(2) may, if the committee thinks fit, do the same where days have been allotted by general agreement notified orally by a minister (i.e. by arrangement between the whips); and

(3) shall report their recommendations to the House.

These recommendations can, however, be debated by the House.

The Labour Government in fact referred all its major Bills to standing committee and secured the passing of a guillotine resolution which was worked out in detail by the business sub-committee under Standing Order 64.[2]

These arrangements have given much greater flexibility to the guillotine procedure. The main difficulty as the guillotine now operates is that too much time is spent on the initial clauses.[3] This difficulty arose on the Government of India Bill, but it was overcome partly by agreement that there should be four days not allocated which could be used if necessary, and partly by the willingness of the Chairman, knowing that he had an agreed scheme, to use the kangaroo. Usually the Chairman hesitates either to use the kangaroo or to accept a closure motion while

---

[1] H.C.189 of 1945–6, p. 50.
[2] See, for instance, Morrison, *Government and Parliament*, pp. 338–47.
[3] H.C. 161 of 1931, Q. 766 (Captain Bourne).

a guillotine resolution is in force.[1] Indeed, the closure sometimes becomes a useless instrument while the guillotine is operating. It can be used to prevent obstruction by a minority but not to prevent obstruction by a majority: but, when a guillotine is in operation, obstruction usually arises from the majority, who can prevent an 'inconvenient' question being raised by obstructing preceding clauses and amendments, knowing that the guillotine will fall at the appointed time.[2] Provision for subsequent modification, too, is essential. It is difficult to say how much time will be taken, especially on technical points. The resolution on the Local Government Bill, 1928–9, for instance, was very badly formulated.[3]

The guillotine, whether formal or informal, is, however, essential if highly controversial Bills are to be passed through strenuous opposition in a reasonable time. As has been mentioned above, it was not used on the Finance Bill of 1909. Mr Lloyd George, who was in charge of the Bill, has said:

We hardly ever went home until one or two, and sometimes six, in the morning, and were there till nine, and, in spite of that, it went on till December. Another Bill of the same kind, where I was responsible, I am afraid, for some of the waste of time, was the Education Bill of 1902. I remember Lord Derby (I think he was then a whip) coming to me. We had been keeping it up until well on into the autumn, and with late sittings, and we had not got very far, and Lord Derby said to me, 'Would you mind telling me quite frankly how long it will take at the present rate?' I said, 'I think you will get through comfortably by April of next year.' He said, 'That is exactly what Mr Balfour thinks.' Then we had the guillotine. They had the same experience exactly as we had.[4]

2. UP TO SECOND READING

It is possible for a Bill to be founded upon resolutions passed by the House. For reasons explained later,[5] this procedure is always adopted for Bills the primary purpose of which is to authorise expenditure or impose taxation. The resolutions are moved in Committee of Ways and

---

[1] H.C. 161 of 1931, Q. 60 (Captain Bourne).
[2] *Ibid.* Q. 951 (Mr Hore-Belisha).
[3] *Ibid.* Qs. 84 and 85 (Captain Bourne). See this resolution in Appendix III.
[4] *Ibid.* Q. 910.   [5] *Post*, pp. 257, 290.

Means and reported to the House, and a Bill is ordered thereon; or the Chairman is directed by the Committee to bring in a Bill (though this method is rarely used).[1] Sometimes, however, resolutions precede other kinds of Bills. The Bill for the suppression of the slave trade in 1833, for instance, was preceded by resolutions, and there are other examples.[2] Sometimes there are preliminary resolutions in committee. The Government of India Bill, 1858, and the Parliament Bill, 1910, were examples.

The reason for this procedure may be examined in relation to three well-known instances, in two of which resolutions were not in fact used. The Conservative Government of 1867 was anxious to produce a Reform Bill because, as Lord Derby put it to Mr Disraeli, it was a good hare to start.[3] Proposals for extending the franchise had, however, been made in 1852, 1854, 1859, 1860, and 1866, and had failed. The Bill of 1866 had, through the defection of the Cave of Adullam, resulted in the defeat of the Liberal Government. The Conservative Government which succeeded had no majority, it was not agreed on the terms to be incorporated in the Bill, and it did not want to be defeated. Accordingly, the Government desired what Mr Disraeli's biographer euphemistically calls 'the co-operation of the House'.[4] Mr Disraeli therefore introduced resolutions. Before these were debated, however, divisions in the Cabinet made considerable modification necessary, and Mr Disraeli is stated to have drafted new proposals in ten minutes; these he explained to the House, though he asked the House to pass the resolutions first. The hostile reception accorded to both resolutions and explanation compelled Mr Disraeli to risk resignations in the Cabinet and to revert to his own scheme of household suffrage in the towns. He withdrew the resolutions and 'gracefully covered his retreat by acknowledging a disposition on the part of the House to afford the ministerial proposals a fair and candid consideration, to secure which was the main object of proceeding by resolution'.[5] Finally, the Bill which 'dished the Whigs' was introduced.

Mr Gladstone was blamed by some for not proceeding by resolution before introducing the Home Rule Bill of 1886. The policy of Home

[1] May, p. 487. [2] Ibid. [3] Life of Disraeli, II, p. 218.
[4] Ibid. II, p. 227. [5] Ibid. II, p. 238.

Rule had been adopted by Mr Gladstone when the result of the election of 1885 was known. Some sections of the Liberal party had opposed the policy; but it is one of the lessons of history that political parties can be converted to the opposite of their policies if they are given time for thought and propaganda. Sir Robert Peel had introduced Roman Catholic Relief in 1829, Mr Disraeli had 'dished the Whigs' in 1867, and, to give a much later example, those who had fought the Government of Ireland Bills of 1912 to 1914 tooth and nail and had violently demanded that the Government secure a mandate, asked Parliament to confer Dominion status upon Ireland in 1921, and without a mandate. This being the general trend of politics, it was arguable that if Mr Gladstone could have proceeded more slowly he could have carried most of the Liberal party with him. Lord Morley gives the case and the answer:

Resolutions, it was argued, would have smoothed the way. General propositions would have found readier access to men's minds. Having accepted the general proposition, people would have found it harder to resist the general application. Devices that startled in the precision of a clause, would in the vagueness of a broad and abstract principle have soothed and persuaded. Mr Gladstone was perfectly alive to all this, but his answer to it was plain. Those who eventually threw out the Bill would have insisted on unmasking the resolutions. They would have exhausted all the stereotyped vituperation of abstract motions. They would have ridiculed any general proposition as mere platitude, and pertinaciously clamoured for working details. What would the resolution have affirmed? The expediency of setting up a legislative authority in Ireland to deal with exclusively Irish affairs. But such a resolution would be consistent equally with a narrow scheme on the one hand, such as a plan for national councils, and a broad scheme on the other, giving to Ireland a separate exchequer, separate control over customs and excise, and practically an independent and co-ordinate legislature. How could the Government meet the challenge to say outright whether they intended broad or narrow? Such a resolution could hardly have outlived an evening's debate, and would not have postponed the evil day of schism for a single week.[1]

The Parliament Bills of 1910 and 1911 were substantially founded upon resolutions as to the relations between the two Houses passed by the House of Commons in 1907.[2] After the rejection of the Finance

[1] *Life of Gladstone*, III, p. 299.
[2] 176 Parl.Deb. 4 s., 909, 1523 (26 June 1907).

Bill of 1909 and the first general election of 1910, the House resolved itself into committee 'to consider the relations between the two Houses of Parliament and the question of the duration of Parliament'.[1] Detailed resolutions, not essentially dissimilar from the provisions ultimately incorporated in the Parliament Act, were then passed by the House in committee.[2] These resolutions were reported to the House,[3] and the Parliament Bill, 1910, was then introduced.[4] The death of King Edward VII and the accession of King George V produced a new situation, and the Constitutional Conference tried to settle the question by agreement.[5] The Government thereupon decided to advise a dissolution in order to secure a mandate for the passing of the Bill and to ask for a 'guarantee' that, in the event of the Government's securing a majority and the House of Lords not passing the Bill, sufficient peers would be created to overcome the opposition of the Upper House.[6] The King insisted that the Bill should first be discussed in the House of Lords,[7] where it was read a first time[8] and discussed on second reading though no division was taken.[9] Obviously, the whole purpose of the resolutions was to enable a full debate on the Government's proposals to take place so that the issue might be submitted to the electorate for a mandate sufficient to ensure the creation of peers. Discussion on resolutions was for this purpose much more convenient than discussion on a Bill; and the resolutions were taken in committee and not in the House in order that a free debate might take place. The resolutions on which the Irish Disestablishment Bill was founded were moved for a not very dissimilar purpose. They were moved by Mr Gladstone in Opposition, and their purpose was to secure that the general election of 1868 should take place on the ground chosen by Mr Gladstone, and not on the ground chosen by the Conservative Government.[10]

These examples show that resolutions are of use only in very exceptional circumstances. To found a Bill on resolutions is merely to add an

---

[1] 15 H.C.Deb. 5 s., 1162 (29 March 1910); 16 H.C.Deb. 5 s., 169 (4 April 1910).
[2] 16 H.C.Deb. 5 s., 718–19 (money Bills); *ibid.* 1493 (general legislation); *ibid.* 1526.
[3] *Ibid.* 1531–47.
[4] *Ibid.* 1547 (14 April 1910).   [5] See *Cabinet Government*, p. 406.
[6] *Life of Lord Oxford and Asquith*, I, pp. 295–8.
[7] *Ibid.* I, p. 298; *Life of Lord Lansdowne*, p. 410.
[8] 6 H.L.Deb. 5 s., 706.   [9] *Ibid.* 777–97.
[10] Cf. H.C. 161 of 1931, Q. 943 (Mr Lloyd George).

extra stage—or, if they are taken in committee, two extra stages[1]—to the legislative procedure. If they are of a general character the debate duplicates the second reading discussion; if they are detailed, they duplicate the committee stage of the Bill itself. Resolutions might be useful if they could take the place of a second reading debate and the Bill could be introduced in a Standing Committee, or referred to it without discussion;[2] otherwise they are, apart from highly exceptional circumstances, of no value whatever.

There are two ways of introducing a Bill, with or without a motion. In either case notice must be given, though notice is prescribed in the latter case by Standing Orders[3] and in the former by the practice of the House.[4] Introduction without a motion is the practice usually followed with Government Bills and with most private members' Bills. When the Bill is presented the title is read by the Clerk at the Table, and the Bill is thus deemed to have been read a first time, and is printed.[5] This method accordingly dispenses with any debate before the second reading or the financial resolution, whichever comes first.[6] If a motion for leave to introduce a Bill is made, there may be a long debate. The famous long sitting of February 1881,[7] was on a motion for leave to bring in the Protection of Life and Property (Ireland) Bill; and such motions were also used for the Government of Ireland Bill, 1886, and the Criminal Law and Procedure (Ireland) Bill, 1887.[8] Such motions may, however, be moved under what is called the 'ten minutes' rule'.[9] On Tuesdays and Wednesdays and, if set down by the Government, on Mondays and Thursdays, motions for leave to bring in Bills may be set down for consideration at the commencement of public business, immediately after questions. If such a motion is opposed, the Speaker may permit a brief explanatory statement from the member who moves and from the member who opposes; and then, without further debate, he may put the question. This method is used by private members who desire to

---

[1] Under the guillotine resolution used for the 1910 resolutions there was no debate on the report stage.

[2] See Jennings, *Parliamentary Reform*, p. 71.   [3] S.O. 35 (2).

[4] May, p. 490. In some cases notice has been dispensed with on the ground of urgency, as in 1914 and 1939: see May, *loc. cit.*, and the Bills mentioned *ante*, pp. 237–8.

[5] S.O. 35 (2).

[6] The Lords' S.O. xxxvii says: 'Bills are seldom opposed at the first reading.'

[7] *Ante*, p. 127.   [8] May, *loc. cit.*   [9] S.O. 12.

give publicity to a measure which they do not expect to pass. In fact, however, there is rapidly growing a convention that the simplest way to deal with such measures is to ignore them. They cannot come up for second reading unless they are unopposed[1]—unless, of course, the member has been successful in the ballot, in which case he does not introduce under the ten minutes' rule—and they therefore die as quickly if leave to introduce is given as they do if it is not.

If leave to present the Bill is given, the member has to present it to the House. For this purpose he obtains from the Public Bill Office a sheet of paper on the outside of which the title of the Bill is written. In accordance with an Order passed on 10 December 1692, he then goes from his place to the bar. The Speaker calls him by name, and he answers 'A Bill, Sir.' The Speaker desires him to 'bring it up'; whereupon he carries the Bill to the Table and delivers it to the Clerk, who reads the title aloud. The Bill is then said to be 'received'.[2] Questions are then put without amendment or debate,[3] and usually without opposition, 'That this Bill be now read a first time', and 'That this Bill be printed.'

When leave to introduce is not sought, but the Bill is presented under the Standing Orders[4] after notice, the sheet of paper obtained from the Public Bill Office is carried by the member from his place to the Table; the short title is read aloud by the Clerk; and the Bill is then deemed to have been read a first time and is to be printed and published.[5] Bills from the House of Lords are read the first time, and a day fixed for the second reading, by a member informing the clerks at the table of his intention to take charge of the Bill and fixing a date for second reading.[6]

The next stage is the second reading.[7] This is the stage in which the principle of the Bill is decided. The member in charge of the Bill moves 'That the Bill be now read a second time.' There is, of course, no 'reading', but a general debate on the merits of the Bill ensues. The method for opposing is usually not just to vote in the negative. Such

[1] *Post*, p. 365.   [2] May, p. 492.
[3] S.O. 35 (2).   [4] I.e. S.O. 35 (1).
[5] A member recently discovered a new method of dealing with such Bills. A Bill having been ordered to be read a first time, a member opposed to it gave 24 July—a few days before the effective end of the session—as the date for second reading: see 324 H.C.Deb. 5 s., 250.
[6] S.O. 35 (3). For the above, see May, p. 494.
[7] For hybrid Bills, see *post*, Chapter XIII.

an opposition, if successful, merely shows that the Bill is not *then* to be read a second time. Consequently, it is usual for an amendment to be moved. This either proposes to leave out the word 'now' and to add the words 'in six months' time', or to add words inconsistent with the principle of the Bill. The former disposes of the Bill for the session, the latter indicates why the Bill should not now be read a second time. For instance, on the Parliament Bill, 1911, Mr Austen Chamberlain moved as an amendment to the motion 'That the Bill be now read a second time'—

To leave out all the words after 'That', and at the end of the Question to insert the words, 'this House would welcome the introduction of a Bill to reform the composition of the House of Lords whilst maintaining its independence as a Second Chamber, but declines to proceed with a measure which places all effective legislative authority in the hands of a Single Chamber and offers no safeguard against the passage into law of grave changes without the consent and contrary to the will of the people'.[1]

Technically, if this amendment had been carried the proposal to read the Bill a second time could have again been made by the Government. In fact, of course, the Government would at once have resigned, as Lord Palmerston resigned on the defeat of the Conspiracy to Murder Bill, 1858. There having been two dissolutions in 1910, the Government would probably not have regarded the alternative of dissolution as available, though Lord Derby's Government advised a dissolution on the defeat of the Reform Bill in 1859 when similar circumstances prevailed.

In the past, more strenuous methods of rejection were occasionally adopted.

On the 23rd January, 1562/3, a Bill was rejected and ordered to be torn; so, also, on the 17th March, 1620/21, Sir Edward Coke moved 'to have the Bill torn in the House'; and it is entered that the Bill was accordingly 'rejected and torn, without one negative'. Even so late as the 3rd June, 1772, the Lords having amended a money clause in the Corn Bill, Governor Pownall moved that the Bill be rejected, which motion being seconded, the Speaker said 'that he could do his part of the business, and toss the Bill over the table'. The Bill was rejected, and the Speaker, according to his promise, threw it over the table, 'several members on both sides of the question kicking it as they went out'.[2]

[1] 22 H.C.Deb. 5 s., 45.   [2] May, p. 506.

Only one amendment may be moved: for it is provided by Standing Orders that:

> If on an amendment to the question that the Bill be now read a second time...it is decided that the word 'now' or any words proposed to be left out stand part of the question, Mr Speaker shall forthwith declare the Bill to be read a second time.[1]

This rule was made in 1919. In effect it restricts the opportunities of third parties and private members, since the amendment put down by Her Majesty's Opposition is always the one moved. Other amendments are often put down, but for purposes of propaganda only, since they cannot be moved. Thus, on the Government of India Bill, 1935, there were really two 'oppositions', the Labour party which thought that the Bill did not go far enough towards the conferment of Dominion status, and the group of Conservative members, led by Mr Winston Churchill, who thought that control of India was being too much relaxed. The only amendment moved was that of the official Opposition.[2] When such an amendment is defeated the Speaker at once declares that the Bill is read a second time, and there is no further debate or division.

3. FINANCIAL RESOLUTIONS

For more than a century the House of Commons had only three Standing Orders, those which are now numbered 78, 79 and 81. Standing Order 79 was passed on 29 March 1707,[3] and has not since been altered. Standing Order 78 was passed on 11 June 1713, but was altered in 1852 and 1866. Standing Order 81 was passed on 25 March 1715, and has not since been altered. These three Orders, together with Standing Orders 80 and 83 to 86, are important in relation to the general question of financial control, and are considered in the next chapter: but since most modern legislation contains financial provisions it is necessary to consider specific problems in this chapter.

---

[1] S.O. 37. Words omitted refer to the third reading.
[2] 297 H.C.Deb. 5 s., 1167.
[3] As a resolution: it became a Standing Order on 29 November 1710. A resolution to the same effect was passed in 1667: Durell, *Parliamentary Grants*, p. 25 n.

For present purposes, the constitutional principles governing financial votes may be said to be the following:

1. Money is granted to the Crown by legislation, even where it is intended that some other authority or body should benefit. For instance, grants to local authorities are made by the Treasury or other department, but they must first be granted to the Crown in order that the department may have them for granting out.

2. 'This House will receive no petition for any sum relating to public service or proceed upon any motion for a grant or charge upon the public revenue, whether payable out of the Consolidated Fund or out of money to be provided by Parliament, unless recommended from the Crown.'[1]

The rule upon which this Order was based was made in 1706 and made permanent in 1713, when the financial practice of government was quite different from what it is now. The old rule was 'That this House will receive no petition for any sum relating to public service, but what is recommended from the Crown.'[2] The practice then adopted was for the Crown to ask for money by means of a message to the House. The House then passed legislation for taxation to meet the sum demanded and appropriated it to the purpose for which it was demanded. The purpose of the rule was thus to prevent a person from petitioning the House for a grant of money without a royal recommendation. The rule was extended 'by the uniform practice of the House, to all direct motions for grants, and to any motion which indirectly involves the expenditure of public money'.[3] This practice was in fact made formal procedure when the Order was amended in the nineteenth century, so that it now prevents any member from moving a motion for a grant to the Crown or to any other person without a royal recommendation.

In the modern practice, authority to spend money is generally provided by permanent legislation (authority is sometimes given by the Appropriation Act, but this method is disliked by the Comptroller and Auditor-General and by the Public Accounts Committee). In a few cases (e.g. the Civil List and the salaries of the judges) this legislation charges the expenditure on the Consolidated Fund. Usually, however, the legislation merely provides that the expenditure shall be met 'out

[1] S.O. 78.   [2] May (1st ed.), p. 325.   [3] Ibid.

of moneys provided by Parliament'. In all such cases it is therefore necessary for Parliament to provide the moneys, and this it does by annual votes which are incorporated into the annual Appropriation Act or into one of the other Consolidated Fund Acts of the year. Further, the Appropriation Act appropriates the money to specific heads. Thus, expenditure on the National Health Service is authorised by the National Health Service Act, 1946, out of 'moneys to be provided by Parliament'. The amount required each year is therefore included in the total voted by the Appropriation Act and is included in the amount appropriated to the Ministry of Health by the same Act.

The money required to furnish the Consolidated Fund with the sums necessary to meet the charges of permanent legislation and the moneys 'provided by Parliament' is raised under a completely different series of statutes. Some of the taxes are levied under permanent legislation, while some taxes are voted every year in the Finance Act. The Chancellor of the Exchequer 'balances the Budget' by proposing changes in taxation or additional taxation in resolutions which are embodied in the Finance Act. If the Budget is not balanced or is balanced by the use of money specially borrowed, the Treasury uses its statutory borrowing powers to add the necessary sums to the Consolidated Fund. The essential point is, however, that the authorisation of expenditure and the authorisation of taxation are effected by different legislation; and it is this change since 1713 which makes the Standing Order so difficult to understand. In terms, it is limited to the authorisation of expenditure. Historically, however, the authorisation of expenditure required the imposition of taxation, and the rule is therefore applied to taxation by the practice of the House, in the sense that no motion for an increase of taxation may be moved except by a minister. Thus, Erskine May says:

The principle that the sanction of the Crown must be given to every grant of money drawn from the public revenue, applies equally to the taxation levied to provide that revenue. No motion can therefore be made to impose a tax, save by a minister of the Crown, unless such tax be in substitution, by way of equivalent, for taxation at that moment submitted to the consideration of Parliament; nor can the amount of a tax proposed on behalf of the Crown be augmented, nor any alteration made in the area of imposition. In like manner, no increase can be considered either of an existing, or of a new or temporary tax for the service of the year, except on the initiative of a minister, acting on behalf of the Crown; nor can a member other than a minister move for the introduction of a Bill framed to effect a reduction of duties, which would incidentally effect the increase of an existing duty, or the imposition of a new tax, although the aggregate amount of imposition would be diminished by the provisions of the Bill.[1]

We are not at present concerned with taxation, which is discussed in the next chapter.[2] It is necessary to emphasise here that the Order applies to every provision in a Bill if that provision authorises expenditure by or on behalf of the Crown, because it is then a motion for a grant or charge upon the public revenue; and this is so even if the money has to be provided subsequently by Parliament; so that the fact that the Bill does not itself provide money is immaterial. If a Bill authorises expenditure a recommendation from the Crown is required at some stage, though the enactment of the Bill will not give the Crown the money to spend. There is nothing in this or any other Standing Order which insists that the Bill shall be introduced by a minister. Motions for the second reading of private members' Bills dealing with Old Age Pensions and Widows' Pensions have been ruled out of order, but the cases appear to come under the Standing Order next to be considered.[3]

3. This House will not proceed upon any petition, motion, or Bill, for granting any money, or for releasing or compounding any sum of money owing to the Crown, but in a committee of the whole House.[4]

This rule, laid down in Standing Orders in 1710 and not since altered, does not specifically say that a Bill which authorises expenditure must begin in a committee. It must be remembered that the old practice was simply to grant money and appropriate it in the same Act. The other case which arose under the old practice was an address to the Crown praying that money be issued or an expense be incurred. This is covered by Standing Order 82, laid down in 1821: 'This House will not proceed

---

[1] May (14th ed.), p. 511.　　　　[2] *Post*, pp. 319–21.
[3] See the cases quoted in May (14th ed.), p. 505, n. 3. The point must be made with some reserve, since some authorities consider that the Standing Order is merely declaratory of an ancient practice or 'common law' of Parliament. It has already been mentioned that the rule as to taxation rests only on practice. See memorandum of Sir Horace Dawkins, then Clerk of the House, H.C. 149 of 1937, p. 3.
[4] S.O. 79.

upon any motion for an address to the Crown, praying that any money may be issued, or that any expense may be incurred, but in a committee of the whole House.' This appears now to apply only to Consolidated Fund Bills (including the Appropriation Bill), which in any case come under Standing Order 79, and to motions (which are never moved) for expenditure out of unappropriated royal revenues. Nevertheless, Standing Order 79 is interpreted to mean that whenever a Bill authorises expenditure a financial resolution in committee of the whole House is necessary. If this interpretation were carried out strictly, there could never be a debate on a Bill until a financial resolution had been passed in committee. In fact, however, it has for long been the practice for Bills which authorise expenditure only incidentally to proceed as far as second reading without a financial resolution. Such a resolution cannot effectively be debated until the purpose of the expenditure is known, and this implies at least publication (i.e. first reading) and perhaps second reading of the Bill. Consequently, the financial clauses are printed in italics (known as 'blanks') and the financial resolution is moved in committee after the second reading debate. The financial clauses may be debated on second reading[1] but the Bill cannot go to committee because this would require a motion that the financial clause or clauses stand part of the Bill.

Where the Bill is primarily concerned with money, however, it is known as a 'money Bill' (a phrase which must not be confused with the definition in the Parliament Act, 1911, which has nothing whatever to do with the present question).[2] In such a case it was necessary until 1938 to move the financial resolution before the Bill was introduced. The test applied in practice to determine whether a Bill was a money Bill was whether there was anything substantial left in the Bill when the financial clauses were abstracted; if there was not, it was regarded as a money Bill.[3] The financial resolution and the Bill thus covered sub-

---

[1] See May, p. 752. It is therefore not quite true to say that the words in italics are treated as if they were not there. For purposes other than debate, however, this is so: 'For the purpose of second reading...I have to look at the Bill without seeing the clauses in italics. Being in italics, they are supposed not to be there, and I look upon them as blank spaces to be filled in later.' 122 H.C.Deb. 5 s., 212 (Mr Speaker Lowther).

[2] See H.C. 149 of 1937, p. 52 (Sir Maurice Gwyer and Mr Granville Ram).

[3] See *ibid.* p. 110.

stantially the same ground, and the debate on the second reading was not essentially different from the debate on the financial resolution. Select Committees in 1932 and 1937 recommended a change in Standing Orders by which *when the Bill was introduced by a minister* the financial resolution might be taken after the second reading. The House accepted the recommendation in 1938 and passed the following Standing Order:

A Bill (other than a Bill which is required to originate in Committee of Ways and Means)[1] the main object of which is the creation of a public charge may either be presented, or brought in upon an Order of the House, by a Minister of the Crown, and, in the case of a Bill so presented or brought in, the creation of the charge shall not require to be authorised by a committee of the whole House until the Bill has been read a second time, and after the charge has been so authorised the Bill shall be proceeded with in the same manner as a Bill which involves a charge that is subsidiary to its main purpose.[2]

This change does not in itself prevent a duplication of debate, since the debate on the financial resolution may be the same as that on the second reading. In the case of a Bill of importance this will clearly be so; but where the Bill is of less importance it is probable that the financial resolution will be let through without debate. While the Opposition would clearly require a debate on a preliminary financial resolution because it was the first opportunity for discussing a proposal, and would probably insist on debating the second reading also, it may be satisfied with a second reading debate and acquiesce in a formal financial resolution.

We have now to relate the two principles, that a motion for a grant or charge requires a Queen's recommendation, and that a motion for a grant (or, by practice, a charge) requires a financial resolution in committee. Under the Standing Orders, two methods of satisfying these principles are permitted. The older method is prescribed by Standing Order 83, whose terms need not be set out, but which allows the making of a motion, without notice, that to-morrow or on some future date the House will resolve itself into a committee 'to consider the making of provision' for expenditure on a subject mentioned.[3] This preliminary

---

[1] See *post*, p. 290.   [2] 331 H.C.Deb. 5 s., 65–103. See now S.O. 80.
[3] See the examples quoted in H.C. 149 of 1937, p. 2. See also the customary resolution for a Civil List Bill: cf. *ibid.* p. 53.

or 'setting-up' resolution receives the Queen's recommendation. The financial resolution is then considered in committee; but since it is the setting-up resolution and not the financial resolution which has the royal recommendation, there is nothing to prevent the committee from amending the financial resolution, even for the purpose of increasing the charge proposed, so long as the terms of the setting-up resolution are not infringed. Standing Order 78 is not broken, because the expenditure is recommended by the Crown; and Standing Order 79 is being obeyed by taking the motion in committee of the whole House.[1] The setting-up resolution was until 1919 drafted in the Public Bill Office of the House and was generally in wide terms, so that there was plenty of scope for the amendment of the financial resolution even if it was very detailed in its terms. On the other hand, when the financial resolution was passed it seems that it bound the House not to increase the charge by an amendment to the Bill, because then Standing Order 79 would be infringed. In other words, if this procedure is used, the setting-up resolution binds the committee on the financial resolution, and both resolutions bind the committee on the Bill.

This method has not been used since 1922, when Standing Order 84 was passed in its present form. This Order, originally drafted in 1919, was designed *inter alia* 'to expedite the business of the House by enforcing the appearance on the paper of money resolutions and thus enabling discussion to take place at once without the stage of the "setting up" resolution'.[2] The financial resolution is put on the paper and, if the Speaker ascertains that it has received the Queen's recommendation,[3] the House resolves itself into committee to consider it. Under this procedure, therefore, no member can move in the debate on the financial resolution to increase the charge, because another Queen's recommendation would be required for his motion; and, of course, any amendment to the Bill must be within the financial resolution, otherwise both Standing Order 78 and Standing Order 79 would be infringed.

---

[1] See ruling of Sir Edward Cornwall, 152 H.C.Deb. 5 s., 1588 (30 March 1922). This 'came as a surprise' to Parliamentary Counsel: H.C. 149 of 1937, p. 54.
[2] H.C. 149 of 1937, p. 5.
[3] The financial resolution is put on the paper with the addition of the phrase 'Queen's recommendation to be signified'. The minister in charge signifies the Queen's recommendation and the House goes into committee.

Under the new procedure, therefore, no member—be he minister or private member—can make any motion to increase the charge as set out in the financial resolution. If that resolution is sufficiently detailed, and the financial provisions of the Bill are those which are really important, the control of the House will be within very narrow limits. With the approval of the Speaker, the task of drafting financial resolutions was transferred in 1919 from the Public Bill Office, which is under the control of the House, to the Parliamentary Counsel to the Treasury, who are of course under the control of the Treasury. Consequently, the Government can, by securing a very detailed resolution, stop the House from discussing any proposal to increase the charge, or to alter the disposition of the expenditure or the purposes for which it is intended.

Consequential difficulties have arisen in respect of many Bills. The Unemployment Bill, 1933, proposed to transfer the task of administering the 'needs test' from local authorities to a new body, the Unemployment Assistance Board. The cost of allowances was to be borne by the Treasury out of moneys provided by Parliament. Apart from the constitutional question as to the composition and control of the Board, the essential question for debate was the terms on which allowances would be granted; but any amendment, for instance by a Labour member, to make the allowances more favourable was necessarily out of order, especially as the financial resolution was very detailed. In other words, the Opposition was prevented from moving amendments in order to contrast its 'generous' policy with the Government's 'harsh' proposals. Also, the Bill proposed to call upon the local authorities to contribute to the cost; but any amendment to reduce this contribution was out of order because it would have increased the cost to the Treasury. Such an amendment would not have increased the actual cost, since it would have transferred it from local taxation to national taxation; but a charge on local taxation does not require a grant from Parliament, so that in a technical sense there was an increase in the 'charge'. In view of opposition from the local authorities, the Chancellor of the Exchequer agreed to make a concession; but in order that this might be done it was necessary to move the Chairman out of the Chair and to introduce a new resolution with a new King's recommendation.[1] The result was that the

---

[1] 284 H.C.Deb. 5 s., 103–4; see the previous discussion, *ibid.* 53–63.

revised amendment came on at 8.30 a.m. after an all-night sitting, owing to obstruction by the Opposition.[1]

The financial resolution for the Depressed Areas (Development and Improvement) Bill, 1934, was so detailed that the attention of the Speaker was drawn to it. The Speaker replied that he had no powers in the matter, but he added:

> It must be evident to all hon. members that under the procedure which has been adopted by this House for some years now, members are very much restricted in their powers to move amendments either on a resolution itself or indeed on the committee stage of a Bill. If I were asked for my opinion on the subject I should say that not only has the limit been reached, but that it has been rather exceeded in the amount of detail which is put in a money resolution.[2]

Many amendments were in fact ruled out, a confused debate took place on the question of procedure, and a motion to report progress was moved.[3] The difficulty was not only that the resolution specified the sum to be spent on the depressed areas but also specified in detail what those areas were. Consequently, Opposition members could neither move to increase the amount, nor even suggest that there were depressed areas in Lancashire, for instance, not covered by the resolution.

As a result of this discussion, verbal instructions were given by the then Prime Minister to the Treasury to the effect that resolutions were to be 'drafted as flexibly as is consistent with the fundamental principle of that underlying Standing Order No. 63'.[4] Though it was stated by Parliamentary Counsel that every effort had been made to give effect to these instructions, difficulties arose on subsequent Bills. Another very detailed financial resolution was drafted for the Tithe Bill, 1936, and the Chairman ruled a number of amendments out of order. The Bill proposed to convert tithe rentcharges into redemption annuities and to make certain grants from the Consolidated Fund. Owing to the detail of the resolution, it was impossible either to increase the charge on the Consolidated Fund, or even to reduce the amounts to be given

---

[1] *Ibid.* 811.   [2] 295 H.C.Deb. 5 s., 1236.
[3] *Ibid.* 1712–58.
[4] H.C. 149 of 1937, p. vii; see also *ibid.* p. 177. The S.O. is now 78.

to the recipients of the annuities (i.e. to reduce the charge on the tithe-payer). As the Chairman said:

> If a financial resolution provides that the money is to be used for the benefit of certain recipients an amendment is out of order which would alter the recipients of the money so as to give it to recipients other than those named under the King's recommendation.[1]

This being the case, a Conservative member moved to report progress. Earl Winterton, a very experienced member, stated that there had been a suggestion that it was the object of every Government to instruct the draftsmen so to draft financial resolutions as to make it almost impossible to amend them, and this remark was received with cheers.[2]

Similar difficulties arose over the Midwives Bill, 1936,[3] the Special Areas Reconstruction (Agreement) Bill, 1936,[4] and the Special Areas (Amendment) Bill, 1937.[5] A debate on the whole question was held on 8 March 1937,[6] on the motion to repeal Standing Order 69.[7] Referring to the last-mentioned Bill, the mover said:

> Look at the present money resolution. There again we have great detail put in, quite unnecessary detail to my mind. We should have had a financial resolution dealing with the money to be provided, and with the purposes in general terms, but if hon. members look at the financial resolution they will find a succession of details. The exact purposes are laid down. The Commissioners [for the Special Areas] may assist in respect of 'industrial undertakings hereinafter established'. Why should they not deal with one already established? You cannot deal with them under the Bill because it has already been settled by the financial resolution. In paragraph (c) there is power to give financial assistance to areas outside a Special Area on conditions which are laid down in detail, which makes it impossible for the House to suggest that there may be other conditions.... Finally, one comes to a remarkable thing to be included in a financial resolution, and that is a definite clause:
> 'Special Areas means the areas specified in the First Schedule of that Act.'
> It is quite unnecessary to put in that definition. It could have been done in the Bill...all those members who are interested in other Special Areas cannot move to have any area put in because of the fact that this definition is

---

[1] 312 H.C.Deb. 5 s., 1138. [2] For the debate, see *ibid.* 1111–48.
[3] 311 H.C.Deb. 5 s., 2017–18. [4] 312 H.C.Deb. 5 s., 90.
[5] 321 H.C.Deb. 5 s., 997–1010. [6] *Ibid.* 815–934.
[7] Now S.O. 79.

in the financial resolution and the resolution has the King's recommendation attached to it.... The whole matter is dealt with in the financial resolution... they draft amendments, but those amendments are out of order. They find that it is no good waiting for the Bill because the Bill is governed by the financial resolution.... That is not fair to the House.[1]

The result of the debate was that the Government agreed to the setting up of a select committee 'to consider the working of the Standing Orders relating to public money and, subject to the unimpaired maintenance of the principles embodied in Standing Orders Nos. 63 to 69 (both inclusive), to report as to whether any or what changes are desirable in Standing Orders Nos. 68 and 69 or in the procedure relating to money resolutions'.[2]

There are, however, two preliminary questions, whether there should be financial resolutions at all, and whether, if there are any, the principles of the existing Standing Orders should be complied with. Sir Courtenay Ilbert, a very high authority on parliamentary procedure, thought that money resolutions should be abolished.[3] Their theoretical purpose, to enable the House of Commons to control national economy, is admirable. In practice—and this is recognised by the Standing Orders—members are more anxious to spend money than to save it. Leaving aside for the present all questions about the annual financial legislation,[4] it must be recognised that the debate on the financial resolution is not a debate on the consequences to the national finances following from the passing of the Bill or the proposed Bill, but a debate on the principle of the Bill itself. It is, indeed, a second reading debate carried on under technical limitations. If a member is fortunate in catching the Chairman's and Speaker's eyes and if (as is not usually the case) a debate takes place on the report of the financial resolution, he may make the same speech three times with nothing more than slight changes of language and emphasis. The minister in charge of the Bill certainly repeats his arguments, and they are replied to by the leaders of the Opposition in

---

[1] 321 H.C.Deb. 5 s., 819. These passages were quoted by the Select Committee, H.C. 149, 1937, pp. vii–viii.

[2] Report from the Select Committee on Procedure relating to money resolutions, H.C. 149 of 1937. S.O. 63 to 69 are now numbered 78, 79 and 81 to 84. S.O. 68 and 69 are now numbered 83 and 84.

[3] H.C. 378 of 1914, Q. 2462. [4] See Chapter IX.

similar speeches. To adapt a phrase of Sir William Harcourt's about the speeches in opposition to the Home Rule Bill of 1893, by the time the Bill goes into committee the speeches begin to sound like old tunes ground out by old hurdy-gurdies.

The essential principle of Standing Order 78 is another matter. It is that the responsibility for financial proposals shall rest with the Government. While it cannot be suggested that private members are not as capable of suggesting means of spending public money as useful as or more useful than those proposed by the Government, there is great danger in allowing private members to do so. There is always temptation for a member to suggest expenditure which will benefit his own constituency or, especially now that members represent interests other than their constituents, his own interest. If such proposals were permitted, there might result a 'you scratch my back and I'll scratch yours' practice, whereby public funds would be diverted to political or private ends. No Government can be prevented from spending money where it can obtain useful political support, and no party can be prevented from pledging itself to do the same if returned to power; but it is at least possible to prevent private members from joining in the scramble for pennies. The Government's opportunities are restricted by the fact that it has to propose means for providing the money and is thus likely to make almost as many enemies as it buys friends. A private member has no such limitation. The rule is so valuable that it has been copied in most of the other Constitutions of the Commonwealth.

If a 'Queen's recommendation' be thus considered necessary, it does not follow that there is any particular sanctity about a committee of the whole House. The origin of Standing Order 79 is to be found in conditions that have long since disappeared. When kings had power and men who opposed them were likely to be cast into outermost darkness, there was some importance in moving the Speaker, the King's representative, out of the Chair, and discussing in private whether the King should have money and, if some was to be granted, whether it should be payable for the benefit of his mistresses or for a war in defence of Protestantism. Such conditions no longer exist. The committee is the House, and the only difference is that discussion is less subject to rigid technical limitations in the one than in the other.

Nor does it follow that the Queen's recommendation should be in such detail that no effective amendment is possible. The assumption that the Opposition can amend a resolution proposed by the Government is of course false. But a debate on an amendment focuses public attention much more effectively than similar speeches on a Government proposal. If the Government proposes that unemployment allowances for dependent children shall be 10s. a week, the Opposition propaganda is far more effective if it can propose that the sum shall be 12s. a week than if it merely says, in opposition to the Government's proposal, that the Government is 'murdering babes'. Moreover, debate on a specific proposal often induces the Government to make a concession to meet the prevailing opinion. Under the practice followed since 1922 this is possible only by withdrawing the financial resolution and substituting another: for the Queen's recommendation is as binding upon ministers as upon private members.

The terms of reference of the Select Committee of 1937 prevented them from discussing either the need for financial resolutions or the principles of the Standing Orders. On the question of the drafting of the resolution it was pointed out that the problem had become important owing to the great increase in the social services. Bills regulating these services 'inevitably require financial provision, and indeed the money is often the very kernel of the Bill. In the past...the natural attitude of the House, representing the tax-payers, was expected to be a desire to cut down the expenditure they contained. But now there is a varying but considerable body of opinion...which wishes to increase the financial provision proposed by the Government for social purposes.'[1] To put the matter in a way different from that adopted by the Select Committee, before 1915 social legislation was usually proposed by a Liberal Government.[2] It was the function of the Conservative party to safeguard the national finances. For instance, the financial resolution of the Old Age Pensions Bill, 1908, could be widely drawn[3]

[1] H.C. 149 of 1937, p. ix.
[2] Conservative Governments before 1900 proposed much social legislation, but the cost usually fell on local taxation. One must not forget, also, the increase of expenditure on education proposed by the Unionist Governments of 1895 to 1905.
[3] 'That it is expedient to provide for Old Age Pensions, and to authorise the payment, out of moneys provided by Parliament, of any expenses incurred for that purpose and

because the main criticism was not that it did not go far enough, but that it destroyed the sturdy independence of the intelligent worker and tended to reduce the nation to bankruptcy.[1] Since 1919, however, both parties have favoured extensions to the social services and, where there has been opposition, the complaint has been that they were inadequate.

This argument, though correct, makes nonsense of the suggestion that the debate on financial resolutions enables the House to control finance, and shows that the stage is useless for the purpose for which it is conceived. On the other hand, it does suggest, given the premises, that the Queen's recommendation should be more narrowly drawn than that of 1908, and this was the conclusion which the committee drew.[2] If, however, the recommendation be drawn in great detail, the function of the House not only in debating the resolution but also in the committee stage of the Bill becomes one of saying yea or nay to the Government's proposals. While in the last resort this is always so, it is so only because the Government gives way to the feeling of the House; and it cannot do this if it is bound by a detailed Queen's recommendation. Accordingly, the committee concluded that greater freedom should be aimed at and that the terms of the resolution should be wider than the terms of a Bill.[3] Since instructions to that effect given by the Prime Minister in 1934 had not been effective, it was recommended that the following resolution should be passed by the House:

That this House, while affirming the principle that proposals for expenditure should be initiated only by the Crown, is of opinion that Standing Order No. 63[4] is capable of being applied so as to restrict unduly the control which, within the limits prescribed by that principle, this House has been accustomed to exercise over legislation authorising expenditure; and that any detailed provisions which define or limit the objects and conditions of expenditure

connected therewith.' 189 Parl.Deb. 4 s., 1127. There was criticism both of the fact that the motion was not put down (as it would now be under S.O. 84) and of the fact that no limitation of expenditure was provided for.

[1] 'While all of us must be anxious that the Pensions Bill...shall not merely relieve the financial burdens of old age, but also be one which does nothing to impair the spirit of thrift, yet there is not a man who does not know that behind these objects the financial questions which the Bill is going to raise, and of which this debate is only the forerunner, are of the most serious kind'; Mr Balfour, leader of the Opposition, 189 Parl.Deb. 4 s., 1134–5.

[3] *Ibid.*

[2] H.C. 149 of 1937, p. ix.

[4] Now S.O. 78.

contained in a Bill should, if and so far as they are set out in a financial resolution, be expressed in wider terms than in the Bill so as to permit amendments
to the Bill, which have for their object the extension or relaxation of such
provisions, and which do not naturally increase the charge.[1]

It was pointed out by Mr Speaker, however, that if such a resolution
were passed, it would naturally follow that Mr Speaker would have to
be responsible for determining whether the financial resolution con-
formed with the standard laid down. He suggested that the question
whether a resolution was or was not too tightly drawn might give rise
to extreme party controversy, and that it might not be desirable to give
him such an embarrassing function.[2] In view of this expression of
opinion, the Government decided not to recommend the resolution to
the House, and instead the following instruction was given to the
departments and Parliamentary Counsel:

I am directed by the Lords Commissioners of His Majesty's Treasury to
invite your attention to the Report of the Select Committee on Procedure
relating to Money Resolutions (H.C. 149 of 1937) and to the reply given by
the Prime Minister to a question in the House of Commons on November 9th,
1937, and in particular to the declaration that it is the definite intention of
His Majesty's Government to secure that financial resolutions in respect of
Bills shall be so framed as not to restrict the scope within which the Committee on the Bills may consider amendments further than is necessary to
enable the Government to discharge their responsibilities in regard to public
expenditure and to leave to the Committee the utmost freedom for discussion
and amendment of details which is compatible with the discharge of those
responsibilities.

I am further to request that the necessary steps be taken to acquaint all
those concerned with the requirement that the terms of any Financial Resolution in the drafting of which they are concerned shall not be so drawn as to
involve undue restrictions and that the Government's declaration shall be
complied with in all cases.[3]

The Speaker described this letter as a 'considerable advance' on the
verbal instructions which had previously been issued.

[1] H.C. 149 of 1937, p. 14.   [2] *Ibid.* p. 175.
[3] 328 H.C.Deb. 5 s., 1595 (9 November 1937).

4. COMMITTEES

The House of Commons knows three kinds of committees, namely, committees of the whole House, standing committees, and select committees. The modern standing committees are a recent innovation and are specially provided for legislative purposes by Standing Orders. The institution of the select committee, consisting of a few members nominated for some specific purpose, goes back to the earliest times of which records exist.[1] In the Parliaments of James I and Charles I, and even later, it was the practice for Bills to be referred to select committees. Members not selected might attend, but had no voice. Sometimes, however, Bills were committed to a committee of the whole House, and the standing committees or grand committees which dealt with privileges, elections and grievances had already tended to become committees of the whole House, except in the case of the Committee of Privileges, which has always remained a select committee. After the Restoration the grand committees (again excepting the Committee of Privileges) were appointed as committees of the whole House, and from 1700 onwards the committee of the whole House became the normal type of committee except for specific matters, for privileges, and for private Bills.

Until 1882, therefore, all public Bills which were not specially referred to a select committee[2] were committed to a committee of the whole House. In the committee the content of the Bill is considered in detail; amendments may be moved and passed so long as they are relevant to the subject-matter of the Bill; such amendments may even go beyond the long title provided that the title is amended and the amendment specially reported to the House. The apparent absurdity of debating minor details in a committee of over 600 members has always been justified on the ground that every member has a right to consider a Bill with special reference to his constituents and to move the changes which he considers necessary. The growth of obstruction, the desire of

---

[1] See the long historical note in Redlich, II, pp. 203–14.

[2] Reference to a select committee (i.e. of fifteen members), is now rare. But cf. the Architects Registration Bill, 1927 (*ante*, p. 197) and the Road Traffic Bill, 1931–2. The purpose is to enable outside parties to give evidence.

members to speak, and the complication of legislation made this system impracticable; and proposals were made from 1854 onwards for the committal of some public Bills to select committees.

The first standing committees were set up as part of a scheme proposed by Mr Gladstone in 1882 for meeting the situation created by Irish obstruction.[1] There was much opposition in the Cabinet,[2] and the proposal was received without enthusiasm in the House.[3] Two standing committees for Law and Trade were, however, established by sessional Order in 1883 and some Bills were submitted to them;[4] but the Orders were not renewed in 1883, and the committees were not again established until they were provided for by Standing Orders in 1888. These committees dealt, the one with law, courts of justice, and legal procedure, and the other with trade, agriculture, fishing, shipping and manufactures;[5] but only comparatively non-contentious matters were referred to them, and nearly all major Bills continued to go to committee of the whole House.

In 1907 a great change was made, and in substance (though there have been subsequent amendments) the present system was established by Standing Orders. Unless the House otherwise orders, all Bills go to standing committees, except:

(a) Bills for imposing taxes and Consolidated Fund and Appropriation Bills.[6]

(b) Bills for confirming provisional orders.[7]

If it is desired that a Bill not within the exceptions shall go to a committee of the whole House, a motion to that effect must be made immediately after the Bill is read a second time and must be decided without amendment or debate.[8] Part only of a Bill may be committed to a standing committee, and the rest to a committee of the whole House.[9] This was done, for instance, with the National Insurance Bill, 1911.[10]

It is sometimes asserted that it was not intended in 1907 that con-

---

[1] Redlich, I, p. 174.   [2] *Life of Sir Charles Dilke*, I, p. 488.
[3] Redlich, *loc. cit.*
[4] The first Bill to be passed through a standing committee was Mr Chamberlain's Bankruptcy Bill of 1883: H.C. 161 of 1931, Q. 2369 (Sir Austen Chamberlain).
[5] Redlich, II, p. 182.   [6] See Chapter IX.
[7] See Chapter XIV.   [8] S.O. 38 (1) (2).
[9] S.O. 38 (3).   [10] *Ante*, p. 243.

troversial measures should be sent to standing committees. The understanding was not quite of that nature. Sir Henry Campbell-Bannerman said that 'the Government had no desire to send the great measures of the session, which almost necessarily were controversial, to Grand Committees. They would still be retained under the control of the House. But there were very many measures, which might be long and elaborate, but which could not only be dealt with by Standing Committees, but had been dealt with with the greatest success by them—Bills such as Factory Bills, full of the most delicate and complicated details, all arousing strong feelings and attacking certain interests.'[1]

This practice was followed until 1945. The reforms of parliamentary procedure worked out by a Cabinet Committee during the war (but not specifically approved by the War Cabinet) and submitted to the Select Committee on Procedure in 1945, provided for reference to standing committees of all Bills except:

(1) Those excepted by the Standing Order;

(2) Bills which were required to be passed with great expedition;

(3) 'One Clause' Bills not requiring detailed examination in committee; and

(4) Bills of 'first-class constitutional importance'.[2]

The proposal was accepted by the Select Committee,[3] and put into operation by the Labour Government. Though no alteration was made in Standing Orders, this represented a fundamental change of practice. The great socialisation measures of the Labour Government and other social legislation like the National Insurance Bill and the National Health Service Bill were all sent upstairs and passed under guillotine resolutions.

The limitation to 'Bills of first-class constitutional importance' was, however, not acceptable to the Conservative Opposition, whose view was that Bills of great social importance such as nationalisation Bills were equally important. Accordingly, the practice since 1951, under Conservative Governments, has been to refer all major Bills to a committee of the whole House. Experience has shown, too, that the Government has had less effective control of standing committees than it had before the reforms of 1945. For the consideration of a particular

---

[1] 171 Parl.Deb. 4 s., 1577.   [2] H.C. 9 of 1945–6, p. xi.
[3] *Ibid.* p. iv.

Bill, a standing committee now consists mainly of the members who have asked to be put on for that Bill. This means that most of the Government members have axes to grind, either on behalf of particular interests or on behalf of their constituents. There is, of course, nothing objectionable in this arrangement, but it does mean that the broader view adopted by the Government (on behalf of the general consumer, for instance) receives less attention than it did, and that there are fewer members ready to obey the whip without question. Though in the last resort the Government can always use the whip, either in the committee or in the House, it is generally found that it has to give way to the 'sense of the committee' more often than it would have to do if it had the docile majority of the House as a whole. Hence ministers prefer to take more complex and contentious Bills on the floor of the House.

The specialist character of the standing committee between 1888 and 1907, such as it was, was abolished by the reforms of 1907. Since then, with the exception of the Scottish Committee mentioned below, all the committees have discussed Bills of all types and have simply been designated Committees A, B, C, D, and E. Until 1939, four committees were established, though three were enough in the average session.[1] As a result of the change in practice in 1945, five smaller committees were set up, but it is still rare for all of them, as well as the Scottish Committee, to be fully employed. At the beginning of the session not enough Bills are ready for second reading, and the predominance of financial business on the floor between February and April or May again prevents the standing committees from being fully employed. Consequently, it seems that the anxiety of the Government and the Select Committee in 1945 to provide enough standing committees was misplaced. The fullest possible use is not being made of those committees.

The Scottish Committee contains all the members for Scottish constituencies, though other members are added up to the maximum provided by Standing Orders. In exceptional circumstances like those of 1922 these rules make the Scottish Committee unusable. Scotland always has a considerable Labour representation but the Scots electors

[1] H.C. 189 of 1945–6, Q. 3014 (Mr Speaker).

are apparently less volatile than the English for they do not 'swing' so easily. Consequently, it is possible to have a Conservative Government in office with a Labour majority in Scotland. This majority may be large enough to make it impossible to give the Scottish Committee a Conservative majority even by adding Conservative members from England. If a Conservative Government is in power in such conditions—and this happened in 1922—all Scottish Bills have to be kept on the floor of the House.

It was suggested by Sir Gilbert Campion, Clerk of the House, in 1945 that the Standing Committee should be given a specialist character.[1] Mr Speaker Clifton Brown opposed this recommendation. He did not think that members could be experts.

> We want to consult experts and then bring our commonsense to bear, and that is why I am frightened of a specialist committee. You get a collection of cranks probably, on most subjects.[2]

'Cranks' is probably a little harsh. There are a few members who may properly be classed as experts, while the rest merely think they are experts. Even so, some attention has to be paid to the special interests of members, and this is always done by adding 'expert' members to the nucleus of the committee and, if need be, even discharging some of the nucleus in order to enable the 'experts' to be added for the consideration of a particular Bill.

The members of each committee are nominated by the Committee of Selection. This committee consists of eleven members nominated by the House at the beginning of every session. Its members are, in practice, private members with long experience and representing all parties.[3] They have to perform certain functions requiring as much impartiality as can be found in a House consisting almost exclusively of partisans; and it is due to their recognition that the parliamentary game must be played according to the rules that criticism of their actions is rare. In nominating members to serve on standing committees they must 'have regard to the composition of the House',[4] and this they interpret to mean that the parties are to be represented as nearly as possible in proportion to their representation in the House itself.

[1] *Ibid.* p. xlii. [2] *Ibid.* Q. 3132.
[3] The Labour party always has a whip as member. [4] S.O. 58.

Each committee consists of a nucleus of twenty members. The Committee of Selection may discharge members from a standing committee for non-attendance or at their own request and nominate others in substitution for those discharged. Also, the Committee of Selection may add not more than thirty members to a standing committee in respect of any Bill referred to it, to serve on the committee during the consideration of that Bill; and in adding such members the committee 'shall have regard to their qualifications'.[1] All this does not apply to the Scottish Committee, which is in a sense specialised. But the result is to make the other committees much more specialised than they would otherwise appear to be. It is true that the nucleus is non-specialised: but a member who is not interested in a particular Bill either does not attend or asks to be discharged. On the other hand, a member who is interested and is not already on the committee asks to be put on for the consideration of that Bill. If, as is not usually the case,[2] there is competition for the thirty possible nominations, it is usually possible to persuade one of the 'nucleus' to resign in order to permit a specialist to be appointed. Thus, where a standing committee is considering an Agriculture Bill, a member who does not know, and does not care to know, the difference between a turnip and a mangel-wurzel, either ceases to be a member or does not attend.[3] Similarly, any honourable and gallant member who is at the moment concerned only with the state of our defences will not be found considering the details of an Education Bill. This specialisation is, of course, based on previous knowledge, friendliness or opposition to the Bill, personal or professional interests, or the interests of constituents. It must be sharply differentiated from such specialisation as occurs in the French *Commissions*. The committee on a Bill is brought together for the consideration of that Bill, and the next Bill on the same subject may be considered by quite a different personnel.

Though the members of the standing committees are chosen by the Committee of Selection, that committee necessarily takes much of its

---

[1] S.O. 58.

[2] The Road Traffic Bill, 1930, was an exceptional case: H.C. 161 of 1931, Qs. 1019, 1020 (Captain Bourne and Mr E. Brown).

[3] Cf. H.C. 161 of 1931, Q. 3887 (Captain Bourne and Sir Horace Dawkins).

information from the whips. It was alleged by Lord Robert Cecil in 1914 that if a member was known not to agree with his party on a particular Bill he was kept off the standing committee to which it was referred,[1] and other unorthodox members have made the same complaint. But the member may always submit his name to the Committee of Selection, which asks the whips for lists of members but is not in any respect bound by the whips' recommendation.

Before the war, the number of members of a standing committee varied from sixty to eighty-five, but the increase in the number of committees in 1945 compelled a reduction, and the usual number is now between forty and fifty,[2] except in the case of the Scottish Committee. The reduction was considered necessary owing to the difficulty of finding enough members to serve. Before the war, a committee usually sat on two mornings a week for two hours on each occasion, though sometimes it was necessary to have afternoon sittings as well. The Select Committee recommended[3] that the committees might sit on three mornings a week. It also recommended that the old Standing Order 49 A, which had been revoked because it was never used, should be revived so that the House could be adjourned to enable standing committees to sit.[4] This has in fact been done,[5] but no use has been made of the power so conferred because both Government and Opposition are anxious to use all the time available on the floor of the House.

The difficulty of finding members prepared to sit on standing committees has two explanations. First, though many Labour members are in fact full-time members living on their salaries of £1000 a year plus any other income they may possess, there is still a large number of members who may be described as part-time politicians. The lawyers, stockbrokers, accountants, insurance brokers and many business men are hard at work every morning and most afternoons and come along to the House after the Courts rise or their offices close. In other words, there is what has been described as 'a House within a House'; a smaller House consisting of those who are willing to work long hours in the House. Secondly, committee work is unspectacular and enjoys little

[1] H.C. 378 of 1914, Q. 804. [2] H.C. 189 of 1945–6, Q. 2705.
[3] H.C. 9 of 1945–6, p. vi. [4] *Ibid.*
[5] S.O. 10.

publicity. The 'Committee Hansard' is read by few and committee discussions are rarely reported in the Press; when they are reported only snippets of information appear. Consequently, a hard-working member secures no kudos in his constituency, and the publicity-monger who appears occasionally to ask a question or make a speech seems to his constituents to be an active and useful member. Even the Prime Minister and the whips, who do not sit on standing committees, rarely give credit where it is due.

There is one limitation on the power of the Committee of Selection not yet mentioned. For the consideration of all public Bills relating exclusively to Wales and Monmouthshire, the standing committee must be so constituted as to comprise all members sitting for constituencies in Wales and Monmouthshire.[1] Such Bills are so very rare that this provision is of no great importance. It does not imply that there must be a Welsh committee as there is a Scottish Committee, but only that when a Bill is referred to one of the Committees A, B, C, D and E, that committee must contain all the Welsh and Monmouthshire representatives.

Subject to these qualifications the standing committees 'upstairs' form miniature parliaments. Recent developments have in fact made them look very like their parent 'downstairs'. The chairman was given closure powers in 1907[2] and kangaroo powers in 1934. Since 1945 guillotine resolutions have been used for all controversial Bills. The chairman also has power to prevent irrelevance and repetition and to refuse to put dilatory motions or to put them without debate.[3] There is even what is commonly called a 'Committee Hansard'—a verbatim report of the proceedings of the committee on a particular Bill. There is no obligation to produce such a document, which in the case of a Bill like the Mines and Quarries Bill, 1954, may run into several volumes, but the committee has the power[4] and usually exercises it.

It follows that the office of chairman is only one degree less important than that of chairman to a committee of the whole House. Until 1934 the procedure was for the Committee of Selection to nominate a chairmen's panel, to consist of not less than four nor more than eight members,

[1] S.O. 58 (1).　　[2] Twenty members must support the closure motion.
[3] S.O. 58 (5).　　[4] S.O. 58 (6).

and this panel appointed from among themselves the chairman of each standing committee.[1] When kangaroo powers were given in 1934, however, it was considered advisable to transfer the power of appointing the chairmen's panel to the Speaker. Accordingly, at the beginning of every session, the Speaker nominates a chairmen's panel of not less than ten members, who act as temporary chairmen of committees of the whole House when requested to do so by the chairman of Ways and Means. In this way they acquire experience of the handling of the whole House in committee. From these temporary chairmen, also, the chairmen of standing committees are appointed by the Speaker.

Thus the standing committees consist of miniature Parliaments of forty or fifty members under a fairly experienced chairman; but on an ordinary Bill the attendance is rarely higher than twenty. The quorum is fifteen, and sometimes the Opposition can obstruct, as it did on the Incitement to Disaffection Bill, 1934, by deliberately staying in the corridor in the hope that a quorum will not be available without them.[2] The minister in charge of the Bill, his parliamentary and private secretaries, and one or both of the Law Officers, are put on the committee. There is often difficulty in securing the attendance of a Law Officer, since both may be engaged in the courts and two or more standing committees may be sitting at the same time. Sir Henry Campbell-Bannerman suggested in 1907 that it might be necessary to appoint a third English Law Officer, such as the Judge Advocate-General, from among members of Parliament. This has never been done; and in practice it might be simpler to increase the salaries of the Law Officers and insist that they undertake no court work on behalf of the Government, as was suggested in the debates on the Ministers of the Crown Bill, 1937.

Usually whips are not appointed to standing committees, so that the parties have less control over their members than in the House. If there is no whip, the whipping is done by the minister's parliamentary private secretary, though not always efficiently. Moreover, a defeat in a standing committee obviously cannot operate as a vote of no-confidence in the Government. What is more, the more informal atmosphere of a com-

---

[1] S.O. 49, now repealed.
[2] If this happens twice with a private member's Bill it goes to the bottom of the list: cf. A. P. Herbert, *The Ayes Have It.*

paratively small committee allows members to be persuaded more readily than by formal speeches in the House. At the same time, defeats of the Government are rare, and, if the minister in charge insists, he can always get the decision reversed in the House on the report stage, or in the House of Lords (provided that the Government has a majority there). In the Standing Committee on the Town and Country Planning Bill, 1932, the Minister of Health was defeated on an amendment requiring the minister's consent to a town and country planning resolution. Such consent had been required under the Act of 1909, but the requirement had been abolished by the Act of 1919. The minister did not ask the House to reverse the decision, with the result that two additional stages were inserted in planning procedure, necessitating delay and additional expense. On the other hand, the Minister of Transport was defeated in standing committee on the Restriction of Ribbon Development Bill, 1935. Conservative members insisted that certain kinds of appeal should go to the courts of summary jurisdiction instead of to the minister. On the report stage the minister succeeded in securing the reversal of this decision.

Also, a certain amount of whipping is done. If, for instance, it appears that the Government is likely to be defeated, the minister's parliamentary private secretary may be sent to scour the corridors in order to find non-attending members of the committee. 'Even in my short parliamentary experience I have been a member of a Grand Committee when, at the last moment, members were imported from another committee to save the minister from defeat.'[1] This statement was confirmed by Mr Asquith.[2] This, however, is exceptional; and while it is the usual practice that most members who vote in committee of the whole House have not listened to much of the debate, the converse is true in standing committees. As Lord Robert Cecil once said:

There is a different spirit from that which exists in the House itself. There is more freedom. There is a genuine feeling on the Grand Committee quite apart from the membership of political parties. There are two main reasons. In the first place, the decisions of a Grand Committee cannot affect the existence of the Government of the day. If the Government is defeated it is beaten only by a section of the House, and it cannot be pretended that it has

[1] 50 H.C.Deb. 5 s., 607 (Mr Goldsmith).   [2] *Ibid.* 614.

lost the confidence of the House itself....It is quite untrue to say that the Government pay no attention to the decisions of a Grand Committee. They have reversed a certain number of decisions of Grand Committees on report stage in this House, but generally speaking they do not reverse them.... But there is another reason why we get better decisions in Grand Committee. Decisions take place the moment discussion is over, and only those who have heard the discussion vote on the question before the Committee[1].... You do not divide yourselves into flocks under the close supervision of the shepherds when you come to divide. There is something in the physical question of voting where you sit instead of having to pass the cold eye of the whip.[2]

Though the Government has control of a Bill whether it is upstairs or downstairs, it does not follow that it usually goes through without amendment. Many amendments are moved by the minister in charge of the Bill. For after it is printed it is subjected to detailed examination both in the Government departments and outside. Though it is a standing instruction to departments to consult all other departments affected before the Bill is brought before the Legislation Committee of the Cabinet—and therefore long before it is published—in practice a complicated Bill requires examination by so many specialists that much of it is done while the Bill is before Parliament. This consultation is designed to prevent debate arising in the Cabinet and therefore deals with major issues. There may be no time to examine all the technical details, and bodies like the Crown Lands Commission, the Forestry Commission and the National Parks Commission may not even be consulted. Thus there may be many departmental amendments of a non-political character. Moreover, even when all the major interests have been consulted there may be others anxious to make representations about detailed provisions. Thus, a local government Bill may have been seen by the associations of local authorities (though they will probably have seen heads of proposals only), but it may still need alteration to bring it into accord with local Acts applying to specific local authorities, or to meet representations made by employees' associations.

Nor must it be forgotten that the draftsmen in the Parliamentary Counsel's office never complete their labours until the Bill is passed.

[1] Cf. 293 H.C.Deb. 5 s., 434 (Earl Winterton).
[2] 50 H.C.Deb. 5 s., 600–1.

They are always working under pressure and have to produce amendments consequential upon amendments, and so almost *ad infinitum*.
The immaculateness of the original conception is marred almost immediately, and as the Bill grows it finds such a host of foster-fathers that
it is almost impossible to answer 'Whose Bill is this?'

In addition, the Bill has to pass through committee. The Government can almost invariably rely on its majority to pass any provision
and to reject any amendment if it insists. But quite often private members
find flaws. Even with the most complicated and technical Bill there are
usually a few members who know something about it—it is said that
only three members of the House in 1928–9 understood the financial
provisions of the Local Government Bill, and two of them were Labour
members (the other was Mr Neville Chamberlain, the minister in charge).
There are others with 'ghosts' to draft amendments, and many with
briefs kindly prepared by interested parties. Even if they do not produce convincing amendments they may ask questions which induce
doubt. The official who 'considers' the matter may think that there is
something in the point or, alternatively, that the point is not important
and life may be easier for the minister if an innocuous amendment is
moved to meet it.

Moreover, the Committee has to be 'managed'. Much of the opposition or criticism is intelligent; and no committee likes to be driven too
hard. An occasional concession sweetens the atmosphere, especially if
the day be hot and the Thames a little odorous. The official in attendance
has to consider two things, convenience of administration afterwards
and ease of passage at the moment. If an amendment will smooth
tempers or allow more difficult matters to go through more easily, and
on the other hand will not complicate administration too much, he will
advise the minister, through his parliamentary private secretary, to
accept an amendment or undertake to propose one on report.

5. REPORT AND THIRD READING

If a Bill is referred to a committee of the whole House and no amendments are there made there is no debate on the report to the House, and
the Bill is ordered to be read the third time forthwith, or a future day is

appointed for the third reading.[1] If on the other hand the Bill has been referred to a standing committee, the Bill has to be considered on report whether or not it has been amended.[2] The reason is that the report stage is an opportunity for further amendment. If there has been no amendment in committee of the whole House, it may be assumed that the House does not desire to amend, and there is no necessity for consequential amendments. But if the Bill has been considered by a standing committee, other members may want to move amendments.

Theoretically, there is no limitation on the amendments which may be moved on report, except that no amendment may be moved which could not have been proposed in committee without an instruction from the House.[3] In practice, however, the Speaker does not select amendments which have been discussed adequately in committee, and he is much more ready to accept a closure motion on a debate which repeats a debate in committee.[4] When the Bill has been to a standing committee, however, the Speaker finds it 'very difficult to curtail the discussion on the report when relatively so small a number of members have had an opportunity of moving amendments, or speaking on them upstairs'.[5] Again, therefore, there is advantage in keeping a Bill on the floor of the House. Amendments are, however, much fewer on the report than in committee. Apart from propaganda amendments by the Opposition and obstructive amendments on behalf of interests, most amendments are moved with a genuine desire to get the Bill altered. It is rarely expected that a minister will accept an amendment after debate, though he may accept it without debate. Ministers realise that Bills are delicate instruments and that if clumsy hands begin meddling with them they are likely to come apart. Accordingly, a debate which convinces a minister usually ends with his promise to 'consider' the point—which means that he will put the suggestion into more expert hands. Such a procedure can be followed more easily in committee than on the report, because points raised on the report can be dealt with, if at all, only in

[1] May, p. 544; S.O. 48. [2] S.O. 49.

[3] S.O. 51. Formerly it was possible to propose any amendment whatever; but S.O. 51 was made in 1888: May, p. 546.

[4] H.C. 161 of 1931, Q. 838 (Mr Arnott and Mr T. Kennedy, chief whip).

[5] H.C. 161 of 1931, p. 406 (Mr Speaker).

'another place'. If in fact the Bill originated in the House of Lords there is no opportunity after the report stage.[1]

Procedure on the report differs in two respects from procedure in committee. In the first place, new clauses are considered first instead of last. No new clause may be offered on the report without notice;[2] and the purpose of the rule is to make any necessary consequential amendments—this being the last opportunity. There is some evidence that new clauses are put down in order to secure priority in the discussion. Whether the House is working under an arrangement between the whips or under a guillotine, the discussion on the later amendments is apt to be scamped. Accordingly, better publicity and (what is perhaps less important) a better debate is obtained by a member who moves a new clause than by one who moves an amendment. Often the Speaker rules that a new clause must be moved as an amendment.[3] Secondly, the procedure differs because if no new clause is put down or amendment proposed there is nothing to discuss. Consequently, if there are no amendments to any clause or any collection of clauses, including the whole Bill, the Speaker simply passes it over. The motion 'That the clause stand part of the Bill' is not put unless an amendment to leave out the clause is made. Accordingly, debates on that motion, which are so common in committee, are rarer on the report, and the procedure is quicker.

As soon as the report stage is concluded, the House may proceed at once to the third reading; and this is often done, though on contentious Bills the report stage is ended by agreement at ten o'clock and another day fixed for the third reading. (This is almost invariably the practice under the guillotine.) On third reading only verbal amendments may be made,[4] and the third reading is in substance a repetition of the second reading debate, though on the Bill as amended. As on the second reading, an amendment may be proposed to the motion that the Bill be now read a third time, and with the same results.[5] If the amendment is

---

[1] 'It is very little good criticising on report stage because you do not give the Department an opportunity of considering the criticisms and considering whether it can meet them': H.C. 161 of 1931, Q. 699 (Captain Bourne).

[2] S.O. 46. This applies also to committee.

[3] H.C. 378 of 1914, Q. 2403 (Sir Courtenay Ilbert, Clerk of the House).

[4] S.O. 53.   [5] *Ante*, pp. 252–3.

rejected, the Speaker declares at once that the Bill is read a third time. It is thereupon carried by the Clerk of the House, or a Clerk at the Table, to the bar of the House of Lords, where he delivers it to one of the Clerks at the Table of that House with the appropriate message.[1]

[1] In 1937 the Ministry of Health Provisional Order (Earsdon Joint Hospital District) Bill was taken to the Lords and there read the first time without having been read for the third time in the Commons. A message was sent requesting their Lordships to be pleased to return the Bill, 'the same not having been read the third time in this House and having been taken to the House of Lords by mistake'. *The Times*, 10 March 1937.

CHAPTER IX

FINANCIAL CONTROL

I. CONSTITUTIONAL PRINCIPLES

In approaching the subject of the financial control exercised by the House of Commons, we reach the borders of a realm where law, parliamentary privilege, and parliamentary custom are almost inextricably intertwined. The principles underlying the procedure of the House were the subject of contests with the Crown and disputes with the peers. The fundamental principle that the Crown has no power to tax save by grant of Parliament is, according to the parliamentary lawyers and therefore according to the law of to-day, to be found in Magna Carta which, as Parliament itself has said, is declaratory of the common law. Good historical arguments may perhaps be found in *Bate's Case*[1] and the *Case of Ship-Money*;[2] but this litigation was adjourned to the field of battle, and the law is not what the courts decided but what Hakewill said in his speech in the House of Commons[3] and what Oliver St John argued in his defence of John Hampden. This is common law, and legislation adds to its force, for the Bill of Rights, 1689, asserts that

Levying money for or to the use of the Crown by pretence of prerogative without grant of Parliament for longer time, or in other manner than the same is or shall be granted, is illegal.

So fundamental is this rule that the courts will infer that a power to tax has not been granted unless there is a clear intendment to the contrary in an Act of Parliament.[4] The Crown may make an agreement to receive payment for a service which cannot be demanded as of right;[5] but it cannot tax except with consent of Parliament.

Taxation, then, requires legislation. It is not the practice of Parlia-

---

[1] (1606) 2 St. Tr. 371. [2] (1637) 3 St. Tr. 825.
[3] *The Libertie of the Subject against the Pretended Power of Impositions* (Ordered to be published by the Committee of the House, 1641).
[4] *Attorney-General* v. *Wilts. United Dairy Co.* (1922), 91 L.J.K.B. 897.
[5] *China Steam Navigation Co.* v. *Attorney-General*, [1932] 2 K.B. 197.

ment to limit the authorisation of taxation to one year, except in one case. Subject to this exception, taxes are granted 'until Parliament shall otherwise determine'. The exception is the income tax.[1] The machinery and principles applicable even in the case of the income-tax are, however, provided for by permanent legislation. Moreover, many other taxes, though provided until Parliament otherwise determine, are modified from year to year according to the needs of the Exchequer and the whims of its Chancellor.

The power to levy taxation and to use the proceeds for the stated purposes may be conferred upon any authority.[2] Local taxation, or rates, is for instance levied by local authorities under permanent legislation, and is used by them for purposes authorised by statutes. But the taxation required by the Central Government is voted to the Crown; and if it be desired to have the money used by some other person or authority, the Treasury is authorised or directed to grant it to that person or body.

So far as taxation is levied for the purposes of the Crown it merely provides the means for making grants of supply to the Crown. Originally, in fact, the two were not distinguished. Taxes were granted to the King to raise and spend as he thought fit. They were an addition to his hereditary revenues and were paid into the Exchequer and withdrawn when required by letters patent or orders under the privy seal addressed to the Treasurer. The distinction between taxation and supply became obvious when the hereditary revenues—other than those of the Duchy of Lancaster, the Duchy of Cornwall, and the Principality of Scotland, which are not properly in that category—were surrendered in return for a fixed Civil List. Then, not merely the produce of taxation but all funds which came into the Exchequer and were not paid out under permanent legislation had to be granted to the King and at the same time—in accordance with a practice begun under Charles II and

---

[1] It was formerly the practice to impose annually one of the customs duties, in order that direct and indirect taxation might be discussed in the House. The duty on tea was usually selected for this purpose, but the duty was abolished by Mr Snowden, and though the extra excise duty on beer is a temporary tax it is not voted every year. Since there is now a complete tariff system, amendments in customs duties are made every year, and there is no fear that the House will lack opportunities for discussing indirect taxation.

[2] See ruling of Mr Speaker Lowther, 122 H.C.Deb. 5 s., 211–16.

developed under William and Mary—appropriated for the specific purposes for which they were intended.

So, in addition to imposing taxation, Parliament has to grant and appropriate supplies. The creation of the Consolidated Fund has made the distinction clear. The produce of taxation and all other public revenues are carried to the Consolidated Fund. A taxing statute, therefore, merely adds to the balances of the Consolidated Fund in the Bank of England and the Bank of Ireland. Out of the Consolidated Fund are paid, first, those amounts which are to be paid out under permanent legislation and which therefore are said to be 'charged on the Consolidated Fund', and, secondly, the supplies granted by Parliament for the current year. The only connection between taxation and supply is that there has to be provided out of taxation a sufficient balance to meet such supplies as are not otherwise and specifically provided for. The legislation providing for the taxation is quite distinct from the legislation providing for supply. But supply is not granted by Parliament merely in a lump sum; it is specifically appropriated to the purposes for which the Crown asks for it. The Crown presents estimates of the amounts required for the various services, in full detail and with full explanations, while Parliament grants the necessary supply and appropriates it according to the heads of the estimates. The main supply is granted by the Appropriation Act, which also appropriates; but that Act also appropriates other items of supply voted in Consolidated Fund Acts either to cover the period between the beginning of the financial year and the passing of the Appropriation Act, or to cover supply granted on Supplementary Estimates required for expenditure in the previous year or years.[1]

Parliament thus grants supply and appropriates it for all services which are not charged on the Consolidated Fund. The former, the Supply Services, require annual legislation;[2] the latter, the Consolidated

---

[1] This and subsequent explanations become clearer if we use dates. Estimates for the year ending 31 March 1956 are called for towards the end of 1954; supply is debated between the spring and summer of 1955; and the Appropriation Act, 1955, authorises expenditure on Supply Services for the year ending 31 March 1956. The Consolidated Fund Acts, 1955, authorise excess expenditure for the year ending 31 March 1955, and also money voted on account for the year ending 31 March 1955, before the Appropriation Act, 1955, is passed in July or August 1955. See also Appendix IV.

[2] As to which, see Appendix IV.

Fund Services, are provided for by permanent legislation. The greater part of public expenditure falls within the Supply Services.[1] In 1954–5 the estimated expenditure was over 4304 million pounds. Of this the Supply Services required nearly 3740 million pounds, or about eighty-seven per cent. Accordingly, Parliament has to vote every year nearly ninety per cent of the sum required for the public expenditure.

So far, then, Parliament has three functions to perform, taxation, supply, and appropriation. There is, however, a function implied in supply which has to be mentioned particularly. Permanent legislation and the Finance Act put the money into the Consolidated Fund. The permanent legislation dealing with Consolidated Fund Services, and the Appropriation Act and Consolidated Fund Acts (dealing with Supply Services), authorise the payment out of that Fund of the stated sums and for the stated purposes.[2] The manner of payment or *issue* is not provided by those Acts but by permanent legislation, the Exchequer and Audit Acts, 1866 to 1921. The manner of making issues from the Fund, as we shall see, gives Parliament a certain control.

Moreover, Parliament usually gives an express authorisation for expenditure apart from the implied authorisation in the Appropriation Act. Strictly speaking, the Appropriation Act grants and appropriates money for a service; it does not say that the service may be provided. Nevertheless, if Parliament by legislation authorises the spending of money on a service, it can hardly be contended that the Crown has no power to establish the service. Usually, the power is conferred by other legislation, and the Appropriation Act merely provides and appropriates the money. For instance, power to pay National Assistance is conferred by the National Assistance Act, 1948, though the money is provided and appropriated by the Appropriation Act. Sometimes, however, the only authorisation is in the latter Act. For instance, for many years before 1937 County Court judges received additions to their statutory salaries, and the only authority for these additions was the annual Appropriation Acts. Again, the Home Office spent money on Air

[1] Many items were transferred from the Consolidated Fund to the Estimates in the middle of last century: Redlich, I, p. 102, quoting Report from the Select Committee on the Public and Private Business of the House, 1861, H.C. 173, pp. viii–ix.
[2] See Appendix IV.

Raid Precautions in 1935–6 and 1936–7 without having any specific statutory powers, and relying only on the Appropriation Acts. The House of Commons, through its organs the Public Accounts Committee and the Comptroller and Auditor-General, dislikes this method of authorising expenditure,[1] and there is even some doubt about its legality, though it has never been challenged in the courts. Consequently, the usual practice is to have special legislation authorising the expenditure. For instance, if Parliament desired to give special gratuities to teachers of constitutional law on account of the valuable public service which they render, a Bill for that purpose would be passed in accordance with the procedure set out in Chapter VIII (requiring a financial resolution). It would then be necessary to grant additional supply and to appropriate it to the particular service; and, if there were not a sufficient balance in the Consolidated Fund to meet this expenditure, additional taxation would be required.

In respect of all these functions—taxation, supply, appropriation, and the authorisation of expenditure—the House of Commons claims pre-eminence. The Commons were summoned to Parliaments, from the end of the thirteenth century onwards, to consider what subsidies should be granted to the King by the Commons of England. The Lords and the clergy separately granted subsidies for themselves; but as the subsidies granted by the Commons became more important, and the Commons became politically stronger, they associated the Lords with their grants; and in 1407 it was stated by Henry IV in an ordinance that subsidies were 'granted by the Commons and assented to by the Lords'.[2] The Lords have always admitted, therefore, that the right of initiation in financial matters has rested with the Commons. The Queen's Speech is addressed to both Houses, but it contains a special financial paragraph addressed to the Commons alone:

Members of the House of Commons: The Estimates for the Public Services will be laid before you.

And at the end of a session:

Members of the House of Commons: I thank you for the provision you have made for the Public Service.

---

[1] For examples, see Epitome, pp. 50, 79, 104–5, 148–9, 167–8, 170, 206, 219–21, 497, 711–12, 723–7, 730–1, 761.   [2] May (13th ed.), p. 520.

Also, though a money Bill is stated to be enacted in accordance with the usual formula (unless it is passed under the Parliament Acts) by the Queen 'by and with the advice and assent of the Lords Spiritual and Temporal, and Commons, in this present Parliament assembled, and by the authority of the same', this is preceded by a preamble which refers to the Commons alone.[1] The Commons propose and the Lords concur if they think fit; and now under the Parliament Acts any money Bill which is sent up to the House of Lords at least one month before the end of the session and is not passed by that House within one month, may be presented for the royal assent without the concurrence of that House.[2]

The Commons claimed not only the right of initiation but also that the Lords had no power to modify the provision made by the Commons, though they have recognised a right to reject. In respect of taxation this was laid down in a Commons resolution of 1671;[3] and it was repeated in respect of supply and appropriation and expenditure generally by a resolution of 1678.[4] Since most Government legislation now contains financial provisions, the effect of this privilege is to cut down very substantially the power of the House of Lords. Where the financial provision is merely incidental, however, the difficulty can be overcome. Occasionally, a Bill containing such a provision is introduced and discussed in the House of Lords. On the third reading in that House, the provisions offending against the Commons' privilege are struck out and the Bill drawn so as to be intelligible after the omission. It is sent to the Commons in that form and so does not offend against privilege. The financial provisions are again printed in the Bill under the order of the House of Commons, but are placed in brackets and

---

[1] I.e. for a taxing statute: 'We, Your Majesty's most dutiful and loyal subjects the Commons of the United Kingdom in Parliament assembled, towards raising the necessary supplies to defray Your Majesty's public expenses, and making an addition to the public revenue, have freely and voluntarily resolved to give and grant unto Your Majesty the several duties hereinafter mentioned.'

For an appropriating statute: 'We, Your Majesty's most dutiful and loyal subjects the Commons of the United Kingdom in Parliament assembled, towards making good the supply which we have cheerfully granted to Your Majesty in this session of Parliament, have resolved to grant unto Your Majesty the sum hereinafter mentioned.'

[2] See on the Parliament Acts, *post*, pp. 414–34.

[3] See the text in May, p. 780. [4] *Ibid.*

underlined with a note indicating that they have not passed the Lords.[1] When passed, the Bill is returned to the Lords with the financial provisions inserted as Commons' amendments. Sometimes, also, the difficulty can be overcome by drafting; for instance, by inserting a provision whose object is to prevent other provisions from creating a charge.[2] Finally, the difficulty that Lords' amendments to Commons' Bills may involve breaches of privilege because they relate to finance is overcome by the Commons waiving their privilege. The Speaker informs the House that the amendment is a breach of privilege. If it is a minor amendment, motion is made that the Commons do not insist on their privilege; and, if passed, it is recorded in the Journals accordingly.

All this relates rather to the functions of the House of Lords than to those of the House of Commons. It is, however, the fact of privilege that has produced the practice of having a single Finance Bill in all ordinary years. Until 1861 the separate items of taxation were dealt with in separate Bills. The Commons had recognised the power of the Lords to reject such Bills, though it had not been exercised. In 1860, however, the Lords rejected the Paper Duty Repeal Bill. The Commons then passed resolutions which asserted, among other things, that 'this House has in its own hands the power so to impose and remit taxes, and to frame Bills of supply, that the right of the Commons as to the matter, manner, measure and time may be maintained inviolate'.[3] What this meant was made clear in 1861, when all the taxation proposals of the year were included in a single Bill. If the Lords rejected that Bill, they deprived the Government of a substantial part of the means required for meeting supply. This practice has since been followed. In 1909, however, the Lords rejected the Finance Bill as a whole,[4] and thus produced, after two general elections and a threat to create peers, the Parliament Act, 1911. Under that Act a Bill certified by the Speaker as a money Bill may secure the royal assent without the consent of the Lords. Nevertheless, the practice of having a single Finance Bill has been followed, except where financial exigencies, as in 1955, require a second Finance Bill; and the privilege is still important, for many Finance Bills

---

[1] May, pp. 783–4.   [2] See the examples in May, pp. 784–5.   [3] May (13th ed.), p. 573.
[4] The necessary money was obtained by borrowing until the Finance (1909–10) Act, 1910, was passed.

are not certified by the Speaker as money Bills,[1] and accordingly cannot be passed without the consent of the Lords.

The imposition of taxation, the grant and appropriation of supply, and the authorisation of expenditure, then, rest with the House of Commons, though they require legislation and therefore the concurrence of the House of Lords unless the Parliament Act, 1911, can be used. The House of Commons, however, does none of these things save at the request of the Crown—that is, of the Government. In Sir Erskine May's famous explanation:

> The Crown demands money, the Commons grant it, and the Lords assent to the grant: but the Commons do not vote money unless it be required by the Crown; nor do they impose or augment taxes, unless such taxation be necessary for the public service, as declared by the Crown through its constitutional advisers.[2]

This rule is laid down in Standing Order 78 so far as it applies to grants and charges on the public revenue, and its application to legislation authorising expenditure has already been considered.[3] The Standing Order applies also to the grants of supply proposed by estimates and supplementary estimates and embodied in Consolidation Fund Bills.[4] In respect of taxation the rule is not embodied in Standing Orders but is part of the ancient practice or common law of the House.[5] Moreover, Standing Order 79, which provides that the House will not proceed upon any motion or Bill for granting any money except in a committee of the whole House[6] is applied strictly to supply, and is extended by the practice of the House to taxation. Supply is considered in the Committee of Supply, and taxation, appropriation and the issue of moneys in the Committee of Ways and Means. These committees are set up at the beginning of each session in response to the statement in the Queen's

---

[1] Between 1913 and 1930–1 (inclusive) eleven Finance Bills were certified and eleven such Bills were not certified: see Hills and Fellowes, *The Finance of Government*, p. 209. Between 1931–2 and 1936–7 (inclusive) *no* Finance Bill was certified. See also *post*, pp. 417–19.

[2] May, p. 446. This is not quite Sir Erskine May's statement, which has been somewhat modified by his editors: see May (1st ed.), p. 324.

[3] *Ante*, pp. 254–6.

[4] The Appropriation Bill is a Consolidated Fund Bill, and in fact bears the title Consolidated Fund (Appropriation) Bill.

[5] *Ante*, pp. 255–6.   [6] *Ante*, pp. 256–7.

Speech that estimates will be laid before the House. The Consolidated Fund Bills (including the Appropriation Bill) and the Finance Bill are founded upon resolutions of the Committee of Ways and Means.

2. ESTIMATES AND SUPPLY

Some ninety per cent of the annual expenditure of the Government has to be voted annually by the House of Commons and authorised by legislation. Detailed estimates of the anticipated expenditure are presented to the House 'by command of Her Majesty' towards the end of February or early in March. They have previously been agreed between the departments concerned and the Treasury,[1] and, if necessary, brought before the Cabinet: they are, therefore, the proposals of the Government. The Navy Estimates, Army Estimates, Air Estimates, and the Estimates for the Revenue Departments, are in separate volumes. The Civil Estimates are published in classes. With the Navy, Army and Air Estimates separate memoranda are usually provided, giving some general account of the three services concerned, and acting almost as very summary annual reports not essentially dissimilar (except in length) from the annual reports presented to Parliament by the Ministers of Health, Labour and Education.

The Defence Service Estimates themselves are far more than lists of figures. The tables invariably give the comparative figures for the previous year; and they are interleaved with pages giving explanatory notes and accounting for the increase or decrease upon the figures for the previous year. Introductory tables explain how far the expenditure on each service is in part to be met out of money provided in other Estimates. For instance, money for payments in lieu of rates on naval buildings is provided not in the Navy Estimates but in the Civil Estimates, where the total payments in lieu of rates on all Government buildings are shown. This is nevertheless part of the cost of maintaining the Royal Navy, and the attention of the House of Commons is drawn

---

[1] See *Cabinet Government*, pp. 142–50. On 1 October 1954, a Circular is sent by the Treasury to the departments, calling for the Estimates for the year ending 31 March 1956. This is submitted to the Treasury by 15 December 1954, is provisionally approved about 15 January 1955, and presented to the House about 15 February 1955.

to the fact that it is being invited to meet part of that cost in another Estimate.

Another table in each of the Service Estimates sets out the actual net expenditure on each vote for the eight preceding years for which the accounts have been audited, together with the estimated expenditure for the preceding year and the current year. The general trend of expenditure on each vote can thus be determined and conclusions drawn as to the line of policy being followed, as for instance that the Admiralty is increasing its expenditure on ships but decreasing its expenditure on men. In the Appendices, too, there is much information —for instance, about ships under construction and undergoing large repairs, the detail of regimental establishments, and the like. Altogether, the three Defence Service Estimates, with indexes, occupy over 1000 pages.

All the Estimates follow common form, except that for convenience of publication and reference the Civil Estimates are divided into Classes. First there is the Vote (Part I), and this (apart from the votes for men, etc., in the Service Estimates) is merely a lump sum.

Next appear the 'Subheads under which this Vote will be accounted for' (Part II). Details are then given (Part III), these being in two degrees of detail in the Civil Estimates, whereas in the Service Estimates further information is given in the notes.

It can hardly be claimed, therefore, that the House of Commons is not given sufficient information. In the Appropriation Act, which will be the outcome of its deliberations, only the votes (Part I) will appear; and even the votes are not entirely sacrosanct for the Service Departments, since the Act will also enable the Treasury in certain circumstances to transfer a surplus on one vote to meet a deficit on another, though subject to subsequent confirmation by Parliament. However, the House of Commons considers that the departments are pledged to the amounts stated in the subheads (Part II), and transfer or 'virement' from one subhead to another in the same vote is permitted only with the consent of the Treasury.[1]

The form of the estimates is technically the concern of the Treasury. They are merely a statement by the Crown of the amount required for

[1] For virement, see *Cabinet Government*, pp. 152–5.

the public service and of the purposes for which it is intended to use that sum. But the House is necessarily concerned, partly because the votes (Part I) will be incorporated in the Appropriation Bill, but above all because, as the Treasury said in 1885, 'the House of Commons has complete control over the public expenditure'.[1] Accordingly, the Public Accounts Committee[2] has ruled that changes in form should be submitted to the House before they are adopted.[3] Moreover, the Estimates Committee[4] is appointed *inter alia* 'to suggest the form in which the Estimates shall be presented for examination'. The function of the House of Commons, through the two Select Committees mentioned, is to secure that there shall be adequate opportunities for discussion and, above all, adequate opportunities for parliamentary control of expenditure. Treasury control, too, goes hand in hand with parliamentary control. If votes and subheads are reduced in number, both parliamentary and Treasury control are diminished, since in the former case virement becomes easier and in the latter case it becomes less necessary, because the Treasury does not in general control expenditure within the limits of a subhead.[5] Also, if a new service is established without opening a new subhead Treasury control over that service is not provided for and, provided that the department does not exceed the amount in the subhead, it can distribute its expenditure within the subhead as it pleases, though it will probably be criticised by the Comptroller and Auditor-General and the Public Accounts Committee when the Appropriation Accounts are examined. For instance, Unemployment Assistance Allowances first appeared in the Estimates in 1935 as Class V, Vote 8 of the Civil Estimates. Consequently, any surplus on that vote could not be used for any Ministry of Labour service except by applying to Parliament with a supplementary estimate. If, however, they had been placed on the Ministry of Labour Vote

---

[1] Epitome, p. 175. [2] See *post*, pp. 332–8.
[3] Epitome, pp. 212–13 (1888); 250–1 (1890); 534 (1911); 559 (1916).
[4] *Post*, pp. 303–16.
[5] *Cabinet Government*, p. 155. Putting the matter in another way, Part I of an Estimate is binding both on the department and on the Treasury, subject to the power of virement conferred by s. 4 of the Appropriation Act in the case of the Defence Services, which requires subsequent ratification by Parliament. Part II is binding on the department but not on the Treasury. Part III is not binding on the department, subject to Treasury control over salaries and works.

(Class V, Vote 7) any surplus could have been used for Ministry of Labour purposes with the sanction of the Treasury. If they had been made not a separate subhead but part of subhead G.–I. of the Ministry of Labour Vote, which dealt with 'Unemployment Insurance, etc.', a surplus on allowances could have been used by the Ministry to meet a deficit on insurance without approaching either the Treasury or Parliament.

The Estimates are considered by the House in Committee of Supply. This is a committee of the whole House set up by the House at the commencement of each session as soon as the address in reply to the Queen's Speech has been agreed to.[1]

The Committee of the whole House on Supply has the name, but has none of the methods, of a Committee. It was established in the days of recurring conflict between Parliament and the Crown as a device to secure freedom of discussion on matters of finance. The debates in the House itself were recorded in the Journal, which was sometimes sent for and examined by the King; and they were conducted in the presence of the Speaker, who in those days was often the nominee and regarded as the representative of the Sovereign. By going into Committee under the chairmanship of a member freely selected, the House of Commons secured a greater degree of privacy and independence.[2]

Twenty-six days in all are allotted for supply, which includes all Estimates and Supplementary Estimates.[3] Under the old procedure any amendment could be moved or question raised when the motion was moved that the House go into Committee of Supply, in accordance with the ancient rule that 'grievances precede supply'—a rule applied with such pertinacity in the reign of Charles I, especially in the Short Parliament of 1640. In 1872 the procedure was modified by allowing amendments only when a new division of the Estimates was being taken.[4] This again was altered in 1879 by providing that on one day a week amendments could be moved and questions raised only on first going into Committee of Supply on the Navy, Army, and Civil Estimates, leaving the rule of 1872 to apply to the second supply day;[5]

---

[1] S.O. 15.
[2] Reports from the Select Committee on National Expenditure, 1918, p. 115.
[3] S.O. 16.   [4] Redlich, I, p. 110.   [5] *Ibid.* p. 114.

and in 1882 the rule of 1879 was applied to all supply days.[1] In 1948 the rule was again amended, on the recommendation of the Select Committee on Procedure of 1945–6. It was recognised that 'Supply days' were no longer means for controlling expenditure but opportunities for the Opposition to criticise the policy of the Government. The theory that money was being voted for administration, however, prevented members from mentioning proposals for legislation. To give some flexibility to this rule it was considered desirable to allow the Opposition to decide whether to ask for a vote to be put down—in which case proposals for legislation could not be mentioned—or to move an amendment to the motion that 'Mr Speaker do now leave the Chair'— in which case greater flexibility was provided by Standing Order. Accordingly, Standing Order 17 now allows the *Government* to initiate a debate on the motion to leave the Chair in order that an amendment to that motion might be moved and debated. This can, of course, operate either when the Opposition asks for it to be done or (as before 1948) when the motion is first moved for going into committee on each batch of Estimates, when private members are allowed to ballot for the privilege of moving amendments.

The function of the Committee of Supply is to examine and consent to the Estimates. In practice it is impossible for a committee of 629 members to do anything of the kind. Indeed, it is impossible for a small committee to consider them with any degree of success, even if they are all prepared to study 1500 pages of figures and explanations and to undertake the long preliminary study which is essential. The Select Committees on Estimates and Public Accounts, which are much smaller, are able with a fair measure of success to exercise not dissimilar functions because they have expert advisers, because their Chairmen are sometimes willing to put themselves to a considerable amount of trouble, and because they are able to summon departmental experts to explain. Such conditions are not practicable in a committee of the whole House.

Accordingly, the Committee of Supply discusses not public expenditure but public policy. Before 1902 the Estimates were put down by the Government and private members raised such questions of policy as were relevant to the votes before the Committee. When the new

[1] *Ibid.*

supply rule was made in 1902 it was agreed that the Opposition should choose the votes to be put down. Accordingly, the Opposition asks to have put down a vote on a department whose policy it wishes to criticise.[1] Since it may want to raise the same question again later, it asks that the vote be not put. If, for instance, a slump is in process and the Labour party is in opposition, there will be a series of debates on unemployment by getting the Ministry of Labour Vote put down time after time. If foreign affairs are the dominant subject, the Foreign Office Vote will be put down. On the last Supply day but one the outstanding votes are put without further debate. Consequently, most of the votes are never put down.

As a Labour member said in 1931 (referring to the tactics of the Conservative Opposition):

> For quite sound reasons of which I do not complain last year the Ministry of Labour Estimates were considered time after time, and when it got to eleven o'clock they were voted on in such a form that they were still kept alive. The Government majority goes down to fifteen so they are put down to the next available occasion, but I am not complaining. . . . If the position in the House were reversed, the other side would have done just the same. Yet, to take one Estimate in which I happened to be very much interested, the Education Estimates were not submitted at all, and they were eventually voted, and they were not challenged at all, by people walking through the Lobbies without a word of discussion.[2]

This statement was made by a member of the Government side. A member of an Opposition party[3] can suggest to his whip that he and some of his fellows would like, for instance, the Education Vote put down. Unless there are more urgent demands, the party leader will probably agree. The right to ask to have a vote put down is divided among the Opposition parties more or less in accordance with their relative strength in the House. Where, as is now usual, the official Opposition has most of the Opposition members, it has most of the Supply days and a substantial group of its members can therefore usually secure the putting down of the vote of the department whose

---

[1] This is so obvious that it hardly needs support; but see, *inter alia*, H.C. 161 of 1931, Q. 1284 (Sir Bolton Eyres Monsell); Q. 372 (Mr Lloyd George); Q. 487 (Mr Ede).

[2] H.C. 161 of 1931, Qs. 487 and 488 (Mr Ede).

[3] Or even a supporter of the Government: see A. P. Herbert, *The Ayes Have It*, p. 77.

policy they wish to criticise. The members of smaller parties, like the Liberal party, have a much smaller opportunity; and the members of groups have none at all. Similarly, members on the Government side must debate such questions as the Opposition chooses to raise. Sometimes, when the Opposition is uncertain which vote to choose the Government whip can say that 'our fellows would like to discuss (say) the Air Votes';[1] but there is sometimes a suspicion that 'our fellows' is a euphemism for some minister who feels that he is not getting enough publicity. An honourable and gallant supporter of the Government who is most anxious to discuss the Fleet Air Arm has to sit in silence—or not to sit at all—while 'those fellows opposite' discuss unemployment, nutrition, the birth rate, and the cost of living.[2] The Post Office Vote is a good example. This is now more popular with the Opposition because sometimes it is desired to criticise the broadcasting system (over which the Postmaster-General has some powers of control), or the decentralised system introduced after the report of the Bridgeman Committee, or the conditions of labour in the Post Office. Formerly, however, this was not so.

Years go by without its being put down, and yet it is a Department which most members, whenever they sit, want very much to criticise in detail; but because such debates have few political repercussions, they are seldom initiated by Opposition leaders.[3]

It is not always easy to choose an appropriate vote on which to hang a debate. For instance, there was formerly no vote for the location of industry because the subject was common to several departments. Sir Edward Fellowes, now Clerk to the House, therefore invented a new form of Supply motion:

That a further sum not exceeding £40 be granted to Her Majesty towards defraying the charges for the following services connected with the location of industry for the year ended 31 March—Class VI, vote 1, Board of Trade, £10; Class V, vote 8, Ministry of Labour and National Service, £10; Class I, vote 24, Ministry of Town and Country Planning, £10, etc.[4]

---

[1] H.C. 378 of 1914, Q. 378 (Mr J. W. Gulland, Government whip).
[2] Cf. H.C. 161 of 1931, Q. 2909 (Captain Crookshank).   [3] *Ibid.*
[4] H.C. 189 of 1945–6, Q. 2324 (Sir Gilbert Campion).

The fact that it was necessary to invent a vote in order that policy might be discussed shows how little debates in Supply have to do with money. It should be added that debate could now take place more easily, under Standing Order 17, on the motion that Mr Speaker do now leave the Chair, the Opposition moving an amendment to regret that Her Majesty's Government had not put forward adequate proposals for the control of the location of industry.

The debate is technically a discussion on proposed expenditure. Its purpose is sometimes said to be to induce economy in the Government; though, as Mr Lloyd George has said, 'it generally ends in a demand that you should spend more money for something or other'.[1] The process is not in fact justifiable on the assumption that it allows finance to be debated. But, because it is assumed that finance is the subject, it is forbidden to discuss any matter that would require legislation; it is in order to suggest that the Minister of Works should provide valets for the pelicans in St James's Park or to criticise him for supporting capitalism by allowing a contractor to charge 6d. for seven minutes on the Boat Pond in Regent's Park, but out of order to suggest a change in the method of administering unemployment assistance. This difficulty has, however, been in large measure overcome by the amendment to Standing Order 17, which allows the Opposition to raise a debate on an amendment to the motion that Mr Speaker do now leave the Chair. When such an amendment is under discussion Mr Speaker may permit such incidental reference to legislative action as he may consider relevant to any matter of administration then under debate, when enforcement of the prohibition (against reference to legislation) would, in his opinion, unduly restrict the discussion of such matters.

For the same reason, also, any member may raise any question relevant to the vote, even if it is not relevant to the debate. This is not an unmixed evil, for the private member's other opportunities for raising minor questions in respect of which he cannot get reasonable answers are extremely limited. Nevertheless, it is apt to make the debates very discursive to find members constantly saying, 'I do not propose to follow the honourable member who has just sat down in his

---

[1] H.C. 161 of 1931, Q. 372. Cf. Mr Gladstone's statement: 'It is more difficult to save a shilling than to spend a million': quoted by Mr J. A. R. Marriott, 95 H.C.Deb. 5 s.,1504.

discussion of the question of   , but would like to raise the question of   '.

For all these reasons debates in Supply are often criticised. Lord Eustace Percy once called them 'the most discursive and futile of all our proceedings'.[1] On the other hand, Sir Austen Chamberlain said:

> I think they [Supply days] are admirable. With the additional occasional vote of censure, they give the private member of the Opposition sufficient opportunities for discussing policy, and I do not believe that you can do more in the House of Commons. I do not think that in these days the House of Commons will ever control the details of expenditure. You have to rely for those upon the Departments whose business it is to control them. The more opportunities you give to the House of Commons to discuss Supply, the more pressure is put upon ministers to spend money.[2]

On the other hand, nobody has a good word to say for the process which is followed at 9 p.m. on the seventh and eighth and the last two days of Supply, of tramping through the lobbies to approve votes which have not been debated. It is followed because members wish to increase the number of divisions in which they vote, and so indicate to their constituents their devotion to duty; and because the Opposition wishes to register a protest against certain items of policy. The former has no public advantage; the latter is quite ineffective because usually nobody knows what are the votes against which the Opposition has divided, and why. In any case, it is useless to divide twice, once in committee against the votes and once on the report to the House against the same votes.[3] Indeed, the report stage is of no utility whatever, though since it has to be taken on one of the Supply days and is not exempted from the ten o'clock rule it does not prolong parliamentary proceedings or serve as an occasion for obstruction.

As a result of the long experience of estimating acquired by the departments and the Treasury, and of the constant pressure of the Treasury and the Public Accounts Committee, the forecasts of the departments are remarkably accurate. Necessarily, there are often slight mistakes made or modifications required in the allocation of

---

[1] *Ibid.* Q. 1886.   [2] H.C. 161 of 1931, Q. 2511.
[3] In 1938 the Labour party decided not to challenge divisions. Instead, they raised questions on the adjournment.

expenditure for other purposes. So long as the variations are within subheads they can be made without approaching Parliament anew. So long as they can be met by virement between subheads or (on the Service Votes) between votes, and the Treasury consents, there is similarly no need to make application to the House. The Treasury does not permit virement where it thinks that its permission may be criticised; and it is not empowered to allow virement between votes unless it may be 'detrimental to the public service' to postpone expenditure 'until provision can be made for it by Parliament in the usual course'.[1] Apart from these cases, every excess of expenditure in a subhead, however small,[2] requires a Supplementary Estimate. A Supplementary Estimate is especially required where some event, such as the outbreak of war between two nations of such a character that British forces must be moved, or civil disturbance in the United Kingdom or one of its dependencies, necessitates expenditure which could not have been foreseen. Any new service or extension of an existing service approved by the Cabinet or the Treasury, whether it needs legislation or not, also gives rise to a Supplementary Estimate. Except in cases such as these, Supplementary Estimates are discouraged. They upset the balance of the budget and allow expenditure to escape from parliamentary control. 'To render parliamentary control effectual it is necessary that the House of Commons should have the money transactions of the year presented to it in one mass and in one account.'[3]

The department must apply to the Treasury as soon as the probability of its expenditure being exceeded is foreseen[4] and the Treasury will decide whether to present a Supplementary Estimate.[5] The practice of postponing payment on an accrued obligation in the hope of avoiding a Supplementary Estimate is sternly forbidden, since the fact of over-expenditure is hidden from Parliament.[6] As the Public Accounts Committee said in 1891:

When the officers of a Department apprehend that the provision that has been voted will be insufficient, their first effort should be to exercise economy by postponing any works or services which can be thus dealt with without

---

[1] Appropriation Act, s. 4 (1).   [2] Epitome, p. 365.
[3] Reports of the Select Committee of Public Accounts 1862, p. 1571 (Mr Gladstone), quoted Durell, p. 48.   [4] Epitome, pp. 139–40, 165, 227, 263–5.
[5] *Ibid.* pp. 165, 227.   [6] *Ibid.* p. 625.

injury to public interests; if that expedient should prove insufficient or impracticable, resort should be had to a supplementary estimate; and in the rare cases which sometimes arise, when the discovery that the grant will be exceeded is not made in time to obtain a supplementary grant, the proper course...will be to make all payments that are due and fully matured and that fall within the general provision of the estimate, rather than avoid an excess by the postponement of such payments.[1]

When a Supplementary Estimate has to be submitted, the Public Accounts Committee requires that provision should be made under every subhead for which there is an anticipated deficit even if there are savings on other subheads in the same vote, which would entitle the Treasury to authorise virement, unless the amount is trivial and the subject appears not to be contentious.[2] This enables the Committee of Supply to consider expenditure under the vote as a whole, by seeing where there have been savings and where over-expenditure has occurred. Sometimes, also, the Treasury insists on a Supplementary Estimate even where there is enough surplus on a vote to cover the deficits. For instance, the Treasury insisted in 1872, on the suggestion of the Public Accounts Committee, that the irregularities in the Post Office should be brought before Parliament by means of a Supplementary Estimate.[3]

Supplementary Estimates are submitted to the Committee of Supply. There are, actually, two kinds of such estimates, those presented before the end of the financial year to meet prospective over-expenditure in that year; and those presented after the end of the year in order to meet excess expenditure in that year.[4] The time occupied by the consideration of all Supplementary Estimates is now included in the Supply days unless they are estimates for war expenditure. This change, which was made in 1948, is a matter of some importance, for it means that debate on Supplementary Estimates cannot now be used for purposes of obstruction.

Even when they were not used for the purpose of obstruction, the debates on Supplementary Estimates were, in normal circumstances, quite useless. As Mr Winston Churchill said in 1931:

I consider the debates on supplementary estimates are the most worthless of any that I have known in my career. They deal with comparatively small

[1] *Ibid.* p. 263. [2] *Ibid.* p. 733. [3] *Ibid.* pp. 36–47, 68–71.
[4] Cf. the two sums provided by the Consolidated Fund Act, 1954, referred to in Appendix IV.

sums of money, that is to say small compared to the annual Budget, and yet very often five or six days are consumed in these debates.[1]

For the purpose of debate, Supplementary Estimates may be divided into two classes. First, there are cases where the excess is due to a mistake in estimating the cost of a service. Here it is not permissible to debate the policy of the original service, except so far as it is brought in question by the excess. Consequently, the debate usually deteriorates into a series of disjointed speeches punctuated by calls to order by the chairman. Secondly, there are Supplementary Estimates due to a change of policy or to a new service. Here the change of policy or the policy of the new service can be debated; but usually that change or new policy is due to recent legislation. Accordingly, the policy of that legislation is discussed yet again. For instance, the Unemployment Act, 1934, was followed by Supplementary Estimates to provide for unemployment assistance allowances. The debate, therefore, was on the 'means test'. That subject had already been discussed on the second reading of the Unemployment Bill for most of three days, on the financial resolution for two days, on the report of the financial resolution for one day, on the guillotine motion for one day, in committee for several days, on the recommittal, on the report for several days and on the third reading for one day. It was then discussed in supply on the Supplementary Estimates for two days and on the report of the resolution for one day. No doubt it was an important subject; and as it happened the debates on Supplementary Estimates were from the point of view of the Opposition most useful, for they compelled the Government to induce the Unemployment Assistance Board to withdraw the 'means test' Regulations. This was, however, the exceptional case; normally the debates are but repetitions of stale arguments.

The exceptional case shows, however, that the debates are sometimes —though rarely—important. Even debates arising out of mistakes in estimating are of value in compelling departments not only to estimate properly but also to keep within their estimates. If Supplementary Estimates passed through as a matter of form there would be great temptation to departments to exceed estimates. The debate is an effective sanction even though it is useless as a debate.

[1] H.C. 161 of 1931, Q. 1527.

3. THE ESTIMATES COMMITTEE

At no time since 1902 has it been suggested that the Committee of Supply has been an effective means of controlling expenditure, or even a body concerned primarily with expenditure. A few members like Mr Gibson Bowles and Sir Frederick Banbury, alarmed at the growth of the social services, have paid particular attention to the Estimates and have insisted on talking about them. In the main, however, the Estimates have been regarded as presented 'for information'; and, as usually happens when information is provided, most members have neglected to inform themselves. Members are always curious until they have the means of satisfying their curiosity. The result has been that, while the Treasury has gained substantial powers of control over public expenditure and has not hesitated to use them, the House has for the most part paid attention to other things. Parliamentary control of finance was never very strong—the praise of times past usually refers to a Constitution that has never existed—but what there was has tended to be transformed into Treasury control.

There was much discussion on this problem in the session of 1887 and 1888. Several select committees were appointed to examine Estimates and to report their observations thereon to the House. In 1887 the Army and Navy Estimates were together referred to a single committee; and in 1888 three separate committees dealt respectively with the Army, Navy, and the Revenue Departments.[1] While this experiment was being tried, another select committee was appointed to consider 'the procedure by which the House annually grants the Supplies to Her Majesty'. Though the time spent in Committee of Supply was considerable and was increasing, the Select Committee had no doubt that the debates had a good effect in preventing increased expenditure, and that the opportunities thus provided were an important and valuable means of raising many questions of policy and administration which might otherwise escape notice. They did not, therefore, think it desirable to dispense with or to limit the functions of the Committee of Supply. They did not favour an annual select committee,

[1] See Eleventh Report from the Select Committee on National Expenditure, 1943–4 (H.C. 122 of 1944), p. 5.

nor a preliminary investigation before the Estimates were considered by the House. It was therefore recommended that as an experiment a third standing committee might be set up to deal with certain classes or votes in place of the Committee of Supply.[1] The main purpose of this proposal, apparently, was to save time in Committee of Supply. It was not, however, adopted, and the experiment then in progress of sending the Estimates to select committees was discontinued.[2]

As a result of criticisms of expenditure incurred during the Boer War, a Select Committee on National Expenditure was appointed in 1902 and reported in 1903.[3] This Committee again pointed out that debates in Supply were really debates on policy and that they left much to be desired from the point of view of financial scrutiny. It was, therefore, recommended that a select committee called the Estimates Committee be appointed on the same lines as the Public Accounts Committee.[4] In order to unify the machinery of financial control, a proportion of members should serve on both the Public Accounts Committee and the Estimates Committee. The latter should consider a class, branch or portion of the Estimates for each year, not exceeding one-fourth of the whole, and the portion to be examined should be selected by the Public Accounts Committee in the previous year. The Estimates Committee would thus, in the course of several years, pass the whole volume of Estimates under review.[5] Once more no action was taken.

The question was, however, raised in the House at intervals, especially when, after 1909, the growing burden of Defence expenditure caused Liberal and Labour members to fear that the expansion of the social services was threatened.[6] In 1912 the House, after debate, agreed

That a Select Committee be appointed to examine such of the Estimates presented to this House as may seem fit to the Committee, and report what, if any, economies consistent with the policy implied in those Estimates should be effected therein.[7]

This decision was quite different from the proposal made in 1888. In moving the motion which became, after an amendment accepted by

---

[1] H.C. 281 of 1888.   [2] H.C. 122 of 1944, p. 6.   [3] H.C. 387 of 1902.
[4] See *post* pp. 332–8.   [5] H.C. 387 of 1903 and H.C. 122 of 1944, pp. 6–7.
[6] E.g. 20 H.C.Deb. 5 s., 399; 21 H.C.Deb. 5 s., 199, 437, 1288; 22 H.C.Deb. 5 s., 1928, 1929, 1944, 2116, 2119, 2123, 2127, 2140, 2150, 2155, 2162.
[7] 37 H.C.Deb. 5 s., 434.

the Government, this resolution, the Chancellor of the Exchequer laid down three principles: that the Government must not be deprived of its responsibility, that the House must not be divested of its authority, and that the Committee must not accept responsibility for policy.[1] Accordingly, the function of the Committee was not to supersede the Committee of Supply but to assist it.

The Select Committee was set up in 1912, 1913 and 1914, and within narrow limits it did good work, though for reasons explained in 1918 and shortly to be set out it was not able to accomplish all that had been hoped. It lapsed with the outbreak of war, because no Estimates were presented. The loss of parliamentary control which resulted from the creation of the War Cabinet and the absence of Estimates was adversely commented on in 1917[2] and as a result a Select Committee on National Expenditure was set up in each of the sessions of 1917–18, 1918, 1919, and 1920 and produced some very useful reports, now of considerable historical value. The Select Committee of 1918 gave particular attention to financial control. In the Seventh Report[3] it suggested a new form of Estimates and Accounts, which has not been adopted; and in the Ninth Report[4] it made a proposal for two select committees on Estimates, for the following reasons:

1. Control in Committee of Supply is not in fact a control over the Estimates.

2. Treasury control, invaluable as it is up to a point, is not a substitute for parliamentary control.

3. Control by ministers is not enough—such a doctrine 'would convert the responsibility of ministers into irresponsibility'.[5]

The Committee considered that the Estimates Committees of 1912, 1913 and 1914 had three defects:

1. The task of examining all the Estimates was too large for any single body to perform, with the result that only a fraction of them were considered

---

[1] *Ibid.* 367.

[2] 92 H.C.Deb. 5 s., 1363–98 (proposals were made, not for the first or last time, for the creation of parliamentary committees like the French *commissions*); 95 H.C.Deb. 5 s., 1493–1569.   [3] H.C. 98 of 1918.

[4] H.C. 121 of 1918. The references are to the consolidated volume, Reports from the Select Committee on National Expenditure, 1918.

[5] Reports, pp. 115–16.

each year and a department whose Estimate was once examined knew that it would be free for the next eight or ten years.

2. They were handicapped by the form of the Estimates, which did not allow of an examination of the total expenditure of any department.[1]

3. Whereas the Public Accounts Committee had the expert assistance of the Comptroller and Auditor-General and his staff, the Estimates Committees had no technical assistance.[2]

The Committee therefore recommended that there should be two Estimates Committees, of fifteen members each, and stated that it might afterwards be desirable to add a third. The Estimates should be allocated to them by the chairman of Ways and Means, and they should examine all the Estimates every year. Though there would not usually be time to allow them to consider Supplementary Estimates, such Estimates might be referred to them in special cases; and in considering Estimates they would pay particular attention to items first introduced as Supplementary Estimates in the previous year. They should not be empowered to make recommendations inconsistent with the policy implied in the Estimates, though it might be proper to propose increased capital expenditure on works, in order to produce economy in annual expenditure. Finally, it was not recommended that the Comptroller and Auditor-General should act as adviser; such a step would introduce complications in his relations with the Treasury and the spending departments. Nor was it desirable to second an officer from the Treasury, whose function it was to meet and answer criticisms and not to supply them. It was recommended, however, that there should be a special officer of the House, called the Examiner of Estimates, whose function should be to advise the committees.[3]

These proposals were not accepted by the Government; but instead a sessional Order was passed in 1919 to refer all Estimates[4] to the standing committees (of which, under the 1919 rules, there were six). The allocation was to be made by the chairman of Ways and Means, and the House was to proceed after report from a standing committee

---

[1] A substantial modification had been proposed in the 7th Report.
[2] Reports, pp. 116–17.
[3] *Ibid.* See also Report of the Machinery of Government Committee, Cd. 9230 (1930 reprint), p. 15.
[4] Except Votes A and 1 of the Army, Navy, and Air Force Estimates.

as if the votes had been reported from Committee of Supply. A minister might move that certain Estimates or Votes should be considered in Committee of Supply; and if this was carried the Estimates or Votes were to be deemed to be withdrawn from the standing committees.[1] In this way it was hoped, first, to provide for adequate consideration of the Estimates and, secondly, to reduce Supply days from twenty to twelve. The latter proposal was, however, given up; with the result that the sessional Order did not in any way save the time of the House.

As a result of further parliamentary agitation, an informal committee was set up to examine the problem, and reported as follows:

1. That an Estimates Committee of 18 should be appointed.

2. That the danger of considerable overlapping of functions rendered it undesirable that the Estimates Committee should sit as a separate body in addition to the Select Committee on National Expenditure and the Public Accounts Committee, and it is therefore proposed that the Estimates Committee and the Select Committee on National Expenditure should be merged into one.

3. That in accordance with the procedure that has been adopted in the past in the case of the Select Committee on National Expenditure there should be one Committee only but power should be given to it to appoint sub-committees.

4. That as in other cases of committees whose functions continue from session to session, e.g. the Public Accounts Committee, the same members, as far as may be possible, should be appointed to serve each session, and leave should be given to the Committee to sit during adjournments of the House if they so desire.

5. That the Committee should have no power to deal with questions of policy or to advocate increased expenditure. Their functions should be to examine Estimates in the light of the Government's policy with a view to discovering any possible economies and any items which appeared to involve or to have involved wasteful or unnecessary expenditure or seemed likely to lead to large increases of expenditure in future years.

6. That the procedure in the House of Commons in regard to Supply should remain unaltered and that on the appointment of the Estimates Committee no hard-and-fast rules should be laid down with the object of securing the postponement of discussions on Estimates in Committee of Supply pending receipt of reports from the Estimates Committee. Rules of this character

---

[1] 112 H.C.Deb. 5 s., 1256–7.

might create considerable difficulties in regard to the business of the House and might also lead, in some cases, to hurried and insufficient consideration of the Estimates by the Committee itself. It is suggested, therefore, that it should be left to the Government, in arranging the order in which the Estimates are to be discussed in the House, to bear constantly in mind the proceedings of the Estimates Committee with a view to meeting the convenience both of the Committee and the House as far as possible....

7. That there should be attached to the Committee an experienced member of the staff of the House of Commons, whose function it would be to prepare material for the Committee deliberations and to render advice and assistance to the Committee and the Chairman in particular. Being a servant of the House, this official would occupy an independent position in relation to Ministers.

8. That this official should not be empowered to call for information from Government Departments except on the instructions of the Chairman of the Committee, nor have the right of access to Departmental papers, but the Committee shall have the ordinary right of sending for persons, papers and records.

9. That no further staff should be appointed at the present time, and that the Committee should decide by experience whether the creation of any additional staff was required.

10. That the selection of the Chairman should be left to the Committee.[1]

The proposal ultimately adopted was somewhat different. The Committee was set up in June 1921, with the following terms of reference:

That a Select Committee be appointed to examine such of the Estimates presented to this House as may seem fit to the Committee, and to suggest the form in which the Estimates shall be presented for examination, and to report what, if any, economies consistent with the policy implied in those Estimates may be effected therein.[2]

The Committee consisted originally of twenty-four members, but it was subsequently increased to twenty-eight members, with a quorum of seven. It was given power to send for persons, papers and records, and to sit notwithstanding any adjournment of the House. Further, it was given power to appoint sub-committees with the full powers of the undivided Committee. Under these terms of reference the Committee

---

[1] 141 H.C.Deb. 5 s., 1692–4.
[2] 143 H.C.Deb. 5 s., 2079–81.

was reappointed annually from 1921 to the outbreak of war in 1939. It will be noticed that no provision was made for an expert adviser. The proposal of the informal committee was a compromise between the views of those who wanted an officer of the status of the Comptroller and Auditor-General (as suggested in 1918 by the Select Committee on National Expenditure) and the views of the Government, and it appears that, as often, the compromise was one of words and not of substance. The Estimates Committee was given a clerk, but it had no expert adviser until 1926, when a Treasury official was seconded to assist the Committee.[1]

This development was due to the First Report of the Estimates Committee in 1926,[2] in which it had recommended a change in the classification and grouping of the Estimates (a change effected by the Government in the following year, subject to emendations), an alteration in the size of the Committee so that it could appoint sub-committees and co-opt to them experts from outside (a suggestion which the Government refused to consider), and a change in the limits of discussion of Estimates in the House of Commons (another suggestion which the Government refused to accept). The Government having thus rejected most of the Committee's suggestions, it was decided by way of a sop to allow the assistance of a Treasury official to be given.[3]

For a short time after its appointment there was some interest in the work of the Committee. Its first chairman, Sir Frederick Banbury, was what Sir Austen Chamberlain once called (when leader of the House of Commons) an 'economy maniac'. He had a very considerable knowledge of financial procedure and of the technique of financial control. He had, also, a deep-seated belief in the futility of nearly all Government expenditure; and with him 'economy' meant not spending more but spending as little as possible. Most members desire more services at less cost; he wanted something more easily obtainable, less cost. In 1922 he secured a debate on the reports of the Estimates Committee,[4] though nothing came of it. After a time, it became difficult to obtain a quorum. In 1930, for instance, only nine members, including the

---

[1] He is usually a Principal Assistant Secretary.
[2] H.C. 59 of 1926.   [3] 198 H.C.Deb. 5 s., 613.
[4] 157 H.C.Deb. 5 s., 1362–1416.

chairman, attended half the meetings. There were frequent changes of chairman and clerk, and generally 'the Committee, not being regarded as one of the major authorities of Parliament, has not been so effective as the importance of its work might require'.[1]

Sir Malcolm Ramsay, then Comptroller and Auditor-General, gave evidence to the same effect in 1931:

> The Estimates Committee has, I am afraid, failed to realise the expectations of those who advocated its establishment. It is true that it has helped to secure certain useful improvements, generally of a minor order. But it has effected no substantial economies, and its results have surely been achieved by disproportionate expenditure of time and labour by members and witnesses, and some at any rate of the matters on which it has made recommendations might equally well have been handled by the Public Accounts Committee (e.g. the regrouping of the Estimates, or the financial control of the Empire Marketing Board).[2]

This, he thought, was due to the difficulties 'which are inherent in any attempt to institute detailed examination and control by the House of Commons without offence to the cardinal doctrine of Cabinet and ministerial responsibility'.[3] These difficulties are of three kinds.

In the first place, expenditure is determined primarily by policy, which the Committee is precluded from examining by its terms of reference. It is difficult enough for the Treasury to control a policy determined by the Cabinet, and the Committee can do less than the Treasury. For instance, if a rearmament programme is determined by the Cabinet, the Treasury cannot do more than regulate contracts and expenses of administration. If the Army Council decides that Sten guns must be superseded by more expensive Sterlings, and the Cabinet agrees (as it is bound to do if the Army Council reports that British armaments would otherwise be inferior to an army against which it might have to fight), the Treasury can make certain that, as far as the nature of the market permits, the guns are acquired through competitive tendering. Also, the Treasury knows something about staffing and insists on a case being made before it consents to any increase, or to

---

[1] H.C. 161 of 1931, Q. 2585 (Sir Herbert Samuel, who had been Chairman of the Select Committee on National Expenditure in 1918).
[2] H.C. 161 of 1931, p. 366.   [3] *Ibid.*

any alteration of grading, or to any new level of salaries.[1] The Estimates Committee is in a less favourable position than the Treasury. Where matters are brought to its attention, the Committee can criticise methods of purchase and disposal, condemn irregularities of practice or by individual officers, and ask whether increases of staff are really necessary. By reason of the fact that it summons officials before it, it can, as a former Speaker said it would be able to do, 'establish a funk' in the Departments.[2] But all this is done by the Public Accounts Committee. Its only advantage over that Committee is that it considers the Estimates and not the Accounts, and so gets in early;[3] but this advantage is offset by two very substantial disadvantages, corresponding to the two other difficulties mentioned by Sir Malcolm Ramsay.

The second difficulty is that of time. The Estimates are not presented to the House until February or March; they are at once referred to the Committee of Supply and some of them have to be considered almost immediately in order that the vote on account[4] and the appropriate Consolidated Fund Bill may be passed before 31 March. The Estimates are passed through Supply by the end of July. The Estimates Committee has first to find out from 1500 pages of detailed figures and explanations some points which may be the subject of questions: it then has to get witnesses before it and examine them; next it has to frame a report; and finally it has to get the report printed. Occasionally it gets out a first report by May; but generally it presents a single report at the end of June. On the one hand it has to hurry its proceedings and cannot obtain full information; on the other hand a report in June is too late for effective consideration by the House, and is also in large part *ex post facto*.

Finally, there is the difficulty of staff. The Comptroller and Auditor-General has a substantial staff working in the departments. They draw his attention, and he draws the attention of the Public Accounts Committee, to any question within his competence. The Public Accounts

[1] On Treasury control, see *Cabinet Government*, ch. VII.
[2] Reports from the Select Committee on National Expenditure, p. 122.
[3] The difference is this: the Estimates Committee considers in, say, 1956 the Estimates for the year ending 31 March 1957. The expenditure authorised by these Estimates comes before the Public Accounts Committee in 1958.
[4] *Post*, p. 316; and see Appendix IV.

Committee thus has a report on which it can set to work. The Estimates Committee is not in that position. The Treasury official who advises them draws their attention to matters of which the Treasury has learned. So far as it can, the Treasury itself proceeds to take the necessary action. What happens in practice is that the Treasury uses the Committee to reinforce doctrines which it lays down for the action of the departments. If, for instance, the Air Ministry will not accept the Treasury ruling as to the making of contracts for supplies, the Treasury official brings the matter before the Committee, which hears the appropriate official from the Ministry and the appropriate official from the Treasury, and probably agrees with the Treasury. Thereupon, the Treasury is pleased to minute that 'The Secretary of State will see that the Committee agrees with the views stated by My Lords in their minute of —— and My Lords trust that he will be able to give instructions accordingly'. The Committee, that is, reinforces Treasury control and does not effect any more economies than the Treasury does. The Public Accounts Committee does the same; and what is more, it can criticise the Treasury itself.

An independent official without a large staff would do much less successfully what the Comptroller and Auditor-General does at present. Moreover, 'the Comptroller deals with Accounts, which are records of fact. Estimates are matters of opinion.'[1] This is over-simplification, since the Comptroller often deals with matters of opinion; but it is largely true. It is, too, 'extremely difficult to see how any officer of the House of Commons, however able, could formulate or express any opinion as regards the requirements of the public service which would be better than that of the Department responsible, or than the conclusion arrived at by the Treasury on behalf of the House after a minute and often prolonged discussion of the details'.[2]

The Estimates Committee disappeared during the war of 1939–45. Estimates give valuable information to the enemy, and, though they were compiled in order that Treasury control might continue, they were not submitted to Parliament, which authorised expenditure under votes of credit. There were thus no Estimates to be referred to a select

[1] H.C. 161 of 1931, p. 367 (Sir Malcolm Ramsay).
[2] *Ibid.*

committee. Instead, the example of 1917 was followed and a Select Committee on National Expenditure was established every year

to examine the current expenditure defrayed out of moneys provided by Parliament for the Defence Services, for Civil Defence, and for other services directly connected with the war, and to report what, if any, economies, consistent with the execution of the policy decided by the Government, may be effected therein.

The Committee presented over one hundred reports,[1] and, under special powers conferred by the House, memoranda on various subjects unsuitable for publication in war conditions were presented to the Prime Minister for the consideration of the War Cabinet.

The Select Committee worked through sub-committees and had a co-ordinating sub-committee or 'steering committee' to allocate functions to sub-committees and avoid overlapping. It had a staff of eleven clerks drawn from the House of Commons offices. It had power, which it exercised regularly, of sending sub-committees to inspect such works as aerodromes. Opinions on the Committee's merits differed considerably. The chairman (Sir John Wardlaw-Milne) and the secretary thought that it exercised a valuable function because it helped to secure that the Government obtained 'value for money'.[2] On the other hand, Mr Speaker Clifton Brown was 'not an admirer' of the Committee because it required a large staff and because there was a risk of its interfering in policy.[3] Mr Herbert Morrison said that it did occasionally stray into the realm of policy and also into the realm of the Public Accounts Committee. Now and again there were clashes.[4] 'They were really overhauling current activities;' he said,[5] 'the Committee got asking questions which in the judgment of some of the Ministers at that time were... running rival with the executive responsibility of the Minister himself'. Later he said that

if the Government or its officers are to be pulled up in the midst of their administration to be examined on current administration before a committee of Parliament, I think it is disturbing, highly inconvenient, and will weaken the efficiency of Whitehall administration.[6]

---

[1] A list of reports and memoranda submitted up to 1944 is given in H.C. 122 of 1944, pp. 12–17.　　　[2] H.C. 189 of 1945–6, Q. 4408 (Sir John Wardlaw-Milne).
[3] *Ibid.* p. 82.　　[4] *Ibid.* Q. 3221.　　[5] *Ibid.* Q. 3229.
[6] *Ibid.* Q. 3345.

The Select Committee did not survive the war, and in 1946 the Estimates Committee was re-established with its old terms of reference, though it was given power to act through sub-committees and to adjourn from place to place. It was, however, obvious from the evidence submitted to the Select Committee on Procedure in 1946 that dissatisfaction with the Estimates Committee continued. Thus Mr Osbert Peake, chairman of the Public Accounts Committee said:

> When the Treasury has agreed with a department that such and such a group of Estimates are reasonable, I do not see what functions the Estimates Committee can usefully perform in going through those same Estimates under the guidance of the Treasury official who has agreed them. It is just doing the work over again.[1]

In answer to another question Mr Peake said that to give the Estimates Committee an adequate machine for checking Estimates would be 'to set up a second Treasury to check the first Treasury, which has checked the department'.[2]

Sir Gilbert Campion, who was then Clerk of the House of Commons, suggested 'that the Public Accounts Committee and the Estimates Committee' should be combined into a 'Public Expenditure Committee' which would have the same framework as the Select Committee on National Expenditure. It would have six investigating sub-committees and one co-ordinating sub-committee consisting of the chairman of the committee and the chairmen of the sub-committees. Four of the sub-committees would divide the departments among them; one would deal with major inquiries; and one would make short-term inquiries into current complaints. He made these suggestions because:

> (1) The work of the Public Accounts Committee and the Estimates Committee overlapped, and the two Committees may (and indeed have) made contradictory reports; and
>
> (2) The field of public expenditure is too wide for any body to cover without a division of labour.

In evidence on these proposals it was also pointed out by some—and denied by others—that there was a 'gap' which neither Committee covered. Thus, in 1959 the Public Accounts Committee would con-

---

[1] *Ibid.* Q. 3924.   [2] *Ibid.* Q. 3927.

sider the expenditure for 1957–8 and the Estimates Committee would consider the expenditure for 1959–60; but neither would cover the expenditure for 1958–9.[1] As we shall see, however, the Public Accounts Committee does project its enquiries into 1958–9 and the Estimates Committee, in considering Estimates for 1959–60, necessarily considers expenditure for 1958–9. What is more, there can be no gaps because the proposed expenditure for 1958–9 was considered by the Estimates Committee in 1958 and the actual expenditure for 1958–9 will be considered by the Public Accounts Committee in 1960. Overlapping is avoided by the practice of making the chairman of the Estimates Committee a member of the Public Accounts Committee. In any event, for the reasons given by Mr Morrison and already quoted the Government was strongly opposed to the setting up of a permanent committee on the lines of the wartime Select Committee on National Expenditure. The Comptroller and Auditor-General, too, objected to the extension of the functions of his office so as to require him to advise on current expenditure, because his staff was composed of accountants engaged in audit and would not be qualified to exercise the wider function.[2]

The Select Committee on Procedure considered

that the functions of the Committee of Public Accounts and the Estimates Committee would be better performed by a single Committee. Such a Committee would have no powers beyond those possessed by the separate committees now, and there would be no change in the position or duties of the Comptroller and Auditor-General either in relation to the Departments or the Committee. The advantage of combining both functions in a single Committee working through sub-committees is twofold. First, the knowledge and experience gained by examination of the Accounts would be brought to bear upon the examination of current expenditure, and vice versa. Secondly, a single committee with sub-committees provides a method for co-ordinating the whole work of the examination of expenditure, for which neither overlapping membership nor any other method of liaison is a satisfactory substitute. The result would be a strengthening of parliamentary control of expenditure and it might be that fewer members would be needed for this work.[3]

The Government refused to accept this recommendation but the Committee's membership was enlarged to thirty-six, and it was em-

[1] *Ibid.* pp. xxxiv–vi.   [2] *Ibid.* p. 188.   [3] *Ibid.* pp. xv–xvi.

powered to appoint sub-committees and to adjourn from place to place. The Committee is therefore able to function much as the Select Committee on National Expenditure functioned during the war. It works through sub-committees, which examine specific items of the Estimates, if necessary at the point at which the expenditure is to be incurred, and report to the main committee, which in turn submits interim reports to the House, where they are frequently discussed in Committee of Supply.

4. APPROPRIATION

The resolutions of the Committee of Supply have, of course, no statutory effect. They merely advise the House to grant supply, and are reported to and adopted by the House. The House in Committee of Ways and Means then resolves to grant out of the Consolidated Fund a sum 'towards making good the Supply granted to Her Majesty'. This is reported to the House and forms the basis of the necessary legislation. The Committee of Ways and Means, like the Committee of Supply, is simply the House in the absence of the Speaker. This stage is, however, pure form, and there have been many suggestions to abolish it; but as it is pure form nobody has bothered.

The Appropriation Act authorises expenditure on the Supply Services for one year only, ending on 31 March next following. The Appropriation Act for the current year is not passed until the end of July. Accordingly, special legislation has to be passed to cover the period from April to July.[1] During March, therefore, the Committee of Supply has to vote enough supply for the period of four months, and the Committee of Ways and Means has to authorise the necessary issues from the Consolidated Fund. So far as the Civil and Revenue Departments are concerned, this is done by a vote on account submitted to the Committee of Supply. It grants a sum on each of the votes in these estimates,[2] and the debate in supply may therefore range over the whole field of administration by the departments concerned. The Committee

[1] I.e. the Appropriation Act, 1957, authorises expenditure to 31 March 1958. Legislation has to be passed to authorise issues from the Consolidated Fund between April 1958 and July 1958, when the Appropriation Act, 1958, is passed.

[2] 'That a sum not exceeding £   be granted to Her Majesty on account, towards defraying the charge for the following Civil and Revenue Department Services...for the year ending on the 31st day of March, 1956.'

of Supply has also to vote supplies for the Army, Navy, and Air Services. In these cases a vote on account is not necessary, for the Appropriation Act will authorise virement between votes for each service. Provided, therefore, that enough money be voted on one vote in each service, this may be applied to all votes until the Appropriation Act is passed. The practice is to approve Vote A (personnel) and Vote 1 (pay, etc.) for each service.

The Committee of Supply having thus granted supply, and this being reported to the House, the Committee of Ways and Means formally authorises the issue of the total from the Consolidated Fund;[1] and this being reported to the House the Consolidated Fund (No. 2) Bill[2] is ordered to be brought in. The second and third reading debates of this measure provide opportunities for raising any question of administration whatever, since it covers all the Government departments.

The Committee of Supply continues to vote the estimates and when they are all voted on the twenty-fifth supply day and reported on the twenty-sixth day the necessary Ways and Means resolutions are passed and reported and the Appropriation Bill ordered to be brought in. This Bill does several things:

1. It authorises the issue of the remaining sums required for supply, and not already voted in the Consolidated Fund (No. 2) Act.

2. It authorises further borrowing powers.

3. It appropriates all the money granted since the previous Appropriation Act.

4. It authorises virements between the votes for the Defence Services.

5. It ratifies virements between such votes made under the Appropriation Act of the last year but one.

---

[1] 'That towards making good the supply granted to Her Majesty for the service of the year ending on the 31st day of March, 1956, the sum of £ be granted out of the Consolidated Fund of the United Kingdom.' This sum will be greater than that in the footnote above, since it will include the pay for the Army, Navy, and Air Services.

[2] The Consolidated Fund (No. 1) Bill, 1955, authorises the issue of money required for Supplementary Estimates for the year ending 31 March 1955, and possibly also some excess votes for the year ending 31 March 1954. Very often the Consolidated Fund (No. 2) Bill 1955 also authorises expenditure on Supplementary Estimates and excess votes. Both Bills also authorise borrowing by the Treasury. The issue clause is: 'The Treasury may issue out of the Consolidated Fund of the United Kingdom and apply towards making good the supply granted to Her Majesty for the service of the year ending on the 31st day of March, 1956, the sum of pounds.' See Appendix IV.

The debates on the second and third readings of this Bill again permit of the raising of any questions of administration.

The appropriation in the Appropriation Act follows the order of the votes in the estimates. It includes verbatim Part I of each vote, but does not give the subheads (Part II) or the detail (Part III). Accordingly, subject to the express authorisation of virement in section 4, which applies only to the Defence Services, Supplementary Estimates become necessary for any excess on any vote. So far as possible, such Supplementary Estimates are presented in the current year; but others cannot be presented until after the end of the financial year, when they become necessary to enable the accounts to be closed and are known as excess votes. Supplementary grants for the current year and the excess votes are included in the two Consolidated Fund Acts; and the sums granted by those Acts are appropriated by the Appropriation Act. Consequently, all the financial transactions of a financial year are completely closed two years later.

For convenience of exposition it has so far been assumed that public expenditure is wholly met out of issues from the Consolidated Fund. In fact, however, there are incidental revenues known as 'appropriations in aid', which are set off against the total sum required, and the amount shown in a supply grant is the net amount. In some cases, in fact, the appropriations in aid are greater than the cost; or, in other words, the income is greater than the expenditure. In such a case a supply grant is nevertheless given in the form of a 'token' vote of £100 or £10 in order that parliamentary control may be effective. For instance, the vote for County Courts in 1936 was £100 and appropriations in aid (due mainly to fees taken) were £780,384. Such appropriations in aid are always included in the Estimates as a separate subhead of the vote and are specifically appropriated by section 3 of the Appropriation Act and the Schedules to that Act.[1] Consequently, if there are extra receipts in any year they cannot be used for extra expenditure without parliamentary sanction. For instance, if the county courts prove unexpectedly popular and an extra £10,000 is obtained from fees, this sum cannot be used by the Lord Chancellor for strengthening the staff of the county courts unless Parliament specifically approves a

[1] By a practice instituted in 1894: see Epitome, pp. 332–4.

Supplementary Estimate. Even the Treasury cannot authorise the extra expenditure by virement; such authorisation would increase both the total of the grant and the total of the appropriation in aid.[1]

5. TAXATION

While this process has been going on, the House has been considering taxation in Committee of Ways and Means and passing the Finance Bill. The Chancellor of the Exchequer knows from the Estimates the anticipated cost of the Supply Services. He also knows the cost of the Consolidated Fund Services. On the other side of the account he knows within narrow limits the actual revenue of the previous year. He considers whether that revenue would alter during the coming year if taxation remained at the same level; if, for instance, trade has improved during the past year, he can presume an increase in the revenue from surtax, since the tax for one year is assessed on the income of the previous year. Putting the two sides of the account together, he finds an anticipated surplus or an anticipated deficit.

He may possibly decide not to propose any change in taxation to alter the situation. The surplus may be used to extinguish part of the National Debt, or the deficit added to the National Debt by borrowing. Even if this is done, it is necessary to move resolutions to reimpose the income tax. Usually, however, modifications are made in some or all of the 'permanent' taxes or in the 'permanent' Sinking Fund. Accordingly, the House goes into Committee of Ways and Means to hear the financial proposals explained by the Chancellor of the Exchequer in his 'Budget statement'.

It is now the practice for the Budget debate to include a debate on the general economic position of the country, and an Economic Survey is published a week or so before the Budget is opened. This enables the Budget proposals to be related to the level of wages and prices. For instance, if there is a fear of inflation a surplus has to be budgeted for in order to remove purchasing power off the market, and extinguish part of the floating debt, while if deflation is to be feared there would no

[1] Or, in other words, the gross estimate would be exceeded, though this figure is not specifically given in the Appropriation Act.

doubt be a Budget deficit. In addition, the Chancellor of the Exchequer gives an account of the income and expenditure (so far as it can be ascertained from issues from the Consolidated Fund[1]) of the previous year. He then indicates the changes in expenditure and, on the existing basis of taxation, in revenue, and produces his surplus or deficit. He then indicates his proposals for taxation for the coming year and moves one of the necessary resolutions. On that resolution the leaders of the Opposition parties make a few complimentary remarks, and it is carried. After that other resolutions are proposed and carried without debate, until the final resolution is reached. This is:

> That it is expedient to alter the law relating to the National Debt, Customs, and Inland Revenue (including Excise) and to make further provision in connection with finance.

On this motion being put, the chief whip moves 'That the Chairman do report progress, and ask leave to sit again.' The Budget debate on subsequent days takes place on the motion thus adjourned, and not on the detailed proposals. It is, in substance though not in form, a second reading debate. The debates on the specific proposals take place in the House, on the report of the Ways and Means resolutions. When they too have been passed the Finance Bill is ordered to be brought in, and the whole question is argued again, both in principle and in detail, on that Bill, which is passed in July.

The reason for the Committee of Ways and Means is the same as the reason for the Committee of Supply; that is, no reason at all, except history. The House being asked to grant supply must find ways and means for meeting the supply. Naturally it goes into committee for the purpose; and a committee being the whole House, the Committee of Ways and Means is the Committee of the whole House. Nothing could be simpler or more logical. The reason for taking all the Ways and Means resolutions, except one, on the same night is quite different. It is to prevent any kind of forestalling. This is particularly necessary with customs and excise duties, since traders have been known to turn a few honest pennies by importing or accumulating stocks in advance of the imposition of duties. Even where forestalling is not easily practicable,

---

[1] *Post*, p. 328

as with death duties and income tax, administration goes on from day to day, and it is desirable to indicate as early as possible what taxes are to be imposed, even though Parliament can always make its legislation retrospective.

For many years before 1913 the Treasury had taken the Ways and Means resolutions as sufficient justification for continuing the imposition of such annual taxes and for making such changes in the permanent taxes as would be imposed and made by the Finance Act when passed. Legally the resolutions gave no such authority, and when the procedure was challenged by Mr Gibson Bowles in 1912 the High Court held that the deduction of income-tax on the alleged authority of a Ways and Means resolution was invalid.[1] The difficulty was resolved by legislation, and the Provisional Collection of Taxes Act, 1913, gives statutory force for a limited period to any Ways and Means resolution varying an existing tax, or renewing for a further period a tax enforced or imposed during the previous financial year whether at the same or a different rate. The Act applies only to duties of customs and excise and to income-tax; the resolution itself must declare that in the public interest it is expedient that the resolution should have this effect; the resolution must be agreed to on report within ten sitting days, and the Bill confirming it read a second time within twenty sitting days and finally become law within four months, from the date of the resolution.

6. THE COMPTROLLER AND AUDITOR-GENERAL

Until 1832 the system of financial control was limited to the methods so far explained in this chapter, subject to the qualification that the control over issues now exercised by the Comptroller and Auditor-General, and therefore postponed to a later section of this chapter,[2] was exercised by the Auditor of the Exchequer.[3] In particular, there was no control over the actual expenditure since no detailed accounts were presented to Parliament.[4] In 1832 it was provided by legislation

[1] *Bowles* v. *Bank of England*, [1913] 1 Ch. 57.   [2] *Post*, pp. 326–8.
[3] Cf. the difficulties caused by the illness of George III in 1811: May, *Constitutional History* (1st ed.), 1, pp. 181–2.
[4] Accounts of (a) the total income, (b) the total payments out of the Consolidated Fund, (c) the charge on the Fund, (d) the net produce of taxation, (e) arrears and balances due from public accountants, (f) exports and imports, (g) shipping registered, (h) public

that the Commissioners of Audit should examine the accounts of naval expenditure side by side with the votes and Estimates for the Naval Service, and present a report to Parliament. In 1846 this was extended to the Army Votes, in 1851 to the Wood and Works Votes, and in 1861 to the Revenue Departments. The Select Committee on Public Moneys of 1857 and the reports of the Public Accounts Committee, first appointed in 1861 and made permanent in 1862, recommended the extension of the system to all public expenditure, and this was carried out by the Exchequer and Audit Departments Act, 1866.[1] In fact, the system thus applied to the Civil and Revenue Departments was more complete than that applied to the Navy and Army, until in 1876, on the representation of the Public Accounts Committee, the Treasury exercised its power under the Act of 1866 to apply a more detailed audit to the accounts of those services.[2]

The result of these reforms was to create an independent officer, the Comptroller and Auditor-General, who was formally described by the Chancellor of the Exchequer in 1885 as 'an officer of the House of Commons'.[3] This description, though accurate, must not lead to the assumption that he is appointed by the House itself, by the Commissioners for the regulation of the House, or by any officer of the House. The reason for the description is that he audits the accounts on behalf of the House[4] and reports direct to the House.[5] He has in fact a status not unlike that of a judge. He is appointed by the Crown; but, unlike other servants of the Crown, he holds office during good behaviour, but subject to removal by the Crown on an address from both Houses of Parliament.[6] He must not hold another office during the pleasure of

expenditure, (i) public funded debt, (j) unfunded debt, (k) disposal of moneys voted, were directed to be presented by the Consolidated Fund Act, 1816, s. 22. But this is very different from an appropriation account.

[1] Accordingly, the votes were for the first time divided into subheads in 1867.

[2] Epitome, pp. 56–63.

[3] *Ibid.* p. 176. Hence the confusion over the report of the informal committee in 1921: *ante*, p. 307. In recommending that the Estimates Committee be assisted by an officer of the House, some members thought that an officer like the Comptroller and Auditor-General was intended, while others thought of the proposed assistant as one of the Clerks-at-the-Table. [4] Epitome, pp. 58, 176. [5] *Ibid.* p. 22.

[6] Exchequer and Audit Departments Act, 1866, s. 3. The tenure is therefore the same as that of a judge of the High Court under the Act of Settlement, as re-enacted by the Supreme Court of Judicature Act, 1925.

the Crown, nor be a member of the House of Commons, nor a peer.[1] He has a salary of £4500 a year which, like that of a judge, is charged on the Consolidated Fund.[2]

The Exchequer and Audit Departments Act unites two offices, the Exchequer and the Audit. The former, which was quite independent of the Treasury, was under the control of a Comptroller-General with a tenure similar to that now possessed by his successor.[3] Its functions, as set out by the Select Committee on Public Moneys in 1857, were 'to provide for the safe keeping and proper appropriation of the public money. For this purpose it is charged with the receipt of the revenues, which are vested in its name, and deposited in its care, until issued under the authority of Parliament for the service of the State; and it is armed with a power of denying its sanction to any demands upon it, from whatever department they may be made, unless those demands are found in accordance with the determinations of the Legislature.'[4] The Audit Office, on the other hand, was more or less dependent on the Treasury, and it audited only such accounts as were referred to it by that department until the legislation of 1832 and 1846 gave the Commissioners power to compare the Naval and Military accounts with the Estimates, and to report the result to Parliament.

Accordingly, the Comptroller and Auditor-General has two functions. He is 'Comptroller-General of the Receipts and Issues of His Majesty's Exchequer' and also 'Auditor-General of Public Accounts'. In the former capacity he controls issues of public money; in the latter he audits the accounts of all the departments and produces 'Appropriation Accounts' which he submits to Parliament. These two functions are discussed later in this chapter,[5] but it is convenient here to give some general account of his functions.

He might be not unfittingly described as the grand protector of red tape. He insists that due formality be observed in everything; not because red tape is attractive in itself, but because it is merely a term of abuse for proper control. Parliament by legislation, the House of Commons by resolution, the Public Accounts Committee by its reports,

[1] *Ibid.*   [2] Exchequer and Audit Departments Act, 1921, s. 7.
[3] 4 & 5 Will. IV, c. 15, s. 2 (1834).
[4] Quoted Todd, *Parliamentary Government* (Walpole's ed.), II, p. 237.
[5] *Post*, pp. 326–32.

and the Treasury by minutes, has laid down a long series of complicated rules whose purpose is to secure responsibility to Parliament and freedom from corruption, waste and inefficiency. The history of financial control in Great Britain is long and tortuous. The present system of control has been developed not by the mere accretion of formality to formality, but as the result of a long experience of abuses. From 1780 to the present day there has been a constant process of reform. Some great statesmen, Mr Burke, Mr Pitt, Sir Robert Peel, and Mr Gladstone, owe their reputations primarily to their financial reforms. Others of lesser rank, like Sir James Graham and Sir George Cornewell Lewis, would be forgotten if they too had not been administrative reformers. Above all, there has been a great host whose names have been almost forgotten, who have sat on committees devising means for protecting the public revenue. Honesty in public administration involves primarily financial probity, and that has been attained. The British Constitution is a system of checks and balances of a kind that Burke did not contemplate. In this sense the Comptroller and Auditor-General is the guardian not of red tape but of the British Constitution.

Primarily, then, he is a referee in the football sense. He sees that the rules are observed. He blows his whistle when he observes an infringement. Though he sends nobody off the field, the Treasury, pressed by the Public Accounts Committee, may.

Even many of those who have studied such matters are hardly aware of the revolution in the public accounts that has taken place under the Exchequer and Audit Act, through the Reports of the Comptroller and Auditor-General, addressed to the House of Commons. These Reports are submitted to the judgment of the Public Accounts Committee, and every irregularity, which in former days would have been judged and buried within the walls of a Department, is examined and reported on, and the financial administration of the Civil Departments is then subjected to public criticism. It may indeed be maintained that, if the First Lord of the Treasury, or a Secretary of State, should order expenditure contrary to Act of Parliament, or to the established rules of the Service, or of the Department over which he presides, the fact is certain to be made known to Parliament by the independent Auditor in his Report upon the Appropriation Account of the Vote to which such expenditure is charged.[1]

[1] Treasury Minute 4800/76, 20 March 1876; Epitome, p. 57.

This statement, written more than eighty years ago, remains true to-day. The Treasury added that the reports of the Comptroller and Auditor-General for 1874–5

testify to a regular and orderly administration of the public money entrusted to the various Departments during the year. If exception be made of certain questions which have stood over from former years, and which are approaching settlement, the irregularities are few, not of an important character, for the most part admitted, and due also for the most part to casual oversight, not to ignorance or inattention.[1]

That statement, too, remains true. The volume of criticism was gradually reduced as the new system became familiar. The exigencies of warfare, as in the Boer War and between 1914 and 1918, compelled a relaxation of the rules. Though there were some respects in which the Select Committee on National Expenditure from 1917 to 1920 suggested changes (particularly in the form of the accounts), their major suggestion was a return to the pre-war practice; since 1920 the volume of criticism has again been reduced and it is somewhat difficult for the Public Accounts Committee to find something to talk about.

The Comptroller and Auditor-General has for his primary task to see that the rules are kept—whether they are in Acts of Parliament, resolutions of the House, decisions of the Public Accounts Committee, Treasury Minutes, or departmental regulations. He has no power within the rules. If an appointment be a 'job' he has no means of criticising it unless the post was not in the Estimates, or was not created after Treasury sanction, or was not filled according to departmental regulations. He is not precluded, however, from suggesting an alteration of the rules. He may make suggestions as to the form of the Estimates even though the duty of deciding is vested by statute in the Treasury.[2] He may suggest means by which frauds may be avoided.[3]

If, in the course of his audit, the Comptroller and Auditor-General becomes aware of facts which appear to him to indicate an improper expenditure or waste of public money, it is his duty to call the attention of Parliament to them.[4]

[1] *Ibid.*
[2] Epitome, p. 172 (1885).
[3] *Ibid.* p. 292 (1892).   [4] *Ibid.* p. 207 (1888).

Successive Comptrollers have interpreted these directions (by the Exchequer and Audit Departments Acts) as going beyond mere audit, and including the duty of scrutinising or criticising improper or wasteful expenditure or indicating where censure or improvements may be required. In this attitude they have been consistently encouraged by the Public Accounts Committee, and the Select Committee on National Expenditure, 1902–3,[1] for the first time formally recognised it, recommending that they should be encouraged in this direction even more than in the past.[2]

I speak as a member of the Public Accounts Committee. I do not say that the Comptroller and Auditor-General exceeds his specific powers, but in my experience during the current session he has pointed out to the Public Accounts Committee certain items where he suggests that the Committee should enquire 'Are we getting value for money?'[3]

Similar evidence was given in 1946:

The Public Accounts Committee has always encouraged the Comptroller and Auditor-General to bring to its notice expenditure which comes before him on his examination and appears to be uneconomical, very likely from comparisons which the auditor is able to make, from his examination of similar expenditure elsewhere. My officers get a knowledge of the public service generally. They are in fact, moved about from one post to another to enable them to be acquainted with the public expenditure generally.[4]

The Comptroller and Auditor-General

is not only concerning himself with the past closed years of account; his officers are situated in the Government departments; they are situated all over the world...and those officers are watching the actual expenditure as it goes along. Important Government contracts are very often shown to them before they are actually concluded. It is not true that there is this hiatus between a closed year of account and a future estimated year of account.[5]

7. THE ISSUE OF PUBLIC MONEY

The Consolidated Fund Acts and the Appropriation Act empower the Treasury to issue the sums stated out of the Consolidated Fund. The sums are however not paid out at once but are withdrawn as required.

[1] H.C. 242 of 1903.
[2] H.C. 161 of 1931, p. 364 (Sir Malcolm Ramsay).
[3] *Ibid.* Q. 2769 (Mr Ede).
[4] H.C. 189 of 1945–6, Q. 4242 (Sir Gilbert Upcott, Comptroller and Auditor-General).
[5] *Ibid.* Q. 3927 (Mr Osbert Peake, Chairman of the Public Accounts Committee).

Though all revenues, subject to statutory exceptions,[1] are by law paid into the Consolidated Fund, this is very largely a matter of account, the principle of practice being that 'Departments use on the spot, and in the manner judged to be the most economical, all the moneys which they collect, but that such use of their moneys is subject to strict account and periodical adjustment'.[2] The Revenue Departments, for instance, pay the cost of collection out of the moneys which they collect, and pay over the balance daily to the Paymaster-General, though they account for the whole. From time to time they submit statements to the Treasury, and then as a matter of accounting the Treasury issues (notionally) a sum out of the Consolidated Fund to cover the cost of administration (provided that it is within the authorised limit) and the department repays (notionally) the necessary balance.[3] The other departments draw on the Paymaster-General for the sums which they require in addition to their receipts, rendering an account every month to the Comptroller and Auditor-General.[4]

The Paymaster-General obtains money from various sources.[5] Though he keeps all his funds in several accounts, he has only one cash balance, and to maintain the balance he draws upon the Exchequer account or Consolidated Fund.[6] He thus uses temporarily for the Supply Services balances of other funds; but periodically issues are made to him from the Consolidated Fund to enable him to restore the balances. From time to time, therefore, as he requires money, and at periodical

---

[1] Only the net revenues of the Crown lands are paid; and other exceptions are draw-backs, bounties, repayments, and discounts: Public Revenue and Consolidated Fund Charges Act, 1854, as amended by 19 & 20 Vict. c. 59; Epitome, p. 4.

[2] Epitome, p. 177.   [3] *Ibid.* p. 176.   [4] H.C. 98 of 1918, p. 109.

[5] Namely,

(1) He receives sums realised by the departments in the course of their administration;

(2) He holds the balance for the time being of the large fund, called the Treasury Chest Fund, established to meet temporarily expenditure abroad (Parliament is asked in the following year to vote the sum necessary to restore the balance);

(3) He holds the Civil Contingencies Fund, established to defray provisionally unforeseen expenditure of a civil character (payments from this also have to be voted by Parliament in the following year);

(4) He also holds large sums on account of what are called Deposit Bonds under the control of different departments of State;

(5) He is supplied day by day, according to his needs, with money from the Consolidated Fund. See Epitome, p. 175.

[6] The Exchequer account is simply the account of the Consolidated Fund at the Bank.

intervals as he repays balances, the Treasury requires payments out of the Consolidated Fund. Such issues from the Fund are, however, under the strict control of the Comptroller and Auditor-General. A royal order under the Sign Manual authorises the Treasury with the concurrence of the Comptroller and Auditor-General to issue from the Exchequer the amounts authorised. From time to time the Treasury requires the Comptroller and Auditor-General to grant 'Credits on the account of Her Majesty's Exchequer'. The Treasury does not specify the services in respect of which the money is required, but the Comptroller and Auditor-General will not authorise in excess of the total of the sums voted by Parliament. Provided the request is within that limit, the Comptroller and Auditor-General writes to the Bank of England or Ireland and 'grants a credit to the Treasury on the account of Her Majesty's Exchequer... to the amount of £   '.[1] Within the amount of that credit, the Treasury requests the Bank to transfer sums from the Exchequer to the Supply Account of the Paymaster-General. The Bank executes the order and transmits it to the Comptroller and Auditor-General in support of the Exchequer account which it has to render to him daily.[2]

This system appears complicated, but it is quite simple in practice. Its purpose is twofold, to secure that large uninvested balances shall not exist, and at the same time to secure that when accounts have been adjusted, no more shall have been spent on any service than has been authorised by Parliament. The latter purpose is secured by the frequent interposition of the Comptroller and Auditor-General. In securing the first object, however, the system prevents any precise relation between the expenditure of the departments and the issues out of the Consolidated Fund. Precautions are taken to secure that the two shall be related as nearly as possible at the end of the financial year. The total of these issues is commonly regarded as the 'public expenditure' of the year, though in fact the actual expenditure cannot be determined precisely until unexpended balances have been surrendered and adjustments made; and this figure is not available until the audited accounts are presented to Parliament in the following year.[3]

[1] H.C. 98 of 1918, p. 109.
[2] *Ibid.* For the duty to render a daily account, see Exchequer and Audit Departments Act, 1866, ss. 13 and 16.
[3] The difference is not very great: cf. the figures for 1880–4: Epitome, p. 177.

8. ACCOUNTS AND AUDIT

Under the Exchequer and Audit Departments Act, 1866, the Comptroller and Auditor-General receives every year from the Treasury a statement of the issues made from the Consolidated Fund in the previous financial year in respect of services charged directly on the Fund; 'and he shall certify and report upon the same with reference to the Acts of Parliament under the authority of which such issues may have been directed; and such reports shall be laid before Parliament on or before the 31st January next'.[1] Thus Parliament receives every year an assurance that the Consolidated Fund is not being used for any charges except those provided for by legislation; and at the same time it receives information about the largest of the charges, that for the National Debt, and the effect of the transactions of the year upon the nominal amount of that debt.

Under the same Act, the departments must submit accounts of the appropriation of the several supply grants authorised by the Appropriation Act; and these 'appropriation accounts' also are laid before Parliament with a report.[2] Every appropriation account is examined by the Comptroller and Auditor-General 'on behalf of the House of Commons'; and in the examination of such accounts he must satisfy himself 'that the money expended has been applied to the purpose or purposes for which the grants made by Parliament were intended to provide and that the expenditure conforms to the authority which governs it'.[3]

The exercise of this function compels an audit by the Comptroller and Auditor-General of the expenditure of the departments. For this purpose he has a large staff engaged continuously, often in the departments, in the process of audit. This is in addition to the system of internal audit which the departments themselves carry out. His functions in this respect were described by the Treasury in 1876:

He is to ascertain, firstly, whether the payments which the accounting Department has charged to the grant are supported by vouchers or proofs of

---

[1] Exchequer and Audit Departments Act, 1866, s. 21. See, for instance, H.C. 30 of 1937. The accounts are published as 'Finance Accounts'.
[2] Exchequer and Audit Departments Act, 1866, s. 22.   [3] *Ibid.* 1921, s. 1 (1).

payment. In so doing he is to test the accuracy of the testing and compilation of the several items of the vouchers, but he may dispense, the Treasury consenting, with this minute examination of the items, if they have been certified as correct by officers of the Department specially authorised to examine them.

He is to ascertain, secondly, whether the money expended has been applied to the purposes for which Parliament granted it. Lastly, the Appropriation Accounts with the Reports of the Comptroller and Auditor-General thereupon, are to be laid before the House of Commons.

It should be added that the Comptroller and Auditor-General is directed to ascertain, at the request of the Treasury, whether the expenditure included in an Appropriation Account is supported by the authority of the Treasury, and to report to the Treasury any portion of such expenditure incurred without that authority, and if the Treasury do not sanction such unauthorised expenditure, the Comptroller and Auditor-General is to report it to the House of Commons as not properly chargeable to the vote.[1]

The Treasury Minute added that this examination 'secures to Parliament the guarantee of a very minute check exercised by an independent auditor, the minuteness of that check being only relaxed to save the needless repetition of the mere clerical labour of casting and computation, when departmental arrangements, in his opinion, and in that of the Treasury, afford sufficient security for the correctness of those operations'.[2]

This minute was written in 1876 to bring to an end a discussion whether the meticulous audit applied to the Civil Departments in 1866 should extend to the Defence Departments in place of the less exacting audit applied to the Navy since 1832 and the Army since 1846. Since each of the two departments already had an Accounts Branch, and the extension of the functions of the Exchequer and Audit Department would involve doubling the staff of that Department, it was decided to have a 'test' audit only of the Defence vouchers. Accordingly, every part of the expenditure of a Defence Department is examined at intervals, the Comptroller and Auditor-General being given a careful discretion as to what part of the Accounts he will audit in detail.[3]

---

[1] Epitome, p. 58; cf. Exchequer and Audit Departments Act, 1921, s. 1 (2) and (3).
[2] Epitome, p. 58.
[3] The test audit was applied to the Army in 1876, to the Navy in 1878, to the Revenue Departments in 1899, and to Old Age Pensions in 1909: see Epitome, pp. 62–3, 85, 423–5, 514.

Moreover, special attention is paid to those parts of the accounts where difficulties are most likely to arise.

We concentrate on the items where we know by experience...there is greatest scope for error or for differences of opinion. Now in every Department a great deal of the money is spent in salaries; the scales are known.... We do not attempt a hundred per cent. check in the larger Departments. When it comes to shipbuilding or payments to contractors, they stand out, and we examine these branches with considerable care....We make a test. We lay ourselves out to cover the whole field of the decentralised expenditure in so many years, we pick out a certain number of establishments every year and we go round and look at them, and examine their accounts. And then we have what I call a general scrutiny of the headquarters expenditure of all the big Departments, because the register of bills paid comes to us very often next day, and our people run down the list. If we find £20,000 paid, say, as compensation to a contractor, then we may draw the papers; if it was only an instalment under a contract we knew about, we pass it, and so on.[1]

The audit is not merely an audit; it involves an examination of legal authority for expenditure and an investigation whether the due forms, such as the requirement of Treasury sanction, have been observed. It is not an 'efficiency audit'. The Comptroller and Auditor-General has no power to suggest that twelve could do the work of fifteen; he can find out whether the Treasury has authorised the employment of fifteen men; and if he finds that it has, he can do no more than suggest privately to the Establishments Branch of the Treasury that the question might be looked at.[2] But on questions of financial administration he does not hesitate to express opinions in the hope that the Treasury, or the Public Accounts Committee, or both, will look into the matter.

Moreover, the departments or sub-departments engaged in manufacturing or trading produce accounts in addition to their appropriation accounts.[3] The Comptroller and Auditor-General was empowered in 1866 to audit such accounts, not being appropriation accounts, as the Treasury might direct;[4] but the Treasury preferred to secure express statutory sanction for the audit of the manufacturing accounts of the

---

[1] H.C. 161 of 1931, Qs. 3777–8.   [2] H.C. 161 of 1931, Q. 3823.
[3] I.e. the Navy Dockyard Accounts and Army (Royal Ordnance Factories) Manufacturing Accounts.
[4] Exchequer and Audit Departments Act, 1866, s. 33.

Army and Navy (dealing with such matters as shipbuilding and the manufacture of arms, munitions, and clothing), and this authority was given by the Army and Navy Audit Act, 1889.[1] These accounts must show 'the cost of labour employed, and the value of stores expended in the several ordnance factories and manufacturing establishments' of the Army and Navy. In other words, their purpose is to determine 'unit costs' by means of which Parliament can compare the cost of production in an official establishment and trade prices.[2] Though there are many difficulties to be faced, particularly the allocation of a percentage for capital charges, the Admiralty and the War Office developed a system of cost accounting which was admitted 'to represent fairly the cost to Government of the articles manufactured',[3]—though they could not be compared precisely with contractors' costs.

The Post Office has since 1912 compiled in addition to its appropriation accounts commercial accounts on the same basis as those of private traders.[4] These are audited by the Comptroller and Auditor-General, who reports to Parliament.[5] The new departments instituted during 1914–18, especially the Ministries of Food and Munitions, made much use of accounts on a commercial basis, and in 1920 trading accounts and balance sheets were produced for all trading services and were reported on by the Comptroller and Auditor-General;[6] this measure received statutory effect in the Exchequer and Audit Departments Act, 1921.

9. THE PUBLIC ACCOUNTS COMMITTEE

Until the Reform Act of 1832 the House of Commons controlled supply through the estimates and issues through the intervention of the Exchequer Department, but, though it appropriated supply grants, it had no means of ensuring that when once these grants were issued to the departments they would be used only for the purposes

---

[1] See Epitome, pp. 211, 222. [2] Ibid. pp. 258–60.
[3] Ibid. p. 583.
[4] For the differences between the appropriation account and the commercial accounts see the evidence of Sir C. King before the Select Committee on National Expenditure in 1918 (9th Report), H.C. 98 of 1918, pp. 74–81.
[5] Under the Telegraph (Money) Act, 1920, s. 2, and the Exchequer and Audit Departments Act, 1921, s. 5. [6] Epitome, pp. 629–31, 680.

set out in the Estimates. The developments of the nineteenth century referred to in the previous section have filled the gap. The accounts are presented to Parliament with the reports of the Comptroller and Auditor-General thereon. The House itself, however, is not a convenient body for discussing the comparatively unimportant questions raised by the Comptroller and Auditor-General. No doubt if some great scandals were unearthed there would be debates in the House, as there were on the Post Office irregularities of 1872 and on the Marconi transaction of 1912. Provision is now made for the consideration of the Reports of the Estimates and Public Accounts Committees on a Supply day;[1] and in any case questions of financial administration can be raised as matters of policy on Supply days, the Consolidated Fund Bills, the Appropriation Bill, the address in answer to the Queen's Speech, long adjournments, and so on. Few of the questions now raised are, however, of that order of importance. Moreover, the technique required is not one of debate, but of examination of official witnesses. It is, in other words, the technique of a select committee and not of a committee of the whole House.

The Select Committee of Public Accounts was set up by Mr Gladstone in 1861 as part of the series of reforms which began with the Select Committee on Public Moneys presided over by Sir George Cornewell Lewis in 1857 and ended with the Exchequer and Audit Departments Act, 1866, passed at the suggestion of Mr Childers. It was set up with very general terms of reference, 'for the examination, from year to year, of the audited accounts of the public expenditure'. The reference was embodied in Standing Orders in 1862, and its terms slightly expanded in 1870 and 1933, so that it now reads 'for the examination of the accounts showing the appropriation of the sums granted by Parliament to meet the public expenditure, and of such other accounts laid before Parliament as the Committee may think fit'.[2] It consists of fifteen members. By convention, it represents the parties of the House in proportion to their voting strength. By convention, also, a member of the Opposition is always elected chairman. Usually, in fact, the Financial Secretary to the Treasury in the last Government formed by the Opposition has been appointed chairman. The reason is that the

[1] S.O. 16 (3).　　　　　　　　　[2] S.O. 90.

Financial Secretary approves such of the Estimates, upon which the Appropriation Accounts are based, as do not in his opinion require the personal consideration of the Chancellor of the Exchequer. A person with experience in that office, therefore, already possesses a considerable knowledge of the detail of public finance. On the other hand, the appointment of such a person is not without its disadvantages. The Financial Secretary to the Treasury stands on the threshold of the Cabinet. When, after a few years of Opposition, some of the former Cabinet ministers have retired from active positions, or have been rejected by ungrateful constituencies, or have died, the Financial Secretary is usually one of the leading members of the Opposition, and therefore almost fully occupied in ordinary political pursuits. He cannot spare the time to pay meticulous attention to financial detail, and he may know just enough about the finance of government to fail to realise that he does not know enough to be chairman of the Public Accounts Committee. A member with some ministerial experience who is willing to spend time in learning the needs of the position and is at the same time a good chairman may become a thorn in the side of every administrator who tries to pass over the slightest irregularity.

There is also a long-standing practice to make the chairman of the Estimates Committee a member of the Public Accounts Committee.[1] This is done in order to secure liaison between the two committees and to avoid overlapping. For instance, in 1928 the Estimates Committee made a recommendation about which the Public Accounts Committee complained in 1929 that it had not been consulted.[2] The liaison between the committees should render such difficulties impossible, and in fact this is the only example known to the Comptroller and Auditor-General[3].

Actually, most of the work is done by the chairman and one or two other members. When there is a change of Government there is at the same time a change in the office of chairman, so that often there is at the right hand of the chairman a former chairman, of the party supporting the Government, probably equally skilled in the many problems

[1] H.C. 189 of 1945–6, Q. 3929.
[2] The Estimates Committee recommended that all capital for the Post Office should be obtained by borrowing. Since 1904 the Public Accounts Committee had laid down that it ought to be provided by annual votes. See Epitome, pp. 708–9.
[3] H.C. 189 of 1945–6, p. 187 (Sir Gilbert Upcott).

raised. At the extreme end of the semicircle sits the Comptroller and Auditor-General, with a group of subordinates from the Exchequer and Audit Department near him. At the other extreme sit the representatives of the Treasury, and in the middle is the witness under examination. For the Committee has the usual power 'to send for persons, papers, and records', and its proceedings usually take the form of the examination of witnesses. Occasionally, the Committee sends for a minister;[1] but more often it examines as witnesses senior officials from the departments.

Accordingly, the procedure is as follows. The Committee has before it the various accounts with the reports of the Comptroller and Auditor-General thereon. The appropriate departmental official, such as the Second Secretary to the Treasury or the Permanent Secretary to the Admiralty or the Director of Navy Accounts is present to answer questions. If members of the Committee find something in the accounts which they do not understand, they ask for an explanation. For the most part, however, their attention is directed to the questions raised by the Comptroller and Auditor-General. Where some statement is not clear, or not entirely accurate, the Comptroller and Auditor-General from one end of the table may interject a remark, and another may come from the Treasury representatives at the other end. Consequently, if a department has committed some irregularity, some senior official has to go hard to defend it. The chairman, already coached by the officials of the House and the Exchequer and Audit Department,[2] asks questions which may not be easy to answer; and it is impossible for the official to presume upon the ignorance of the politicians, for the Exchequer and Audit Department and, possibly, the Treasury, have chapter and verse at hand ready to confute him. Nor is the Treasury itself necessarily free from criticism. If it has condoned a fault on the ground that it was 'only a very little one', the chairman, or the Comptroller and Auditor-

---

[1] H.C. 161 of 1931, Qs. 3765–6 (Sir Malcolm Ramsay, Comptroller and Auditor-General).

[2] The Committee meets on two afternoons a week during the second half of the session. Each meeting is preceded by a consultation, lasting two hours or more, between the chairman and the Comptroller and Auditor-General during which the chairman studies 'the weak spots in the departmental defences': H.C. 189 of 1945–6, Q. 3929 (Mr Osbert Peake).

General, or both, may point out that it raises an issue of considerable practical importance.

The Committee reports to the House from time to time. It publishes also most of the evidence which it receives. It does not publish all, because certain information is given to the Committee in confidence. For instance, before it was decided in 1937 to publish at regular intervals information about the Exchange Equalisation Fund, the average monthly holding of gold and foreign exchange held to the account during the year covered by the Appropriation Accounts was made known to the Committee but not published; and details about Government contracts or guarantees under the Trade Facilities Acts are often given by the Treasury on condition that they are not published in the minutes of evidence.

Whether the reports and the evidence are read by other members is another matter. No doubt if anything of real importance were discovered it would form the basis of a debate. Often, too, a member of the Committee asks a question in the House, either to elucidate a point not cleared up by the expert evidence, or to draw public attention to a criticism by securing an admission from the responsible minister. In any case, the effectiveness of the Committee is to be measured not by the attention which its reports receive in Parliament, but by the attention which they receive in the departments. Of the value of its work in this respect there can be no doubt. The Select Committee on Expenditure reported in 1903:

> Every witness bore testimony to the increasing value of the Committee as a check on wasteful expenditure.

The Select Committee on National Expenditure in 1918 said:

> It is recognised on all hands that the work of the Comptroller and Auditor-General and of the Public Accounts Committee...is highly efficient and useful.[1]

Its most important result is the state of mind which it induces in the department. Mr Speaker said in 1918 that Government departments had 'a wholesome dread' of the Public Accounts Committee.[2] Knowing

---

[1] Quoted by Sir Malcolm Ramsay, H.C. 161 of 1931, p. 365.
[2] Report from the Select Committee on National Expenditure, 1918, p. 122.

that they will be called to account not only by the Treasury but by the Comptroller and Auditor-General and the Public Accounts Committee, the departments are very careful to prevent irregularities.

One example, quoted in 1946,[1] will suffice. There had been misuse of army petrol for two years in succession. In the second year the allegation related to four tins of petrol. The chairman of the Public Accounts Committee (Sir A. M. Samuel) told the accounting officer for the War Office 'that if this occurred again, he would have the Commander-in-Chief of the Army before the Public Accounts Committee'.

If members could see, as I do, the papers, it does not matter of what Department, they would see frequent references to the way that the Comptroller and Auditor-General and the Public Accounts Committee would be likely to regard any particular transaction which is debateable. I have found this in the War Office, the Admiralty, the Treasury themselves, the Air Force—all the big Departments.[2]

It is still true, as Mr Gibson Bowles said in 1903, that 'there is ground for believing that the Spending Departments stand more in awe of the Public Accounts Committee than of the House itself, probably because there is less chance of escaping its close scrutiny'. The mere fact that the Committee exists, and that the Comptroller and Auditor-General can invoke its assistance, fortifies the Accounting Officers against temptation to stray from the path of economy, or of financial regularity; further, it enables the Comptroller and Auditor-General to dispose at once, and in his stride, of many matters of which Parliament never hears.[3]

The development of the present honest and incorruptible system of financial administration has in fact been due to the collaboration of the Treasury, the Comptroller and Auditor-General and the Public Accounts Committee. The reports of the Committees, the memoranda of the Comptroller and Auditor-General, and the Treasury minutes form, to use a phrase of the Select Committee on National Expenditure in 1918,[4] a body of 'case law' of such importance that the more

---

[1] H.C. 189 of 1945–6, Q. 3942 (Mr Osbert Peake).
[2] H.C. 161 of 1931, Q. 3759 (Sir Malcolm Ramsay).
[3] *Ibid.* p. 365. 'Without the Public Accounts Committee I would be quite ineffective, or more ineffective than I am now. They are the sanction on which it all depends': *ibid.* Q. 3758 (Sir Malcolm Ramsay, Comptroller and Auditor-General).
[4] H.C. 98 of 1918, p. iv.

permanent recommendations are published from time to time in the *Epitome of the Reports of the Committees of Public Accounts*,[1] the standard text-book of financial administration.

10. FINANCIAL CONTROL IN GENERAL

'It is with no disrespect to this House', said Mr Austen Chamberlain, Chancellor of the Exchequer, in 1919, 'that I say that it is not an efficient body for checking expenditure, and that it does not help the Chancellor of the Exchequer of the day, be he whom he may, to exercise control over expenditure. It is quite true that one section of members calls for economy here, and another section calls for economy there, and so on over the whole sphere, but at any given point there is always a majority for spending more, not less.'[2]

Expenditure depends primarily on policy, and the most efficient form of financial control can do no more than secure that due economy is observed in the execution of policy. The maintenance of such economy in a community like Great Britain, where the reforms of a century and a half have eradicated any tendency towards serious corruption, involves minute examination of small items of expenditure. Such a task could not be borne by the House itself even if it wished. The main principles of financial control have been laid down by legislation and resolution. Within the limits of those principles, control is maintained by the Select Committees on Estimates and of Public Accounts, by the Comptroller and Auditor-General, and above all by the Treasury.

The major constitutional principles have already been explained.[3] No taxation is levied and no supply is granted, except by authority of Parliament. The subsequent explanations show that at every stage in the normal finance process there is an element of control. The demand for supply is made in great detail in the form of estimates, and after the sanction of the Treasury has been obtained. No money is issued except on the request of the Treasury and with the sanction of the Comptroller and Auditor-General. The Treasury, the Comptroller and Auditor-General and the Public Accounts Committee secure that no expenditure is incurred outside the limits of the votes of Parliament or even outside

---

[1] See H.C. 161 of 1927 (first edition); H.C. 154 of 1938 (second edition).
[2] 116 H.C.Deb. 5 s., 257.   [3] *Ante*, pp. 283–91.

the limits of the subheads, except in the one case with the consent of the Treasury and of Parliament, and in the other case with the consent of the Treasury. Money voted but not used remains in or has to be surrendered to the Exchequer, whence it goes as the 'Old Sinking Fund' to reduce the National Debt.

The normal process of expenditure is thus subject to rigid control. There are, however, kinds of expenditure which have escaped from some at least of the shackles.

In the first place, Parliament has tended to give the Treasury much wider discretion in respect of borrowing money. Until 1914 every kind of loan was specifically authorised by legislation, and for a specific purpose. The exigencies of war made such a system impossible, and wide borrowing powers were conferred by the War Loan Acts, 1914–19, the National Loans Acts, 1939–44, and other emergency legislation, parts of which have become a permanent part of the law. The Exchange Equalisation Account, originally established in 1932 to maintain sterling after it went off gold, was subjected to stringent conditions which disappeared under the Currency (Defence) Act, 1939; and in this respect that Act is still in force.

In the second place, the more common use of grants in aid has considerably diminished parliamentary control. As the Public Accounts Committee said in 1896:

Grants in aid furnish an exception to the general rule that the expenditure within the Parliamentary votes must be accounted for in detail by the Accounting Officer; the appropriation of the money examined by the Comptroller and Auditor-General, and that any unexpended balance disclosed thereby must be surrendered to the Exchequer. These grants in aid, being in the nature of subscriptions or contributions for purposes not directly under the control of the Administration, may, it is true, be paid away within the year by the Accounting Officer; but the receipt in full which he obtains from the grantee or grantees is his sufficient discharge; the expenditure is not necessarily followed in detail by the Comptroller and Auditor-General; and any unexpended balance remains with the recipients.[1]

Sometimes the receipt is a full discharge; sometimes accounts have to be presented to the Treasury or the Comptroller and Auditor-General;

[1] Epitome, p. 390.

sometimes there is a complete audit by or on behalf of the Comptroller and Auditor-General.[1] Normally the grant in aid, not being accounted for in detail, is not set out in detail in the Estimates, and to that extent parliamentary control is restricted. The establishment of separate Funds for quasi-independent authorities, and fed by grants in aid, is part of the process of taking the subject-matter 'out of politics'; being out of politics means being out of control.[2]

Finally, a large part of public expenditure is now determined by permanent legislation, with the result that the Treasury, the Comptroller and Auditor-General, and the Public Accounts Committee have no jurisdiction except to see that the statutory conditions are observed. For instance, the expenditure on National Insurance and the National Health Service depends not on the state of the Budget but on the state of the population. This applies also to the grants in aid of local government, such as the General Exchequer Contribution under the Local Government Act, 1929, as amended, and the grants towards education and police expenditure. Less important financially, though more important constitutionally (because they lend themselves more easily to log-rolling) are the grants in aid of various industries.

These are complications arising out of the growing complexity of the administrative system.[3] Generalisation is at present difficult because the process is comparatively new; and experimentation is proceeding not only as to the relations between the departments and the newer authorities, but also as to the relations between such bodies and Parliament. When the Public Accounts Committee considered the question of grants in aid in 1896, it refused to lay down inflexible rules. Sometimes, as in the case of the universities, there are excellent reasons for preventing such a grant in aid as would confer a right of financial control. In other cases, as in respect of most local authorities, an indirect control is provided by a different system of audit. In yet other cases it is very desirable to confer authority on the Comptroller and Auditor-General to report to Parliament and thus secure control by the Public Accounts Committee.

[1] See the memorandum, Epitome, pp. 393–5.   [2] *Ibid.* pp. 709, 771.
[3] See *Cabinet Government*, ch. IV.

CHAPTER X

THE NATIONALISED INDUSTRIES

Nationalised industries are not new in the British Constitution. The royal dockyards, the ordnance factories and the Post Office are of such respectable antiquity that even in the great days of *laissez-faire* it was never suggested that they be handed over either to 'private enterprise' or to autonomous corporations. On the other hand, their constitutional position is by no means peculiar. They are represented in Parliament by ministers, the First Lord of the Admiralty, the Secretary of State for War, and the Postmaster-General; their employees are all on the civil establishments of the Crown and are therefore 'civil servants'; they are subject to the full panoply of Treasury control; and their actions are as fully open to Parliamentary scrutiny as the actions of the Home Office.

The idea of a body of commissioners empowered by the Crown or incorporated by statute to undertake specific functions, too, is not new. The offices of Lord Treasurer and Lord Admiral have been in commission for centuries. The Commissioners of Woods and Forests and the Commissioners of Works have disappeared, but we still have with us the Commissioners of Inland Revenue, the Commissioners of Customs and Excise, the Forestry Commission, the Prison Commission, and others. They, too, were or are under parliamentary control through responsible ministers. On the other hand, commissioners may be autonomous and have no responsible minister; the oldest are the Commissioners of Assize, Gaol Delivery and Oyer and Terminer, who have not received an order from a minister for three centuries and would be very much on their dignity if they did.

Nor, again, is the idea of an autonomous corporation, empowered by royal charter or Act of Parliament, a new one. The universities and colleges of Oxford and Cambridge, the ancient grammar schools, and the older municipal corporations are almost as ancient as Parliament itself. Many of the trading corporations of the seventeenth and eighteenth centuries, of which the East India Company was the greatest and most famous, had powers of government by grant from the Crown and were controlled by Parliament, if at all, only because Parliament had ultimate legislative power.

These were the precedents which came to mind when, in the later period of what is generally known as the age of collectivisation, 'the State' (an entity not known to the law) came to be regarded as capable of managing industries. The system developed almost unawares. The municipal corporations were independent chartered corporations exercising governmental and even commercial functions. When in the eighteenth century it was desired to build turnpike roads, provide sewers, drain fenlands, operate canals, supply water and, at a later stage, operate railways and provide gas and electricity, the chartered or statutory corporation, exercising monopoly and other powers by Act of Parliament, was the obvious constitutional method. The Port of London Authority, the prototype of the modern nationalised industry,[1] was merely a late example of this method of providing services, an obvious development from these older statutory undertakers. Between the wars there were established the Forestry Commission (now once more under ministerial control), the Central Electricity Board, the London Passenger Transport Board, the Coal Mines Reorganisation Commission, the Agricultural Marketing Boards, and other bodies of the same type. The Labour party was especially interested in these bodies because they supplied precedents for the nationalisation of great industries like coal mining, the production and supply of gas and electricity on a national scale, the production of iron and steel, and the provision of public transport services.[2] It was desired to bring these industries under national control, to secure their operation for the public benefit and not for private profit, but at the same time to enable them to function like private industries freed from the meticulous control which had grown up in the departments for which ministers were responsible to Parliament. When the Labour party assumed office in 1945 a committee of ministers was established by the Prime Minister,

---

[1] See Chapter II of *Public Enterprise*, mentioned in the next note.
[2] See S. and B. Webb, *Statutory Authorities for Special Purposes*; H. Morrison, *Socialisation and Transport* (1933); and *Public Enterprise*, edited for the New Fabian Research Bureau by William A. Robson (1937).

under the chairmanship of Mr Herbert Morrison, with a parallel committee of officials as a working party to feed the ministerial committee and to report on matters remitted by that committee.[1] The principle of the public corporation was accepted by the committee and was applied, with considerable variations of detail, to a number of industries. It must, however, be remembered that the principle is independent of the function. It had already been applied to the British Broadcasting Corporation and it could be applied to corporations controlling art galleries, museums, theatres, cinemas, independent schools and other services which it might be thought desirable to place under the control of an autonomous national authority.

The essential characteristics of a service carried on by a Government department may perhaps be described as follows:

(1) The service is carried on in the name of the minister, who is completely responsible for it to Parliament, and who may therefore be questioned on any aspect of the service, or be criticised in the debate on any motion on which debate on the service is relevant: e.g. in Supply, on a Consolidated Fund Bill, on the Queen's Speech, on the adjournment, or on a specific motion for which time has been found.

(2) The income of the service is paid into the Consolidated Fund and the expenditure is paid out of the Consolidated Fund, and accordingly the complete panoply of financial control described in Chapter IX of this book and Chapter VII of *Cabinet Government* applies to it. This means in particular that:

(a) the expenditure has to be estimated in detail, included in one of the Supply votes submitted to Parliament, and therefore made liable to debate in the Committee of Supply and examination by the Select Committee on Estimates;

(b) Treasury sanction has to be obtained for all changes in the staff employed, salary scales and wage rates are determined by the Treasury, and Treasury sanction has to be obtained for all variations in the estimates;

(c) Parliamentary sanction has to be obtained for all expenditure not covered by the estimates, even though there is no loss to the public revenues because the appropriations in aid (i.e. the income of the service) have also been increased;

(d) an appropriation account has to be prepared for audit by the Comptroller and Auditor-General, who may report thereon to Parliament, drawing

[1] H. Morrison, *Government and Parliament*, p. 247.

343

attention not only to any defect in accounting or loss of public funds, but also to any expenditure not authorised in a proper manner, or any extravagance or waste of money to which the auditors draw his attention; and this appropriation account may be examined and reported on by the Public Accounts Committee.

These tight constitutional restrictions are designed to bring public administration under public control and to prevent misuse of public funds. Since they involve checks and balances in the administration, require that all decisions and the reasons therefor be recorded in writing so that they can later be defended, and demand a substantial staff engaged very largely in preparing answers to questions and criticisms, they are expensive, dilatory and restrictive of initiative. Though inaction will be criticised, unsuccessful action is likely to arouse the more criticism. The restrictions have therefore to be removed or modified for the nationalised industries, so that something of the elasticity, rapidity and cheapness of ordinary industrial administration may be achieved. The making of profits is not the sole objective of a nationalised industry, and so the ordinary criteria of private industry are not applicable; but a business which seeks to cover its costs, or even to make a profit, while keeping its prices low must be operated differently from, say, the Royal Navy, whose efficiency cannot be measured in such terms. There are obviously two ways of lightening the restrictions on public corporations, by limiting ministerial control, which necessarily involves limiting parliamentary control, and by according greater financial autonomy, which also limits parliamentary control.

The public corporation is a device for vesting responsibility not in a minister but in a body of persons called a board, commission, court of management, or otherwise. It will be convenient to call it a 'board' even if that is not its official title. The minister usually appoints the members of the board, and the present discussion relates to boards all or most of whose members are so appointed, for different considerations apply to profit-making public utilities and boards elected by producers or traders which are given public functions. Since the purpose of nationalisation is to secure that the service be provided in the national interest and there are other aspects of the national interest under the control of the Government, it is usual to give the appropriate minister the power to issue general directions to the board, which the board is bound to observe, though the responsibility for detailed administration is vested in the board and not in the minister. Further, certain kinds of decisions may require his sanction, such as the fixing of the charges to be paid for the service. Since the minister or the Government may require information about the board's operations in order to formulate policy in cognate fields, and since members of Parliament may require information about matters affecting their constituents, the minister is usually empowered to require the board to supply such information. Finally, the board is almost invariably required to have its accounts audited (usually by auditors appointed by the minister) and to present them to the minister with an annual report. The accounts and the report are laid before Parliament by the minister.

As Mr Herbert Morrison has pointed out,[1] the legislation passed while the Labour Government was in office from 1945 to 1951 gave more powers to ministers than the pre-war legislation establishing the Central Electricity Board, the London Passenger Transport Board, and the British Broadcasting Corporation. 'We thought', he says, 'that the pre-war ministerial powers were insufficient if the boards were to be made properly accountable and if they were to conform to the Government's economic and social policy'. One consequence of this increased accountability to the ministers was increased accountability to Parliament. Exactly how this arises, however, needs further elucidation:

(1) Questions asked by members of Parliament may seek information only. Usually such questions, if asked about nationalised industries, are in order, because under most of the recent statutes ministers have power to obtain information from the boards. On the other hand, ministers are not bound to answer, and they often refuse to answer on the ground that the question relates to a matter within the jurisdiction of the board and that interference by Parliament with administrative details is undesirable. If similar questions are again put down, the Clerks-at-the-Table may rule them out of order. The Speaker has directed, however, that the rule be waived where the matter is of sufficient 'public importance'.[2] There is, too, an easier way of obtaining information, namely, to ask the board to supply it. For the sake of 'public relations' the boards are almost invariably anxious to satisfy members

---

[1] *Government and Parliament*, p. 251.   [2] 451 H.C.Deb. 5 s., 1632-3.

of Parliament, and the chairman of the British Transport Commission told the first Select Committee on the Nationalised Industries that his correspondence with members of Parliament averaged 1700 letters a year.[1] It may be, of course, that the member is anxious not for information but for the publicity which shows his assiduity on behalf of his constituents.

(2) Questions are, however, rarely asked for the sake of the information that the answers will produce. On the one side they are, more often, polite intimations that the members would like the grievances of their constituents examined; on the other side they are usually pegs on which to hang supplementary questions critical of the policy of the Government. As such, they are in order only if the minister questioned has responsibility for the action taken or the action sought. The minister cannot be blamed for any action or omission of a board unless his consent thereto was required by law, or he has power to overrule the decision. Usually, under the statutes relating to the nationalised industries, neither is true. It is usually possible to put a question in the form whether the minister will issue a direction to the board concerned, but the answer will probably be that the minister does not desire to give directions in matters of administrative detail. As Mr Herbert Morrison has pointed out,[2] other formulae may be used in order to make certain that the question is in order and therefore to get it on the order paper. On the other hand, the member is unlikely to receive a satisfactory answer. One of the reasons for giving the nationalised industries the form of the public corporation was that they should not be subjected to the same parliamentary supervision as, for example, the Post Office. The use of the parliamentary question in the like manner as it is used to criticise and control ordinary administration would be inconsistent with this objective, and the minister is usually justified in refusing to allow indirect methods to be used to establish a control which Parliament deliberately sought to take away. The first Select Committee on the Nationalised Industries[3] examined the question of increasing the opportunities for parliamentary questions and came to the conclusion that it would not be practicable without amendment of the statutes by which the corporations were empowered.

(3) There is nothing to prevent members from criticising the functioning of the nationalised industries in any debate on which the subject is relevant. In the debate on the Queen's Speech anything would be relevant. In debate on a Consolidated Fund Bill or on an adjournment motion anything other than a proposal for legislation would be relevant. In Committee of Supply there would have to be a relevant vote, but under the modern procedure it

[1] H.C. 332 of 1952.
[2] *Government and Parliament*, pp. 260–1.
[3] H.C. 332 of 1952.

would be possible to have a vote put down, or to raise the matter on the motion that Mr Speaker do leave the chair, or to have the adjournment moved forthwith. Private members' motions and Bills taken on Fridays would also provide opportunities for members successful in the ballot. Thus, the nationalised industries (like the universities) are not exempt from parliamentary control. They are exempt only from the process of parliamentary nagging which is part of the process of parliamentary control of the Government.

The degree to which a nationalised industry is subjected to financial control depends upon the degree to which and the manner in which the industry is subsidised from public funds. In evidence before the second Select Committee on Nationalised Industries[1] the clerk to the Select Committee on Estimates classified the corporations then existing (there have been certain changes since) as follows:

(i) The corporations which are financially independent unless resort has to be had to the Treasury guarantee of the principal (either stock or temporary loans), and the payment of interest thereon, e.g. the British Transport Commission; the British Electricity Authority, including the Area Electricity Boards; the Gas Council, including each Area Gas Board; the Iron and Steel Corporation; and the North of Scotland Hydro-Electric Board.

(ii) The corporations responsible for raising their own capital (with Treasury guarantee) but drawing deficiency payments from voted moneys, e.g. the British Overseas Airways Corporation and the British European Airways Corporation (and formerly the British South American Airways Corporation).

(iii) The corporations which are not subsidised from voted moneys but derive the whole or part of their capital from advances made out of issues from the Consolidated Fund, e.g. the National Coal Board; the Colonial Development Corporation; the National Film Finance Corporation; and the Raw Cotton Commission. (The Overseas Food Corporation was in this class until the passing of the Overseas Resources Development Act, 1951.)

(iv) The corporations which derive their capital from the Consolidated Fund as in (iii) above, and in addition may receive grants from voted moneys, e.g. the New Towns Development Corporations in England and Scotland and the National Research Development Corporation.

(v) The corporations which derive the whole of their capital and operating income from voted moneys, e.g. the British Broadcasting Corporation and the Overseas Food Corporation.

[1] H.C. 235 of 1953, p. 1.

These variations, together with the terms of the statutes, determine the limits of Treasury control. When capital or income is voted the Treasury must be satisfied that the vote is necessary, and when a Treasury guarantee is required for a loan the Treasury must be satisfied that a loan is required. In so far as the nationalised industry finances itself from its own revenue there is no Treasury control; nor does such control extend to the expenditure of a grant-in-aid as it extends to expenditure detailed in the Estimates. One of the main purposes of corporate autonomy is to remove the necessity for the meticulous examination of proposals for expenditure, salary scales and wage rates, and changes of staff, to which Government departments are subject.

Generally speaking, the nationalised industries are not covered by the terms of reference of the Select Committee on Estimates. They are within its jurisdiction only if they are subsidised, in whole or in part, from voted moneys which appear in the Estimates.[1] Thus, the Committee can examine the proposed expenditure on the Airways Corporations and the British Broadcasting Corporation, and has in fact done so. The great nationalised industries, coal, electricity, gas and railways, are not within the Committee's jurisdiction.

The accounts of the public corporations are audited not by the Comptroller and Auditor-General but by professional auditors, who are usually appointed either by or with the approval of the appropriate minister. On the other hand, the accounts are always presented to Parliament, either as part of the annual report or otherwise. These 'White Paper accounts' (as they are called to distinguish them from the appropriation accounts presented on behalf of Government departments)[2] are not reported on by the Comptroller and Auditor-General.[3] On the other hand, they are within Standing Order 90 and therefore within the terms of reference of the Public Accounts Committee.[4] This means that, though the Committee may examine, and on a number of occasions has examined,[5] the accounts of public corporations, it has not the assistance of the Comptroller and Auditor-General. He is present

---

[1] H.C. 235 of 1953, p. 2.   [2] *Ibid.* p. 4.
[3] *Ibid.* pp. 6 and 10. The statement to the contrary on p. 4 is incorrect; see p. 10, where it is corrected.   [4] *Ibid.* p. 1.
[5] See the lists for 1947–8 to 1951–2: *ibid.* p. 2.

at the meetings, and may draw attention to any point which occurs to him, but he has taken no part in the audit and made no report. Accordingly, he cannot give the assistance which he renders in respect of appropriation accounts.[1] The difference between audit by the Comptroller and Auditor-General and a professional auditor are considerable:

The Comptroller and Auditor-General would go a good deal further than any commercial accountant. He writes really what amounts to an efficiency audit. He would comment if he thinks money has been wasted, though it has been spent perfectly properly, for the purpose for which it was appropriated by the House. If he thinks it is wastefully expended he will say so in his comments, which a commercial auditor will not do.[2]

The demand for greater parliamentary control of the nationalised industries has been persistent, particularly from the Conservative benches, though it has not always been clear whether the members wished to control the policy that an industry was following or merely to exercise over it the kind of check which the Public Accounts Committee exercises over a Government department. The Public Accounts Committee does not control policy, but it helps the Comptroller and Auditor-General to see that the formalities of Government expenditure are observed and that the audited expenditure shows a close relation to the detail of the estimate submitted to Parliament. A nationalised industry does not, however, submit an estimate to Parliament, nor does it observe the formalities which have been developed over a century by the interaction of the Treasury, the Comptroller and Auditor-General, and the Public Accounts Committee. The case for further control was perhaps most clearly expressed before the second Select Committee on Nationalised Industries by Mr Hugh Molson, Parliamentary Secretary to the Ministry of Works, speaking for himself and not for his ministry:[3]

I think that the existence of State-owned monopolies makes periodic inquiries necessary because in the first place all competition has been eliminated; secondly, the taxpayers have now replaced the shareholders and are entitled to some account of how their affairs are being run; and, thirdly, the advocates of nationalisation have usually supported it on the ground that the nationalised industries were too important to be left in the hands of private individuals. I think that must apply equally even if the individuals administering them now have been appointed by the Government. They should

[1] *Ibid.* pp. 9–10.   [2] *Ibid.* p. 7.   [3] *Ibid.* p. 38.

not cease to be accountable during the whole of their tenure of office. Parliamentary questions I am sure would be quite inadequate for this purpose. They would usually be casual, capricious, superficial and inconclusive.

Mr Molson went on to say that it was not easy to reconcile the principle that the policy of the industry should be in harmony with national policy with the principle that the industry should be free from political interference, but he went on to suggest that there should be a committee of members of the House of Commons, with an officer like the Comptroller and Auditor-General, which should 'elucidate...deep problems of policy' while avoiding day-to-day interference with detail. He then gave four examples of the matters which such a committee would want to consider:

First, there is the question of closing uneconomic lines on the railways. As I see it one of the effects of nationalisation is that the accounts are now so large that they do not show the profitability or otherwise of particular units. Secondly, it might well be thought that, over a period of years, in the case of the coal mines, for example, an excessive amount had been devoted to welfare and various benefit schemes and so on of the miners as compared with lower paid workers in other industries. Thirdly, there is the competition of the electricity board and the gas board, and the possibility of encouraging the use of solid fuel. Fourthly, there is perhaps the productivity in the coal industry.

It will be seen that these examples are, for the most part, matters on which the officials of the boards, and possibly the officials of the ministries concerned, would have some technical knowledge and experience. Others outside the nationalised industry and the Government might be able to reach useful conclusions on them. It is, however, a little difficult to see why a committee of members of Parliament should be required. If they are matters of national policy they are matters for the Government; if they involve technical issues they are matters on which the Government should be advised by a Royal Commission or Departmental Committee; they have no relation to the matters which are discussed by the Public Accounts Committee.

Lord Hurcomb, then chairman of the British Transport Commission (who had had experience of the work of the Public Accounts Committee as a civil servant) put the case rather differently:[1]

[1] *Ibid.* p. 63.

If there was some sort of relationship, not of investigation or probing into financial detail, or in which challenge to efficiency were its main object, but designed to know what the undertaking was doing, what it was at, what its policy was in major directions, being able to suggest to the chairman of the body concerned what were the points in the committee's own mind as to where the body might be giving insufficient weight to some trend of public opinion, or, perhaps, overlooking some important public aspect of its work, or not giving it enough emphasis—if one could establish that sort of relationship, so that the organisation did not feel itself perpetually under the harrow, but was having an opportunity of explaining its policy and its endeavours, and answering any challenge that might be put to what it had done, including its financial results, I think in a broad way that would be extremely helpful to the organisation, and ought to go a long way towards informing the mind of Parliament.... One of the great handicaps under which anyone in my position suffers is that he gets no opportunity of stating his own case or of explaining what are his difficulties direct to members of Parliament.

Thus Lord Hurcomb regarded the problem as one of public relations, which could presumably be equally well met by a periodical explanation to the appropriate committees of private members—committees which, because they have no official status, could not put any organisation under the harrow. That the chairman of the Select Committee did not appreciate what Lord Hurcomb's problem was became at once apparent, for he proceeded to draw an analogy with the Public Accounts Committee. There was of course no analogy, and Lord Hurcomb correctly pointed out that 'if you subject one of these public corporations to the full scrutiny of the Public Accounts Committee such as it gives to a Department you are really going to destroy its financial autonomy and independence and you are going to convert it into a public Department'.

Lord Reith, who had had experience of two public corporations as well as experience as minister, and Mr Herbert Morrison, who was more than any other person responsible for the form taken by the Labour party's nationalisation proposals, opposed the proposal. As Lord Reith said:[1]

I should have thought the appointment of a select committee, *ad hoc*, on a nationalised industry was in effect a negation of what Parliament deliberately

[1] *Ibid.* p. 75.

did in setting it up. Parliament passed a sort of self-denying ordinance, taking from itself the right of direct interference, as with Government Departments. Unless there is to be a revision of attitude, I would have thought it was contrary to the principle of what was done that you should set up a committee, whether of one House or both.

What Lord Reith recommended was a Royal Commission, which would secure some uniformity among the public corporations in respect of accountability, intervention, and so forth, and give greater satisfaction to Parliament. From further answers it was clear that Lord Reith intended not a running commentary, which might result in regular criticism, but a single examination of the principles governing public corporations.

Mr Herbert Morrison recognised that there must be periodical accountability, and he suggested[1] that there should be an inquiry every seven years, not by a select committee, but by such committees as those which examined the working of and made recommendations about the British Broadcasting Corporation before its charter was renewed. Its members would not consist only of members of Parliament. A select committee, he pointed out, could not be expert in industrial efficiency, and in any case an annual examination would have a harmful effect on the public corporations by developing in them a 'red-tapeish, unadventurous and conventionally civil service frame of mind'.

In spite of these strong arguments, the second Select Committee on Nationalised Industries decided that there ought to be a standing select committee in order so to enlarge the field of public accountability as to provide the House of Commons with the information which it requires without interfering with or jeopardising the efficiency of the nationalised industries. The committee would set up a tradition which would result in its being not an enemy or a critic of the nationalised industries, but a confidant and a protection against irresponsible pressure as well as a guardian of the public interest. It would examine the reports and accounts of the industries and obtain further information as to the general policy and practice. It should have on its staff a person of the status of the Comptroller and Auditor-General, who should be an officer of the House of Commons with high administrative

[1] *Ibid.* p. 49.

experience, and there should also be on its staff at least one professional accountant.

This recommendation did not close the debate. Mr Herbert Morrison was not convinced.[1] There was evidently discussion in the Government, for no decision was taken until May 1956, when it was decided to appoint a committee with modified terms of reference, which would in effect merely enable it to scrutinise and seek explanations about the annual reports and accounts of the nationalised industries. There was, of course, a major premise which was not made articulate in the Select Committee because such bodies, by long tradition, do not debate issues from a party point of view. Most of the nationalised industries were nationalised by the Labour Government against the opposition of the Conservative party. This being a select committee under a Conservative Government, it contained a Conservative majority. There is no evidence that the Committee divided along party lines, but there was an implication in the questions asked that private enterprise is efficient because *ex hypothesi* it has to stand competition, and even suggestions, which one would have thought contrary to experience, that shareholders are able to control policy and ensure efficient management. In present political conditions the attitude of any select committee with a Conservative majority would be the same. In other words, the select committee might be a confidant and a protector when it had a Labour majority—though even that is doubtful, for Labour back-benchers like Conservative back-benchers always think that they know better than those on the Treasury bench—but it is unlikely to happen with a Conservative majority. There is clearly a case for fairly broad ministerial powers which do not impinge on detailed administration. There is probably a case for a periodical investigation of the kind suggested by Mr Herbert Morrison, an investigation not by politicians with axes to grind but by persons with the necessary knowledge and experience, especially those acquired in the practice of large-scale private industry and in Government departments. As *The Economist* put it:[2]

politicians are no more qualified to teach good management, Blue book in hand, than they are qualified, pick in hand, to teach miners how to dig coal.

[1] *Government and Parliament*, p. 265.
[2] 'Under Public Control?' p. 667 (May 19, 1956).

All experience suggests that the best instruments for 'efficiency audits' are bodies like the Fleck and Herbert committees—groups of independent experts who can collect information informally as well as round the official witness table, divide fields of inquiry between their members, and compile a report that looks eventually at the wood instead of at the trees. There is no similarity between wide-ranging special inquiries of this sort and a select committee of the Commons—which is a group of some twenty or so politicians, carefully chosen to secure proportionate representation of the parties, dealing only with evidence that is formally presented, trying to justify its existence by finding some cocktail party on which too much has been spent, poking about terrier-like among the bills

—and, be it added, trying to find some stick to beat the other side or the politicians on the Front Bench.

CHAPTER XI

THE PRIVATE MEMBER

1. SHEPHERDS AND SHEEP

It is obvious from the emphasis which has been given in the preceding chapters to the Government and the whips that the private member plays no very obvious part in the proceedings of the House of Commons. He and his fellows are, so to speak, the House; the Standing Orders contain very few provisions which distinguish between official and private members; the theory behind the procedure is that all members are equal; yet so different is the practice that it has been suggested that members, and especially members on the Government side, 'have nothing to do except to get into mischief'.[1]

The time of the House is almost wholly taken by the Government.[2] Only twenty Fridays are available for private members' motions and Bills. If the pressure on Government time is great, however, all or any of these days may be taken by the Government on a resolution passed, after debate, by a simple majority; for this motion as for nearly all others the whips are put on and the Government supporters shepherded into the 'Aye' lobby. Private members may raise matters on the evening adjournment—which usually means in practice not more than half an hour between the division taken just before ten o'clock and the rising of the House at 10.30 p.m.[3] When the House first goes into committee on each of the four groups of Estimates, private members may move amendments.[4] On the address in reply to the Queen's Speech at the beginning of the session any matter may, in theory, be raised by any member who catches the Speaker's eye; on the Estimates, any member may, in theory, raise any question relating to the administration of the department covered by the vote before the House; and on the larger adjournments and the Appropriation Bill and the Consolidated Fund Bills any matter of administration may, in theory,

---

[1] H.C. 161 of 1931, Q. 729 (Mr Ede). [2] *Ante*, pp. 75, 121–2.
[3] *Ante*, pp. 116–18. [4] *Ante*, p. 295.

be raised. On any other question any member may, in theory, raise any relevant issue. But the use of the words 'in theory' shows that these privileges are not always as extensive as they appear to be.

If the debate on a motion is to take all day, the first two and the last two speeches will be made by front bench speakers. If the occasion is important, Privy Councillors, who have precedence by courtesy, will desire to make observations; and in any event at least one speech must be heard from the third party. In the result three, or perhaps four hours, will be available for ordinary private members, and these will be the worst of the evening; for speeches at dinner-time are rarely listened to, and speeches afterwards are barely reported. Even the process of 'catching the Speaker's eye' is not carried out without assistance from the whips. While the Speaker or Chairman would resist any attempt to dictate to him what orators he shall call upon, it is convenient for him to know beforehand as many as possible of those who may wish to speak, so that he can secure an orderly debate and enable all points of view to be met. Of this many examples could be given; but one from the debate on Palestine on 21 July 1937 will suffice. During the course of the debate Mr Winston Churchill strangely managed to 'catch the Deputy-Speaker's eye' though he had not risen for the purpose. In answer to protests, the Deputy-Speaker said:

Perhaps I may be allowed to say that information is conveyed sometimes through the usual channels to the occupant of the Chair as to certain intentions of hon. and right hon. members, intentions which probably are not known to other members of the House but which do have some effect on the mind of the occupant of the Chair as to what would be for the convenience of the House as a whole.[1]

It does not follow that the member who takes an independent line unpopular with the whips is excluded from debates; there is, indeed, evidence that the 'crank' is often preferred to the straight party man because he is less likely to act like an 'old hurdy-gurdy grinding out old tunes'.[2] It is said to be the invariable practice of the whips to put down all the names of members who wish to speak, and to make no kind of selection. In any case a member can always inform the Speaker or Chairman personally. But there is no doubt that sometimes members

[1] 326 H.C.Deb. 5 s., 2340-1.   [2] *Ante*, p. 63.

are asked to speak by the whips and that on other occasions members are asked not to speak. The whips do not control the order of debate, but they have some influence in suggesting it.

Private members may put down their own amendments to Government Bills, but their opportunity of speaking to them is limited by several factors. Only one amendment is taken on second and third readings; and in committee or on report an amendment may not be 'selected' by the Chairman or Speaker, so that the member is left to make his point, if he is permitted to, on an amendment not essentially dissimilar proposed by another member or (in committee) on the motion that the clause stand part of the Bill. The whips have no control over the exercise of the kangaroo; but the Chairman or Speaker is aware of the arrangements made between the whips for bringing the debate to a close. These arrangements, too, effectively bind the private members. They are gentlemen's agreements which the leaders do their best to carry out, and the obstructive member who does not obey becomes unpopular both with his leaders and with his fellow members. If the 'hope' is expressed that the amendment will not be put or pressed, the line of least resistance is to consent. If the member proves obstreperous there is always the closure and, though it is rarely used, the original kangaroo closure—that the clause stand part of the Bill. There is evidence, too, that many amendments put down by private members are in fact drafted by the whips. This is particularly true of the Labour party.[1]

While there is nothing to prevent an Opposition member from putting down such amendments as he pleases, the main discussions in committee and on report are 'wrecking' amendments in the sense that, if carried, they would go to the root of one of the principles of the Bill. They are neither carried nor expected to be carried, but they provide that basis for public criticism which is the essential function of an Opposition. Accordingly, amendments are drafted by or on behalf of the Shadow Cabinet or, in the case of the Labour party, the executive committee of the parliamentary party, and are distributed among the members.[2]

[1] See *ante*, p. 182.
[2] *Mr T. Kennedy* (Chief whip): 'As a matter of fact, with regard to the great majority of members, their amendments are prepared for them by their party organisations and put on the paper.... *Captain Bourne*: I hesitate to express an opinion as to what

The debates on the Estimates, the Appropriation Bill, the Consolidated Fund Bills, the address in reply to the Queen's Speech, and the long adjournments, are similarly organised. The subject for each day's discussion is arranged between the whips and, though a private member may raise any question he pleases so long as it is in order, in practice he is expected to follow the lead given by the first speaker. If the Post Office Vote is put down, for instance, a member may make a speech about the absence of telephone facilities in Little Muggleton, an important (or unimportant) village in his constituency. If the official in the box or the Postmaster-General's parliamentary secretary can telephone to the General Post Office to find out the answer, it is possible that the Assistant Postmaster-General will say a few soothing words about 'having the matter under consideration' when he comes to make the closing speech: but if the Opposition has decided to discuss broadcasting on this vote, this little interchange of compliments will be irrelevant to the main course of the discussion. The member can again raise the question on the Consolidated Fund Bill; but it requires some courage to talk of Little Muggleton while the rest of the House is discussing the bombing of Arcadian towns by the Utopian air force. The debate on the address may last a week, and any member may raise any question from calendar reform to the provision of canvas covers for battleship funnels; in fact, however, the subject for each day's debate is arranged between the whips, and the appropriate ministers are present with the appropriate officials in the box. It is of little use to raise the question of conditions in Dartmoor prison when the minister present has with him a dossier on anti-submarine precautions.

As the 'Prince of Obstructionists' who has now gone to another place has said:

At all times one is subject to the working of the machine; business must be got through; the whips come to arrangements—no doubt in many cases admirable and convenient to the whole body of members—and, as a result, the back bencher is left to fend for himself. He has a constituency grievance,

---

may happen in your party, but I can assure you that except in the case of big Bills that is not what happens with us, and the private members put down their own points. *Mr T. Kennedy*: So do all of us, I should say.' H.C. 161 of 1931, Qs. 701–2. There is more organisation in the Labour party, but otherwise there is no distinction.

or he has by his diligence unearthed some administrative mistake, and yet he finds no opportunity of bringing it before the House. He might, it is true, get the occasion on a Supply day or on the adjournment, but the Supply for which it is appropriate may never be taken, or unless he is personally popular and has a large circle of friends who will help him, he fails to keep a House on the adjournment;[1] members of the 1924 Parliament will remember a particularly notorious case of this when a member was repeatedly counted out, until it became a standing joke.[2]

The private member supporting the Government is in a worse position even than the private member in opposition. If the latter makes a nuisance of himself he annoys the Government more than the leaders of the Opposition. While factious opposition or obstruction has been rare since 1914, the Opposition is less concerned than the Government with the orderly progress of debate. The chief whip is not particularly anxious for commendatory speeches; he wants to get his business through; but he certainly does not want criticism from his own side. If there is a 'ginger group' in the Opposition it may annoy the leaders of the Opposition a little—as the 'fourth party' annoyed Sir Stafford Northcote—but it annoys the Government still more. A 'ginger group' on the Government side is a rebellion. As Mr Winston Churchill said:

Even in a period of political activity there is small scope for the supporter of a Government. The whips do not want speeches, but votes. The ministers regard an oration in their praise or defence as only one degree less tiresome than an attack. The earnest party man becomes a silent drudge, tramping at intervals through lobbies to record his vote, and wondering why he comes to Westminster at all. Ambitious youth diverges into criticism or even hostility, or seeks an outlet for his energies elsewhere.[3]

Mr Balfour said the same thing in less picturesque but more sardonic language:

The most obvious duty (I do not say the only duty) of any individual member of a parliamentary majority is, speaking generally, to assist Government business, to defend Government action, and in particular to be found

---

[1] Actually, it is not the practice to demand a count on the evening adjournment.
[2] H.C. 161 of 1931, Q. 2909 (Captain Crookshank).
[3] *Life of Lord Randolph Churchill*, I, pp. 69–70.

in the Government lobby whenever the House divides. He may further these ends by his eloquence. He may do so even more effectually perhaps by his silence.[1]

2. PRIVATE MEMBERS' MOTIONS

In the spacious days of a century and a century and a half ago, the great parliamentary debates took place on private members' motions. Mr Fox, Mr Burke, Mr Whitbread, Mr Brougham, in one generation, Sir Robert Peel, Lord John Russell, Sir James Graham, Mr O'Connell in the next, moved resolutions that were the talk of the clubs for weeks before and after, and great efforts were made to get the country gentlemen to come to Town. It is significant of the speeding up of the process of government after the Reform Act that the private member's motion was less important when Sir Robert Peel, Lord John Russell, or Mr Disraeli faced the Prime Minister than when Mr Fox or Mr Tierney led (or failed to lead) the Opposition. As the nineteenth century proceeded, debate became more and more a matter of defence and criticism of Government measures. As likely as not, the great debate in which Mr Pitt answered the oratory of the most brilliant team that ever poured out golden words, Mr Fox, Mr Burke and Mr Sheridan, the subject under discussion had not proceeded from the Government, had never been considered in Cabinet and, perhaps, led Mr Pitt and his principal lieutenants into opposite lobbies at the end. When Mr Gladstone sat stolidly on the Treasury Bench watching Mr Disraeli's handkerchief rise to his lips to mark the pause preceding the carefully prepared 'impromptu' sarcasm, and saving up his righteous indignation till it could flow in a torrent of glorious but empty words, the issue was a clause drafted by Mr Gladstone himself with all the assistance of an expert civil service. Even so, Government business had precedence on two days a week only, and private members' business was not without its importance. To-day, private members' motions are taken only on ten Fridays during a session, alternating with private members' Bills. They thus give an opportunity to members to spend the week-end in their constituencies, to catch up on their correspondence, to pay some attention to their professions or businesses, or to spend a day with their families.

[1] A. J. Balfour, *Chapters of Autobiography*, p. 134.

It must not be thought that there is no competition for the honour of moving motions. Though the Press usually gives little space to the debate, the opening speaker secures more publicity than an intervention on a Government motion at dinner-time or late in the evening (which is too late for the editions of London newspapers designed for the provinces). He may even secure the paragraph in the evening papers which is commonly given only to the notorious and the famous. Moreover, a parliamentary private secretary or a junior whip may tell a friend, who may tell a minister, who may tell the Prime Minister, that 'X made a good speech yesterday'; and if X becomes more than an algebraic symbol or a name in a division list he may, in due course, take the first step to office and fame. Further, the whips encourage their men to take part. The privilege is allotted by ballot. Those members who wish to compete place their names on a numbered list at the beginning of the session, and a ballot is taken before the chairman of Committees of as many members as entries are made. Members may then put down motions which will be taken in the order of the ballot. Thus, a single Communist member has as much chance of proposing a motion which he alone would support as a Conservative has of proposing a resolution for which an enormous majority would vote if only they could be persuaded to attend. But if all the Labour members put down their names and no Conservatives take the trouble, every Friday will be occupied in attacking the Government. This situation would never arise, because few members can resist the opportunity of a little publicity which would do them good in their own constituencies if not elsewhere; but since the luck of the ballot is likely to favour that party which puts down the most names, the whips urge all back-bench members to do so. 'We are always told that we must all ballot or the other side will get too many places.'[1]

It does not follow, therefore, that a member puts down his name because he is simply bursting with a grievance which, when he explodes, will shake the foundations of the State. When he ballots he probably has not the least notion of the subject which he desires to raise. If he is successful, a friend may help him. Perhaps the friend has spent the time between two divisions in thinking out a really magnificent speech.

[1] H.C. 161 of 1931, Q. 3975 (Sir Basil Peto).

If unfortunately he is unsuccessful in the ballot, he has either to consign his notes to the usual depository or suggest to a more fortunate member that the subject is well worth raising and he, the speaker, would be very glad to second. In any case there is always that guide, philosopher and friend, the whip, who in the stores of his experience or the pigeon-holes of his desk has a hard-baked chestnut which has not recently seen the light.[1] Here, as elsewhere, the Labour party's organisation proves superior; and often the subjects are determined beforehand by the executive committee in order that serious debates may take place when Labour members are successful. It must be remembered, however, that whether the whip compiles a list out of his own head or obtains it at a committee meeting, private members may have been consulted beforehand or may have shown by intervention in debate that some interest is taken in a particular question.[2] Nor is there anything to prevent any member from riding his own hobby-horse—if the House will listen to him.

The fortuitous character of the results of the ballot usually prevents private members' motions from being used to raise 'grievances'. They are sometimes defended on that ground;[3] but this is an example of the use of an historic phrase without understanding that its meaning has completely changed. Grievances in the historic sense date from the time when the King governed and the Commons granted supplies. Before granting supplies the Commons insisted that their grievances— the grievances of the commons of England in the widest sense—be remedied. To-day, the commons of England—or, rather, of the United Kingdom—themselves govern; and a Government that did not remedy common grievances would very soon find its place in history. Grievances of a party character, including sectional and class grievances, are raised by the Opposition not on motions made by private members, but as part of the normal process of opposing Government proposals. Private grievances which raise political or constitutional issues are similarly

---

[1] 'I dare say that you have noticed that when the ballot is taken, in ninety-nine per cent of cases the members in all parts of the House whose names are read out as successful get up and read off a formula off a piece of paper which has been supplied to them by the whips.' H.C. 161 of 1931, Q. 1258 (Mr R. Morrison).

[2] *Ibid.* (Sir Archibald Sinclair).

[3] E.g. H.C. 161 of 1931, Q. 290 (Mr Hacking).

raised, and if they arise suddenly the proper and effective technique is an urgency motion for the adjournment.[1] Private grievances of a more personal character, such as refusals of pensions, insurance benefit, unemployment allowances, and the like, are taken up by members in direct correspondence with ministers; if no satisfactory reply is forthcoming, a question is raised; and if that proves unavailing the question can be raised 'on the first suitable occasion'—such as the evening adjournment, the appropriate Supply Vote, or the Consolidated Fund Bill or long adjournment. Members successful in the ballot do not give notice that they will raise the question of the refusal of an old age pension to Mrs Jones, of Merioneth Street, Cardiff, and move a motion. Mrs Jones will get her pension if she is entitled to it, but not by a private member's motion.

Private members' motions from the Government side are usually completely useless;[2] when they come from the Opposition they are usually in substance Opposition motions. There is, it is true, inadequate opportunity for an Opposition to discuss its legislative proposals. It can raise such questions on the address in answer to the Queen's Speech; and it can state its alternatives to the Government's programme. In respect of administration it can use all the other opportunities for debate —Supply, the Appropriation Bill, Consolidated Fund Bills, adjournments—but it cannot on these occasions debate any question which requires legislation. But if private members' motions are to become Opposition motions they should become so in fact, and not depend on the luck of the ballot for the selection of the persons to move them and for the opportunity to move them at all. There are occasionally subjects which cut across party boundaries and on which the Government has not made up its mind. Such were proposals for the full enfranchisement of women before 1928 and the provision of a contributory insurance system for widows', orphans' and old age pensions before 1925. Private members' motions then are part of the technique of propaganda. They enable 'the opinion of the House' to be taken. The 'opinion' need not be representative, for the attendance may be small; and in any case it is

---

[1] *Ante*, pp. 111–16.
[2] A notable exception was the motion which resulted in the appointment of the Cadman Committee on Civil Aviation in 1938.

easy to prevent a division on the substance, either by moving a dilatory amendment, such as referring to a committee, or by simply talking it out. They are thus of some value, though the value is not great. For the most part, the only value of private members' motions is that they enable ministers to put in half-a-day's work on administrative business.

3. PRIVATE MEMBERS' BILLS

It has been explained already that, technically, private members' Bills follow the same procedure as Government Bills.[1] Any member can introduce any Bill he pleases, subject only to the qualification that a money Bill requires a preliminary resolution to which the Queen's recommendation is attached.[2] The Queen's recommendation is in fact the Government's recommendation; and if the Government recommends expenditure it introduces the Bill. It is not true, as is commonly alleged, that a private member cannot introduce any Bill authorising expenditure. Like a minister, he can introduce a Bill containing the financial clauses in 'blanks' or italics; but it cannot proceed beyond second reading without a financial resolution with a Queen's recommendation. In practice, therefore, private members do not introduce such Bills; and if they did the Government would no doubt oppose the motion to introduce (where that method was used) or the second reading.

Subject to the one qualification as to money Bills, there is no difficulty whatever about introducing a Bill. It may be introduced after notice and read a first time without debate;[3] or a motion for leave to introduce may be put down for discussion under the 'ten minutes' rule';[4] or a motion for leave to introduce may be put down as an order of the day. In practice private members use the first method if they expect the Bill to pass, and the second if they do not. The first method gives an automatic first reading and printing at the public expense. It is sometimes used even if the Bill is not expected to proceed further; for the member thus indicates to the appropriate department that it is required and hopes for Government 'adoption'; or he satisfies the

---

[1] *Ante*, pp. 236–7. [2] S.O. 64 and 65, and *ante*, pp. 254–6.
[3] S.O. 32 (2). [4] S.O. 10; *ante*, pp. 250–2.

'interest' which he represents in the House that he is doing something for its benefit; or he circulates copies to other members in the hope that later on he may get an opportunity of carrying it further; or he indicates to his constituents that he has taken at least the first step towards becoming a legislator. In practice, however, introduction under the ten minutes' rule secures greater publicity. If anyone feels energetic enough to oppose, there is a short debate which gets a few lines in the newspapers; and even if the member does not want publicity for himself, he may want it for his cause. There used to be a Blasphemy Bill for which leave was sought year after year, and which was as regularly defeated. No one doubts that the present blasphemy laws are a disgrace to the nation. They would be seriously oppressive if anyone took the idea into his head of enforcing them. This Bill, therefore, drew attention to the danger in the hope that at long last Parliament might be induced to remedy it. The third method, introduction by leave on a motion placed on the orders of the day, is never used except by ministers, and then only for very exceptional Bills like the Parliament Bill.

The difficulty arises not with the first stage but with the second. If a Bill is so non-contentious that not a single member takes the trouble to oppose, there is no technical difficulty, for the second reading may be taken as unopposed business after 10 p.m. The Bill then goes to a standing committee,[1] and the report stage and third reading, if unopposed, may similarly be taken after 10 p.m. But any single member may object, and so stop the Bill altogether unless it has precedence on a Friday. Since there are members who object to all legislation, believing that Parliament passes too much, the prospects of a Bill which has not precedence on a Friday are not rosy. It may even get as far as the report stage before an obstructionist wakes up.[2]

Thus, a Bill approved by ninety-nine per cent of the members has no chance of success unless it secures precedence on a Friday. As has been explained,[3] private members' Bills have precedence on ten Fridays in each session unless a motion has been carried to take part or the whole

---

[1] But if it is believed that no amendment will be moved, so that the committee stage will be purely formal, the member will move to commit the Bill to the whole House, and then the committee stage comes on after ten o'clock.

[2] Cf. H.C. 161 of 1931, Q. 3067 (Sir Dennis Herbert).

[3] *Ante*, p. 121.

of private members' time. After Easter, if the session begins in the autumn (as it usually does), or after Whitsuntide if it begins in the new year, private members' Bills are taken in such order as to give priority to those most advanced: that is, a Bill which has already been to the House of Lords and amended there takes precedence over those requiring a third reading, which precede those requiring consideration on report,[1] and these precede Bills requiring second reading.[2] The result of this rule is that eight Fridays are given to second readings and the rest to later stages. In practice, not more than two Bills are likely to be debated in a single sitting, or sixteen altogether. More than this number are in fact introduced for debate on Fridays, since three Bills are put down for each day, though the third is rarely reached.

For the honour of moving second readings on Fridays, members have to ballot. The system operates in the same way, and with much the same results, as balloting for motions.[3]

About 250 members have put down their names in the book; about twenty attend the 'draw'. Not many more than twenty are eager to 'win a turkey' for themselves, being pregnant with a particular reform. The rest go in to give a friend another chance, or as a party duty, for the whips have always a few Bills ready for a Friday. Sometimes one of the Departments wants to get some small measure through for which there is no room in the Government programme.[4]

There is, however, not quite so much reliance on the whips. Apart from the departmental Bills there are hardy annuals which the whips take from the pigeon-holes at the request of those members who are anxious to legislate but do not know what to legislate for. These are, however, the exception rather than the rule, chiefly because there are many outside interests which desire legislation to be passed. For instance, the law for the protection of animals is gradually becoming more and more stringent owing to the activities of the Royal Society

---

[1] But only if the report stage has not been entered upon. Accordingly, if the report stage is obstructed one week or the House is counted out, the Bill is postponed to all other Bills, which usually means that it lapses. Thus a Bill may easily be talked out on report by putting down so many amendments that, even with the use of the kangaroo and closure, it cannot be dealt with in one sitting.

[2] S.O. 5. Bills in committee take precedence over Bills requiring second reading; but in practice most private Bills go to standing committees.

[3] *Ante*, p. 361.   [4] A. P. Herbert, *The Ayes Have It*, p. 68.

for the Prevention of Cruelty to Animals. When the Society finds a gap in the law it has the necessary Bill drafted. If one of its representatives in Parliament is successful in the ballot, he introduces the Bill. If no representative is successful the Society may be able to persuade some other member to take up the Bill.[1] Again, the Early Closing Association, the Lord's Day Observance Society, and other bodies, are anxious to secure the early closing of shops and the closing of shops on Sundays. Temperance societies wish to limit facilities for the sale of alcoholic liquor, and 'the Trade' to extend them. Professional associations wish to secure regulation of their professions rather on the lines adopted long ago for physicians, surgeons and lawyers; nurses, architects, journalists, osteopaths, and the like have therefore 'promoted' public Bills. Associations of public officials, such as asylum officers, firemen, and local government officers generally have sought to obtain by legislation compulsory superannuation.

This is merely one aspect of a system whose operation has already been examined.[2] Indeed, it applies not only to balloted Bills but to all Bills. For the introduction of a Bill, even if there be no hope of its passing, is one of the methods of propaganda by which it is hoped, in due course, to obtain Government support for legislation. If a Bill is introduced by any means at all, the opposition interests are organised. If, for instance, an association of local government officers seeks advantages for its members, the associations of local authorities proceed at once to consider their attitude. The officers' association learns from the minutes of the local authorities' associations whether there is any prospect of agreement. It is reasonably certain that the Government will not 'bless' the Bill unless the interests are substantially agreed. If the 'blessing' is obtained it may go through unopposed, or it may be adopted as a Government Bill, or it may be passed through as a balloted Bill. The proceedings preliminary to the Local Government Superannuation Act, 1937,[3] provide an excellent example.

If an interest is serious in desiring the introduction of a balloted Bill, it is useless merely to hope that one of the interest's 'representatives' in Parliament will be successful in the ballot. It is desirable to obtain

---

[1] Actually, most of the Society's Bills go through after ten o'clock.
[2] See Chapter VII.   [3] *Ante*, pp. 215–20.

as many chances in the ballot as possible. Accordingly, the association concerned may circulate all likely members in the hope of securing promises to introduce the Bill if success in the ballot is obtained. Thus on one occasion the Association of Conservative Clubs secured promises from over 200 Conservative members that, if successful in the ballot, they would introduce a Bill for lifting licensing regulations in clubs. The Bill was in fact introduced but, being objected to by the Government, it was defeated, the Government promising to consider Government legislation.[1]

Sir Alan Herbert secured consideration for his Marriage Bill by persuading a successful member, Mr De la Bere, to take it over. Sir Alan was not exactly an 'interest', though he conducted his propaganda at least as efficiently as most interests, and he adopted the same technique. Failing to secure a place in his first ballot, he approached more successful members. Two members 'were by no means willing to be the foster-fathers of divorce'. Another member had entered by mistake, thinking that he was balloting for seats in the Strangers' Gallery, but he could not be found.

Then a friend said: 'What about X—? He's won a good place, and is going about asking what on earth he's to do with it.' I bustled about and found X— at last. He said: 'Divorce? Good God, no! I was in the Navy.' I did not immediately follow the reasoning, and had no opportunity to inquire about it. For he rushed across the Lobby to the whips' office, where he was, I believe, provided with a Bill.[2]

In his second session Sir Alan was again unsuccessful in the ballot. Labour members had been fortunate, but the Labour members could not help him: 'I was kindly told that there were plenty of Bills for Labour members.'[3] He therefore tried the successful Conservative and Liberal members. One had a Bill which became the Summary Procedure (Domestic Proceedings) Act, 1937. 'Others had their own Bills or were not at home or were entirely dependent on the support of the Roman Catholics, or were in conference, or simply spluttered at the word "divorce".[4] At last, he met Mr De la Bere.

---

[1] See also *ante*, pp. 192–3.   [2] *The Ayes Have It*, p. 70.
[3] *Ibid.* p. 82; for the reason, see *ante*, pp. 361–2.
[4] *The Ayes Have It*, pp. 82–3.

Two other members, with Bills in their beaks, descended on us and tried to carry him off. But I was able to claim priority and bullied them away. He, too, already had a Bill in his hand, an innocent little thing about municipal elections, which the whips had given him. My heart sank when I saw that: but I did not know Mr De la Bere.[1]

In fact, in spite of opposition from his whips, Mr De la Bere undertook to introduce the Bill, which now provides much work for members of the profession of which Sir Alan Herbert is a grass widow, as the Matrimonial Causes Act, 1937.

It will be seen from this example, unusual though it is, that not all balloted Bills originate from outside interests. There are many branches of the law where minor amendments are desirable, and if a member's attention is drawn to them he may decide to introduce a Bill whenever he secures the opportunity. For instance, many members take an interest in motor traffic. Compulsory third-party insurance, the abolition of the rule that sharing a taxi fare is an offence, and the limitation of all future driving licences to special classes of vehicles, were all the product of private members' Bills, though there is no evidence that they were produced by interests.[2] Again, the repeal of the rule which made 'sleeping out' an offence, the Act authorising the supply of meals to schoolchildren, and the Summary Jurisdiction (Domestic Proceedings) Act, 1937, were passed as a result of private members' actions.

Though Friday is a private members' day, the Government remains in control. The Cabinet considers its attitude to all private members' Bills and a minister explains the Government's decision. The whips are in attendance and will be put on if the Government considers that the Bill ought not to pass. If this is done it is certain that the Bill will be defeated. Accordingly, the Government's 'blessing' or neutrality is essential. More than blessing or neutrality is, however, required. For even in such a case the whips are not put on in favour of the Bill. The member in charge of it must secure two things, a House and a

[1] *Ibid.* p. 84. The Ministry of Health had been trying to get 'the innocent little thing' before the House for some time. It became the Local Authorities (Hours of Poll) Act, 1938—thanks to a private member who resisted importunities.
[2] Compulsory third-party insurance was ultimately embodied in a Government Bill, the private member's Bill being withdrawn.

majority. It is not easy to keep a House, partly because many members are not interested, partly because Friday is apt to be part of the week-end, and partly because it is a convenient day for members to visit their constituencies. It is known to local parties that no Government business is taken on Fridays, that the House rises early, and that members have free travelling facilities. Saturdays and Sundays being unfavourable for political meetings, Friday has become the usual propaganda day. Many members are thus miles from Westminster, on their way to remote constituencies, when private members' Bills are under discussion.[1] The member must thus undertake some private whipping. If his Bill arouses some interest, or if he has friends, he may be able to keep a quorum; but often the House is counted out on a Friday, and sometimes members in the precincts deliberately fail to respond to the bell which summons them for a count, as the simplest way of defeating the Bill.

Moreover, unless the Bill is first on the order paper it is easy to talk it out by debating the preceding Bill at length. Sir Alan Herbert's Marriage Bill came up on report as the first Bill on the order paper; but so many amendments were proposed that it could not be completed and came up again as the fifth Bill on the last Friday allotted to private members. Before it was a Road Traffic Bill which was quite non-contentious and which had passed through committee in half an hour, and a Shops Bill which sought to restrict the sale of ice-cream on Sundays. In order to talk out the last-named Bill, members occupied the whole day in debating the Road Traffic Bill, with the result that not only the Shops Bill but also the Marriage Bill lapsed for want of time,[2] and only the Government's assistance permitted the passing of the Marriage Bill.[3] Any member can move the closure, but it is difficult to closure two Bills in a short sitting, and still more difficult to closure a report stage when numerous amendments have been put down.

Finally, it is necessary to secure a majority. Though the member in charge may be able to do some private whipping, so may the opposition

---

[1] 'The pressure from the constituency is getting so much greater, with free railway travelling, that most members find it essential to go off on Friday.' Captain Crookshank, H.C. 161 of 1931, Q. 3020.

[2] A. P. Herbert, *The Ayes Have It*, pp. 154–65.

[3] *Ibid.* pp. 166–8.

to the Bill. The rival contestants may in fact be the representatives of rival interests, and these will whip in their supporters. Seeing that the House is necessarily thin on a Friday, it may be merely a matter of chance whether supporters or opponents are more numerous.[1]

These are not the only difficulties, for the Bill has to pass through a standing committee. Usually one committee only is used, though the Government will sometimes consent to allocation to another committee if there is no fear of holding up its own Bills. If a number of Bills are passed on the earliest Fridays they become 'piled up' there and the later Bills have little chance of getting through.[2] Much amendment may be necessary; for, apart from amendments required to allay opposition, the Government may take a hand. The Bill will have been drafted privately, and both the department concerned and the Drafting Office may insist on changes. Also, the delay of one Bill necessarily involves the delay of all the rest, and a dozen Bills may be held up merely because it is desired to prevent one Bill from becoming law. When the Bills have passed through committee they have still to secure a place for report and third reading on one of perhaps four days allotted for that purpose. If one is 'sticky' it holds up the rest.

In spite of these difficulties, some Bills get through. In the session 1924–9, private members introduced 430 Bills, and sixty were passed. Of these sixty Bills, twenty-nine were balloted Bills, though 119 Bills were introduced under the ballot.[3] The number of Fridays occupied by private members in that Parliament was fifty-four. It should be noted, however, that more private members' Bills, namely thirty-one, were passed without taking private members' time than were passed on Fridays. The Bills were in fact of essentially the same type; for the difficulty of securing the passage of a Bill on a Friday is so great that, exceptional cases like the Marriage Bill (for which the Government found time) apart, only essentially non-contentious Bills are passed under either procedure.

The private member can, however, usually be certain that he will not

---

[1] It has been said that the Government whips sometimes secure a count when the Government wishes to destroy a Bill without opposing it: cf. H.C. 161 of 1931, Q. 2986.

[2] It was stated in 1931 that fourteen Bills were at that moment piled up before Standing Committee A: H.C. 161 of 1931, Q. 248.

[3] See the figures *ante*, p. 236.

fall at the last ditch. If his Bill has gone so far that it would be a waste of parliamentary time to let it fall merely because there is not an hour or two of private members' time left for its last stage, the Government will usually 'star' it as a Government Bill so that it may be taken in Government time. This happened not only with the Matrimonial Causes Bill, 1937, but also with the Local Government and Other Officers' Superannuation Bill, of which some account has been given elsewhere.[1] Similarly, the Government found time for two private members' Bills in the session of 1937–8, the Divorce and Nullity of Marriage (Scotland) Bill[2] and the Architects Registration Bill.[3]

Reforms are not necessarily the less valuable because they are non-contentious. The presumption falls the other way. Yet so many are the divergencies of interest and opinion that any proposal for substantial reform arouses opposition somewhere. It would be impossible to remove much of the nonsense of the common law by private members' Bills; for there are always lawyers in the House who think the common law perfect. Most successful Bills are not reforms, but create additional restrictions or powers of a minor character. Moreover, they must be short and simple, otherwise they will get held up in committee. Consequently, many private members' Bills are mere skeletons whose flesh has to be provided by departmental regulations.

Drafting, too, is a highly skilled art which the advisers of private members do not necessarily possess. Usually, Parliamentary Counsel do their best to put private members' Bills into shape, but difficulties constantly arise. The Isolation Hospitals Act, 1893, originated in a private member's Bill. It was a very convenient measure whose powers were much used before it was repealed (prospectively) by the Public Health Act, 1936. It provided an administrative system, however, which was cumbersome and fitted badly into the county council organisation established in 1889. It contained many provisions which were quite unnecessary—for instance, hospital committees were empowered to provide not only buildings, but also 'tents, wooden houses or other places for the reception of patients' and required that every hospital should 'so far as practicable be connected to the telegraph system'. It

[1] *Ante*, pp. 217–20. [2] *The Times*, 12 July 1938.
[3] *Ibid.* 15 July 1938.

was not specifically provided that every bed should 'so far as practicable be furnished with bedclothes'; but no doubt the draftsman forgot that.[1]

For these reasons there is some doubt whether private members ought to be encouraged to propose legislation. Sir Winston Churchill, for instance, said that 'there ought to be a very effective procedure for making it difficult for all sorts of happy thoughts to be carried on to the statute book'.[2] Mr Ramsay MacDonald, as Prime Minister,[3] wanted to take away two or three of the days given to second readings because 'every session there are six or seven admirable Bills that really the House of Commons wants to get through, and they have not got the ghost of a chance, not even if they are balloted for, unless they get the first place, or the second place'.[4] Mr Thomas Kennedy, as chief whip, thought that 'the time spent on private members' Bills under the present rules of procedure is...very largely wasted'.[5] On the other hand, Mr Ernest Brown, referring to the sixty Bills passed in the Parliament of 1924–9, thought that 'there would have been a great loss to the House and to the country if those private members had not had an opportunity of getting these Bills through'.[6] Mr Lloyd George emphasised that 'the time you give to private members is not so much a contribution to legislation, because very little legislation has ever come out of it, but it is rather an opportunity for discussing new ideas and new proposals upon a variety of topics'.[7]

The criticisms are perhaps exaggerations. Much useful non-controversial legislation is carried through by private members, though it is rarely so heroic as the Marriage Bill of 1937. The fact that much Government legislation is either vote-catching or of a departmental character renders desirable the provision of time for other measures.

[1] See Second Interim Report of the Local Government and Public Health Consolidation Committee, Cmd. 5059/1936, pp. 61–2.

[2] H.C. 161 of 1931, Q. 1530.

[3] It has already been pointed out that Mr MacDonald's evidence in 1931 contradicted the evidence which he gave in 1914.

[4] H.C. 161 of 1931, Q. 131.   [5] *Ibid.* Q. 718.   [6] *Ibid.* Q. 893.

[7] *Ibid.* Q. 1072. An example mentioned was the private member's Bill which several years later induced the Government to propose equality of franchise for men and women: cf. *ibid.* Q. 1267 (Sir Archibald Sinclair).

4. LOST SHEEP

The circumstances set out above show that the position of the private member is rarely one of importance or even of great interest. We must not forget the dull though, under present conditions, necessary work performed on standing committees, select committees, and Private Bill Committees; but in the House itself the assistance chiefly required is that of voting. Private members on the Opposition side are in slightly better case than their opponents, for they are encouraged, so long as they follow the tactics of their leaders and do not act as 'ginger groups', to make nuisances of themselves within the recognised limits of parliamentary opposition. Making allowances for these qualifications, it is still true that some members find time hanging heavily on their hands as they wait about for the division bell.

The result has been the development since 1918 of a regular warren of private members' committees, sometimes containing members of one party only, but often cutting across party boundaries. They are quite unofficial, though they are so far noticed by the whips' office that summonses to meetings of party committees may be sent out with the daily whip, and often ministers are invited to attend to give their views on a question under discussion.

The first of these committees was, apparently, the Unionist Agricultural Committee, which was established before 1914 and met once a fortnight during the session.[1] It was re-established after 1918, and has always been powerful because of the strength of the agricultural interest in the Conservative party. It has close relations with the three Farmers' Unions and the Country Landowners' Association; it is used, for instance, by the National Farmers' Union to bring pressure to bear upon the Government to adopt the Union's agricultural policy. This committee formed the model for several others, such as committees dealing with each of the three armed forces. When the Conservative party went into opposition the committees were converted into more or less official opposition committees. The former ministers being now relieved of responsibility, they were generally elected as chairmen of the appropriate committees, and other committees were formed to watch

[1] H.C. 161 of 1931, Qs. 3448–9 (Earl Winterton).

the actions of the respective departments.[1] The chairmen were usually members of the Opposition Policy Committee, the Conservative 'Shadow Cabinet'. When the Conservative party came back into office at the end of 1924, the committees went back to an unofficial status, and the former ministers returned to the Cabinet. Some of the committees then went out of existence owing to lack of support. Others, like the Agricultural Committee, the three committees on the armed forces, the Foreign Affairs Committee, the Imperial Affairs Committee, the Finance Committee, and the Trade and Industry Committee, continued or were re-established. The same process was followed in 1929, when the Conservative party again went into opposition, and in 1931, when the party came back into office. The committees were re-established when the Conservative party went into opposition in 1945 and were continued when Mr Winston Churchill's Government was established in 1951. In 1952 there were fourteen Conservative committees, covering most aspects of government.[2] They do useful work in enabling members interested in particular branches of Government policy to make themselves familiar with the problems involved. In Opposition, they enable members to develop criticisms of the Government's policy, and normally the chairman is an ex-minister who is a member of the Shadow Cabinet. When the Conservative Government is in office, they enable criticism of the Government's policy to be discussed privately and, in most cases, settled.

One of the best known of the committees is the Conservative Private Members' Committee, or '1922' Committee. This was established after the general election of 1922 to hold weekly meetings at which eminent people, including ministers, but often persons like bankers from outside the House give addresses and allow themselves to be cross-examined by such members as choose to attend. The committee is not in any sense a party meeting, and its importance has been exaggerated. If a Prime Minister is being attacked by a section of his party, as Mr Baldwin was when the 'Empire Free Trade' agitation was at its height, he calls a party meeting. The 1922 Committee is more like a glorified political discussion group, though its meetings are usually more interesting and therefore more popular than the debates in the House.

[1] See *ante*, pp. 180–1.   [2] R. T. McKenzie, *British Political Parties*, p. 57.

The appropriate committees are often in touch with the outside interests which support the Conservative party. The relations between the Agricultural Committee and the agricultural interests have been emphasised because they are of particular importance. The Federation of British Industries, the Association of British Chambers of Commerce, and similar bodies are, however, in close touch with the Finance Committee and the Trade and Industry Committee. Frequently, the active members of the committee are the representatives of the particular interest in the House. This statement is equally true where there are no profits to be obtained. The Navy League and similar bodies necessarily have close relations with the committees devoted to special study of the armed forces.

There is no Labour committee corresponding to the 1922 Committee, since the Parliamentary Labour party has weekly meetings while in opposition and meetings in alternate weeks when there is a Labour Government. There are, however, 'functional' committees, formally organised by the Parliamentary party, to keep members in touch with the various aspects of Government policy and, when the party is in opposition, to enable criticism of Government activity to be directed. During the Labour Government of 1945–51, too, there were regional committees.

Any group of members can, of course, form any kind of committee they please. Such committees are therefore springing up and dying the whole time. Each needs only a chairman and a secretary; and often if the secretary is rejected by his constituency, or is made a junior minister, or is called to 'another place' in either sense of that term, the committee just disappears. Many committees, too, deal with ephemeral questions and therefore live and die like the May-fly. Committees need not be party committees and there are many which include representatives of all parties. Sometimes there are committees representing particular areas. For practical purposes the Welsh parliamentary party is a committee of this kind, and there is also a Lancashire Members' Group. If such committees are to contain Labour members, they must be strictly non-political in the commonly accepted sense; for unorthodoxy is frowned upon by the Parliamentary Labour party; and, though there is no express prohibition against joining non-party committees, Labour members are expected to consult the party secretary before they allow their names to be used.

The device of the non-party committee is particularly useful for an interest—particularly a philanthropic society, but including many of the professional associations—which is not associated with the party organisations but is anxious to secure legislation of a particular kind. For instance, when a group of societies led by the Councils for the Preservation of Rural England and Rural Scotland came to the conclusion that agitation should be conducted to persuade the Government to provide money for National Parks, their first step was to set up a representative committee. It persuaded the Government to appoint a Departmental Committee; and when that committee reported in favour it conducted further agitation. One of the methods adopted was the setting up of a non-party parliamentary committee on National Parks. Sometimes, indeed, these parliamentary committees contain representatives of outside interests as well as members of Parliament, and some contain peers as well as members of the House of Commons. Nor can more political interests neglect the device of the parliamentary committee. Thus, the Federation of British Industries used to have a parliamentary committee, and there is in existence a parliamentary committee of the National Farmers' Union.

While the committees of Government supporters are entirely unofficial, they naturally request the assistance of ministers where their conclusions appear to be contrary to ministerial policy, and on their part ministers are anxious to retain the support of their majority and to that end ask to be allowed to address the appropriate committee.[1] Sometimes, a committee sends a deputation to the minister; sometimes, even, a Bill is drafted to embody the committee's conclusions. The following quotations illustrate the technique:

The Conservative Agricultural Parliamentary Committee at its meeting last week expressed grave anxiety at the serious position of the poultry industry, and it was unanimously decided to ask the Prime Minister to receive a deputation at the earliest possible moment. Mr Baldwin has now

---

[1] Note that, as a committee is quite unofficial, a peer may address it: e.g. Lord Halifax, Foreign Secretary, addressed the Foreign Affairs Committee: *The Times*, 24 June 1938.

intimated that he will be prepared to receive the deputation at 4 o'clock this afternoon.[1]

In view of the difficulties in the poultry industry the Conservative Parliamentary Agricultural Committee has decided to introduce a private member's Bill to amend the Agricultural Marketing Act, 1933, in so far as it affects poultry and poultry products. Mr Turton, the chairman of the Poultry Sub-Committee will introduce the Bill under the ten minutes' rule.[2]

Sir John Reith, the Director-General of the British Broadcasting Corporation, was present at a largely attended meeting of the Conservative Members' Committee, at which the whole question of the alleged bias of the B.B.C. in the presentation of news and in certain recent educational talks was fully and frankly discussed.[3]

An emergency meeting of the Parliamentary Committee of the Empire Industries Association has been called for next Tuesday to consider the proposed Anglo-American Trade Agreement. On the following day there will be a meeting of the Tariff Policy Group of M.P.'s, at which Captain Wallace, Parliamentary Secretary to the Board of Trade, and Mr R. H. Hudson, Secretary of the Department of Overseas Trade, will discuss the question of trade agreements. It is hoped that this meeting will be a preliminary to an interview with the Prime Minister.[4]

About a hundred M.P.'s attended last night's meeting of the Conservative Private Members' Committee at which Mr Hore-Belisha, Secretary for War, listened to suggestions for improving recruiting for the Regular Army.... He would consider carefully every suggestion put forward and he would welcome further suggestions.[5]

Of particular interest in this connection was the sequel to Mr Chamberlain's speech at Kettering in July 1938. Mr Chamberlain seized the occasion of an ordinary political speech on 2 July to give his views on the home production of agricultural products as part of the technique of defence. The 1922 Committee met on 4 July (*The Times* significantly

---

[1] *The Times*, 24 February 1937.

[2] *Ibid.* 18 June 1937 (the Bill proceeded no further).

[3] *Ibid.* 16 March 1937 (Sir John Reith later attended a similar meeting of Labour members).

[4] *Ibid.* 4 June 1937. *The Manchester Guardian* adds: 'I learn that the Association has persuaded the Dominions Prime Ministers to come to the House of Commons to have a talk with them as soon as the final reports of the Imperial Conference have been drafted': 9 June 1937. (It seems that there was Dominion opposition to a trade agreement which sought to lower tariffs against American products.)

[5] *Ibid.* 20 July 1937.

explained that 'owing to the Royal Show at Cardiff the Conservative Agricultural Committee does not meet this week'),[1] and *The Times* reported: 'The 1922 Committee is not normally a critical body, but speeches made at this meeting by responsible backbenchers were in line with the statement of the N.F.U. given below.' This statement by the National Farmers' Union was as follows:

The references to agricultural policy in the Prime Minister's speech at Kettering have created considerable astonishment in agricultural circles. It is impossible to believe that his statement represents the Government's last word on agricultural policy before the General Election: yet that is how the speech is being interpreted. The patent insecurity of the farmer's position, the present condition of our soil, the continued drift of workers away from agricultural employment, all emphasise the need for further legislative action if the home farmer is to play any real part at all in the defence programme. The situation is so disquieting that it should be cleared up at once, and the N.F.U. has made prompt representations on the subject to the Minister of Agriculture.[2]

The Times further announced that 'in view of some misunderstanding which seems to have arisen among agriculturists in the House of Commons after the Prime Minister's speech at Kettering on Saturday, it is understood that Mr Chamberlain has invited a number of supporters of the Government who represent rural constituencies to meet him to-morrow afternoon (i.e. 6 July)'. A meeting was accordingly held at the House of Commons on that date, the Prime Minister being accompanied by the Minister of Agriculture, and the unusual step was taken of issuing a long communication to the press.[3]

---

[1] *The Times*, 5 July 1938.   [2] *Ibid.*

[3] *The Times*, 7 July 1938. It is worth noting that the Warwickshire branch of the National Farmers' Union sent a telegram to the members for the county: 'Warwickshire farmers dismayed and disgusted by insult to home agriculture in the Prime Minister's Kettering speech; what are you doing about it?': *The Times*, 7 July 1938. Other branches of the same body took action as effective and immediate. Indeed, some branches requested their officers to find out the policies of the other parties. The loss of the farmers' vote would be a serious matter to a Conservative Government. The Milk Bill, 1938, was defeated by the Conservative Agricultural Committee and the National Farmers' Union in combination, for it was never read a second time. An 'agricultural' candidate supported by the N.F.U. was put up against the Liberal National candidate for the East Norfolk by-election in January 1939, but withdrew at the personal request of the Prime Minister. A few days later, the Minister of Agriculture resigned.

In addition, several committees took a conspicuous part in the discussions which resulted in the withdrawal of the original proposals made in 1937 for a National Defence Contribution.[1] Here, as often, it was difficult to distinguish the private committees from outside interests; for obviously those members most interested in taxation upon commerce and industry are those with connections with the Federation of British Industries, the Association of British Chambers of Commerce, the Chamber of Shipping, and many other bodies. It is in any case clear that among Conservative members, at least, these committee discussions arouse more interest than the average debate in the House. As Sir Austen Chamberlain said in 1931:

> When I have said, 'But why are there so few fellows on our benches', I have been told, 'Our Committee on India is meeting', or something of that kind.[2]

Mr Winston Churchill's evidence was to the same effect:

> I am very struck by how the House of Commons likes committee work. You see these unofficial committees are always crowded...the House empty and unofficial committees full.[3]

Earl Winterton added:

> When I first got into the House, with regard to a member of our party... provided that he attended the divisions, nobody took the slightest interest in him or cared what he did with his time. He was never approached to serve on any committee except occasionally a Private Bill Committee. The result is that he was inclined to sit in the House to learn all about it, and this went on for the first two sessions. The member now finds so many things to do that he does not get in the habit of sitting in the House at all.[4]

The sheep escape from the fold and assemble in flocks of their own choosing, but they can always be called back by the division bell.

---

[1] *Ante*, p. 145.   [2] H.C. 161 of 1931, Q. 2369.
[3] *Ibid.* Q. 1359.   [4] *Ibid.* Q. 3426.

CHAPTER XII

THE HOUSE OF LORDS

I. ARISTOCRACY

Some continental writers continue to speak of the House of Lords as the 'aristocratic' element in the British Constitution. An acute French public lawyer, Professor Achille Mestre, speaks of 'the survival of a certain aristocratic element', and adds that, in spite of the rise of the Labour party, 'English democracy continues to feel the need of a directing *élite* whose economic independence guarantees its probity'.[1] Names, of course, matter little; and 'aristocratic' may be a term either of abuse or of commendation according as one follows the tradition of the French Revolution or of Burke. But if the use of the word suggests that the House of Lords has not essentially altered its character since Mr Pitt waged war against the French Republic it is not desirable to use it; for there have been changes great indeed.

During the late eighteenth century the system of Government was based essentially on 'property', which meant property in land. The landowners nominated and elected members of Parliament in nearly all counties and boroughs. The great families were the main support of the various sections of Whigs and Tories. Property filled the livings of the Church and the higher ranks of the Army. Justice was administered locally by country gentlemen, though strange to say the superior courts were much more open to the talents. Peerage and property were not quite synonymous, especially because titles descended only in tail male (or, in the case of the few baronies by writ, to heirs general) and not to all descendants or even to all male descendants. But the practice of entailing resulted in lands being tied to titles; and where property was held apart from a title, as where it passed to the heir general, or where it was purchased by a Nabob or a merchant, it was the natural ambition of the owner to receive a peerage, and the natural desire of the political groups to obtain his 'influence' by gratifying his ambition. Accordingly,

---

[1] Preface to P. H. Siriex, *Le Régime parlementaire anglais contemporain*, pp. iii, iv.

it is generally true that property governed Great Britain, whether the Prime Minister was a landless younger son like William Pitt or a noble nonentity like the Duke of Portland. Property, too, was not the monopoly of one party, though the French Revolution and the attitude of Fox and Sheridan had tended to make the Tories the hope of property and the Whigs the hope of radicals. This tendency for Toryism and property to go together was accentuated when the second Earl Grey allowed himself to be carried along on the crest of the Reform movement of 1830. Even so, the Whigs still relied largely on the great families, like those of Cavendish and Russell, and fifty Whig peers would have given the Whigs a majority sufficient to secure the passage of the Reform Bill in 1832.[1]

This condition was substantially altered by the Industrial Revolution and its political counterpart, the Reform Act of 1832. The former made industrial capital more important than land, and the latter to a considerable degree transferred political influence from the country gentlemen to the newer kind of capitalist, the Whig, dissenting manufacturer. While the House of Lords for the time being still represented property, a more substantial section of the House of Commons depended on the votes of the newer middle class. Sir Robert Peel, himself the son of a manufacturer, was able between 1834 and 1841 to attract enough of the new 'influence' to give the Conservative party, still based essentially on property, a majority. The repeal of the Corn Laws in 1846, however, decreased the influence of property by lowering rents, increased the influence of the newer capitalists by lowering costs of production and increasing trade, and at the same time split the Conservative party. The immediate result in the House of Lords was that for the first time since 1789 the Tories were almost balanced by a combination of Whigs and Peelites. In the House of Commons the country gentlemen went into opposition under the combined leadership of a scion of the house of Bentinck (a Whig family which was converted to Toryism by the French Revolution) and a political adventurer named Disraeli. The Conservative party did not again obtain a majority in the Lower House

---

[1] The Bill was defeated on second reading by 199 votes to 158, a majority of forty-one. Of the 357 peers who voted, seventy-nine voted by proxy. See Molesworth, *History of England*, I, p. 192. The House of Lords then contained about 400 peers.

until 1874, by which time Disraeli had converted it into a 'party of resistance' not to attacks on rent but to radicalism. In the meantime, however, the natural tendency of hereditary legislators to move to the right had long before recreated the Conservative majority in the House of Lords. By 1855 peers were again moving into opposition to the Coalition Government.[1] This process was accelerated by the Reform Act of 1867 and the growing radicalism of the Liberal party under Mr Gladstone. In 1869 Lord Granville reported to Queen Victoria that the Liberals had a majority against them of between sixty and seventy, not including bishops or alleged Liberals who more often voted with the Conservative Opposition than with the Liberal Government.[2]

In spite of the many Liberal creations, the adoption by Mr Gladstone of the policy of Home Rule for Ireland caused another large defection. On the Home Rule Bill of 1893—the first to go to the House of Lords— in a House of 560 peers, forty-one voted for the Bill and 419 against it.[3] From 1895 to 1905 Unionist Governments were in power, and naturally most of those ennobled were good Unionists. Sir Henry Campbell-Bannerman created twenty-one peers; but in 1910 Mr Asquith said that of the 600 peers twenty-six were bishops and of the remainder 500 were Unionists.[4] The Budget of 1909 was defeated by 350 votes to 75;[5] and the Government of Ireland Bill, 1912, by 326 votes to 69.[6]

The majority no longer consisted, however, of the 'country gentlemen' in the sense of 1846. The primary test of nobility, at least for purposes of ennoblement, was still wealth. In their recommendations to Queen Victoria the Prime Ministers of the nineteenth century always emphasised that the proposed recipient of royal favour was able to 'support' the title, but this became not a specific statement as to the size of the rent roll but a general allegation. The rent roll was by no means the sole source of wealth and other sources of income were more important. The repeal of the Corn Laws and the rapid development of commerce and industry had shifted the incidence of wealth. Of the vast numbers who thus became able to 'live like a lord', only

---

[1] *Life of Lord Granville*, I, p. 495.   [2] *Ibid.* II, p. 16.
[3] *Life of Gladstone*, III, p. 504; *Letters of Queen Victoria*, 3rd series, II, p. 311.
[4] Lord Oxford and Asquith, *Fifty Years of Parliament*, II, p. 41.
[5] 4 H.L.Deb. 5 s., 1341–6.   [6] 13 H.L.Deb. 5 s., 813–16.

comparatively few were ennobled; and peerages were created for what have been known since 1921 as 'political and public services'.

Judging from the Honours Lists issued since 1945, wealth as such seems to have little claim. The award of peerages to the managing directors or chairmen of directors of the great industrial, commercial and financial combines must no doubt be regarded as a tribute rather to merit than to wealth, and is comparable with awards to distinguished lawyers, scientists, medical men, diplomats, civil servants, trade unionists and officers of the armed forces. There have been a few awards for 'political and public services' to persons whose lights had previously shone under bushels, but the bushels perhaps had some close connection with the Conservative Central Office; and, probably, these awards are similar to those made during the Labour Government for distinguished service to the Labour movement. Service in the House of Commons is still the easiest path to the House of Lords. It was noted in 1938 that of the 137 peers created between 1922 and 1936, seventy-four were or had been members of Parliament.[1] The proportion has been much the same since: of the 188 peers created between 1937 and January 1956, eighty-one had been members of the House of Commons.

The peerage could not in any case be an aristocracy of wealth, for death duties, income-tax and surtax have heavily reduced inherited wealth and made its accumulation extremely difficult. The 'great houses' have nearly all been closed, given to the National Trust, or put on exhibition as museums. On the other hand, the House of Lords cannot be regarded as representative of an impoverished aristocracy, once wealthy, but now victim of the Welfare State. Over half the peerages in existence in 1955 dated from 1906 or later. Of 925 peerages, excluding life peerages, only 603 were held by peers of the third or later generation; and to the 312 peers of the first or second generation must be added the thirty-five bishops and lords of appeal. It appears, therefore, that about one-fifth of the members of the House of Lords (excluding peeresses and minors) have been appointed to that House by reason of their own merits; but, since they normally reach that House towards the end of their careers, the majority of them are unable to take an active part in its work. The remainder are peers of the second and

[1] 1st ed., p. 368, n. 3.

subsequent generations, the majority of whom never attend after their formal introduction. Nor is there any particular reason why they should attend. Merit, particularly political merit, is not heritable; nor are the peers now representative of any section of opinion whatever.

2. COMPOSITION

In examining the 'aristocratic' basis of the House of Lords, we have necessarily considered its composition. On 31 October 1955 it consisted of 803 hereditary peers of the United Kingdom, sixteen representative peers of Scotland, four representative peers of Ireland, nine Lords of Appeal in Ordinary, and twenty-six Lords Spiritual.

The peers of the United Kingdom are the successors of the lords who were summoned to the *Curia Regis* by the Norman and Angevin kings. The great lords were the great landowners; and since land descended to heirs, the heirs also were great landowners. When, after the Restoration, attendance became a privilege and not a duty, it did not require much falsification of history to assert that a writ of summons followed by attendance conferred a hereditary right. Accordingly, there are a few 'baronies by writ' which go back to the Middle Ages. The other peerages—the vast majority—have been created by letters patent, and these were held to confer a right of attendance. Peerages of England created before the Act of Union with Scotland, 1701, therefore confer upon their holders for the time being membership of the House of Lords. After the Act of Union, new peerages were created in the peerage of Great Britain; and after the Act of Union with Ireland, 1800, new peerages were in the peerage of the United Kingdom. Thus, the hereditary peers summoned to the House are the successors of the peers entitled by writ of summons, by letters patent in the peerage of England and by letters patent in the peerage of the United Kingdom. Peerages by writ descend to heirs general, whereas peerages by letters patent descend according to the limitations of the letters patent, which are usually to heirs in tail male. Peerages by writ may thus descend to females; and occasionally a woman is entitled to a peerage either by special grant, or by a special limitation. Such peeresses in their own right are not entitled to sit in the House of Lords. But any other holder of a peerage of England or the United Kingdom is entitled to a seat provided that he is of full age and takes the oath (though there have been many cases of peers sitting and voting without taking the oath).

The peers of Scotland are not as such entitled to sit in the House of Lords. If they also hold peerages of the United Kingdom (as many do) they are entitled to sit in that capacity. Those who do not elect sixteen of their number for the duration of each Parliament. As no new peerages of Scotland can be created, and the number of peers of Scotland without peerages of the United Kingdom has now been reduced to thirty-three, the peers of Scotland now have a substantial measure of representation. The peers of Ireland were entitled to elect twenty-eight of their number, each of whom sat in the House of Lords for life. New peerages of Ireland can now be created for every peerage which becomes extinct. But in fact there have been no recent additions to this peerage, and it may be assumed that there will be none. Also, the machinery for election was destroyed by legislation consequential upon the creation of the Irish Free State. The number of representative peers of Ireland has in consequence been reduced gradually by death, and it may be assumed that the representatives of the peerage of Ireland will have disappeared from the House of Lords by 1980.[1]

The Lords of Appeal in Ordinary are given peerages for life in accordance with legislation passed since 1876 in order to strengthen the House of Lords in its judicial aspect. Most of them take no part in ordinary political debates, though they assist in the more technical branches of legislation. The Lords Spiritual sit in the House of Lords only so long as they hold their sees. They are the Archbishops of Canterbury and York and the Bishops of London, Durham and Winchester, and twenty-one other bishops according to seniority of appointment (the Bishop of Sodor and Man excepted). Until 1868 all bishops, except the Bishop of Sodor and Man, sat in the House; but as new bishoprics were created the number of Lords Spiritual has not been increased; and in fact it was decreased as a result of the disestablishment of the Welsh Church.

From the Government point of view, it is more important to learn the political sympathies of the Lords Temporal. The Lords Spiritual,

---

[1] There were five left in 1955, one of whom has a United Kingdom peerage.

the Lords of Appeal in Ordinary, and those judges (other than the Lord Chancellor) who hold hereditary peerages, do not disclose their sympathies. Including these, there are 285 peers who give no information. Of the rest, 484 are Conservative, or Liberal-Nationalist, or National Labour, or plain 'National'. In opposition are 51 Liberals and 51 Labour Peers. Thus, even if the doubtful votes were given against the Government, the Government would still have a majority of over seventy per cent in a House of 850 Lords. Such an attendance would be impossible; but it is evident that on all political issues a Conservative Government has an enormous majority, and that no Government formed by the present Opposition could have anything but a small minority.

The effective majority of the Conservative party is not to be determined only by political affiliations. For even when political issues of the utmost importance are being debated the attendance is not large. On no occasion since 1919 have half the peers taken part in a division. Taking the period of fifteen years from 1922 to the end of the session in 1936, there were 456 divisions in the House of Lords. The number voting was as many as 200 on ten occasions only, and as many as 100 on ninety occasions only (including the occasions when more than 200 peers voted). At the other extreme, there were ninety-eight divisions in which less than fifty-one peers voted; and in twelve of these less than thirty-one peers voted. The average vote per division was less than eighty-three, or about one-ninth of the membership of the House, and it is worth noticing that while the average under Conservative (or National) Governments was eighty-one, that under Labour Governments was ninety-two. By 1945 there had been a substantial increase in the size of the House of Lords, but the figures from 1945 to 1955 were no better. There were 172 divisions, in four of which over 200 peers voted, and in twenty-three of which more than 100 peers voted. There were fourteen divisions in which the vote was under fifty-one, though in only one of them was the vote under thirty-one. The average vote per division was just under seventy-nine, or less than one-tenth of the total membership of the House. There was, however, very little difference in the attendance from 1945 to 1951, when there was a Labour Government, and between 1951 and 1955, when there was a Conservative Government. The slight falling off might be attributed to the decrease in the number of Labour peers attending, no doubt owing to age. Nor are these figures indicative of the interest and excitement of the proceedings, for the number of divisions is very low (only thirty a session on the average before 1945 and only seventeen afterwards), and there are many sittings at which no vote is taken. The quorum is only three, and there are many sittings for legislative business when a few ministers and a handful of Opposition peers alone are present. Nor must it be forgotten that the figures are somewhat swollen by divisions early in the afternoon. The House of Lords rarely sits for more than three hours at a time; but even then the attendance falls off rapidly. Thus, on 30 May 1934, there were 109 peers at the first division, and sixty-two at the third. On 8 November 1934, the House sat all day. There were 107 peers at the first division and sixty at the last. On 22 April 1931, there were 143 peers at the first division, and ninety-three at the last. Since 1945 the tendency has been for the first division to be less well attended than the second, after which the attendance falls off. Thus, on 12 July 1954 there were eighty-nine at the first division and 101 at the second, but only sixty-nine at the last.

Nor are the peers amenable to the whip. They have no fear of losing their seats. A dissolution holds no terrors for them. They have no constituents to call them to order or to press them to take an active part. They accept the whip because they want it, not because the party label is the essential passport to Parliament. Few of them can be called professional politicians. Some are ministers and others hope to be ministers. A number are promoted members of the House of Commons who find that they cannot live without a moderate diet of oratory. The rest attend only because they are interested, intellectually or materially, or because duty calls them to assist in the government of the country or to protest against dangerous innovations or, as that good Conservative, Queen Victoria, put it, 'subversive measures'.[1] They will not undertake the humdrum task of discussing ordinary legislation; still less will they attend merely to vote when votes are not required either to support the Conservative party or to act as a public protest. The greater the Conservative majority, the less their attendance is necessary.

[1] *Life of Sir Henry Campbell-Bannerman*, I, p. 171.

It does not need an attendance of 500 to outvote the 51 Labour peers, any more than it requires a sledgehammer to swat a fly. There are other things to do; estates require attention, foxes must be hunted, justice dispensed in petty sessions, and boards of directors attended (though on his quarterly visit to London a director might just 'look in to see if anything is doing').

Above all, it is quite useless to sit through a debate that does not promise to be interesting. The subject itself may attract an audience. The debate on the Prayer Book Measure in 1927 attracted the largest audience since 1919 not merely because the bishops were professionally concerned, nor because most peers are pillars of the Church, but because the discussion promised to be interesting. Nearly one-half, 329, of the votes available were cast in the division. Similarly, since 1945, the only debates other than those on the Parliament Bill which more than 200 peers have voted were those on the suspension of the death penalty in 1948 (when the whips were taken off and 209 peers voted), and the debate on the proposal to set up an independent television authority, when 244 peers voted. Political controversy may stimulate interest. The only other occasion when over 300 peers voted was on the motion to approve the Report of the Joint Select Committee on Indian Constitutional Reform in 1934 when 301 peers took part in the division. Similarly, 291 peers voted on the second reading of the Government of India Bill, 1935. Here the Conservative party was divided: it was not known whether there was a majority in the House of Lords; and all the 'big guns' available were brought into action. There was similarly a division of Conservative opinion over television policy in 1953, and 244 peers voted on 26 November. Even on the second reading of the Television Bill on 1 July 1954, there were 194 peers in the division lobbies.

Again, the peers are necessarily interested in the future of their own order. Most of them resent the 'clipping of wings' to which they were forcibly subjected in 1911. They are anxious to restore some of the power which the Parliament Act took away from them. They recognise that by way of compromise some modification of the composition of their House may be necessary as a *quid pro quo*. On a motion for the reform of the House of Lords in 1927, 266 peers voted in a division;

and 253 voted on a Parliament (Reform) Bill in 1933. Even the question of admitting to the House peeresses in their own right brought 206 peers into the division lobbies in 1926. On the three Parliament Bills of 1948 and 1949, there voted respectively 258 peers, 238 peers and 147 peers.

Sometimes, again, it is necessary to protest against 'confiscatory' legislation. On the Licensing Bill, 1908, 272 peers voted against and ninety-six in favour; and on the Finance Bill, 1909, 350 voted against and seventy-five in favour. But here political controversy made the subject interesting, the need to 'damn the Radicals' was urgent, and the pockets of peers had to be protected. Such a combination has not been common, but there were three divisions on the Coal Mines Bill, 1930, in which over 200 peers took part, and there was a large attendance when the Lords emasculated the Agricultural Land (Utilisation) Bill, 1931. More often, one or two of the motives alone are present. Discussions on agriculture are often well attended because the 'landed interest' is still strong in the House.[1] The Drink Trade is particularly well represented; and a worthy bishop can achieve fame by advocating 'temperance' even when he knows that no measure he introduces can pass the House of Commons.[2] Coal Mines Bills[3] and Bills regulating the supply of electricity[4] (provided that there was some attack on vested interests) used to show that peers derived their revenues from sources other than land and liquor; but there were only two divisions on the Coal Industry Nationalisation Bill, 1946, and the higher vote against the Bill was only fifty-five; while there were again only two divisions on the Electricity Bill, 1947, the higher vote against the Government being sixty-five. On the other hand, 119 peers voted against the

[1] E.g. Agriculture Bill, 1919; Allotments Bill, 1922; Exportation of Horses Bill, 1922; Importation of Horses Bill, 1922; Agricultural Wages (Amendment) Bill, 1925; Wild Birds Protection Bill, 1926; Ecclesiastical and Glebe Lands Bill, 1927; Agricultural Land (Utilisation) Bill, 1931. On the other hand, the House is not particularly interested in Agricultural Marketing; see the Bills of 1931 and 1933.

[2] Cf. Public House (Improvement) Bill, 1924; Liquor (Popular Control) Bills, 1924, 1927 and 1928. Presumably the Betting and Lotteries Bill, 1934, belonged to a like category.

[3] E.g. Coal Mines Bills, 1926 and 1930; Mining Industry Bill, 1926. Cf. the Petroleum (Production) Bill, 1934.

[4] Electricity (Supply) Bills, 1919 and 1926.

Government in a vote on general economic policy in March 1947, and there was a moderate attendance, rather larger than usual, on the Transport Bill of the same year and the Iron and Steel Bill of 1949. On the motion to insist that the date of vesting under that Bill be postponed, 103 peers voted against the Government.

It is plain that the Parliament Acts have clipped the wings of the 'backwoodsmen' and that they no longer turn out in force to defend their economic interests, because the only way to defend them is to secure the election of a Conservative Government; and, from the point of view of those who still remember when the wealthy were not impoverished by taxation, such a Government is probably only slightly better than a Labour Government because it must for electoral reasons maintain the Welfare State and full employment. The blame ought to be attributed to Benjamin Disraeli who first enfranchised the working-class, though oddly enough nobody ever does so. There is a small band of hard-working Conservative, Liberal and Labour peers, who do their best to keep the machine working; some forty or fifty others are sufficiently politically-minded to turn out for the equivalent of a three-line whip; and another hundred can be induced to attend a particularly interesting debate, such as those on the Prayer Book Measure, the Government of India Bill, the Parliament Bill, capital punishment, and television policy. The maximum attendance, however, is about one-quarter of the House. Though in 1910 there were about 300 peers fewer than there are at present, the attendances at the political debates were much higher than they have been since. The Liberal Government could rarely rely on more than 50 votes, yet between 1906 and 1910 the Conservative Opposition facing them reached 150 or more on 18 occasions. The Education Bill, 1906, secured an attendance of 312, the Licensing Bill, 1908, an attendance of 368, and the Finance Bill, 1909, an attendance of 425.

With the Labour Governments of 1924 and 1929–31 such exemplary attention was unnecessary. The Governments were more conservative than those of Sir Henry Campbell-Bannerman and Mr Asquith. They had far fewer representatives, and much less able representatives, in the House of Lords. Mr Lloyd George, Mr Bonar Law, and Mr Baldwin had accustomed Conservative lords to legislation which would have caused the previous generation to call out the militia. For other reasons the temperature of the political atmosphere was much lower—and it needs a forest fire to bring out the inhabitants of the political jungle. Accordingly, though the attendance was greater than it has normally been before and since, it was by no means so great as between 1906 and 1910. Apart from the Coal Mines Bill, 1930, and the Agricultural Land (Utilisation) Bill, 1931, only the Unemployment Insurance (No. 2) Bill, 1930, the Education (School Attendance) Bill, 1931 (when the Lords rejected a Bill whose essential principle was passed without a division in 1936), and the Representation of the People (No. 2) Bill, 1931, produced attendances which might be regarded as 'large'.

The number of Labour peers rose to a maximum of sixty-three in 1953, owing partly to creations under the Labour Government of 1945–51 and partly to the 'bipartisan' Honours List issued at the Coronation of Elizabeth II. The highest Government vote between 1945 and 1951, the Conservative peers opposing, was the eighty-one who voted for the second reading of the Parliament Bill in June 1948, when the Liberals supported the Government. There was a Labour vote of thirty-seven on the Parliament Bill, 1949, when the Liberals voted against the Government, but there was no other occasion on which so many Labour peers voted, and usually the Labour vote was between twelve and twenty-five. It was therefore unnecessary for the Conservative peers to turn out in force. The solid core of forty or fifty hard-working Conservative peers was all that was necessary to put the Government in a minority, and this was done on 113 occasions. Since the Conservatives rarely insisted on their amendments if the House of Commons objected, the process of putting the Government in a minority was part of the game of politics. The Government was put in a minority in the hope that the electorate would be persuaded that a Conservative Government would be much better. In other words, the House of Lords was merely part of the political machinery of the Conservative party, and it was unnecessary to call out the legions from the back of beyond, or even from the City of London and Mayfair.

The Conservative peers almost always vote Conservative. A Liberal or Labour motion secures scant support. But this does not mean that

Conservative peers always obey the Conservative whip. In the Lords the right wing is far more obvious than it is in the Commons. Having no fear of being deprived of the label—indeed, according to their own views it is the right wing and not the Conservative party that is truly Conservative—Conservative peers do not hesitate to vote against the Government. One effect of the Reform Act of 1832 was to complete the understanding that the Government was responsible to the House of Commons alone. George III thought in 1783 that he could overthrow the Fox–North Coalition by persuading the peers to reject Fox's India Bill. He did not succeed; but neither did the House of Commons overthrow Mr Pitt in 1784 by voting against him. Certainly Mr Pitt could not have carried on after 1784 merely because he secured a majority in the House of Commons at the general election. But from 1832 to 1874, from 1880 to 1885, and from 1893 to 1895, it was the usual experience for the Government to find itself in a minority in the Lords.

When the House of Lords voted in 1839 for a Select Committee on the Government of Ireland, Lord John Russell sought a vote of confidence from the House of Commons. Executive government, he said, must be carried on according to one principle or the other, and the principle should be that of the House of Commons.[1] A similar procedure was followed when the Government was defeated in the House of Lords in the Don Pacifico debate of 1850.[2] In 1882 the House of Lords appointed a Select Committee to investigate the working of the Irish Land Act of 1881. Mr Forster refused to attend, and the House of Commons passed a resolution, on the Government's motion, that inquiry was inexpedient.[3] Since 1886, however, the support of a Liberal or Labour Government in the House of Lords has been so small that, on the one hand, it has never thought of resigning or even of asking for a vote of confidence from the House of Commons; and, on the other

---

[1] 47 Hans.Deb. 3 s., 9–10; *Life of Lord Melbourne*, p. 472. On the other hand Lord John Russell decided to resign in 1849 if the Bill repealing the Navigation Acts was rejected by the House of Lords: see *Later Correspondence of Lord John Russell*, I, p. 195. But Lord Palmerston thought otherwise and gave cogent reasons showing that the situation would then become impossible: *ibid.* pp. 193–4.

[2] Greville, *Memoirs of the Reign of Queen Victoria*, III, p. 344.

[3] *Life of W. E. Forster*, II, pp. 389–90.

hand, the House of Lords has rarely resorted to a vote of censure.[1] A debate on a motion in the Upper House is wholly academic; and though the rejection or amendment of a Bill may cause a dispute between the two Houses and may compel the Government to dissolve Parliament, there is no longer any suggestion that the Government is responsible to the House of Lords.[2]

While on the one hand this makes the Government independent of the House of Lords, on the other hand it makes the House of Lords independent of the Government. Accordingly, even a Conservative Government can be defeated with impunity, and any other Government is beaten regularly. The peers vote as their consciences or their pockets indicate—though, of course, the conscience resides so near the pocket that it is rarely possible to separate them.[3] This means that the 'die-hards' constantly find themselves opposing the Government; and as the Government has no means of compelling the attendance of its more orthodox supporters it often finds itself in a minority. Between 1906 and 1910 the Liberal Government was defeated in 113 divisions out of 134, between 1929 and 1931 the Labour Government was defeated in fifty-three divisions out of eighty-six and between 1945 and 1951 the Labour Government was defeated on 113 occasions. The Conservative strength is so overwhelming that it is necessary only to

[1] Such a vote was moved and passed when Mr Asquith announced in 1911 that the King had been advised and had consented to create enough peers to secure the passage of the Parliament Bill. A similar motion was rejected in the House of Commons; and nobody paid any attention to the peers.

[2] 'The Government of the day, the House of Commons of the day, would treat with derision any vote passed by the House of Lords condemning a particular ministry or a particular member of a ministry'—Mr A. J. Balfour, 176 Parl.Deb. 4 s., 928 (24 June 1907).

[3] 'The present political battle is fiercer than you would ever guess. The Lords feel that they are sure to be robbed: they see the end of the ordered world. Chaos and confiscation lie before them': Walter A. Page (American Ambassador to the Court of St James), 24 August 1913: B. J. Hendrick, *Life and Letters of Walter A. Page*, I, pp. 140–1. Heavy taxation and regulation of property may reasonably be called 'robbery' by one side and 'justice' by the other. Property owners did not want to be 'robbed'; and their consciences would not let them be 'robbed', for if civilisation and order are based on property, 'robbery' brings barbarism and anarchy. On the other side, it was considered that civilisation and order were based on 'justice'; and obviously Radical consciences must insist upon a more 'just' distribution of the national income, for only in that way can civilisation and order be established and maintained. Both arguments were right— assuming that both premises were correct.

put on the whip. But Conservative Governments are not immune from defeat. In 1922 and 1923 the Government was defeated seven times; from 1925 to 1929 it was defeated eight times; and between 1931 and 1936 the 'National' Governments were defeated eleven times.

The truth is that the House of Lords is always a little more to the right than a Conservative Government. The Government exists by reason of its votes, many of which must be derived from sections of the population which take but a small portion of the national income. The peers are not completely representative of 'property', but they can hardly be said to be a fair cross-section of the national life, especially when the aspects of life that matter are economic interests. Their view of the national interest, therefore, does not necessarily coincide with that of a Government which is very susceptible to movements of opinion among a much wider section of the population. No serious difficulty results. The peers do not defeat Conservative measures but amend them. If the amendments are small, the Government, and therefore the House of Commons, accepts them. If they are important they are rejected by the House of Commons, and when they return to the House of Lords with the Commons' reasons for disagreement, the motion, 'That this House do not insist on the amendment', is carried without opposition. With a Labour or Liberal Government the situation is different; but this leads us to a consideration of the functions of the House of Lords.

3. FUNCTIONS

Relics of history confer upon the peers functions which a Second Chamber does not usually possess. They are not merely hereditary legislators but hereditary advisers of the Crown. They possess individually the right to request an audience with the Queen. Since the Queen no longer determines policy, the function is of no importance. It was discouraged by Queen Victoria[1] and is now never exercised. The Queen's function is not to discuss the matter, but to hear what is said;[2] and no doubt she pays much less attention to what is said formally than

[1] Who thought it 'extremely inconvenient': *Letters of Queen Victoria*, 1st series, I, p. 421.

[2] Lord Brougham, *Life and Times*, III, p. 95; *Letters of Queen Victoria*, 1st series, I, pp. 117–18.

to what is said informally on some social occasion. 'It is only for the Sovereign to say that he is convinced of the good motives which have actuated the step, and that consideration will be given to the matter and arguments which have been stated.'[1]

The House of Lords is also a court of record. It hears appeals in civil matters from the (English) Court of Appeal with leave of the Court or of the House;[2] in a criminal matter from the (English) Court of Criminal Appeal if the Attorney-General certifies it is of exceptional public importance,[3] and from the Court of Criminal Appeal of Northern Ireland in similar circumstances;[4] from the Court of Appeal of Northern Ireland;[5] and, in civil cases, from the (Scottish) Court of Session.[6] In certain cases, however, the right has been taken away altogether or limited to appeals for which the inferior court gives leave.

Technically, the House of Lords in its judicial capacity is the same as the House in any other capacity.[7] An appeal is brought by way of petition to the House, praying that the matter of the order or judgment appealed against may be reviewed 'before Her Majesty the Queen in her Court of Parliament'.[8] The only legal limitation is that an appeal may not be heard and determined by the House unless there are present not less than three 'Lords of Appeal'. These consist of the Lord Chancellor, the nine Lords of Appeal in Ordinary, and such peers of Parliament as hold for the time being or have held 'high judicial office', which includes the office of Lord Chancellor, of judge of any of the superior courts, of Lord of Appeal in Ordinary, and of member of the Judicial Committee of the Privy Council.[9] This does not prevent other peers from sitting and taking part in the judicial work of the House.

---

[1] Viscount Melbourne to Queen Victoria, *Letters of Queen Victoria*, 1st Series, I, pp. 431–2.

[2] Appellate Jurisdiction Act, 1876; Administration of Justice (Appeals) Act, 1934.

[3] Criminal Appeal Act, 1907; Supreme Court of Judicature Act, 1925.

[4] Criminal Appeal (Northern Ireland) Act, 1920.

[5] Irish Free State (Consequential Provisions) Act, 1922.

[6] Appellate Jurisdiction Act, 1876, s. 3.

[7] Hence the 'legislative assembly' cannot sit until the 'court' has adjourned. In 1948, however, the House resolved (while building operations were going on and it was inconvenient to sit in the Chamber) that appeals might be heard by an Appellate Committee, which reported to the House.

[8] Appellate Jurisdiction Act, 1876, s. 4.

[9] *Ibid.* ss. 5, 25; Appellate Jurisdiction Act, 1887, s. 5.

During the seventeenth and eighteenth centuries there were many cases in which lay peers took part in the proceedings.[1] In Titus Oates' case, for instance, the House affirmed by 35 votes to 23 the decision in the court below, contrary to the unanimous opinion of the nine judges who attended. Since 1793, however, the practice has grown up that lay peers do not take part in the proceedings. In 1806 lay peers attended the decision in *Seymour* v. *Lord Euston* at the instance of the Prince of Wales; but when in O'Connell's case[2] lay peers attended, Lord Wharncliffe warned them that they ought not to intervene, so as not to diminish the authority of the Court, and they did not vote. Lord Denman spoke in *Bradlaugh* v. *Clarke*,[3] but did not vote. The sittings are in fact quite distinct, and when the House adjourns its resolution excludes judicial business. Legislation authorises sittings for judicial business not only after a prorogation but also after a dissolution.[4] The assimilation of legislative and judicial business is thus purely theoretical.

The House of Lords is also a court for the trial of persons impeached by the Commons for 'high crimes and misdemeanours'. Where a peer is impeached for high treason, a Lord High Steward is appointed by the Crown on the address of the House of Lords. On other occasions the Lord Chancellor or Lord Speaker presides. In either event all the peers may take part. In fact, however, there has been no impeachment since that of Lord Melville in 1805, and the procedure may now be regarded as obsolete. Impeachment in the seventeenth and early eighteenth centuries was a means for 'liquidating' opponents. The ballot boxes are now available for political opponents and the criminal courts for criminals.

Finally, the House has a statutory right to determine all questions as to the validity of Irish peerages, and all claims to Scottish peerages in respect of which no vote has been questioned since 1800.[5] It has also a right to determine whether a person is entitled to sit and vote as a peer, though it determines questions as to the validity of an English peerage or a United Kingdom peerage only on the reference of the Crown.

[1] See the examples quoted in May (13th ed.), p. 357.
[2] *O'Connell* v. *R.*, 11 Cl. & Fin. 155 (1844).
[3] (1883) 8 App. Cas. 354.
[4] Appellate Jurisdiction Act, 1876, ss. 9, 10.
[5] Anson, *Law and Custom of the Constitution*, I, p. 247.

These functions are of no political importance. The real work of the House of Lords consists in the debating of motions and the enactment of legislation.

Speaking generally, there is much less debate in the House of Lords than in the House of Commons. Not only is the attendance much less, but also there is no urge from constituents for frequent intervention in debate. The fact that the House of Commons is representative, that most of the ministers and most of the leading members of Opposition parties are in that House, and that the Government is responsible to that House alone, gives the Commons a great preponderance of authority. The great forum of political discussion is therefore in the Lower House. It cannot be said that the debates in the 'gilded sepulchre' are without interest and importance. Sometimes, as on matters of foreign or colonial affairs, there is a better debate in the Upper Chamber. There are in that House a few members of considerable diplomatic and administrative experience; they are not overburdened with daily business, as are the ministers in the House of Commons; they have more time to consider the manner and the matter of their speeches. Also, the debate is of short duration, it is carefully brought to an end so that noble lords may enjoy their dinners, and comparatively few of the speeches are made because the orators want to make them rather than because anybody wants to hear them. There are more bores and less intelligence in the Lords than in the Commons; but in the former they are usually absent or dumb. The result is that there are two or three debates a year which at least bear comparison with similar debates in the other place. The quality of these debates is usually quite high and, by reason of their rarity, it tends to be exaggerated. It is frequently explained, too, as a result of an absence of party spirit. The truth is, however, that most of the speakers belong to one party only and the debate sounds more interesting because the speakers start from the same premises and argue within the sphere thus confined. In the Commons, on the other hand, differences are more often due to divergencies about fundamentals. Accordingly, the newspapers favourable to the majority in the House of Lords describe the debate as free from party spirit; while the other newspapers regard it as 'academic'.

The House of Lords, too, has much more time for debates on motions as distinct from debates on Bills. Though every Government does its best to introduce a proportion of its legislative proposals in the House of Lords, it finds difficulty in doing so. Those Bills which depend upon party policy must be introduced in the House of Commons, because it is there that the political issue will be debated and the reactions of public opinion made manifest. Most Bills, too, contain financial provisions, and while it is possible in some cases to avoid difficulties of privilege by fictions,[1] such devices are not practicable where the financial element is substantial and important. Consequently, few Bills are ready for the House of Lords near the beginning of a session, and these few are usually technical and substantially non-controversial. Bills of a similar character are introduced by peers detached from the Government, but most of the time early in the session is available for motions. These may be specific, or they may be merely a means of securing information. Questions are comparatively rare in the House of Lords, and to a degree the House follows the practice adopted in the House of Commons before time became almost the monopoly of the Government and private members had to be content with questions. A peer raises a subject and, after a speech, moves for papers. A Government spokesman replies, and a few other lords take part; and then the motion for papers is withdrawn. Occasionally, the debates are instructive and the attendance large. More often the attendance is small and the discussion of no great public interest. Most of the newspapers barely mention it, while others give much less space than is accorded to the concurrent debate in the House of Commons.

Some of the major Bills of the session reach the House of Lords about the middle of the session, and many are crowded together at the end, so that the House has often to suspend standing orders in order to secure their passage. Though complaint is often made, there is no solution to this difficulty; for such Bills cannot be introduced in the House of Lords, and they cannot leave the House of Commons until they have been fully discussed. In the last days of the session not only are these new Bills coming up but also the Commons' answers to Lords' amendments to previous Bills are brought up and have to be disposed of quickly. With a Liberal or Labour Government it would be simple to obstruct

[1] *Ante*, pp. 288–9.

legislation by discussing it as fully as it deserves; but the House has not used this device, and has adopted the more honest technique of rejecting or radically amending what it does not like.

Though many amendments are moved in the House, few of them are insisted on by the House itself. Government amendments are many, and are rarely opposed. They arise out of the continued study which is given to Bills in Government departments, out of decisions by the minister in charge to accept representations made by outside interests, out of promises made in the Commons to 'consider' questions 'in another place', and out of the needs of drafting consequent upon amendments in the House of Commons. Peers also move amendments; but generally if the Government refuses to accept them they are withdrawn. Divisions are challenged on the average about thirty times a session; but some of these are in the nature of Opposition demonstrations when a Conservative Government is in power. With a Liberal or Labour Government the situation is different, since the House generally does not reject—it amends out of existence.

Debate is carried on much as in the House of Commons. Amendments may, however, be made on third reading;[1] there are no standing committees;[2] and above all there is no closure. The House can, of course, regulate its own procedure. It could, therefore, adopt a closure or a guillotine, after debate, though there is nothing in the Standing Orders about either. In 1926, however, Lord Cave accepted a closure motion and refused to allow it to be debated. The House proceeded at 6.30 p.m. to consider the Coal Mines Bill on its third reading. Seven speeches, four from the Government side and three from the Opposition, were made within an hour. But it was then dinner-time, and when another Labour peer rose to speak he was interrupted with cries of 'Divide!' Two more Labour peers then spoke; but the second had not proceeded far when the leader of the House, the Marquis of Salisbury, interrupted, and moved 'that the Question be now put', on the ground that the speeches were 'an abuse of the traditions and privileges of this House'. Though it is contrary to the traditions and privileges of the House for one noble

---

[1] But notice must be given: Lords' S.O. 43.
[2] A standing committee was set up in 1888, but it became the practice to 'negative the standing committee' and the Standing Orders were revoked in 1910: May, p. 466.

lord to interrupt another, except for the purposes of personal explanation and elucidation, the Lord Chancellor accepted the motion; and though any motion may, in accordance with the traditions and privileges of the House, be debated, he refused to allow a debate on the closure motion, which was carried by 44 votes to 4. The time was then 8.15 p.m., so that the debate had lasted for less than two hours, on a Bill which had required two whole days for the second reading and two more days for the third reading in the House of Commons. It was subsequently alleged by the Lord Chancellor (and supported by many others) that there was 'concerted action' to obstruct the passage of the Bill, though this was denied by the acting leader of the Opposition, and in any case four peers could not obstruct for long, especially when three of them had already spoken and the fourth was engaged in making his speech. To put the motion without debate was in fact contrary to Standing Order XLV.[1] A motion which was in substance a motion of censure was rejected subsequently by 113 votes to 10; but the Lord Chancellor said that he did not consider that his action established a precedent, and it has not since been followed.[2]

Among the Bills which reach the House late in the session is the annual Finance Bill. It is often certified under the Parliament Act, and in such a case it will pass whether the Lords consent or not. Even if it is not certified, the Lords have no power of amendment, since the House of Commons insists on its privilege in this respect. In truth, however, the procedure is no different whether the Bill is certified or not. No Finance Bill since that of 1909 has been opposed. In fact, it was the practice from 1911 to 1914 not to debate the Bill at all. The Marquess of Crewe, in moving the second reading in 1914, made a general explanation, but the Opposition refused to debate because their opportunities for amendment were 'virtually non-existent'.[3] Since 1919 the peers have been more reconciled to their lot, and there is generally a debate on the second reading, though it ends without a division. No attempt at a 'Budget speech' is made: indeed, there was growing up a practice

[1] See now Lords' S.O. 23.
[2] For the closure, see 64 H.L.Deb. 5 s., 994; and for the subsequent debate, see *ibid.* 1090–1141.
[3] 17 H.L.Deb. 5 s., 303 (Marquess of Lansdowne).

that the Government speaker should move the motion without a speech. The Labour Government in 1924 did not follow this practice, presumably through ignorance; and though it was adopted again in 1925 and 1926 it has now become understood that a general statement is to be made. A few other peers make remarks, but the debate rarely lasts more than an hour. The Committee is then negatived, or made purely formal,[1] Standing Orders are suspended, and the Bill is read a third time without discussion.

4. DIFFERENCES BETWEEN THE HOUSES

It will be clear from the preceding explanation that the problem of the relations between the two Houses of Parliament arises in a serious form only when the Government is not supported by the Conservative party. Amendments are made to Government Bills even when the Conservatives are in power; but if the House of Commons disagrees the peers either do not insist on their amendments or accept compromises suggested by the Government. The position is otherwise when the Conservative party is in Opposition. Even then, the right wing is prominent and challenges divisions which are not called for by the whips; but often the whole weight of the Conservative party is thrown against the Government.

Though the Reform Act of 1832 by implication vested ultimate authority in the House that was more representative of the people, the precise relationship of the two Houses did not come in question until after the middle of the century. It was early recognised that a Government supported by a majority in the House of Commons need not bother about an adverse majority in the House of Lords.[2] On the other hand it was recognised that that House had a perfect right to reject legislation, though Lord John Russell pointed out in 1839 that if that right were carried to extremes—if, for instance, the peers rejected a Consolidated Fund Bill—'the whole country would be thrown into confusion'. Lord John added:

So far as to the right of legislation. What, then, is the practical conclusion and understanding to which all parties have come, for a long period, with

---

[1] In 1920 there were two speeches on the motion to commit, but there was then no discussion on the second reading. [2] *Cabinet Government*, pp. 454-5.

respect to that subject? It is this—that if a Bill were sent up from this House, of a very important nature, with regard to which there are considerable numbers of persons both on one side and on the other, and in favour of which there was only a small majority, the House of Lords might properly say, 'It appears that the representatives of the people are very nearly divided on the subject. We do not think that the country has made up its mind to this change. Let it be considered another year, and let us know whether it is a change called for by general opinion.' If a Bill, however, were sent up repeatedly from this House by large majorities declaring the sense of the country, then I think it is usual for the House of Lords, even though holding an opinion against the Bill, and having an abstract right to reject it at once, to exercise a wise discretion, and say, 'We will not oppose the general sense of the country, repeatedly expressed, but we will confirm the opinion of the House of Commons, though in the abstract it differs from ours.'[1]

This was, perhaps, an idealisation of the attitude of the House of Lords to the measures of the Governments of 1830 to 1841.[2] It indicated, however, the attitude of those Governments to the House of Lords, and it gave that House a thesis upon which to justify its opposition. The House of Commons being the representative House, the Lords could resist only so long as it was not certain that the Commons expressed the public will. This principle was set out by Bagehot in 1861:

Since the Reform Act the House of Lords has become a revising and suspending House. It can alter Bills; it can reject Bills on which the House of Commons is not thoroughly in earnest—upon which the nation is not yet determined. Their veto is a sort of hypothetical veto. They say, 'We reject your Bill for this once, or these twice, or even these thrice; but if you keep on sending it up, at last we won't reject it.' The House has ceased to be one of latent directors, and has become one of temporary rejectors and palpable alterers.[3]

The Duke of Wellington, as Bagehot added, presided over the change,[4] and for the most part the House of Commons acquiesced until after the second Reform Act in 1867. Even in 1860, however, Mr Gladstone was by no means content with this doctrine, and had he not been restrained

---

[1] 47 Hans.Deb. 3 s., 9.
[2] See Emily Allyn, *Lords versus Commoners*.
[3] Bagehot, *English Constitution* (World's Classics edn.), p. 88.
[4] See the letter to Lord Derby, quoted *ibid.* pp. 89–92.

by his colleagues he would have taken stronger measures than the resolutions on the Paper Duties Bill.[1]

When the Conservative party had once obtained predominance in the House of Lords, the claim to reject such measures as were not clearly 'desired by the people' became in fact a claim to insist on a general election whenever a Liberal Government was in power. As Sir Charles Dilke said, referring to the virtual rejection of the Irish Land Bill of 1881:

> The claim of Lord Salisbury to force us to 'consult the country' is a claim for annual Parliaments when we are in office and septennial Parliaments when they are in office.[2]

It was, in fact, an absurd principle, since it assumed that Conservative peers who had not to fight elections and were responsible to no constituents knew 'the mind of the country' better than the House of Commons who had recently been elected and were anxious to be re-elected shortly. The Conservative peers who thus thought themselves capable of weighing public opinion impartially were not only biased politically, but often were likely to be prejudiced materially by the legislation to be passed. As Lord Morley pointed out, the House of Lords which in 1880 rejected the Bill for compensating dispossessed tenants in Ireland did not contain a single representative of the Irish Nationalist party, though it did contain plenty of Irish landlords.[3]

It could no doubt be argued that during the course of seven years it was possible for members to lose touch with their constituencies. But the members who passed the Irish Church Bill in 1869 and those who passed the Irish Land Bill in 1881 had only just been elected, while the difficulties over the Reform Bill of 1884 arose not because the 'mind of the people' was against reform but because the Conservative party feared that the constituencies would be gerrymandered by the consequential Redistribution Bill. Moreover, as the franchise was extended and the elections made more real by the institution of secret voting and the imposition of heavy penalties against corrupt and illegal practices,

---

[1] *Letters of Queen Victoria*, 1st series, III, pp. 510–14.
[2] *Life of Sir Charles Dilke*, I, p. 371.
[3] Lord Morley, *Recollections*, I, p. 172.

members became more and more dependent on public opinion and less and less upon 'influence'; accordingly, the process of 'nursing' a constituency had to be carried out throughout the life of a Parliament, and this meant listening to every wind that blew. Thus, the radicalisation of the Liberal party proceeded side by side with a much closer dependence of the members upon their constituencies. This is evidenced not only by the 'pilgrimages of passion' which Mr Disraeli began and Mr Gladstone developed, but also by the local party organisations that Mr Disraeli began and Mr Joseph Chamberlain developed. On the one hand, therefore, the House of Commons became more closely related to public opinion; and on the other hand the growing democratisation of the electoral system and the radicalism of the Liberal party sent more and more peers to the right and therefore far away from the people who gave Mr Gladstone his majorities. In truth, the only effect of the doctrine, though an important one, was to reduce considerably the opposition of the House of Lords, because at least it was recognised that there was a point at which the House must give way. That House passed much that it disliked, and it was often possible for Mr Gladstone to make compromises with the Conservative leaders, sometimes with the assistance of the Queen.[1]

Mr Bright suggested in 1880 that the doctrine of the 'second bite' should be formalised by legislation, so that if the peers rejected a Bill once, and it was again passed in the next session by the House of Commons, it should receive the royal assent and become law without the consent of the House of Lords.[2] This suggestion had been made thirty years before by James Mill, but received no effective support; for what the Conservative peers wanted was not merely to delay Radical legislation but to compel a Liberal Government to go to the country upon it, thus giving the Conservative party the opportunity to redress its defeat. Even Queen Victoria supported this point of view. Thus,

[1] E.g. on the Irish Church Bill, 1869: *Life of Gladstone*, II, p. 275 *et seq.*; on the Irish Land Bill, 1870: *Letters of Queen Victoria*, 2nd series, II, p. 222; on the Education Bill, 1870; *Life of Lord Ripon*, I, pp. 226–8; on the Ballot Bill, 1872: *Letters of Queen Victoria*, 2nd series, II, p. 223; on the Reform Bill, 1884: *Life of Gladstone*, III, p. 130 *et seq.*; *Letters of Queen Victoria*, 2nd series, III, p. 577; Guedalla, *The Queen and Mr Gladstone*, II, pp. 280–1. For the Queen's assistance, see *Cabinet Government*, pp. 355–63.

[2] Lord Morley, *Recollections*, I, p. 198.

when the Reform Bill of 1884 was defeated in the Lords she suggested that the Government ought to dissolve Parliament, but Mr Gladstone replied:

At no period in our history...has the House of Commons been dissolved at the call of the House of Lords, given through an adverse vote;...the establishment of such a principle would place the House of Commons in a position of inferiority, as a legislative Chamber, to the House of Lords.[1]

This is the kind of statement—strictly accurate in fact but untrue in its implications—which Mr Gladstone made with remarkable skill. The doctrine of the 'second bite' was good Whig doctrine. An adverse vote had not in fact caused a dissolution because Whig and Liberal Governments had acquiesced in their defeat—as Mr Gladstone had been compelled to acquiesce in 1860. At the same time, the underlying idea of Mr Gladstone's statement was the necessary result of the three Reform Acts if not of the first two of them. The Constitution was in course of transition between 1832 and 1884. Before 1832 the House of Commons was only slightly more 'representative' than the House of Lords. The Reform Act made it much more representative; but the combined effect of new peerages and of the growing commercial and industrial interests of peers through the exploitation of minerals, the increase of urban rents, and the practice of investment in joint stock companies, was that the House of Lords, while still heavily weighted in favour of 'land', did in part represent other kinds of property. The interests most partially represented during this period were those of Ireland since the Irish landlords were strong among the peers and the Catholic and nationalist sentiment of the mass of the Irish voters was not represented at all. So far as Great Britain was concerned, the enfranchisement of the working classes shifted the balance between the two Houses. After 1867, and still more after 1884, candidates of all parties had to appeal to a mass of opinion which was quite unknown in the House of Lords; and as 'influence' gradually had less and less interest after 1872 the members of the two Houses came to speak different languages. In substance, the House of Lords represented one class interest and one party; it was much less representative than the Conservative party in the House of Commons.

[1] *Letters of Queen Victoria*, 2nd Series, III, p. 518.

It is sometimes urged that an appeal to the country can never be undemocratic. The assertion is theoretically attractive but ignores practical issues. Elections are determined by a small floating vote which has no fixed political allegiance and which can be swayed by purely temporary issues. Every Government takes some decisions which would not be approved on a referendum. Given a reasonable period of office, it hopes to show that its decision was right. It appeals to the people not on a particular issue but on its whole political record. Particularly is this true of a reforming Government, since the fruits of its legislation or administration cannot immediately be gathered. It might reasonably be claimed that an interval of seven years between elections was too long—it was reduced to five years by the Parliament Act, 1911—but if government is to be effective there must be a reasonable period. The power of dissolution is a means by which the Government can appeal to the people against the House of Commons. It may of course be used in a period of excitement to continue in power a Government which would not long survive, as was done in the 'khaki' elections of 1900 and 1918; but 'smart' tactics are apt to bring their own retribution; it required another war to bring the Conservatives back after 1905, and Mr Lloyd George never obtained office after 1922.

It is in fact reasonable that the Government, which is on the defensive, should choose its own time to dissolve within the legal limits; it is quite unreasonable to suggest that a dissolution should always take place at the moment selected by the Conservative party. Yet such would be the result of a power in the House of Lords to compel a dissolution by voting against the measures of 'progressive' Governments.

The solution to the difficulty of the relations between the two Houses could be sought only in a limitation of the powers of the Lords, or in a reform of the composition of their House, or in both. Any such solution required the assent of the peers, and the only remedy available to a Liberal Government was that threatened in 1832, the creation of enough new peers to compel the House of Lords to give way. For this purpose a clear and firm support had to be obtained from the country. Mr Joseph Chamberlain in an attack on the House of Lords in 1884 said that 'the cup is nearly full'; and ten years later, as the white-haired boy of the Unionist alliance, he described 'filling up the cup' as 'the latest electoral device'.[1] Whether Lord Rosebery's Government deliberately 'ploughed the sands' in order to 'fill up the cup' does not definitely appear. Lord Rosebery himself was more concerned with the reform of the House of Lords than (to use yet another of the hackneyed metaphors) with the clipping of its wings. He had raised the subject in 1884 and 1888, and he discussed it with Queen Victoria in 1894.[2]

The resignation of the Liberal Government in 1895 deprived the question of its actuality for another ten years. In 1906 the Liberals adopted the practice of sending as many controversial Bills as possible to the House of Lords at the same time, believing that the peers dare not reject them all.[3] The Conservative leaders in the House of Lords, for their part, collaborated with the Conservative minority in the House of Commons.[4] Mr Balfour, who announced that it was the bounden duty of his audience to see that 'the great Unionist party should still control, whether in power or whether in Opposition, the destinies of this great Empire',[5] advised Lord Lansdowne in tactics. He assumed that the more 'moderate' members of the Cabinet would assent to legislation in a more 'extreme' form and trust to the House of Lords to cut out or modify the most 'outrageous' provisions, while the left wing of the Cabinet would be consoled by the reflection that they were accumulating a case against the House of Lords. This should be met by making serious modifications in important Government measures. If it were done with caution and tact, the peers would not do themselves any harm, but might strengthen themselves as the rejection of the Home Rule Bill of 1893 had done. All points of importance should be fought stiffly in the House of Commons, and the House of Lords should be made the theatre of compromise.[6] This, as Lord Newton has said, was

---

[1] *Life of Lord Oxford and Asquith*, I, pp. 78, 94.

[2] *Letters of Queen Victoria*, 3rd series, II, pp. 385–8, 390–1, 429–30. The Queen communicated this last letter to Lord Salisbury asking, *inter alia*, whether she should warn Lord Rosebery that she would require a dissolution before allowing the Cabinet to make a proposal, and whether the Unionist party was *then* ready for a dissolution: *ibid*. pp. 430–1. Lord Salisbury replied that she ought, and it was: *ibid*. pp. 433–4. Lord Salisbury and the Queen both admitted the need for reform.

[3] *Life of Sir Henry Campbell-Bannerman*, II, p. 277.

[4] *Life of Lord Lansdowne*, pp. 353–4.

[5] Lord Oxford and Asquith, *Fifty Years of Parliament*, II, p. 39.

[6] *Life of Lord Lansdowne*, pp. 354–5.

admirable diagnosis and equally admirable advice; 'its only flaw is the quite unfounded expectation that the House of Lords might emerge from the ordeal not only unscathed but in greater strength.'[1] It illustrates the dangers of arguments drawn from history. There is no proof whatever that the rejection of the Home Rule Bill strengthened the House of Lords; but even if it did the situation was quite different. The Liberal Government of 1893 petered out through internal dissensions; in 1906 the Opposition, not the Government, was divided, and the Government had just obtained an enormous majority.

However, the Conservative peers accepted the advice and, perhaps at the instigation of Mr Balfour,[2] mutilated the Education Bill of 1906. The House of Commons, on the advice of the Cabinet, rejected the amendments en bloc,[3] and paid no attention to a resolution in the House of Lords protesting against this 'constitutional innovation'.[4] Attempts to reach a compromise broke down,[5] and the Bill was dropped. In his funeral oration Sir Henry Campbell-Bannerman announced:

> The resources of the House of Commons are not exhausted, and I say with conviction a way must be found, and a way will be found by which the will of the people, expressed through their elected representatives in this House, will be made to prevail.[6]

The House of Lords proceeded to defeat the Plural Voting Bill and radically to amend the Agricultural Holdings Bill and the Town Tenants (Ireland) Bill; but 'in deference to their respect for organised labour', as Campbell-Bannerman's biographer put it,[7] or because the ground was 'unfavourable', as Lord Lansdowne put it,[8] the 'far more dangerous'[9] Trade Disputes Bill was passed.

Not all the Unionist peers thought that the Unionist party could continue to govern 'this great Empire' through an unreformed House of

---

[1] *Life of Lord Lansdowne*, p. 355.   [2] *Life of Randall Davidson*, I, p. 528.
[3] *Life of Sir Henry Campbell-Bannerman*, II, p. 306; 166 Parl.Deb. 4 s., 1576–1646; 167 Parl.Deb. 4 s., 153–244, 379–472.
[4] 167 Parl.Deb. 4 s., 915–39, 1370–1412.
[5] *Life of Lord Lansdowne*, pp. 356–7; *Life of Sir Henry Campbell-Bannerman*, II, pp. 307–11.
[6] *Ibid.* II, pp. 311–12; 167 Parl.Deb. 4 s., 1740.
[7] *Life of Sir Henry Campbell-Bannerman*, p. 312.
[8] *Life of Lord Lansdowne*, p. 359.   [9] Lord Newton's phrase, *ibid.* p. 358.

Lords, and in 1907 Lord Newton introduced a Bill to reform the House, for reasons which he has himself described:

The failure of the Unionist party to recognise the necessity of reforming the House of Lords when they had the opportunity during their ten years' period of office from 1895 to 1905 is one of the most curious oversights in *party tactics*[1] imaginable. The House of Lords positively invited attack. Overgrown, unrepresentative, and unwieldy, when the Unionists were in office it was expected merely to act as a kind of registry office, and to pass without amendment, and occasionally without discussion, any measure sent up to it at the last moment. When, however, a Liberal Government was in power, it was expected to come to the rescue of a discomfited Opposition. Although the House of Lords has occasionally shown itself to be a more correct interpreter of public feeling than the House of Commons, its gigantic and permanent Conservative majority deprived it of any appearance of impartiality, and, unfortunately, it had not shown any sign of independence by throwing out any Conservative measure.[2]

The Bill 'merely embodied the various proposals made from time to time in the past for a reduction in numbers and better representation of minorities'.[3] 'Qualified' hereditary peers were to sit, these including ministers, former ministers, former viceroys, former ambassadors, former judges, Irish peers, peers of the first generation, and peers who had been twice elected to the House of Commons. The 'unqualified' peers were to elect one-quarter of their number for each Parliament under a system of proportional representation. There was also to be a reduction of the spiritual peers, and the Government was to be allowed to create life peers with the right to sit and vote. The Bill was, however, withdrawn, and it was agreed to set up a select committee, which reported in 1908 and in substance approved of the provisions of the Bill.[4]

---

[1] Present writer's italics. [2] *Life of Lord Lansdowne*, p. 360.

[3] *Ibid.* p. 361. The previous history is as follows. Lord Rosebery's motion for a committee in 1884 was defeated by 77 to 38 votes. A similar motion in 1888 was defeated by 97 to 47 votes. In the same year Lord Dunraven withdrew a Bill on an assurance from Lord Salisbury that he would deal with the matter. Accordingly, Lord Salisbury introduced two Bills, one for the creation of life peers, and the other (the 'Black Sheep Bill') to discontinue writs to those who did not take their seats. These Bills were read a second time but were then withdrawn owing to threatened opposition in 'another place'. In 1889 Lord Carnarvon introduced another 'Black Sheep Bill' which was defeated by 73 votes to 14.

[4] See Cd. 3824.

The King's Speech in 1907 had already declared the intention of the Government to propose a solution of the difficulty. The Cabinet decided, however, that it would be dangerous to touch the composition of the House of Lords until the question of its powers had been settled.[1] A Cabinet Committee produced a plan under which a hundred peers (including the ministers) would debate and vote with the House of Commons in the event of disagreement, the decision of this body being final.[2] Sir Henry Campbell-Bannerman objected strongly to this plan, and circulated a memorandum criticising it and suggesting an alternative.[3] Ultimately, the Cabinet came back to Mr Bright's idea of a suspensory veto.

The resolution passed by the House of Commons (by 432 votes to 147) with a view to its principle being incorporated in a Bill was:

> That, in order to give effect to the will of the people as expressed by their elected representatives, it is necessary that the powers of the other House to alter or reject Bills passed by this House should be so restricted by law as to secure that within the limits of a single Parliament the final decision of the Commons shall prevail.[4]

The plan sketched by the Prime Minister in his Cabinet memorandum[5] and his speech to the House[6] was that in the event of a disagreement there should be a conference between representatives of the two Houses; if that failed, the Bill should be introduced again after an interval.[7] If the peers again refused to pass it, it should be capable of becoming law with the consent of the House of Commons alone. The Bill to which the resolution was a preliminary was never introduced; but, with the addition of special provisions for money Bills and the shortening of the duration of Parliament, the resolution formed the basis of the Parliament Act, 1911.

The truth is that the cup was not quite overflowing until the House of Lords rejected the Budget of 1909. On the motion of Mr Asquith,

---

[1] *Life of Sir Henry Campbell-Bannerman*, II, p. 350. [2] *Ibid.*
[3] For the text, see *ibid.* pp. 351–5. [4] 176 Parl.Deb. 4 s., 1523.
[5] *Life of Sir Henry Campbell-Bannerman*, II, pp. 353–5.
[6] 176 Parl.Deb. 4 s., 921–3.
[7] In the next session according to the memorandum; after six months, 'unless in cases of great urgency', according to the speech.

the House of Commons passed (by 349 votes to 134) a resolution on
2 December 1909:

> That the action of the House of Lords in refusing to pass into law the
> financial provision made by this House for the service of the year is a breach
> of the Constitution, and a usurpation of the rights of the Commons.[1]

Thereupon Parliament was dissolved.[2]

In the new Parliament resolutions designed to form the basis of the
Parliament Bill were passed and the Bill read a first time. The second
resolution was based essentially on the resolution passed in 1906 at the
instance of Sir Henry Campbell-Bannerman, though it was more precise
in its drafting. To this it was necessary, as a result of the defeat of the
Finance Bill, 1909, to add a resolution enabling a money Bill to be
passed in a single session without the consent of the House of Lords;
and a third resolution approved the reduction of the duration of Parliament from seven to five years.[3] The next step was delayed by the death
of Edward VII and the accession of George V. It was thought desirable
to make an attempt to settle the problem by agreement, and a Constitutional Conference was set up in June 1910.

Though there was, as the Prime Minister said, 'an honest and continuous effort' extending over six months to arrive at a settlement,[4] the
conference broke down on the major difficulty, whether a Home Rule
Bill could be passed over the veto of the Lords, and, if so, how;[5] and

---

[1] *Life of Lord Oxford and Asquith*, I, pp. 260–1; Lord Oxford and Asquith, *Fifty
Years of Parliament*, II, p. 77; 13 H.C.Deb. 5 s., 578.

[2] In this election the peers took part as propagandists for the first time: *Life of Lord
Lansdowne*, p. 384. See the debate on this, 14 H.C.Deb. 5 s., 15 *et seq.*

[3] It is illustrative of the continuity of British history that the same proposals had been
made by the Cabinet Committee which drafted the Reform Bill of 1831, but had been
rejected by the Cabinet.

[4] *Life of Lord Oxford and Asquith*, I, p. 286.

[5] Mr Balfour made a statement to a meeting of Unionist leaders. The following summary was drawn up by Sir Robert (Lord) Finlay, and is reprinted from the *Life of Lord
Lansdowne*, pp. 402–3:

'Legislation was to be divided into ordinary, financial, and constitutional legislation.

'1. *Ordinary Legislation.*

'If a difference arose on two occasions in two sessions, in two years, between the
Houses of Parliament, it was to be settled by a joint sitting of the two houses. The joint
sitting was to consist of the whole of the House of Commons and 100 peers, 20 of them

also (apparently) on the question of the reform of the House of Lords, which the Government refused to discuss.[1] The Government therefore decided to proceed with its own proposals for legislation and (after the King's contingent consent to the creation of peers had been obtained and, at his request, the Parliament Bill introduced into the House of Lords for discussion) Parliament was dissolved. In the next Parliament the Bill was passed by threatening to create peers to 'swamp' the Unionist majority in the Lords.[2]

During the previous session, however, Lord Rosebery had raised once more the question of the reform of the House of Lords, and in March 1910 that House had resolved,

1. That a strong and efficient Second Chamber is not merely an integral part of the British Constitution, but is necessary to the well-being of the State and to the balance of Parliament.[3]

2. That such a Chamber can best be obtained by the reform and reconstitution of the House of Lords.[4]

members of the Government and 80 to be selected on a system of proportional representation.

'2. *Financial Legislation.*

'The Budget not to be rejected by the Lords unless in case of tacking.

'Legal tacking presents no difficulties, but in the case of "equitable" tacking, the Government proposed that such a Bill should be treated like ordinary legislation.

'3. *Constitutional Legislation.*

'The Prime Minister stated that no differentiation was possible between that and ordinary legislation.

'But the Government were willing that Bills affecting the Crown or the Protestant Succession or the Act which is to embody this agreement should be subject to special safeguards. If the two Houses differed, the Bill would drop; if they agreed, there should be a plebiscite.

'On October 16, the Conference broke off on the difficulty of Home Rule. Mr Balfour proposed that if a Home Rule Bill was twice rejected by the House of Lords, it should go to a plebiscite. Mr Lloyd George, while admitting the reasonableness of this, said it was impossible for the Government to assent.

'Subsequently the Government proposed a compromise, viz. that a general election should intervene on the next occasion on which a Home Rule Bill, having passed the House of Commons, was rejected by the House of Lords—but only on this one occasion; and that Home Rule Bills if introduced afterwards should be treated like ordinary Bills.'

(By 'equitable tacking' is apparently meant the making of fundamental political changes by way of legislation which was in truth financial; cf. Lord Lansdowne's memo: *ibid.* p. 398.)

[1] *Life of Lord Lansdowne*, p. 402.   [2] *Cabinet Government*, pp. 401–11.
[3] 5 H.L.Deb. 5 s., 413–22 (passed unanimously).
[4] *Ibid.* 422–3 (passed unanimously).

3. That a necessary preliminary of such reform and reconstruction is the acceptance of the principle that the possession of a peerage should no longer of itself give the right to sit and vote in the House of Lords.[1]

After the failure of the Constitutional Conference, the House agreed unanimously to two further resolutions:

1. That in future the House of Lords shall consist of Lords of Parliament:
   A. Chosen by the whole body of hereditary peers from among themselves and by nomination of the Crown.
   B. Sitting by virtue of offices and of qualifications held by them.
   C. Chosen from outside.
2. That the term of tenure for all Lords of Parliament shall be the same, except in the case of those who sit *ex officio*, who would sit so long as they held the office for which they sit.[2]

5. THE PARLIAMENT ACT AND ITS CONSEQUENCES

In accordance with the resolutions of the House of Commons, the Parliament Act, 1911,[3] contained three sets of provisions. It must first be noticed that the preamble asserts

Whereas it is intended to substitute for the House of Lords as it at present exists a Second Chamber constituted on a popular instead of hereditary basis, but such substitution cannot be immediately brought into operation.

'Immediately' was certainly correct; for 46 years later the intention has not been carried out. The truth is that while the members of the Liberal Cabinet were agreed on the proposals for restricting the powers of the Lords, they were not agreed as to the method of reconstructing the House.[4] In the Liberal party itself the problem was regarded as even wider; the problem, that is, of 'ending or mending'.

In view of the increased powers given to the Commons and the destruction of the Lords' power to insist, in substance, upon a dissolution, the maximum duration of Parliament was reduced to five years. In practice this involves a reduction to four years. A Prime Minister will necessarily choose the moment for dissolution most favourable to his

---

[1] 5 H.L.Deb. 5 s., 423–50, 459–94 (passed by 175 votes to 17).
[2] 6 H.L.Deb. 5 s., 714–58.
[3] The text as amended in 1949 is set out in Appendix V.
[4] *Life of Lord Oxford and Asquith*, I, p. 276.

own party. Certain months of the year, December and January, and July to September, are difficult months because of Christmas festivities and absences on holiday. The need for financial legislation makes any month from February to June almost impossible without collaboration from the Opposition. This leaves October and November, though other months are not absolutely ruled out. But international complications may render an election at a particular time undesirable; and in any case the Government dare not leave the date to be determined by the Parliament Act lest it be at that moment more unpopular than usual. Accordingly, Parliament is usually dissolved at the end of the fourth year, if not earlier.[1]

In respect of money Bills the Act provides:

If a money Bill, having been passed by the House of Commons, and sent up to the House of Lords at least one month before the end of the session, is not passed by the House of Lords without amendment within one month after it is so sent up to that House, the Bill shall, unless the House of Commons direct to the contrary,[2] be presented to His Majesty and become an Act

---

[1] Duration of Parliaments, 1911–55.

Met	Dissolved	Years	Days
31 Jan. 1911	25 Nov. 1918*	7	299
4 Feb. 1919	26 Oct. 1922	3	265
20 Nov. 1922	16 Nov. 1923	–	361
8 Jan. 1924	9 Oct. 1924	–	266
2 Dec. 1924	10 May 1929	4	159
25 June 1929	7 Oct. 1931	2	105
3 Nov. 1931	25 Oct. 1935	3	356
16 Nov. 1935	15 June 1945*	9	212
1 Aug. 1945	3 Feb. 1950	4	187
1 Mar. 1950	5 Oct. 1951	1	219
31 Oct. 1951	6 May 1955	3	188

* Prolonged by emergency legislation.

[2] The Land Settlement (Scotland) Bill, 1934, was certified by the Speaker as a Money Bill, and was sent to the House of Lords on 30 May. It was not read a second time in that House until 4 July, and was passed without amendment on 5 July. It ought, therefore, to have been presented for the royal assent without the consent of the House of Lords on 1 July. The delay was due not to opposition but to an oversight by the minister in charge in the House of Lords. Accordingly, on 5 July the Lord President of the Council moved in the House of Commons: 'That, in pursuance of the Parliament Act, 1911, this House directs that the provisions of section one, sub-section (1), of that Act shall not apply to the Land Settlement (Scotland) Bill.' The motion was agreed to and communicated to the House of Lords; the Bill then received the royal assent as an ordinary Bill passed by both Houses. See 291 H.C.Deb. 5 s., 2202–4; 93 H.L.Deb. 5 s., 457, 534.

of Parliament on the Royal Assent being signified, notwithstanding that the House of Lords have not consented to the Bill.

As has already been explained,[1] this provision fits into a group of privileges and conventions which sharply distinguishes the attitude of the House of Lords to financial legislation and to general legislation. In that House, no distinction is made between Finance Bills which are technically 'Money Bills' and those which are not. The Act says:

A Money Bill means a Public Bill which in the opinion of the Speaker of the House of Commons contains only provisions dealing with all or any of the following subjects, namely, the imposition, repeal, remission, alteration or regulation of taxation; the imposition for the payment of debt or other financial purposes of charges on the Consolidated Fund, or on money provided by Parliament, or the variation or repeal of any such charges; supply; the appropriation, receipt, custody, issue or audit of amounts of public money; the raising or guarantee of any loan or the repayment thereof; or subordinate matters incidental to these subjects or any of them. In this subsection the expressions 'taxation', 'public money', and 'loan' respectively do not include any taxation, money or loan raised by local authorities or bodies for local purposes.

There shall be endorsed on every Money Bill when it is sent up to the House of Lords and when it is presented to His Majesty for assent the certificate of the Speaker of the House of Commons signed by him that it is a Money Bill. Before giving his certificate, the Speaker shall consult, if practicable, two members to be appointed from the Chairmen's Panel at the beginning of each Session by the Committee of Selection.

Any certificate of the Speaker of the House of Commons given under this Act shall be conclusive for all purposes, and shall not be questioned in any court of law.

Lord Ullswater, who was Mr Speaker Lowther from 1905 to 1921, has said that this clause was so carefully drafted that he never had any difficulty in deciding whether a Bill came within it.[2] He said, too, that the Finance Bill, 1909, the *fons et origo* of this clause, would not have come within it, no doubt because it did not deal *only* with the 'imposition, repeal, remission, alteration, or regulation of taxation'. On the other hand, the Finance Bill, 1931, which contained Mr Snowden's land tax proposals, was certified by Mr Speaker Fitzroy. The Import Duties Bill, 1932, was also certified, though the Income Tax Bill, 1918, and the

[1] *Ante*, pp. 287–9. [2] Lord Ullswater, *A Speaker's Commentary*, II, p. 103.

Ottawa Agreements Bill, 1932, were not. The Import Duties Bill imposed an *ad valorem* customs duty and empowered the Treasury on the advice of an advisory committee to impose certain other duties. It enabled a revolution to be effected in British fiscal policy, and it was in fact described by Viscount Snowden (Lord Privy Seal but also an opponent) as 'the most important measure dealing with trade and commerce which has been before Parliament for nearly a century'. Mr Snowden's Bill of 1931 was described by its opponents in the House of Lords as 'confiscation'.

Thus a change in financial policy of real importance may be effected by the House of Commons alone in one session; but if a financial measure contains new administrative machinery or administrative powers other than those specifically set out in the definition, it cannot be certified. Of the 29 Finance Bills between 1913 and the end of 1937, only twelve were certified as money Bills.[1] The list of titles of Bills certified between 1913 and 1930, given by Hills and Fellowes,[2] shows that

---

[1] *Finance Bills Certified*: 1913, 1914, 1914–15 (No. 1), 1916 (New Duties), 1919, 1920, 1922, 1925, 1926, 1928–9, 1930–1, 1930–1 (No. 2).
Finance Bills not Certified: 1914–15 (No. 2), 1914–15 (No. 3), 1916, 1917–18, 1918, 1921, 1923, 1924, 1927, 1928, 1929–30, 1931–2, 1932–3, 1933–4, 1934–5, 1935–6, 1936–7.
[2] *Titles of other Bills Certified*, 1913–30:

1913   Provisional Collection of Taxes.
        Government of Soudan Loan.
        Public Buildings Expenses.
        Isle of Man (Customs).
        Telegraph (Money).
1914   Anglo-Persian Oil Company (Acquisition of Capital).
        East African Protectorates (Loan).
        War Loan.
        Death Duties (Killed in War).
        Superannuation.
1914–16 War Loan Extension.
        Police Magistrates (Superannuation).
        American Loan.
1917–18 Army Annual Act, 1916, Amendment.
1918   Government War Obligations.
1919   Representation of the People (Returning Officers' Expenses)
           Civil Contingencies Fund.
        Disabled Men (Facilities for Employment).
        Retired Officers (Civil Employment).
        Superannuation (Prison Officers).
1920   Resident Magistrates (Ireland).
        British Empire Exhibition (Guarantee).

Mr Speaker at once took a very restrictive view of the definition clause.[1] The Bills certified may in fact be classed as follows:

(1) Finance Bills which deal only with taxation and not with machinery;
(2) Consolidated Fund Bills;
(3) Isle of Man (Customs) Bills;
(4) Bills imposing customs and/or excise duties, but without 'machinery' clauses;

1921   Mr Speaker's Retirement.
      Housing (Scotland) (No. 2).
      Land Settlement Amendment.
      Safeguarding of Industries.
      Irish Railways (Settlement of Claims).
1922   Diseases of Animals.
      Anglo-Persian Oil Company (Payment of Calls).
1924   West Indian Islands (Telegraph).
      Old Age Pensions.
1924–5   Irish Free State Land Purchase (Loan Guarantee).
      War Charges (Validity).
      China Indemnity (Application).
1926   Palestine and East Africa Loans (Guarantee).
1928–9   Overseas Trade.
      Pensions (Governors of Dominions).
      Unemployment Insurance.
1929–30   Air Transport (Subsidy Agreements).
      Highlands and Islands (Medical Service), Additional Grant.

This list is taken from Hills and Fellowes, *The Finance of Government*, pp. 209–10. It is not complete in the sense that it includes every Bill. It excludes Consolidated Fund Bills (including Appropriation Bills), and where Bills with the same titles have been certified on more than one occasion they are included only once: e.g. Isle of Man (Customs) Bills, Telegraph (Money) Bills, etc. The list in the next note (for which I am indebted to Sir Edward Fellowes, Clerk of the House of Commons) therefore gives a more complete picture.

[1] *Bills endorsed with Mr Speaker's Certificate as Money Bills under Parliament Act, 1911*, 1931–7:
1931–2   Abnormal Importations (Customs Duties).
      Consolidated Fund (No. 1).
      Consolidated Fund (Appropriation).
      Horticultural Products (Emergency Customs Duties).
      Import Duties.
      Isle of Man (Customs).
      Isle of Man (Customs) (No. 2).
      Transitional Payments Prolongation (Unemployed Persons).
1932–3   Austrian Loan Guarantee.
      Consolidated Fund (No. 1).
      Consolidated Fund (No. 2).

(5) Bills authorising grants to colonies, local authorities, independent statutory bodies, agricultural interests, etc., and nothing more;
(6) Bills authorising loans, including Post Office Bills;
(7) Bills dealing with the remuneration of Government officials;
(8) Bills authorising Treasury guarantees.

          Consolidated Fund (Appropriation).
          Exchange Equalisation Account.
          Isle of Man (Customs).
          Local Government (General Exchequer Contributions).
1933–4 British Hydrocarbon Oils Production.
          Cattle Industry (Emergency Provisions).
          Consolidated Fund (No. 1).
          Consolidated Fund (Appropriation).
          Isle of Man (Customs).
          Land Settlement (Scotland).
          Overseas Trade.
          Rural Water Supplies.
          Statutory Salaries (Restoration).
1934–5 Cattle Industry (Emergency Provisions).
          Cattle Industry (Emergency Provisions) (No. 2).
          Consolidated Fund (No. 1).
          Consolidated Fund (No. 2).
          Consolidated Fund (Appropriation).
          Isle of Man (Customs).
          London Passenger Transport (Agreement).
          Post Office and Telegraph (Money).
1935–6 British Shipping (Continuation of Subsidy).
          Cattle Industry (Emergency Provisions).
          Consolidated Fund (No. 1).
          Consolidated Fund (No. 2).
          Consolidated Fund (Appropriation).
          Isle of Man (Customs).
          Pensions (Governors of Dominions, etc.).
          Railways (Agreement).
          Unemployment Assistance (Temporary Provisions) (Extension).
1936–7 Beef and Veal Customs Duties.
          British Shipping (Continuance of Subsidy).
          Consolidated Fund (No. 1).
          Consolidated Fund (No. 2).
          Consolidated Fund (Appropriation).
          Defence Loans.
          Empire Settlement.
          Exchange Equalisation Account.
          Export Guarantees.
          Isle of Man (Customs).
          Post Office and Telegraph (Home) Statutory Salaries.

Of the Bills (other than Finance Bills) certified, only the Safeguarding of Industries Bill, 1921, was of real political importance. They include none of the important Bills establishing new social services or measures of 'socialisation' or public control over industry or agriculture. Bills dealing with such matters cannot come within the definition unless they merely increase Governmental contributions to social services or are in relief of industry or agriculture.

The common notion that by 'tacking' provisions to a money Bill the House of Commons could pass 'extreme' legislation in a single sitting without the consent of the House of Lords is therefore false. It derives from Unionist propaganda in 1911 and since[1] and is not justified either by the terms of the Act or by the practice of forty-five years. Certainly the House could enormously increase the amounts given to existing social services (though it probably could not alter the method of distribution) or to industries at present subsidised (though most of the subsidies are temporary and the Acts could not be re-enacted as money Bills). It could, too, raise the tariff wall as high as it pleased or, alternatively, abolish it altogether. Further, it could 'soak the rich' by a large increase in death duties, income-tax, and surtax. These powers are no doubt 'dangerous' from one point of view; but they would arise under any reasonable interpretation of the Parliament Act, and not through 'tacking'.

The allegation about tacking is, in fact, an allegation that a Speaker might be found ready to pervert the meaning of the definition in the interests of a 'progressive' Government. All the traditions of the office are against any such method of decision. Mr Speaker in matters such as this regards himself as a judge; he takes care to free himself from all party association and to achieve as near impartiality as is humanly possible. Accordingly, he follows precedents as carefully as a court of common law. The precedents have now been made and, with the exceptions mentioned, it would be impossible for 'revolutionary' legislation to be regarded as a money Bill unless the office of Speaker became very

---

[1] Cf. Mr Baldwin at Perth on 25 October 1924: 'The present regulation with regard to financial Bills seems to open the door to far-reaching changes being carried when they are not really financial changes but only camouflaged as such': quoted by the Duke of Sutherland, 60 H.L.Deb. 5 s., 689 (25 March 1925).

different from what it is now. Moreover, in case of real difficulty the Speaker always consults the two members from the chairmen's panel prescribed by the Act. One of these is always a member of the Opposition; and it is certain that, if Mr Speaker so far forgot the traditions of his office as to give a biased interpretation to the definition, his position would become intolerable. The establishment of a joint committee presided over by Mr Speaker, as has been proposed, would do no good and might do harm. However carefully chosen, the members of such a committee would tend to regard themselves as advocates for their respective Houses. They would act not as judges but as partisans, wrapping their content in legal phrases, and the Speaker would become less a judge than an arbitrator. On the other hand, the transfer of the function to a High Court judge would not be a better solution. Interpretation in this instance requires a knowledge of parliamentary procedure which a judge possesses only if he has a political past; and there is no evidence that judges lose the bias of their youth more easily than Speakers.

During the past forty-five years, the transfer of financial power to the House of Commons alone has had little noticeable effect. The power to reject Finance Bills was a reserve power for use in exceptional cases only, since it is in essence a power to refuse supplies, and that is, in constitutional theory, a power to overthrow the Government or compel a dissolution. The events of 1909 showed that a battle on a Finance Bill is apt to be represented as a contest between 'the Dukes' and 'the people', and is not favourable ground for the Conservative party. The practice on Finance Bills since 1919 has not been different from the practice before 1909. The Bill is passed without a Committee stage and without a division whether it is certified as a money Bill or not. The procedure on the Finance Bill, 1930, which was not certified because it dealt with the valuation of properties in London, differed in no respect from the procedure on the Finance Bill, 1931, which was certified. It is reasonably certain that the Conservative party, for tactical reasons, would not have sought to defeat the Bill of 1931. Having always a majority in the Lords, the Conservative leaders can choose the ground most favourable to themselves, and taxation of the rich (for so an 'extreme' Finance Bill would be represented) is not unpopular except among the rich.

Nor has the Act had any real effect on the procedure on other certified Bills. The Import Duties Bill, 1932, was certified, and the Ottawa Agreements Bill, 1932, was not. They were, however, equally strenuously opposed,[1] and the difference in the attendance is to be accounted for by the fact that the Liberal peers abstained from voting on the former and the Labour peers on the latter. In view of the narrow statutory definition, it is unlikely that many Bills of political importance, apart from Finance Bills, will be certified. In short, the provision as to money Bills is not of great political importance.

The Parliament Act does not apply at all to private Bills, to Bills confirming Provisional Orders, and to Bills containing any provision to extend the maximum duration of Parliament beyond five years. Other Bills come within section 2 which as originally enacted was as follows:[2]

(1) If any Public Bill (other than a Money Bill or a Bill containing any provision to extend the maximum duration of Parliament beyond five years) is passed by the House of Commons in *three* successive sessions (whether of the same Parliament or not), and, having been sent up to the House of Lords at least one month before the end of the sessions, is rejected by the House of Lords in each of those sessions, that Bill shall, on its rejection for the *third* time by the House of Lords, unless the House of Commons direct to the contrary, be presented to His Majesty and become an Act of Parliament on the Royal Assent being signified thereto, notwithstanding that the House of Lords have not consented to the Bill:

Provided that this provision shall not take effect unless *two years have* elapsed between the date of the second reading in the first of those sessions of the Bill in the House of Commons and the date on which it passes the House of Commons in the *third* of those sessions.

(2) When a Bill is presented to His Majesty for assent in pursuance of the provisions of this section, there shall be endorsed on the Bill the certificate of the Speaker of the House of Commons signed by him that the provisions of this section have been duly complied with.

(3) A Bill shall be deemed to be rejected by the House of Lords if it is not

---

[1] The Import Duties Bill was read a second time by 129 votes to 12, and the Ottawa Agreements Bill by 139 votes to 34. While it may be assumed that the same Conservative peers were interested, only 66 peers voted with the majority on both occasions, and there was no cross-voting. 243 peers took part in the two divisions, and only 71 in both. The Finance Bill, 1909, was rejected by 350 votes to 75.

[2] The words amended have been italicised. For the present version, see Appendix v.

passed by the House of Lords either without amendment or with such amendments only as may be agreed to by both Houses.

(4) A Bill shall be deemed to be the same Bill as a former Bill sent up to the House of Lords in the preceding session if, when it is sent up to the House of Lords, it is identical with the former Bill or contains only such alterations as are certified by the Speaker of the House of Commons to be necessary owing to the time which has elapsed since the date of the former Bill, or to represent any amendments which have been made by the House of Lords in the former Bill in the preceding session, and any amendments made by the House of Lords in the *third* session and agreed to by the House of Commons shall be inserted in the Bill as presented for the Royal Assent in pursuance of this section:

Provided that the House of Commons may, if they think fit, on the passage of such a Bill through the House in the *second or third* session, suggest any further amendments without inserting the amendments in the Bill, and any such suggested amendments shall be considered by the House of Lords, and, if agreed to by that House, shall be treated as amendments made by the House of Lords and agreed to by the House of Commons; but the exercise of this power by the House of Commons shall not affect the operation of this section in the event of the Bill being rejected by the House of Lords.

As in the case of money Bills, the Speaker's certificate is conclusive and may not be questioned in any court of law.

The need for three separate sessions was not a substantial limitation, since the Government could by prorogations make the sessions as short as it pleased, and would no doubt feel justified in rigidly limiting debate in the second and third sessions by guillotine resolutions. The operative provision was the two years' limitation. The three sessions need not be in the same Parliament. It was 'one of the primary and most clearly avowed purposes of that Act to...abrogate the power of the House of Lords to force a dissolution',[1] or in other words to abolish the doctrine of the second bite. But with five-year Parliaments a general election had to intervene unless the Bill was introduced well within the period of three years after the previous general election. In 1912–13, for instance, it was necessary to introduce and pass with great rapidity the Government of Ireland Bill, the Welsh Church Bill, and the Trade Disputes Bill, since the Parliament was due to end in 1915.[2] The Trade Disputes

[1] *Life of Lord Oxford and Asquith*, II, p 33.
[2] *Ibid.* I, p. 355.

Bill was assented to by the Lords, but the others were passed under the Parliament Act.

Experience of the operation of this section before the war was limited to the period of 1912–14, since the outbreak of war in 1914 suspended domestic politics and the House of Lords was in agreement with the Government for the whole period between 1919 and 1945 except during the short Labour Governments of 1924 and 1929–31. Between 1912 and 1914 the procedure of the Parliament Act was adopted for two Bills, the Government of Ireland Bill, and the Established Church (Wales) Bill, both of which became law in 1914. The procedure was also followed in 1912 and 1913 for the Temperance (Scotland) Bill; but a compromise in 1913 enabled the Unionist peers to pass the measure into law. The Plural Voting Bill, which was rejected by the Lords in 1913, was again introduced and again rejected in 1914, but the outbreak of war prevented its being introduced for the third time.

Of these four Bills the Government of Ireland Bill was the most controversial. In the House of Commons in 1912 it was discussed on its introduction for three days and on second reading for seven days. The financial resolution was debated for four days (there were two resolutions owing to a defeat of the Government), and the Bill itself was in committee for six days before a guillotine resolution was proposed. The debate on the guillotine resolution occupied two days, and under the resolution it was discussed in committee for twenty-six days more, on report for eight days, and on third reading for two days. It passed its third reading by 367 votes to 267, but was defeated on second reading in the House of Lords by 326 votes to 69. The Established Church (Wales) Bill had similarly been examined at length for more than thirty days and rejected by the House of Lords on the motion for second reading. The Temperance (Scotland) Bill had been passed by the House of Lords, but with amendments which the House of Commons would not accept.

In the following session the three Bills were again introduced and read a second time in the House of Commons. The Prime Minister then moved, and the House passed resolutions, to the following effect:

1. To make the Committee stage on each Bill purely formal.
2. To limit the debate on the financial resolution on the Government of

Ireland Bill to one day and on that of the Established Church (Wales) Bill to three hours.

3. To make the report stages of the financial resolutions purely formal.

4. In each of the above cases to suspend the eleven o'clock rule.[1]

The result of making the committee stage purely formal was to make the report stage also purely formal. Thus, the House had no opportunity to amend the Bills; and the Prime Minister stated that this was done because the Parliament Act required that (subject to formal and Lords' amendments) the Bills when presented for the second and third time to the Lords must be identical Bills. The proviso to section 2 (4) of the Act certainly contemplates that suggestions for amendments may be made; and Mr Asquith explained that if amendments intended to improve any of the Bills (i.e. not wrecking amendments) were put down the Government would consider them and, if they thought them amendments within the principle of the Bill, would find time for them. These amendments would be put down as resolutions, and not as formal amendments to the Bill in question. Such resolutions should be put down before the third reading in order that, if approved, they might be submitted to the Lords with the Bill. It was thought necessary to have a debate on the financial resolution appropriate to the importance of the financial clauses; these were important in the Ireland Bill, and so a whole day was allotted, whereas three hours were considered sufficient for the Welsh Church Bill.

The three Bills were read the third time and sent to the Lords. There the Government of Ireland Bill and the Established Church (Wales) Bill were again refused a second reading. The Temperance (Scotland) Bill had not been rejected in the previous session, but merely amended. The Unionist leaders were therefore prepared for a compromise. The Parliament Act made the position of the Government much stronger (for they were assured of securing the Bill in 1914 as passed by the House of Commons in 1912) than they could have been before the Act was passed. Accordingly, the compromise was not at all favourable to the Opposition, but was accepted by them as the 'best terms that we could get'.[2] The Bill was read a third time, as amended, without a division, and the House of Commons accepted the amendment.

[1] 54 H.C.Deb. 5 s., 815–942.
[2] The Marquess of Lansdowne, 14 H.L.Deb. 5 s., 1572.

In 1914 the Government of Ireland Bill and the Established Church (Wales) Bill were introduced for the third time, and the Plural Voting Bill (which had been refused a second reading in the House of Lords in 1913) for the second time. After the second reading in each case, the Prime Minister proposed a further procedure resolution.[1] This resolution differed in three respects from that passed in the previous year. In the first place, the Government had in 1913 neglected to take steps to prevent instructions from being moved on the motion to go into committee, and this omission was rectified. In the second place, it was no longer thought necessary to debate the financial resolutions on the Ireland and Welsh Bills (there were no financial clauses in the Plural Voting Bill). And in the third place the eleven o'clock rule was not suspended. During the course of the debate, however, the Prime Minister agreed that the provision as to financial resolutions should follow the precedent of 1913, because proposals had been made in the Budget which might affect the finance of Home Rule.[2]

The Plural Voting Bill was again defeated in the House of Lords;

[1] 62 H.C.Deb. 5 s., 948–1082.

[2] The resolution of 12 May 1914, which may be regarded as the precedent, was as follows:

'That on the Committee stage of the Government of Ireland Bill and the Established Church (Wales) Bill and the Plural Voting Bill the Chairman shall forthwith put the question that he do report the Bill, without Amendment, to the House without putting any other Question, and the Question so put shall be decided without Amendment or Debate, and when an Order of the Day is read for the House to resolve itself into Committee on any of those Bills, Mr Speaker shall leave the Chair without putting any Question, not withstanding that Notice of an Instruction has been given.

'On any day on which the Committee stage of any Financial Resolution relating to the Government of Ireland Bill is put down as the first order of the day, the Chairman shall at 10.30 p.m. on that day, or if that day is a Wednesday at 8.15, or if a Friday at 4.30, bring the proceedings on that stage (if not previously concluded) to a conclusion.

'If the proceedings on the Committee stage of any Financial Resolution relating to the Established Church (Wales) Bill are not brought to a conclusion before the expiration of three hours after their being commenced the Chairman shall, at the expiration of that time, bring those proceedings to a conclusion.

'On the Committee stage of any Financial Resolution relating to the Government of Ireland Bill or the Established Church (Wales) Bill the Chairman shall forthwith put the Question upon the Resolution without putting any other Question, and the Question so put shall be decided without Amendment or Debate; and on the Report stage of any such Financial Resolution the Speaker shall forthwith put the Question that the House doth agree with the Committee in the Resolution without putting any other Question, and the Question so put shall be decided without Amendment or Debate.' See 62 H.C.Deb. 5 s., 1081–2.

but a motion for adjourning the second reading debates on the other Bills was carried against the Government. Lord Ullswater has pointed to the difficulty of certifying that a Bill is 'not passed' in the third session, because until the session is over or the Bill is rejected it cannot be assumed that the Bill will not be passed.[1] As Speaker, however, he certified both Bills, and they received the royal assent just before the King's speech proroguing Parliament.[2]

There had been a period of more than two years between the second readings in the House of Commons in the first session and the third readings in that House in the third session. In the interval circumstances had entirely changed. The avowed intention of Ulster to resist Home Rule by force of arms if necessary induced the Government to agree to the exclusion of several counties of Ulster from the scope of the Government of Ireland Act. For a long time it was hoped that an agreed compromise could be reached. The method of 'suggestion' contemplated by the proviso to section 2 (4) of the Act seemed to the Government to be, in Mr Asquith's phrase, 'no use'.[3] Accordingly, after the second reading in the House of Commons in the third session but before the third reading in that session, the Prime Minister announced that a Bill to amend the Government of Ireland Bill would be introduced.[4] Actually, agreement proved impossible, and the Government of Ireland (Amendment) Bill was introduced into the House of Lords on 1 July 1914, before that House was asked to read the original Government of Ireland Bill a second time. It was a Bill entitled 'an Act to amend the Government of Ireland Act, 1914', though of course there was no Government of Ireland Act, 1914, at that time in existence. This Bill was passed by the House of Lords, but so amended that the Government could not accept it. On 20 July 1914, the King on the advice of the Government summoned a conference at Buckingham Palace, at which the representatives of the four parties concerned—the Government, the Opposition, the Irish Nationalist party, and the Ulster Unionist party—under the presidency of Mr Speaker, sought to reach agreement. No agreement was reached; but before the Amendment

---

[1] Lord Ullswater, *A Speaker's Commentary*, II, pp. 112–15.
[2] 17 H.L.Deb. 5 s., 743.   [3] 62 H.C.Deb. 5 s., 955.
[4] *Ibid.*

Bill came up for second reading the deterioration in the international situation made postponement necessary, and no further steps were taken.

'Suggested amendments for the consideration of the House of Lords' had been put on the paper after the Established Church (Wales) Bill had been read a second time in the House of Commons in 1914. The Government refused to give time for their consideration, on the ground that they conflicted with the principle of the Bill. But the outbreak of war compelled a suspension of both the Government of Ireland Bill and the Welsh Church Bill. Accordingly, a Suspensory Bill was passed through both Houses suspending, as events happened, the application of both Bills for the duration of the war. This Bill in fact became law before the other Bills, since these other Bills were not passed by the House of Lords. The Government of Ireland Act, 1914, never came into force, being repealed by the Government of Ireland Act, 1920. The Established Church (Wales) Act, 1914, was brought into force, with substantial amendments, by the Welsh Church Act, 1919.

The circumstances of the time were wholly peculiar, and it is no criticism of the Parliament Act that it became necessary to suspend the operation of the two Acts which had been passed under section 2. Nevertheless, it is clear that the provision had substantial defects. The minimum period of two years was very long. Its justification was, no doubt, that it prevented the rapid passage of 'extreme' legislation and so gave public opinion time to form and express itself. On the other hand, we have seen[1] that 'extreme' legislation such as the conversion of a free trade system into a high tariff system, or *vice versa*, or taxation which was in substance a capital levy, could be passed through in little more than one month as a money Bill. Two years for even the most controversial legislation was an unconscionably long time.

The consequences of the Parliament Act became evident when the Labour party came into power in 1945, when for the first time since 1914 the party with a majority in the Commons had a minority in the Lords, while the Opposition party in the Commons had a majority in the Lords. It was clear that the Lords' veto could not obstruct legislation passed by the Commons during the first two sessions of the Parliament, since it would in any case come into force under the Parliament Act.

[1] *Ante*, pp. 417–18.

Moreover, if the Conservative party insisted even on using the delay authorised by the Parliament Act, a Bill to abolish the House of Lords would probably be passed under that Act. On the other hand, the Conservative party could hope to obstruct legislation passed in the third and subsequent sessions in such a manner as to compel the Government to go to the country on that legislation, though if the Conservatives did so they ran the risk of the abolition of the House of Lords if the Labour party won the election of 1949 or 1950. Accordingly, though Government defeats on Bills were numerous during the first two sessions, the Lords did not insist on their amendments if the Commons resisted them. Also, the Lords' House could be used for debates on policy, in which the Government would necessarily be defeated, and which would have the effect of weakening the hold which the Labour party had in the country. In consequence, the Government was defeated eight times during the session of 1945–6 and twenty-five times during the session of 1946–7. On the other hand, it was able to get enacted a number of controversial Bills without using the Parliament Act. Among them were the Bank of England Bill (nationalising the Bank), the Trade Disputes and Trade Unions Bill (repealing the Act of 1927 passed after the 'General Strike'), the Coal Industry Nationalisation Bill, the Transport Bill (nationalising the railways and the system of goods transport by road), the Town and Country Planning Bill (placing considerable restrictions on taking profits from land development), and the Electricity Bill (nationalising electricity production and distribution). On the second reading of the Parliament Bill, 1947, it was pointed out by Sir David Maxwell Fyfe, for the Conservative Opposition,[1] that on the Transport Bill the Government proposed eighty-six amendments in the House of Lords on their own initiative and fifty-three amendments to meet Opposition criticisms, and accepted ninety-one amendments moved by Opposition peers. On the Companies Bill, which was not controversial, the House of Lords made 360 amendments. On the Town and Country Planning Bill there were 289 Government amendments and forty-seven Opposition amendments, while on the Electricity Bill there were 107 Government amendments and eighty-one Opposition amendments.

[1] 444 H.C.Deb. 5 s., 56.

Though Sir David did not point the moral, it was plain enough that this large volume of amendments justified the changed attitude of the Labour party to the House of Lords. In 1935 the Labour party programme had included a proposal to abolish the Second Chamber. It was, however, plain by 1945 that this proposal, by itself, was unsatisfactory, because some machinery had to be substituted for the exercise of the function of cleaning up Bills which had left the Commons in an unsatisfactory condition. It might be machinery within the Commons, or it might be a reformed Second Chamber. The House of Lords, as it operated, could not be justified and was not sought to be justified by either party. On the other hand, it would be dangerous for the Labour party to reform the House of Lords, for the next Conservative Government might then increase the powers of that House, and at the same time amend its composition, in such a way as to enable the Conservative party to control Labour legislation as it had controlled Liberal legislation before 1911. In other words, it was better for the Labour party to continue the tradition that the House of Lords should not be reformed except by agreement with the parties, but at the same time to provide for a reduction of the powers of the Lords so that they could not compel a Labour Government to go to the country on controversial legislation which passed the Commons in the second half of a Parliament. Hence the party programme of 1945 merely asserted that obstruction by the House of Lords would be dealt with.

Though in fact the House of Lords had not obstructed during the first two sessions, it was necessary to contemplate the possibility of obstruction in the remaining sessions of the Parliament, particularly because a bill for nationalising the iron and steel industry was contemplated. It was not possible to wait for the obstruction to develop, because a Bill to amend the Parliament Act or in the alternative to abolish the House of Lords, if introduced in (say) 1948 could not be passed under the Parliament Act until 1950, and the Government would probably want to go to the country in the spring of 1950, if not the autumn of 1949. In 1947, therefore, the Government brought in a Bill to reduce from three to two the number of sessions in which a Bill under the Parliament Act must be passed and from two years to one year the minimum period during which such a Bill could be delayed. It was assumed that the Bill would be rejected by the House of Lords, and accordingly its operation was made retrospective in such manner that any Bill rejected a second time by the House of Lords before the royal assent was given to the new Parliament Bill could be presented for assent and become law.

The Parliament Bill was read a second time on 11 November 1947, and was supported by 345 votes to 194. It was read a third time on 10 December by 340 votes to 186. When the Bill came up for second reading in the House of Lords, Lord Salisbury on behalf of the Conservative party moved the rejection, but stated that he would withdraw the amendment if the Government agreed to the summoning of a conference to consider both the composition and the functions of the Upper House. A suitable formula having been found, the Government agreed to the postponement of the Bill. At the conference[1] agreement was reached, subject to reference to the parties, on the principles governing the composition of the House, but no agreement could be reached on the subject of powers. The Government was willing to allow a period of twelve months from the second reading in the House of Commons or nine months from the third reading, whichever was the longer, thus meeting the argument that the proceedings in the House of Commons might be so delayed that the 'suspensive veto' of the House of Lords would be a mere form. It was not prepared to go further because any longer period would jeopardise the effective use, for legislative purposes, of the fourth session of a Parliament; and it was argued for the Government that the greater the powers given to the reformed Upper House the greater would be the necessity for the Prime Minister to attempt to redress the adverse political balance by advising a creation of peers, and the greater the danger that the Lords might become a rival to the Commons. The Conservatives, on the other hand, considered that sufficient time should be allowed to enable the electorate to be properly informed of the issues involved and to enable public opinion to crystallise and express itself; the year's delay contemplated by the Parliament Bill was largely illusory because it might take eight months for a Bill to pass through Parliament; hence the Government's proposals were a formidable step towards single-chamber government,

[1] Cmd. 7390.

which was an especial danger in Britain because there is no written Constitution and fundamental constitutional changes could be made by ordinary legislation. The Opposition would have been willing to accept, as part of a comprehensive arrangement, eighteen months from the second reading in the House of Commons or one year from the third reading, whichever was the longer. The Liberals were prepared to accept the Government's compromise proposal and regretted that the conference should break down on a mere difference of three months.

The difference of three months might, however, make all the difference. The fourth session of the Parliament of 1945–50 would normally begin in November 1948. If a Bill was read a second time that month and a third time in February 1949, it could become law under the Labour proposal in November 1949 and there could be a general election in the spring of 1950. Under the Conservative proposal the Bill could not become law until July 1950, and a general election in the spring of 1950 would be fought on the Bill, which had not been enacted. If, however, the Bill was complicated and was not read a third time until July 1949, it could become law under the Labour proposal in April 1950 and there could be an election in May. Under the Conservative proposal the Bill would become law, as before, in July 1950, and again a spring election would be fought on the Bill. No doubt both parties had in mind that the Parliament of 1945–50 was due to expire on 31 July 1950, and so the Conservative party was trying to force the Labour party either to dissolve in the spring of 1950 without having its Iron and Steel (or any other controversial) Bill enacted, or to dissolve in July, when conditions would no doubt favour the Conservative party. Since general elections in July are unusual because, first, many electors are on holiday and, secondly, the register is stale, the Parliament of 1945–50 was a special case, but the Labour case would become even stronger with a Parliament beginning in the spring; and if a Parliament began in the autumn it would probably end in the spring. Hence the difference between the parties was a difference of principle.

The parties having failed to agree, the Parliament Bill was again brought up in the House of Lords on 8 June 1948 and was defeated by 177 votes to 81. Thereupon the Government decided to have a special short session in September 1948 in order to get the Bill passed a second time for the purposes of the Parliament Act, 1911. The Bill was read a second time on 20 September by 319 votes to 192. On the following day the committee stage was taken, the Government moving that the Bill be reported without further amendment or debate. It was then read a third time by 323 votes to 195 and carried to the Lords, where it was defeated on second reading by 204 votes to 34. The third session for the purposes of the Act began in November 1948 but, since the Bill could not be passed until 12 November 1949, it was not read a second time until 31 November 1949, when the second reading was carried by 333 votes to 196. On 14 November a motion was carried in Committee to report without further amendment or debate and the Bill was read a third time by 340 votes to 18. On 29 November the Bill was defeated on second reading in the House of Lords by 110 votes to 37, but received the royal assent under the Parliament Act on 16 December 1949.

Opposition to the Parliament Bill by the Conservative party and the House of Lords was not due entirely to the belief that public opinion ought to be given an opportunity to crystallise and express itself on the measure; but it was noticeable that public opinion took no great interest in the matter. Though preparations for a general election were already being made by both parties and the dissolution of Parliament followed within six weeks after the royal assent was received, the Bill was not mentioned as an issue by the commentators on the election.[1] As a political issue the House of Lords is already dead; and one result of the long delay in reaching party agreement in the matter is that no public outcry would follow if the House were decently buried. That the Bill has strengthened the hands of a Labour Government became plain in the discussions on the Iron and Steel Bill, which received the royal assent on 24 November 1949. It was not opposed on second reading in the House of Lords, but thirteen amendments were carried against the Government by majorities ranging from 77 to 28; but when the Bill went back to the Lords those amendments which had not been accepted by the Commons were not insisted upon, save an amendment postponing the vesting date for the properties concerned from 1 May 1950 to 1 July 1951. 'That the Lords do insist on this amendment' was

[1] H. G. Nicholas, *The British General Election of 1950.*

carried by 103 votes to 29, though it had been defeated in the Commons by 285 votes to 137. The purpose was, of course, to postpone the vesting date until after the general election. The Government had, however, already decided to dissolve Parliament early in 1950, and so the vesting date would be after the general election in any case (though the Conservative Opposition was not aware of the fact). Moreover, the Government had the last word, because the Parliament Bill would become law within a month and the clause providing for retrospective effect would enable the Iron and Steel Bill to be enacted forthwith, for it had been read a second time on 17 November 1948. It was therefore easy to reach a compromise. Incidentally, however, the fact that the Iron and Steel Bill took over a year to enact shows that the period of twelve months from second reading now provided by the Parliament Acts of 1911 and 1949 is a little short. The period of nine months from third reading, suggested by the Labour party during the negotiations, would have been better, and it is a pity that the Conservative party did not accept it, for the more difficult problem of reforming the House of Lords would then have been solved also.

6. END OR MEND?

Before 1911 Conservative peers were content to defend the House of Lords as it existed. The proposals which became the Parliament Act, 1911, convinced them that reform was the only alternative to the substantial mutilation of their powers or their complete abolition, and they assented to Lord Rosebery's drastic proposals[1] without substantial opposition. After 1911 there was additional incentive to reform in that it was an obvious preliminary to the restoration of the powers taken away by that Act, but since 1945, and particularly since the enactment of the Parliament Act, 1949, modification rather than restoration seems to have been the policy of the Conservative party.

In 1917 the Coalition Government took the first step towards redeeming the promise made in the preamble of the Parliament Act, and a conference of thirty members drawn from all parties, under the presidency of Viscount Bryce, met to examine the situation. As might have

[1] *Ante*, pp. 413–14.

been expected, the conference could not agree, but the chairman summarised the results of the discussion in a letter to the Prime Minister.[1]

It was agreed at the outset that the hereditary peers should form only a minority of the Second Chamber, and that there should be no property qualifications. Proposals for selecting the majority of the Chamber fell into four classes:

1. Direct election by large constituencies on the plan of the Australian Senate and the New Zealand Legislative Council (now abolished).

2. Nomination—for a small proportion only—of persons of eminence not connected with party politics.

3. Election by local authorities grouped together in geographical areas, somewhat like the system adopted in France.

4. Election by the House of Commons.

The first plan was soon abandoned, for it was not intended that the Second Chamber should be coeval with the House of Commons, and it was felt that a directly elected House of Lords would compete with the House of Commons. The second proposal also disappeared as a practical plan, because it was realised that persons eminent in other walks of life would not necessarily be good legislators, and that very quickly the nominated members would become mere political supporters of the Government in power.[2] To the third plan it was objected that local authorities were not elected for parliamentary purposes, and that the proposal would introduce an irrelevant consideration into local elections. The Liberal and Labour parties also objected that county councils were almost wholly Conservative, and in any case it was felt that an elected assembly would compete with the House of Commons on a footing of equality.

The last proposal, election by the House of Commons, therefore secured most approval. As Dr Lees-Smith has said:[3]

Its merits are that it creates a Second Chamber which has no claim to become a rival to the first, and that it avoids the expense, labour and confusion of a second series of popular elections. On the other hand, an equally

---

[1] Cd. 9038/1918. No other record was published, but a summary of the minutes and memoranda has been published by H. B. Lees-Smith in *Second Chambers in Theory and Practice* (London, 1923), ch. XI, from which the following account is taken.

[2] Cf. the experience of Eire.

[3] *Second Chambers in Theory and Practice*, p. 221.

obvious result is that it is certain to be elected on party lines, to reflect the prevailing composition of parties in the Lower House, and to be used largely as a consolation for politicians who have grown tired or who have been defeated in the election for the more popular Chamber.

To avoid the difficulty of party elections, it was suggested that nominations might be made by a Committee of Selection of about twenty members, half from the House of Commons and half from the new Second Chamber; but the suggestion did not meet with the support of a majority of the conference. This left the proposal for direct election by the House of Commons. To secure representation of minorities, it was agreed without dissent that the election should be by proportional representation; but, in order to prevent manipulation by a small group of members, it was agreed by a substantial majority that Great Britain should be divided into thirteen areas, and that election should be made by the members of the House of Commons sitting for constituencies within each area.

The most acute divergencies were revealed when the question of the powers of the Second Chamber was discussed. Some desired that disputes between the two Houses should be settled by a joint sitting; others wanted a referendum. Ultimately, agreement was reached on a 'free conference' of sixty members, thirty from each House, meeting in secret. If a Bill were rejected by this conference, it would not pass; if the conference altered it or accepted it, it was to go back to the Houses, in which case it could be rejected or accepted, but not amended; if one House accepted and the other rejected, it would again go back to the free conference; if the conference again accepted it by a majority of at least three, the Bill could be passed by either House without the consent of the other.

After the failure of the Bryce Conference to reach agreement, the Government introduced resolutions into the House in 1922 as follows:

1. That this House shall be composed, in addition to peers of the Blood Royal, Lords Spiritual, and Law Lords, of
   (a) Members elected, either directly or indirectly, from outside;
   (b) Hereditary peers elected by their order;
   (c) Members nominated by the Crown;
the numbers in each case to be determined by statute.

2. That, with the exception of peers of the Blood Royal and the Law Lords, every other member of the reconstituted and reduced House of Lords shall hold his seat for a term of years to be fixed by statute, but shall be eligible for re-election.

3. That the reconstituted House of Lords shall consist approximately of 350 members.[1]

To these were added resolutions to the effect that the decision as to what was a money Bill should be left to a standing joint committee of both Houses, consisting of the Speaker and seven members from each House, and that the Parliament Act should not apply to a Bill altering the constitution or powers of the House of Lords.

It is obvious that these resolutions raised more questions than they solved. They did not state the system of election; they did not determine the proportion of elected members; and they did not indicate the period of office. Above all, and this was the fundamental Conservative objection, they did not substantially increase the powers of the House of Lords. They were received so coldly that they were not proceeded with.

In 1923 the Labour party became the official Opposition, though it was almost unrepresented in the House of Lords. The advent of a Labour Government in 1924 suggested that a Labour majority might not be remote, and it was foreseen that no Labour Government could for long leave the hereditary privileges of the Conservative peers untouched. The programme drawn up by the Conservative Shadow Cabinet, *Looking Ahead*, declared in the same year that the Unionist party 'recognises [that] the establishment of an effective Second Chamber means a reconsideration of the composition and powers of the House of Lords in the light of modern conditions'. In March 1925, a Conservative peer raised the question in the House of Lords with 'the ardour of youth and the buoyancy of a man experienced in aerial navigation',[2] and the Government decided to appoint a Cabinet Committee to consider the matter.[3] In 1927, the question was raised again, and the Lord Chancellor announced the Government's tentative conclusions.[4] They may be summarised as follows:

[1] 51 H.L.Deb. 5 s., 536–7.
[2] The phrases of Lord Oxford and Asquith, 60 H.L.Deb. 5 s., 701.
[3] 60 H.L.Deb. 5 s., 685–727.   [4] 67 H.L.Deb. 5 s., 778–87.

1. The question whether the Bill is a money Bill should be settled by a joint standing committee representing the two Houses equally; this committee should consider not merely the form, but also the substance.

2. No Bill to alter the powers or composition of the House of Lords should be capable of being passed under the Parliament Act.

3. The Crown should have the power to add a limited number of members on the nomination of the Government; these would sit for twelve years, one-third retiring every four years.

4. The hereditary peers should elect a number of their own order to sit as representative peers; these would sit for twelve years each, one-third retiring every four years.

5. The House should contain not more than 350 members, excluding peers of the Blood Royal and Lords of Appeal.

The House passed by 212 votes to 54 a motion welcoming a reasonable measure limiting and defining membership of the House and dealing with the defects of the Parliament Act, but the Government's proposals were not put to the vote. In fact, they received no great welcome, and were never elaborated or proceeded with.

On 11 December 1928, the Earl of Clarendon tried his hand, and moved a resolution:

1. That it is desirable that early steps should be taken to limit the number of members of the House, and to make suitable provision for an elective representation of the peerage, and for such other representation or nomination as would ensure to each political party a fair position in the House.

2. That the following constitution of this House would in the opinion of this House fulfil these conditions:

(a) 150 peers to be elected by proportional representation or the cumulative vote in each Parliament by the whole body of peers, to sit and vote in the House;

(b) 150 persons to be nominated by the Crown in proportion to the parties in the House of Commons in each Parliament, to sit for the life of each Parliament;

(c) the Crown to have the power to appoint a limited number of life peers in each Parliament.[1]

Assuming that the life peers cancelled each other in a political sense, the 'fair position' thus accorded to the Conservative party was a per-

[1] 72 H.L.Deb. 5 s., 484.

manent majority, since under any system of proportional representation nobody but a Conservative peer would secure a quota, whereas there would be some Conservatives elected by the House of Commons. However, it was not for that reason that the House refused to accept the second part of the resolution. With the substitution of 'reduce' for 'limit', the first part was carried by 52 votes to 8.[1] It is worthy of notice that this resolution did not propose the amendment of the Parliament Act.

In December 1933, the Marquis of Salisbury introduced a Bill to reform the House of Lords. His proposals were, shortly, as follows:[2]

1. A more restrictive definition of 'money Bill'. This to be interpreted by a joint select committee of both Houses, with the Speaker as chairman.

2. No Bill other than a Money Bill should be passed under the Parliament Act until *after* a dissolution.

3. The peers should elect 150 of their own order.

4. Another 150 should be added from outside, according to a method to be prescribed by resolutions of both Houses of Parliament.

5. These, together with the Peers of the Blood Royal, the Lords of Appeal, and a few bishops, would make a House of 320.

The Bill was read a first time by 84 votes to 34, and a second time by 171 votes to 82, but proceeded no further.

Subsequently the enthusiasm of the reformers became somewhat damped. There was, however, another method of effecting a slight reform. A peerage is an honour—or a burden, according to opinion— which cannot be destroyed otherwise than by Act of Parliament so long as male heirs exist. There would be less hesitation to create and to accept peerages if they could be conferred for life only. It appeared to Liberal statesmen of the middle of the nineteenth century that this method would enable the solid Tory phalanx created by Mr Pitt and his successors and by the tendency of Whig lords to turn Tory after 1832 to be outnumbered without resorting to the method of 'swamping' by hereditary peers. There were, however, no recent precedents except those 'made in favour of ladies of dubious reputation in the days of the later Stuarts and the early Georges. But these ladies, it had to be admitted, had never claimed to sit in Parliament, even in their most

[1] 72 H.L.Deb. 5 s., 656.   [2] 90 H.L.Deb. 5 s., 597–613.

adventurous moods.'[1] In 1851 a life peerage was offered to Dr Lushington, in order to strengthen the legal talent of the House of Lords, but he declined it. The same object was put forward in 1855, when a life peerage was conferred on Sir James Parke, a judge whose legal eminence was considered in 1855 to be greater than it is considered to-day. The patent contained an express provision that Lord Wensleydale, as he called himself, should be entitled to a writ of summons. There was, however, considerable opposition for several reasons. It was feared by some Liberals that the effect of admitting life peers would be to strengthen the House of Lords at the expense of the other House. On the other hand, it was feared by Conservatives that once the precedent was established the Conservative hegemony in the House of Lords would be destroyed—and there was no doubt that the peerage was conferred with this intention. It was also thought that the Prince Consort—then most unpopular—desired to have 'literary and scientific peers'. The leader of the Conservative party, Lord Derby, 'had a special dread of literary and scientific peers, though, as he does not appear to have suggested that hereditary peers should be prohibited from gaining distinction by translations from the Greek and Latin poets, it must be assumed that the difficulties which he anticipated were of a character attributed to the Prime Minister in a modern play, when he suggests that his private secretary should attempt to discover some person, the appearance of whose name in a Birthday Honours List would at least not excite general disapprobation'.[2] For these reasons, the House refused to consult the judges as to whether the patent conferred the right to a writ of summons, but decided for themselves that it did not. Lord Wensleydale was then given a hereditary peerage.

The decision of the House is not binding on it, but has some legal merit, and for political reasons would probably not be reversed. Legislation authorising life peers to sit and vote might possibly be passed, and in 1935 the House gave a second reading, by 44 votes to 14, to a Bill for that purpose, though it proceeded no further. Such a solution

---

[1] *Life of Lord Granville*, I, p. 159.

[2] *Ibid.* pp. 158–9. The point may be put more shortly. Presumably Lord Derby thought that the peerage, like the Order of the Garter, should have 'no damned merit about it'. These are degenerate days; for some peers have been known to be learned, and even the Garter has been conferred for merit—though never for learning.

might have satisfied Gladstonian Liberals, but it would not be accepted by either side to-day. On the other hand, the two sides have moved nearer than they have ever been. The Conservatives have a fear that the House of Lords will be allowed to die of atrophy. In the last two sessions of the Parliament of 1951–5 there were thirty-eight divisions. The debates on television apparently brought out some of the Conservative and Liberal 'backwoodsmen', and if they be excluded there were twenty-seven divisions. The average vote on the Conservative side was forty-five, while the average Labour vote was seventeen. Of the Conservative peers, twenty-one held ministerial offices or political offices in the Royal Household, while nearly all the Labour peers had held office under the Labour Government of 1945–51. It is of course easy to keep the Government side of the machine working with a solid bloc of twenty or more office-holders. To keep an Opposition functioning through two Parliaments with a handful of ageing ex-ministers is by no means so easy. There have been suggestions, apparently of an official character, that a batch of Labour peers should be created in order to strengthen the Opposition and meet the wastage due to old age. It is, however, not easy to find persons of the right quality who can devote three afternoons and evenings a week for thirty-six weeks in the year, at their own expense, to parliamentary business. Enquiries among Labour members in the House of Commons, the most likely source of recruitment to the peerage, showed that few were willing or able to exchange £1000 a year and the excitement of political debate for the dull and unrewarded task of opposition in the House of Lords, even with the prestige of a peerage. Nor, indeed, is it certain that the Labour party would accept the proposal. It would be opposed by all who thought the House of Lords to be a useless institution, by many who thought that the Labour party should cease to support the hereditary principle by continuing to recommend Labour peers, and by others who thought that the quickest way to compel the Conservative party to reform the House of Lords was to withdraw all Labour opposition in that House. The institution of a daily allowance of £3, suggested from the Conservative side, would overcome some of these difficulties, but the Labour party has yet to be persuaded that some advantage is to be gained by enabling the Conservative party to keep its majority. The gradual fall in the

Conservative vote in the House of Lords is no doubt due to the fact that peers, like other people, have now to earn their living, that those who live outside the London area cannot afford to stay in London for two nights a week, and that many of those who live in London cannot spare time for more than casual attendance. Thus, though a daily allowance would help the Labour party to keep opposition going, if it wanted to do so, it would also help the Conservative party to maintain the relics of hereditary rule.

Mere inactivity will not solve the problem. As the law now stands the House of Lords has important work to do, and it must continue to function. That work will not be effective unless there is an Opposition, so that running the machine with a score of ministers and lords in waiting and a handful of company directors and retired officials living in London will not do. Moreover, if no action is taken the next Labour Government will have to find some twenty peers to hold office and yet will be faced with the prospect of a Government defeat every time the Conservatives choose to oppose a Government proposal or to move a motion criticising Government policy. Hence both parties desire some reform, though they are not quite agreed as to the form which it should take. Meanwhile, a peerage has ceased to be regarded as an office and attendance on parliamentary business is no longer regarded as a duty. A peerage is, in fact, a mere 'honour' carrying a social status higher than that of a baronetcy, with the same curious characteristic that it descends to heirs male of the body of the person who merited it.

At the Annual Conference of the Labour party in 1934, the National Executive Committee submitted a report on 'Parliamentary Problems and Procedure' which was endorsed by the Conference, and which contained the following paragraphs:

A Labour Government meeting with sabotage from the House of Lords would take immediate steps to overcome it; and it will, in any event, take steps during its term of office to pass legislation abolishing the House of Lords as a legislative Chamber.

If the Party obtained a mandate from the people in support of its policy, the Labour Government would regard it as its duty to carry that policy through by the necessary legislation and administrative action. The Party will, therefore, at the next General Election, make it clear to the country that in placing its policy before the people, it was also asking for a mandate to deal forthwith with any attempt by the House of Lords to defeat the will of the people by rejecting, mutilating or delaying measures which formed an essential part of the programme approved by the electorate.[1]

In moving the adoption of the Report, Mr J. R. Clynes said: 'in our view the House of Lords is an institution which cannot well be reformed; it cannot be amended, it must be ended.'[2] The only criticism of the policy proposed was that it was not decided to take immediate action, by the creation of peers, to pass legislation to abolish the House of Lords—a policy which appeared to the majority to be 'unwise strategy'. Accordingly, the Labour party manifesto for the general election of 1935 ended with the sentence: 'Labour seeks a mandate to carry out this programme by constitutional and democratic means, and with this end in view it seeks power to abolish the House of Lords and improve the procedure of the House of Commons.'

In 1945 this precise statement became less precise: 'We give clear notice that we will not tolerate obstruction of the people's will by the House of Lords.' This represented the maximum of agreement between the two wings of the party. The left wing maintained the old Radical objection to any Second Chamber; the right wing thought that, if the powers of the Lords were diminished a little more, the issue would be of no political importance. As it happens, neither in 1935 nor in 1945 was there any public interest in the matter;[3] and in the Parliaments of 1945 to 1951 the only action taken by the Labour Government was to reduce to one year the delay imposed by the Parliament Act, action which in turn produced no reaction in public opinion.[4] The problem has thus become almost a technical one, how the functions now performed by the House of Lords can best be performed. This question was discussed at the inter-party conference which followed the first passing of the Parliament Bill by the House of Commons in 1948. The following propositions were agreed *ad referendum*:[5]

(1) The Second Chamber should be complementary to and not a rival to the Lower House and, with this end in view, the reform of the House of

---

[1] Report of the Thirty-Fourth Annual Conference of the Labour Party, 1934, p. 263.
[2] *Ibid.* p. 148.
[3] For 1945, see R. B. McCallum and Alison Readman, *The British General Election of 1945*, where the subject is not even mentioned. The present writer is able to support this negative evidence from a contemporary analysis of the London Press made by him.
[4] *Ante*, pp. 428–34.   [5] Cmd. 7390.

Lords should be based on a modification of its existing constitution, as opposed to the establishment of a Second Chamber of a completely new type based on some system of election.

(2) The revised constitution of the House of Lords should be such as to secure as far as practicable that a permanent majority is not assured to any one political party.

(3) The present right to attend and vote based solely on heredity should not by itself constitute a qualification to a reformed Second Chamber.

(4) Members of the Second Chamber should be styled 'Lords of Parliament' and would be appointed on grounds of personal distinction or public service. They might be drawn either from hereditary peers, or from commoners who would be created life peers.

(5) Women should be capable of being appointed Lords of Parliament in like manner as men.

(6) Provision should be made for the inclusion in the Second Chamber of certain descendants of the Sovereign, certain Lords Spiritual, and the Law Lords.

(7) In order that persons without private means should not be excluded, some remuneration would be payable to members of the Second Chamber.

(8) Peers who were not Lords of Parliament should be entitled to stand for election to the House of Commons, and also to vote at elections in the same manner as other citizens.

(9) Some provision should be made for the disqualification of a member of the Second Chamber who neglects, or becomes no longer able or fitted, to perform his duties as such.

Finally,

the representatives of all three parties were united in their desire to see the House of Lords continue to play its proper part in the Legislature, and in particular to exercise the valuable function of revising Bills and initiating discussions on public affairs: it was regarded as essential, moreover, that there should be a legislative body composed of men of mature judgment and experience gained in many spheres of public life.

Since the parties failed to agree on the period of delay to be allowed to the Second Chamber, this agreed statement was not put to the party organisations for their approval. The statement does, however, represent a considerable change in the policy of the Labour party, due no doubt to eleven years' experience in office. It was indeed obvious that the complicated legislation passed by the Labour Government of 1945–51 needed a Second Chamber, more efficient and less politically-minded than the House of Lords, to undertake the complicated task of 'cleaning-up' the Bills after the House of Commons had dealt with them. The task could no doubt be undertaken by a drafting committee of the House of Commons itself, but it would be unreasonable to impose such a heavy burden upon its members, and it would be carried out more efficiently by a properly composed Second Chamber.

Since the Labour party has never proposed the abolition of the judicial functions of the 'House of Lords' (which is, in reality, a completely different body), we may exclude them from consideration; in addition, the future of impeachment and the determination of claims to peerages requires no consideration. In the Bryce Conference of 1917–18 there was general agreement that the following were the functions of a Second Chamber:

1. The examination and revision of Bills brought from the House of Commons, a function which has become more needed since, on many occasions, during the last thirty years, the House of Commons has been obliged to act under special rules limiting debate.

2. The initiation of Bills dealing with subjects of a practically non-controversial character which may have an easier passage through the House of Commons if they have been fully discussed and put into a well-considered shape before being submitted to it.

3. The interposition of so much delay (and no more) in the passing of a Bill into law as may be needed to enable the opinion of the nation to be adequately expressed upon it. This would be specially needed as regards Bills which affect the fundamentals of the Constitution or introduce new principles of legislation; or which raise issues whereon the opinion of the country may appear to be almost equally divided.

4. Full and free discussion of large and important questions, such as those of foreign policy, at moments when the House of Commons may happen to be so much occupied that it cannot find sufficient time for them. Such discussions may often be all the more useful if conducted in an assembly whose debates and divisions do not involve the fate of the executive Government.[1]

It is by no means certain that these propositions would have secured the same unanimity thirty years later. The relations between elected representatives and the electorate are far closer than they were in 1914,

---

[1] Cd. 9038/1918, p. 4; Lees-Smith, *Second Chambers in Theory and Practice*, pp. 32–3.

and the policy of the Government is far more effectively determined by public opinion. On the other hand, the House of Lords is even more remote from the 'opinion of the country', and it would be very difficult to secure a reformed House which could exercise all four functions. Moreover, there is a substantial element of ambiguity in the four propositions, and especially in the third, which alone made agreement possible. The debates of 1906 to 1914, as well as the difficulty of securing agreed proposals for reform, show that the members of the Conference agreed to the formula but did not agree to the substance. To prove this, it is necessary only to ask if a Second Chamber ought to have passed the Government of Ireland Bill in 1912—or, for that matter, in 1893.

There can be no doubt that some interesting debates are held in the House of Lords. Among its members are able persons who have held high office in the service of the Crown, who have acquired experience in many parts of the world, and who are able to place their knowledge and experience at the disposal of the public. For this reason it is wise not to over-emphasise the small attendances; the peers present change from day to day according to the subject under discussion, and apart from the leaders on both sides noble lords do not intervene unless they regard themselves as experts. Moreover, the House of Lords is an effective 'home of rest' for semi-retired politicians. Statesmen of experience, like the late Lord Balfour, the late Lord Morley and the late Lord Oxford and Asquith, were able to take part in affairs of State without involving themselves in the labour of representing large constituencies and of working for long hours in a pressed House of Commons. Sometimes, the Government is thus able to retain the services of such persons as ministers. Disraeli found it necessary to go to the House of Lords. Lord Balfour and Lord Morley could never have continued as ministers if they had been compelled to serve in the House of Commons. But, whether they remain as ministers or not, their contributions to debates are of considerable value. It is certainly true, also, that the fact that no vote of the House of Lords compels the resignation of the Government results in a greater freedom of debate in that House.

The functions of the House of Lords as a legislative assembly are far less important. An examination of the number of amendments made by the House of Lords and accepted by the House of Commons produces what some regard as a surprisingly large number. The explanation, however, is simple. Modern Bills are extremely complicated and technical. However carefully and ably drafted they may be, difficulties are constantly being met with. While they are in the House of Commons they are being subjected to constant examination by the draftsmen and by the officials of the appropriate departments. Outside bodies subject them to a rigorous dissection and make known their conclusions to the Government. Other people examine them with such expert knowledge as they possess. Members of Parliament, too, examine Bills from the points of view of their constituents, of the outside bodies with which they are connected, and of their own interests.

The result is a host of amendments moved or accepted by the Government. It is not uncommon for a Bill to be increased in length by one-third during its passage. Many, indeed most, of these amendments are made in the House of Commons. Frequently, however, difficulties are discovered too late for them to be dealt with in that House. Frequently, too, a point is made in the House of Commons which the Government undertakes to study. Moreover, amendments in the House of Commons frequently involve consequential amendments. Amendments of these kinds are made in the House of Lords. By far the greatest number of House of Lords amendments are in fact Government amendments. Occasionally a Lord of Appeal makes useful proposals; occasionally some other lord with technical knowledge proposes amendments of value. But these are comparatively rare; and in general it may be said that, with a Conservative Government in power, nearly all changes are proposed by the Government.

It is not impossible to suggest a device whereby the House of Commons could deal with such technical and detailed amendments, for instance by the establishment of a drafting committee.[1] It is, however, certainly an advantage to have the House of Lords available for technical and drafting amendments. The advantage would be far greater if pressure on parliamentary time led to limitation of opportunities for raising small points in the House of Commons, as has sometimes been proposed. On

[1] Jennings, *Parliamentary Reform* (London, 1934), pp. 96–9.

the other hand, there is no agreement as to what further functions are implied in 'examination and revision'. The Conservative peers thought in 1931, and continued to think, that they had 'improved' the Agricultural Land (Utilisation) Bill, whereas Labour ministers thought that they had 'mutilated' it. What one side regards as common sense the other considers to be blatant politics in the worst sense.

There are, however, two legislative functions which the House of Lords performs well and, in part, better than the House of Commons. Strangely enough, these functions are not mentioned by its defenders. Nor have they yet been mentioned in this book, for they appear in subsequent chapters.[1] They are, the consideration of Private Bills and Provisional Order Bills, and the consideration of special orders. Though the House of Commons now passes far fewer private Bills than it did in the railway boom, there is considerable pressure on the House. Bills are now much more fully considered, and they take up a considerable time in the Opposed Bill Groups and the Unopposed Bill Committee. It is not easy to find members to perform the exacting tasks required, since so many members have other activities in the mornings and assiduity brings no reward, even in the political sense. The Private Bills and Provisional Order Bills are divided between the two Houses in more or less equal proportions. Often, as will be explained later,[2] a Bill opposed in one House is not opposed in the other. Accordingly, the abolition of the House of Lords would involve almost the doubling of the functions of the House of Commons in this respect. Again, it is generally much easier to secure peers to go to Edinburgh or Glasgow to sit on parliamentary panels for Scottish Provisional Orders, than it is to find members of the House of Commons to perform the same function.[3] Members of the Lower House are fully occupied in Westminster or in their constituencies. Many peers, on the other hand, are willing to perform a public service without remuneration or publicity.

When a Conservative Government is in power, there is little if any advantage in having a private Bill considered by the House of Commons first; nor is there any advantage in having members of that House to

[1] Chapters XIII and XIV. [2] *Post*, p. 470; and see Appendix VI.
[3] See *post*, pp. 485–6.

form the parliamentary panel for Scottish Provisional Orders. With a Labour majority it is easier to secure additional powers for local authorities from the House of Commons, though they are likely to be obstructed by the House of Lords. This is, however, a consideration which affects debate on the second reading, and has nothing to do with the committee stage. It would no doubt be easy to invent devices for the performance of the functions which the peers now exercise. Scottish Provisional Orders could be dealt with by the extra-parliamentary panel. In the opinion of many, it would be a decided advantage to extend very considerably the power of making provisional orders for England and Wales, and to create extra-parliamentary panels for cases when members of the House could not be found. It is, however, essential to remember that any proposal for the abolition of the House of Lords must bring with it consequential proposals for dealing with Private Bills and Provisional Orders.

The second function is the consideration of special orders as defined by the House of Lords.[1] Such orders were not until recently effectively considered in the House of Commons, whereas they are considered, and very effectively, in the House of Lords. The procedure is of limited importance and if it were abolished it would not add to the functions of the House of Commons. It would, nevertheless, extend in practice the powers of ministers over delegated legislation and withdraw one of the most important methods of parliamentary control.

The formula in which the third function was defined by the Bryce Committee causes the greatest difficulty. No proposal so far made would be considered by members of the Labour party as tending towards the creation of a Second Chamber which would be a better judge of the 'opinion of the country' than a House of Commons elected on adult franchise. It is, probably, universally admitted that under our system of representation (or any other) a general election cannot produce a clear expression of opinion on any particular issue. Though Home Rule was the chief item of Liberal policy from 1886–93, Unionists denied that Mr Gladstone had a mandate for it; and it was still more strenuously denied that Conservatives secured a mandate for general tariffs in 1931. Even if no 'lies' are used to secure a majority—and allegations of that

[1] *Post*, pp. 509–12.

kind are made after nearly every general election[1]—the manifesto of any party contains so many items, and there are so many cross-currents of opinion, that it cannot definitely be said that there is a majority for every item. Even if it could be so asserted, it could not be claimed that the Bill founded upon the 'mandate' would necessarily prove acceptable. Party manifestos contain general statements which are often nothing more than formulae concealing differences of opinion; a perfect citizen, like a good lawyer, should see the full text before he gives a firm opinion. Acceptance of a general proposition does not necessarily mean agreement upon the details of a measure founded upon that proposition. We might indeed go further; agreement upon legislation does not necessarily involve agreement upon the spirit with which it is administered.

The working of a democratic system under modern conditions is a more complicated process than the theorists of the middle of the last century (inspired, however little they knew it, by the French Revolution) were able to foresee. Government is a continuous process inspired either by purely material and interested motives (whether they be the motives of a class or of individuals) or motives of public policy, and those motives may be roughly classified as 'conservative' or 'progressive', 'left' or 'right'. These, too, are merely general formulae, and their meaning can be determined only by the general tendencies of proposals and decisions. The policies put forward by the respective parties differ more in spirit than in substance; and it is the spirit which is chosen by the electorate, not merely on the basis of the proposals made, but also on the basis of past performance.

It is quite impossible to say that when the electorate gave a vast majority to the Liberal party in 1905–6 it gave a specific mandate for the Education Bill, the Trade Disputes Bill, the Licensing Bill, or the 'People's Budget'. It is equally impossible to say that when a reduced majority was given to the Liberal Government in 1910 a mandate was given for Home Rule or Welsh Disestablishment or the war of 1914; or that the election of 1918 gave a mandate for the settlement with

[1] E.g. 'pro-Boer' in 1900; 'Chinese slavery' in 1905; that the Unionists intended to abolish old age pensions in 1910; 'hang the Kaiser' and 'helping the enemy' in 1918; the 'Red Letter' in 1924; the 'Savings Bank lie' and the 'doctor's mandate' in 1931; and 'no great armaments programme' (not to speak of 'supporting the League of Nations') in 1935. For subsequent elections see the Nuffield College series.

Ireland; or that the election of 1931 gave a mandate for general tariffs; or that the election of 1935 gave a mandate for a vast armament programme; and it would be extremely difficult to say what were the contents and implications of the 'socialism' which the electorate supported in 1945—it was certainly not the nationalisation of industries, which has never caught the public imagination. It is not contended that if these questions had been submitted to the referendum they might not have been carried.

Obviously, every question of legislation and administration upon which there is any dispute cannot be submitted to a general election or a referendum. The Liberal Government of 1914 or the Chamberlain Government of 1939 could not hold up its ultimatum to Germany while it consulted the people; yet both in their immediate results and their ultimate consequences the declarations of war were far more important than the Budget of 1909, the Parliament Bill, or Home Rule. Governments must often take decisions in advance of the approval of the House of Commons and almost always in advance of the approval of the electorate. This does not mean that a party can deny its electoral pledges (except in a very extreme case) where no new circumstances have arisen. If Mr Gladstone had pledged himself in 1892 not to introduce Home Rule, he would have committed a gross breach of constitutional propriety if he had used his majority to propose it; and the House of Lords or any other body would have been justified in rejecting it. Similarly, if Mr Baldwin had introduced general tariffs in 1925 a more impartial Second Chamber than the House of Lords would have been justified in demanding an appeal to the people.

One might even go further, and assert that there are certain kinds of proposals which are quite inconsistent with the operation of democracy and which ought not to be accepted without the most specific consent of the people. These include—and as far as can be foreseen include only —legislation to interfere with freedom of elections, freedom of party association for democratic purposes, freedom of constitutional opposition, and regular appeals to the people. Any proposal short of this can be reversed by a vote at a general election. Even Home Rule could have been reversed if it had been carried, though it would have been difficult. Even if the Union was a 'fundamental of the Constitution', it does not follow that the Second Chamber would have been justified in rejecting Home Rule. It is really beside the point to argue whether or not the Liberal Government had a mandate for it in 1910. If that doctrine were to prevail there would be an election every six months. According to it, when the Liberal Government had secured a mandate for the Budget in 1910, it ought then to have secured a mandate for the Parliament Bill (as it did); it ought then to have dissolved Parliament in order to secure a mandate for Home Rule; after that it required a mandate for Welsh Disestablishment, another for the abolition of plural voting, and yet another for the declaration of war. The truth is that anybody who voted Liberal in 1910 knew perfectly well that he was running the risk of everything which accorded with Liberal 'philosophy', and especially of Home Rule, which had been an article of Liberal faith since 1886.[1]

The truth is that the mandate conferred by a general election is a mandate to govern according to democratic principles and in the light of a particular 'philosophy' or 'ideology'. Burke's argument that the member of Parliament must decide according to his political principles and the need of the moment has been converted not into the doctrine that everything requires the express approval of a majority of the electors, but into the thesis that the Government must decide according to its political principles and the needs of the moment, subject however to the consent of the House of Commons, and subject to the constant warning that the last word rests with the electorate. The result is a system of administration which has not always in particular issues a majority in the country, but which accords far more closely with public opinion than at any other time in the history of these islands and (it is believed) than in any other country in the world.

If this is so, the need for a Second Chamber to exercise the third function, the delaying of measures until the 'opinion of the nation' can be adequately expressed, does not exist; and it is unnecessary to ask

[1] Anyone who studies the literature of the Budget Protest League in 1909–10 will be aware that the Unionists did not *fight* the first election of 1910 on the land tax, but on 'beer and baccy'. The argument that by attacking capital the Budget was undermining employment was gradually dropped, and emphasis laid on the fact that English beer, spirits and cheap tobaccos were being heavily taxed, while the rich man's champagne, cigars, and lager beer were escaping lightly. The general attack just before the election might be described as 'tariff reform *versus* Socialism'. What, then, was the mandate conferred?

whether the Parliament Acts provide too much or too little delay, or how the opinion of the nation is to be expressed, or how it is possible to get a Second Chamber which is more capable of determining whether the opinion of the nation has been expressed than members of Parliament who owe their seats to the opinions of their constituents, or any other of the score of questions raised by this ambiguous formula.

CHAPTER XIII

PRIVATE BILL LEGISLATION

I. PRIVATE BILLS

As Redlich points out,[1] the control which Parliament exercises through private Bill legislation and similar means has essentially the same purpose as the 'tutelle administrative' of continental countries. The abolition of the Court of Star Chamber and the jurisdiction of the Council left justices of the peace and other local authorities free from any kind of control save that of the courts on the one hand and Parliament on the other; and the tradition that wide powers ought not to be left in the hands of the Crown prevented the growth of any substantial powers of administrative control until 1834 and has retarded its development since.[2] Though wide powers were conferred upon the Government from 1834 onwards and with increasing rapidity since 1870,[3] Parliament still retains in its hands many functions which elsewhere would be regarded as administrative in character.

The purpose of a private Bill is to secure powers additional to or in derogation of the general law. Such Bills are defined as 'Bills for the particular interest or benefit of any person or persons'.[4] But a public Bill which affects the rights of a particular person or group of persons, even if introduced by the Government (such as a Bill to regulate Crown lands or to acquire property for the Post Office) is regarded as a 'hybrid' Bill and is treated like a private Bill after second reading.

Private Bills are divided into three classes. Personal Bills deal with estates, names, naturalisation, divorce, and include other Bills not specified by the House of Lords as 'local Bills'. Such Bills must be

---

[1] *Recht und Technik des englischen Parlamentarismus*, p. 732. (This chapter is not in the English edition.)

[2] See Holdsworth, *History of English Law*, XI, p. 615, though the author appears to consider that the tradition (called by him the 'rule of law') is wholly admirable.

[3] For the development, see Jennings, 'Central Control' in *A Century of Municipal Progress* (ed. Laski, Jennings and Robson); and for the modern law see Jennings, *Principles of Local Government Law*, ch. v.

[4] May, p. 833.

introduced in the House of Lords, but they are not now common. Estate Bills were directed largely to the breaking of settlements and the determination of uncertain titles; but the Settled Land Acts on the one hand and the stricter practice and the less rigid law of conveyancing on the other hand have rendered them infrequent. Naturalisation Bills are uncommon because of the provisions of the Naturalisation Act, 1870, and the British Nationality Act. The creation of judicial methods of divorce and the separation of the Irish Free State have removed the need for divorce Bills; and informal marriages may be validated by Provisional Order.

Apart from a few Bills regulating charities and other special trusts, most Bills are either promoted by local authorities or regulate public utilities, but since most of the public utilities were nationalised by the Labour Government of 1945–51 the corporations administering the nationalised industries have become more frequent applicants than public utility companies. Thus, in spite of the growth of administrative powers, including the powers of making Provisional Orders, the primary function of private Bill legislation is to regulate or confer powers upon local authorities or other statutory undertakers. It is significant of the position of these administrative and quasi-administrative authorities that, unlike similar bodies in other countries, they have the right to approach Parliament direct. The mere suggestion in 1930 that their opportunities should be cut down[1] met with opposition. 'Local authorities attach great importance to their undoubted right to approach Parliament, whenever they consider it necessary, and they would resent any attempt to interfere with that right.'[2] Though new methods of obtaining powers, especially by local authorities, have been conferred, so that procedure by Provisional Order, Special Procedure, adoption of adoptive provisions, or consent of a Government department, is often appropriate, no limitation (except a population limit in respect of applications for county borough status)[3] has been placed upon the power to approach Parliament.

[1] See Report from the Select Committee on Private Bills, 1930 (H.C. 158 of 1930), pp. 18–19.   [2] *Ibid.* p. 19.

[3] Local Government Act, 1933, s. 139, re-enacting s. 1 (2) of the Local Government (County Boroughs and Adjustments) Act, 1926, which was enacted on the recommendation of the Royal Commission on Local Government, First Interim Report (1925).

Private Bills originate, therefore, with outside interests, especially local authorities and other statutory undertakers, and a special procedure is prescribed. The procedure cannot be avoided by securing a private member to introduce a public Bill; for if such a Bill deals with private interests it will be objected to on that ground. In considering the enactment of private Bills Parliament recognises that they are for the benefit of outside interests, that other interests may be affected, and that Parliament must hold the balance evenly between the private interests. Accordingly, detailed rules are laid down by Standing Orders in each House and, except on the floor of the House, a special procedure is followed.

Private Bills in some respects follow a procedure older than that used for public Bills. Individual petitions for the redress of grievances were submitted to the King in Parliament before the common petition, or petition 'pur toute la commune', became usual, and long before it became the practice to put such petitions in the form of an Act. It is still necessary for private Bills to be originated by petitions deposited by the promoters in the Private Bill Office. Exceptional cases apart, the opportunity arises once a year only, for every step in the procedure before the first reading is determined by Standing Orders. The pivotal dates for this purpose are 27 November, the last date for the deposit of the petition and the Bill,[1] and 30 January, the last day for the presentation of petitions against the Bill.[2] These dates give both Houses the time to consider all Bills presented before the Houses rise or the session ends in July.

It is assumed that the Bill will seek powers or privileges to which other people will object. All the preliminary procedure is therefore directed to securing that persons likely to object receive adequate notice and are given the opportunity to petition against the Bill or any part of it. In the case of local authorities' Bills there is even an earlier stage directed to securing that the electors have adequate notice of the intention to promote and, in the case of Bills promoted by borough and urban district councils, have actually consented to it at a town's meeting or on a poll.[3] The absurdity of trying to hold a meeting of all local

---

[1] S.O. (C.) 38; S.O. (L.) 38.
[2] S.O. (C.) 129; but it is 6 February in the case of House of Lords Bills: S.O. (L.) 101.
[3] Local Government Act, 1933, ss. 254 and 255 and 9th Schedule.

government electors in a city like Birmingham and the cost involved in meetings and polls have often been pointed out,[1] but they remain part of the law; and not infrequently the proposals of a borough council are defeated at this stage.[2]

In respect of all Bills notice of the intention to promote must be given by newspaper advertisements and Gazette notices, and individual notices must be given to owners, lessees and occupiers of lands and houses affected by the proposals.[3] The result is that all interested parties have, or ought to have, notice of the intention, and knowledge that they may be affected. Plans, sections, maps and other documents have to be deposited with the clerks of county councils and town clerks in the area covered and in the Private Bill Office. In some cases documents have also to be deposited with the appropriate Government departments, conservancy boards, catchment boards, and local authorities. Finally, the petition and the Bill itself must be deposited in the Private Bill Office, where they are open to inspection. Printed copies must also be left at the Vote Office of the House of Commons for the use of members, the Office of the Clerk of Parliaments and at the appropriate Government departments.[4] Thus the whole world, so to speak, knows whether it is to be affected and makes its plans accordingly. In fact, however, the whole world cannot bother to read advertisements and examine Bills, and in practice groups of interests have Bills watched on their behalf by parliamentary agents. Nearly every collective organisation, including such bodies as the Federation of British Industries, the associations of local authorities, and associations of employees, pays fees to have its interests watched.

It is necessary for Parliament to ascertain that all the preliminary steps required by Standing Orders have been complied with. For this purpose there are Examiners appointed by Mr Speaker and by the House

---

[1] Royal Commission on Local Government, 1923–9, Final Report (Cmd. 3436), pp. 50–6; Local Government and Public Health Consolidation Committee, 1933, 1st Report (Cmd. 4272), p. 60.

[2] Interests sometimes organise opposition for this purpose. Cf. the opposition organised by the National Farmers' Union against proposals for compulsory pasteurisation of milk: 1st ed., p. 219.

[3] S.O. (C.) 4–25; S.O. (L.) 4–23.

[4] S.O. (C.) 26–44; S.O. (L.) 26–44. Certain other requirements have to be satisfied in some cases; see S.O. (C.) 45–7; S.O. (L.) 45–7.

of Lords.[1] Two Examiners, one in respect of each House, begin to examine all petitions on 18 December.[2] Notice of the examination is given to the promoters, who must appear, otherwise the petition will be struck out. The promotion and opposition is in fact carried out by members of a specialised profession, that of parliamentary agents, who appear at the examination. Seeing that the provisions of some seventy-five Standing Orders have to be satisfied, the examination is by no means cursory. But, unless the Examiners certify that Standing Orders have been complied with, the Bill cannot proceed without an order of the appropriate House. Any person may send in memorials complaining that Standing Orders have not been complied with, and may appear in person or by agent and produce witnesses.[3] Memorials are, however, becoming increasingly rare, and proceedings before the Examiners usually consist of the handing in of affidavits by the promoters' agents, and personal evidence as to other facts by those responsible for the preparation of Bills, notices, etc.[4]

The Examiners have identical powers conferred upon them by both Houses, and report to both Houses. If their report is favourable, the chairman of Ways and Means (or Counsel to Mr Speaker) in conference with the Lord Chairman of Committees (or his Counsel) decides on or before 8 January in which House the respective Bills shall first be introduced.[5] Henceforth a Bill allocated to the House of Commons is under the control of the chairman of Ways and Means. Petitions against the Bills will already have been presented, since they are required on or before 30 January.[6] But permission to oppose is not granted to everyone: a person has no right to be heard unless he has a *locus standi*. 'Generally speaking, it may be said that petitioners whose property or interests are proved to be directly and specially affected by the Bill have a *locus standi*.'[7] This is a generalisation of a mass of precedents formulated, until 1864, by the committees which examined private Bills. In 1864 special courts were established to deal with objections in the House of Commons on the ground of *locus standi*. The chairman of Ways and

---

[1] S.O. (C.) 9; S.O. (L.) 69.   [2] S.O. (C.) 70; S.O. (L.) 70.
[3] S.O. (C.) 75; S.O. (L.) 76.   [4] H.C. 158 of 1930, p. 48.
[5] S.O. (C.) 87; S.O. (L.) 91.   [6] S.O. (C.) 129; S.O. (L.) 101.
[7] May, p. 888.

Means, the deputy chairman, Counsel to Mr Speaker, and not less than seven members of the House are 'Referees of the House on Private Bills'. They sit in one or more courts, and three at least are required to form each court; and the courts determine the right to be heard.[1]

When the Examiner reports that Standing Orders have been complied with the Bill is presented by being laid on the Table of the appropriate House and is deemed to be read a first time. If the Examiner reports that any Standing Order has not been complied with, his report is referred to the Standing Orders Committee. This consists in the Commons of the chairman of Ways and Means, the deputy chairman, and not less than two members selected from time to time by the chairman from a panel appointed by the Committee of Selection. In the Lords it consists of the chairman of Committees and forty lords, though the quorum is three.[2] The Committees interpret the Standing Orders when a special report for that purpose is made by the Examiner, and also they report in any case whether compliance with the Standing Orders can be dispensed with.[3] Between the first and second reading the Bill is examined in the Private Bill Office as to its conformity with the rules and Standing Orders of the House.[4]

The second reading is the first opportunity given to the House itself to discuss the general principles of a Bill. In the House of Commons the order for second reading is put down by the chairman of Ways and Means and is taken as unopposed private business before questions. If, however, the Bill is opposed and continues to be opposed, it is set down for second reading at 7 p.m. on an evening selected by the chairman and a debate takes place, thus interrupting public business. Until comparatively recently, private Bills were opposed only when some outside opponent drew the attention of a member to provisions which the opponent regarded as objectionable. This is still the most fruitful source of opposition; and one of the reasons for the practice whereby economic and other interests secure representatives in the House of Commons is the desire to oppose private Bills. For instance, many local authorities have sought powers for regulating or restricting posters more strictly than is possible under the general law. The British Advertising Associa-

---

[1] S.O. (C.) 89–91.

[2] S.O. (C.) 103; S.O. (L.) 84, 85.

[3] S.O. (C.) 104–8; S.O. (L.) 87–9.

[4] S.O. (C.) 197.

tion with the assistance of the Federation of British Industries has 'briefed' a member to oppose—though of course the member opposes in what he considers to be the public interest and receives no payment, which would in any event be a gross breach of privilege.[1] Occasionally, however, another kind of opposition has developed. A few members have obtained from the Vote Office copies of all private Bills and have opposed those which they regard as 'socialistic'. Also there is a tendency to oppose private Bills for reasons which are really irrelevant. Thus, a London Passenger Transport Board Bill was opposed in 1938 because the Board did not give sufficient encouragement to its employees to join the Territorial Army.[2] In the result, while most Bills go through the House itself without opposition, a few are obstructed every year, and time has to be found for debate. The opposition may take the form either of moving that the Bill be read a second time six months hence (which, if carried, is equivalent to a direct negative), or of moving instructions to the committee to delete certain provisions or to insert certain limitations, conditions or qualifications.[3]

2. COMMITTEES

The Committee stage is the most important stage of the Bill. It is there that the case for conferring the powers and privileges has to be made out, and it is there that the contest between promoters and opposers has to be fought out with all the paraphernalia of a court of law. The parties are represented by counsel, and witnesses are examined and cross-examined. There is, however, the important difference that the Government departments affected—which have already received and studied copies of the Bill—will give their views on the desirability or otherwise of the powers sought. This stage may therefore become dilatory and expensive. Accordingly, the promoters do their best to meet opposition

---

[1] The West Yorkshire Gas Distribution Bill, 1938, was opposed on behalf of local authorities; *The Times*, 8 July 1938.

[2] *The Times*, 9 March 1938.

[3] In certain cases the Bill, after second reading, has to be referred again to the Examiner to ascertain that certain Standing Orders have been complied with. In other cases the Bill stands referred to the Committee of Selection in the House of Commons or, in the House of Lords, to the Committee of Selection if opposed and the Lord Chairman of Committees if unopposed.

beforehand by undertaking to insert protective clauses, to qualify the powers sought, and generally to reach a compromise. From the moment when the Bill is deposited they will be in consultation with the prospective opponents, the Government departments affected, and the chairman of Ways and Means. The first will inform them what changes will induce them to withdraw their opposition; the second will explain what amendments are required to secure their support; and the chairman will advise about the practice followed by committees in the conferment of new powers.

Thus, the period between the deposit of the Bill and its consideration in committee is really of supreme importance. Amendments will be proposed to meet all criticisms that are not based on the principles of the Bill or any of its clauses. Such amendments will be incorporated in the 'filled-up' Bill which is deposited in the Committee and Private Bill Office, and copies of such amendments must be supplied to those opponents who ask for them.[1] They usually succeed in meeting most of the criticisms put forward by opponents. Protective clauses cover the interests of parties affected, and modifications are made in response to criticisms of Government departments. In the result, whereas only about six per cent of House of Commons Bills are unopposed in the first instance, about fifty per cent of them are unopposed by the time that they reach the committees.[2] One of the Bills eventually unopposed in both Houses in 1927 had twenty petitions against it on its deposit.[3] These figures provide 'a striking measure of the amount of progress that can be made towards settlement by private negotiations before the Bill is actually brought into Committee'.[4]

In the Commons the Bills stand referred after second reading to the Committee of Selection.[5] This committee, consisting of eleven members, allocates the Bills, either singly or in groups, to the appropriate committees. A Bill is regarded as opposed if a petition is presented against it in which the petitioner or petitioners have prayed to be heard, or if the chairman of Ways and Means reports to the House that in his opinion it ought to be treated as opposed.[6] Every such Bill is referred

---

[1] May, p. 733.
[2] H.C. 158 of 1930, p. 13. See also Appendix VI, Tables I and II.
[3] *Ibid.*   [4] *Ibid.*
[5] S.O. (C.) 109.   [6] S.O. (C.) 111 (2).

by the Committee of Selection to a chairman and three members 'not locally or otherwise interested therein'.[1] Every unopposed Bill is referred to the Committee on Unopposed Bills, which consists of the chairman of Ways and Means (who is chairman *ex officio* of the Committee), the Deputy Chairman, and three members from time to time selected by the chairman of Ways and Means from a panel appointed by the Committee of Selection at the commencement of every session. This Committee has the assistance of Counsel to Mr Speaker.[2]

The function of an Opposed Bill Group or of the Committee on Unopposed Bills is to determine whether it is in the public interest that a Bill should pass and if so in what form it should pass. There is thus a preliminary question, whether the Bill ought to be passed at all. The House itself has determined, by reading it a second time, that there is at least a case for examination; but the Committee may decide, on its own motion, or on account of an adverse report from a Government department, or (in the case of an opposed Bill) on the petition or oral argument of an opponent, that the Bill as a whole ought not to pass. It does this by finding the preamble not proven. But if it finds the preamble proved, it may still decide that particular provisions should be deleted or modified or protective clauses inserted. In the case of an opposed Bill, this involves argument by counsel and, probably, the examination of witnesses. Thus an Opposed Bill Group looks very like a court of law, though the arguments tend not towards the determination of the application of law to facts but towards a proof that certain changes in the law are desirable or undesirable. Hence the requirement that each member of the Committee shall declare:

That my constituents have no local interest, and that I have no personal interest, in any Bill included in the said Group, and that, in the event of any Bill being added to the said Group in which my constituents or I have any such interest, I will disclose the fact; and that I will never vote on any question which may arise without having duly heard and attended to the evidence relating thereto.[3]

For many years special provision was made for legislation conferring local government powers. Local legislation has been the great laboratory of local government law, and there is scarcely a function exercised

[1] S.O. (C.) 119.   [2] S.O. (C.) 132 (1).   [3] S.O. (C.) 120.

462

by local authorities under general legislation which is not the generalisation of some special power originally conferred by local Act. In some places the town council sought powers even before 1835 to effect 'improvements' in their towns. In others, citizens banded themselves together to approach Parliament with a view to their incorporation and the conferment upon them of special powers. Incorporated guardians of the poor were in existence before the Poor Law Amendment Act of 1834. A 'watch' was often provided before the Municipal Corporations Act of 1835. Highway boards existed before the Highway Act, 1835. Above all, nearly all public health powers, such as those dealing with paving, lighting, sewering, refuse collection, and water supply, were based originally on local Act provisions.[1] Even when the general public health statutes began in 1848 the general law lagged behind the special laws of the more progressive authorities. A large number of the powers set out in the Public Health Act, 1875, were mere generalisations of local Act powers; and the amendments in the Public Health Acts of 1890, 1907, 1925 and 1936 were derived almost entirely from local experience.[2]

The extent to which other powers had become usual even before the Public Health Act, 1848, is shown by the numerous provisions of the Clauses Acts of 1845 and 1847.[3] These Acts, running in the aggregate

---

[1] See S. and B. Webb, *Statutory Authorities.*

[2] 'The Public Health Acts of 1890, 1907 and 1925, which comprise in all 234 sections, are derived from, and based on, local Act clauses. Their diversity of origin shows itself unmistakably in discrepancies of language not only between the different Acts but between different sections of the same Act. It is perhaps less generally recognised that the great Public Health Act of 1875 is itself a consolidation of a large number of different and overlapping Acts.... Moreover, the parent Act of 1848 was largely based on clauses which had become more or less stereotyped in local Acts in the early part of the nineteenth century.' Local Government and Public Health Consolidation Committee, Second Interim Report, 1936, Cmd. 5059, p. 11. For an example in which the sins of the fathers were visited on the children, see Jennings, 'Judicial Process at its Worst', *Modern Law Review,* I, pp. 111–31.

[3] The following are the 'Clauses Acts': the Companies Clauses Consolidation Act, 1845; the Companies Clauses Consolidation (Scotland) Act, 1845; the Lands Clauses Consolidation Act, 1845; the Lands Clauses Consolidation (Scotland) Act, 1845; the Railways Clauses Consolidation Act, 1845; the Railways Clauses Consolidation (Scotland) Act, 1845; the Markets and Fairs Clauses Act, 1847; the Gasworks Clauses Act, 1847; the Commissioners Clauses Act, 1847; the Waterworks Clauses Act, 1847; the Harbours, Docks, and Piers Clauses Act, 1847; the Towns Improvement Clauses Act, 1847; the Cemeteries Clauses Act, 1847; the Town Police Clauses Act, 1847. A few later Acts have been passed.

to many hundreds of sections, are applicable only when incorporated by reference in other statutes. Being in a form already approved by Parliament, it was necessary only to prove that they were needed and such need being proved it was unnecessary to argue about their details. Thus they saved some of the expense of promotion, and were readily granted once a reasonable case had been made out. Some of them, it is true, related to other aspects of economic development than those of local government—the incorporation of companies, the making of railways, the supply of gas and water—but for the most part they contain provisions made necessary by the rapid development of local government, especially after 1834.

Though the enactment of general legislation, especially after the formation of the Local Government Board in 1871, made application to Parliament less necessary, the flood of local legislation has never seriously abated. New powers such as those relating to housing, town and country planning, the regulation of advertisements, and the restriction of ribbon development, were largely founded on local experiments. Often it is possible to trace a particular provision to its source in some interesting and valuable experiment. Moreover, a successful experiment receives the compliment of imitation before it is adopted into the general law. Particular provisions are known as 'Birmingham clauses' or 'Surrey clauses'. When Parliament has granted a new power its action forms a precedent; and if there is something in the idea it is adopted by others. A select committee in 1936 'passed in review some 200 clauses which are of frequent occurrence in local legislation Bills'.[1]

Sometimes the grant of new administrative powers is opposed. For instance, the British Poster Advertising Association, assisted by the Federation of British Industries, has consistently opposed extension of control over advertisements. Generally speaking, however, new local government powers do not affect industrial or commercial interests, and the question for Parliament is whether they are intrinsically desirable. It was formerly thought that this question should be determined by a special and more or less expert committee. In the session of 1882 all

[1] Report of the Committee on Common Form Clauses in Private Bills, H.C. 162 of 1936, p. 2. Of the 173 'common form' clauses specifically referred to, none is earlier than 1926, though no doubt some were based on earlier precedents.

private Bills promoted by local authorities and relating to police or sanitary regulations were referred by order of the House to a select committee specially constituted by the Committee of Selection; and, except in 1901 and 1902, this Police and Sanitary Committee was re-appointed annually from 1886 to 1908. In 1909 the reference was extended so as to include all Bills promoted by local authorities by which it was proposed to create powers relating to police, sanitary or other local government regulations in conflict with, deviation from, or excess of the provisions of the general law; the Committee was then known as the Local Legislation Committee, and it was reappointed annually until 1930.[1]

The Committee consisted of fifteen members who gradually acquired a very wide experience of the development of local government problems and were able to 'settle' clauses which became precedents not only for subsequent local legislation but also for the general law. The Public Health Acts of 1890, 1907 and 1925, and many of the amendments made in the Public Health Act, 1936, were founded upon their decisions. The rapid urbanisation of the country, the general acceptance of the principle of public regulation of social and economic life, the growing efficiency of local government after the great reforms of 1875, 1888 and 1894, altered the balance of private Bill legislation. The grant of public utility or monopoly powers and the conferment of local government powers became the essential purposes of local Acts. The former has always been the more important; but between 1919 and 1929 the Local Legislation Committee considered twenty per cent of all private Bills.[2] These were not necessarily composed wholly, or even mainly, of local government clauses. The eighteen local legislation Bills promoted in 1927 contained on the average only twenty-nine per cent local legislation clauses, and only one Bill contained as many as fifty per cent.[3]

The Committee was authorised to divide into two sections, but with the growth of local legislation it became a bottleneck. Local legislation Bills were delayed, were more expensive than other Bills, and often, at the end of a session, were inadequately considered. The Ministry of

[1] May (13th ed.), p. 731.　　[2] H.C. 158 of 1930, p. 40.
[3] *Ibid.*; and see Appendix VI, Table III.

Health and the local authorities' associations (except the Urban District Councils' Association) were nevertheless in favour of its continuance. Indeed, the Ministry of Health considered that all local authorities' Bills should be sent to the Committee. This would have required a considerable addition to its personnel; and the Select Committee of 1930 doubted whether enough members could be found to do the work.[1] The Committee therefore recommended that the Local Legislation Committee should not be reappointed, and that all Bills should go to the Opposed Bill Groups or the Unopposed Bill Committee; and this recommendation was carried out in the session of 1931.

The result was that there was no longer any body of members expert in matters of local legislation. The increase in the work of the Unopposed Bill Committee made impossible that detailed consideration of new proposals which is necessary if local legislation is to develop along sound and uniform lines. In the Opposed Bill Groups the local legislation clauses were usually unopposed, so that attention was directed primarily to the opposed clauses and insufficient examination made of the local legislation clauses. Above all, the advantage of uniformity had been altogether lost. To some extent the difficulty was overcome in 1936 when a special select committee was set up to consider recent 'common form clauses'.[2] This committee divided 173 clauses into five groups; the first contained sixty-eight clauses which could normally be accepted without special proof; the second contained thirty-eight clauses which could similarly be accepted, but subject to amendments set out in detail; the third contained twenty-five clauses which should not be accepted without proof of local needs; the fourth contained nine clauses which should not be allowed, except in very special circumstances; and the last contained thirty-three clauses which would become, and have now become, unnecessary when the Public Health Act, 1936, came into operation. These clauses were subsequently published as Standard

---

[1] H.C. 158 of 1930, p. 42. It may be pointed out that this difficulty would be overcome if the Committee were charged not only with local legislation but also with all questions relating to local government, whether raised on private Bills, public Bills, or administration. For then it would perform a function of great public importance, the examination of the relations between Parliament and the local authorities.

[2] Report of the Committee on Common Form Clauses in Private Bills, H.C. 162 of 1936.

Clauses, a revised edition being issued as the result of a session's experience in 1937.

We thus have a new device not essentially dissimilar from a 'Clauses Act'. It is true that provisions of a Clauses Act are incorporated simply by reference, while the Standard Clauses are specifically set out, but the result is not very different. The Standard Clauses are for the most part closely followed by promoters who seek special powers in the matters covered by them. 'Generally, the House of Commons refused to accept departures from the standard forms unless satisfactory reasons for the proposals were forthcoming. Clauses which the Committee regarded as requiring evidence of local need were in each case reviewed in the light of the evidence put forward, and in the result about one-quarter of these clauses were not allowed by Parliament.'[1]

The number of local legislation clauses was reduced through the efforts of the Local Government and Public Health Consolidation Committee. That Committee had by 1938 produced three draft Bills which had been enacted by Parliament as the Local Government Act, 1933, the Public Health Act, 1936, and the Food and Drugs Act, 1938. Part of the work contemplated by its terms of reference was handed over to a new committee set up, at the suggestion of the Local Government and Public Health Consolidation Committee, to deal with the law of highways and streets; but the rest of public health law remained within the jurisdiction of the Committee. It was expected that there would be three more Acts of the kind already passed but these efforts necessarily came to an end in 1939.

The effect of modernising the public health law, in the matters covered by the Act of 1936, has already been reflected in local legislation. The first, and obvious, effect has been to render unnecessary many provisions which hitherto had had to be specially obtained in private Bills—these being provisions which are now covered by the new Act. But the effect has been wider than this; the recent review and recasting of much of the public health law has had the effect of reducing any local feeling that there were defects in the general law requiring local redress and so of limiting the demand for further provision on subjects falling within that review. The advantages of adherence to a single code of procedure in public health matters have also been

[1] Nineteenth Annual Report of the Ministry of Health, 1937–8 (Cmd. 5801), pp. 140–1.

recognised, and the Bills have tended to make use of definitions and provisions governing procedure which are contained in the new Act.[1]

In spite of these changes, there was still some criticism of the results attendant upon the abolition of the Local Legislation Committee. In 1937, therefore, another select committee was set up to examine anew the question of local legislation clauses.[2] The Ministry of Health and the Home Office were again insistent that greater uniformity was desirable, especially with opposed Bills. The Opposed Bill Groups are not entirely without guidance, since the appropriate department makes a report to the Committee; and often negotiations proceed with the promoters after deposit in order to meet criticisms before the Bill goes to committee;[3] but it was made clear in evidence that the position was not entirely satisfactory,[4] and the Select Committee agreed that 'there was a greater lack of uniformity in regard to local legislation clauses than the application of the Standard Clauses would obviate or than differences in local needs demanded'.[5] The change proposed was that opposed local legislation clauses should continue to go to the Opposed Bill Groups, but that unopposed local legislation Bills and clauses should go to special groups. The Committee of Selection should appoint a chairman and nominate a panel of members, four members of that panel sitting with the chairman to consider Bills and portions of Bills referred to them. Bills containing local legislation clauses should be divided by the chairman of Ways and Means at his discretion, and the group would have power to hear counsel in exceptional circumstances. This proposal was not adopted in the session 1937–8, but a new Sessional Order was adopted by the House under which each of the Opposed Bill Groups,

[1] *Ibid.* p. 142.

[2] Report from the Select Committee on Private Bill Procedure (Local Legislation Clauses), H.C. 112 of 1937.

[3] In 1937–8 the Minister of Health made reports on twenty-three of the forty-six Bills promoted by local authorities and other authorities connected with the Ministry. 'The number of reports would have been much greater but for the success of negotiations with the Agents for the Bills. These negotiations not only reduce the scope of the Minister's reports to Parliament but also result in a reduction of the time required for the Committee stage, so reducing both the pressure upon the members and the labour and expenditure of the promoters': Nineteenth Annual Report of the Ministry of Health, 1937–8 (Cmd. 5801), p. 142.

[4] H.C. 112 of 1937, pp. 57–67.

[5] *Ibid.* p. iv.

though continuing to deal with all unopposed clauses in the Bills before them, has the assistance and advice of Counsel to Mr Speaker when local legislation clauses are involved.[1]

Further, Standing Order 156 provides in the Commons that in the case of a Bill promoted by, or proposing to transfer powers on, a local authority, the Committee on the Bill shall consider the clauses of the Bill with reference to the following matters:

(*a*) whether the Bill gives powers relating to police, sanitary or other local government regulations in conflict with, deviation from, or excess of, the provisions or powers of the general law;

(*b*) whether the Bill gives powers which may be obtained by means of bye-laws made subject to the restrictions of Public General Acts already existing;

(*c*) whether the Bill assigns a period for repayment of any loan or for the redemption of any charge or debt under the Bill exceeding the term of sixty years, or any period disproportionate to the duration of the works to be executed, or other objects of the loan, charge or debt; and

(*d*) whether the Bill gives borrowing powers for purposes for which such powers already exist, or may be obtained under any Public General Acts, without subjecting the exercise of the powers under the Bill to the consent of a Government department.

The Committee is instructed to report to the House:

(i) In what manner any clauses relating to the above matters have been dealt with by the Committee, and in particular whether a period for the repayment of any loan or for the redemption of any charge or debt under the Bill exceeding the term of sixty years has been allowed and the reasons therefor; and

(ii) whether any report from any Government department has been referred to the Committee; and, if so, in what manner the recommendations (if any) in that report have been dealt with by the Committee; and

(iii) any other circumstances of which, in the opinion of the Committee, it is desirable that the House should be informed.

The House of Lords appears not to have felt any such difficulty, perhaps because the greater leisure of the peers enables them to consider private Bills more at length. Opposed Bills are referred each to a select committee of five lords appointed by the Committee of Selection.[2]

[1] Nineteenth Annual Report of the Ministry of Health, 1937–8 (Cmd. 5801), p. 141.
[2] S.O. (L.) 111–12.

Unopposed Bills are referred to the Lord Chairman, who may either direct that they be treated as opposed (and so referred to a select committee), or deal with them in his own committee. It should be remembered that the Lord Chairman has not to sit in the House itself for long hours, and is thus able to devote more time to private Bills. The House takes its full share of local legislation, and if it were abolished some arrangements would have to be made to meet the extra pressure upon the House of Commons.[1]

There is nothing to prevent opposition in both Houses. But the purpose of the committee stage of an opposed Bill is as much to find an equitable arrangement between promoters and opposers as to safeguard the public interest. Consequently, the proportion of Bills opposed in both Houses is comparatively small. No figures are available as to the number of Commons' Bills which are subsequently unopposed in the Lords; but between 1919 and 1929 only fifty of the 506 Lords' Bills were opposed in the Commons.[2] A sample of fifty-three Bills taken in 1927 showed that ten Bills were eventually opposed in one House only, and eleven were opposed in both Houses.[3] These figures do not quite lead to the conclusion formulated by the Select Committee of 1930 that 'in the main opponents are satisfied with the treatment they receive... from...committees in the first House, and do not usually need to incur further expenses, to both sides, by fighting again in the second House';[4] but they do show that the committee stage in one House substantially reduces the number of opposed Bills in the second House. Also, approval by the one House usually leads to approval by the other. Of 481 Commons' Bills, forty-five were withdrawn or rejected in the Commons and only one in the Lords; while of 506 Lords' Bills, forty-four were withdrawn or rejected in the Lords and only five in the Commons.[5]

Private Bills are not passed without cost to the promoters nor are they opposed without expense to the petitioners. The long and detailed initial proceedings, the fees payable to the two Houses, the expenses of Parliamentary agents, the printing of Bills and amendments, the ex-

---

[1] See *ante*, pp. 448–9.
[2] See Appendix VI, Table I.
[3] H.C. 158 of 1930, p. 13.
[4] *Ibid.* p. 14.
[5] See Appendix VI, Table I.

penses of witnesses, and (where necessary) the fees of counsel, make promotion an expensive luxury. A Bill which is strenuously contested in both Houses, such as a Bill to create a new county borough, may cost anything up to £30,000.[1] An analysis of fifty-five Bills in 1927 showed that twenty-two unopposed Bills cost on the average £1587 each; that seven unopposed local legislation Bills cost on the average £3167 each; that ten Bills opposed in only one House cost on the average £4452 each; and that eleven Bills opposed in both Houses cost on the average £7448 each. Averages in such cases are apt to be misleading. Of the unopposed Bills ten cost less than £1000 each, while two cost over £4000 each. No local legislation Bill cost less than £1000 and no opposed Bill cost less than £2000. On the other hand, one Bill opposed in only one House cost over £8000; and one Bill opposed in both Houses cost over £16,000.[2]

In the case of an unopposed Bill, about forty-six per cent of the cost goes in legal and professional charges, about twenty-one per cent in House fees, about twenty-five per cent in advertising and printing, and the remainder in miscellaneous expenses. With other Bills there is a sharp fall in the proportion (though not, of course, in the amount) of House fees, but there are substantial increases in legal charges (especially for counsel) and in railway fares and expenses.[3]

Of the report stage and third reading little need be said. In the House of Commons the Bill is ordered to lie upon the Table if it is amended in committee or if the committee report that the allegations contained in the preamble have not been proved or that the parties providing the Bill have stated that it is not their intention to proceed with it. If, however, the Bill is approved without amendment it is ordered to be read a third time.[4] An amended Bill has to be printed and copies delivered to the Private Bill Office for the use of members, so that amendments may be moved in the House; in fact, however, this stage

---

[1] See Royal Commission on Local Government, Minutes of Evidence, I, pp. 186–90. The Middlesbrough and Stockton Extension, 1913, which was by Provisional Order, cost £26,275. The cost of the Birmingham Extension, 1910–11, is stated to have been over £32,200. It is believed that the total costs incurred in respect of the Leeds, Bradford and Sheffield proposals, 1920–1, exceeded £100,000.

[2] See Appendix VI, Table IV.   [3] See Appendix VI, Table V.

[4] S.O. (C.) 178.

is a pure formality. In nearly all cases, too, a Bill is read a third time without debate. All Bills are reported in the House of Lords, but again this is a formality. In neither House may amendments be moved (though this is limited to amendments proposed by the promoters in the House of Commons) unless they have been submitted to the chairman of Ways and Means or the Chairman of Committees, as the case may be.[1]

[1] S.O. (C.) 182–3; S.O. (L.) 148.

CHAPTER XIV

DELEGATED LEGISLATION

I. METHODS OF DELEGATION

Suspicion of governmental powers was a characteristic of the Constitution from the opening of the seventeenth century until the close of the nineteenth; and even with a Government which owes its authority only to a majority in Parliament, based on a free demonstration of public opinion, it has not wholly disappeared. If the King could legislate and tax otherwise than in Parliament he could govern without Parliament, and it was therefore a cardinal doctrine of the Parliamentary party that the King had no such powers. It was asserted by Coke with his usual force in his statement in 1605 that 'the law of the realm cannot be changed but in Parliament'[1] and by the opinion in the *Case of Proclamations*[2] that the King could not by his proclamation alter the law or create new offences. The Petition of Grievances in 1610 had already insisted on 'the indubitable right of the people of this kingdom not to be made subject to any punishments that shall extend to their lives, lands, bodies, or goods, other than such as are ordained by the common laws of this land or the statutes made by their common consent in Parliament'.[3] Even the right to dispense with law 'as it hath been assumed and exercised of late' and the right to suspend a law were deemed illegal by the Bill of Rights; and the same instrument, not for the first time, denied the right to tax without consent of Parliament.

These principles became fundamental to the Constitution and have never since been denied. The conflicts of the seventeenth century, however, produced a principle no less important, though it was not expressed in statutory form. The fear of 'prerogative' extended even to a fear of statutory powers, and the experience of Cabinet government under George III did nothing to dissipate it. In the nineteenth century it joined with the general disapproval by the new Whigs of the Peelite

---

[1] Tanner, *English Constitutional Conflicts of the Seventeenth Century*, p. 36.
[2] (1610) 12 Co. Rep. 74; 2 St. Tr. 723.   [3] 2 St. Tr. 524–6.

and (early) Gladstonian school of all kinds of restriction to produce the conclusion that governmental power was inherently obnoxious. The Whigs' constitutional lawyer, A. V. Dicey, laid it down that the 'rule of law' which 'forms a fundamental principle of the Constitution, excludes the existence of arbitrariness, of prerogative, *or even of wide discretionary authority* on the part of the Government'.[1]

Yet English law has always tolerated some powers of legislation outside Parliament. The right of the Crown to legislate for conquered or ceded territories has always been regarded as subsisting, though it disappears when a local legislature is set up unless the right to legislate is reserved.[2] The right to act as the Crown pleases outside British territory and against foreigners follows from principles of the common law; and orders may be made so as to bind even British subjects in territories which are not part of the dominions of the Crown, such as protectorates, trust territories, and other places where the Crown has jurisdiction, in accordance with the Foreign Jurisdiction Act, 1890. The Crown may also legislate for settled colonies under the British Settlements Acts. The discipline of the Army is provided mainly by Queen's Rules and Regulations. The procedure of the courts is governed by Rules of Court. The Church Assembly passes its own measures subject to subsequent Parliamentary sanction.

These exceptions apart, neither Crown nor Government has received general powers of legislation. There is no power to issue regulations 'in execution of the laws' as there is in democratic countries which follow the French tradition. Such a power is necessarily restricted, since there must first be laws before regulations can be issued for their execution; with us there must be not only laws but also specific power to issue regulations. Numerous powers of this kind have been conferred; but express authority for their exercise must always be shown; and so powerful is the tradition that powers of law-making (except by courts) are inherently dangerous that protests are often raised even against the narrowly defined powers which are frequently conferred upon ministers.

Such express delegation of legislative powers is in fact very common.

---

[1] Dicey, *Law of the Constitution* (1st ed. 1885), p. 217; (9th ed. 1915), p. 198; cf. Jennings, *The Law and the Constitution* (4th ed.), pp. 41–60, 289–301.

[2] *Campbell* v. *Hall* (1774), 1 Cowp. 204.

Even before the Reform Act of 1832 Parliament conferred upon commissioners or other authorities power to make rules for special purposes.[1] Various factors have produced an increase both in the scope and the importance of delegated legislation.

It is convenient that rules of a local character or applying to a particular statutory monopoly should be made under authority conferred by Parliament rather than by Parliament itself. The burden of private Bill legislation has always been onerous, and much of the content of local legislation must depend upon a knowledge of local conditions which Parliament does not possess. Borough councils were given in 1835 power to make by-laws, with the consent of the Secretary of State, for the 'good rule and government' of their towns; and similar powers have been conferred upon other local authorities and for other purposes.[2] Similar powers were given also to railway companies, tramway companies, gas, water, and electricity companies, and other statutory undertakers. The modern 'scheme' system, whereby private rights are affected by clearance orders, town and country planning schemes, and the like, after confirmation by the Minister of Health, produces the same result. Except where a scheme or order has to be laid before both Houses, when Parliament has conferred the powers it no longer has any control, save such control as it inevitably exercises over any responsible minister.

Even in respect of provisions for new administrative organisation, or new powers, or the compulsory acquisition of land, Parliament has delegated some or all of the powers which would otherwise be exercised by control over private Bills. The Provisional Order system, which originated with the Public Health Act, 1848, and was extremely popular

---

[1] Committee on Ministers' Powers, 1932, Minutes of Evidence, p. 34 (Sir W. Graham-Harrison, K.C.B., K.C.). The following figures of Acts conferring legislative powers were given for selected years:

1819–20	10 Acts	1835	10 Acts
1825	20 Acts	1850	27 Acts
1831	12 Acts	1860	33 Acts
1832	14 Acts	1870	24 Acts
1833	24 Acts	1880	7 Acts
1834	14 Acts	1890	17 Acts

[2] See the list in Jennings, *The Law relating to Local Authorities*, pp. 320–1; and see the following statutes since enacted: Restriction of Ribbon Development Act, 1935; Housing Act, 1936; Public Health Act, 1936; Public Health (Drainage of Trade Premises) Act, 1937; National Parks and Access to the Countryside Act, 1949.

until 1919, results in a devolution to Government departments of control over the initial procedure for securing publicity and reducing opposition, and enables each House to dispense with a long committee
stage unless opposition continues after second reading.

Since 1919, however, there has been a tendency to replace Provisional
Orders, which need confirmation by Parliament and, if opposed, a com-
mittee stage similar to that on a private Bill, by simple orders, made by
a Government department, which require either a simplified procedure,
or a simple resolution in both Houses, or no action at all by Parliament.
A generalised procedure was formulated in the Statutory Orders
(Special Procedure) Act, 1945, and Chapter VIII of the Standing Orders
(Private Business).

Parliament has similarly delegated powers which avoid the necessity
of legislation by public Bill. The details of legal procedure have for long
been determined by rules of court made by the judges themselves.[1]
Articles of War, now called Queen's Rules and Regulations, have been
made by the Crown on statutory authority for the government and
discipline of the army since 1717.[2] Legislative powers were conferred
on the Commissioners of Customs and Excise during the late eighteenth
century.[3] Once the principles of legislation have been settled, the administrative and technical details can be determined without recourse to
Parliament. The 'spoils system' having died with 'Old Corruption'
and been superseded by an incorruptible civil service, whose numbers
are authorised every year by Parliament, administrative details are an
administrative matter; and Parliament has not the time, nor the knowledge, nor the inclination, to concern itself with technical details of no
great importance. Parliamentary Counsel, from Lord Thring in 1869
to the present day, have deliberately attempted, with encouragement
from ministers and no serious opposition, to leave such matters for
ministerial regulation or Orders in Council, now known generally,
under the Statutory Instruments Act, 1946, as 'statutory instruments'.[4]

---

[1] Cf. Committee on Ministers' Powers, Minutes of Evidence, 1932, p. 34.
[2] Report of the Committee on Ministers' Powers, Cmd. 4060, 1932, p. 11.
[3] *Ibid.*
[4] Lord Thring, *Practical Legislation* (1st ed.), p. 12; Ilbert, *Legislative Methods and
Forms*; Committee on Ministers' Powers, 1932, Minutes of Evidence, p. 33 (Sir W.
Graham-Harrison).

In many cases, indeed, Parliament has gone even further. The central poor law authority had power from 1834 to 1948 to determine the essential principles of poor relief; and it is an accident of history that some of the least important provisions of the poor law were in the Poor Law Act, 1930, and some of the most important in the Public Assistance Order and the Relief Regulation Order issued by the Minister of Health. The Defence of the Realm Acts, 1914–16, gave the Crown power to do almost anything for the prosecution of war except spend and tax; the Emergency Powers Act, 1920, gives wide, though temporary, powers for making laws for the protection of essential services during industrial disputes; the emergency legislation of 1931 enabled the Government to meet the economic crisis by exceptional measures; the Import Duties Act, 1932, gave the Treasury powers to alter the burden of some kinds of indirect taxation; and the Emergency Powers (Defence) Acts, 1939 to 1944, gave enormous wartime powers, not all of which have disappeared.[1]

Leaving aside these exceptional cases, it is clear that powers to make delegated legislation must grow in number as the scope of governmental powers increases through the development of 'collectivism'. Though, as has been said,[2] they were not unknown in the eighteenth century and not uncommon early in the nineteenth century, they have grown in number and importance with the development of the 'period of Collectivism' which is usually said to begin about 1870.[3] For the most part, the earlier developments were in the cognate fields of local government and public utilities, and much delegated legislation of a general character still regulates these services. Since 1906, however, the Central Government has been given many direct administrative functions, and there has consequently been an increase in the statutory instruments issued by departments to supplement the legislation applying to their own centrally administered services.

The practice of delegation is now inevitable. The Committee on Ministers' Powers, whose members had no particular bias towards collectivism, stated in 1932:

In truth whether good or bad the development of the practice is inevitable. It is a natural reflection, in the sphere of constitutional law, of changes in our

[1] Cf. Report of the Committee on Ministers' Powers, 1932, pp. 31–6.
[2] *Ante*, p. 475.   [3] Cf. Dicey, *Law and Opinion in England*, ch. VIII.

ideas of government which have resulted from changes in political, social and economic ideas, and of changes in the circumstances of our lives which have resulted from scientific discoveries.[1]

For this opinion they gave cogent and exhaustive reasons:

1. Pressure upon Parliamentary time is great. The more procedure and subordinate matters can be withdrawn from detailed Parliamentary discussion, the greater will be the time which Parliament can devote to the consideration of essential principles of legislation.

2. The subject matter of modern legislation is very often of a technical nature. Apart from the broad principles involved, technical matters are difficult to include in a Bill, since they cannot be effectively discussed in Parliament. . . .

3. If large and complex schemes of reform are to be given technical shape, it is difficult to work out the administrative machinery in time to insert in the Bill all the provisions required; it is impossible to foresee all the contingencies and local conditions for which provision must eventually be made. The National Health Insurance Regulations, and the Orders setting up Trade Boards, illustrate particularly well this aspect of the problem.

4. The practice, further, is valuable because it provides for a power of constant adaptation to unknown future conditions without the necessity of amending legislation. Flexibility is essential. The method of delegated legislation permits of the rapid utilisation of experience, and enables the results of consultation with interests affected by the operation of new Acts to be translated into practice. In matters, for example, like mechanical road transport, where technical development is rapid, and often unforeseen, delegation is essential to meet the new positions which arise.

5. The practice, again, permits of experiment being made and thus affords an opportunity, otherwise difficult to ensure, of utilising the lessons of experience. The advantage of this in matters, for instance, like town planning, is too obvious to require detailed emphasis.

6. In a modern State there are many occasions when there is a sudden need for legislative action. For many such needs delegated legislation is the only convenient or even possible remedy. No doubt, where there is time, on legislative issues of great magnitude, it is right that Parliament itself should either decide what the broad outlines of the legislation shall be, or at least indicate the general scope of the delegated powers which it considers are called for by the occasion. But emergency and urgency are matters of degree; and the type of need may be of greater or less national importance. It may

[1] Cmd. 4060, p. 5.

be not only prudent but vital for Parliament to arm the executive Government in advance with almost plenary power to meet occasions of emergency, which affect the whole nation—as in the extreme case of the Defence of the Realm Acts in the Great War, where the emergency had arisen; or in the less extreme case of the Emergency Powers Act, 1920, where the emergency had not arisen but power was conferred to meet emergencies that might arise in the future.... There is in truth no alternative means by which strong measures to meet great emergencies can be made possible; and for that reason the means is constitutional. But the measure of the need should be the measure alike of the power and of its limitation. It is of the essence of constitutional government that the normal control of Parliament should not be suspended either to a greater degree, or for a longer time, than the exigency demands.[1]

To these six reasons must be added a seventh, which may be expressed in the words of Sir William Graham-Harrison, First Parliamentary Counsel to the Treasury in 1930:

I should like also to emphasise a side of the question which appeals to me particularly as one who has drafted, not only a large number of Statutes, but also a very large number of Statutory Rules and Orders, viz., the superiority in form which, as a result of the different circumstances and conditions under which they are respectively prepared and completed, delegated legislation has over Statutes. In most cases the time available for drafting Bills is inadequate, and their final form when they have passed both Houses is generally unsatisfactory. On the other hand, Statutory Rules can be prepared in comparative leisure and their subject matter can be arranged in a logical and intelligible shape uncontrolled by the exigencies of Parliamentary procedure and the necessity for that compression which every Minister (however much in debate he may use the draftsman as a whipping-boy) invariably requires in the case of a Bill.[2]

2. PROVISIONAL ORDERS

Power to make Provisional Orders has been conferred upon most Government departments and, in a few cases, upon local authorities.[3] The system originated with the Public Health Act, 1848, and was continued and developed in the other Sanitary Acts which were consoli-

[1] Cmd. 4060, pp. 51-2.
[2] Committee on Ministers' Powers, Minutes of Evidence, p. 35.
[3] For the list of such powers, see May, pp. 991-3.

dated in the Public Health Act, 1875; but it has been extended to many fields of social control. The order is scheduled, either alone or with other orders of the same kind, to a Provisional Orders Confirmation Bill, which is introduced by the appropriate minister as a public Bill, but is subsequently treated much like a private Bill. Accordingly, the Standing Orders governing the introduction of a private Bill, with a few exceptions, do not apply. The preliminary procedure is in the hands of the minister, whose function it is to determine that there is adequate publicity and notification to interested parties, and who also determines whether there is a case to be laid before Parliament. The fact that there is power to ask for a provisional order does not prevent any authority or person from proceeding by private Bill; but the minister is generally able to compromise the claims of prospective opponents before the order is scheduled to a Bill, the proportion of opposed Bills is small, and the cost is generally less.

The exact procedure varies from statute to statute, but there is a general provision which is applied by many statutory provisions, and it will be convenient to take that provision as an example.

Section 285 of the Local Government Act, 1933, provides as follows:

(1) Where the Minister is authorised to make a provisional order under this Act, or under any enactment passed after the commencement of this Act, the following provisions shall have effect:

(a) before a provisional order is made, notice of the purport of the application therefor shall be given by the applicants by advertisement in the London Gazette and in one or more local newspapers circulating in the area to which the provisional order will relate;

(b) the Minister shall consider any objections to the application which may be made by any persons affected thereby, and shall, unless he considers that for special reasons an inquiry is unnecessary, cause a local inquiry to be held, of which notice shall be given in such a manner as the Minister may direct and at which all persons interested shall be permitted to attend and make objections;

(c) the Minister may submit the provisional order to Parliament for confirmation, and the order shall have no effect until it is confirmed by Parliament;

(d) if while the Bill for the confirmation of the order is pending in either House of Parliament a petition is presented against the order, the petitioner shall be allowed to appear before the Select Committee to which the Bill is referred, and oppose the order, as in the case of a private Bill;

(*e*) any Act confirming a provisional order may be repealed, altered or amended by a provisional order made by the Minister and confirmed by Parliament;

(*f*) at any time before submitting a provisional order to Parliament the Minister may revoke the order, either wholly or in part;

(*g*) the making of a provisional order shall be prima facie evidence that all the requirements of this Act in respect of proceedings required to be taken before the making of the order have been complied with. . . .

(2) The reasonable costs incurred by a local authority in promoting or opposing a provisional order, and of the inquiry preliminary thereto, or in supporting or opposing a Bill to confirm a provisional order, as sanctioned by the Minister, shall be deemed to be expenses properly incurred by the local authority interested or affected by the order, and shall be paid accordingly, and a local authority may borrow for the purpose of defraying such costs.

The public notification required under this provision is less than that required under the Standing Orders relating to private Bills. It is, in fact, less than that required under older provisions authorising the issue of provisional orders.[1] It is, however, adequate. Individuals likely to be affected acquire knowledge, directly or indirectly, through the local newspaper; and though the circulation of the *London Gazette* does not compete with that of the popular newspapers, it is read carefully by persons acting on behalf of large interests like the nationalised industries, other statutory undertakers, and local authorities. The local inquiry is held by an official of the ministry and is very like a court of law, though the official gives no decision and merely reports to the Minister. Accordingly, the provisional order procedure interposes an additional quasi-judicial hearing and may add to the cost.

The fact that, where procedure by provisional order is an alternative to procedure by private Bill, petitioners usually proceed by provisional order, shows that nevertheless there are advantages in that procedure.[2] The most obvious is that if the minister concerned refuses to make the order, the great expense of promoting a Bill is thereby avoided. It is

[1] E.g. Public Health Act, 1875, ss. 297 and 298, and Local Government Act, 1888, s. 87. The change was deliberately made: see Local Government and Public Health Consolidation Committee (First) Interim Report, Cmd. 4272, p. 100.

[2] Cf. the evidence of Mr I. G. Gibbon, on behalf of the Ministry of Health: Royal Commission on Local Government (1923), Minutes of Evidence, I, pp. 118–19.

true that, where a Bill is promoted, the minister generally gives an indication that he will be compelled to make an adverse report on it to the committee of the House, and so enables the promoters to withdraw the Bill. Expense will, however, already have been incurred; and in any case the promoters cannot always be certain that when the minister has not said that he will report adversely he will not in fact do so. Secondly, the local inquiry gives an opportunity for the promoters to be informed of the case for the opposers. In order to minimise the expense they will, as far as possible, meet objections. The inspector at the local inquiry or the officials of the ministry afterwards are often able to act as arbitrators, and to suggest a compromise which more or less satisfies both sides.[1] This is equally true where the principles of the order are disputed, for the scope of the controversy may be limited to the principles and incidental objections can be met.

Even in hotly contested cases there may be eliminated once and for all at this early stage a good deal of contentious matter which might otherwise be left to be fought out at much expense before one or both Committees of the Houses. In this connection, it should be noted that, if any part of a proposal is rejected by the Minister, the issue is settled as regards that part, and it cannot be raised again before committees.[2]

Finally, when the opponents have had their say and the minister has nevertheless made the order, they must realise that the chances of opposition in Parliament are not very great. Consequently, the number of Provisional Order Bills opposed in Parliament is very small, and the costs of the promoters consequently reduced.[3]

There are, also, public advantages, apart from advantages to the promoters and opposers, to be obtained. A parliamentary committee has to take decisions far from the locality where the decision will be put into effect. The Chairman of the Police and Sanitary Committee (the pre-

---

[1] '*Mr Pritchard*: You have had cases, have you not, where the whole matter has been settled to the satisfaction of everybody at the local inquiry? *Mr Gibbon*: Many cases have been of that kind': Royal Commission on Local Government (1923), Minutes of Evidence, I, p. 119.
[2] *Ibid*. p. 118 (Mr I. G. Gibbon).
[3] From 1905 to 1914, out of forty-four Orders for the extension of boundaries, only twenty-three were opposed in Parliament; of these twenty-three, only five were altered in respect of area, and only one (which was defeated on second reading) failed to pass: *ibid*. p. 119.

decessor of the Local Legislation Committee),[1] speaking in the House of Commons in 1893, quoted a case in which, after Parliament had fixed a boundary, he had visited the district and found the boundary to be such that 'no one visiting the locality could have approved it, after even a short and hasty inspection'. The Select Committee on a Bradford Bill in 1903 expressed the opinion that it would have been better if a local inquiry had been held and the corporation had proceeded by provisional order.[2] The inspector who holds the inquiry has experience of the kind of proposal which is being made. He is able to inform himself of the local circumstances and the conditions in which the proposal will have to be carried out, and thus to recommend not merely whether the proposal should be approved in principle, but also whether, and if so in what particulars, it should be modified.

It is nevertheless true that in hotly contested cases the local inquiry may add to the expense. It was for this reason that the Royal Commission on Local Government (1923) recommended that proposals for the creation of county boroughs—the most expensive of all proceedings in Parliament[3]—should always be made by private Bill; and this proposal was carried out by legislation in 1926.

In certain special cases the House of Commons requires a deposit of documents as for a private Bill.[4] In other respects, however, the House knows nothing of a provisional order until the Bill is introduced by the minister. Such Bills are set down on each day in a separate list immediately after private business, and are rarely opposed.[5] After the first reading they are referred to Examiners, who are instructed to report whether Standing Orders are complied with;[6] but as there are no Standing Orders, apart from the special cases just mentioned, this procedure is purely formal. Normally, therefore, the procedure on confirming Bills is purely formal until after second reading, when the Bill is referred to the Committee of Selection, and thenceforward the Standing Orders relating to private Bills apply.[7] If petitions have already been deposited the order is referred to an Opposed Bill Group; if not, it goes

---

[1] Quoted *ibid.*
[2] *Ibid.*
[3] See *ante*, p. 471.
[4] S.O. (C.) 212; S.O. (L.) 179.
[5] S.O. (C.) 218.
[6] S.O. (C.) 214; S.O. (L.) 181.
[7] S.O. (C.) 217; S.O. (L.) 184–5.

to the Committee on Unopposed Bills. Thus, a provisional order comes into the private Bill procedure after the second reading. Moreover, the precise dates fixed for private Bills do not apply, though no confirming Bill may be read a first time after 15 May.[1] The same principles apply to confirming Bills introduced in the House of Lords.

Power to make provisional orders is conferred upon ministers having jurisdiction in Scotland as well as on ministers having jurisdiction in England. There is, however, a general power conferred upon the Secretary of State for Scotland to make an order upon the petition of a public authority or person desiring to obtain parliamentary powers in regard to any matter affecting public or private interests in Scotland for which a private Bill could have been promoted before the power was conferred. This power was conferred originally by the Private Legislation Procedure (Scotland) Act, 1899, and is now to be found in the Private Legislation Procedure (Scotland) Act, 1936. The procedure is so unusual that it repays a little examination. The details are in part Standing Orders, but in the main in General Orders issued by the Lord Chairman of Committees and the chairman of Ways and Means acting jointly with the Secretary of State.[2]

The petition is presented to the Secretary of State, praying him to issue a provisional order in accordance with the terms of a draft order submitted to him, or with such modifications as may be necessary.[3] A printed copy of the draft order must be deposited in the office of the Clerk of Parliaments, in the Private Bill Office of the House of Commons, and at the Treasury and the offices of the Government departments.[4] Notices and deposits must be made in accordance with General Orders, which follow the lines of the Standing Orders applicable to private Bills. The Chairmen examine the draft order, and if they report that some or all of its provisions relate to matter outside Scotland to such an extent, or raise questions of public policy of such novelty and importance, that they ought to be dealt with by private Bill and not by provisional order, the Secretary of State must refuse to issue the order.[5] Thus, there is a check at the outset exercised on behalf of the House of

---

[1] S.O. (C.) 216; S.O. (L.) 182.
[2] Private Legislation Procedure (Scotland) Act, 1936, s. 15.
[3] *Ibid.* s. 1 (1).   [4] *Ibid.* s. 1 (2).   [5] *Ibid.* s. 2 (2).

Commons so as to prevent the power being abused. The notices already issued serve as notices for a private Bill, though notice must be given of the intention to proceed by private Bill, and such additional notices as may be required by Standing Orders must be served.[1] If, however, the Chairmen's report is not adverse, the order may proceed, though the Examiner—who is generally one of the examiners for private Bills—will ascertain whether General Orders have been complied with.

If there is opposition to the draft order, or if in any other case he thinks fit, the Secretary of State will direct an inquiry by commissioners.[2] These are chosen, if possible, from 'parliamentary panels' consisting of not more than fifteen peers chosen by the Lords' Committee of Selection and of not more than twenty-five members of Parliament chosen by the Commons' Committee of Selection.[3] The Chairmen choose two members from each panel; but if this is not possible—so the Act says, but what it means is, if two peers and two members of Parliament willing to act cannot be found—three of the commissioners or all of them may be chosen from one of the panels. If even this cannot be done, the requisite number of commissioners is made up by the Secretary of State from an 'extra-parliamentary panel' of twenty persons qualified 'by experience of affairs' nominated for periods of five years by the Chairmen acting jointly with the Secretary of State.[4] Evidence was given before the Select Committee on the Private Legislation Procedure (Wales) Bill in 1904[5]—which was instructed to consider the application of the Scottish Provisional Order system to other parts of the United Kingdom—that there was often difficulty in getting peers or members of the House of Commons to act as commissioners.[6] In the case of members of the House of Commons, attendance at the House requires so much time and attention, and constituencies require so much care, that reluctance to serve is natural, particularly because there is no publicity to be obtained from such service. It is understood, however, that it is usually possible to obtain peers willing to serve.

The commissioners sit in public in some appropriate place in

---

[1] *Ibid.* s. 2 (4). [2] *Ibid.* s. 3 (1).
[3] S.O. (L.) 190; S.O. (C.) 228.
[4] Private Legislation Procedure (Scotland) Act, 1936, ss. 4, 5.
[5] H.C. 243 of 1904. [6] *Ibid.* p. 2 (Lord Balfour of Burleigh).

Scotland. It was hoped that this place would be the locality from which the draft order originated. Evidence before the Select Committee of 1904, however, indicated that usually it was found more convenient to sit in Edinburgh or Glasgow. In consequence, not all the saving of expense contemplated had been effected. Nevertheless, the scheme provides a measure of devolution to Scotland, since the commissioners follow the procedure of a parliamentary committee. This, indeed, was the main intention, namely, 'to secure the greatest amount of devolution without impairing the real and effective control of Parliament'.[1] It was for this reason, also, that the Bill of 1904 was introduced, to give the same measure of devolution to Wales. The Committee advised against any such extension, and also reported that they did not consider that 'any widespread or matured desire exists in England for an extension thereto of the Scotch system'[2]—a remark which was no doubt correct because the number of persons in England who knew, or know now, about the Scottish system can be counted on the fingers of one hand.

Under the Scottish system, if there is no opposition to the order, or if opposition is withdrawn before an inquiry is ordered, the Secretary of State may make the order as prayed, or with such modifications as may be necessary having regard to the recommendations of the Chairmen and of the Treasury and other departments. If, however, modifications are made, printed copies must first be deposited at the office of the Clerk of Parliaments, the Private Bill Office of the House of Commons, and the Treasury and other departments, and a time allowed for recommendations. When the order is made, it is scheduled to a confirmation Bill, which is deemed to have passed through all its stages up to and including committee. Thus, it requires only report and third reading in each House.[3]

If there is opposition to the order and the opposition is not withdrawn, or if the opposition has been withdrawn after the inquiry, or if an inquiry has been held although there was no opposition, the action of the Secretary of State must depend on the report of the commissioners. If they report against the order, he must refuse to make it. If they report in favour, he may make the order, with or without such

[1] *Ibid.* p. 1 (Lord Balfour of Burleigh).   [2] H.C. 243 of 1904, p. v.
[3] Private Legislation Procedure (Scotland) Act, 1936, s. 7.

modifications as appear to be necessary having regard to the recommendations of the commissioners, the Chairmen, the Treasury, and the other departments. But if modifications are made, printed copies must be deposited as before.[1] The confirming Bill is then introduced; but if a petition be presented against an order, any member may, after the Bill has been read a second time, move that it be referred to a joint committee of both Houses. If the motion is carried, the joint committee acts like a committee on a private Bill. But if no such motion is moved and carried, the Bill is deemed to have passed the committee stage, and is ordered to be considered as if reported by a committee. The same steps may be taken in the second House.[2]

Thus, the Scottish provisional order system is primarily an attempt to secure a form of devolution. It is, at the same time, a method of saving some of the expense of a private Bill, since some part of that expense is the cost of bringing witnesses and officials to London.[3] It cannot add an additional inquiry to the procedure, and so add to the cost, as sometimes happens with an English provisional order; for there can be at most two committee stages—the inquiry and the joint committee stage—whereas an English order may be dealt with at a local inquiry and before committees of each House. In addition, the procedure may be somewhat shortened; for there is no second reading for an unopposed order, and no committee stage, apart from the inquiry by the commissioners, for an opposed order unless a motion for a joint committee is carried.

It is therefore obvious that the procedure cannot cost more than procedure by Bill and may cost less. The Select Committee of 1904 stated that some witnesses had agreed that there had been a saving of expense, especially for small opponents, while others said that there was a saving in small local matters, but not otherwise.[4] Actually, the evidence was rather more positive. While the English Parliamentary Bar, without giving particulars, was doubtful if there was any saving (though no doubt the Scottish Bar could reply that there must be saving if promoters and opposers had to pay the fees of Scottish counsel and not the

[1] *Ibid.* s. 8.
[2] Private Legislation Procedure (Scotland) Act, 1936, s. 9.
[3] See Appendix VI, Table V. [4] H.C. 243 of 1904, p. iii.

higher fees of English counsel), those who gave particulars were clear that there had been a saving. For instance, one witness compared the cost of a Glasgow Police Order with that of a Renfrew Harbour Order and Bill which he regarded as of much the same degree of complication; the former cost £579 and the latter £773.[1] Also, a witness for the Caledonian Railway Company, which was much concerned with opposition to Bills and Orders, stated that between 1898 and 1900 the cost of forty-three Bills was £32,940, while between 1901 and 1903 the cost of ten Bills and thirty-four Orders was £12,814. In other words, their average costs per annum had been reduced by the new procedure from £10,980 to £4271.[2] No other witnesses gave evidence to refute these figures. Comparisons are, however, always difficult, since no two Bills or Orders are alike. There appears to have been no subsequent investigation, and the general impression seems to be that the Scottish system is less expensive than the private Bill system, and probably less expensive than the English provisional order system.

The Select Committee of 1904 recognised that the Scottish system had in other respects been a success,[3] and their arguments for not extending it were not convincing. Indeed, they threw out the suggestion that all provisional orders should be taken by joint committees of the two Houses. Select Committees in 1902 and 1918 came to the same conclusion.[4] On the other hand, the Consultative Council on Local Health Administration came to the opposite conclusion:

The method of consideration by two Houses gives opportunity of adjustment and satisfaction of various interests which could not be guaranteed by the decision of a joint committee; and the evidence which we have received tends to show that in only a minority of cases does opposition in the second House arise, and when it does arise it is generally limited in practice to matters of important detail. Therefore, the consequent expense is not great enough to justify a departure from the original procedure.[5]

---

[1] *Ibid.* p. 205.　　　　　[2] *Ibid.* p. 207.　　　　　[3] *Ibid.* p. iv.
[4] Royal Commission on Local Government (1923), Minutes of Evidence, p. 119.
[5] *Ibid.*

3. SPECIAL PARLIAMENTARY PROCEDURE

The procedure by way of provisional order is somewhat complicated, and there has been a tendency—referred to in subsequent paragraphs—to replace provisional orders by orders taking effect by ministerial action only. Under the Statutory Orders (Special Procedure) Act, 1945, a new procedure known (somewhat unhappily) as 'the Special Procedure' has been developed. It applies only to legislation enacted since 1945, to the Town and Country Planning Act, 1944 (now virtually superseded by the Act of 1947) and the corresponding Scottish Act, and the Water Act, 1945. The preliminary procedure is laid down by the Act in question. An order is then laid before Parliament by the appropriate minister, and the procedure laid down by the Act of 1945 is followed. Petitions are referred to the Lord Chairman of Committees and the chairman of Ways and Means, who report whether they may be received. If a resolution to annul the order is passed by the House, no further action is required. If no such resolution is passed, the petitions are referred to a joint committee of both Houses. The joint committee may then listen to argument and suggest amendments to the House. If no amendment is suggested, the order takes effect when the joint committee reports. If amendments are suggested the order takes effect as so amended on such date as the appropriate minister may determine. On the other hand the minister may, if he pleases, withdraw the order. If the joint committee advises that the order be not approved, it does not take effect unless it is confirmed by Act of Parliament. A Bill for this purpose is treated as a public Bill.

It will be seen that the purpose of this Act is to give a shortened procedure for orders which might otherwise have to be passed as provisional orders. Effectively it vests control in a joint committee of both Houses.

4. STATUTORY INSTRUMENTS

One way to avoid the necessity of recourse to Parliament for additional powers is to confer them by general legislation. The request of a local authority or statutory undertaker for special arrangements dependent upon local conditions cannot be anticipated; but sometimes there are economic changes which require general legislation, and in the absence of such legislation Parliament is flooded with private Bills or provisional orders. Recent examples are the invention of trolley-buses and the need for aerodromes. While the railway boom was met—rather late in the day—by Clauses Acts, nothing was done to relieve Parliament from the extra business involved by the invention of the internal combustion engine. It is, however, in the realm of local government that the need for general legislation becomes most apparent. Though legislative developments have been rapid, particularly since 1919, some local authorities have always been in advance of them. Direct economic changes such as the movement of population and the development of a new salaried semi-professional section of the middle class have had their influence; and these and other causes have given rise to new developments in political intervention. In spite of frequent general legislation, especially in housing and town and country planning, local authorities have been the most persistent seekers of private Acts and provisional orders.

The device adopted in Public Health law was the collection of local Act clauses into general legislation; but most of these clauses were made 'adoptive', so that the local authority had to adopt them at a special meeting, and often to secure also the consent of the Local Government Board or the appropriate minister. Thus, the Infectious Disease (Notification) Act, 1889, might be adopted by any urban or rural sanitary authority until it was made compulsory in 1899; the Infectious Disease (Prevention) Act, 1890, might similarly be adopted until most of it was incorporated into the Public Health Act, 1936; the Public Health Acts Amendment Act, 1890, might be adopted by any urban authority, while certain portions might be adopted by a rural authority, and other portions might be extended to a rural authority by the Local Government Board; the Public Health Acts Amendment Act, 1907, might be extended to any local authority by order of the Local Government Board made on the application of the local authority; and the Public Health Act, 1925, applied in part to an urban authority on adoption, though in some cases the consent of the Minister of Health was required, while a rural authority could adopt some parts but required an order from the Minister of Health for adopting the rest.

The value, or lack of value, of this procedure was examined by the Local Government and Public Health Consolidation Committee in 1936. The Committee pointed out that there were two kinds of procedure for adoption:

(1) A procedure under which, apart from difference in detail, a local authority have power to adopt an Act, or a part of an Act, or a particular section of an Act, without reference to the Central Department, but only after complying with a special procedure designed to give publicity to the proposal to adopt, and (2) a procedure under which the decision whether the Act or enactment is to come into operation in any particular area lies with the Department.[1]

The Report then continued:

There is no doubt that both procedures have in the past proved themselves, and in certain circumstances still are, convenient legislative methods. To take an example outside the Public Health code, if a council wish to take advantage of the enabling provisions of the Local Government and Other Officers' Superannuation Act, 1922,[2] and establish thereunder a superannuation scheme for their staff, it is clearly right that a decision of such importance should not be taken by a chance majority of members attending the ordinary meeting of the council. Again, as regards the power of the Minister to bring enactments into operation by order, it is convenient in view of the widely different circumstances of different local authorities and the wide variations in their financial resources and in the types of district under their control, that Parliament should sometimes confer powers or impose obligations in general terms, leaving it to the Minister to decide whether in any particular case the circumstances require that a particular authority should be entrusted with the discharge of the functions in question. It is also to be remembered that the Public Health code is largely the outcome of local experiments sanctioned by Parliament in local legislation, and that, as already pointed out, much of the present general code consists of these local Act provisions re-enacted in a generalised form. Thus, a system under which the application of the particular enactment to any given locality is left to the discretion of the Department represents a natural transition from the method—still in active operation—of Parliament itself conferring by local Act additional powers required by particular authorities.

[1] Local Government and Public Health Consolidation Committee, Second Interim Report, Cmd. 5059, 1936, p. 13.
[2] Now superseded by the Local Government Superannuation Act, 1937, a compulsory Act.

None the less, when all this is said, our examination of the Acts has led us to the conclusion that the method of proceeding by way of 'adoption' has in the past been overdone. Not a few cases of patent absurdity can be found....
Again, there are a number of provisions which at present require adoption but might well have been formed as enabling clauses, operating without adoption if and in so far as the local authority think fit to exercise the powers.[1]

Accordingly, the principle of adoption was almost completely removed from the Public Health Act, 1936, which was the first result of the labours of the Committee in the field of public health.

This process of developing general law is, however, extremely slow. Many of the provisions incorporated in the Public Health Act, 1936, were granted originally by local Act clauses in the early years of the nineteenth century. Some were then incorporated in the Public Health Act, 1848, or subsequent legislation, and consolidated with other provisions in the Public Health Act, 1875. Local Act clauses continued to manufacture new powers, extensions of old powers, and amendments of the general law. Many of these were incorporated in the adoptive provisions of the Public Health Acts of 1890, 1907 and 1925. The enactment of these provisions was followed by further local Act clauses, extending, modifying, and often repealing them. Thus there was in 1935 a chaos of competing legal principles. There were contradictions in the Act of 1875 because of the diversity of its origin; there were contradictions between the Act of 1875 and the later Acts; there were adoptive provisions in force in some places and not in others, and there were local Act clauses which had to be read with general law and adoptive provisions.[2] The Public Health Act, 1936, resolved some of these difficulties, but the Local Government and Public Health Consolidation Committee had not completed its work at the outbreak of war.

Moreover, the enactment of general law has lagged behind the need. Though there was a Public Health Act in 1925 and considerable additional powers were conferred by the Local Government Act, 1929, the Committee on Common Form Clauses was able to mark sixty-eight clauses as 'Clauses which can normally be accepted without special proof'—clauses, therefore, which really required no specific Parlia-

---

[1] Report, Cmd. 5059, p. 14.   [2] Cf. *ibid*, pp. 10–15.

mentary sanction; and only five of these were covered by the Public Health Act, 1936.

Basic principles must necessarily be sanctioned by Parliament; but it is quite clear that the general and, in principle, wholesome tradition against delegated legislation has compelled Parliament to undertake a closer supervision than is necessary. This is a statement of universal application, but it is particularly evident in respect of matters of purely local concern. If it is necessary to secure the assent of Parliament, it is not always necessary that Parliament should always undertake the process of amendment which is the essential purpose of the committee stage. Consequently, Parliament has in many cases authorised the 'special order' and 'scheme' methods of procedure, requiring only its assent, express or implied, to the provisions made or approved by a department.

The term 'special order' is not one of art. In the House of Lords it means, subject to exceptions, 'any order in council, departmental order, rules, regulations, scheme or other similar instrument...presented to or laid in draft before the House where an affirmative resolution is required before the Order or any part thereof becomes effective or is made or as a condition of the continuance in operation of the Order'.[1] This use of the term has been 'regretted' by a former Parliamentary Counsel to the Treasury as tending to cause confusion.[2] In the statutes the term is used for departmental orders which take the place of provisional orders.[3] Such 'special orders' are now included in 'statutory instruments' as defined by the Statutory Instruments Act, 1945, but the latter is a wider term embracing also what were formerly known as 'rules, regulations and orders'.

Until 1919 all extensions and modifications of the powers of statutory undertakers were carried out either by local Acts or by provisional orders. The Electricity (Supply) Act, 1919, departed from this tradition.[4]

[1] S.O. (L.) 212 (1).

[2] Report of the Committee on Ministers' Powers, 1932. Cmd. 4060, p. 28.

[3] In the Schedule to the Electric Lighting (Clauses) Act, 1899, however, 'special order' means a *provisional order* made under the Electric Lighting Act, 1882.

[4] Exactly why is not clear. The change was made in standing committee, and it has been suggested (rather obliquely) that the undertakers wanted to avoid the fees required for provisional orders: see Royal Commission on Local Government (1923), Minutes of Evidence, II, pp. 341–3 (Sir Ernest Moon).

It provided in section 26 that anything which under the Electric Lighting Acts might be effected by a provisional order confirmed by Parliament might be effected by a 'special order' made by the Electricity Commissioners and confirmed by the Board of Trade. Before making the order notice of the proposal had to be made, objections considered and, if the objections were not withdrawn, a local inquiry held.[1] Special orders under this section could not come into force, however, 'unless and until approved, with or without modifications', by a resolution passed by each House of Parliament;[2] but the Act provided for other special orders which had only to be laid before Parliament for thirty days and which did not take effect if an Address was presented to that effect within that period.[3]

Similarly, section 10 of the Gas Regulation Act, 1920, empowered the Board of Trade to make a special order to effect anything relating to gas which might be effected by provisional order under the Gas and Water Works Facilities Act, 1870. Publication, consideration of objects, and if necessary a local inquiry, were required as under the Act of 1919. The special order had to be laid in draft before both Houses of Parliament; and the order could not be made unless both Houses by resolution approved the draft, either without modification or addition or with modifications or additions to which both Houses agreed.[4]

Water undertakers were not at first so successful in securing a relaxation of parliamentary control. Under the Gas and Water Works Facilities Act, 1870, and the Water Act, 1945, most water orders had to be provisional until confirmed by Parliament. But, as we have seen, the special procedure under the Act of 1945 now applies to them.[5]

The 'scheme' procedure is in substance the same, but its develop-

[1] See the Factory and Workshop Act, 1901, ss. 80 and 81, applied by the Electricity (Supply) Act, 1919, s. 35 (2).
[2] It is not easy to see how either House could modify the order, except by moving an amendment to the order to the effect that it be considered by a select committee.
[3] Electricity (Supply)Act, 1919, s. 35 (3).
[4] Gas Regulation Act, 1920, s. 10. The powers were extended by the Gas Undertakings Act, 1929, s. 7, and the Gas Undertakings Act, 1934, s. 17.
[5] In his evidence to the Royal Commission on Local Government (1923), Sir Ernest Moon, Counsel to Mr Speaker, stated that he regarded the water order system under the Act of 1921 as the best, since it avoided the necessity for bothering Parliament where there was no opposition, but gave objectors the right to make their case in Parliament. See Minutes of Evidence, II, pp. 341–2.

ment has proceeded further, especially in the law of Housing and Town and Country Planning. The Artisans' and Labourers' Dwellings Improvement Act, 1875, provided for the making of improvement schemes for dealing with unhealthy or slum areas. After some amendment it was incorporated in the Housing of the Working Classes Act, 1890. The schemes were made by local authorities and publication was necessary, but to become effective they required an order of the Local Government Board. The Board held a local inquiry and then made a provisional order which, of course, required confirmation by Parliament.[1] The Act of 1890 also enabled the local authorities to make 'reconstruction schemes', but the necessary order of the Local Government Board was provisional only if there was opposition.[2] The Housing of the Working Classes Act, 1903, abolished the need for a provisional order for improvement schemes in certain cases, including cases in which such notice of the draft order had been served or was required for a provisional order, and there was no opposition.[3] In substance, therefore, improvement schemes and reconstruction schemes were put on the same basis. The Housing, Town Planning, etc., Act, 1909, then abolished in both cases the need for confirmation by Parliament.[4] The Act of 1909 also introduced 'town planning schemes'. These did not require confirmation by Parliament; but if objections were made, the scheme had to be laid before Parliament in draft, and no further proceedings could be taken if either House presented an Address to the Crown against the draft.[5] This qualification was, however, repealed by the Housing, Town Planning, etc., Act, 1919.[6] The 'clearance order' procedure established by the Housing Act, 1930, was again no concern of Parliament's, except for the minister's general responsibility. The more extended 'town and country planning schemes' authorised by the Town and Country Planning Act, 1932, had to be laid before Parliament and might be invalidated by resolution of either House. If they provided for the suspension of statutory enactments affirmatory resolutions were necessary; and if

---

[1] Housing of the Working Classes Act, 1890, ss. 7 and 8.
[2] *Ibid.* s. 39 (this was new in 1890).
[3] Housing of the Working Classes Act, 1903, s. 5.
[4] Housing, Town Planning, etc., Act, 1909, s. 24.
[5] *Ibid.* s. 54. But see footnote 1, p. 496.
[6] Housing, Town Planning, etc., Act, 1919, s. 44.

they authorised the acquisition or appropriation of any land forming part of any common, open space, or allotment, they were provisional only.[1] In many cases provisional orders were necessary even under the Town and Country Planning Act, 1944, until the Statutory Orders (Special Procedure) Act, 1945, was enacted.

Provisions for the compulsory acquisition of land have followed the same evolution. It is unnecessary to trace it in detail, but an outline will show that Parliament has gradually relaxed its control. In the early years of the nineteenth century, powers for compulsory acquisition were required primarily by railway companies, canal companies, turnpike trustees, and other statutory undertakers. Such powers could be obtained only by local Acts. After 1845 the details could be left out and the Lands Clauses Consolidation Act, 1845, incorporated. From the middle of the nineteenth century onwards, powers were conferred upon ministers, especially on the application of local authorities, for the making of provisional orders. For the purposes of their older functions, therefore, local authorities, like statutory undertakers, can still acquire land compulsorily only by provisional order. On the other hand, for the purposes of allotments, education, housing, public libraries, road improvements, small holdings and town and country planning, they can now acquire land compulsorily without recourse to Parliament.[2] The result is that the Local Government Act, 1933,[3] contains both kinds of powers, though there is no reason why an authority should have to secure Parliamentary consent to the acquisition of land for a convalescent home and not for a school.

These examples show on the one hand that Parliament has to a substantial degree delegated to ministers its function of conferring powers, and on the other hand that the present practice has no consistency. General legislation is necessarily concerned with special problems. In relation to each problem the department concerned considers whether a general power may be conferred directly, or whether the minister should be given power to consent to 'adoption', or a power to make

[1] Town and Country Planning Act, 1932, 1st and 3rd Schedules. The latter requirement was originally enacted in the Housing, Town Planning, etc., Act, 1909, s. 73.

[2] Local Government and Public Health Consolidation Committee, (First) Interim Report, 1933, Cmd. 4272, p. 46.

[3] Local Government Act, 1933, ss. 160 and 161.

provisional orders, or special orders, or other statutory instruments; and, in the last case, whether an affirmative resolution in both Houses, or laying before Parliament with powers to annul, should be required. The department is naturally in favour of the procedure which is cheapest and most expeditious, and which occupies no Government time. It knows, also, that affirmative resolutions are rarely opposed, and that resolutions to annul are seldom proposed.

The problem has therefore never been adequately discussed from the parliamentary angle. Local legislation is a great burden on members of the two Houses. It confers no glory upon those who are condemned to sit on committees; it has no political importance; and where the function is delegated to a minister the usual parliamentary methods of criticism are effective. A member who receives a complaint from his own constituency never hesitates to take any steps which may gain him a few votes. If he discovers a real misuse of power he finds substantial support in the House of Commons. He can question ministers and, if necessary, raise the matter on the adjournment. On the other hand, he can rarely secure enough support to oppose an affirmatory resolution or to secure the passage of a resolution to annul, particularly if the question is of local concern only. Indeed, it is undesirable that the time of the House should be occupied by local matters which raise no general issues.

Most delegated legislation is of the kinds mentioned above. If enactment by Parliament were required, it would be enacted in private Bills. Every year, however, some hundreds of statutory instruments, of a kind which, if enacted, would be found in public general Acts, are issued by Government departments under statutory powers.[1] It is in respect of them that the problem has primarily arisen, and it was to them that the Committee on Ministers' Powers, set up in 1929 because of complaints, mainly directed its attention. Apart from delegated powers which it regarded as 'normal', the Committee considered that certain powers must be regarded as 'exceptional', namely:

(i) Powers to legislate on matters of principle, and even to impose taxation.

(ii) Powers to amend Acts of Parliament, either the Act by which the powers are delegated, or other Acts.

[1] See Table V.

TABLE V

The following figures give the numbers of rules registered under the Rules Publication Act, 1893, s. 3, between 1894 and 1929, inclusive:

Year	Annual total	General	Local	Year	Annual total	General	Local
1894	1015	—	—	1912	1919	342	1577
1895	950	246	704	1913	1406	414	992
1896	1229	197	1032	1914	1914	522	1392
1897	986	168	818	1915	1241	406	835
1898	1151	200	951	1916	941	508	433
1899	1000	223	777	1917	1383	753	630
1900	995	174	821	1918	1825	1204	621
1901	1042	156	886	1919	2241	1091	1150
1902	980	161	819	1920	2475	916	1559
1903	1196	170	1026	1921	2110	727	1383
1904	1899	143	1756	1922	1450	430	1020
1905	1379	162	1217	1923	1624	366	1258
1906	986	165	821	1924	1601	426	1175
1907	1058	231	827	1925	1461	466	995
1908	1349	256	1093	1926	1745	448	1297
1909	1528	205	1323	1927	1349	445	904
1910	1368	218	1150	1928	1132	415	717
1911	1336	172	1164	1929	1262	391	871

The figures were given by Dr C. T. Carr, in his evidence before the Committee on Ministers' Powers: Minutes of Evidence, II, p. 205. The distinction between 'General' and 'Local' follows that adopted between public Acts and local and personal Acts of Parliament: see the Treasury Regulations of 1894, reprinted in Report of the Committee on Ministers' Powers, 1932, Cmd. 4060, p. 120. The following qualifications must, however, be made:

(1) The lists do not include 'provisional rules' made under s. 2 of the Act of 1893 on the ground of urgency: these are usually, though not always, made statutory subsequently. They are usually of a 'general' nature, and thus would increase slightly the proportion of 'general' to 'local'.

(2) Only rules of a legislative, not of an executive character, are registered: most of the latter are 'local'.

(3) Rules 'made' by some other body, such as a local authority, statutory undertakers, or an independent statutory authority, but 'confirmed' by a Government department, are omitted. Most of these are of a local character, and they are very numerous.

(4) Only rules relating to courts or made by the Privy Council, the Judicial Committee, and Government departments, are registered. The lists therefore exclude some rules made by statutory authorities which are not Government departments.

(iii) Powers conferring so wide a discretion on a minister, that it is almost impossible to know what limit Parliament did intend to impose.

(iv) Limited powers which have, however, been taken out of the control of the Courts.[1]

It should be emphasised that these are exceptional both in the nature of the powers and in the circumstances in which they are conferred. The

TABLE VI

The following table gives similar particulars for the years 1937 to 1945, inclusive, and is taken from Sir Cecil Carr's evidence before the Select Committee on Procedure (H.C. 189 of 1945–6, p. 243):

Year	Annual total	General	Local
1937	1231	644	597
1938	1661	831	830
1939	1946	1336	610
1940	2222	1626	596
1941	2157	1590	567
1942	2937	1901	1036
1943	1788	1333	455
1944	1483	1082	455
1945	1706	1179	527

These figures of course give evidence of wartime inflation.

In his evidence before the Select Committee on Delegated Legislation (H.C. 301 of 1953, p. 2), Sir Cecil Carr commented as follows:

'If a graph were constructed from the statistics of registration, it would show that the local normally outnumber the general instruments, sometimes in the proportion of more than four to one. The annual total of local instruments is sometimes noticeably swollen by the passing of a particular enabling statute; in 1904, for instance, an upward leap of 700 in the total of local instruments was due to a flood of orders under section 11 of the Education Act, 1902, appointing foundation managers for schools. In the case of the general orders the annual totals would be seen to exhibit remarkable steadiness from 1894 to 1911 and again, at a rather higher level, from 1922 to 1932. They climb steeply during a world war and for a time outnumber the local instruments. The total of 1204 general instruments in 1918 was almost three times the total for 1913; the total of 1901 in 1942 was almost three times the total for 1937. Since 1948, when the total was 1508, there has been what some will regard as healthy annual decline; the figure fell to 1379 in 1949, to 1211 in 1950, to 1166 in 1951, and to 1087 in 1952. The annual total of all instruments has never exceeded 3000; the annual total of general instruments has never exceeded 2000. To estimate the total of all instruments in operation today would be mere guesswork.'

[1] Report of the Committee on Ministers' Powers, 1932, Cmd. 4060, p. 31. For examples, see *ibid.* pp. 31–41.

great majority of statutory instruments are issued under powers which the Committee classified as 'normal'. As usually happens when abuses become the subject of public discussion, public opinion tends to assume that the exceptions are the rule. In this instance some of the exceptions were used by a Lord Chief Justice of England as ammunition for a broadside against 'the new despotism',[1] and this support from high authority has naturally not been completely over-weighted by the much more balanced judgment of the Committee on Ministers' Powers.[2] The most that can be said is that Parliament sometimes delegates powers in unnecessarily wide or vague terms, that occasionally a temporary power is given to amend public general Acts (though a good case can be made in each instance)[3] and, more often, a power to amend or repeal local Acts, that occasionally the jurisdiction of the Courts is excluded (usually because the right of challenge in the Courts may hold up for a long time the necessary administrative action, or even destroy the efficacy of action already taken), and that in exceptional political and economic conditions very wide powers are sometimes conferred.[4]

To prevent any possible development of abuses, the Committee recommended that:

1. The precise limits of the law-making power which Parliament intends to confer on a Minister should always be expressly defined in clear language by the statute which confers it: when discretion is conferred, its limits should be defined with equal clearness.

2. The use of the so-called 'Henry VIII Clause', conferring power on a Minister to modify the provisions of Acts of Parliament (hitherto limited to such amendments as may appear to him to be necessary for the purpose of

---

[1] Lord Hewart of Bury, *The New Despotism*.

[2] 'We dispose, in passing, of the suggestion, unsupported as it is by the smallest shred of evidence, that the existence of such provisions [i.e. the exceptional provisions under (ii), p. 497] in certain Acts of Parliament is due directly or indirectly to any attempt or desire on the part of members of the permanent Civil Service to secure for themselves or for their Departments an arbitrary power.... The power has been asked for and granted but rarely, and always subject to conditions limiting the period of its operation and defining the purposes for which it may be used': Cmd. 4060, pp. 59–60.

[3] This is the so-called 'Henry VIII Clause', though it has about as much relation to Henry VIII's Statute of Proclamations as a Dogs Act has to Magna Carta. The Committee found nine instances, all exceptional and temporary, between 1888 and 1929: see Cmd. 4060, pp. 123–7.

[4] There were no special circumstances to justify the Import Duties Act, 1932; but there is much to be said for a flexible tariff under proper safeguards.

bringing the statute into operation), should be abandoned in all but the most exceptional cases, and should not be permitted by Parliament except upon special grounds stated in the Ministerial Memorandum attached to the Bill. . . .

3. The 'Henry VIII clause' should

(*a*) never be used except for the sole purpose of bringing an Act into operation;

(*b*) be subject to a time limit of one year from the passing of the Act.

4. The use of clauses designed to exclude the jurisdiction of the Courts to inquire into the legality of a regulation or order should be abandoned in all but the most exceptional cases, and should not be permitted by Parliament except upon special grounds stated in the Ministerial Memorandum attached to the Bill. . . .

5. Whenever Parliament determines that it is necessary to take the exceptional course mentioned in the last recommendation and to confer on a Minister the power to make a regulation whose validity is not open to challenge in the Courts:

(*a*) Parliament should state plainly in the statute that this is its intention.

(*b*) A period of challenge of at least three months and preferably six months should be allowed. Apart from emergency legislation, we doubt if there are any cases where it would be right to forbid challenge absolutely.

6. Except where immunity from challenge is intentionally conferred, there should not be anything in the language of the statute even to suggest a doubt as to the right and duty of the Courts of Law to decide in any particular case whether the Minister has acted within the limits of his power.[1]

Apart from its general control over the administrative actions of ministers, Parliament usually—or at least frequently, for the powers are so numerous that a quantitative analysis is difficult—retains some control over delegated legislation of a general character. While there is no general statute which requires rules or regulations to be laid before Parliament, the delegating statute in many cases itself requires the regulation to be so laid. The requirement takes different forms in various statutes, classified by the Committee on Ministers' Powers as:

(i) Laying—with no further directions.

(ii) Laying—with provision that, if within a specified period of time a resolution is passed by either House for annulling (in some cases for annulling or modifying) the regulation, the regulation may—or shall—be annulled or modified, as the case may be, by Order in Council.

[1] Cmd. 4060, p. 66.

(iii) Laying—with provision that the regulation shall not operate until approved by resolution; or shall not operate beyond a certain specific period, unless approved by resolution within that period.

(iv) Laying in draft for a certain number of days.

(v) Laying in draft with provision that the regulation is not to operate till the draft has been approved by resolution.[1]

The Report adds: 'It is impossible to discover any rational justification for the existence of so many different forms of laying or on what principle Parliament acts in deciding which should be adopted in any particular enactment.'[2]

In evidence before the Select Committee on Delegated Legislation in 1953,[3] Sir Alan Ellis, K.C.B., Q.C., Senior Parliamentary Counsel, reduced the classes to three, those which required an affirmative resolution in each House, those which required no resolution but could be annulled by motion—usually called a 'prayer', because the motion prays that the instrument be annulled—and those which were laid simply for information. In each case the decision is taken on the responsibility of

---

[1] Cmd. 4060, pp. 41–2. Examples are given in the references. A fuller analysis was made by a Select Committee of the House of Lords in 1934 (H.L. 13 of 1934), whose work is referred to *post*, p. 510. Orders were divided by this Committee into the following five categories:

Class I. Those which are laid, in draft or otherwise, with the provision that the Order shall not be made or operate unless approved by resolution. This class is covered by S.O. (L.) 212, referred to *post*, pp. 511–12.

Class II. Those which are laid with no further directions, i.e. without a provision for an address or resolution, adverse or affirmative, thus giving Parliament no direct power over them. Seven such orders were laid in 1932.

Class III. Those which are operative when made, but are subject to annulment by adverse address. This is by far the most numerous class, and 374 such Orders were laid in 1932.

Class IV. Those which are laid in draft for a period of days with provision for an adverse address or resolution. There were seventy such Orders laid in 1932.

Class V. Those which are operative when made but which cease to have effect unless confirmed by resolution within a prescribed time. There were no such Orders laid in the House of Lords in 1932, but the class includes some of the most important kinds of delegated legislation, including regulations under the Emergency Powers Act, 1920, and orders under the Henry VIII clause. It also includes orders issued under the Import Duties Act, 1932, and other taxing statutes, which usually have to be laid before the House of Commons alone. This class was not within S.O. (L.) 212 as first drafted, but the S.O. was extended to the class on the recommendation of the Select Committee.

[2] *Ibid.* p. 42.

[3] Report from the Select Committee on Delegated Legislation, H.C. 310 of 1953, pp. 31–2.

the minister concerned, and if Parliamentary Counsel are not given instructions on this point at the outset they seek such instructions. No express rules for the exercise of the choice are in existence, and Sir Alan thought that it was undesirable to lay down such rules because the circumstances were almost infinitely various. Analysis of the relevant statutory provisions then in force showed, however, that as between the affirmative procedure and the negative or 'prayer' procedure, the latter was normal. The affirmative procedure had generally been used for:

(1) Powers the exercise of which would substantially affect provisions of Acts of Parliament, whether by alteration of their effect, or by increase or limitation of the extent or duration of their effect (but consequential adaptations are normally left to negative procedure);

(2) Powers to impose financial charges (e.g. purchase tax) or to make other forms of financial provision;

(3) Skeleton powers, i.e. powers to make schemes and so forth where only the purpose is fixed by the enabling Act and the whole substance of the matter will be in delegated legislation (e.g. Development Council Orders under the Industrial Organisation and Development Act, 1947); and

(4) Other powers of an exceptional or politically important nature (e.g. the Highway Code, the regulation of the importation of livestock under the Livestock Industry Act, 1937, restrictions under section 29 of the Road and Rail Traffic Act, 1933).

The purely informative procedure had become very unusual in modern legislation, at least as regards powers of a legislative as distinct from a purely administrative character. In older statutes the cases were very diverse, extending from the broad power to make safety regulations for coal mines under the Coal Mines Act, 1911, to matters dealing with the internal organisation of Government departments.

In some of the cases covered by classes (i) and (ii) of the classification made by the Committee on Ministers' Powers, antecedent publicity was provided for by section 1 of the Rules Publication Act, 1893. This applied to statutory rules which had to be laid before Parliament, but not to those which had to be laid or laid in draft for any period before they came into operation. Nor did it apply to rules made for Scotland or by the Minister of Health, the Board of Trade, or the Revenue Departments, or by or for the purposes of the Post Office or to rules made by the Minister of Agriculture and Fisheries under the Contagious Diseases (Animals) Acts. Where the section did apply, forty days' notice of the proposal to make the rules, and of the place where copies of the draft rules might be obtained, had to be published in the *London Gazette*. Any public body might obtain copies on payment, and representations or suggestions had to be taken into consideration before finally settling the rules.

The provision was thus subject to considerable limitations, not all of which have been mentioned, but the whole Act was repealed by the Statutory Instruments Act, 1946. This Act applies to subordinate legislation passed after the date on which the Act came into operation and to rules to which the Act of 1893 applied. It provides for the numbering, printing, publication and citation of statutory instruments. Where a copy has to be laid before Parliament, it must be laid before the instrument comes into operation unless it is urgent. Where a statutory instrument can be annulled by Parliament, forty days are allowed for the annulment proceedings. Where the instrument has to be laid in draft, forty days are again allowed before the instrument is brought into operation, unless a specific period is prescribed.

According to the evidence which the chairman of Ways and Means laid before the Committee on Ministers' Powers, the procedure of moving an Address to annul or disapprove a rule or order was 'quite ineffective'; and the other form under which an affirmative resolution was required was 'little if at all more effective'.[1] The same opinion had been expressed eight years before by Counsel to Mr Speaker, who was referring especially to the special orders under the Electricity and Gas Acts:

Experience has shown that the statutory requirements for parliamentary approval of these special orders do not provide genuine safeguards, and that it is difficult to secure proper criticism of a draft order under the Standing Orders of the House.[2]

One difficulty is that members have not always an opportunity of seeing the regulation. By direction of Mr Speaker the departments have been notified on several occasions that such documents ought to be

[1] Committee on Ministers' Powers, Minutes of Evidence, p. 229.
[2] Royal Commission on Local Government (1923), Minutes of Evidence, II, p. 341.

sent in duplicate, and this is usually done, though occasionally it is neglected. When it is done, one copy is filed and placed in the Library for inspection. As the custody and preservation of the document is important, the other copy is locked up, and a member who wishes to see it must ask the librarian or clerk to produce it. If only one copy is presented, this is locked up and a special request is necessary for inspection.[1]

Nor is it easy for a member of the House of Commons to oppose a regulation. Where an affirmative resolution is required, a Government motion is necessary and time has to be found for it. Sometimes, as on National Assistance Regulations or an Import Duties Order, a long debate takes place. Even here, however, there is the difficulty that usually no provision for amendment is made. A spelling mistake in the Unemployment Assistance Regulations of 1934 compelled the Government to withdraw the Regulations and to produce another and corrected set. On many points in these Regulations there might have been substantial agreement on some amendments; but the Regulations had to be either accepted or rejected as proposed by the Minister of Labour.

Such resolutions are, however, 'exempted business' for the purpose of the ten o'clock rule. They can, therefore, be taken after the close of ordinary business. They are in fact so taken unless the Opposition specifically asks for them to be put down at a more convenient time— that is, if they are of political importance. The members representing the particular interest concerned have therefore to persuade enough of their friends to stay in the House in order to oppose the order:

If the discussion has to take place, as it now has, under the Standing Orders of the House of Commons, after 11 o'clock, it is perfectly impossible for anyone who objects, to get his friends to wait in the House in order to support him. Of course the Department have always got the Whips at their disposal and they can keep a House, and keep a House which will vote according to

[1] *Ibid.*; as qualified in the Report, Cmd. 4060, p. 43. In the Minutes of Evidence, at p. 233, Sir Dennis Herbert gave a specific example. A draft order under the Census Act was officially laid on the Table on 28 October 1930. About ten days afterwards a member inquired for it, but found that it could not be seen. The draft laid on the Table was the only one supplied, and that had to be sent to the printers. It had to lie on the Table for twenty sitting days, but the prints were not received until 17 November, the fourteenth sitting day, and it was notified on the 'pink paper' on 19 November, the sixteenth sitting day. That left four days for the Address to annul, if any; and notice of that had to be given for two days.

the desire of the Minister who is head of the Department. But the unfortunate opponent could never get anybody to stay, or at any rate he could get very few people to stay; he would have no chance.[1]

What should be done when a member wished to oppose on behalf of his constituency was discussed on a Gas Order for Barnsley in 1923. Mr Speaker ruled that it was in order for a member to move an amendment to the motion, to the effect that the order should be referred to a select committee.[2] Accordingly, the member for Barnsley moved to strike out the word 'approved' and to add words whose effect was to refer the matter to a select committee of four members. The committee was to report whether the order should be approved with or without modifications, setting out the modifications, if any, which they proposed. The proceedings of the committee were to be conducted as in the case of a Provisional Order Confirmation Bill, and opponents were given a right of being heard provided that they deposited notices of objection within a fixed time. If no statement of objection was deposited the order of reference was to be discharged.[3] In a subsequent case in which objection was taken privately by a member, the original motion was moved in this form by the Government.[4] The threat of opposition is in fact sometimes enough to induce the minister to accept amendments, so that the order is moved with the amendments. This was, apparently, not a very successful procedure, as the member in question subsequently pointed out:

I warn the House of the danger of doing otherwise than remitting these orders as a whole to these committees. Only a few months ago I had to move a similar amendment, but under the threat—if I may so call it—the minister in charge was good enough to meet my wishes, and he agreed to accept a long string of amendments to the order. These were largely consequential, and merely meant the leaving out of one district, and they were settled most carefully by the Government Department. Ultimately, however, it was ascertained that if the order had been passed in that form, they would have created chaos, and it was only the fact that the town clerk of Watford discovered these mistakes which caused the matter to be put right in time.[5]

[1] Royal Commission on Local Government (1923), Minutes of Evidence, II, p. 343 (Counsel to Mr Speaker).	[2] Ibid.
[3] 164 H.C.Deb. 5 s., 1921–34.	[4] 176 H.C.Deb. 5 s., 179.
[5] 189 H.C.Deb. 5 s., 406.

Since in the case of special orders under the Gas Regulation Acts and in the case of certain other orders or draft orders the House is empowered to pass the orders with or without modification, it is permissible for a member to move an amendment of substance. This is, however, a dangerous method; for if the House accepts the amendment the order takes effect, and there is no report stage to make consequential amendments or ascertain that the order as amended makes sense. If, for instance, a member moves an amendment to prevent a gas-holder (which may be, as one member has said, designed according to a precedent set by the Temple of Vesta in the Forum, but is nevertheless not always a thing of beauty and a joy for ever) from being set down in the middle of a village, the House is likely to be affected by his plea. At the same time, there is no opportunity for amendments to be moved to permit of the building of the holder in some less obtrusive place; and the result of the amendment may be to prevent the gas company from carrying out its statutory duty of supplying gas. Accordingly, the usual practice is for the minister to enter into negotiations with the member to induce him to accept either a general reference to a select committee, or a special reference of the particular objection that he wishes to raise.[1] Amendments may also be moved by the minister himself where the Select Committee of the House of Lords, to which reference will presently be made, reports that those amendments ought to be made and the amendments are accepted by the House of Lords.[2]

Such a procedure is possible only where the House has power to pass the orders with or without modifications. In many cases, however, the House can do no more than accept or reject. Orders under the Import Duties Act, 1932, for instance, which are of profound importance because they involve changes in taxation, are recommended to the Treasury by the Import Duties Advisory Committee, an independent body, and are laid by the Treasury before the House. In order to prevent lobbying of members by outside interests, no power of amendment is given to the House. Accordingly, the orders give rise to ordinary political debates on motions which cannot be amended and which are supported by the Government whips. Defeat of the motion would be

---

[1] 189 H.C.Deb. 5 s., 403–6.
[2] 197 H.C.Deb. 5 s., 2043–8.

defeat of the Government, and probably the Government would resign. Effectively, therefore, such orders are outside the control of the House.

Where the statutory instrument requires no express resolution but can be annulled on Address within a certain period, the motion for the Address has to be put down by the member who desires to oppose. Such a motion is 'exempted business' and so can be taken after 10 p.m. whether the ten o'clock rule has or has not been suspended. Being a private member's motion, however, it is postponed to Government business on all days when Government business has precedence. Government orders, other than exempted business, are taken and postponed at ten o'clock when the rule is in force; and the chief whip can move that the House do adjourn. If the adjournment is moved it is invariably carried, and so the procedure would enable the Government to obstruct all 'prayers' until the time for them had lapsed. The power of obstructing is, however, rarely used[1] and it would probably be used only where a group of members was using the procedure of the 'prayer' to obstruct the business of the House. If, however, the member does move his motion for an Address, the whips can be put on against him, and he will find it very difficult to keep a sufficient number of members to enable him to defeat the whips. Moreover, he probably will not be able to move at all if the ten o'clock rule has been suspended, since Government business will continue to enjoy precedence.

In spite of the difficulties in the procedure, however, use has been made both of opportunities to debate affirmative resolutions and of the procedure of the 'prayer'. In the session of 1951–2 there were fifty-three affirmative resolutions, and the total time taken in debate was 14 hours 34 minutes, one of the resolutions being debated for 2 hours, one for 2½ hours, and five for shorter periods of more than 45 minutes. In the same session there were thirty-six 'prayers' and the total time taken in debate was over 25 hours. A group of six, relating to the National Health Service, was debated for 5 hours, and even then the closure was used. In the earlier part of the session of 1952–3 there were twenty-nine affirmative resolutions, debate on which occupied over 18 hours, and five 'prayers' debated for 9 hours.[2] It would, however, be wise not to regard these figures as necessarily typical. The extent of

---

[1] H.C. 310 of 1953, p. xx.   [2] H.C. 310 of 1953, pp. 40–4.

debate either on an affirmative resolution or on a 'prayer' depends upon the extent to which the subject is politically controversial. For instance, orders relating to food rationing were not at all controversial during the war of 1939–45; but as 'normality' was approached public opinion began to hope for acceleration in the process of 'derationing', and it became politically worth while to court popularity by putting down 'prayers'. Again, one sometimes finds a member, or a group of members, paying particular attention to delegated legislation and using all available methods for imposing a check on it. All that can be said, therefore, is that debate on delegated legislation has become a good deal more common since 1945 than it was before 1939. The fact that, as we shall see, both Houses now have 'scrutiny committees' for delegated legislation, concerned with form rather than policy, perhaps encourages members to study the policy also and to use the appropriate procedure for criticising it.

Where the statutory instrument is merely ordered to be laid before the House and no provision is made for annulment on Address, the member can do no more than put down a motion. Such a motion will not be exempted business and cannot, therefore, be taken after 10 p.m., but can be made only on a day on which private members' motions have precedence; that is, it can be moved only on a Friday and by a member who has been successful in the ballot. Fridays are never used for this purpose, since it would be impossible to keep a House and members must choose subjects of more general interest. The member's only remedy, therefore, is to raise the matter, without a motion, on the adjournment, the appropriate Supply vote, or the Consolidated Fund Bill.

The new system of special orders was disliked by many of the peers when it was introduced into the Electricity Supply Act, 1919, and from time to time protests were made in the House of Lords when Gas and Electricity Orders were before the House because there was no real control over them. In a debate in May 1924, the Marquess of Salisbury suggested that possibly the procedure under the Ministry of Transport Act, 1919, might be followed. That Act was passed when the Coalition Government was unable to make up its mind whether to maintain the railways under national control or not; and 'with a view to affording time for the consideration and formulation of the policy to be pursued' (the only time, probably, that differences of opinion in the Cabinet have actually appeared in a statute), the minister was empowered to make orders for the temporary control of the railways. These included power to authorise the taking of land compulsorily. It was provided by section 29 (3) of the Act, however, that on publishing a notice of his intention to make such an order, the minister should send a copy of the draft order to the Lords' chairman of Committees and the Commons' chairman of Ways and Means; and if either of them reported that the order ought not to be proceeded with except with the authority of Parliament, the order was not to take effect until it had been approved by resolution in both Houses. Further, if either House by resolution directed the proposals to be dealt with by private Bill, the notices should be regarded as published and served for a private Bill. The Lord Privy Seal, on behalf of the Labour Government, suggested that the matter should be referred to a select committee. The House of Lords agreed, and later appointed a select committee.[1]

The committee was reappointed in the following session, and in its report in 1925[2] it recommended that a standing committee, to be called the Special Orders Committee, should be appointed, and that every regulation, order, scheme, or similar rule requiring an affirmative resolution of the House in order to become effective should stand referred to it. Provision was to be made for separate methods of treatment according as the order would, but for some Act of Parliament, have been required to be enacted by private Bill, hybrid Bill, or public Bill respectively. A Standing Order was made accordingly. In 1933 another select committee was set up to consider the amendment of this Standing Order. In its report[3] the committee recommended that no special procedure should be adopted for orders which merely had to be laid before the House, and which remained in force (subject, of course, to repealing legislation) unless annulled whether any resolution were passed or not. The classes of orders which could be annulled or not brought into force

---

[1] For the debate, see 57 H.L.Deb. 5 s., 645–58.

[2] Report by the Select Committee of the House of Lords on Legislation by Special Orders, etc., requiring affirmative Resolution by both Houses of Parliament, H.L. 119 of 1925.

[3] Report by the Select Committee of the House of Lords on Proceedings in Relation to Special Orders, H.L. 13 of 1934.

by adverse resolution were very numerous, and sometimes of a technical and administrative character, and no special procedure was recommended for them. It was recommended, however, that the Standing Order should be amended so as to include orders which took effect immediately, but ceased to have effect unless confirmed within a prescribed time.[1]

The special orders with which the Special Orders Committee is concerned, therefore, include 'any order in council, departmental order, rules, regulations, scheme or other similar instrument (hereinafter referred to as Orders) presented to or laid, or laid in draft, before the House where an affirmative resolution is required before the Order or any part thereof becomes effective or is made or as a condition of the continuance in operation of the Order or any part thereof'. The following Orders are, however, excepted: (*a*) measures under the Church of England Assembly (Powers) Act, 1919;[2] (*b*) any regulations made under the Emergency Powers Act, 1920;[3] and (*c*) any orders made under the Sunday Entertainments Act, 1932.[4]

The orders to which the Standing Order applies stand referred to the Special Orders Committee as soon as they are laid on the Table. If the Committee has any doubt whether the order is *intra vires*, it must report to the House accordingly. In the case of an order which, but for the provision of the Act authorising it, would have required to be enacted as a public Bill, the Committee must report:

(i) Whether the provisions raise important questions of policy or principle.

[1] That is, the committee recommended that, in addition to orders in Class I in the classification set out *ante*, p. 502, orders in Class V also should be referred to the Special Orders Committee.

[2] This Act, which contains the only real 'Henry VIII clause' on the statute book, provides a special procedure. Measures passed by the Church Assembly stand referred to a statutory committee called the Ecclesiastical Committee, consisting of fifteen members from each House selected by the Lord Chancellor and Mr Speaker respectively. The Committee reports to Parliament stating the nature and legal effect of a measure and its view as to the expediency thereof, especially with relation to the constitutional rights of all Her Majesty's subjects. To give the measure legal effect resolutions must be passed in both Houses directing that the measure be presented to Her Majesty for the royal assent.

[3] Presumably these are excluded because of their urgency and because in any case they will be discussed in both Houses.

[4] These orders are not made unless there has been a favourable poll in the districts concerned, and are presumably excluded for that reason.

(ii) How far the special order is founded on precedent.

(iii) Whether, having regard to the answers to the two preceding questions and to any other relevant circumstances, the order can be passed by the House without special attention or whether there ought to be any further inquiry before the House proceeds to a decision upon the resolution, and, if so, what form that inquiry should take.

If, on the other hand, the order would, but for the provisions of the Act, require to be enacted by a private or hybrid Bill, petitions may be deposited against it and will be referred to the Committee. If such petitions are presented the Committee must report:

(i) Whether the petition discloses substantial grounds of complaint.

(ii) Whether the matter has been so dealt with upon a departmental inquiry that further inquiry is unnecessary.

(iii) Whether the submissions in the petition could have been brought before a local inquiry or not.

(iv) Whether, having regard to the answers to the preceding questions and to the findings, if any, of these inquiries and to the other circumstances of the case, there ought to be a further inquiry by a select committee, to be appointed by the Committee of Selection.[1]

It will be seen that the Special Orders Committee really has two functions to perform, to consider whether the House should debate an order which is of the nature of a public Bill, and to determine whether an order which is of the nature of a private Bill should be treated as if it were an opposed private Bill. The former function may be useful to prevent such delegated legislation as is assumed to exist by those who think in terms of a 'New Despotism'. There is no evidence that there has been any such delegated legislation, but no doubt the existence of the Special Orders Committee is useful in preventing it in those cases where an affirmative resolution is necessary. The Committee's main task, however, is to consider orders of the type which would, before 1919, have been scheduled to Provisional Orders Confirmation Bills. In other words, it gives opponents who have failed to convince the minister the opportunity of convincing a committee of peers. It is doubtful if the power of opposing Provisional Orders is genuinely in the public interest; but, if it is, it is desirable that those interests which have been able to secure the substitution of the special order method for the

[1] S.O. (L.) 212.

provisional order method should be subject to the same kind of parliamentary control.

Until 1944 the House of Commons had no comparable procedure. In consequence of a debate in that House on a private member's motion on 17 May 1944,[1] the Government agreed to propose the setting up of a Select Committee on Statutory Rules and Orders, and the Committee was set up by resolution on 21 June 1944.[2] It has since been set up sessionally under the name of the Select Committee on Statutory Instruments, and its terms of reference have been slightly expanded. The Committee has now to consider every statutory instrument or draft of an instrument laid before the House with a view to determining whether the special attention of the House should be drawn to it on any of the following grounds:

(i)   that it imposes a charge on the public revenues or contains provisions requiring payments to be made to the Exchequer or any Government Department or to any local or public authority in consideration of any licence or consent, or of any services to be rendered, or prescribes the amount of any such charge or payments;

(ii)   that it is made in pursuance of an enactment containing provisions excluding it from challenge in the courts;

(iii)   that it appears to make some unusual or unexpected use of the powers conferred by the statute under which it is made;

(iv)   that it purports to have retrospective effect where the parent statute confers no express authority so to provide;

(v)   that there appears to have been unjustifiable delay in the publication or in the laying of it before Parliament;

(vi)   that there appears to have been unjustifiable delay in sending a notification to Mr Speaker under the proviso to subsection (1) of section 4 of the Statutory Instruments Act, 1946, where an instrument has come into operation before it has been laid before Parliament; and

(vii)   that for any special reason its form or purport calls for elucidation;

and, if they so determine, to report to that effect.

The jurisdiction of the Committee at first extended only to statutory instruments for which an affirmatory resolution was necessary or against which a member might move a 'prayer'. This was a comparatively small proportion of the instruments actually issued. The Committee

---

[1] 400 H.C. Deb. 5 s., 202-99.   [2] 401 H.C.Deb. 5 s., 310-11.

first sat in July 1944, and out of 1483 statutory rules and orders issued in that year 291 came up for scrutiny. The enactment of the Supplies and Services (Transitional Powers) Act, 1945, increased the volume of work: thus 118 documents were up for scrutiny at the meeting of the Committee in January 1946, compared with twenty-one in January 1945. Up to May 1946, when Sir Cecil Carr gave evidence to the Select Committee on Procedure, no report had been made under the first head (imposition of a charge) or the second (exclusion of the jurisdiction of the courts). There had been few reports under the third head (unusual or unexpected use of statutory power) or under the last (obscurity). Most of the reports came under the fifth head and drew attention to delay in laying before the House or in publication. Sir Cecil reported that 'a marked improvement in punctuality is now visible'.[1] There were also five special reports dealing with particular aspects of the making, laying and publishing of statutory rules and orders; but until complaint was made these were apparently not circulated to the departments.[2]

Sir Gilbert Campion suggested in 1946 that the Select Committee's order of reference might be extended to cover:

(1) The merits of a statutory instrument as an exercise of the power delegated, but not the merits of the Act by which the power was conferred; and

(2) Grievances arising out of instruments actually in operation, whether or not the statutory period during which the control of the House could be exercised had expired.[3]

The Select Committee on Procedure considered, however, that this proposal went beyond the scope of their investigation and suggested that an *ad hoc* committee, or a joint committee of both Houses, should be set up to examine the proposal.[4] No action has been taken on this recommendation.

Sir Cecil Carr gave further figures in his evidence to the Select Committee on Delegated Legislation in 1953.[5] From its establishment in 1944 to the end of January, 1953, the Select Committee on Statutory Instruments examined nearly 7000 statutory instruments. This number represented about 70 per cent of all the statutory instruments of general

---

[1] On all the above, see H.C. 189 of 1945–6, pp. 243–4.
[2] *Ibid.* Q. 4659.   [3] *Ibid.* pp. xliv–xlv.
[4] *Ibid.* pp. xi–xii.   [5] H.C. 310 of 1953, p. 6.

application—those of local application which are, as we have seen, usually more numerous, are not examined by the Committee. Incidentally, this figure shows what a large part of delegated legislation is subject to parliamentary control, either by affirmative resolution or by 'prayer': but the Select Committee is not the body to exercise that control. Its duty is to consider whether, from the point of view of form, the delegated legislation is a proper use of the power conferred on the department concerned. It has therefore adopted the procedure of asking the department concerned to explain any use of the power which prima facie seems objectionable, and where the Committee is not convinced it annexes the department's answer in its report to the House. During the period which Sir Cecil Carr's evidence covered, the Committee had so reported on only ninety-three statutory instruments, or 1·7 per cent of the instruments referred to it.[1]

The Committee consists of eleven members, and it has become a convention to elect a member from the Opposition as chairman. It usually meets fortnightly, though more frequent meetings are summoned when necessary. Even so, it does sometimes happen that the report is too late to be of use to the House, particularly where there is delay in setting up the Committee at the beginning of the session or in receiving replies from the departments concerned. The Select Committee on Delegated Legislation made proposals for overcoming these difficulties, but they appear not to have been accepted.

The Committee on Ministers' Powers recommended that in each House there should be a standing committee charged with the duty of scrutinising every Bill containing any proposal for conferring legislative powers on ministers, as well as every regulation made in the exercise of such powers and required to be laid before Parliament. They would be assisted by Counsel to the Lord Chairman and to Mr Speaker respectively.[2] In the case of a Bill, the function of the Committee would be to report to the House whether the Bill was in all respects normal, or whether there were exceptional provisions which ought to be reported to the House, and particularly whether there were provisions which appeared to offend against the rules as to delegated legislation laid down by the

[1] *Ibid.* p. xxii.
[2] Report of the Committee on Ministers' Powers, Cmd. 4060, p. 63.

Committee.[1] Such consideration would be given after the first reading, and the Bill could not then be proceeded with on second reading, or at least in Committee, until seven days after the report had been circulated.[2]

In addition, the Committee on Ministers' Powers recommended the amendment of the Rules Publication Act, 1893, so as to remove some of the exceptions. It was also recommended that Standing Orders should require that every Bill proposing to confer law-making power on the minister presenting it should be accompanied by a memorandum drawing attention to the power, explaining why it was needed, how it would be exercised, and what safeguards there were against abuse.[3]

Effect has not been given to these recommendations. The Rules Publication Act, 1893, has been repealed by the Statutory Instruments Act, 1945, but it was not thought necessary to give effect to the second proposal. The Select Committee on Delegated Legislation considered the first proposal and rejected it. 'Individual members and unofficial committees of members are vigilant and can be relied upon to take close interest in any proposal in a Bill to delegate power to legislate.'[4] The Select Committee also examined, and rejected proposals to:

(1) have a memorandum attached to every Bill drawing attention to the nature and extent of the proposed delegation of powers, and in particular to any proposal therein to give power to impose a tax, or to a power which would have retrospective effect or which would protect the delegated legislation from judicial review; and

(2) have proposals for delegation side-scored or printed in special type.

The truth is that the delegation of legislative powers is no longer regarded with the disfavour which attached to it in the 1920's, largely through the propaganda of persons whose main objection was to the growth of the Welfare State and who therefore disliked both the cause and the consequence of the delegation of legislative powers. Their propaganda had, however, the effect of drawing the attention of members of Parliament to the danger that such powers might be abused. The mere existence of the two Select Committees in the two Houses renders such abuse unlikely, and the vigilance of members prevents proposals being made for unnecessarily extensive delegated powers.

---

[1] *Ante*, pp. 497–9.　　　　[2] Cmd. 4060, pp. 67–9.
[3] *Ibid.* pp. 66–7.　　　　[4] H.C. 310 of 1953, p. xxiv.

CHAPTER XV

PARLIAMENTARY DEMOCRACY

A survey of the working of the British Parliament necessarily involves an examination of much that is technical. It requires a consideration of the labour that goes on behind the scenes, of the hard work performed by members in committees that never receive the glare of publicity, and of the business which is called 'formal' because no one makes a song and dance, or even a speech, about it. Parliament is a hard-working institution, and a false impression is conveyed by 'anecdotal histories' and lobby correspondents—an impression of emotional debates, humorous and dramatic 'scenes' and personal intrigues, which make up part but not the whole of the life of Parliament. It is, nevertheless, a living institution. It has indeed more life than any of the institutions that have been set up more or less in imitation of it. It is not a very dramatic place, but it holds an essential position in the very centre of the constitutional structure. It holds that position partly because of its great traditions. It has fought kings and dismissed them. It raised up an army to destroy a king and was itself destroyed by its army, only to recall another king and to rise up again on the site of its own destruction. It has been modified and reformed to meet the changes of centuries. It has been led by the greatest men that the country has produced—Pitt the Elder and Pitt the Younger, Sir Robert Peel, Disraeli, Gladstone, Lloyd George and Winston Churchill; it has seen the greatest wits and orators in opposition to each other; it has, above all, achieved the pinnacle of freedom by listening to men like Charles James Fox, Sir Henry Campbell-Bannerman and Mr Ramsay MacDonald who dared to be unpopular and, in the cant phrase, 'unpatriotic', because they insisted on speaking the truth as they understood it. It has taught more lessons than any similar institution has ever learned. It is not only the mother of Parliaments but their preceptor. It teaches, too, by example.

While therefore it is necessary to emphasise the importance of detail and technicality and to descend into a multiplicity of particulars, it is equally necessary to let the broad outlines stand clear. The outlines, it is true, are not determined by a rigid framework within which the matter must be confined; on the contrary, the shape is determined by the content, and that content is precisely that mass of detail and technicality. For that reason it has been necessary in this book to enter into detail, to explain, for instance, the nature of financial resolutions and the procedure for special orders. The whole is but the sum of its parts and cannot be understood without them. The time has now come to survey the whole as a whole.

We may begin by putting aside the House of Lords. While from time to time the peculiarities of that institution have been referred to, it receives in this book but a single (though lengthy) chapter. It is placed, so to speak, between Private Members and Private Bills. Its wings have been clipped a little more since the first edition of this book was published. It was, however, never an eagle, and the fact that it can no longer claim to soar above the mountains is of no importance. What is important is that, the parties having failed to reach agreement in 1948, the House of Lords is dying on its feet. Since 1938, its membership has increased by 150, while the average attendance, which was already low, has decreased by ten. The functions of the House of Lords are not the less useful because they are pedestrian; they are indeed so evidently useful that the Labour party, which was once pledged to 'end' the House of Lords, was ready to agree in 1948 to quite a reasonable scheme for 'mending' it. The Conservative party, with the fine careless rapture which produced the first Parliament Act, gazed on the prospect of an Iron and Steel Bill, failed to seize the psychological momentum, refused to agree to a scheme which enabled a Government to pass legislation in the fourth session of a Parliament without an appeal to the people, and therefore authorised the Labour party to get such legislation through an unreformed and increasingly incompetent Second Chamber without such an appeal. Now the existence of the House of Lords is dependent on the continued willingness of a score of Labour peers to suffer regular defeat at the hands of a slightly larger Conservative majority. It was discovered long ago that the House of Commons could not function without an Opposition; it is not the less necessary in the House of Lords.

Those who have had experience of single-chamber government do not like it much, not because a Second Chamber can reverse the errors of the electorate (and indeed there is no criterion by which the electorate can be judged) but because a single Chamber cannot be expected to undertake all the heavy labour that modern conditions impose upon the legislature of a highly industrialised country. The House of Commons has been so devised by history that it needs the House of Lords to complete and supplement its work. The latter House could continue to function if all the Labour peers were withdrawn either by death or by deliberate abstention, but its effectiveness would disappear and it would no doubt be abolished as soon as there was a sufficient Labour majority in the House of Commons.

When 'democracy' and 'Parliament' appear in the same sentence, however, the latter means the House of Commons. That House sits longer and more often than the other. It has, indeed, far more to do. Strangely enough, it nearly always appears to do something which is quite different from what it really is doing. Apart from the question hour, those Fridays when a few private members are listening to debates on motions (the rest, like most of the ministers, being engaged on their lawful business elsewhere), and a few other occasions, the House appears to be legislating. It is discussing whether a Bill shall be read a second or third time, whether words shall be there inserted, whether a clause shall stand part of a Bill, whether it is expedient that a sum be granted (*scil.* by legislation) to Her Majesty. What it is really doing is defending and criticising the Government.

Bagehot, with his incomparable capacity for seeing into the truth of things, placed the legislative function last among the functions of the House. Its main function, he said, was to choose a Prime Minister. We must now modify his analysis. It is not the House but the electorate that chooses the Prime Minister. It is true that the electorate's choice is limited. It has to choose, for instance, between Sir Anthony Eden and Mr Attlee. It does it, too, without choosing either. What the elector has to do is to choose between Sir John Blue and Mr Red; but because there are elected as a result four hundred Blues and two hundred Reds, the leader of the Blues becomes Prime Minister. Most of those who voted for Sir John supported him because he supported Sir Anthony. Had he changed his colour they would have rejected him with equal enthusiasm. The electors decide, by majorities in a majority of constituencies, that Sir Anthony shall be Prime Minister. Nevertheless, the Prime Minister is not just a nomadic chieftain whose rank is determined by the number of sheep that bear his brand. In a sense the sheep brand the shepherd. Sir Anthony was chosen apparently because he was recommended by Sir Winston Churchill; but he was recommended because it was thought that all the sheep, both inside and outside the House, who had an aversion from red, would follow him. That most of them would do so was shown by the fact that the most important of them—the members, peers and candidates of his own party—subsequently elected him unanimously. Unanimous election does not necessarily imply that they all wanted to follow him; when Mr Balfour resigned some wanted to follow Mr Austen Chamberlain and some Mr Walter Long, so they unanimously elected Mr Bonar Law. It does show, however, that they were prepared to follow at least *faute de mieux*.

This function, then, is no longer that of the House of Commons. It is no longer true to say with Bagehot:

No matter that a few months since it was chosen to support Lord Aberdeen or Lord Palmerston; upon a sudden occasion it ousts the statesman to whom it at first adhered, and selects an opposite statesman whom it at first rejected.[1]

If the modern Lord John Russell wishes to upset the coach he does not propose a resolution in the House of Commons; he holds private converse with a press lord and calls a meeting in the Carlton Club.

In truth, the real function of the House is that which Bagehot broke up into three elements, to 'express the mind of the people', to 'teach the nation what it does not know', and to make us 'hear what otherwise we should not'.[2] It does it by defending and criticising the Government. The technique varies from time to time, and the process involves the three elements mentioned by Bagehot; but the essential principle is that which underlies the whole of the British Constitution, the principle of democracy.[3]

---

[1] *English Constitution* (World's Classics ed.), p. 116.
[2] *Ibid.* pp. 117–19.　　　　　　　　[3] *Cabinet Government*, ch. 1.

It is easy to be cynical about the interests and ambitions of politicians. Indeed, a political observer, if he is to observe correctly, must be a cynic. Bagehot was one of the greatest of political scientists because he was not misled by shibboleths, nor impressed by sentimental refrains, nor diverted by the claims of the patriots that everything was for the best in the age and country of Queen Victoria. A writer who can discuss how 'the actions of a retired widow and an unemployed youth' become important is a great man indeed. No doubt he would have modified his language ninety years later. The extent to which one can be unconventional depends upon the strength of the convention. A writer must clothe his thoughts more or less in the style of the time. The present fashion being to talk of royalty in terms of sickly adulation (which the recipients must dislike more than anybody), even a Bagehot must at least be polite.

Let us, then, not assume that members of Parliament are all high-souled, public spirited, conscientious, single-minded representatives of the people, intent only on the people's good, and without reference to their own prestige. There are no such people outside the Saints' Calendar; and if there were they could not take part in the rough and tumble of political life. Nevertheless, the worst that can be said about members is that they are ordinary people with a fair slice of ambition; and—the question has been asked before—is ambition a sin? In truth, what the democratic system does is to harness a man's ambitions, if they lie in the right direction, to the national dog-cart. The horse will go of his own volition because he wants to get somewhere, and perforce the cart will follow; by choosing the right horses the nation will arrive at its chosen destination. The horse chooses the destination, but the nation chooses the horse; and—it is here that a dictatorship differs—the horse can always be changed, in mid-stream if necessary.

If he requires sweet stimulation in the form of ribbons and titles, no harm is done. A guinea is no less gold because it has a stamp, nor is a horse the slower because he appears in the stud-book. There is, indeed, advantage to be obtained from the system of distributing medals and prizes. It induces many to take the road of public service who might otherwise remain in the stable. Moreover, a title confers prestige only because there are many who cannot separate merit and distinction.

Prime Ministers are better as plain right honourables,[1] but ordinary members look more impressive if they are baronets and knights. Government implies mutual respect between the governors and the governed; and if the governed have more respect for governors with ribbons the process is made easier. The man of the people may possibly engage in politics because he likes to meet eminent people and to be considered eminent himself; the eminent persons may like to meet still more eminent persons; and the very eminent persons may feel flattered by the respect which their eminence induces in ordinary people. So everybody is happy, like the three men in O'Henry's story, each of whom wanted to shake another of them by the hand.

Let us, then, praise famous men because they are famous; but let us also remember that they are compelled to do something for the public in order to become famous. Ambition is a virtue, not a vice, and the world would be infinitely poorer without it—even learned men like to be thought learned. Political ambition in a democratic state lies high in the scale of virtues because it cannot be achieved save by a devotion to the common good. High office is not achieved by the flattery of adventurers, nor by lying denunciation of competitors, nor, above all, by mixing poisons for modern Borgias; it can be achieved only by persuading plain people of the righteousness of one's cause, the honesty of one's opinions, and the capacity of one's intellect. Nor, indeed, can motives be separated. It is not possible to distinguish the desire to advance the public weal from the desire to receive public approval for advancing the public weal. If any fact appears clearly from the examination of the more technical parts of parliamentary government in certain parts of this book, it is that men and women can be found ready to perform the hard, exacting and uninteresting tasks that receive no publicity and no public recognition. Who knows of the work done by an Opposed Bill Group? Even here, of course, motives are mixed. Lord John Russell, in his *Essay on Government*, said that unpaid magistrates are highly praised for disinterestedness; but, he added, 'They have power, however, for their trouble, and a power which the barons of old struggled so hard to possess and exercise.' Members of Parliament have not much

---

[1] Though the Garter is not inappropriate now that the Queen awards it of her own volition.

power; but they have some, and they like the feel of it. It is not unpleasant to be able to cross-examine the most eminent civil servants and to contradict the leaders of the Parliamentary Bar.

It may appear that we have wandered far from the essential function of Parliament. In truth we have not. If it can be shown that there are reasons for seeking membership of Parliament, and if it is true, to quote Mr Kirkwood (who cannot be accused of material motives or obsequiousness to authority), that 'the first concern of an M.P. is to keep his seat',[1] it follows that the contacts between members and their constituents must be close indeed and the relations between public opinion and the feeling of the House of the most intimate character. In five years at most the member must seek a new franchise, and if he wants it renewed he will do all he can in the meantime to maintain the confidence of his constituents. Naturally there are devices whose public advantages seem not to be great; the subscriptions to local sports clubs and charities, the garden parties where plain people shake hands with a marchioness, the organised joy-rides to the seaside, the heart-to-heart talks in the lobbies,[2] are not essential parts of the British Constitution and are seldom described by the learned. They are, however, the sugar coating, and the main task of the member is to forward the interests and support the policies of as many of his constituents as he can.

For this purpose he must maintain close contact with his constituency. It has already been pointed out that the British Parliament differs from many legislatures (including the Congress of the United States and the Parliaments of other Commonwealth countries) in that every member can visit his constituency during the week-end. There is no need for the 'telegraphic lobby', though that device is sometimes used by organised interests. The members for Sheffield are soon informed of the desires of the steel manufacturers and the engineering trade unions; the member for Swindon is necessarily interested in the progress of British Railways and

---

[1] *My Life of Revolt*, p. 220.

[2] Just a little side-light. I was between the two main lobbies recently when two ladies sent in a green card to fetch out their member. When the member arrived the door-keeper asked if he knew them. 'I ought to', he replied. Thereupon, the door-keeper stood behind him in the entrance to the members' lobby and unobtrusively pointed them out. A shilling having passed from hand to hand, the member walked up to the ladies and greeted them effusively. How happy they appeared, to be recognised among so many!

the views of the railway trade unions. These are extreme and therefore obvious examples; it is, however, true as a general principle that the member must maintain close relations with all the organised opinions of his constituents. Every member receives individual protests and requests for assistance; every member maintains the closest contact with his local party committee which is, in turn, if the party be well organised, in contact with a large body of local opinion.

The relationship works both ways and the inspiration is mutual. Primarily, it enables the member to understand what the people want and what they will not stand. Members can return from their constituencies convinced, for instance, that something must be done about the cost of living. On the other hand, they can go down to their constituencies to explain why the plans of Mr Macmillan ought to be approved. On foreign affairs particularly, members can speak with an emphasis which no Cabinet minister, whose views will be quoted abroad, dares to use. Often, indeed, private members grossly exaggerate in their political speeches. They are apt to put everything into black and white, though most things are grey. Their influence is not great; few listen to their speeches and not many more read them; but they exercise an informative function of importance.

Such reports as they make are only partially in evidence in the House itself. Far more important than the speeches that they make are the conversations that they hold. There is a lobby opinion which is more important even than the opinion of the House. Both directly and indirectly they impress the whips, and the whips impress ministers.

The Cabinet is subjected to these influences from private members because it, too, wants to keep office. The most honest and self-sacrificing member—Mr Baldwin, say, or Sir Austen Chamberlain—really likes the feeling of power that ministerial office gives. It is in other respects a thankless and wearing task; nobody would do it for long unless he liked it; and it is part of the technique of propaganda to persuade people that he is there only for the public good. So, in a very real sense, he is. Certainly the only material advantage to be gained from Cabinet office is the salary, and many ministers leave office poorer than when they entered it. There are only four advantages to be obtained from Cabinet office: the sensation of power, the respect of the masses, the interest of the work, and the consciousness of public-spiritedness. These advantages are, however, great indeed, and there are few who would not be Cabinet ministers if they were given the opportunity.

This being so, few Governments are anxious to be defeated. There may come a time when internal dissensions make the task so anxious that ministers may be willing to give up. Lord Rosebery's Government in 1895 was only too glad to seize the opportunity of a defeat on a snap vote; and Mr Balfour's just petered into futility. These are, however, the exceptions. Moreover, we must not ignore the great importance of conscientiously held opinions. Not all Cabinet ministers place their opinions before their prospects; some have suited their opinions to their forecasts of trends in political weather. Most, however, really believe in the ideas that they support and propagate. They believe that their policies are essential to the public interest and that the opinions of the Opposition are noxious.

They can forward those policies only if they are in power, and in order to achieve and maintain power they must obtain and keep a parliamentary majority. On the one hand, they must give way to public opinion so long as the essential principles of their policies are maintained; on the other hand they must do their best to persuade public opinion to their point of view. No Government hesitates to do what it considers to be necessary merely because it appears to be presently unpopular. It believes that free people are open to persuasion and that ministers can justify themselves in Parliament and on the platform. If they are mistaken they can do no more than go out of office. Often they are not mistaken; they can make a great effort to justify themselves, and usually they succeed. The British system of government is government by party, and the party is a huge propaganda machine one of whose parts is the House of Commons itself.

On the one hand, therefore, we find that the Government is very susceptible to public opinion; on the other hand we find public opinion very susceptible to persuasion by the Government. Parliament is not the only instrument available. The Prime Minister is leader of a party, and general movements of opinion are brought to him through the party machine as well as through members of Parliament. The most important efforts of propaganda are conducted through the national party machines and their local branches and through the Press. We are not at the moment concerned with these instruments. Important though they are, they are dependent in the last resort on Parliament. It is not merely an assembly of 630 persons in close contact with local movements of opinion, it is also one of the greatest propaganda instruments in the world.

It is, to use one of Bagehot's favourite phrases, a dignified assembly. It is dignified not only in the sense that it conducts its proceedings with decorum and restraint, but also in the sense that it enjoys a prestige which no institution in the world can surpass. Only a small proportion of the people has ever attended its debates. Few have heard the call 'Speaker' ring through the lobbies. But all know about Parliament and read something about its discussions for two-thirds of the year. It has occupied the centre of the political stage for centuries. So much of the history of freedom is part of the history of Parliament that freedom and parliamentary government are often considered to be the same thing. It enjoys such a prestige that it has been called the finest platform in England. It is the place where the primary defence of the Government's policy must be made—and, we must add, though it is a point to be left for later emphasis, where the primary attack on the Government's policy must be made. While it is true that a plea that convinces a well-disposed audience may be received more coldly at the next general election, the first step is to persuade the ministerial majority; and through the Press and the members themselves something is done to persuade the rest.

In speaking of public opinion, however, we make use of one of those generalisations which are apt to lead to false conclusions. On certain issues one can discern a general or popular tendency. The Hoare-Laval proposals were received with almost unanimous disapproval. Usually, opinion is more evenly divided, even on such general issues as the abdication of Edward VIII or the attack on the Suez Canal in 1956. Most issues, however, are not of such wide appeal and consequence. Superannuation for local government officers, the provision of houses, subsidies to farmers, and the like, provide the ordinary texture of parliamentary discussion. They affect people generally as users of public services and consumers of goods; but this is a remote relationship, and people as users and consumers can express their views only through the casting of votes once in four or five years on a multitude of accumulated proposals and performances. The public servants and the producers concerned, or, to generalise, the 'interests' concerned, are far more directly and immediately affected. They are, accordingly, far more vocal. What is called 'public opinion' is often nothing more than the views of a group of special interests. When Sir John Simon withdrew the first National Defence Contribution it was not because the general body of electors expressed any views about it, but because the group of interests known as 'the City' objected to it. Similarly, the battle over the Coal Mines Bill in 1937–8 was one in which the people as consumers took no part. The fight was a series of conflicts in which the Mining Association, the Mineworkers' Federation, the public utilities, and the co-operative societies (the nearest approach to the consumers) were engaged. Nor are such interests necessarily concerned with profits. The local authorities' associations are as influential as any, and on some kinds of legislation the philanthropic societies have the most weighty views to express.

This aspect of the matter has already been fully considered. It is most important in respect of legislation. Its result is that much legislation derives from organised interests, that most of it is amended on the representations of such interests, and that often parliamentary opposition is in truth the opposition of interests. No further emphasis is required; but it is essential to remember that public opinion is often merely the sum of the opinions of minority groups, that members represent such groups as well as their constituents, and that matters of general concern are comparatively few.

Much of this might equally be true of a dictatorship and its tame 'legislature'. Every dictator has for his primary aim the maintenance of his own power and must, therefore, follow the whims of such public opinion as exists. Dictators are not merely, to use Milton's expressive phrase, 'the masters and the patrons of a banditti'. Certainly they begin as such, but when they have achieved power banditry becomes the official governmental policy, an 'ideology' which its philosophers are expected to justify and other nations to respect. Much can be done with public opinion if a doctrine is repeated often enough and the contrary cannot be asserted in public. There are, however, substantial limits; for though any individual can be induced to accept any general principle he may not like its application to himself; and if there are enough of him there may arise that suppressed murmur that precedes revolution. The whole nation may salute its chief with a mighty 'Hail! Robber', but everybody thinks that the other fellow ought to be robbed. One may rob Peter to pay Paul provided that there are few Peters and many Pauls; but all the Pauls in office cannot maintain themselves if the rest of the population is made up of Peters. The Pauls, too, are a gigantic vested interest, the only highly organised interest that remains. The banditti insist on their share of the plunder, and a leader who does not give it risks deposition. Other interests are, however, organised within the party. The financial interests state their case against the agricultural interest; the winegrowers of one part of the country make demands that are repudiated by the winegrowers of another district. They all fall into the party line, they all lift up their hands in the same salute, but they ask for different things. The leader has to placate public opinion in general and selected portions of it in particular.

The real difference between Britain and the dictatorship countries is that with us there is not one faction seeking to maintain itself in power by persuasion, fraud or force, but at least two factions each trying to achieve and maintain power by persuasion. These factions are based on different views of the national interest, and each appeals to public opinion to uphold its policy. To a substantial degree these different views are dependent on personal and economic motives; yet each seeks to appeal to the people as a whole. The Conservative party believes that it can persuade the great mass of the people that State-controlled private capitalism produces the optimum benefit; the Labour party believes that that benefit would best be obtained by State capitalism or socialism. These are, however, the differences of principle, and in their application to immediate and pressing problems they differ only in emphasis. They are no greater than the differences that separated Tories and Whigs or Conservatives and Liberals during the last century. Naturally the organised capitalist groups are on the one side and the organised workers' groups on the other. But the appeal is to the whole, and because it is to the whole the immediate differences cannot be fundamental. The purpose of a general election is to persuade the uncertain element in the electorate to step over the one side or the other of the line that separates the one party from the other. It does not need much change of opinion for a person to leave one party to support another if he considers merely the immediate issues.

There may be and are other and smaller parties appealing to particular groups of opinion, but though sometimes these parties break the simplicity of the two-party system, there are so many tendencies towards its restoration that in the end it returns. As a result, the whole Constitution, from the electoral process to parliamentary procedure, assumes the two-party system; and because it assumes that system it assists in maintaining it. There are, in reality, only two ways of voting, for and against the Government. There are only two lobbies in the House of Commons. Parties will not obtain much support unless they have some opportunity of putting their policies into practice. They will be unable to build up strong organisations unless they can show their ability and their prospect of forming a Government. Parties without organisation are unable to appeal effectively to an enormous electorate. Each of them, too, has a long and not inglorious history, a history which induces loyalty in its members; that loyalty, too, becomes a personal matter, the loyalty to those who are believed to embody the spirit of Pitt or Disraeli or the Tolpuddle Martyrs. It therefore takes a long time to create a party. The facility for compromise, which is all that the British 'genius for government' means, enables minor differences of opinion to be submerged in major principles of agreement. The Peelite, Radical, Liberal Unionist, Liberal National and National Labour members and candidates ultimately find their places in one or other of the two great parties. Little coteries of rebels may for a time maintain their independence, but financial considerations, the desire of electors to give a straight vote for or against a possible Government, and the natural ambitions of men to put their policies into action, ultimately wipe out their differences.

There is nothing to prevent any person from creating what party he pleases; but anyone who wishes to secure the adoption of a policy must either spend a generation in organisation and propaganda or persuade one of the two great parties. The House of Commons is the oratorical battleground of those parties. The one supports and the other opposes the Government. The one defends a policy and the other puts forward another. Any defect of administration, any weakness of principle or defect of practice, any blunder of politics, is soon brought to light and exhibited to the world.

The functions which Bagehot described are thus exercised through the competition of Government and Opposition. The 'mind of the people' is expressed in different ways and through different forms because it is not and cannot be a single mind. Political education is real education because at least two points of view are always being put, and the elector has to choose between them. The other side has power to speak and therefore can and must be heard. The Opposition demands that policies be formulated openly and consequences of policies revealed. Parliament compels the Government to defend itself by open and rational argument; but it also compels the Opposition to state what is the alternative and, if that alternative be plausible, to attempt to carry it out.

It does not, however, produce only a choice of alternatives. It compels either choice to be adopted and put into execution with reasonable consideration for individuals. The majority does not override the minority roughshod, because the habits of centuries have created a free people, disliking oppression even of minorities. Members of Parliament, to quote Milton again, know the people of England to be a free people, and themselves the representatives of that freedom. It is their business to discover and secure the reprobation of injuries to that freedom. British history has witnessed most of the dangers to which constitutions are subject. Masters and patrons of a banditti, religious and racial persecution, martial law, censorship of the press, suppression of opinion, suppression of trade unions, overweening military officers— are they not all in the history books? There is nothing in the technique of modern dictatorship, except perhaps its brutality, that has not been tried and rejected in this country long ago. British constitutional history is a story of resistance to oppression, often temporarily unsuccessful, but ultimately resulting in its abolition. Magna Carta (at least as it is now interpreted), the Petition of Right, the Act of Settlement, the Habeas Corpus Acts, bear witness to the legal devices that have been made to destroy oppression and maintain freedom.

Legal devices are not and cannot be enough. In Great Britain, in particular, they are wholly ineffective as against a Parliament. For, as Lord Burleigh said, 'England can never be ruined but by a Parliament'; and when the House of Commons tried to exclude the member for Middlesex Junius wrote:

We can never be really in danger till the forms of Parliament are made use of to destroy the substance of our civil and political liberties: till Parliament itself betrays its trust, by contributing to establish new principles of government; and employing the very weapons committed to it by the collective body to stab the Constitution.[1]

In the last resort all legal principles and all constitutional checks depend on the proper exercise of the 'transcendent and absolute' power of Parliament.

The whole constitutional machine is, however, impregnated with the principles of democratic parliamentary government. At the peak stands Her Majesty's Opposition, ready and able to pounce upon injustice and oppression even more readily than upon defects of policy. In that it does not stand alone, for the Government not only does not dare but does not want to act oppressively. If there is in any Government department any military officer or other person who thinks that government might be easier if he could suppress a few of the 'undesirables', there is always a minister to explain, first, that the House of Commons will not stand it, and secondly and above all, that he will not permit it. Moreover, the power of the Opposition itself rests only on sufferance. There is nothing whatever in the constitutional machinery that prevents an Opposition from being suppressed. Nor is there anything effective to prevent the power of the Opposition from being completely destroyed by the destruction of free elections. The Opposition cannot outvote the majority, it can only carry out Canning's threat to defy it and appeal to the people. But if there is no appeal to the people the threat is as empty as the House is on a Sunday. Even if there is an Opposition and freedom of elections there is no effective appeal if there is no freedom of assembly and organisation. The checks and balances are mutually interdependent. One alone cannot be overthrown and, so long as they remain, it is the function of the Opposition not only to see that they operate but also to prevent gradual and insidious encroachments.

[1] *Letters of Junius* (Everett's ed.), p. 158.

In the last resort the sanction of all constitutional principles is the threat of revolution. It is a threat which need not be used and is seldom heard. For, in truth, the whole system is a free system, impregnated with ideas which are the product of centuries of constitutional development, and dependent in the last analysis on the will of the people to be free. So, the constitutional structure not only contains the necessary laws to make it work freely, but also is riddled with practices and conventions which are even more a part of the national life than the laws themselves. In the House of Commons, which is the focus of the whole apparatus, Her Majesty's Government is assisted by Her Majesty's Opposition. Preceding chapters have shown how important are the arrangements 'behind the Speaker's Chair', and how even more important is the atmosphere in which parliamentary proceedings are conducted. The Opposition has rooms allotted to it in the House. Its leader has a salary charged, like those of the judges, on the Consolidated Fund, and a room in the same corridor as the rooms of the Secretaries of State. He is, perhaps, sworn of the Privy Council on the advice of his chief opponent. He stands side by side with the Prime Minister when the Queen opens Parliament.

These are the symbols of freedom. The right honourable gentleman, the member for South Leeds, is in his place on the Front Opposition Bench to exercise a function which is almost as important as the function of the right honourable gentleman opposite. The one permits the other to govern because the second permits the first to oppose, and together they lead their parties in the operation of the constitutional machine.

APPENDIX I

HOUSE OF COMMONS

Analysis of Time spent on Business on the Floor of the House

	1929–30		1928–9		1928		1927		1926		1924–5		1936–7	1937–8
	Full days	Fridays or equivalents	Full days	Fridays or equivalents	Full days	Fridays or equivalents	Full days	Fridays or equivalents	Full days	Fridays or equivalents	Full days	Fridays or equivalents	Days	Days
Preliminaries	3	—	—	—	1*	—	—	—	—	—	3	—	—	—
Private Members	13	19	—	—	8	15	9½	13	7	13	10½	13	23½	27
Opposition	5	—	—	—	2½	—	7½	—	1½	—	6	1	10½	14½
Address	6	1	6	1	4½	1	4	1	4	1	5	—	6½	6
Adjournment for Recess	—	4	—	1	—	2	—	3	3	—	—	3½	3½	4
Financial Business	56¾	3	31	4	38½	4½	42½	3	53½	1	46½	2½	45½	44
Routine Business	1½	—	½	1	2	—	1½	—	2	—	1½	—	1	1½
Government Motions	2	—	—	—	—	—	—	1	1¼	—	1½	—	—	—
Government Bills	61¼	12	42½	13	31¼	1½	48	9	40¼	10	44	11	61½	62
Special occasions	1†	—	—	—	3‡	—	1§	—	9½	4	—	—	3‖	—
Adjournment (S.O. 8)	—	—	—	—	¼	—	—	—	—	—	—	—	—	—
Sitting days	149½	39	80	20	91	24	114	30	119	32	118	31	155	159

* Election of Speaker. † Death of Statesman. ‡ Prayer Book Measure and Death of Statesman.

§ Prayer Book. ‖ Abdication and Accession.

For the figures from 1924–30, see H.C. 161 of 1931, p. 438. The 1936–7 and 1937–8 figures are from *The Times*, 31 July 1937, and 30 July 1938. There Fridays are counted as whole days, and Opposition and Government motions and motions under S.O. 8 are not distinguished.

WHO MADE THE LAWS IN 1936-7?

Ch.	Short title	Introduced by	Source
1	Merchant Shipping (Carriage of Munitions to Spain) Act, 1936	Board of Trade	Cabinet policy
2	Railway Freight Rebates Act, 1936	Ministry of Transport	Agreement between railway companies and associations of local authorities, accepted by Government
3	His Majesty's Declaration of Abdication Act, 1936	Prime Minister	The King on the advice of the Cabinet and in consultation with the Dominions
4	Expiring Laws Continuance Act, 1936	Treasury	Government (annual)
5	Trunk Roads Act, 1936	Ministry of Transport	Department, after consultation with local authorities. Matter of public debate for some years
6	Public Meetings Act, 1936	Attorney-General	Cabinet policy, arising out of public discussion
7	Consolidated Fund (No. 1) Act, 1937	Treasury	Government (annual)
8	Beef and Veal Customs Duties Act, 1937	Treasury	Government policy adopted in 1934 on pressure from agricultural interests but contested by importing interests and (apparently) Foreign and Dominions Offices on political grounds (i.e. Argentine and Australia). Policy at length carried out under pressure of Conservative Agriculture Committee and non-parliamentary committee, and National Farmers' Union
9	India and Burma (Existing laws) Act, 1937	India and Burma Office	Departments (consequential)
10	Unemployment Assistance (Temporary Provisions) (Amendment) Act, 1937	Ministry of Labour	Department (consequential)
11	Public Works Loans Act, 1937	Treasury	On behalf of the Public Works Loans Board (annual)
12	Firearms Act, 1937	Home Office	Departmental on the recommendation of a Departmental Committee
13	Defence Loans Act, 1937	Treasury	Cabinet policy
14	East India Loans Act, 1937	India Office	Department, on behalf of Government of India
15	Geneva Convention Act, 1937	Board of Trade	Department, to ratify international convention, and with consent of Commonwealth of Australia
16	Regency Act, 1937	Home Office	Cabinet policy and royal message
17	Reserve Forces Act, 1937	War Office	Department
18	Empire Settlement Act, 1937	Dominions Office	Department—consequential on lapse of temporary Act

Ch.	Short title	Introduced by	Source
19	Merchant Shipping (Spanish Frontiers Observation) Act, 1937	Board of Trade	Cabinet policy
20	Consolidated Fund (No. 2) Act, 1937	Treasury	Department (annual)
21	British Shipping (Continuance of Subsidy) Act, 1937	Board of Trade	Department: subsidy continued for one year at request of shipping interests
22	Local Government (Financial Provisions) Act, 1937	Ministry of Health	Department after consultation with associations of local authorities. Necessitated by temporary provision
23	Merchant Shipping Act, 1937	Board of Trade	Department: in part because of an observation by a judge; in part on recommendation of Sea-Fish Commission
24	National Health Insurance (Amendment) Act, 1937	Ministry of Health	Department—drafting amendment to Act of 1936
25	Education (Deaf Children) Act, 1937	Private member (Mr R. Duckworth)	Board of Education and National Union of Teachers
26	Army and Air Force (Annual) Act, 1937	War Office	Department (annual)
27	County Councils Association Expenses (Amendment) Act, 1937	Private member (Lieut.-Col. Acland-Troyte)	County Councils Association (unopposed)
28	Harbours, Piers and Ferries (Scotland) Act, 1937	Scottish Office	Based on draft Bill published in 1934 and submitted to harbour authorities for observations
29	Local Government (Financial Provisions) (Scotland) Act, 1937	Scottish Office	Department after consultation with associations of local authorities. Necessitated by temporary provisions
30	Maternity Services (Scotland) Act, 1937	Scottish Office	Department of Health for Scotland, after consultation with associations of local authorities
31	Special Areas (Amendment) Act, 1937	Ministry of Labour	Department, on recommendation of Commissioners for the Special Areas
32	Civil List Act, 1937	Treasury	Select Committee of the House of Commons, after message from the Crown
33	Diseases of Fish Act, 1937	Ministry of Agriculture and Scottish Office	Based on recommendation of Departmental Committee in 1929. Bill of 1934 failed to pass because of opposition and lack of time. Opposition removed by negotiation with fish farmers
34	Sheep Stocks Valuation (Scotland) Act, 1937	Private member (Col. Sir Charles MacAndrew)	Based on report of Departmental Committee and obtained from Scottish Office through Whips' Office
35	Statutory Salaries Act, 1937	Treasury	Department, on the representations of the Comptroller and Auditor-General, supported by Select Committee of Public Accounts
36	Local Government (Members' Travelling Expenses) Act, 1937	Private member (Sir G. Bowyer)	Urban District Councils' Association (entirely unopposed)

Ch.	Short title	Introduced by	Source
37	Children and Young Persons (Scotland) Act, 1937	Lord Advocate	Parliamentary Counsel to the Treasury and Statute Law Revision Committee (consolidation)
38	Ministers of the Crown Act, 1937	Home Office	Two select committees of the House of Commons and Cabinet policy
39	Widows', Orphans' and Old Age Contributory Pensions (Voluntary Contributors) Act, 1937	Ministry of Health	Cabinet policy (King's Speech) after public agitation on behalf of 'black-coated workers' and consultation with the Consultative Council of Approved Societies
40	Public Health (Drainage of Trade Premises) Act, 1937	Ministry of Health	Joint Advisory Committee Report, followed by Bill drafted by Central Council for Rivers Protection and subsequent amendments agreed by Ministry of Health, local authorities' associations, Federation of British Industries, British Waterworks Association, Institute of Sewage Purification, etc.
41	Exchange Equalisation Account Act, 1937	Treasury	Cabinet policy
42	Exportation of Horses Act, 1937	Private member (Mr E. A. Radford)	Member, assisted by the League for the Prevention of the Exportation of Horses for Butchery, the Royal Society for the Prevention of Cruelty to Animals, and Our Dumb Friends' League
43	Public Records (Scotland) Act, 1937	Lord Advocate	Departmental
44	Road Traffic Act, 1937	Private member (Sir A. Pownall)	To reverse a judicial decision; suggested by Ministry of Transport through Whips' Office
45	Hydrogen Cyanide (Fumigation) Act, 1937	Home Office	Departmental
46	Physical Training and Recreation Act, 1937	Board of Education	Department, after some public agitation
47	Teachers (Superannuation) Act, 1937	Board of Education	National Union of Teachers, the British Council and Scottish Institute of Education
48	Methylated Spirits (Sale by Retail) (Scotland) Act, 1937	Private member (Miss F. Horsbrugh)	Member, as a result of publicity by Salvation Army, Church Army, etc.
49	Trade Marks (Amendment) Act, 1937	Board of Trade	Departmental committee, on recommendation of Trade Marks, Patents, and Designs Federation, after consultation with Federation of British Industries
50	Livestock Industry Act, 1937	Ministry of Agriculture and Fisheries	See ch. 8 above, this being part of the same policy
51	Post Office and Telegraph (Money) Act, 1937	Post Office	Department
52	Chairmen of Traffic Commissioners, etc. (Tenure of Office) Act, 1937	Ministry of Transport	Department
53	Agricultural Wages (Regulation) (Scotland) Act, 1937	Scottish Office	Representation of Central Executive of Farmers and Farm Servants, but opposed by National Farmers' Union. Departmental Committee reported in favour
54	Finance Act, 1937	Treasury	Department (annual)

Ch.	Short title	Introduced by	Source
55	Appropriation Act, 1937	Treasury	Department (annual)
56	Coal (Registration of Ownership) Act, 1937	Board of Trade (Mines Department)	Cabinet policy (election programme)
57	Matrimonial Causes Act, 1937	Private member (Mr De la Bere)	Another private member (Mr A. P. Herbert)
58	Summary Procedure (Domestic Proceedings) Act, 1937	Private member (Mr M. Petherick)	Private member's Bill in 1934, followed by Departmental Committee
59	Cinematograph Films (Animals) Act, 1937	Private member (Sir R. Gower)	Royal Society for the Prevention of Cruelty to Animals and National Canine Defence League
60	Rating and Valuation Act, 1937	Ministry of Health	Department, after consultation with local authorities' associations
61	Export Guarantee Act, 1937	Overseas Trade Department	Department: to continue and extend expiring powers and consolidate legislation
62	Coal Mines (Employment of Boys) Act, 1937	Private member (Mr C. S. Taylor)	Mines Department
63	Nigeria (Remission of Payments) Act, 1937	Colonial Office	Department
64	Isle of Man (Customs) Act, 1937	Treasury	Manx Legislature (annual)
65	London Naval Treaty Act, 1937	Admiralty	Cabinet policy
66	Milk (Amendment) Act, 1937	Ministry of Agriculture	Continuation and extension of temporary Act passed in part satisfaction of agricultural interests, pending permanent legislation on lines recommended by Milk Reorganisation Commission
67	Factories Act, 1937	Home Office	Department, after years of consultations with representatives of industry and organised labour
68	Local Government Superannuation Act, 1937	Ministry of Health	Based on Bill promoted by National Association of Local Government Officers but modified in agreement with Ministry of Health, General Council of the Trades Union Congress, and associations of local authorities
69	Local Government Superannuation (Scotland) Act, 1937	Scottish Office	Based on Bill promoted by National Association of Local Government Officers but modified in agreement with Ministry of Health, General Council of the Trades Union Congress, and associations of local authorities
70	Agriculture Act, 1937	Ministry of Agriculture and Fisheries and Scottish Office	Government policy, on pressure from agricultural interests

THE SHADOW CABINET, 1956

Mr Clement Attlee having been raised to the peerage, Mr Hugh Gaitskell was elected leader by the Parliamentary Labour party and thus became *ex officio* Leader of the Opposition in accordance with the Ministers of the Crown Act, 1937. Mr Herbert Morrison having resigned his position as Deputy Leader, Mr Griffiths was elected in his place. Mr Gaitskell then requested other members of the Parliamentary Labour party to pay particular attention to the affairs of the several ministries in accordance with the following list, which is taken from *The Times* of 15 February 1956:

Agriculture, Fisheries and Food: T. Williams, F. T. Willey, A. J. Champion.

Colonial Office: Aneurin Bevan and Arthur Creech Jones.

Commonwealth Relations: Arthur Creech Jones.

Defence: R. R. Stokes.

Admiralty: L. J. Callaghan.

Air Ministry: G. de Freitas.

War Office: J. Strachey.

Ministry of Supply: G. Brown.

Education: M. Stewart and Miss Herbison.

Foreign Office: A. Robens and K. Younger.

Fuel and power and atomic energy: L. J. Callaghan and H. Neal.

Health: Dr Edith Summerskill and A. Blenkinsop.

Home Office: K. Younger and A. Greenwood.

Housing and Local Government: G. R. Mitchison and G. S. Lindgren.

Labour and National Service: G. Brown and F. Lee.

Law Officers: Sir Lynn Ungoed Thomas.

Pensions and National Insurance: H. A. Marquand and T. Steele.

Post Office: Ness Edwards and C. R. Hobson.

Scottish Office: T. Fraser and A. Woodburn.

Transport and Civil Aviation: G. Strauss and E. Davies.

Treasury and Board of Trade: H. Wilson, Douglas Jay, A. Bottomley, and P. Gordon Walker.

Works: A. Greenwood.

The 'Shadow Cabinet' is, strictly, the parliamentary committee of the Parliamentary Labour party, which includes the Leader, the Deputy Leader, the chief whip, and the members elected by the parliamentary party.

THE ANNUAL FINANCIAL LEGISLATION
AS ILLUSTRATED BY THE LEGISLATION
FOR THE SESSION 1953-4

(1) *The Consolidated Fund (No. 3) Act, 1953.*

Enacted on 18 December 1953, for the following purposes:

(*a*) To authorise the issue of a sum out of the Consolidated Fund for the service of the financial year ending on 31 March 1954. This sum is required to meet expenditure above that provided by the Appropriation Act, 1953, as set out in Supplementary Estimates.

(*b*) To authorise the Treasury to borrow by Treasury Bills or otherwise the amount referred to in the previous paragraph. This is a matter of precaution in case the amount to the credit of the Consolidated Fund at any given moment is not sufficient to cover the issues authorised by the present Act.

(2) *The Consolidated Fund Act, 1954.*

Enacted on 26 March 1954, for the following purposes:

(*a*) To authorise the issue of a sum out of the Consolidated Fund for the service of the financial years 1952–3 and 1953–4. So far as 1952–3 is concerned, this completes the authorisation of the expenditure of the year by authorising the issue of the sums necessary to meet excess expenditure during the year. So far as 1953–4 is concerned, the purpose is to authorise the issue of funds to meet another set of Supplementary Estimates.

(*b*) To authorise the issue of a sum out of the Consolidated Fund for the service of the financial year 1954–5. This year has not begun at the moment of enactment, but the Appropriation Act, which contains the main authorisation for the issues of the year, will not be passed until the end of the session. Accordingly, the House passes a vote on account which is estimated to cover the issues necessary between the beginning of the financial year and the enactment of the Appropriation Act. This vote takes effect under the present Act.

(*c*) To authorise the Treasury to borrow by Treasury Bills or otherwise the amounts referred to in the two previous paragraphs. Again this is a matter of precaution.

(3) *The Finance Act*, 1954.

Enacted on 30 July 1954, for the following purposes:

(*a*) To make alterations in the customs and excise duties, to impose any new customs and excise duties which may be considered necessary, and to continue any temporary duties which it is thought desirable to continue.

(*b*) To authorise the levy of income tax for the year 1954–5, to fix the standard rate, and to make such alterations in its incidence and administration as may be thought necessary.

(*c*) To make such alterations in other taxes or to impose such additional taxes as may be thought necessary.

(*d*) To make any alterations in the administration of the National Debt as may be considered necessary.

Note: the Finance Act is not annual legislation of the same kind as the other Acts mentioned. But for the fact that the income tax is authorised for one year only and that other alterations are in fact always proposed, annual legislation would not be necessary. Taxation, other than the income tax, is levied by permanent legislation. That is, the House insists on voting supplies out of the Consolidated Fund annually; but, apart from the income tax, the funds necessary to meet those supplies pass into the Consolidated Fund under permanent legislation.

(4) *The Appropriation Act*, 1954.

Enacted on 30 July 1954, for the following purposes:

(*a*) To authorise the issue of a sum out of the Consolidated Fund for the service of the financial year 1954–5; i.e. to complete the authorisation of the supply contained in the estimates of the year, part of which has been authorised by the vote on account embodied in the Consolidated Fund Act.

(*b*) To authorise the Treasury to borrow by Treasury Bills or otherwise the amount referred to in the previous paragraph. Again this is a matter of precaution.

(*c*) To appropriate to the specific heads set out in Schedule B of the Act (occupying 53 pages of the *Law Reports* edition) the sums voted by the Consolidated Fund (No. 3) Act, 1953, the Consolidated Fund Act, 1954, and the Appropriation Act, 1954, and also to authorise the appropriation in aid of the specific services the sums set out (e.g. fees, etc., not authorised as taxation).

(*d*) To authorise 'virement' between the aggregate grants for the armed forces (see *Cabinet Government*, pp. 152–4).

(*e*) To ratify the exercise of 'virement' by the Treasury in the financial year 1952–3.

(*f*) To provide for a declaration where a person receives sums of a certain kind.

PARLIAMENT ACT, 1911
[1 & 2 Geo. 5, C. 13]

AS AMENDED BY THE PARLIAMENT ACT, 1949
[12, 13 & 14 Geo. 6, C. 103]

An Act to make provision with respect to the powers of the House of Lords in relation to those of the House of Commons, and to limit the duration of Parliament. [18th August 1911.]

𝖂𝖍𝖊𝖗𝖊𝖆𝖘 it is expedient that provision should be made for regulating the relations between the two Houses of Parliament:

And whereas it is intended to substitute for the House of Lords as it at present exists a Second Chamber constituted on a popular instead of hereditary basis, but such substitution cannot be immediately brought into operation:

And whereas provision will require hereafter to be made by Parliament in a measure effecting such substitution for limiting and defining the powers of the new Second Chamber, but it is expedient to make such provision as in this Act appears for restricting the existing powers of the House of Lords:

Be it therefore enacted by the King's most Excellent Majesty, by and with the advice and consent of the Lords Spiritual and Temporal, and Commons, in this present Parliament assembled, and by the authority of the same, as follows:

1. [*Powers of House of Lords as to Money Bills.*] (1) If a Money Bill, having been passed by the House of Commons, and sent up to the House of Lords at least one month before the end of the session, is not passed by the House of Lords without amendment within one month after it is so sent up to that House, the Bill shall, unless the House of Commons direct to the contrary, be presented to His Majesty and become an Act of Parliament on the Royal Assent being signified, notwithstanding that the House of Lords have not consented to the Bill.

(2) A Money Bill means a Public Bill which in the opinion of the Speaker of the House of Commons contains only provisions dealing with all or any of the following subjects, namely, the imposition, repeal, remission, alteration, or regulation of taxation; the imposition for the payment of debt or other financial purposes of Charges on the Consolidated Fund, or on money

provided by Parliament, or the variation or repeal of any such charges; supply; the appropriation, receipt, custody, issue or audit of accounts of public money; the raising or guarantee of any loan or the repayment thereof; or subordinate matters incidental to those subjects or any of them. In this subsection the expressions 'taxation', 'public money', and 'loan' respectively do not include any taxation, money, or loan raised by local authorities or bodies for local purposes.

(3) There shall be endorsed on every Money Bill when it is sent up to the House of Lords and when it is presented to His Majesty for assent the certificate of the Speaker of the House of Commons signed by him that it is a Money Bill. Before giving his certificate, the Speaker shall consult, if practicable, two members to be appointed from the Chairman's Panel at the beginning of each Session by the Committee of Selection.

2. [*Restriction of the powers of the House of Lords as to Bills other than Money Bills.*] (1) If any Public Bill (other than a Money Bill or a Bill containing any provision to extend the maximum duration of Parliament beyond five years) is passed by the House of Commons in two successive sessions (whether of the same Parliament or not), and, having been sent up to the House of Lords at least one month before the end of the session, is rejected by the House of Lords in each of those sessions, that Bill shall, on its rejection for the second time by the House of Lords, unless the House of Commons direct to the contrary, be presented to His Majesty and become an Act of Parliament on the Royal Assent being signified thereto, notwithstanding that the House of Lords have not consented to the Bill: Provided that this provision shall not take effect unless one year has elapsed between the date of the second reading in the first of those sessions of the Bill in the House of Commons and the date on which it passes the House of Commons in the second of those sessions.

(2) When a Bill is presented to His Majesty for assent in pursuance of the provisions of this section, there shall be endorsed on the Bill the certificate of the Speaker of the House of Commons signed by him that the provisions of this section have been duly complied with.

(3) A Bill shall be deemed to be rejected by the House of Lords if it is not passed by the House of Lords either without amendment or with such amendments only as may be agreed to by both Houses.

(4) A Bill shall be deemed to be the same Bill as a former Bill sent up to the House of Lords in the preceding session if, when it is sent up to the House of Lords, it is identical with the former Bill or contains only such alterations as are certified by the Speaker of the House of Commons to be

necessary owing to the time which has elapsed since the date of the former Bill, or to represent any amendments which have been made by the House of Lords in the former Bill in the preceding session, and any amendments which are certified by the Speaker to have been made by the House of Lords in the third session and agreed to by the House of Commons shall be inserted in the Bill as presented for Royal Assent in pursuance of this section:

Provided that the House of Commons may, if they think fit, on the passage of such a Bill through the House in the second session, suggest any further amendments without inserting the amendments in the Bill, and any such suggested amendments shall be considered by the House of Lords, and, if agreed to by that House, shall be treated as amendments made by the House of Lords and agreed to by the House of Commons; but the exercise of this power by the House of Commons shall not affect the operation of this section in the event of the Bill being rejected by the House of Lords.

3. [*Certificate of Speaker.*] Any certificate of the Speaker of the House of Commons given under this Act shall be conclusive for all purposes, and shall not be questioned in any court of law.

4. [*Enacting words.*] (1) In every Bill presented to His Majesty under the preceding provisions of this Act, the words of enactment shall be as follows, that is to say:

'Be it enacted by the King's most Excellent Majesty, by and with the advice and consent of the Commons in this present Parliament assembled, in accordance with the provisions of the Parliament Acts, 1911 and 1949, and by authority of the same, as follows.'

(2) Any alteration of a Bill necessary to give effect to this section shall not be deemed to be an amendment of this Bill.

5. [*Provisional Order Bills excluded.*] In this Act the expression 'Public Bill' does not include any Bill for confirming a Provisional Order.

6. [*Saving for existing rights and privileges of the House of Commons.*] Nothing in this Act shall diminish or qualify the existing rights and privileges of the House of Commons.

7. [*Duration of Parliament.*] Five years shall be substituted for seven years as the time fixed for the maximum duration of Parliament under the Septennial Act, 1715.

8. [*Short title.*] This Act may be cited as the Parliament Act, 1911.

[This Act and the Parliament Act, 1949, shall be construed as one and may be cited together as the Parliament Acts, 1911 and 1949; see section 2 (2) of the Parliament Act, 1949.]

STATISTICS OF PRIVATE BILLS

(SEE H.C. 158 OF 1930)

TABLE I. *Private Bills promoted in Sessions* 1919–29

Sessions	1919	1920	1921	1922	1923	1924	1925	1926	1927	1928	1929	Total
Total no. of Bills	86	139	87	76	77	74	88	80	82	96	102	987
Originating in Commons	45	63	41	36	38	35	41	38	42	48	54	481
Originating in Lords	41	76	46	40	39	39	47	42	40	48	48	506
Divorce Bills	4	7	5	4	—	—	—	—	—	—	—	20
Bills suspended	2	—	—	—	—	4	1	—	—	—	6	13
Commons Bills												
Opposed in Commons Committee	6	20	17	13	6	16	13	9	8	7	14	129
Unopposed in Commons	14	23	8	11	20	8	14	15	20	19	16	168
Lords Bills												
Opposed in Commons Committee	1	14	6	5	1	5	5	2	4	2	5	50
Unopposed in Commons	31	40	23	23	28	20	26	27	26	33	27	304
Referred to Local Legislation Committee												
Commons Bills	6	13	10	10	10	8	13	8	10	12	10	110
Lords Bills	2	10	5	5	7	6	10	9	8	9	2	73
Referred to joint committees												
Commons Bills	13	—	3	—	—	—	—	—	—	8	6	30
Lords Bills	—	—	4	—	—	—	—	—	—	2	1	7
Referred to a select committee												
Commons Bills	—	—	—	—	—	—	—	—	—	—	2	2
Commons Bills												
Withdrawn or rejected												
In Commons	4	8	4	3	2	2	5	6	4	2	5	45
In Lords	—	—	—	—	—	—	—	1	—	—	—	1
Lords Bills												
Withdrawn or rejected												
In Lords	3	6	5	3	3	4	3	4	2	3	8	44
In Commons	1	1	—	—	—	1	2	—	—	—	—	5

The following Bills must be deducted from the totals as they are shown twice above:

	1919	1920	1921	1922	1923	1924	1925	1926	1927	1928	1929	Total
Bills rejected or withdrawn after Committee stage	1	3	3	1	—	—	4	1	—	1	—	14
Totals	86	139	87	76	77	74	88	80	82	96	102	987

NOTES

Divorce Bills. These ceased in practice after the establishment of the Irish Free State.

Suspended Bills. These Bills were introduced in one session and suspended to the following session.

Unopposed Commons Bills. These exclude Bills containing Local Legislation clauses, which under the practice up to 1931 were referred to the Local Legislation Committee. Since 1932 they have followed the ordinary procedure.

Select Committees. Two Bills were referred to a select committee for consolidation.

TABLE II. *Commons Bills originally unopposed during Sessions* 1922–9

Sessions	1922	1923	1924	1925	1926	1927	1928	1929	Total
No. of Commons Bills	36	38	35	41	38	42	48	54	332
No. originally unopposed	3	6	2	1	1	2	1	4	20

TABLE III. *Local Legislation Clauses*

Local Legislation Bills, 1927	No. of L.L. clauses	No. of other clauses	Total no. of clauses
Aberdare U.D.C.	36	119	155
Buxton Corporation	90	47	137
Chepping Wycombe Corporation	83	126	209
Coventry Corporation	40	102	142
Croydon Corporation	30	106	136
Fleetwood U.D.C.	89	95	184
Grimsby Corporation	14	97	111
Leeds Corporation	6	102	108
Liverpool Corporation	35	194	229
London County Council (General Power)	30	32	62
Matlock U.D.C.	50	206	256
Newcastle-upon-Tyne Corporation	1	16	17
Pontypool U.D.C.	13	38	51
Salford Corporation	20	53	73
Sunderland Corporation	87	183	270
Swansea Corporation	49	63	112
Wallasey Corporation	25	161	186
West Bridgford U.D.C.	25	30	55

TABLE IV. *Net cost in £1000's of promotion of fifty-five Bills by classes*

Class of Bill						Total net cost in £1000's												Total no. of Bills	Average cost per Bill in £'s
	0	1	2	3	4	5	6	7	8	9	10	11	12	13	14	15	16		
1. Unopposed	10	6	4	—	2	—	—	—	—	—	—	—	—	—	—	—	—	22	1587
2. Unopposed Local Legislation	—	2	2	1	—	2	—	—	—	—	—	—	—	—	—	—	—	7	3167
3. Opposed in First House only	—	—	3	2	2	1	—	1	1	—	—	—	—	—	—	—	—	10	4452
4. Opposed in both Houses	—	—	1	—	1	3	1	2	—	—	2	—	—	—	—	—	1	11	7448
5. Bills that did not become law	—	2	2	⋯	—	1	—	—	—	—	—	—	—	—	—	—	—	5	—

TABLE V. *Average cost per £1000 for each Category of Expenditure*

	Class of Bill			
	1 Un- opposed	2 Un- opposed Local Legisla- tion	3 Opposed in First House	4 Opposed in both Houses
A. Legal and Professional Charges				
(1) Local solicitors, Town Clerks, etc.	89	64	92	14
(2) Agents	272	297	159	130
(3) Counsel	16	74	216	281
(4) Experts	82	86	113	108
(5) Shorthand writers	—	10	11	15
Total	459	531	591	548
B. House Fees				
(1) Lords	110	51	43	25
(2) Commons	101	43	39	32
Total	211	94	82	57
C. Printing charges, etc.				
(1) Advertising	62	50	27	22
(2) Bill	145	175	71	55
(3) Evidence	—	35	87	114
(4) Other documents	15	11	19	27
(5) Plans, maps, books, etc.	28	24	38	56
Total	250	295	242	274
D. Miscellaneous expenditure				
(1) Notice to owners	6	1	1	6
(2) Poll of electors	13	—	—	3
(3) Railway fares and expenses	22	51	54	76
(4) Other expenses	39	28	30	36
Total	80	80	85	121
Grand total	1000	1000	1000	1000

INDEX

Special Orders, meaning (*cont.*)
504–9; reference to select committee,
506–7; modification of in House of
Commons, 506–9; frequency of
debate, 508–9; examination in House
of Commons by Select Committee on
Statutory Rules and Orders, 513
Special Orders Committee, 510, 511–12
Special Procedure, 489
Speeches, numbers of, 148; length of, 148;
Government attitude to, 149; effect
on voting, 161; reporting of in the
press, 163–6; reading of, by ministers,
165
Standard Clauses, 466–7
Standing Committees, nomination of
members, 61; appointment of chairmen, 72, 275–6; impartiality of, 73;
closure in, 128–31, 275; seating
arrangements, 232; origin of, 269–
70; reference of Bills to, 269–70; controversial Bills in, 269–70; reforms of
1945, 270–1; decrease in Government control of, 270–1; loss of
specialist character, 271–2, 273; the
Scottish Committee, 271–2, 273, 274;
nomination and composition of, 272–
5; numbers of members, 274; hours
of sitting, 274; difficulty of finding
members for, 274; closure, Kangaroo
and guillotine in, 275; and Bills
relating exclusively to Wales and
Monmouthshire, 275; reports of proceedings, 275; powers and importance of chairmen, 275; attendance
and quorum, 276; obstruction in,
276; Law Officers in, 276; whipping
in, 276–7; defeat of Government in,
276–7; atmosphere of, 277–8; amendments in, 278; criticism of Bills by
private members, 279; humouring of,
279; report stage in, 280; private
members' Bills in, 371; in House of
Lords, 400
Standing Orders, protection of minorities
by, 59, 60–1; suspension of, 59–60;
arrangement of business under, 75
Standing Orders Committee, 459
Star Chamber, Court of, effect of its
abolition, 454
Statutory Instruments, 476, 489–516; *see
also* Delegated Legislation, Special
Orders
Statutory Undertakers, *see* Public Utilities
Statutum de Tallagio non concedendo, 237
Stock Exchange, political influence of, 171

Sueter, Rear-Admiral Sir M., 195
Sugar Commission, questions on, 11
Supplementary Estimates, when required,
300; application to Treasury for, 300;
submission to Parliament, 301; debate on, 301–2; kinds of, 302; sums
voted by Appropriation Act, 318
Supplementary Questions, 106–7
Supply, separation from taxation, 284–5;
granted by Consolidated Fund Acts,
285, 291; *see also* Committee of
Supply
Supply Rule, waiving of, 60; origin of,
123; nature of, 124, 294–5
Supply Services, nature of, 254–5, 285–6

Tacking, 412–13 n., 420–1
Talking out, 86; relation to closure, 130;
talking out private members' Bills, 370
Taxation, influence of on composition of
Commons, 51–2; authorisation of,
255; royal recommendation required,
255–6; requires legislation, 283–4;
distinction between taxation and
supply, 283–4; permanent Acts
generally used, 284; local, 284; pay-
ment of revenues into Consolidated
Fund, 285; enacting formula, 288;
generally, 319–21
Ten Minutes' Rule, 98, 149, 193, 236, 365
Ten o'clock rule, and exempted business,
59–60, 75, 116–117, 149, 505, 508
Third reading, 281–2
Thring, Henry (Lord), 225, 476
Time, analysis of time spent in business on
the floor of the House of Commons,
533
Town planning schemes, 495–6
Trade boards, 188
Trade Marks, Patents and Designs
Federation, and legislation, 192
Trade Unions, political influence of, 31,
171; and nomination of Labour
Party candidates, 35–6; representa-
tion in Parliament, 43; pressure on
Labour Governments, 140, 146; as
pressure groups, 187–8; consulted by
Government, 209; and local govern-
ment superannuation, 219
Trades Union Congress, General Council
of, consulted by Government, 209
Tradition, importance of in House of
Commons, 13–15
Transport, representation in Parliament,
42; transport interests as pressure
groups, 186–7